Over 50 The Definitive Guide to Retirement

A FRANK E. TAYLOR BOOK

Chilton Book Company · Radnor, Pennsylvania

Over 50

The Definitive Guide
to Retirement

AUREN URIS

To the men and women who have found
joy and fulfillment in retirement.
From their example we get the exciting idea
that we can go forth and do likewise.

Copyright © 1979 by Auren Uris
All Rights Reserved
Published in Radnor, Pennsylvania, by Chilton Book Company
and simultaneously in Don Mills, Ontario, Canada,
by Thomas Nelson & Sons, Ltd.

Library of Congress Catalog Card No. 79-3107
ISBN 0-8019-6714-7

Designed by Arlene Putterman
Manufactured in the United States of America

A Frank E. Taylor Book
3 4 5 6 7 8 9 0   8 7 6 5 4 3 2 1 0

PREFACE

I have been a writer, editor and researcher almost all my adult life. In addition to my job at the Research Institute of America, I have written over thirty books on subjects ranging from effective executive behavior to successful job hunting.

A year before my retirement from RIA I was asked by Chilton to write a book about retirement. Then a funny thing happened. Midway through the project I officially retired from the Institute. And even though I was asked to stay on at RIA for an extended period, and had every reason to be reassured about my future, I suddenly developed the shakes. My anxiety didn't last long and was highly educational. I learned how strong the emotional impact of retirement can be, no matter how well fixed you are. Ending a lifetime of associations and habits for a new and uncertain phase of your life is a double trauma. Thus I realized that in addition to facts and information, it was essential to include in my book the insights, understanding and case histories that would reassure and better prepare those planning their lives after 50.

And so I continued to broaden and deepen my coverage through personal interviews, contacts with experts and organizations concerned with retirement, and the available literature. Retirees and preretirees at all levels in all types of companies were interviewed. These people discussed personal histories, problems and solutions, and ideas they thought would be helpful to others before and after retirement.

My research included attendance at seminars, contacts with city, state and federal offices concerned with problems of aging, and the staffs of organizations such as the American Association of Retired Persons (AARP), Action for Independent Maturity (AIM), and the National Council of Senior Citizens (NCSC). Professionals in both business and academia made valuable contributions which broaden the scope of this reference book. Consultation with individuals involved in developing and administering company benefit programs was helpful in fleshing out the range of preretirement and postretirement programs—benefits as well as limitations.

Over 50 also profited from contributions by a group of my friends and colleagues on the staff of the Research Institute of America. These highly qualified people, duly noted in the Acknowledgments, contributed first drafts of important chapters. Their help greatly strengthened the work.

My hope is that *Over 50* will bring to those thinking about retirement—whether they expect to retire early, late, or not at all—and to their concerned relatives and friends, useful information and the reassurance that there is, indeed, life after that last regular paycheck signals entry into a new and challenging period of adulthood.

ACKNOWLEDGMENTS

The magnitude and detail of this work necessarily involve contributions by many people, including friends, colleagues, experts and those super experts, retirees and preretirees, the individuals whose firsthand experience illuminates essential areas as no other source can. I have expressed my gratitude to all individually. While it is difficult to mention every collaborator here, public appreciation is due those whose help has been extensive and continuing. This group includes people who have assisted in developing the manuscript by hand-holding, encouragement and criticism and, in some cases, all three.

To colleagues at the Research Institute of America who contributed first-draft versions of key chapters: David Beck, Jane Bensahel, Cecelia Dobrish, Bert Gottfried, C. B. Hayden and Louise Trenta.

And to colleagues whose help was less specific but equally appreciated: Joseph Ardleigh, Ruth Burger, Al Caruso, Mary Ann Jung, Marjorie Noppel, Thomas L. Quick and Barbara Whitmore.

For library services and guidance: Madeline Cohen, Joy Elbaum, Inese Rudzitis Gruber, C. B. Hayden and Nancy Rock.

For outstanding help with one phase or another in the physical preparation of the manuscript: Charlotte Braunhut, Morna Douglas, Doris Horvath, Ann LoMele, Winifred Mathie, Fay Rossi and Ellen Taylor.

Professionals contributed to this work in many ways, and most of these people have been linked with their contribution as it appears in the text. These men and women deserve my particular appreciation: Maya Anyas, Phoebe Bailey, Michelle Barnett, Gladys Gassert, Herbert Golden, William Rutherford, Ray Tannenbaum, Dr. Harry Taube, John Thummel and L. W. Tieman.

To Doris Reichbart, my special thanks for a continuing willingness to read early chapter drafts and to give me the benefit of her criticism and suggestions for improvement.

And finally, to my children—"mature offspring" cuts closer to the reality—Mary, Victoria, Bettina and Daniel, who insist on keeping me young, open-minded and on the ball: three assets for anyone's retirement.

CONTENTS

I

Retirement: A New Beginning

1
THE ULTIMATE
PROMOTION

Retiring? You're lucky, because these days retirement promises more fulfilled living than ever before. People over 50 today are decidedly different from their grandparents at the same age. The new fifties are youthful and vital at a stage in life that used to be thought of as middle age. Actuaries tell us that a man of 65 today has a life expectancy that a 53-year-old had in the 1920s. Putting it another way, a man of 65 has a life expectancy of 78.7; for a woman, it is 83.1. And that expectancy is constantly rising. By the year 2000, it will reach 80 for men and 84.5 for women. And, for the wise-living individual, the average can be surpassed.

The implications of this development are exhilarating. Today's retiree—let's say, retiring at 65—is not looking forward to a few brief years but, on the average, more than a decade for men and several years longer for women. As a result of increased longevity, the over-65 group is expected to number almost 30 million by the year 2000. That adds up to a lot of individuals with the potential for a whole new life experience. Look for a society shifting from a youth orientation toward one favoring the interests and values of mature adults.

Not only will you live longer, but those added years will see you in more robust health, with physical capacity at 70 equal to a 50-year-old of yesterday. My own memory confirms this development. I remember my parents both had complete sets of dentures in their forties. Their contemporaries were by and large sober, settled-down people. Over-fifties were supposedly headed for the grave. A man or woman of that age carrying a tennis racket would have been hooted off the street. Fun, enjoyment—that was for kids. Today, reviewing my friends and acquaintances of all ages, I find that the happiest people are in their early sixties. Nowadays, people retain their vitality and drive decades longer. You have what it takes, at 60, 70, 80, to assert yourself. Brother and sister, you count as a person of worth, a person to reckon with socially, and as an individual.

You now have some political power, and will have more in the future. The age group to which you belong is growing both in numbers and as a percentage of the total population. This means:

VOTES. Meaningful pressure on politicians to pass legislation recognizing your contribution to and status in society.

PURCHASING POWER. Manufacturers and style setters must cater to your wants and needs.

A STRONG CULTURAL VOICE. Books, movies, TV programs, will now reflect your tastes, interests, and numbers.

A NEW SOCIAL FORCE. You are, for heaven's sake, *for* yourself—and can act to win your desired status in your community and in the country at large.

How can you move to help other seniors gain their rightful place and influence?

Take pride in your status, be aware of your group and its goals, and become an activist—social and political—to the extent you would like.

● *Life Begins at . . .*

A popular book some decades back announced that "Life Begins at Forty." Then, as succeeding generations discovered to their pleasant surprise that people remained youthful at 50 and over, a variety of titles, mostly magazine articles, bemused the public: "Life Begins at Fifty-five," "Life Begins at Sixty," and so on. Peter Drucker, the well-known economist and management expert, titled a piece of his "Here I Am Fifty-three and I Still Don't Know What I Want to Do When I Grow Up."

"Life Begins at Forty" was author Walter Pitkin's idea of the age at which he had reached that high plateau known as maturity. In the case of each of the other "Life Begins . . ." type of article, it was the author's personal idea of the time at which the world and life take on a new look.

Retirement is certainly a logical milestone for marking the start of a new life. You may assume the author's privilege and select for yourself the age at which "life begins." It may be next year when you're about to retire or, if you've already retired, it may be that life begins tomorrow—after a today when you've been able to do the thinking out of which emerges a new design for living. In considering your new life, remember: *No one exactly like you has ever retired before.* Therefore, no one else's idea about life and living is necessarily yours. For the period in life known as *retirement* you must develop your own approach. True, the experience of others, and your adaptation of that experience, can be helpful. And the more you know about retirement—its problems, pleasures, and opportunities—the better off you will be.

Regardless of others' views of what retirement is and should be, however, *you* are your own ultimate expert, your own authority. The lifestyle you design should be the one that gives you the greatest rewards and the fewest problems within the framework of *real* limitations—not fancied ones which can be the greatest joy-killers of all. You must draw a picture of yourself in surroundings that optimize your strengths and minimize handicaps.

When I was in my thirties, I worked as a production foreman at the Celanese Plastics plant in Newark, New Jersey. Gary Whitby, one of the best people in the training department, ran management meetings for the edification of department heads. Scarcely a meeting went by in which he didn't sound his favorite theme at least once: "Use what you have to get what you want." It's an attractive and encouraging principle. It suggests that most of us have resources adequate for our needs. But Gary's personal solution can be improved upon. You can certainly expand the "what-you-have" element. You can add *new* information, *new* insights, *new* understanding, all capable of making you more potent. To the "get-what-you-want element," you can add your personal objectives, the targets that you aim for in your day-to-day living.

A GREAT NEW ATTITUDE

Here are some quick tips to help you maximize the benefits of your retirement.

Don't let them retire you. Even if, in the literal sense, you are taking retirement unwillingly, try to minimize that fact in your thinking. As long as an individual feels that he or she is being "forced" to take an action, it becomes less easy to take it with good grace. Some authorities say, "Don't retire *from* a job, retire *into* something." It's a constructive thought and can be translated into positive feelings more easily if you accept the following point.

Regard retirement as the ultimate promotion. View the "something" into which you retire as a new phase of your career, the phase in which you can go on to win greater satisfactions and greater rewards, material as well as emotional. Viewed as a *promotion*, retirement takes on an entirely different aspect. You can view your retirement life not as a withdrawal, but as a new kind of job that has an especial virtue—this time you can write your own job description!

Be excited by the opportunities. This is a key element in viewing retirement in a constructive way. Now admittedly, retirees face problems. They may have a belt-tightening income, lose the comfort of affiliation with an established organization, or miss the benefits of a structured workday. But with retirement comes the end of a number of restraints, gentle though they may be. Now you have a freedom of thought and action that may have been previously impossible.

One man about to retire told me, "I've been giving myself a preview of the days ahead, and you know one of the things that I'm most pleased about? I feel I no longer have to be an open advocate of the establishment. Don't get me wrong—it's not that I'm opposed to it, either. It's just that as long as you hold a typical kind of job, whether you think much about it or not, you become an active supporter of the system. I guess for a long time I've been a closet dropout. Now I'm going to have a chance to liberate those repressed feelings. It's a great adventure and I can scarcely wait to see what happens."

Not all of us can be so candid and so insightful. But perhaps, if you think about it, you'll find all kinds of restrictions that the average working life places on you, not only in terms of work and time, but also in thought and values. Shedding those restrictions can bring a new freedom.

Don't be surprised if ideas and opinions that you have suppressed come to the surface as you retire. Another person I talked to, retired for less than a year, said, "As a youngster I was always interested in reading science fiction. As I grew up, that interest simply got swamped by the rush of everyday activities. Suddenly, with retirement, that interest came surging to the surface. Now I'm up to my ears in reading and collecting books and old magazines in the science-fiction field. And I find myself involved in a whole new and absorbing activity. The fact that I'm making money in trading science-fiction materials is obviously an added plus."

Whether it's a bottled-up interest in science fiction, a repressed lust for travel, or any one of a hundred other activities, be on the lookout for the opportunity to latch onto interests that you've kept under wraps. These opportunities may be just what it takes to make you feel better about retirement and see it in its proper perspective—as your passport to an exciting world.

NEW FREEDOM

In addition to individual matters, there is a general approach that can affect your feelings about your new situation. A retired high school principal who left a New York suburb for Falls Church, Virginia, expresses it this way:

"The great thing about retirement," Hy Burton told me, "is that you can refocus your sights, put your efforts where they bring the most immediate rewards. The way I see it, I have a great new responsibility, and it's to *myself*. I can shuck off responsibilities I've had ever since I was a kid of 14, when I had to start working to help my mother support our household.

"At long last I can stop worrying about the ills of the school system in general and the specific grinding problems of my own school. And our kids are all grown up and are on their own. We love to spend time with them—occasionally. But Mary and I love it here in our new apartment and we've already started to build a new life for ourselves. Imagine that! We're like social pioneers."

For many people, retirement means the end of some responsibilities. Remember Burton's concept of retirement as an unshackling. Of course, in some cases, one cannot be as single-minded. Some responsibilities may remain—for a handicapped child or, for younger retirees, aging parents. But even so, using Burton's idea of responsibility for yourself may help you rethink your obligations so that new arrangements may ease the burden.

ADDING UP YOUR ASSETS

Now, put the key ideas in this chapter together and see how they make the future glow:

1. People who retire—at any age—will live and retain their youthful vigor longer than any previous generation.

2. Over-50s, becoming a larger percentage of the population, will pack more clout, so that society at large will become more senior oriented, more strongly emphasizing your needs and interests.

3. Retirement, for some people, can mean a chance to undertake new ventures, new challenges, in the form of a second career.

4. Old aspirations and interests may revive and offer new pleasures and satisfactions.

5. Now it can be your turn to put your wishes to the fore, since your great new responsibility is you, yourself!

6. Consider retirement as an unshackling, a liberation that can free you for active service—of your own choosing.

● *Banishing Misconceptions*

With the many benefits of retirement promising a happy future, why do some people hang back? Putting it even more bluntly, why does the very thought of retirement terrify some, and make most others uneasy?

The answer was suggested to me by a man who "hadn't slept for weeks before his last day on the job," and then several months later reported, "I'm having a ball." His explanation: "It's fear of the unknown."

I believe he's right. Misconceptions about retirement are barriers on the road to progress. Spotting these obstacles, knowing them for what they are, can greatly smooth the transition. And this clear-eyed, informed approach is a major element in the new preparation for retirement.

FOURTEEN FEARS

I don't like negative ideas. Over years of dealing with ideas and people, I've become aware of the essential drag on spirit, energy, and motivation exerted by negatives. My conversations with retirees and people about to retire convince me that many difficulties result from their downbeat feelings about themselves and their circumstances. The pages ahead may help you identify and eliminate any that may be handicapping you.

Read each item carefully. Ask yourself, "Is this me? Is this the way I think or feel?" Then check the answer that best applies to you. Unearthing just *one* threat that is bugging you can help you make an adjustment in your thinking that may mean clearing the air, freeing you to enjoy the positive benefits of a new life.

Remember, if you let them, negative ideas will nibble the future to death for you. Fortunately, this need not be the case. Consider the paragraphs and pages that follow as an exposé of the fears that threaten to spoil a good thing.

1. "I'm afraid of the word." Retirement is very much handicapped by semantics. The very word *retirement* gets you off on the wrong foot. Consider some of the negative implications: to retire means to withdraw; to retire means to go to sleep; to retire means to retreat, to fall back, to recede.

Consider those senses of the word and you can understand why people instinctively cringe at the thought of retirement. Is the semantic threat a factor in your thinking?

( ) Not at all   ( ) To some extent   ( ) Bothers me a lot

2. "I'm over the hill." A typical example: The setting is a cocktail party. A stranger, making small talk to get a conversation started, says, "I'm an engineer at the Taylor company. What do you do?"

"I'm retired."

A person who designates himself as a retiree may seem to be saying, "I'm an idler, I have ceased making a contribution to society." The fact is, the only hill that retired people are over is one that exists in their own minds.

Even if not intended, the phrase "I'm retired" suggests something undesirable. Some preferred answers: "I'm pursuing a second career." If you want to be specific, say "as a consultant," or whatever it is you feel is most significant in your present activity. Has this question of status been in your mind?

( ) Not at all   ( ) To some extent   ( ) Bothers me a lot

3. "I'm old." True enough, the average age of people who are retired is going to be higher than that of people who have not yet done so. But *old*? What does that mean? The French say, "You're as old as you look." Americans say, "You're as old as you feel."

In general, functional age varies greatly from chronological age. Many people will tell you they feel younger at 65 than they felt at 55.

Another key point: In addition to how you feel about yourself, an important aspect of age is how old you appear to others. Satchel Paige, the legendary black baseball player, posed a revealing question: "How old would you be if you didn't know how old you are?"

Have you been linking the idea of growing old with retirement?

( ) Not at all   ( ) To some extent   ( ) Bothers me a lot

4. "Retirement will kill me." Before we understood the right and wrong way to retire, the sudden change from being a productive, wage-earning member of society one day and a separated at-loose-ends person the next day, proved a tremendous shock to many people. A shock which the human system often couldn't stand very well. And it's true that the physical and emotional upset of the unprepared retiree noticeably cut down longevity, as evidenced by high mortality rates.

But these days you don't have to worry about the scare stories that suggest that retirees fade quickly. Current statistics explain why: The health of retired people is often better than that of similar age groups of nonretired individuals.

Despite evidence to the contrary, do you feel your health or longevity is threatened by retirement?

( ) Not at all   ( ) To some extent   ( ) Bothers me a lot

5. "I'll be bored to death." This is a common fear especially of the traditional high-pressure, hard-driven executive but can affect anyone who is deeply involved in a job. Supposedly, such a person will be lost without an organizational affiliation and without the tasks and objectives that fall to the lot of the executive. Employees at all levels share this worry.

But with the proper preparation, the most driven executive who ever lived, the most dedicated worker can learn how to apply the very same energies and devotion to other causes and other goals, self-selected and self-designed.

Even though your reason tells you otherwise, are you haunted by fears of idleness, time hanging heavy on your hands?

( ) Not at all   ( ) To some extent   ( ) Bothers me a lot

6. "I'll lose my friends." For those who have many good friends and

colleagues at work, there is a fear that the relationships terminate the day retirement begins.

Of course this needn't be the case at all. You needn't drop contacts with those people on the job whose friendship you value. As a matter of fact, job-wise people will tell you that in many cases people whose friendship you prize have had to be held at arm's length because of the demands of a job. For example, Oscar Green was head of a research and development department for a plastics manufacturer. He liked and admired quite a number of the men and women who were his subordinates. Yet he hesitated to develop intimate friendships because of the fear that these relationships might interfere with work. He might be accused of favoritism if he promoted a friend or granted some other privilege.

But Oscar Green as a retired person could now pick up with a select few and actually improve the quality of the relationships. For the first time there could be the amount of socializing that he had hoped for before, but hesitated to develop.

Has this been a retirement-tarnishing concern of yours?

( ) Not at all   ( ) To some extent   ( ) Bothers me a lot

7. "I can't face it." I have talked to dozens of people who have retired. One of the most common statements they make: "I was unprepared for retirement." And then they add "I just wasn't foresighted enough. As a result I wouldn't bring myself to plan until six months before, and by then it was too late."

Being unprepared for retirement, whether it's in the emotional or practical aspects, generally means that the individual has been unable to face up to the facts of life. Fearing an uncertain future and resisting the need to plan in advance, people keep coming up to the day of retirement in disbelief that the event is really happening. The result is that instead of stepping forward bravely, embracing the opportunities of retirement, they hang back and create a self-fulfilling prophecy—they "know they're not going to enjoy retirement"—and make that inevitable by not making provision for it. Is this your view?

( ) Not at all   ( ) To some extent   ( ) Bothers me a lot

8. "I'll be a victim of the unexpected." This is the other side of the lack-of-preparation coin. One former executive says, "I had seen colleagues of mine retire successfully. My brother is the best example I

know of someone who found retirement to be a ball. So I assumed there was nothing to it. But I had failed to anticipate some of the hidden changes. I was a person who always had a couple of subordinates around who did everything from make coffee for me in the morning to doing my personal shopping at Christmastime. Suddenly they were all gone and I felt both alone and helpless."

It's unrealistic to assume that in retirement everything remains exactly the same except that you don't have a job. There are changes you must make. To think of these necessary adjustments as "problems" is wrong. Many of the new things in the life of a retiree are perfectly obvious and easily coped with. Everything from devising a daily schedule of activity to finding new friends can be handled. Are you shortchanging yourself with this approach?

( ) Not at all   ( ) To some extent   ( ) Bothers me a lot

9. "I'll face problems I can't solve." Darkening the retirement horizons for many is the fear that some aspect of their new life is going to represent a massive and continuing difficulty. It may be the fear that the financial situation will automatically become disastrous, or that one will never be able to fill in the activity gap that results from the loss of a job. Basically this attitude is reinforced by an unspoken feeling: "I can't cope."

The antidote to this is to be reminded of your creativity and ingenuity in the past in solving problems, in analyzing and dealing with situations, and in meeting challenges. You've met them before. By and large, you're more capable, more mature, more experienced. This means that you're better able to face up to the "unsolvable" problem and deal with it effectively. Is this fear likely to hamstring you?

( ) Not at all   ( ) To some extent   ( ) Bothers me a lot

10. "I'll be stuck in front of the TV." Men and women alike are susceptible to this tender trap. In the absence of an ongoing, constructive program, people are lured by the Lorelei appeal of the electronic tube. They have seen it happen to others, why not to them? As a matter of fact, the TV-hypnotized person is a contemporary stereotype. Can one escape?

It is not the intention here to denigrate television. Many creative people are involved in providing the news and entertainment of this versatile and important medium. But to retired people, it may promote passivity and a certain amount of psychic deterioration if TV-watching becomes an overinflated part of the daily schedule. At best, it cuts down on other desirable activities.

Self-regulation can help. Confine viewing to a reasonable part of your schedule. Be selective. Keep track of time spent in front of the magic box. If it's more than three hours a day, start looking for other things you enjoy that can be allotted some TV hours. Is TV a menace for you?

( ) Not at all   ( ) To some extent   ( ) Bothers me a lot

11. "I'll start living in the past." Memories, fond memories, are an important legacy. No wonder that, to some extent, we all hang onto the past. The job is usually an important part of our recollection. When people leave an employer, they usually leave behind a successful experience. Even aside from possible career high points—where you've pulled off one or another triumph in completing an assignment or project—for most people the job represents a period of achievement. If that weren't true, you probably wouldn't have remained with the organization.

At best, leaving an assured success for an uncertain future is a risk, so it's no wonder that many people are emotionally hooked to the past. Some retirees are compelled to dwell on those great days when their performance seemed at its best and status and self-esteem were at a peak. But those who live in the past tend to neglect the present. And even worse, the present tends to neglect them. No matter how devoted friends and family are, tolerance of other people's nostalgia tends to be limited. Is this your hangup?

( ) Not at all   ( ) To some extent   ( ) Bothers me a lot

12. "I'm afraid of the future." Some people fear confronting an unknown tomorrow. When people are young, the future is where the action will be. For the most part, young people perform in the present for future benefits. They undertake tough tasks and deny themselves many things in the expectation that they will reap rewards tomorrow, next month, or next year.

But some retirees hesitate to commit themselves to major expenditures of time or energy in the hope of future return. This is both short-sighted and self-defeating. The average retiree should have the same attitude toward the present as a 25-year-old go-getter. Two benefits derive from this tack. First, it makes the present a livelier and more creative period. Second, it reinforces a future-mindedness that makes for a dynamic attitude out of which achievement and satisfaction grow. Are you being held back by this attitude?

( ) Not at all   ( ) To some extent   ( ) Bothers me a lot

13. "My days of growth are over." People at nine or ninety have two kinds of resources—those that are developed and those that are still latent. One of the major rewards of retirement is that you have more time and freedom to develop your potential to grow. The individual who figuratively makes a date with the undertaker, or marks time by some soporific pastime, will grow hair and little else.

On the other hand, the person who vaults into the saddle and seeks "the one thing I've always wanted to do" or undertakes the exploration summed up in the phrase "for the first time in my life I'm going to see what's on the other side of the mountain" is open to a happy and exciting period of growth.

Are you bothered by the feeling that your inner resources will dry up when you retire?

( ) Not at all   ( ) To some extent   ( ) Bothers me a lot

14. "Retirement is the end." It is an understandable weakness: some people see retirement as "the end of a glorious career;" "the conclusion of my personal contribution to society;" "the last milestone before the cemetery."

These negative views combine the worst elements of self-pity and lack of understanding. The positive view—and the one that makes sense in terms of your future health and happiness—is that the termination of your formal working years opens many doors for new experience, satisfaction, and even deeper levels of mature wisdom.

And retirement is not a conclusion in another, more literal, sense. You may decide, as many people have, that you want to continue to work. If you feel this is desirable, and it may be for a number of reasons (see Chapter 16, Another Job), more power to you.

As desirable as another job may be, remember that to some extent it is just a postponement. True, later on you may be in a better frame of mind. But if the same wariness exists, then it may still be difficult to collect the rewards of retirement.

Best antidote: do a bit of sleuthing. Ask around for cases of happy retirees, and seek them out, talk to them. Chances are they will be glad to share their experiences with you. In their success lies proof that retirement can be an introduction to the best time of your life.

Consciously or unconsciously, and you'll have to probe your own psyche on this, do you fear that the end of your job means the end of the line?

( ) Not at all   ( ) To some extent   ( ) Bothers me a lot

OVERCOMING OBSTACLES

Now look back at the ratings you've indicated to the items in the questionnaire. If you indicated "not at all," you can *forget* the threat.

Items rated "to some extent" deserve your attention: *Think* about them. When do they bother you? Does the reaction appear when you are feeling down, or does some specific situation trigger the response? In either case, the implication is that the sensitivity occurs when your defenses and your normal self-confidence are down. Recognize the timing, and you will realize that, like a bad dream, the fear will disappear when you put the spotlight of reality and common sense full upon it.

Items rated "bothers me a lot" can dim the glow of the most promising retirement. The fear of loss of status, of the end of your regular working days as the end of the line, can place an unnecessary pall over your spirits.

Any item that got this rating warrants top priority. As a matter of fact, it may very well be absorbing more of your attention than you want to give it. One recommendation: Don't try to sweep it under the rug. Remember that in every case, you're up against an exaggeration. You feel you'll be at loose ends, bored to death? Nonsense! Now that you are aware of your mini-phobia, *you can take action.* This action consists of being aware of the feeling that is bothering you; realizing that it is a feeling based, for the most part, on a distortion of reality, not on reality itself; and supplying the evidence and counter-arguments that help cancel the fear. For example, are you afraid you will lose friends? Or that you lack the inner resources to cope with some of the circumstances of the retired life? Those are fears, not facts. For one thing, you don't know how your friends will feel. For another, a large part of the way your friends react to your retirement will be a reflection of your own behavior. The person who turns morose will induce negative feelings in others. The person who makes retirement a take-over operation, with matters under control and going splendidly, will have to beat off the mob who would like to have a piece of the action, if only in a reflected way.

The threats to effective retirement discussed in the questionnaire are by no means comprehensive. In addition to these aspects, you may be able through your own self-analysis to uncover other ideas that may upset the apple cart for you. Treat these self-discovered items the same way you would any of the items listed. Consider to what extent the threat is serious, and if it is, remember that detecting the problem is half the cure. The other half comes from supplying the evidence and counter-arguments that help cancel them out.

● *Know yourself*

Even when an individual seems prepared, even eager, to retire, problems can still arise that may spoil that person's new way of life. For example, Pam Gibbs, at the age of 58, could hardly wait to retire. She had eagerly contemplated a future as a retiree for the past four or five years. "I've always loved vacations, travel, seeing new places," she said. "I've got dozens of plans I'm going to work on the minute I get my last paycheck." But Pam, like most of us, didn't know herself as well as she might. After six months of a life of leisure, she was half-mad with boredom. She had been in a high-powered job, working intensively with a group of bright, creative people. After the first few weeks of winding down, the loose, unstructured life she had chosen became intolerable.

Many people in the same situation arrived there from an opposite tack. Henry Karras, a foreman for a construction company, resolved that when *he* retired, he wasn't going to let down. "I love activity and pressure," he asserted. "And that's the way I want it to the end."

Because of his experience and skills, Henry Karras had no problem finding a second career. He was hired as a field instructor by a road building concern. His organization was involved in a considerable number of state projects and Henry, at the age of 65, found himself on a very tight schedule involving a lot of travel.

"Henry," his wife told him, "slow down. We don't need the money that much and I'm not ready to be the next widow on the block."

Henry didn't enter the hereafter as a result of his activity, but he did have a minor heart attack. Strangely enough, his enforced slowdown, once he got used to it, was surprisingly easy to take.

He told his wife ruefully, "Just as it says in the ads, leisure can be fun." He learned the hard way, but he learned.

When people decide prematurely that they know what they're going to do when they retire, there's always the possibility of misjudgment. One of the virtues of retirement is that it gives you the opportunity to learn about yourself, to discover what you really want, what you really like to do, who you really are, and to make adjustments as you go.

● *Retirement Readiness Quotient*

You've had an opportunity to consider a number of threats to a well-balanced, constructive approach to leaving your job. These factors give you a chance to think about your real feelings concerning this important career step. Now you are ready to try to pin down, in an even more personal way, your attitude toward retirement.

Take the quiz that follows with an open mind, answering the questions as honestly and accurately as possible. Be tough with yourself. The more you work at coming up with the answers, the more useful the results can be. You may want to compare the picture of readiness that emerges from your rating of the factors above with your scoring of the quiz that follows.

A SELF-RATING QUIZ

Let's say you're 40 years old, and retirement seems pretty far off. In that case, this quiz may put some strain on your imagination, and it is possible that the rating you get will be more interesting than truly useful. But if you are over 55, and retirement is something you have already been thinking about, your score on this quiz may give you some insights—and surprises—that can assist in your adjusting to the future. Answer the questions as accurately as possible; if necessary, do a little role-playing to put yourself in the suggested situations.

1. If you were retiring today, right this minute—
   a. What would you miss most in your job? _____
   b. What would you miss least? _____
2. You're well fixed financially, and your boss comes along and says, "I

know you're all set to quit and gather the rosebuds of retirement, but the organization needs you. How about staying on in your old job for another couple of years?" Would you say—
a. No, thanks. ( )
b. Yes. ( )

3. Say the word "retirement" and—
   a. Your mind is filled with a dozen ideas of exciting things you want to do. ( )
   b. Your heart sinks. ( )

4. Whenever you discuss your retirement with your spouse, friends, or other family members—
   a. You speak enthusiastically. ( )
   b. You speak gloomily. ( )

5. In thinking about your retirement—
   a. You already have made a number of satisfactory plans and decisions. ( )
   b. Your mind is mostly a vacuum. ( )

6. You think of retirement—
   a. As a beginning. ( )
   b. As an end. ( )

7. You have one or more major projects or activities you plan to tackle in retirement that you never could fit in while you were working.
   a. Yes ( )
   b. No ( )

8. You like to read about retirement, discuss it, and investigate its many aspects.
   a. True ( )
   b. False ( )

INTERPRETING YOUR ANSWERS

Question 1, "What would you miss in your job," can be particularly revealing. For example: two people on whom the quiz was tested both answered with the same word, "structure," but one said he would miss it *most*, the other, *least*. The person who would miss the structure, regularity, and schedules imposed by a job would obviously be well advised to set up fairly strict programs for his day-to-day retirement activity. For the person who would be glad to minimize structure, spontaneous programming would be one of the benefits of retirement.

In general, people who miss elements rooted in the work itself—the challenge of a tough assignment or contacts with colleagues—should try to duplicate these elements in their retirement activity. For example, take on a tough problem that has been plaguing your community and look for groups with which you would enjoy working.

For the other seven questions, "a" answers indicate a readiness or favorable disposition toward retirement and "b" answers suggest reluctance. If your replies have all been the "a", you have a positive outlook toward retirement that augurs well for you and your future. If one or more of your choices in questions 2 through 8 have been the second alternative, go over these and rethink your answers. *Why* do you think or feel the way you do? If the answer doesn't come readily, don't worry. Somewhere in the pages ahead you'll find answers that may put a problem into a more favorable perspective.

EVALUATING YOUR ATTITUDE

There is a right and a wrong way to contemplate retirement. The wrong way is to approach it with the grim, stolid terror of the person who fears going to the dentist but knows he has to, anyway. The right way requires an attitude based on some time-honored qualities.

UNDERSTANDING.   See retirement as just one link in a life-long chain.

KNOWLEDGE.   Prepare as well as you can for retirement.

FLEXIBILITY.   In some things—like a daily activity schedule—be prepared to remove one element and substitute another until results are satisfactory.

OPENNESS.   Be ready for new experiences, new relationships, and the development of new attitudes that represent a deepening of your maturity and wisdom.

Perhaps the single most constructive statement I've ever heard about the post-job period was made by Phoebe Bailey, National Training Director of AIM (Action for Independent Maturity), at the end of a lunch devoted mostly to talking shop, with a few asides about our respective children and grandchildren. Phoebe is the most "in" person I know in the field. Her experience includes countless conversations with retirees pre- and post-, from rank-and-file employees to presidents, and discussions and lectures on most aspects of retirement. "You know, Auren," she said, "in the long run, the most important thing about retirement is that it be *a time in which you feel good about yourself and what you are doing*. Of course, this requires an individual formula for each person. . . ."

The next chapter and those that follow aim to help you put together the elements of your own personal retirement formula, based on your needs, your preferences, and your potential for growth.

2
THE BEST TIME
TO RETIRE

Let's assume that the time of your retirement lies ahead, and also that you have some freedom of choice. *When* should you retire? Every working person confronts this question sooner or later, and answers vary widely.

For example, Bobby Orr, the defenseman whose rushing style changed the face of hockey, quit the Chicago Black Hawks at the age of 30. His decision to retire was based on physical injuries—six operations to his left knee had failed to bring his performance up to a level he could accept.

Child movie stars have quit at the age of 8 or 10 when the qualities that put them before the cameras were beginning to disappear at the approach of puberty.

Pablo Picasso, who died at the age of 92, never retired, although his art made him a very wealthy man.

Joseph Zoram, a Denver machinist, retired at 75. He had been able to retire financially earlier, but his employer was perfectly willing to have him stay on. "Joe is the best model maker in the shop," he said. Zoram quit work when his eyesight began to fail.

Which is the best age for your retirement?

● *Preliminary Considerations*

The Self-Appraisal Questionnaire in this chapter is a tool that may help you arrive at a decision as to your own best time to retire. And, if the answer indicates that you are not yet ready, you can then, again with the help of the Self-Appraisal Questionnaire, pinpoint the factors to work on that can bring you to your retirement date, whenever it is, in the best possible shape.

Before using the questionnaire, there are some preliminary considerations that may clarify the timing question for you.

What factors should you weigh in arriving at this key decision? The answer needn't be a blind guess. Still less should it be based on some of the advice, however well-intentioned, of colleagues, friends, family, and so on. Authorities in the field of retirement, correctly understanding the timing of retirement as a key step, have developed a number of rules.

1. *"Hold on to your job as long as you can."* This expert supports his view by pointing out that if you enjoy your work and the companionship of colleagues, why give that up hastily? He goes on to say that even if you're not in a dream job and experience occasional tensions, even upsets, at least these are familiar situations that you have dealt with before and can be coped with again. The expert concludes by saying that retirement is a new job and might entail even more tension. Why rush from a better situation into a worse one?

But this concept of holding on reinforces the destructive idea that retirement is necessarily a bad thing, to be delayed as long as possible. In some cases, of course, this may be true. *But is it true for you?*

2. *"Retire at the earliest possible moment."* Some individuals jump the gun. They leave their jobs at an extremely early age. A book written some time ago was entitled, "How to Retire at Forty-one." It was a first-hand account of a failure. The man eventually returned to work. That author's experience aside, for a person to quit a job so early and embark on a life that could even vaguely be called retirement makes little sense for the average person.

While there's nothing wrong with quitting a job at 41, or any other age, and looking for another occupation, unless you're independently wealthy, there are several reasons why this kind of super-early retirement may be unwise. Unless you have a call in a specific direction, different from the one you've been following, such a move suggests confusion and indecision rather than considered judgment.

Quit too early, and you miss the opportunity to bring to your vocation the wisdom, maturity, and experience that mark the years of most people's peak effectiveness. You may miss out on what for many are the most rewarding years of their working life.

3. *"Work until they throw you out."* More elegantly, this move is de-

scribed as, "Work until the mandatory retirement age." Recent legislation has changed this from 65 to 70, but prolonged deferment of retiring may overlook some cogent factors.

For example, are there activities—physically strenuous ones—that you might have to perform in the next five or ten years that would be beyond your capabilities if you work until seventy? Traveling for a 50 or 55-year-old person, with or without spouse, is likely to be a considerably different experience from the same travel when one is 65 or 70.

4. *"Retire when you're fed up."* Every once in a while, a job gets to be too much. An unreasonable boss, an unfavorable working situation, a long commute, or overly demanding or unpleasant assignments can make people want out. But individuals who jump into retirement for this reason alone may find that they have permitted one factor to outweigh many others—everything from financial considerations to lack of emotional and practical preparation.

5. *"Give the youngsters a chance."* John G. Kemeny, president of Dartmouth College, pointed out that if college teachers with tenure as a group extended retirement age from 65 to 70, they would create hardships for the new Ph.D.s entering the teaching profession. As Dr. Kemeny put it, "If the retirement age were extended, the unemployment rate for Ph.D.s would skyrocket." As a result, he saw many potential faculty members driven out of the profession because of lack of job opportunities.

But remember, the decision about when to retire should be based on *your* needs, *your* desires, *your* interests. Never was benign selfishness a better principle by which to decide.

SPECIAL SITUATIONS

Sometimes fate steps in and dictates your retirement decision, as the following cases illustrate.

A WINDFALL. Olga and Sam Birkett stopped into a local tavern to have a couple of beers after a fishing trip. On their way out, and paying for their drinks, they bought a lottery ticket. It proved to be a winner—a million dollars worth! What were they going to do with the cash paid out by the New York State lottery? During an interview, Sam Birkett said he was definitely going to retire. One of their post-retirement plans: since they were outdoor people, they were planning to spend a lot of time canoeing in Minnesota and exploring the wilderness of the uninhabited west.

Sometimes a cash windfall—an inheritance, a gift, or as happened to the Birketts, winning a lottery—makes it possible to consider quitting the world of work, permanently.

HEALTH.   A sudden ailment or more slowly developing handicap may make retirement a must, especially when sound medical advice recommends it.

FAMILY TIES.   "Phyllis needs us," Nell Parmenter said to her husband. "Even though Greg left her fairly well provided for, it's going to be a struggle with three kids. If you take early retirement, even though money may be a bit tight, we'll be able to get an apartment nearby, and help Phyllis get back on her feet. I know you don't like moving back east, but it would mean so much to her. And she suggested it. . . ."

In some crucial situations, the needs of loved ones may suggest a move that may not be convenient, but may be tolerable. And you may, out of love or conscience, decide to make that move.

A SUDDEN RESOLVE.   George Gruber and his wife Alice had just come back from the funeral of his brother, and George had been deeply moved.

"Alice," he said, "I stood at the graveside, looking down at that coffin, and I decided life is too short to just let things take their course. For the past few years we've talked of living in Alaska. I'm not sure how practical it is, but we've got enough to carry us for several years. And after we settle in, I'm sure I'll be able to figure out some way to add to our resources. . . ."

People like the Grubers let themselves be swept along by strong feelings into making the retirement decision. In some cases, it works out well. In others, it means disaster. It is important to understand this kind of crisis, recognize it if it should ever arise for you, and be prepared to face up to pressures to which you will be subject. No one else can say, in general, whether retirement is wise or unwise for you. You must be your own counselor. But do try to think through at least the immediate practicalities, and those of the near future. If the outlook is even fairly promising, at least you will have time later to reconsider and plan for the long haul.

CONFLICT. An individual may have a falling out—with a boss, a colleague, or the organizational establishment. Out of personal pride, or a matter of principle, he or she may decide to leave, premature though this may be. Frank Glynn was vice president of an electricity-producing utility that was guilty of some rate practices Frank felt were unethical. He finally decided that the situation was not tolerable. He wrote a letter to the head of the company, protesting what had been done, and at the same time put in for early retirement.

In writing that letter, Frank knew that his stand would make it impossible to continue in his job, and took what to him seemed a necessary step. This kind of move, courageous though it is, obviously must be made either with the intention of seeking another means of self-support, or with the knowledge that present finances will be adequate.

The sudden-decision situations just considered are the exceptions. For the most part, you have plenty of time to think about the timing of your departure from the organization. You can compare advantages and disadvantages of one course versus another.

And now, to help put the question, "When should I retire?" into perspective, here is the promised tool to help you arrive at the best answer.

● *Self-Appraisal Questionnaire*

This questionnaire has been devised to help guide your considerations about when to retire along practical lines. Using factors that influence your decision, you're asked to read a number of statements and check off the one that comes closest to describing your situation.

Note that each statement has a number, or score, assigned to it. The purpose of this is to weight your answers, that is, to give them their relative importance not only in relation to other items concerning the same subject but also in relation to other factors entirely.

For example, *finances* is clearly a vital factor in your decision. If you can't afford to retire early, then you just have to forget it, no matter how favorable other factors might be. Accordingly, the items relating to finances are weighted very heavily. There are many other crucial factors in addition to finances that must be considered if your retirement is to be a happy and productive experience. Even if you are able, financially, to retire early—at 55 or somewhere short of a mandatory retirement age—you may have to think seriously about whether it is wise and practical for you to do so.

Of course, with the passing of time your situation in relation to the factors listed may change. You can then take the quiz over again and the new score you get may suggest a different decision.

Go through each of the factors below and check off the one statement in each group that most closely approximates your situation. Make your responses accurate and honest. The usefulness of your score at the end depends heavily on how carefully you do this. After the last factor, you'll find scoring directions and an interpretation of your total score.

FINANCES

−50	( )	I don't have enough reserves on hand to make it now.
5	( )	I have just enough to scrape by, but I'm not sure about inflation.
10	( )	I can make it if I live "cheaply" and cut back on extras.
15	( )	I'm OK for the foreseeable future at my present level of living.
25	( )	I will do fine in almost any event.
50	( )	Money is no consideration.

HEALTH

− 5	( )	My work keeps me zipping along, gives me exercise, and forces me to watch my diet and personal habits.
5	( )	I feel that my work favors my health in that it keeps me busy and on a regular schedule.
15	( )	My work generally leaves me dragged out at the end of the day. If it weren't for weekends, I'd be in a bad way.
50	( )	My work is a terrible strain. It drains my energies, keeps me on edge, and doesn't let me sleep nights.

RELATIONSHIPS

− 5	( )	If I retire now, I suspect my personal relationships will suffer badly—for example, I expect my wife and I will get on each other's nerves, I will lose some of my job friends, and so on.

0   ( )   I'm not sure if I have enough, and good enough, friends to make for a satisfactory social life if I stop work now.

10   ( )   I've never depended very much on people I met on the job for socializing, and I have a well-rounded group of friends and relatives who always have and will continue to make for a full social life.

25   ( )   The minute I stop working I'll be able to improve and devote more time to practically all of my relationships.

EMOTIONAL OUTLOOK

−10   ( )   I'm emotionally unprepared to stop work. If I retire now, I won't be able to make the many adjustments that are necessary.

5   ( )   I don't believe retirement is going to be much of a threat for me. I'm pretty flexible.

15   ( )   I find the prospect of retirement kind of exciting, an attractive adventure.

30   ( )   I can hardly wait for retirement. There are so many things I want to do.

HOUSING

−5   ( )   If I stop working now, I'll have to give up my present living arrangements for something much less desirable.

5   ( )   My retirement won't affect my housing arrangements much one way or the other.

15   ( )   I expect benefits from my retirement: I'll be able to do a lot of work around the house that I've been putting off for years, which will mean not only enjoyable activity but also an increase in the value of the place.

20   ( )   If I retire now, I'll be able to move to another site in another part of the country (or whatever) that will give my whole life a lift.

WORK

−15   ( )   I would miss it terribly. There is so much more I want to achieve before I quit.

0	( )	Work? I can take it or leave it.
15	( )	I'm proud of my work record. However, I feel my job achievement is behind me.
25	( )	The day I leave the job will be one of the happiest of my life.

ACTIVITIES

−10	( )	I know I'll never find anything else to do that I will enjoy as much as I do my job.
5	( )	I enjoy my life on the job as much as anything I might do on the outside.
10	( )	I like the idea of getting into new things.
20	( )	There are any number of things I've been eager to do and, when I leave my job, I'll finally have enough time to get to them.

EVALUATING YOUR SCORE

In a moment, you'll be able to total your score and see what the implications are for you. But first, a word about the weighting. It's an attempt to make the score realistic. For example, consider the money factor. As was mentioned earlier, many other things might favor retirement, but if your financial situation is unsatisfactory, early retirement might be a catastrophe. That's why the money factor gets the highest value and why, if you put a check by the first of the statements suggesting that you are financially unprepared to stop work, other items would have to be very, very strong to compensate.

And somewhat the same thinking explains the weighting of the health item. If your health is going to suffer if you continue in your job, it becomes a strong reason for retirement. And so on.

Now, go back over all your checkmarks (it's assumed you've made a choice for each factor) and total up your score.
Total Score: _____.

If your score is over *100*, chances are you are both practically and mentally ready to consider early retirement. But don't act on the results of this questionnaire alone. Double-check such a move by an approach from a different perspective. Using the facts that you have in effect pinned down by using this tool, you can now discuss the move with interested parties—spouse, family or possibly a counsellor provided by your employer.

If your score is between *80* and *100,* the decision is up in the air. There seem to be advantages and disadvantages to the move that pretty well balance each other. Continue to explore the situation further. You can start by reconsidering the answers you checked off above. Make sure that they represent what you *really* think and feel. If no significant changes are made, then you may want to explore some of the key factors. In one case it may be your health; or perhaps your own financial picture isn't altogether clear. You may want to reexamine your net worth (see Chapter 9, Finances), or any of the other factors that you feel may deserve reexamination.

If you scored below *80,* indications are you are definitely not ready for retirement at this time. If this decision seems reasonable to you, you may want to let matters rest as they are for the moment. However, if you're really interested in retiring early, you may want to take steps that can improve the retirement possibilities for you. I've already emphasized the importance of the financial factor, but if, for instance, the matter of housing is particularly important, you may want to consider the actions that can change the picture so that your situation in this respect will be satisfactory well before you reach mandatory retirement age.

Finally, keep in mind that the situation with respect to one or more of the factors may well change. You may want to come back and recheck the factors. Where your situation has changed significantly, you will come up with a new score that may suggest the time is ripe to retire.

3
RETIREMENT
PROGRAMS

Most companies, aware of the problems faced by retiring employees, try to supply some help by way of preparation for the move. The phrase "most companies" suggests that there are some organizations that make no such efforts. They perhaps feel that their employees, having benefited from their paychecks over the years, are capable of taking care of themselves when they end the employee-employer relationship. Their preretirement "program" might then be considered a certain amount of separation pay, possibly a gold watch or other such token, and a handshake.

Fortunately, few companies take this outdated view. The majority try to prepare employees facing the retirement phase of their lives by supplying a pension, financial information, and one or more items from a whole range of services.

● *Plans for the Self-Employed*

Before getting into the particulars of company retirement benefits, consider a group of individuals in a special situation. They are the self-employed: professionals such as doctors, lawyers, architects, freelance artists, and writers. In the same category are those who own an unincorporated business such as a gardening or snow-plowing service. The owner of an incorporated activity is likely to be the president, is an employee of the corporation, and is taxed accordingly.

Self-employed people, of course, may qualify for social security benefits, just as regular employees do. The former pay a self-employment tax which is usually about 1½ times as much as the employed person pays. For example, employees pay (in 1979) about 6 percent, which is matched by the employer. Self-employed persons in a sense are getting a bargain, because for their 9 percent they get the same coverage as employees get for 12: 6 from the employee, 6 from employer.

The same taxable income limit ($22,900 in 1979) is set for both employees and self-employed individuals. People who earn $400 a year or more and are employed may have to pay both forms of tax, if their earnings as employees do not reach the full taxable limit.

Self-employed individuals can add to social security benefits by setting up an Individual Retirement Account (if they work for an organization that has no retirement plan) or a Keogh Plan (if they are self-employed).

But for the large group of people working for an employer, benefits may go considerably further than those furnished by social security.

● *Corporate Programs*

To give you an idea of benefits that organizations provide and to help you put your benefit program in perspective, this chapter describes the offerings of several retirement programs. By learning about the efforts these organizations make to prepare those who are ending their working careers, you get a better idea of what your own needs might be. Also, it can be helpful to compare your organization's procedures to others to better appreciate what your program affords. And don't be disappointed if your employer's benefits are less than others. Benefits are part of a total "package." You may have been compensated in other ways—a larger paycheck, for example.

Bear in mind that organizations have their own needs and values and usually design their preretirement programs in line with these. And don't think that the size of an organization is a major factor in how little or how much effort and expense go into their retirement preparations. Small companies may do a good deal, large ones less.

The following descriptions will give you some idea of company planning.

EXXON CORPORATION

Exxon, a vast corporate entity with operations centered in oil and related products, offers the following information about the program for its office and affiliates located in New York City. Other affiliates use somewhat similar approaches with minor modifications.

Information and benefits brochure

Each year a benefits statement is prepared for every employee, outlining coverage under the various company plans. This statement includes an estimate of what their retirement income would be at normal retirement time. In addition, an employee may request a confidential estimate of his or her retirement income for a specific date—i.e., age—from the local benefits office. The staff of the benefits office is available to answer any questions that an employee may have in this regard.

Exxon also provides their employees with a clearly presented and illustrated brochure entitled, "How Your Benefits Work For You." Included in this general benefits brochure is a section on "When You Retire," which explains—and illustrates by means of charts—what the employee might expect if he or she were to retire at age 50 up to 64. Since mandatory retirement has been moved up to 70, Exxon, along with many other employers, will be updating this material.

Financial and tax information

When the decision is made to retire, the employee has an intensive session with a plan administrator to review the annuity income worksheet and the various options available. In practice, this is a question-and-answer period to make sure that the employee is aware of what his or her monthly income will be—apart from social security payments—and what alternatives he or she may elect with respect to this income. The employee continues to meet with the plans administrator until retirement plans are final.

Exxon also assists its employees in the area of taxes. Employees are given the option to meet with an attorney in the tax department who specializes in the benefits area. The tax situation relative to the company benefit plans is reviewed.

Medical review

The employee has a preretirement examination by the company physician. Any specific health questions or conditions are discussed and the employee is counseled on obtaining assistance, medication, and so on.

Postretirement statement

After the employee retires, a brochure is prepared based on the individual's own situation, including further tax information, health insurance information, and a summary of insurance coverage under the Exxon program.

AN EXXON SPOKESPERSON COMMENTS:

Our experience has been that the employee's concerns focus on a few major topics: survivor protection, continuing medical coverage and tax questions, particularly if they are retiring from overseas service. In addition, we often are asked about Social Security benefits and Medicare, and we provide booklets outlining these programs to the employee. We find we are asked relatively few questions about leisure time activities, lifestyle changes or second careers. Generally, our employees have their plans well-established in these areas and the decision to retire has been an integral part of this planning.

A PUBLISHING COMPANY

An organization considerably smaller than Exxon has a retirement program in keeping with its policies and traditions. Here are the elements that make up the preparation.

Preliminary letter

In advance of retirement—about six months—the employee is reminded of the specific date. Prior to this time, employees have the privilege of contacting the personnel department to make inquiries about the projected amount of pension payable at various retirement ages. This would hold for vested employees only. As a follow-up to the formal notification, the head of the personnel department sends a personal letter to the employee:

> Dear Bill:
> I've been advised that you will be retiring as of December 1, 19___, and although it is still a long way off, I want to extend my best wishes for a happy retirement.

Al Williams will be in touch with you shortly to outline and explain relevant details. He will be available to answer any questions you may have, and you should feel free to contact him at any time.

December is still a long way off, but even at this early date, I'd like to express my thanks for your years of service and dedication to the company. A large measure of the respected image of this organization is due to your efforts and achievements and each of us who now benefit from that, thank you.

Best regards,
Fred

Notification of benefits

The individual in charge of the benefits program in turn sends a letter detailing the benefits the employee will receive or the options from among which choices must be made. This letter is presented in full because it spells out typical provisions and choices available to the retiree.

Mr. William Newell
78 Queen Street
New York, N.Y. 10047

Dear Bill:

I'd like to follow up on Fred Metzger's letter to you dated June 9. Further, I'd like to echo the sentiments of thanks and admiration that I'm certain I share with everyone at the Institute.

What follows is a fairly complete outline of the relevant matters connected with your official retirement as of December 1. If any questions arise concerning the items covered here, please feel free to contact me.

Pension. You may elect either a regular pension, called Life Annuity, or one of four other options. All five options are detailed in the enclosed "Definition of Pension Plan Optional Forms of Payment." I have estimated your pension under the various options, based upon Mrs. Newell being named your contingent annuitant, projecting your earnings through the month of November, and assuming your Social Security retirement benefit will be $430 monthly. Since you are the beneficiary of the Retirement Plan's minimum benefit formula, the last named item is rather important: your Life Annuity will decrease by 75% of your Social Security benefit in excess of $430 monthly, and the various options likewise will be lowered proportionately. Although I was careful to estimate your pension as accurately as present data permits, all my figures are subject to final verification by the Pension Plan administrators and trustees.

Pension Option	*Estimated Amount*
Life Annuity	$840/month
10 Years Certain & Continuous	775/month
50% Contingent Annuitant	645/month
75% Contingent Annuitant	580/month
100% Contingent Annuitant	525/month

Your first pension check covering the month of December 19___ should reach you on or about January 1. Subsequent check mailings are timed to arrive around the beginning of each month thereafter.

At your early convenience, please send me your birth certificate. If you select an option other than Life Annuity, send me your beneficiary's birth certificate too. And if your beneficiary or contingent annuitant is Mrs. Newell, I'll also need your marriage license or certificate. All of these documents must be "official;" i.e., they must be embossed with a raised seal by the issuer. These documents will be returned to you shortly after you retire.

Enclosed are two forms for you to complete, sign, and return to me. One of them requires the signature of a witness, a function I'll be happy to fulfill if you wish. The items are fairly self-explanatory, and some have been filled in for you. Any item that calls for an amount to be paid should be left blank at this time, since the final confirmed figure will have to be entered. The two forms are:

1. Trustee Notification of Payment
2. Option Selection

Social Security retirement benefits. About 2½ to 3 months prior to December 1, ask your nearest Social Security office for a determination letter that states what your Social Security pension will be as of December 1. When you receive it please forward that letter to me. It must be submitted to the Retirement Plan officials along with the other documents.

Medicare. During your visit to the Social Security office, be certain to apply for *both* Part A *and* Part B of Medicare. Part B requires a small monthly payment and is not granted automatically. This is especially important since our group health coverage is integrated with all of Medicare. In other words, our coverage will pay for otherwise covered expenses only after the application of *both* parts of Medicare, even if you have only *Part A.* Although it is many years off, the same applies to Mrs. Newell when she reaches age 65.

Health coverage. The group health insurance that you have now for yourself will be continued after your retirement at no cost to you. You also may continue group health coverage for Mrs. Newell by paying the group premium for dependent coverage. These payments are made in advance for periods no shorter than a calendar quarter. Your cost would always be the actual group cost, and would increase or decrease as the group cost changed. You will be notified of payments due and whether the cost has changed. The current group cost is $59.80 per month. If you want dependent coverage on Mrs. Newell to continue, your check for $59.80 to cover the remainder of 1978's last quarter, should be forwarded at the end of November.

Life and Accidental Death and Dismemberment (AD&D) insurance coverage. AD&D stops when you cease to be an employee on November 30. Group life insurance stops after your last day worked, too, except for a 1-month period of extended coverage. During this 1-month grace period you may convert your group life coverage into an individual policy. If you wish to avail yourself of this conversion feature, let me know and I'll be happy to provide the required forms.

LTD. Your Long Term Disability (LTD) Income Protection Plan stops automatically on your 65th birthday, and there is no conversion feature.

To summarize briefly:

1. Complete and sign the two pension forms as soon as possible, and return them to me.
2. Send me your birth certificate at your earliest convenience. If you select other than the Life Annuity, also send me your beneficiary's birth and marriage certificates.
3. Apply for your Social Security retirement benefits some time in September in order to generate an entitlement letter.
4. Be certain to apply for *both* parts of Medicare in September.
5. Let me know if you'll be continuing dependent group health coverage for Mrs. Newell. If so, let me have your check for the remainder of the year before your retirement date.
6. If you are interested in converting your group life insurance to an individual policy, let me know before the end of the grace period.

Thank you for taking the time to review these matters. Timely responses regarding the items detailed in this letter will help assure that your wishes are carried out and that payments to you will be made promptly when due. And if you have any questions, I'll be happy to answer them for you.

Cordially,

Manager,
Compensation & Benefits

Pension options

Of special interest are the choices the retiring employee has as to the particular form in which pension payments are to be made.

The choices as given below obviously have different appeals for different people. Here are the five options the publishing company makes available, and some explanation of their benefits and disadvantages.

LIFE ANNUITY.   The largest amount payable; pays the retiree for life; no payments to anyone following retiree's death unless in the form of refund of unused employee contributions.

TEN-YEAR CERTAIN & CONTINUOUS.   Pays less than life annuity for the lifetime of the retiree; if retiree's death occurs before 120 monthly payments have been made following early or normal retirement, the remainder thereof will be paid to the retiree's beneficiary.

50% CONTINGENT ANNUITANT.   Pays less than 10 C & C for the retiree's lifetime; after retiree's death continues payments to a designated contingent annuitant for his/her lifetime in an amount equal to 50 percent of what the retiree was receiving.

75% CONTINGENT ANNUITANT.   Pays less than 50 percent C.A. for the retiree's lifetime; after retiree's death continues payments to a designated contingent annuitant for his/her lifetime in an amount equal to 75 percent of what the retiree was receiving.

100% CONTINGENT ANNUITANT.   Pays less than 75 percent C.A. for the retiree's lifetime; after retiree's death continues payments to a designated contingent annuitant for his/her lifetime in an amount equal to 100 percent of what the retiree was receiving.

A discussion with the administrator of your company's program will help you decide which option is best in your case. As a matter of interest, the most popular choice is the ten-year Certain and Continuous.

JOSEPH E. SEAGRAM & SONS

Joseph E. Seagram & Sons, distillers and nationwide distributors, have an interesting combination of in-house and outside materials provided for preretirees.

Seagram started rethinking its retirement program in 1970—although its pension plan has been in effect since 1933—and eventually developed procedures for the entire corporation, which has about 9000 employees and about 210 to 220 retirees each year.

In conversations with Employee Benefits Administrator L. W. Tieman, these figures were provided: Seagram in 1978 had 2650 retirees. This group breaks down as follows:

DISABILITY RETIREMENTS. People who stopped working because of physical or other disabilities.

EARLY RETIREMENTS. Individuals who stopped working in advance of mandatory retirement age.

SPECIAL EARLY RETIREMENTS. This is an interesting category. Seagram's made it possible for individuals to retire at a point where the combination of age and years of service totalled 85 years, as long as there was a minimum of 25 years of service. In other words, if an individual worked for Seagram for 25 years, at which point he or she is 60, he or she can retire with a full pension. Similarly, the combination of age and service could be 30 years of service at age 55, and so on.

VESTED TERMINATION. These are employees who had worked for the company at least ten years and had reached retirement age.

Basically, the Seagram program consists of brochures explaining the financial and insurance benefits provided for retirees. Any questions individuals may have about their retirement situation are handled by personal interviews with people in the benefits department.

In addition to the organization's own procedures and materials, Seagram's sends to retirees a program procured from an outside source entitled, "The Retirement Planning Workshop." This outside program is intended to provide information in key areas involved in preretirement planning and living.

The three letters sent out by L. W. Tieman to employees who are approaching retirement offer further information to help retirees think through their individual situations.

Communication I

Dear Mr./Ms. _____:

As each enrolled member of the Pension Plan approaches age 60, the Company prepares retirement information for his benefit. The following is to remind you that:

1. Your normal retirement date is _____. Our records indicate your date of birth to be _____ and the date of your continuous service with the Company as _____. If there are any questions about these dates, the problem must be resolved promptly.

2. We estimate your normal retirement pension, without options, will be approximately $____ per year or $____ per month. We will be glad to do estimates with options if you wish. To do so, we need the name and birthdate of the beneficiary.

3. During retirement, Life Insurance in effect[*] will be:

$_____ @ Present Coverage
$_____ @ _____
$_____ @ _____
$_____ @ _____
$_____ @ _____

4. At age 65, you will be eligible to participate in the Retirement Major Medical Plan. Prior to age 65, the annual premium is $200 per year for you and your spouse, payable to Joseph E. Seagram & Sons, Inc. At age 65, the premium is reduced to $100 per year for each and is deducted from the remaining Life Insurance in effect.

Retirement Major Medical is designed to pick up expenses not covered by Medicare and, therefore, will not duplicate any benefits paid for or provided by any local, State or Federal medical program.

You should read the Retirement Group Life Insurance and Retirement Medical Program sections of "Your Benefit Program Manual." Please pay particular attention to the Life Insurance Conversion Privilege under the Group Insurance coverage.

All other Group Insurance coverage, except those mentioned above, terminate at the end of the month in which your termination of employment occurs.

5. We are also enclosing a booklet; "Social Security Benefits" which explains additional information regarding Social Security and Medicare benefits.

If you have questions regarding the above, please do not hesitate to let us know.

Very truly yours,

Supervisor, Employee Pensions

---

[*]This chart gives the employee the amounts by which coverage decreases at designated ages.

Communication II

Dear

To assist you in planning for your retirement years, the Company has enrolled you in the Retirement Planning Workshop. This free program, which consists of a series of mailings over a one-year period, is designed to provide you with specific information necessary in planning for your retirement. [It is published by the Bureau of Business Practice, a division of Prentice-Hall.]

The mailings will cover five major areas: MONEY, HEALTH, ACTIVITIES, LIVING ARRANGEMENTS and PERSONAL GUIDANCE.

You will receive a Program binder and the first installment of the subscription in September. In addition, a permanent reference section containing important information about Social Security and taxes will be included.

We feel you will find this Program of value, particularly since it will answer many of your questions and assist you in developing your retirement plans in an organized manner to meet your personal needs. If you have any questions after receiving the initial information or any time during the coming years, please feel free to let us know.

Very truly yours,

Employee Benefits Administrator

Communication III

Dear Associate:

As previously advised, the Company has enrolled you in the Retirement Planning Workshop. This Program is intended to provide you with an organized approach to planning for your retirement.

Enclosed is the Workshop binder and initial portfolio. Over the next two years you will also be receiving additional portfolios. As you read and use the Workshop, you will find it an invaluable aid in planning for your retirement years.

If you should have any questions or need any assistance in using the Workshop, please feel free to contact this office. Also, we would welcome hearing your opinion of the Program.

Sincerely,

Employee Benefits Administrator

Although Seagram has long experience in the benefits area, and its program seems to be working well, as suggested earlier, it continues to explore ways to improve coverage, especially services that can help retirees make it across the goal line better prepared for their post-retirement life.

SANDOZ, INC.

Sandoz, Inc., a pharmaceutical and chemical company headquartered in East Hanover, New Jersey, offers a unique service to its pre-retirement employees—comprehensive counseling aimed at providing a clear picture of their finances. This includes projections—two years, five years, and so on—into the future, based on income as available at those times.

In addition to the counseling element, the entire preretirement program at Sandoz consists of three elements: (1) seminars, (2) literature service, and (3) financial counseling.

Seminars

In the seminars, relevant subjects are presented to stimulate awareness on the part of the preretirees of what lies ahead. These subjects include health in retirement, Social Security and Medicare benefits, legal affairs, financial planning, and psychological adjustment to retirement. AIM (Action for Independent Maturity) booklets are given to all seminar participants as background reading material. Both lectures and discussions are used, as the Administrator considers appropriate.

Literature service

The literature service consists of a broad range of materials, dealing with all aspects of retirement. Books, brochures, and pamphlets are augmented by clippings from newspapers and magazines. All this material, catalogued and filed, is made available to employees on request.

Financial counseling

The financial counseling program (initiated by John Thummel, formerly Senior Vice President and Chief Financial Officer of Sandoz, and now the Financial Counselor) goes into a broad spectrum of personal financial situations. And since no two personal financial situations are identical, the approach must be tailored to the individual being counseled.

Since a complete financial analysis requires disclosure of personal information not otherwise available to any company official, and to create rapport between the employee and the financial counselor, Sandoz has provided an organizational structure that insures confidentiality. This necessitates separating the financial counseling function from any influence by or reporting to corporate officials and/or headquarters. Therefore, Sandoz has an independent Financial Counseling Office, separated from the corporate structure, guaranteeing employees that their personal information will remain confidential. Employees may, on their own initiative, approach the counseling office without the knowledge of the employer. This gives the employee the freedom to ask questions that otherwise might be held back—such as the possibility of early retirement. Retirement at any age can now be investigated without fear of repercussions.

With employees having access to a counselor who will spell out in clear terms their present financial situation, with projections into the distant future, they can plan for that future, making informed judgments concerning the *time* of retirement.

The counseling consists of three parts:

1. General information on financial matters. Employees are told of their vested rights in benefits.

2. Direct consideration and review of the individual's situation, present and future. Every aspect of personal finance of interest to the employee is discussed.

3. As a result of financial counseling, areas of interest may be disclosed that are outside the financial counselor's activity. If the employee likes, outside professional experts may be engaged, such as an insurance broker, investment counselor, attorney, or tax expert.

The Sandoz program—especially the financial counseling portion—is considered highly successful. Its effectiveness seems to be based on three factors:

1. It is voluntary. (Perhaps the location of the Financial Counseling Office explains its popularity. It is on company premises and available during, as well as outside, working hours.)

2. It is available to employees at all levels, from rank-and-file to management.

3. It is unique in providing financial understanding that can be a major assist to employees seeking financial preparedness before leaving the company.

EQUITABLE LIFE ASSURANCE SOCIETY

This insurance organization, which operates throughout the United States, administers its retirement program through the Career Planning Division. Essentially, Equitable uses a two-phase program:

Phase I

Here is the description as provided by Carol Van Sickle, Director of the Career Planning Division:

This part of the program, provided by our Benefits Administration Division, covers specifics regarding the employee's Equitable benefits. Employees are initially contacted at age 52½, at which time they are advised of their right to elect the Pre-Retirement Survivor Benefit. At age 59½, and again at 61½, they are furnished with estimates of their retirement income at age 65 (based on their current salary), as well as group insurance information; this is repeated approximately 4 months prior to age 65, with the addition of Investment Plan data including a description of the optional forms of pay-out available for Investment Plan funds and an explanation of the Federal Income Tax rules applicable to each type of pay-out.

Benefits Consultants conduct personal interviews with Home Office employees. Employees located outside New York are encouraged to write or call the Consultants if they have any questions. All correspondence and consultations are treated as highly confidential.

Another source of individualized benefit information is the annual Benefit Report issued to all employees. The Benefit Report is a large computer-printed form which provides specific figures under a variety of headings: annual salary; estimated annual average cost to Equitable for your benefits (This item included cost of vacations, personal days and holidays, cost of group insurance program, retirement plan, investment plan, and Social Security, and a miscellaneous item. These fringe benefits to the employee paid for by Equitable represented in one case about 30 percent of an employee's annual salary.); health insurance; projected monthly retirement income; death benefits; and investment plan accounts.

Employees are encouraged to contact the Career Planning Division for clarification of any items on the Benefits Report.

Employees who are interested in early retirement may request benefit information pertinent to the date of their choice. Last year a total of 178 employees retired; 96 were early retirement.

Employees continue to maintain contact with the Benefits Consultants after retirement. Last year there were 2400 post-retirement inquiries concerning a variety of subjects: lost checks, change of address, beneficiary changes, Medicare claim procedures, etc.

Phase II

Equitable offers its preretirees a retirement planning seminar which is produced by an outside organization, AIM (Action for Independent Maturity) which is an affiliate of AARP (American Association of Retired Persons).

The AIM program gives the preretirees the opportunity to participate and discuss problem areas or areas of their interest. These discussions—conducted by a trained leader—are with people who have similar concerns and interests.

The AIM program covers eight aspects of retirement:

1. The Challenge of Retirement
2. Health and Safety
3. Housing and Location
4. Legal Affairs
5. Attitude and Role Adjustments
6. Meaningful Use of Time
7. Sources of Income
8. Financial Planning

This is strictly a voluntary program, available to employees age 50 or over, in the home office or in locations outside New York. The discussion leaders are Equitable people, principally retirees, who have been trained by AIM. Resource authorities on the various topics include Equitable specialists and representatives of outside agencies such as the Social Security Administration.

Director Van Sickle says, "On the whole our employees seem to like the AIM program. In locations outside New York we get quite a lot of spouse participation. For some reason, this doesn't happen in our New York Office."

The Equitable retirees seem to particularly appreciate the presence of resource authorities who can be called on for specific information and guidance in any one of the eight areas that are covered.

However, AIM has instructed the Resource people to encourage participants to seek out experts, authorities, or professionals to help them with specific problems in their own communities rather than accept their statements as the last word.

"Finally," Director Van Sickle says, "our discussion leaders for the most part are retired employees. This has two advantages: It gives several retirees an interesting assignment, and it allows people nearing retirement a chance to hear from someone who is already experiencing that lifestyle."

● *Your Options and Responsibilities*

TAKING ADVANTAGE OF YOUR COMPANY'S PROGRAM

Whether the organization that employs you has a limited or extensive program, or one that is somewhere in between, make the effort to get maximum mileage from whatever is offered. Here are some of the things you can do.

Learn what is offered

It's a wise move, regardless of your age, to get some idea of what your organization offers in the way of a preretirement program and retirement benefits.

Many companies have printed material that tells pretty much the whole story. Get the brochure or other material, read it, and ask for clarification of any parts of the program you don't understand.

In some cases, an employee handbook describes retirement benefits in general terms. Thinking about your own situation and interests, project yourself into the retirement situation and pinpoint questions that the handbook doesn't spell out: What happens to your health insurance on retirement? What about life insurance? Does the organization have any postretirement benefits or services?

Participate early

One or two decades ago, even organizations with relatively advanced ideas considered six months or a year sufficient time for employees to actively start thinking about retirement. But the trend has been to increase the period—to two, three, or five years. When the retirement age was still 65, many firms invited employees at the age of 55 to start, at least in a preliminary way, their preretirement indoctrination. With the mandatory retirement age boosted to 70, it is likely that 55 will still be a popular age at which to get employees to start retirement preparation. Among other reasons, this advance briefing makes it possible for those who are considering early retirement to give this option some realistic thought. One benefits administrator I talked to told me "We've had people under 30 asking permission to attend our financial seminars. We're glad to have them."

Early participation is advisable because it encourages hard-headed thinking about your finances, frequently *the* key to retirement planning. If the organization, through printed material, lectures, or seminars, covers the subject of finances, it can help you firm up your plans for making retirement at whatever age practical. It may suggest changes in your saving practices, or a new tack in investments.

Other areas covered—health, housing arrangements, and family considerations—also can be brought into focus, and thought through in terms of anticipating problems and offsetting them, as opposed to trying to wrestle with them only when they confront you and have become crucial because they are at your doorstep, here and now.

Keep up-to-date

Changes may take place in two areas: the nature of the organization's retirement program, and in your own status. In the latter instance, for example, you may get a promotion and a higher salary. This usually means a higher pension and possible shifts in your planning.

Organizations that alter programs these days usually add features, services, and benefits. While such improvements will no doubt be publicized among all employees, again there may be some aspects that affect you personally that you may want to get clarified. Don't hesitate to ask either your boss, or if he or she suggests it, the appropriate person in the Benefits Department, who can spell out just what the changes mean in your case.

Meetings, seminars, lectures

A benefits administrator told me, "We ran a series of lectures for our preretirees. Attendance was voluntary, and the notice was run in our house organ. I was startled to find, among the fifty or so people who attended, a young engineer of twenty-eight. He told me he was interested because his father was about to retire, and he wanted to know what the whole business was about. But he made no secret of the fact that he was also interested for himself. 'I'm going to retire some day,' he said."

The fact is that people who haven't been exposed to retirement—either because a member of the family or friend has retired, or through reading—may have only the foggiest notion of what it means in practical terms. The earlier you get a clear idea of the kind of things a preretirement program covers, the better you will be able to adjust your thinking as retirement becomes a consideration for yourself or a member of your immediate family.

Counseling

If your organization provides a counseling service that can help you start thinking about your plans, by all means take advantage of it. In most cases, the counseling will be limited to financial matters, social security, pensions, taxes and so on. These, of course, are vital, and getting expert opinion can make your preparations just that much more effective.

There are some areas where the average person definitely can benefit from guidance. How will you take your pension payments? Some people, because of their financial situation, have opted for a lump sum, and have had approval from the organization. More often, the choice lies among these: Life Annuity; Ten-Year Certain and Continuous; 50 percent Contingent Annuitant; 75 percent Contingent Annuitant; 100 percent Contingent Annuitant. Each of these pays out different monthly sums, and each has advantages and disadvantages. Which is best suited to your needs? The benefits administrator or someone on the staff can explain the pros and cons so that you can make the most suitable choice.

In some organizations, counseling may take in other important matters, such as health, housing, possibly family relationships, and any emotional problems that may be aggravated by the retirement situation. Counseling help lies as much in providing the individual with an opportunity for clarifying questions and problems as it does in getting positive guidance. As a matter of fact, most counselors see their role as supportive and problem-spotting, rather than in "telling people what to do."

Resolving problems

Few retirements, or preretirement periods, are problem-free. As mentioned, finances and health are two major factors that may force you to make a retirement decision different from that anticipated. Keep a sharp eye out for developments or complications that may influence your thinking. And, as much as possible, use your organization's personnel and services to help you minimize difficulties.

For example, George Hirsch planned to retire at 67. He and his wife lived in a mortgage-free home in a neighborhood that they had been a part of for years. A combination of pension benefits and Social Security, plus savings, promised to take care of their money needs. But catastrophe struck in the form of a devastating fire that destroyed their home. Insurance only covered part of the loss, and personal belongings—clothes, furniture, and so on—couldn't be replaced.

George had a couple of interviews with his boss and the head of personnel, and it was arranged that he would continue working at his old job for at least a couple of years, a move that would improve their finances and assist them in working out a new living arrangement.

For another example, Greta Hynes' husband retired a year before she did, just long enough for her to realize that both of them being home at the same time would be difficult. "We'd be fighting all the time," Greta told the company counselor.

To reassure her, and alleviate the problem over the long haul, the counselor suggested that she plan to stay in her job for another six months. And during that period, he helped her work out a system for planning her and her husband's time in order to minimize possible friction.

Optimizing your work time

Both your boss and people in personnel are interested in seeing to it that you wind up your job on a high note. "I'd rather go out with a bang than a whimper," is the way one preretiree put it.

Nothing can be as enervating and uncomfortable for an active person who has been a good worker, than to not have sufficient work to be kept busy. From the employer's viewpoint, this situation is doubly undesirable: not only is someone being paid a full salary for partial work, but also the example can be demoralizing for other employees.

So for your own sake—your own feelings of self worth and your image in the eyes of long-time colleagues—try to arrange for a satisfactory workload and meaningful contribution right up to the end. Don't let some well-intentioned, but misguided, boss feel it is a kindness to let you "take it easy." Boredom isn't easy. Having nothing to do can be the hardest of all.

Partial retirement

If you're interested, explore options for "partial" retirement. When you retire, your pension is payable no matter what you do or don't do in the way of work, but if your earnings are substantial, your Social Security payments will be affected.

With this financial situation in mind, you may nevertheless be interested in continuing some form of employment with your present organization. It would be wise to discuss the matter well in advance of retirement. For one thing, company policy may prohibit such an arrangement, in which case you should know about it and consider alternative plans. Another consideration: if you are not to continue in your old job, but in either a tailored version of it or possibly a job elsewhere in the organization, arrangements may have to be made in advance.

Again, your boss and other people in the organization should be consulted, so that you can get enough information to understand what you can be offered, and weigh its attractiveness against other options. The following section examines some possibilities.

● Continuing to Work

Some people may—for good and sufficient reason—want to defer full retirement. The extension of the mandatory retirement age from 65 to 70 may put more individuals in this category, and the likelihood that eventually there will be no mandatory retirement age gives the employee even greater leeway in planning for retirement. If you are interested in remaining a wage earner past what might otherwise be considered a retirement point, here are some possibilities.

STAYING ON

Your present employer agrees that you continue on the payroll past the traditional retirement age. The organization policy may be, "We shall feel free to keep in their jobs employees whose services cannot be easily replaced, or who, for one reason or another, it is mutually desirable to continue in employment."

This has been the rationale that makes it possible for one company to retain the services of a virtually irreplaceable marketing vice president; another to keep on the roster a mechanic and model-maker who has been working wonders in its research and development shop for decades; another to retain the manager of the cafeteria, who is as much a part of the organization as the foundation stone. "We'd never find another Helen Valenti," the personnel director says. "She has been keeping us all healthy and happy for years. We all want that to continue."

PHASED RETIREMENT

This approach is becoming increasingly popular. Sears, Roebuck & Co., along with many other companies large and small, is trying out programs in which employees over 65 work reduced hours. From the organization viewpoint, phased retirement eases the transition to full retirement, and creates more opportunities for less-experienced workers.

In some cases, the phasing starts well before the mandatory retirement age. In addition to reduced hours in the work week, organizations also modify responsibilities, which has the effect of easing the load. For example, a west coast advertising agency had been looking into ways in which it could keep copychief Rick Wade on the job, but relieve him of some of the job pressures. Eventually they agreed that he would continue to write copy for some key accounts and be available to join in planning sessions for new campaigns. However, his responsibilities as department head, including that of supervising the other copy writers, would be transferred to a new person who would be put in charge.

INDEPENDENT CONTRACTING

Some organizations enforce their retirement policy strictly. To avoid controversy and ill feeling, they make no exceptions. Retirement is mandatory—for clerks, department heads, executives, and the president as well—at age 70. A few of these companies have developed a policy that makes it possible for some people whose services are considered highly desirable to remain past retirement doing work similar to their old jobs. They stay not as company employees, but as independent contractors. The sample commitment following illustrates how one company proceeds.

Mr. Peter Rovenna
Home Address
Chicago, Ill.

Dear Peter:

The following describes our agreement whereby The X Engineering Company engages you in an independent contractor capacity as design engineer and consultant on related engineering matters.

We agree that you will render services in this capacity during the period of this agreement for not less than 909 hours or more than 1,364 hours, except that the minimum will be reduced upon mutual agreement or the event of your illness or incapacity.

Except for brief project-related conferences and consultations, your presence will not be required on company premises. Your hours of work and place will be of your own choosing. No supervision of your work is contemplated. However, for your convenience, office space and access to library and other materials and services will be provided at our home office.

We agree that your fee is $21.33 per hour, subject to increase by that percentage by which the maximum salary paid your job category is next increased. Any such increase shall, in your case, become effective for services performed on or after the Monday following announcement of maximum salary increase. Your fee shall be paid within one week after your billing.

You will not serve in any capacity for any enterprise in direct competition with our organization or its affiliates, but your other employments or relationships shall not be considered inconsistent with this agreement.

This agreement is effective December 1, 1980 and will terminate November 30, 1981, and is renewable subject to mutual agreement.

Your acceptance by signing in the space below will constitute our agreement.

Very truly yours,
The X Company

Accepted:

_____ by_____

Employee   Department Head

ANOTHER JOB

Some people want to continue to work, but the choice of continuing with their present employer is blocked for any one of a number of reasons.

The employee himself or herself may not want to continue the association in any form, or the prospect of a job with another organization may be "too good to refuse." Or the company may have a mandatory retirement policy that it doesn't want to modify, for fear that once exceptions are made, or precedents set, the policy will become impossible to enforce.

Whatever the reason, the retired person wants to continue in a money-earning activity. In some cases, this may be seen as a second career, a name and concept that is very attractive to those whose feelings—and they can range all over the lot—may be summed up by the sentence, "I'm just not ready to retire."

For people in this category, the following considerations may be useful and relevant.

If you believe it is possible for you to get a high-paying position that, along with your pension, will permit you to live in a more desirable way than you could with a pension and Social Security (which you won't be able to collect if your earnings are substantial), then you are on the right track.

Perhaps your real reason is a true love of work. I have always maintained that the world of work has a tremendous amount to offer in the way of meaningful and rewarding challenges, as well as stimulating activity and contacts with people.

A certain number of people see in retirement a termination of many desirable things, and the possible start of a less satisfactory kind of life. Let's be realistic. For some people it may be. A small number of people—even at this late date, when so much more is known about successful retirement—fail to find all the ingredients of a full life in their post-working years. But this is a small group and, for the most part, they are the ones who have failed to prepare adequately for the change. And another job may simply postpone the crisis.

If you or any friend or relative falls into this category, reassure him or her that most fears of this type are unfounded. There is no difficulty that results from retirement alone that cannot be eliminated or minimized by some action developed by an enlightened approach. To those who hesitate on the threshold of retirement, beset by doubts and fears, a reassuring note summed up in a comic line popular some years ago: "Try it, you'll like it."

4
LEAVING YOUR JOB

Feelings about the last days on the job will vary widely. Some retirees will scarcely be able to repress their joy; others will have difficulty disguising their gloom. (Let's hope that latter group is a small minority.) Chances are, most people's feelings will lie somewhere in the middle range. This group also includes a number who, if they were honest, would have to admit that they're not sure how they feel or how they're supposed to feel.

In addition to your mood on the last of your working days, the nature of your job and your relationships with your colleagues are also factors. But whatever the situation, there are two ways in which you can sever your occupational bonds: You could ease out quietly. There's certainly nothing wrong with this course. Many people take it. They "don't want to make a fuss," feeling that it's no big deal. They make minimum preparations for their departure and simply leave after taking care of the formalities.

On the other hand, some people, because of their feelings and situation in the company, feel their leaving is an event which requires a good deal of activity on their part.

You needn't make a choice between these two courses of action. Obviously you will favor the one that is most appropriate for you, if you have strong feelings. A compromise—pulling out *half* the ceremonial stops—may be for you.

However, the actual business of separating yourself from the organization with which you've been affiliated—probably for many years—does have many elements, and certainly you don't want to leave behind any unfinished business.

Accordingly, view the items below as suggested points for you to consider. Apply the ones that are appropriate, and modify or adapt them as your situation dictates.

● *Final Considerations*

Your organization will want to "process" you. This usually means one or more visits to personnel, the benefits office, and so on. (Aspects of this subject have been covered in Chapter 3 and you will find related information in Chapter 9.)

Be sure to give the meetings and procedures involved in finishing your employment all the time and attention required. It's not just a matter of being cooperative, but of being sure you're not missing any bets. These matters tended to, you can now turn to everything else.

A PERSONAL LEGACY

Your work

Perhaps your workload has tapered off and your responsibilities officially ended sometime before D (Departure)-Day. If this hasn't been the case, make sure that there are no matters that you have failed to turn over to your boss or replacement. For your own sake as well as theirs, it's nice to be able to leave with the feeling that you have cleaned things up in an orderly and satisfactory way.

Everyone has something special that he or she brings to the job or has developed over the years. It may be a unique way of doing things—special methods, insights, ways of handling particular problems.

In some cases your special ways may have been recorded in the form of workbooks, personal procedure manuals, and so on. Give some thought to what you want to do with these ideas or materials. Perhaps you may decide to have these go with you. But if you make the opposite decision, then plan to take the steps that will get the materials or ideas to the people who will benefit from them most.

Expressing appreciation

Over the years you have probably acquired a group of "fans," or at any rate people who worked with you, for you, were on your side, perhaps pushed your interests in the organization. You may want to send individual notes or memos to these individuals. Or perhaps you just want to stop in at their desks or offices to express your gratitude, good wishes, and so on.

Smoothing over rough spots

Perhaps in your relationships there were some who were less than friendly. There may even be some individuals with whom you've had some hard words, and towards whom you still feel somewhat antagonistic. Should you, at the moment of leave-taking, try to settle old scores, get in a last word, or possibly do the more constructive and reasonable thing of making it clear that bygones are bygones?

Let me put it to you this way. If your impulses are in the latter category—that is, if you feel that you can smile, shake hands, and say something like, "Well, George, it's too bad we weren't better friends . . ."—by all means act on that impulse. But if at this late date you still harbor a grudge, possibly for the best of reasons, you may decide to signal your displeasure one way or another—snubbing the individual in a chance encounter in the corridor, for example. If that's your mood and intention, think twice before taking action. Here's why:

One of the good things about retirement is that you can leave an organization with a happy feeling of closure. You leave with a reputation well established, or at the very least, you have wiped the slate clean. Harboring ill will at this stage of the game, and making it clear that you do, is only warranted if the affronts or event which caused your feeling is absolutely unforgivable. You be the judge.

Confirming friendships

The average person has developed a whole range of relationships. There are people—even after years of working in an organization—with whom you may only have a nodding acquaintance; there are those to whom the phrase "a good acquaintance" applies; then there are friends; and then there are very good friends, those you hope to continue to see after you leave. It's perfectly acceptable and even desirable that you personally see all the individuals with whom you have worked over the years. In some cases you need spend only a minute or two with them, time enough for only a handshake and a few pleasant words. Other relationships may suggest a longer visit. And then for the people that you hope to continue to see—and ex-colleagues and friends can be an important group in the social life of a retiree—you want to build bridges. Make it clear that you hope to keep up the contact and continue to see them off the job. What you say to these people is direct and sincere, quite different from the traditional general statement that retirees usually make and which is expected, although not necessarily, to be carried out.

Farewells

There are probably a number of individuals with whom you may not have worked directly but still had occasional, friendly contact, such as a secretary, an elevator operator, or a supervisor who is known only as a voice at the other end of a telephone line. It can be a very warm and welcome gesture to either visit or, if that's not convenient, to at least pick up a phone and call these people and say good-bye personally.

Odds and ends

Are there any formalities or obligations—usually minor—that you want to be sure to take care of before your actual departure?

Have you concluded all your business with personnel? Everything from final separation arrangements to providing your new address, if you are about to move?

Did you pay the cafeteria manager the dollar or so you owe for coffee on the cuff? Do you owe the office anything for personal phone calls? Does anybody owe you money?

Are there any people you meant to say so long to, but haven't as yet? Have you collected the home phone numbers and addresses of the people you would like to look up but for whom you don't have this information?

In raising all these questions and suggesting final touches you might want to consider, I haven't intended that you prolong the leavetaking. As Shakespeare said, "Stand not on the order of your going, but go at once." When you are ready to go, go. A big future is waiting for you out there.

PERSONAL BELONGINGS

Spend years on any job, and you can't help but accumulate all kinds of items. Some you use in your work, some are for office decoration, and others are purely personal mementoes you've brought in to add your own touch. Now that it is time to clear out you want to make a clean sweep.

A wise move is to start weeks in advance of the actual time of leavetaking. This helps you make unpressured decisions about key items and avoids a last-minute panic. The following system for your disposal problems may be of some help to you.

Keep

There are family pictures, your pipe rack, sports trophies, desk items, and knicknacks for the bookcase that you set store by or expect to use. If there are a number of these, and some are bulky, make the arrangements that will get them packed and shipped home.

Toss out

There are things that have no value to you or anybody else. They may be old records, reports, letters, or interoffice communications. Dump them. If there is any doubt—you may want to retrieve the letter of praise from the president for the way you stepped in and solved a problem that ended a vast organization headache—fish that out from your interoffice files, *then* dispose of everything else. Under this heading goes everything broken, unrepairable, of no interest, or obsolete. This category may involve some tough decision-making. Can you bring yourself to junk the report that brought you so much praise? And what about all those witty cartoons you have thumbtacked onto your bulletin board? It's your decision—but a word of advice: into the wastebasket. You don't want to start the new phase of your life overloaded with reminders of the past, no matter how glorious. Leave room for the new glories!

Return

Shakespeare advised, "Neither a borrower nor a lender be," but like so much good advice, it is often ignored. Ordinary business intercourse forces us to be both borrowers and lenders, and at clean-up time, you're almost sure to find a number of things that belong to colleagues. Books are especially likely candidates for this category. Usually no decisions have to be made: you simply return the item to the original owner.

And the Shakespearean quote does suggest a move you may want to make: recall all the loans *you've* made. If in the past you have handed over a prized ashtray and it has not been returned, now is the time to retrieve it and any other things you'd like to have returned.

Give away

This category also can hit the high numbers. Plants, books, pictures, or office equipment you may have purchased for your own use and no longer have a need for are candidates to be passed along to others in the office.

In some cases, a gift will be particularly appropriate for the beneficiary. Says one retiree who is cleaning up: "Charlotte, you have always liked that Matisse reproduction. Would you like to have it?" In another instance an executive handed over her attache case to her assistant: "Vera, now that your job has become important enough for you to develop brief-case-itis, perhaps you'll accept this case of mine. . . ."

One warning: don't let impulsive generosity prompt you to offer something to an individual who may be less than pleased to receive it. For example, think twice before offering an ailing plant. Or, the attache case mentioned above should not be tendered if it is in bad shape.

Sell

There may be things you want to dispose of that are surely good enough not to throw away, and for which you see no natural recipients as gifts. One art director put a sign on the wall outside his office door: "Garage Sale." And he had a number of things with price tags laid out on his drafting table. The sale turned into a lively occasion, where a good time was had by all, and the director ended up a few hundred dollars richer.

A caution here: though the sale idea can work well in some organizations, it would be frowned on in others. You judge whether the climate in your place would be conducive to selling some of your belongings. Of course, you needn't advertise. One mechanic who had tools in duplicate that he was willing to trade for cash simply let his colleagues know that he was willing to sell some of his tools, and business was brisk, friendly, and mutually satisfactory.

Buy

Consider the case of Joe Hawley of Linden, New Jersey. With his organization for thirty years, his desk was the same one he had when he started. He felt it practically belonged to him, and wanted to take it along with him. It was company property, but Hawley was attached to the "old oaken bucket," as he called it, and asked his boss if he could buy it from the company.

The answer he got was a smile and, "Joe, I can imagine the many associations you have with that old piece. Forgive me if I say, as an objective observer, that we should have replaced it for you ten years ago. If you want it, it's yours for the price of one dollar. And we'll be making a profit on the deal."

You may have some items that belong in the same category as Joe Hawley's desk: a piece of sculpture, a typewriter, or piece of furniture. Again, organizations and situations vary. If you think it is appropriate, ask for the item, or offer to pay for it if you feel that would be a consideration.

If, after you've gone as far as you can in the clean-up there are still some things left behind, such as files, furniture, or company-owned decorations, you may, as a courtesy, spend a few minutes with the person who is the next tenant in the office or workstation. In addition to handing over the office and its remaining contents, it is a gracious gesture to pass along keys for desk or file drawers, or for the entrance door to the office itself. Any tips you can give that will help anticipate difficulties will be welcome.

● *Last Days on the Job*

I talked to a number of people who were within a year or less of retirement. In our conversations, it became clear that in some cases a problem of idleness—being underloaded in terms of assignments— often arises.

While I had the impression that for most people, having nothing to do was an annoyance, tastes may differ. Certainly for the individual who enjoys relaxing on the job, who doesn't find a light workload unacceptable, this presents no problem. Just thank your lucky stars and your boss, and enjoy it.

But as I said, I had the strong impression that most people want to keep on going right up to the wire. They find a slack schedule wearing on the nerves. For these, then, some suggestions.

First, how does this come about? In some cases a well-meaning but miscalculating supervisor may precipitate this undesirable situation. In other instances, the employee may trigger the situation by sloughing off.

In this case his boss may think, "No point in cracking the whip for another few months. . . ."

Whatever the cause, the individual who faces the prospect of being at loose ends for several months, or even weeks, may become bored or frustrated by inactivity.

If this undesirable fate befalls you, here are some of the counter-measures you may want to consider to keep yourself active, involved, and happy during the months before your retirement.

Don't let your boss assume that you want to spend your last days on the job in idleness. Call your supervisor's attention to your need for a fuller schedule. One woman told her supervisor, "I know you think you're doing me a favor, Mr. Davis, but if I don't have something better to do than sit around, I'm not going to last to my retirement day."

If you want a fuller workload, you make a stronger case by suggesting specific tasks you would like to undertake: "That group working to develop a new filing system seems to have run into trouble. Do you think maybe I could lend a hand?"

If you seem to have trouble in contacting your boss or communicating your dissatisfaction, take on a task that you know needs doing. As long as it doesn't interfere with anyone else's work or step on toes, you'll have the satisfaction of developing your own pet project with all the interest and sense of achievement that such activity can bring.

"I was eager to help the person who was taking my job to catch on fast. I happened to know who it was and wished him well," said one of the preretirees with whom I discussed the problem. "My boss had expected to have me work with the replacement but had only assigned a few days to the training. I suggested that I could do a much more thorough job and there was really a lot to communicate, and so suggested a longer breaking-in period. My boss agreed, and I really enjoyed training that young fellow. To some extent it made me feel as though I was leaving a constructive part of myself behind, a kind of monument."

Another person I talked to said that his problem had come about because his boss had made arrangements for his departure somewhat prematurely. The result was there really *wasn't* anything left for him to do in the department.

"But then I suggested that I could pick up some of the liaison work, work with some of the other department heads in areas where there had been problems of communication and cooperation, and that gave me three months of new, challenging work that was really great."

One preretiree said, "I don't mind soldiering a bit on the job. I was going into another line of work and appreciated the rest, but I certainly didn't want to hang around, watching my old buddies working and feeling out of it. So, with my boss's permission, I just took off. After just a few hours on the job I'd take afternoons off, have lunch in the park, feed the pigeons, and then take in an early movie."

Several factors play a part in what you do about the closing weeks of your regime. Part of it depends on your own feelings, your need for activity or, for that matter, taking it easy. However, another part depends on how you want to look to your colleagues and others on the work scene. One such consideration showed up in the mind of a man who was retiring at the age of 69. "Funny thing, I'd been with the company many, many years and was always a good worker. But I felt that if my last days on the job were spent goofing off, that was the impression that I'd leave behind. And I'm darned if I wanted to ruin a reputation I'd built up over thirty years."

● *The Retirement Ceremony*

The business world has its own established ceremonies. Many of them are rites of passage. Like all rituals, these signal an event, either the beginning or the end of a particular cycle. For example, promotions also tend to have their ceremonial rite of passage—gatherings marked by eating, drinking, and speeches of greater or lesser length and color.

Perhaps of all the company ceremonies, those marking retirement can be the most emotional. Certainly for the retiree this is likely to be true. He or she stands firmly at the crossroads looking back at a long, memorable worklife, looking ahead to an unpredictable future, but one that will surely be different from the past.

When you stand at this crossroad you will be feeling your own emotions, thinking your own thoughts, and don't be surprised if the things you feel and think are quite different from what you expected. The actuality in this, as in most other things, is different from the expectation. It is hoped that your feelings will be positive and warm toward the organization and the people you are leaving. If this is the case you will find it a lot easier to fill the role which is yours, that of being the center of the retirement ceremony.

You probably will be the guest of honor at one or more celebrations. The people with whom you worked most closely may want to take you to lunch or dinner. The organization may want to celebrate the event by a cocktail party, dinner, or both.

Depending on the size of the organization, the guests may be limited to the department in which you worked, the division, or possibly the entire company roster. And some companies use the occasion of a retirement ceremony to invite past retirees, members of a 25-Year Club, and so on.

Most people who are about to leave are expected to fall in with the company tradition and plan, and most do, but you may have a choice of what ceremonies you want or don't want.

For example: Gene Cullen has worked for his organization for 20 years. His boss, head of the department, has told Gene he'd like to have a departmental lunch a few days before his departure, to celebrate. Gene is delighted and expects to enjoy the lunch to the utmost.

But then Gene is also approached by the personnel director, who suggests a cocktail party on the Wednesday night of his last week on the job. "We'll invite everyone in the division," he explains, "and we'll also invite some of the old-timers. . . ." But Gene has attended several events of this kind himself and has developed a rather dim view of them. For one thing, he has noticed that a certain percentage of the people show up just for the free drinks and buffet. Several he knows just stop in to kill time—they're taking a late train or going to the theater. And so, of all the people there, only a small percentage seem to really appreciate the ceremony for what it is. As a result, the atmosphere, as pleasant as it seems to be, is somewhat unconvincing. The hilarity and good fellowship have a kind of hollow ring. And so Gene decides to back off. He thanks the personnel director for the kind thought and suggests that if the PD feels the need for some kind of ceremony, it be smaller, more informal. "Fine," says the director, "we'll arrange for a get-together in Mr. Smith's office—just some old-timers. . . ." This is much more to Gene's taste.

AN EMPLOYER'S SPEECH

If there is to be some kind of ceremony which the brass will attend, it is customary and proper for a speech to be delivered, usually by the top person. The latter may give precedence to someone else if that person happens to have particularly close ties to the retiree.

At Sandoz, Inc., a retirement party was given for John Thummel, who had been chief financial officer of the organization. As leave-taking time approached, Thummel was asked to stay on doing the job he had requested—shaping the company's benefits program, with special attention to individual financial counseling for preretirees—a much-needed and gratifying service for those about to end their employment at Sandoz.

The eulogy for John Thummel was given by Dr. Albert Frey, President and Chief Executive Officer of Sandoz. Here it is in full, a good example of its kind:

Honored guests, friends, colleagues, ladies and gentlemen:

It is indeed a pleasure for me to be with all of you this evening and above all, to pay tribute to John Thummel in the presence of his lovely wife, Rosa, and their children, Gabriella, Randolph, and Carl.

Tonight we honor John as he steps from the active ranks to a new phase of life. We usually refer to this phase as "retirement," but that would hardly be the word in John's case. The fact is that he simply changes his activities from one major subject to another. As we all know, he has diligently prepared himself for this, in the famous Thummel style: Not to leave anything to chance and to plan ahead—not fearing, but welcoming change, as he always did!

As most of you already know, John will continue to stay within our ranks, in a consultant role, to assist and counsel other members of our company to prepare for this inevitable but important step in life—prudently—in a positive manner—and with pride. Who could do this better and with more understanding and stature than John? That he is willing to do this for our Company beyond the normal time frame deserves special mention and our most sincere thanks.

This prospective activity of John's will be the crown on top of an active and highly successful life which he has spent at the helm of Sandoz, U.S. We all know, without going into detail, that John has done outstanding work and we can also safely say, without exaggeration, that we would not be where we are today without John Thummel's outstanding contribution to this Company. In addition, and most importantly, John has achieved this in a most extraordinary way. The living proof of it is assembled right here in this room tonight—he achieved his goals through happy and satisfied people, whom he did not only treat as equal members of an effective team—but truly as his friends!

And here we all are, John, your friends, to express with this modest gathering how much we love you and how much we enjoyed working with you.

The human aspects of the business have always been John's highest priorities. No wonder that he was the leading architect of the fine benefit plans we enjoy today at Sandoz. He created them with diligence over the years—and sometimes against considerable odds. What he has done just in this segment for the good of every employee of Sandoz—and in doing so for the good of the Company—we shall never forget. Therefore I am sure you will agree with me that this is a very opportune occasion to express our special thanks to John for his untiring and successful efforts in this important segment.

John always had the vision to intelligently plan for the future and he was always stimulating change. Now here he is, facing a major change in life himself. We know he will master it brilliantly and state an example for us how to do it. Nevertheless, he will always remain a "manager." When I saw him organizing Rosa's Art Exhibit in New York just a week ago, I knew that John would never cease to be an entrepreneur—all he is doing now is changing his field of activity.

So it is with gratitude and a sense of regret that we see John take leave of our ranks. Gratitude—for his long and productive years of service—a record of which he can well be proud! Regret—because we shall lose him now as an active part of Sandoz.

John, once more our grateful thanks for your untiring efforts, your devotion to your colleagues and your Company, and for your many contributions which contributed so much to the well-being of us all.

Best wishes for your coming years of well-earned leisure—a lot of enjoyment—and best of health!

YOUR FAREWELL ADDRESS

Washington gave one, so why shouldn't you? If you are the guest of honor at any type of celebration, it's likely that there will be a certain amount of ceremony. Typically, there's a speech by your boss or other executive—laudatory, of course—and most likely the presentation of one or more gifts. Then, don't be surprised to find that you're the next speaker on the program. How should you respond?

Observing organizational celebrations over the years, it becomes clear that guests of honor have a unique opportunity to express their feelings in a way that will be pleasing to the audience and rewarding to themselves.

Typically, the guest of honor listens to the encomiums, accepts the gift, mutters a "Thank you very much," and the party continues. But such a response is often disappointing to an audience that would really like to feel the warmth of interaction with a departing colleague. And often the person being honored realizes in retrospect that an opportunity has been missed. Granted, if you are too overcome with emotion or intimidated by the situation (as a result of inexperience as a public speaker) the "thank you" response will just have to do. But if you are sufficiently at ease to speak up, the situation is made to order for a talk that can add to the warmth and spirit of the occasion.

For example, friends and colleagues of Beth Whalen have been invited to a party to celebrate her retirement. Her boss makes a warm speech about Beth Whalen's splendid service and her contributions to the company. This is followed by the presentation of a gift. She's urged to open it, and when she does, it turns out to be an expensive camera. "For your travels," the boss explains.

Someone in the audience calls out "Speech!" and others pick up the request. What should Beth say? Beth and all people in the same situation have a range of choices, and here they are:

Short version

This is for people who are either overcome by emotion or don't like to speak in public: "It's been wonderful working with you all. I'll never forget my years here, the many heart-warming things that happened. Thank you for the lovely gift. I'll surely keep in touch. I love you all."

Medium version

This is recommended for people who want to do a little bit more than just express their warm feelings toward coworkers. In addition to the expressions of warmth and gratitude, you might want to add: (1) some words about the organization as "a good place to work"; (2) expressions of thanks to those who have been of help; and (3) for an individual who has been of special help, special praise, to wit—"But of course it was Mr. Henley who encouraged me to get the training and technical background I needed to qualify for my management job. And Helen Bartley is the best boss a person could work for."

Long version

This is for the person who feels a longer speech is required to do justice to the occasion. If you have the impulse to give the occasion full treatment, you certainly have that prerogative. The points made above all apply, but here are some additional ones: You may want to recall old times, the first day you started work, and so on. Or special, memorable incidents: the day the power went off; the day the new building opened, and so on. Of particular interest, especially for newer people, would be your recollections of "the way things used to be," what's different today, and so on. This theme is particularly welcome if it avoids the suggestion that the olden days were the golden days that make the present seem depressing or otherwise undesirable. A tinge of the "good old days," is fine, but don't overdo.

There's one impulse above all others that a guest of honor should avoid, regardless of how justified it may seem. This is the voicing of old resentments, a "paying off of debts" to enemies, and so on. There may be a certain irony in the eyes of the guest of honor to the smiles and cheers that in his or her mind cover over some pretty rocky and unpleasant incidents. For those people who have something to be bitter about, a perfectly practical suggestion. Make the acid comments in private to friends and faithful colleagues. That way one can ease the load on one's chest without ruining a pleasant event.

One way to make a speech sound fresh and spontaneous is to direct it to the immediate and unique aspects of the gathering. One might say, for example: "I doubt that any room has ever held so many people of goodwill . . ." Or, "As Mr. Jones handed this wonderful gift to me, I must confess to feelings of bewilderment. I thought, They're rewarding *me* for my pleasant years working with the nicest bunch of people anywhere on the planet . . . !"

As much as possible, avoid the cliches that are often dragged out on such occasions. "I'm happier than I can say . . ." "I'm overwhelmed . . ." "What can I say? . . . ." Of course, experienced speakers sometimes use cliches to add a certain amount of camp humor. A veteran of the podium who starts off with "Unaccustomed as I am to public speaking . . ." usually wins a hearty chuckle.

One rule supersedes all others: if you speak from the heart, anything goes (except the negative or hostile churnings mentioned earlier) and, of course, it shouldn't go on too long. Conserve your energies and the audience's for the festivities.

Here's a "farewell address" that reaches out to the audience, and avoids any sticky or phony elements:

> Dear friends, as you know, my wife and I have been planning my retirement for some time and I'm really looking forward to our

new design for living. I can assure you that even if retirement really turns out to be my best years, as the books say, I'd still be leaving with real regret.

I've worked in this organization for twenty-seven years. To be altogether frank, I'd have to say, as would be true of any job, that there were ups and downs. For my part, I made some mistakes, and every once in a while things would happen that I could have done without. But almost every job is like that. And I want to assure you that the things I'm taking away with me are fond memories and a strong sense of achievement in working for a worthwhile and mature organization.

But best of all are the personal relationships I had in working with a fine bunch of colleagues. I know that my friendship with some of you will never end. I hope we'll be seeing a great deal of each other from time to time. But even with those people I didn't get to know well, there was always a pleasant and professional working relationship. By and large, people seem to like working here and take their jobs seriously. I can assure you that I never would have gotten the promotions I did— from supervisor to division head isn't bad, is it?—if it hadn't been for the excellent training and experience and, most of all, the high standards with which work is performed here.

And so I want to thank you all individually and as a group for your help over the years. It's been a learning and maturing experience for me, and you've all contributed. For that, my thanks once again and continuing gratitude. I love you all.

II

Evaluating Your Prospects

5
POSTRETIREMENT LIFESTYLES

What is your life going to be like after retirement?

The question is both fascinating and intimidating, as is anything that touches on the future. The menace of the question can, fortunately, be minimized without lessening the fascination by the application of both logic and imagination.

This chapter includes descriptions of patterns of living that are possible for you in the days ahead. In reading about them you accomplish two purposes.

1. You contemplate the future, your future, and some of the possible ways you will be spending your time.

2. You start thinking in specific terms about what you would *like* to do, and get going on the planning that can get you more directly into the lifestyle best suited to your plans.

● *Breaking with the Past*

Before you can begin effective lifestyle planning, you may first have to deal with a factor that may otherwise hinder you. Where it exists, it limits freedom to look ahead, make assessments, and dwell on the future with the relish it deserves. This hindrance is the pattern of feelings about work and/or your job that may distort your ability to contemplate the future constructively.

RESTRICTIVE ATTITUDES

Take a look at people you know who are newly retired. Chances are, you can group them into categories in terms of their attitude toward working.

Continuation syndrome

Even when it is not financially necessary, some people want to keep on working in the same field without losing a day. While in some cases, such dedication to one's vocation may be exemplary, often these people simply find it difficult to change the work habit. They like to stick with what they've been doing because the future is an unknown quantity and they hesitate to contemplate a change. As sympathetic as one may be with this attitude, it leads to an undesirable result—failure to gain the benefit of the many advantages of retirement.

"Out of the frying pan . . ."

Other people are so eager to start a second career that they miss the opportunities that a more considered view of the future might yield. For example, an accountant I know decided he wanted to go into the men's clothing business after retirement. At 65 he became a retail salesman, and two years later, part-owner of the store. You may think this is a success story until you listen to his wife: "Harold jumped from the frying pan into the fire. He was so happy to get away from the pressures of his job, I expected great things from his retirement. But that store of his gives him twice the headaches he used to have. And we don't need the money. Harold made some wise investments. . . ."

Perhaps people like this should never leave the world of work. They may not be comfortable in any other milieu. But it's too bad they can't explore other possibilities, not only for their own sakes but for their spouses'. The accountant's wife said, "I had hopes that Harold and I would travel and see the world. But we haven't gone more than a hundred miles from home since he began work at the store."

Avocation

To others, a life worth living means keeping busy. Ideal, you may say. And it might be, except that these people plunge themselves into their sport, or hobby, or craft without giving enough consideration to other possibilities. And usually, without giving a spouse or other family members a chance to discuss their ideas for the future.

Marking time

Doting on the past, some people fall into a rut. Bewildered by the whole business of retirement, they flounder a while and then give up. The world of leisure and unstructured time is as alien to them as land is to the white whale. They *feel* beached, out of action. Sadly, many of them simply wait to keep their date with Charon.

Bitterness

Then there are those who are bitter about retirement and angry at the world. They continually scold fate, the system, their previous employer, and Father Time for their retirement. And they're lonely, since most people, not surprisingly, don't relish hearing that complaining litany over and over again.

OVERCOMING THOSE ATTITUDES

Whether a person becomes a *continuer* or *second-careerist*, an *avocationist* or *seeker*, a *mark-timer*, or a *berator* depends on his or her temperament and flexibility. The value of these categories to you lies in becoming aware to what extent, if any, these feelings about work may linger on and in easing them into the past as expeditiously as possible. Then the road becomes clear for progress toward the important objective: starting the preliminary planning that will give you the optional retirement lifestyle in the years ahead.

As you start this adventure, remember that whatever factors influence your choice—and these include finances, where you live, your relationships, what gives you your "kicks"—no one can tell you how you should live your life. This is a one-person decision, though consultation with others is obviously not ruled out.

Four exercises

At no time in history have people of retirement age had the possibilities before them that you do today. The enormous range of free and low-cost programs, the ease of travel, the breaking down of barriers between different groups mean that you can have a lifestyle that enriches, delights, and satisfies—provided you choose wisely and plan well.

I'll have more to say about planning at the end of this chapter—why it's advisable and how to go about it. But in picking a lifestyle that will suit you, it can be helpful to think about yourself, about the kind of person you are.

This kind of thinking is more fruitful if structured in some way. What I'm going to suggest are four exercises—games, if you like—that psychologists have developed to help people make decisions about their future. These exercises have been tested on thousands of subjects. They're simple, they're fun, and they work.

EXERCISE #1.   Start thinking about everything you've ever done that made you feel good about yourself. Go right back to early childhood, if you can. Keep thinking until you can write down *at least* twenty accomplishments. These should not all be work-related, by any means. Include anything that *you* did—not that others, or fate, did for you—that made you feel proud or just plain pleased with yourself. For example, forcing yourself to speak to a stranger at age 15 may have been just as great an achievement as getting on the debating team or winning a promotion. All three might be on your list.

One caution: You have undoubtedly been praised and rewarded for accomplishments that really didn't mean much to you personally. *Don't* include them. It's what you did that made *you* feel good that counts.

Accomplishments that gave pleasure were listed by an about-to-retire film editor from Chicago. Following is her list.

1. Making a career for myself in a man-oriented profession long before "women's liberation."

2. As a child, making order of my mother's dresser drawers semi-annually.

3. Renting a car and driving to the beach from the city, the day after finally getting a driver's license . . . scared silly the entire time.

4. In post-World War II Britain, I remembered to share an offering of two eggs brought to me as a gift by a new English friend (who hadn't herself had an egg for years).

5. Passing my Life Saver Instruction examination.

6. Being invited back as a camp counsellor for season after season.

7. Editing my first film—after several years as an assistant film editor.

8. Dipping my hand to the bottom of the pickle barrel to come up with a choice and large specimen.

9. I made leather sandals by hand and wore them for years.

10. I plan, cook for, and enjoy entertaining both large and small parties at home.

11. Making old and new photo montages—collages that are meaningful to the recipients.

12. Going abroad several times alone, not knowing a soul and not very good at languages, and ending up with new, lifelong friends.

13. Going abroad for business and making my way through foreign production problems and completing the job "on time and within budget"—and well.

14. As a Girl Scout at camp, making my first stew using a large tin can as a pot over a campfire.

15. Got along with, and got to "almost like" an impossible client.

16. Gave a talk about "Life in Hollywood" to a group of club members.

17. Answered a newspaper ad for a fourth roommate when I had no place to live, met three strangers, and am still friends with them 30 years later.

18. Baked my first batch of cookies as a child.

19. I've supported myself since I was 14 years old.

20. I've finished this list.

EXERCISE #2. Now take another sheet of paper and write down everything you like about yourself. This is for your eyes only, so don't be modest. If you like the color of your hair, say so. If you like the way you can make people laugh, put that down. The vital thing is: *no negatives*.

Here is the soon-to-retire film editor's list:

These are the things I like about me:
My sense of humor.
The way I tell a story.
My face when I use makeup.
The way I wear clothes.
My eyes when I'm happy.
My height.

Making order out of disorder.
I go out of my way to search out the "right" gift.
I take pleasure in color, shape, and size of objects.
I am a loving, caring, and thoughtful friend and relative.
I am a good homemaker.
I've turned into a swan from being the ugly duckling.

You may not finish these first two lists at one sitting, but you'll be hanging on to them anyway, since you'll need them when you plan. Keep adding to them as new points come to mind.

EXERCISE #3. Now for comparison, thought, and analysis. Look over the things you've done in life and the things you like about yourself. Try to spot the activities that brought out what you like in yourself *and* gave you a feeling of satisfaction. For example, on list 1, you may have noted the time in childhood when you were the penpal of a handicapped youngster your own age. And, on list 2, you may have put down, "Caring, loving." Or you may have recalled how good it felt when the local paper published a photograph you took thirty years ago. On list 2, correspondingly, you may have written that you like your feeling for beauty, your eye for the unusual.

Make a checkmark by each entry on list 1 that corresponds, however tenuously, with an entry on list 2. There are several such points in the lists of the Chicago film editor: straightening out her mother's dresser drawers and making order out of disorder; sharing eggs with friends in postwar Britain and being a loving friend; giving a talk to a group of club members and enjoying telling a story. These overlap areas are particularly suggestive of areas of interest and capability to be tied into lifestyle selection later on.

EXERCISE #4. You don't really have to do this next exercise on paper, unless you feel like it. All you need do is sit back, close your eyes, and fantasize for a few minutes.

You are now 90 years old. You are just as healthy and vigorous, mentally and physically, as you were before you closed your eyes. Any yogurt manufacturer would love to hire you for a television commercial (whether or not you eat yogurt), as an example of a long-lived person who can think, work, talk and play as well as any 50-year old.

Now, what have you been doing for the past decades, in the years since retirement? What is your daily life like? What kind of people are around you and which ones do you like to pass your day with (and which ones do you avoid)? Remember, it's *you* who have survived to 90, not all your contemporaries. What plans are you making for the next five years—since, after all, someone in your good shape can expect to live for at least that long?

The point of this exercise is to free your mind to come up with thoughts as richly developed and in as much detail as possible.

Use the past to shape tomorrow

When done properly, these exercises can improve your contact with your inner self and give you a better perspective on choices that lie ahead.

Put your two lists where they'll be handy, so that you can add to them and refer to them before you start to plan, and ask the person you'll be sharing your retirement with, if there is one, to play the same games. It might be a good idea to compare notes afterwards. But even if you'd rather not, you'll both have a better basis for discussing a satisfying lifestyle—and for compromising, if necessary—if you both know where you stand before you start.

Following are your options, examples of postretirement lifestyles that can suggest directions you may want to explore, both in your planning and by actual trial.

● Sample Lifestyles

BEARING THE TORCH

What image comes to mind when you think of a torchbearer? Is it of someone lighting up the darkness? Or a marathon runner passing on the flame to the person who must run the next lap?

An increasing number of retired people are becoming torchbearers—in both those senses—and their hearts are as full as their days. Working as volunteers, some of them bring light into lives that are deeply shadowed. Others dedicate themselves to passing along their wisdom and skills to the generations who will carry on into the twenty-first century.

As a lifestyle, says 70-year-old Wilbur Grant, helping others to help themselves is the most rewarding he could have chosen. In the last year before his retirement, his company paid him to work with a special group of new employees several hours a week. These were young people from disadvantaged homes who needed remedial reading and writing in order to function in their jobs. He went on tutoring after he left the company and then, through his church, helped set up a program to aid school-age boys and girls in impoverished neighborhoods.

"Many of them need more than help with their schoolwork," Grant reports. "They need someone who cares, who respects them, who worries about what they've had for breakfast and lunch, what they want to be when they grow up. We give them that—as well as a place to come after school so they won't get into mischief—and in this day and age, that mischief is a lot more serious than it used to be."

There is more in such work than the satisfaction of doing what is desperately needed. When Winnefred Baker visits the Rehabilitation Center in Auburn, New York, she knows that she brings more than a cheery presence and comforting smile. "Besides being 81 years old," she says, "I have arthritis. A lot of people in the Rehabilitation Center are much younger than I, but they get discouraged and they think about giving up. So, maybe I'm an example to them, and I know that that keeps me young and keeps me trying."

By banding together in volunteer groups—or just plain getting into politics—older citizens can also help one another get a fair shake. The Gray Panthers are becoming a formidable influence that few elected officials can afford to ignore. (If you're interested, you can contact them at 3700 Chestnut Street, Philadelphia, PA 19104.) And Los Angeles's Howard Jarvis is the epitome of what retirees can do if they set their minds to it.

Jarvis, the father of Proposition 13, planned an extended vacation when he retired. But when some of his neighbors asked his advice on what they could do about high taxes, he was off, down a road that saw him addressing at most a dozen people when he began his campaign. He persevered despite all the discouragement. Finally, when he was 75 years old, he saw California lead the nation in putting the lid on property taxes, a campaign that swept the country, especially benefitting men and women on pensions, Social Security, and fixed incomes who stood in danger of losing their homes.

Not all *torchbearers* go out in the world. Though sociologists write of the "nuclear family," without grandparents, aunts, uncles, cousins, and bemoan the passing of the "extended family," where relatives were close and always on call, the fact is that there are many older Americans who today cherish traditional family values. Men and women alike care for their grandchildren—even their greatgrandchildren. They take some of the load off their own working children, help with the cooking and cleaning, teach the toddlers how to get dressed, and pass on to the preteens the lore of wood and stream. "So long as you wait to be asked," notes Georgia's Mary Chisholm, "so long as you don't interfere and sound off as though you know everything, you'll be wanted." And her husband, with a grandson at his side waiting for a game of dominoes, nods in agreement.

Choosing a commitment

Granted, a lot needs to be done in this world, and you've got the time to do it. But for a torchbearing lifestyle to give you the glow you're looking for, you can't just volunteer willy-nilly. You want to look for: work that you'll enjoy; a group you'll like to work with; an idea you can give a real commitment to; and a feeling of accomplishment you will relish.

Without those, you could risk going from place to place, carrying a load of guilt with you because you *said* you'd help—and then found you really didn't want to. That doesn't mean you shouldn't leave a group if it's not offering what you want. But for this way of life to give maximum satisfaction, you shouldn't leave too many. Instead, try scouting around before committing yourself too deeply.

Where to look? You might, of course, start by asking friends. This can be easier for women than for men. Volunteering was long thought of as "woman's work," but no longer. Today, men of all ages are donating their time and energies. If you're a man whose community hasn't caught up with the trend, don't let that discourage you.

Your church or synagogue, your union and local clubs, hospitals, and all the organizations in the United Fund or Community Chest are logical places for both men and women to investigate. But if you don't find something that really calls you, try making a call yourself to the National Center for Voluntary Action. The number is (202) 467-5560. The address is 1214 16th Street, NW, Washington, DC 20036, if you'd rather write. Someone there will put you in touch with the nearest Volunteer Action Center, of which there are some 300 throughout the

U.S. You'll find a plethora of programs to look into. What's more, if there's nothing that appeals to you but you see a need that should be met, you can ask the National Center to help you start your own project and perhaps guide you through the building of a brand-new community group.

Another number to jot down is the toll-free (800) 424-8580. That's where you get ACTION, the government's helping hand to those in need, which itself needs volunteers to make it effective while keeping down tax-paid costs. ACTION has programs open to any senior citizen—and some special ones just for those in low-income brackets. Some of the best known programs are described below.

RETIRED SENIOR VOLUNTEER PROGRAM.   If you can put in from two to forty hours a week *without* getting paid for your work, the Retired Senior Volunteer Program has from 100 to 200 different jobs. They range from helping in a local hospital to tutoring in schools, from serving in school lunchrooms to putting your talents to work for the city or county, from counseling youngsters to serving as an advocate for other people your age. (You can also learn about these RSVP positions by contacting your state bureau of social services.)

PEACE CORPS AND VISTA.   If you're adventure-minded, what about the Peace Corps or Vista? Both of these, incidentally, pay your basic expenses, allow you to collect Social Security while you're volunteering, and give you a "bonus" when your tour of duty is over. On leaving the Peace Corps, you get $125 for every month worked; on leaving Vista, $50 for every month you were on the job. For complete details, you should get in touch with ACTION, but briefly here are the basic facts.

The Peace Corps serves in 63 countries and 11 percent of its volunteers are over 50 years of age. Some, in fact, are in their seventies and eighties. (That famous Peace Corps alumna Lillian Carter, President Carter's mother, was 68 when she went as a volunteer nurse to India.) The Corps needs skills in the fields of health, education, and village development. It is constantly being asked to send skilled technicians, doctors, nurses, teachers, and engineers to developing nations. *But* it will also train "generalists" without such skills who are eager to serve. To be eligible, you need good health, a willingness to lead a rugged life for two years (that's the minimum commitment), trainability, and a desire to help.

Vista is our domestic equivalent of the Peace Corps. Volunteers are asked to give a one-year commitment, during which time they work—and live—in low-income communities and on Indian reservations. All kinds of skills are needed, particularly those that enable community-betterment programs to get off the ground. The prerequisites are the same as for the Peace Corps, with living expenses based on what people in the community you're stationed in have to meet their basic daily needs.

FOSTER GRANDPARENTS AND SENIOR COMPANIONS.   For older volunteers who can't afford to serve without some financial help, there are two ACTION programs of particular interest: *Foster Grandparents* get a modest hourly wage ($1.60 an hour in January, 1979). They also are given an annual physical checkup and a hot meal on any day they work. Each foster grandparent serves 20 hours a week on a regular schedule, working with two children, 10 hours with each. The children are physically or mentally handicapped and they are in institutions, so the help and love they get from these foster grandparents is of great importance to them. Guidelines as to who is eligible to serve vary from state to state and year to year—ACTION has the details.

Senior Companions do the same kind of work with elderly people who are housebound. The aim is to help them remain independent, in their own homes, instead of going into nursing homes. Companions receive the same benefits as Foster Grandparents.

SERVICE CORPS OF RETIRED EXECUTIVES.   Retired business people can put their experience to valuable use as members of SCORE, the Service Corps of Retired Executives, which is sponsored by both ACTION and the U.S. Small Business Administration. Through SCORE, they assist ailing businesses, putting in a set number of hours each week. For further information, write 1441 L Street, NW, Wasmington, DC 20416 or phone (202) 382-5558. There are nearly 300 SCORE groups in operation, but if your locality doesn't have one, and you can find other retirees interested in joining, contact your nearest SBA office to see about setting one up.

Creating a commitment

A point for any would-be torchbearer who can't find just the right organization to work for: consider going "independent." You may need to look no further than your own neighborhood. Would a day-care center for working parents be an asset? How about a neighborhood newspaper? Can you think of something to keep idle teenagers off the streets? Could your town use a mediation center to settle local feuds, like the one citizens started in New York State's Coram, Long Island? Is there a group of pediatricians who might help you start a Dial-a-Grandma service to dispense practical advice to the parents of newborns, like the one Lanie Carter founded with the help of a La Jolla, California, doctor? Are there invalids to visit, newcomers in town to greet, funds to raise, or new laws that need passing?

Talk up any need you see to get others interested. Ask advice from anyone who might be useful—your clergyman, your doctor, the principal of the nearest school, and the National Center for Voluntary Action. You have a tremendous amount to give the world—and it really is better to give than to receive. If torchbearing is the lifestyle you choose, your retirement will be a reaching out that may live in others' memories for decades to come.

BLISSFULLY AT LEISURE

To many people, retirement and leisure are virtually synonymous. Look at the communities with names like "Leisure Village" or "Leisure Springs." Even the dictionary definition carries that same connotation. Websters defines retirement as: "1: freedom provided by the cessation of activities, esp. time free from work or duties; 2: ease."

The word leisure itself comes from the Latin *licere*, "to be permitted." That's exactly what retirement can mean to you: to be permitted to do *what* you want, *when* you want it. No more getting up in the morning and looking out at a driving rainstorm or blizzard with the knowledge you *have* to go out in it. No more living by other people's schedules. No more tasks that must be done whether you like them or not. Finally, you'll be permitted to enjoy the fruits of your labor. As a retired Boston Red Sox coach put it on a recent TV show: "I'm gardening, I'm fishing, and I'm having a hell of a good time."

Choosing leisure as your retirement lifestyle means that you can mix in activities from the other lifestyles—you just won't be *committed* to any one of the activities. You'll be able to do a lot of other things, too. In other words, freedom is the keystone of this lifestyle.

But note the title of this section. You want to be *blissfully* at leisure if you're going to build a way of life around it. Those people you see in photographs now and then, sitting morosely on a beach in Florida or California, staring into space, not talking to one another, know nothing but leisure. And they look as though they're suffering instead of basking in the sunshine and gleaning the rewards of their long years of work.

What makes the difference between a retirement of leisurely enjoyment and one of painful, aimless boredom? Just one thing: knowing exactly where the pitfalls lie—and avoiding them. If you know you can't avoid them, you'd be better off, right from the start, picking a different lifestyle for your retirement years.

What are the major points you should consider before deciding on a life of leisure?

Feelings

When Esther Hagler, who is in her eighties, appeared on the "Over Easy" PBS television show, she spoke of her retirement years as her "harvest time." She said she had thoroughly enjoyed her earlier life as a garment industry worker, union organizer, and shop steward. But when it came to retiring, that was all right, too. It meant not so much leaving her job as gaining the opportunity to meet new people, stroll on the beach near her Santa Cruz, California, home, and take in the sun and sea breeze.

If you, like Esther Hagler, feel in your bones that the time has come to let go of what you're doing and go on to more relaxed activities, then you've definitely got one of the qualities that you need for blissful leisure time ahead.

If, on the other hand, you haven't accomplished all that you want to, if the urge to work more or learn more or contribute more is strong, you couldn't relax and enjoy day after day without a set purpose. So don't risk the unease you'd feel in trying to take it easy when there are so many other lifestyles to choose from.

Work

If you've been relinquishing bits and pieces of your job for some time now, and finding other things to do at work without brooding about the loss of those old responsibilities, you've been gliding into retirement. It won't be a big jolt for you. So, since you're accepting it, you will probably be pretty relaxed about having all that freedom, too.

But if you are still working harder than ever at retirement time, chances are an abrupt change to total, unstructured leisure would be psychologically and physically harmful to you. You might suddenly feel useless or unwanted, and you'd probably be unable to enjoy the many pleasures your retirement could hold for you. It would be better for you to choose a lifestyle that would keep you busy for at least part of every day. Some people just aren't cut out for the life of leisure.

Location

Ever since the 1920s, many people associate a leisurely retirement with moving to the sunny areas in the South and West. In Chapter 10, I've explored the questions to consider before making such a move. Now, look at it strictly from the point of view of being blissfully at leisure.

On the pro side, the climate gives you more days outdoors for sports. It will also lessen the chance you'll be out of action with a respiratory illness during the winter. And—though housing costs are high and food costs about the same—the money you save on winter clothing, winter driving expenses, winter heating, and so on can go to those leisure-time activities you want to enjoy.

And you may develop a more positive approach to life if you're in a new place than if you're in an old familiar one and "not going to the office anymore." Meeting new people and getting into a different swing of things can be enormously vitalizing. And many—probably most—of the friends you make will also be retired. You won't be around so many people who are busy from nine to five and then, in the evening, talking about activities that you don't take part in, instead of the ones you do.

But consider the pros of staying where you are, as well. You have old friends and neighbors, probably family, too, nearby. Loneliness is almost certainly *not* going to blight your leisure hours. You have an established place in the community and know of ways to put your time to good use. You probably have a paid-up or nearly paid-up house, leaving you more money for pleasure. And you won't have to spend time and energy building up a new support network—you already have a doctor, dentist, banker, broker, auto mechanic, and tradespeople you know and trust.

In other words, you've got the base from which to operate. You don't have to start from scratch, not knowing if you'll like what you're getting into a year or two from now. And then, too, you could be one of those men and women who need a change of season to "recharge their batteries" throughout the year.

So, if the pros of moving elsewhere don't clearly outweigh the pros of staying put, why not try this tactic: Before you retire, take a couple of vacations, visiting the places you're thinking of moving to. Then, in the first couple of years after your retirement, spend your winters in the place you and your mate feel you like best. Don't make a final move until you're sure this is the setting for that lifetime of leisure you've earned. If it isn't, there are countless other localities to choose from—and you've got the leisure to explore them.

Companionship

If you're single—whether unmarried, divorced, or widowed—a retirement that is totally uncharted can very quickly become lonely. *But not necessarily.* If you are gregarious by nature, full of ideas for what you want to do, thrilled at the chance—at last—to do them, and satisfied with your state in general, then you've got nothing to worry about on that score.

Neither married people nor friends living together can take for granted that they'll always get along well together. Many couples assume that because they have lived together for years, quarrel seldom, and have both benefitted from the life they've led to date, their marriages will take any strain that retirement may impose. But in some cases, as divorceé Mackey Brown phrased it, "We simply marched, in lockstep, like creatures on their way to Noah's Ark."

With retirement, at least one of the two will no longer be marching down the accustomed path, and the change in pace can mean encountering problems that were hidden when both were preoccupied with their separate problems and apart for a large part of the day.

Take the case of Evan Brandon, who retired three years ago after many years as a successful business executive. It had been literally decades since he and his wife spent more than an occasional evening alone together. They entertained frequently, went out to dinner at least three times a week—always with other people—traveled with friends or, when the trip was a business one, spent their time away with new and old acquaintances. On those few nights when both were home alone, they were occupied with their own interests.

Then Evan retired with a generous pension and savings and investments that many another retiree might envy. He looked forward, he thought, to the leisurely times before him. But he quickly found himself a man in a woman's world. Bette had long since formed a circle of friends with whom she passed the day. And though they greeted him affectionately as they looked up from their bridge hands or stopped by to exchange gossip, he felt increasingly out of place.

What's more, the woman whose world now surrounded him was a stranger to him. He had never realized before how *executive* his wife had become. She ran garden shows, raised money for her alma mater, and headed committees. If she wasn't entertaining friends in the house, she was off doing things in which, again, he had no part.

It didn't take long for Evan to begin asserting himself—or so he saw it. He was lost without a secretary, and tried to turn Bette into one. Every time she started out the door, he had an urgent task for her to do—for him. He'd call her when she was out, drag her out of a meeting, and ask her to go out of her way to buy or locate something for him. He was irked when he caught a flash of annoyance in her voice and hurt when she finally suggested that, since he had so much time on his hands and she didn't, maybe he could start doing things for himself.

Evan "solved" his problem by meeting a widow who gave him the attention he craved. She wanted marriage, so he asked Bette for a divorce. Her terms: a financial settlement that would leave her well-off and him living, with a new wife to support, on a much lower standard than he'd ever known. What's more, his own lawyer made it clear that after forty-odd years of marriage, Bette would probably get what she wanted in the courts. Then the widow, facing financial realities, had second thoughts. Now, Evan is once again back with the wife he doesn't know—facing a future of bitterness and unease.

Fortunately, most couples who reach retirement age together are on firmer ground in their relationship than Evan and Bette. Fortunately, too, for those who do run into trouble, now that they're in each other's pockets all day long, there's help.

One book—*The Mirages Of Marriage*, by William J. Lederer and Dr. Don D. Jackson (Norton, $10)—has helped innumerable troubled couples. For others, the services of a marriage counselor may be called for. And a great many husbands and wives, of all ages, have rediscovered each other—and the way to communicate together—through the marriage encounter movement, sponsored by churches and synagogues throughout the country.

The point is, marriages can be affected by retirement, and if either husband or wife has too little to do, trouble is almost certain to follow. When both partners recognize this, and strive to maintain their unity, any temporary strain passes relatively quickly. But it's something to take seriously into account in planning your retirement lifestyle—and another reason why, of all the options open, choosing a life of leisure can be the most hazardous, the one that has to be most carefully thought through.

It does, though, have those two big advantages to offer—all that freedom, after years of living by other people's rules, plus the chance to combine, in whatever mix you choose, activities from all the other lifestyles.

TRAVELING

Any retiree who wants to go on the road, through the skies, across the seas—or all three—can work out ways to satisfy that wanderlust. You've got the time. With today's low-cost travel opportunities, you've probably got the money. All you need is the right mix of planning and imagination to take off.

First, of course, you want to be sure this *is* the lifestyle for you. Don't mistake the enjoyment of getting away on a brief vacation for the solid satisfactions you want to get from your retirement. Unless you're a seasoned traveler, with a very clear idea of where you want to go and a thorough knowledge of what you'll find there, keep your options open. Learn from the experiences—good and bad—of those who have taken this path before you. That way, you can slip into or out of a traveling lifestyle with ease.

Basic principles

Bob and Mary Caster had been dreaming for years about going to Europe. They had gone on one of those seven-capitals-in-two-weeks whirlwind tours eighteen years ago. Twice after that they were back on more leisurely trips. Now, with Bob's retirement and both of them in fine health, they were ready for a good long stay abroad.

They pored over their travel agent's brochures and suggestions, full of anticipation. Then reality set in. At these prices, with the dollar slipping, there would be no money to spare—no shopping sprees or dinners in famous restaurants, none of the spur-of-the-moment side trips they'd been looking forward to.

"But if we don't go . . ." Bob began.

And Mary finished: "We'll feel just like a couple of kids who have been told there won't be any Christmas."

The Casters soon discovered a solution to their problem. It involved some basic principles that anyone considering the traveling lifestyle must be aware of.

When Bob and Mary had talked to the travel agent, they'd made no reference to the fact that money was now much more of a factor than it used to be. And she, naturally, assumed they wanted the same type of arrangements and accommodations that they had in the past. Now they asked her to come up with some budgetwise trips more suited to their present income. Bob and Mary also asked for suggestions from a former schoolteacher who did a lot of traveling on a tight income.

GATHER INFORMATION. Among other things, the teacher advised them to consult the public library. There they found a number of useful books, such as: *World Travel Planner,* by Bob and Joan Watkins; *How to Double Your Travel Funds,* by Charles E. Planck; *Travel at One-Half the Price,* by Peter J. San Roman; *How to Beat the High Cost of Travel,* by Betty Ross; *Bargain Paradises of the World,* by Norman D. Ford; *Pan American's World Guide;* and *World Traveler's Almanac,* published by Rand-McNally.

As their friend had warned, some of these were several years old. The U.S. dollar doesn't stretch the way it used to and inflation has driven up prices in almost every foreign country. But Bob and Mary still found the books full of good suggestions and one in particular—*World Traveler's Almanac*—extremely valuable. (If your public library doesn't have a book you want, ask if it can be ordered. If not, ask a bookstore to get it for you.)

At the library, the Casters also consulted the *Reader's Guide To Periodical Literature,* to find travel articles that described the countries they wanted to visit. And they found out that *The New York Times,* which is kept on microfilm in most libraries and is indexed, carries a big travel section every Sunday, with articles by people who have recently visited the areas they write about.

They picked up a lot of interesting facts in their reading, such as the fact that Canada, France, the Scandinavian countries, Spain, Germany, and Austria give discounts to travelers of any nation who are over 65. In this country, similar discounts are given by the National Park Service, the Kentucky state parks, some Marriott, Sheraton, Holiday Inn, Treadway Inn, Howard Johnson Inn, and Rodeway hotels and motels.

Newport, R.I., has reduced-rate weeks for older people, and Hawaii offers special low-cost activities for senior citizens.

They also learned there are tour operators and organizations specializing in trips for the retired, among them the National Council of Senior Citizens; American Association of Retired People; The Retired Officers' Association; Senior Travelers, Inc., of Flint, Mich.; Gadabout Tours, Palm Springs, Cal; Senior Citizens International Club, Hempstead, L.I., N.Y.; Kasheta Travels, East Rockaway, N.Y.; and Young Israel Tours, New York, N.Y.

Armed with this information, the Casters set about making their plans for Europe, looking for the cheapest possible air and ground fares that would still allow them to do pretty much as they pleased.

BE FLEXIBLE. It's doubtful that you want to become a complete nomad—in fact, that's something I'd advise against. If you want to preserve the privilege to "fold up your tent" and move on whenever you want, try to build flexibility into all your plans to the maximum extent feasible.

Time is a prime consideration. Unless there's pressing business to return to, buy an open-end air ticket or take a freighter, with no return booked on any special date. (Do, however, always *keep* a return ticket or enough money to buy one in case an emergency at home requires your immediate attention.)

You don't want to lock yourself into too many fixed reservations on the ground, either—hotel bookings that require you to be in such-and-such a place at such-and-such a time. That's one reason why off-season travel is the only one that makes sense for most retirees. Have a room booked at your first destination, so that you can recover from jet lag and cushion the culture shock, but don't commit yourself for more than a few days. Part of the fun of this lifestyle is deciding to stay longer in any place you really like. And if, again, you go off-season, you can have that freedom easily.

The Casters, for example, decided on a no-frills flight to London, as their gateway to Europe. They wrote ahead to book five days at a "B and B"—a small, private hotel which includes "bed and breakfast" in the same low price, having learned from friends that they'd get both comfort, a personal touch, and a morning meal that would be so hearty they'd require only a light lunch each day. Once the five days were up, they were free to make plans in the light of what they learned on the spot.

Money is another area where you want to maintain flexibility. Once you've made up a travel budget, make it a rule of thumb to add at least one-third more to it. Travel is always more expensive than you anticipate.

But if you keep your eyes peeled for savings as you go, you may never have to touch that reserve fund. For example, small villages are often far cheaper—and more charming—than towns and cities, especially popular resorts. Also make it a cardinal point not to splurge until you're near the end of your trip. Postpone any gift shopping till then, put off luxuries till you're on the last lap, cut corners until you're almost within sight of the airline terminal that will be your take-off spot for home.

Bob and Mary made their money more flexible by hanging loose in another way many novices travelers overlook—they committed themselves to a minimum of ground travel plans, which don't have to be booked ahead if you go off-season. The Casters knew, for example, that they could save on fares if they bought a British Rail Pass and a Eurail Pass before leaving the U.S. (neither is sold abroad). And both can mean marvelous savings if they suit your purpose. But once you begin to use either one, you are committed to the time limit on it. For a two-week—or even three-month—pass to pay off, you have to do the most traveling possible in that period of time. Bob and Mary wanted to keep a more leisurely pace, so, this trip, decided against them.

What they did do was look for bargains they hadn't heard about beforehand, such as an inexpensive, all-inclusive bus tour leaving England for Greece. This gave them the chance to make friends with their British traveling companions while crossing the Channel, France, Italy, the Adriatic and, finally, Greece. They had a wonderful time, but probably would never have considered it had it not been for their flexible frame of mind.

Attitude is one of the greatest assets you can bring to a traveling lifestyle. Ideally, this means taking in life without preconceived ideas of what it *ought* to be. To be a real traveler, you may have to forego your daily shower sometimes, a private bathroom many times, plus such old favorites as hamburgers and hot dogs. You'll consider staying in private homes that rent rooms, thus saving money and getting a slice of native life in the bargain.

And you'll go far—in all senses—if you're "cool" enough to learn from the nomadic young. These days, they're often the most experienced travelers around. In fact, one of the most invaluable guidebooks you can pack with you, wherever you go in the world, may be one of the student guides from the Institute of International Education, 809 United Nations Plaza, New York, N.Y. 10017. Write their publications department to see what they have available before planning *a trip anywhere.* Their books will give you a host of useful tips, from where to find a laundromat in Rome to local bus fares in Mexico City. Travel, at its best, is always a learning experience, and you're never too old to study human nature, as well as the world about you.

LEARN LOCAL CUSTOMS. You can do this best by studying the language of the countries you'll visit ahead of time. In most cases, half a dozen lessons in conversation give you the basics, as can self-teaching from a book. But if, like Bob and Mary, you don't want to take the time until you know if this lifestyle is for you, you can still get more out of your travels by following these guidelines:

Always touch base with the local tourist office, and don't be shy about asking questions, expressing your interests, and seeking advice. In most countries, tourism is a big business and governments have bureaus fully staffed to do everything from finding you low-cost accommodations to telling you the climate in some remote region you'd like to visit.

Observe the way people who live in a place carry out their daily lives. If you carry out the old "when in Rome" maxim, you won't, for example, go rushing around in the early afternoon, when Romans are resting. You will, on the other hand, save money by buying fresh fruits, a slice of cheese, and just-out-of-the-oven bread in a street market for your lunch. Wherever you go, watching how the people who live there get along will save you money and make your visit more enjoyable.

Find some way to communicate, even if it's just through sign language or playing with a child. Once you've made friends, they'll often *show* you—even without knowing English—how to get along.

Try to settle down for a while. You might consider renting an apartment in a place you enjoy, taking a language course, or studying at one of the American-sponsored art or history courses that abound in many countries throughout the world. This gives you an exposure to another culture you'll never get, just passing through—plus a base of operations from which to broaden your travels without spending money on hotels.

That's what the Casters did on their first trip after Bob's retirement. By now, they've decided to go back to Europe for an even longer stay, this time in Italy, where they're renting a large apartment for a year with two other couples. They've spent a fascinating winter at home, learning Italian and boning up on the places they want to drive to from their new "home" in Florence. And if Italy palls, or becomes too expensive, they've decided to explore South America, totally content, by now, with the traveling lifestyle they eased into without pain.

A cautionary tale

In contrast to the Casters, take a look at Edgar and Eunice Black. They, too, wanted to travel in retirement, and since they'd enjoyed camping with their children years ago, they decided to take to the open road.

Appalled at the $350 a week rental for a mobile home, they thought they'd save by buying one. Their next—mistaken—step was to burn their bridges behind them. They sold their house and sank a good portion of the money into a mobile home with every conceivable convenience, a new car to haul it, and the finest camping equipment they could find. And off they went to what was to be a life of fun for several months.

By now, however, it's another story. They're lonesome for their friends in a campground where everyone else is a nomad, too. But they have a feeling they'll look "defeated" if they go back home. They're bored with the lifestyle they've chosen, which was a lot more fun when they were young and the kids were along. And they're sitting in an Arizona campground because they've lost the energy to move on. Eunice starts reading or watching TV as soon as the breakfast dishes are done. Edgar starts drinking beer at 10 A.M.

It's not that Europe is a better choice for roaming than the U.S.— there are plenty of expatriate Edgars and Eunices, too. And in this day when the dollar doesn't go so far, and no Medicare benefits are paid in foreign lands, sticking to this country makes good sense for many, many retirees.

But to make a traveling lifestyle enjoyable, heed the following advice:

1. Don't commit too many resources to it right off the bat.

2. Leave yourself the option of coming home if and when you want to. (That's showing flexibility, too.)

3. Learn about the places you're going to ahead of time.

4. Keep learning when you get there—primarily by making friends.

You'll find more on travel—places, procedures, costs and opportunities—in Chapter 15.

CONTINUING EDUCATION

You don't have to take up a traveling lifestyle to discover new worlds—you can do it right in your own hometown. What's more, this particular kind of exploration will give you a sense of youthful vigor you may never have expected to feel again. It will improve your memory and keep your mind in trim, just as exercise helps keep your body fit.

What am I talking about? A lifestyle built around learning. Brains need a daily workout just as much as muscles do. Going back to school—as countless retirees are discovering—is the way to get that workout.

Some of them take up courses they never dreamed of enrolling in before: Jeanne Hahn of Elyria, Ohio, was in her sixties when she first went to flying school. She now has logged over 100 hours in the air and is part-owner of two planes. Thousands of retirees attend bird-watching classes, music courses, acting school, and art workshops. Robert Anderson, a former assistant high school principal, took up painting after he retired in 1963 and has been studying—and selling his work—ever since.

Others improve the skills they already have by studying everything from bridge to woodcarving. Mabel Levin attributes her winning the golf club championship two years in a row to the fact that she's never stopped working with a pro. Dr. Bennett Kraft attends classes with his wife at New College, a branch of the University of Southern Florida, but also, on his own, takes courses to keep his medical knowledge up to date, even though he no longer practices.

For some men and women, retirement means a chance to go back to studies they had to give up in order to earn a living. I. F. Stone, for example, was a philosophy major when he dropped out of college and took the first steps in a career that brought him fame as a journalist. At age seventy, he was back on campus studying the Greek and Roman classics. At New York's Brooklyn College, eighty-two-year-old Irving Kanter is fulfilling a lifelong dream. He had never been in a school in his life until he enrolled in night high-school classes after his retirement. In the Eastern European village where he was born, Jews weren't eligible for public education and he had only private tutors. Then, on coming to this country, he had to work. For him, the key to his retirement lifestyle is pursuing an opportunity he had been yearning for all his life.

The fact is that universities and colleges all over the country are making it as easy as possible for retired people to take courses and, if they want, work for an undergraduate or a graduate degree. Many of them will give reductions in tuition to students over sixty-five. Others give degree credits for "life experience"—an accountant, for example, would be allowed to take course exams in mathematics without enrolling in any course. On passing, he or she would automatically get credits for those courses. Some programs allow older students to earn college credits at home.

If learning is the lifestyle you choose, naturally you'll look into what nearby colleges have to offer. But if the curriculum there isn't what you want, don't sign up for something that doesn't appeal to you just because the campus is convenient. Learning isn't a joy unless you're intrigued by the subject, and a joyous retirement, after all, *is* your ultimate goal.

One possibility is to write to colleges and universities asking what courses they give in the field that interests you, explaining your age and financial condition. Then, if you decide to enroll and are accepted by one of them, move to that city and make it your retirement home.

But if that is out of the question—or you're not absolutely sure you want this lifestyle—consider the following options.

External degree programs

Most of these require you to go occasionally to the college campus for seminars and for meetings with your faculty adviser. You have to complete the same requirements as any other college student to get a degree, but you study on your own, at home, under long-distance faculty guidance. You can usually speed up the process of getting your degree with credits for life experience and college-level courses you've passed in earlier years. Some external degree programs also let you advance at a faster pace if you pass proficiency exams in courses you haven't taken.

University without walls

Colleges which take part in this program also give credits long-distance. You work out a "learning contract" with your faculty adviser, agree to complete a certain study program, and the university agrees to give you a degree when you've finished it. For the names of participating institutions, write UWW, Union For Experimenting Colleges and Universities, 106 Woodrow Street, Yellow Springs, Ohio, 45387.

Two states—California and New York—also have exceptionally good programs for older adult students. For information on them, write: The Extended University, University of California, Office of the President, 650 University Hall, Berkeley, CA 94720; or Regents External Degree Program, State Education Dept., Dept. 1919 AM, 99 Washington Avenue, Albany, NY 12210.

You can get more information on all these study opportunities by going to the reference desk of your public library and asking to consult the *National Directory Of External Degree Programs,* by Alfred Munzert. It's almost certain to be available, but if for some reason it isn't, ask your librarian's help in learning where you can take courses in the field of your choice.

Alternatives to formal study

It could be that studying appeals to you, but you really don't want to go back to school in the formal sense. In that case, look into a workshop in whatever subject or skill you'd like to master. Workshops of all kinds are sponsored by churches, public high-school evening programs, community colleges, senior citizen centers, YMCA and YWCA, the American Association of Retired People, and many other groups. All you have to do to find one is ask around, keep your eyes open for notices in your local paper, or write to be put on the mailing list of sponsoring organizations.

But if you can't find one that attracts you, why not start your own? Say, for example, that you're interested in archeology, but not so much so that you want to enroll in a college-level course. In that case, try writing the head of the archeology department at the nearest university about the possibility of setting up a weekly study group in your town on the subject. Ask if there's a graduate student who would conduct such a class and, if so, for what fee. Then when you've found a teacher, map out a rough program for the course. Next step? Contact your local paper and see if they'll run an article to attract other would-be amateur archeologists. If not, take out a classified ad. Put up signs on bulletin boards in churches, senior citizens' meeting halls, clubhouses, and supermarkets. Chances are, you will find enough people to make it worth the teacher's while to come.

And for some subjects, of course, you don't need a professional educator. If, for example, you'd like to learn more about antiques, you can ask the most knowledgeable dealer around to suggest a person to run a course. Or, from the *Encyclopedia of Associations* in your public library, you can find the names of antique-dealer and antique-amateur groups. Through them, you might find someone in your vicinity who is qualified and interested in starting the program you have in mind.

Another possibility is to look for a way to exchange skills. Figure out what you know best that another person might like to learn. And don't underestimate your talents. Out there, there *will* be someone who would like to know how to write a business letter, darn a sweater, cook a

Southern-style meal. Again, take out an ad and put up bulletin-board notices, such as: "Experienced business-letter writer will exchange lessons in this field for someone who will teach him French." It's a wonderful way to meet people, while picking up the know-how you'd like to have.

Concerns

One aspect of going back to school or of studying in any group that includes younger people is the difference in age. Will the kids snicker if you show up on campus? Will the younger members of the garden club course leave you out in the cold, like some burlap-wrapped plant in wintertime?

It *does* take some initial courage. But, as Brooklyn College's oldest student, Irving Kanter, put it, "I figured if other people can do it, I can do it, too." Keep reminding yourself of all those "other people" who've paved the way, but also be prepared for a pleasant surprise. You may be an object of curiosity at first, but your fellow students are there to learn, not stare, and you'll probably find yourself smothered with consideration, then accepted as just another one of the group, before two weeks have passed.

You will, though, make it easier for everyone to welcome your presence if you don't try to match the wisdom you've accumulated over the years with that of the teacher. By all means, take part in class discussions. But if you think the professor's wrong, take issue with what has been said and state why you disagree, rather than imply that you "know best" because of your years. You, too, are there to learn; don't lose track of that essential point.

Another aspect of going back to school that may concern you is that slippage in memory that so often comes with age. How will you take exams if you can't even remember where you put your keys last night? Take heart! For one thing, studying will wake up brain cells that you may have been neglecting. Also, you can figure out ways to record and refer to essential facts you need in your course. Don't forget—if you'll pardon the pun—that you can always ask for a private interview with your teachers, in which you can bring up this particular difficulty. Chances are strong that, in a world where "absent-minded professors" of *all* ages abound, someone will have some tips to help you out.

The fact is that the "infirmities of age" have often been a *help* in getting people involved in a new interest in life, so long as their curiosity has been kept alive. Grandma Moses took up painting at age 76 precisely because her arthritic hands needed exercise—and went on to live till 101 as one of America's most renowned artists. A friend of mine who loved food too well acquired high blood pressure and was put on a strict diet. Now, at age 69, he's the graduate of a Cordon Bleu Cooking School. He can only sample the masterpieces he turns out—but he's giving lessons and cooking gourmet dinners for his friends. He still enjoys food, but at a safe distance from his arteries.

If this lifestyle appeals to you, believe me, the love of learning will see you through most of the fears you have at the start.

PASSIONS NEW AND OLD

In the introduction to this chapter, I suggested you think back to the things you'd done, throughout your life, that gave you a good feeling about yourself. Now before describing this particular lifestyle, I'd like to ask you to jot down the occasions that have most interested you, that have made you feel especially alive, curious, and involved. They could center around a sport, a hobby, or a whole range of activities through which, if you think about it, there almost certainly runs a common theme: being around people, laughing, winning, or almost anything.

If the notes you make point to travel, learning, helping others, or just watching the world go by, other lifestyles I've described may be suited to your needs. But if the activities in your notes don't run in any of those directions, consider rekindling an old enthusiasm or finding a new one that will revive those same lively feelings.

A lifestyle built around something that passionately interests you will make you forget your age, the working companions you have left at the office, and the daily activities you once may have thought you couldn't live without. You won't be able to *wait*, each day, to get busy—and if you're the kind of person who loves to be occupied, this could well be the way of life for you.

Options

What kind of interests do I mean? As thousands of retirees can attest, the range is virtually limitless. Take, for example, retired high-school counselor Howard C. Litton. His burning interest in local history has led him to delve into days gone by in Jefferson County, Missouri, where he lives. As a result, he's published—and is selling—a history of Festus-Crystal City compiled from photostats and typed transcriptions of old newspaper articles and advertisements going back more than a century. In it, readers get the feel of what it was like in the "twin cities" when steamboats plied the Mississippi and one neighboring town prided itself on consisting of "a mill, a store, a blacksmith shop, and four dwelling-houses."

Or, consider the courtroom buffs across the nation. Every day they're at the local courthouse, following trials, chatting with the lawyers, and, since they gain an enormous amount of legal expertise, often giving a bit of free advice when they think it's needed. As *The Wall Street Journal* put it, they are "spectators to drama that is endlessly diverse, always real, and free of charge." Nor do all of them merely watch. Out in California, they've formed a Santa Monica Courtwatchers Club, which gives a monthly lunch with guest speakers from the judiciary, police department, and legal community.

The hum of history or the buzz of a courthouse corridor doesn't appeal? Then what about bees? There are between 200,000 and 300,000 beekeepers—apiculturists—in the U.S. today and many of them are collecting all that honey just for the love of it—although, as with many passionate interests, what starts as a hobby could turn into a second career later on. As an example of how easy it is to start a hobby, an under-$100 investment plus the know-how you can get from two government handbooks, *Beekeeping For Beginners* (Home and Garden Booklet, no. 158, 35 cents) and *Beekeeping In the United States* (Agricultural Handbook no. 335, $2.65) can get you started in beekeeping. Both can be ordered from the Superintendent of Documents, Government Printing Office, Washington, D.C. 20402. And for more help with the hive, there are monthly magazines that will steer you to other apiculturists as well as courses and clubs: *The American Bee Journal*, published by Dadant & Sons, Inc., Hamilton, Ill. 62341, and *Gleanings In Bee Culture*, put out by A.I. Root Company, P.O. Box 706, Medina, O. 44256.

Limitations

Money is obviously a limiting factor in pursuing interests like those just outlined. But what if the activity that has always intrigued you most involves spending more money than you can afford now that you're retiring? Suppose, for example, you've always loved auctions, outbidding the dealers and building up a small but fine collection of Chinese porcelains. Now that you won't have the salary you're accustomed to, you've dropped out of the market.

For the time being—though not necessarily forever—your collecting days may be over. But your interest is still there, and you can find ways to weave your lifestyle around it. Learn even more than you know now by reading everything you can about the subject, either through books you buy, at the public library, or in the nearest school of fine arts. Continue to haunt the auctions and watch from the sidelines, even though you can't be in the action at the moment. An added bonus here: you'll be keeping abreast of the value of your collection. Get to meet other collectors by talking to them at auctions, advertising for people in your area who have the same interest (if you don't know them already), and giving dealers your name and asking them to put you in touch with other *cognoscenti*. Together, you might form a study club. Or try keeping in touch with collectors elsewhere, via a letter-writing network.

Consider writing on the subject—articles, or maybe even a book. Or give classes, either gratis or for a fee.

You could also consider branching out. For instance, you've been collecting expensive porcelains. In the course of pursuing your hobby, though, you've picked up a lot of knowledge about china in general. What about investing a small amount of money in American and European pieces and joining the flea market circuit? This is one way that many retirees are having fun these days and getting to meet people while they make a bit of money on the side. (Just keep your eyes open for the announcements of flea markets in your region or check out-of-town newspapers at your library, for those held in your state.)

That's one way to keep your passion alive without spending more than you can now afford. But what if the avocation you most enjoy requires more physical activity than you now feel up to? The same principle applies. Look for new ways in which you can increase your knowledge, feed your interest, and make this hobby the center of your life.

Retiree Alfred Treen and his wife, for example, felt that dog breeding required more work than they were able to do. They learned to be dog judges instead, and now travel all around the country with their expenses paid and a host of new acquaintances to visit wherever they land.

Al Centro can no longer play tennis. When he got the news from his doctor, it almost broke his ailing heart. For a while, he stayed away from the courts, but then he forced himself to watch others playing as he wished he could himself. He went back to checking out equipment in the sports shop he'd frequented and got the idea of setting up a small restringing business. For him, it's strictly a hobby—he doesn't need the money. But he meets a lot of interesting people of all ages. Even though he can't play any more, his days still revolve around the game he loves.

Developing interests

Suppose that when you wrote down the activities that most intrigued you throughout your life you discovered, in the end, they were all work-related. And now you're retired. You envy the people who have already formed outside interests that they can devote themselves to full-time. But you didn't do that. You've made some investigations into other people's hobbies, and you know they're not for you.

It's true, as researchers at the Ethel Percy Andrus Gerontology Center have found, that avocations developed early in life carry over best into the later years. The same team also discovered that hobbies taken up after retirement often fail to satisfy because they are looked on as poor substitutes for a job. If you suspect that's the case with you, why not try this? Analyze very carefully what you have most enjoyed in your years of work.

Is it the feeling of accomplishment that finishing a particular project brings? Before you give up on finding something to intrigue you now, look to hobbies that give you a chance to *make* things: models, jewelry, sculpture, fly-tying, candlemaking, refinishing furniture, building doll houses, gourmet cooking, or better mousetraps. Once you master this new skill, you'll have a constant source of satisfaction just as you have gotten from your work (and you'll probably win more plaudits from your friends than you ever got on the job).

Are the daily social contacts the thing you'll miss most when you retire? Collectors have those, too—they get out talking to dealers, fellow collectors, buyers, and in some cases museum curators and other specialists. Try volunteering—maybe you'll find that "bearing the torch" is really the lifestyle for you. But anything that brings you out of the house and into a group of friends every day—whether it's a folk-dancing class, a bridge game, or simply a leisurely check on how the fish are running—will keep you stimulated. And if the weather where you live is bad, or your health poor, consider getting into short-wave radio, so that you can keep in touch *without* leaving your home.

Is running things what you've liked most on the job? Now you can run everything from a garden to a civic project to a gathering of the clan (by seeking out your roots and unknown relatives). Could be, too, that whatever you've worked at to date you're a field marshal at heart. Military history may be what you're looking for, and with it a chance to meet others interested in this field, maybe even build up a strategic planning center where you refight the battles of the past.

These aren't, of course, all the satisfactions you may have found in working. But you can probably figure out for yourself what you'll miss most and what opportunities you want to duplicate. If you can't, this amazing country of ours now has a new industry. It's called Leisure Consulting and the practitioners in the field, for a relatively modest fee, will give you the aptitude tests and counseling you need to find the avocation that's just right for you.

Who knows? As a Los Angeles client of Constructive Leisure's Patsy B. Edwards discovered not so long ago, what you really need isn't a job after all but a sailboat, with all those navigational skills and the challenges of wind and weather to master from now on.

● *A Personal Plan*

OUTLINING OBJECTIVES AND OBSTACLES

Now that you've examined these sample retirement lifestyles, take out the lists you drew up of the accomplishments that have most gratified you in life and of the things you like best about yourself. In choosing what to center your days around, try to chart a way that will give you more opportunities to bring out the qualities in yourself that give you the most pride and pleasure.

Remember, too, that you can combine lifestyles now in a way that may have been impossible when you were working. For example, before retirement, Dr. Leonard Greenberg was the ever-busy chairman of the Preventive Medicine Department at Albert Einstein University in New York. Now, at age eighty-five, he works on the Sarasota, Fla., Environmental Protection Advisory Board, plays golf regularly, and attends weekly lectures and case presentations at nearby Memorial Hospital—a mix, in other words, of the torchbearing, leisurely, and learning lifestyles.

Or consider this quotation, in *Retirement In American Society*, from one of the people over sixty-five studied by Cornell University researchers Gordon F. Streib and Clement J. Schneider, S.J.: "Retirement means everything to me. I'm so happy with the whole set-up. . . . On Monday I gardened. On Tuesday I played eighteen holes of golf. On Wednesday I did yard work all morning. On Saturday I went fishing. I read a lot. In the winter I go to my lodge and play cards. . . . I've read the Bible through twice in less than a year since I retired. I pray a lot. . . . I'm so thankful. . . . It's very *nice*."

To get that kind of satisfaction from retirement is everybody's aim. You'll increase you own odds enormously if you tailor your plans to your individual circumstances. Some questions that will help you map out your personalized program follow.

Have there been a lot of changes in your life of late? This question is vitally important for medical reasons. Through studying thousands of people, Drs. Thomas Holmes of the University of Washington Medical School, Richard H. Rahe of the U.S. Navy, and their colleagues have found that undergoing too many changes—bad *or* good—in a relatively short period of time can adversely affect the health.

You can use the "life change" scale, reprinted from *The Journal Of Psychosomatic Research*, to judge how many points you've accumulated in the past two years. If you score over 300, it would be wise not to make any more radical changes than are absolutely necessary during the coming two-year period—put off moving, for example, or making a major investment that could cause you worries. (Even if you score over 300, that's no set prediction you'll become ill. It is, however, a warning sign to be kind to yourself and avoid strain wherever you can.)

THE SOCIAL READJUSTMENT RATING SCALE
(LIFE CHANGE SCALE)

Life Event	Mean Value
1. Death of spouse	100
2. Divorce	73
3. Marital separation	65
4. Jail term	63
5. Death of close family member	63
6. Personal injury or illness	53
7. Marriage	50
8. Fired at work	47
9. Marital reconciliation	45
10. Retirement	45
11. Change in health of family member	44
12. Pregnancy	40
13. Sex difficulties	39
14. Gain of new family member (a birth, adoption, oldster moving in)	39

THE SOCIAL READJUSTMENT RATING SCALE—CONTINUED

Life Event	Mean Value
15. Business readjustment (e.g., merger, reorganization, bankruptcy, etc.)	39
16. Change in financial state (a lot worse off or a lot better off than usual)	38
17. Death of close friend	37
18. Change to different line of work	36
19. Change in number of arguments with spouse (either a lot more or a lot less than usual, regarding child rearing, personal habits)	35
20. Mortgage over $10,000 (e.g., purchasing a home or business)	31
21. Foreclosure of mortgage or loan	30
22. Change in responsibilities at work (promotion, demotion, or lateral transfer)	29
23. Son or daughter leaving home (e.g., marriage, attending college)	29
24. Trouble with in-laws	29
25. Outstanding personal achievement	28
26. Wife begins or stops work	26
27. Begin or end school	26
28. Change in living conditions (e.g., building a new house, remodeling, deterioration of home or neighborhood)	25
29. Revison of personal habits (dress, manners, associations, etc.)	24
30. Trouble with boss	23
31. Change in work hours or conditions	20
32. Change in residence	20
33. Change in schools	20
34. Change in recreation	19
35. Change in church activities	19
36. Change in social activities (e.g., clubs, dancing, movies, visiting)	18
37. Mortgage or loan less than $10,000 (e.g., purchasing a car, TV, freezer)	17
38. Change in sleeping habits (a lot more or a lot less sleep or change in part of day when asleep)	16
39. Change in number of family get-togethers	15
40. Change in eating habits (a lot more or a lot less food intake, or very different meal hours or surroundings)	15
41. Vacation	13
42. Christmas	12
43. Minor violations of the law (e.g., traffic ticket, jay-walking, disturbing the peace)	11

Remember, if your score totals more than 300 over the past two years, you may be under an emotional strain without knowing it. Cooling it for a reasonable time into the future is probably a good idea.

Are you exceptionally well-off financially? Rich retirees have special problems. They may have financial security and the chance to indulge in all sorts of luxuries. But when the whole world's your oyster, one more pearl doesn't mean much. They can become prematurely world-weary because they don't have enough challenges. They meet the same kind of people all the time, no matter where they travel. Too much is done for them.

If you fall into that category, consider combining lifestyles in a way that gives you what money can't buy. For instance, instead of yet another cruise, why not learn authentic Greek weaving—including how to make dye from plants and how to spin wool—at Woolworks, a studio run by American Naomi Cassagnol, in Athens and the Greek isles? Or, you could join an Earthwatch expedition and get a tax benefit at the same time. On the field trips Earthwatch sponsors, you get to work with scientists studying everything from guanacos in Patagonia to prehistoric stone circles in Scotland. For further information, write Earthwatch at 10 Juniper Road, Box 127, Belmont, Mass. 02178. In other words, let your money work to give you a greater variety of experiences.

Are you exceptionally strapped for funds? It's too bad you and a rich retiree can't get together on that problem, but if you can't, don't yield to the temptation to say you can't afford the lifestyle you want. Every one of the ones I've reviewed can be indulged in by a person with no more income than a Social Security check—provided you make up your mind to have it.

There are stipends available for adult students. Hundreds of thousands of the "passionately interested" earn extra income through their hobbies, while enjoying them for their own sake. If you scale your ambitions to reality, you'll find many ways to be blissfully at leisure. And many torchbearers give such valuable service that they are gladly paid.

Even would-be travelers can build a lifestyle around that interest by: (1) studying the language of the country they hope to visit in public school night courses and records from the public library; (2) reading in the library every book available on the land that interests them—its history, art, architecture, industries, politics, famous figures, and so on; (3) methodically hoarding a small sum every month earmarked only for that hoped-for trip; and (4) making a point of seeking out people from that country who have emigrated here. And they can even get in touch with people *there* by finding English-writing pen pals—a hobby that's not just for children anymore. You can contact them through The International Friendship League, Mt. Vernon St., Boston, Mass., 02108, and Letters Abroad, 209 East 56th Street, New York, N.Y.10022.

Do you live alone? If so, your retirement lifestyle should be one that allows you daily contact with other people. Say that you're drawn to a learning lifestyle and to one of the study-at-home programs I've mentioned. That's fine, but don't devote so much time to your education that there's none left to be out around people.

Many retirees who live alone do so involuntarily; they have lost their mates or close friends. So, they must contend not only with loneliness but with grief and depression as well. For them, psychological counseling at a community mental health center, to help them get through this difficult period, is often a *must*. To commit themselves to any particular lifestyle before "working through" their feelings would be a mistake. They would be better off merely keeping active in ways that lead them to new acquaintances for the time being.

How's your health? If you're in topnotch condition, then the only caution you need is: "Keep away from boredom." Choose a lifestyle that really engages your interest. Follow the example of ninety-nine-year-old Welthy Fisher, who recently told *The New York Times* she attributes her longevity to "deep breathing exercises and a good mental attitude. I could never manage to feel as I was supposed to about my chronological age. Maybe I was too busy. The future always seemed limitless and I have never stopped expecting something to happen, some invitation for another adventure."

And if your health is less than perfect? The same advice holds: A lifestyle so intriguing that it keeps your mind off your problems, even though you may have to lead it at a slower pace. As Dr. Hans Selye, the seventy-one-year-old President of Montreal's International Institute of Stress—and victor in a personal battle against cancer—puts it in *Stress Without Distress:* "Few things are as frustrating as complete inactivity, the absence of any stimulus, any challenge, to which you could react. As a physician, I have seen innumerable instances of this in patients. . . . Those who sought complete rest suffered most . . . whereas those who managed to go on being active . . . gained strength. . . ."

For you to go on being active could mean meeting only mental challenges. No matter—it's the stimulus and the activity that counts.

Canadian Dr. Hans Selye, the world authority on stress, has developed the concept of the Racehorse and Turtle in connection with two commonly observed attitudes toward self-programming.

"Some people," says Dr. Selye, "are like racehorses. They like the hectic life, seem to thrive on full schedules, rapid movement, and if they had a personal slogan it could be summed up in the words, 'Keep moving.'

"Then there are the turtles. These people prefer a slow pace. They are perfectly capable of relaxing in the sun for a while, enjoying the experience of inactivity. This type of program," Selye points out, "would drive the racehorse type out of his or her mind."

While the racehorse and turtle are two extreme types—most of us would fit somewhere in between—they still are important in helping us think through our own needs and preferences in terms of activity and the use of leisure.

To begin with, understand that there's no particular virtue in being a racehorse rather than a turtle, or vice versa. The real point is that whichever type you are, you fashion a pattern of activity best suited to that type.

There's a good reason for this move, aside from the fact that it *sounds* right. Dr. Selye, as an expert on stress, points out that just as the turtle type of individual would cave in under the stress created by the kind of schedule that would be appropriate for the racehorse, the latter would suffer the penalties of stress if forced to adopt a slow-paced, relaxed, turtle pattern. It seems odd to think that an individual lying on a clean white beach under a warm sun could possibly suffer stress from such an occupation, yet that is exactly the point that Selye makes. And it's a great insight and an assist to those who ask themselves the question, "What kind of lifestyle should I design for myself?" "What kind of daily schedule should I devise?" "What kinds and how much of a range of activities should I include in my daily program?"

Remember, it can be disastrous for a natural "turtle" to plunge into excessive activity in order to avoid feeling "out of things." And it can be just as bad for racehorses to take it too easy.

Whether you are naturally fast-paced or slow, keep the following points in mind when choosing your lifestyle.

1. Slip into it gradually, keeping your options open—after all, even racehorses walk to the starting gate.

2. Examine it from the point of view of how it suits *you,* not your family's expectations of what retired people should do or your friends' plans for *their* futures.

3. Hold off any major financial commitment till you know you like the lifestyle you've planned.

4. Always keep in mind that key word to a successful retirement: enjoy!

6
WHEN WOMEN RETIRE

Although most concerns of male and female retirees are the same, women do have some problems and opportunities unique to them. In spite of the many strides taken by women in recent years, certain inequities still exist, under the law and in the minds of many people, both male and female. It is to be hoped that, in the very near future, this chapter will become obsolete.

● *Attitudes*

I talked to a number of women who were within five years or less of retirement. As with a similar group of men, feelings and opinions varied considerably. The concerns of these women were different from those of their male counterparts, not as a result of biology, but because of differences in the patterns of their working experience.

Here is what they said, and equally important, why they said it. Those women who face retirement in the near future may want to see to what extent their own views are expressed here.

For some women, the world of work had become a happy refuge from what they regarded as the drudgery of housekeeping and homemaking. "I could hardly wait to get back to work after my youngest became of school age," one interviewee said. "Compared to the diaper and cooking routine, the office was an interesting and pleasant diversion." For people of this mind, leaving the workscene often meant deprivation of a valued social milieu.

On the other hand, many women were less fearful of the unstructured life that looms after the job is finished. For many men, the workday solves all their problems of order, schedule, and activity. With the prop removed, they weren't sure how they were going to fill the gap. But the group of women interviewed in depth for this chapter saw no problem in organizing their time and filling it productively.

Some women feel at sea in dealing in larger, long-range money matters—savings, investments, and so on. And many in the group feel less employable than men, particularly at age 55 and over. To some extent this seemed to stem from being less assertive. They felt less capable of selling an employer—in pursuit of a second career, or just additional income—on their experience and capabilities. And they didn't have the idea that some men have, of creating a job opportunity for themselves, going into one-person business ventures, and so on.

Women are resigned to less remunerative work. Women who felt they would be retiring with inadequate income counted on earnings from pick-up jobs like baby-sitting, department-store sales-clerking Saturdays and Sundays, and so on. "Just enough to help me get by," was the way one person put it. I had the feeling that this view reflected attitudes of women current in previous years.

Women expect to do more volunteer work. For men, volunteering usually comes out of failure elsewhere, or a need to "do something." For women, volunteering was incorporated into their postretirement programs. "I expect to do church work," one interviewee said. "I've been looking forward to it for some time."

Few women feel that leaving a job means a loss of power. For men, particularly those in the executive echelons, retirement suggests they are being shorn of power. (One man told me of a dream he had, in which his retirement ceremony was like a movie scene in which the hero, discharged in disgrace from the army, has his sword broken in full view of the regiment.) Few women share this sense of loss, in part for the obvious reason that few have had high-power jobs. But there may be a psychological factor involved, reflecting more realistic, modest power needs.

● *Advantages*

In some respects, women are more fortunate than men when it comes to developing a rewarding retirement lifestyle. Several examples follow.

TEAMING UP. For a wide variety of reasons, women seem to find it easier to team up with other women for travel, for lunch, for entertainment, than men. How often do you see older women together on group excursions, taking a shopping trip, out for a walk, etc.? It's not often that you see men getting together as often, or as easily. Are women more sociable? more gregarious? easier to satisfy? more needing of companionship? Women needn't be too concerned about the cause, but they should try to exploit the opportunity. You're wise to take advantage of this tendency, whether you team up with old, comfortable friends, or take the opportunity to cultivate new ones.

FINDING THINGS TO DO. Is it because so many women have had years of household and family responsibility that they seem to have little trouble in keeping busy with projects—whether independent or mutual efforts? I think it has something to do with that—and something to do with the fact that they have often been alone for a good part of their lives, with husbands at work and children at school, learning to manage on their own. Men—at least in the past—went from being taken care of by mothers straight to being taken care of by wives, without much, if any, time to be seriously responsible for themselves. It seems to have made a difference.

LIVING LONGER. Women enjoy a longer and longer life span as medical and scientific advances continue. The latest figures show that women at age 65 now have an average life expectancy of 83 years, while for men it's closer to 80 years. You can expect it to increase in the future, too. That's why it is wise now to consider, quite carefully, how you want to spend your retirement. If you retire at 65, you can expect 15 years at least—more than enough time for a new career, new friends, new home base, or new spouse! The choices are yours—make them, don't just leave them to chance.

FINDING WORK. If you're looking for parttime work or are interested in volunteering, statistics again come up on your side. The percentage of women working parttime, for example, is always greater than men, and you can expect the same statistics to hold true after you retire.

In general, women's greater familiarity with volunteering helps them in that area. There is more and more organizational interest in job-sharing and those extra years you're likely to have after retirement help to insure that you can find work if you want.

The increasing importance of women on the work scene is suggested by a series of articles in *The Wall Street Journal* under the running title, *Women at Work*. In one piece originating in Morton Grove, Illinois, the increase in working wives was described. Editorialized the *Journal:* "Once a small minority, American women who hold paying jobs soon may outnumber those who stay at home."

Another column detailed the extent to which management practices are being changed to accommodate women employees: more flexible hours, greater opportunity for promotion, and for that matter, for getting hired in the first place.

And, in keeping with its generally realistic approach, the *Journal* reported that marital relationships are often strained when wives get jobs—as might be the case when a husband retires, and his spouse takes over wage-earning to keep the wolf from the door. It's a negative factor to be figured into any decisions you may make. Over all, the *Journal*'s series indicated more women are working at more kinds of jobs than ever before.

● *Finances*

Although at present women spend about 75 percent of the consumer dollar, there is a great difference between handling finances and dispensing shopping and household funds. In the traditional family unit in which the man earned the money and the woman stayed at home, women typically found themselves unable to cope with financial matters following divorce or death of a spouse. Not only the problems of developing a continuing income, but also those of family budgeting, tax decisions, and investment matters were thrust upon women completely unprepared for them.

Fortunately, many books and articles have begun appearing in the last few years aimed at assisting women in dealing with the financial responsibilities for which their traditional education and experience have left them unprepared. As women of all ages continue to rethink their roles in society, it is to be hoped that more help of this kind will become available.

INEQUITIES IN THE SYSTEM

Despite recent improvements in the lot of women, there still exist inequities in matters such as Social Security payments. The government is making major efforts to see that payments to women will soon duplicate those paid to men. Modifications in the rules are aimed at slowly eliminating the discrimination to which women have been exposed for many years.

Women will be at a disadvantage for pensions for some time to come. It's not that pension plans intentionally discriminate, but that women's pensions are smaller because generally they have been receiving lower salaries. Although the procedures in Social Security payments are being more and more equalized, people whose payments are based on lower earnings—generally true for women—will be getting smaller Social Security income.

Conversations with bankers who have some experience with the investment practices of both men and women, suggest that women tend to be more conservative, which is both an advantage and a limitation. The advantage is that money kept in savings tends to be highly secure. On the other hand, in an economy suffering from an increasing inflation rate, return on savings in the form of interest is being outstripped by inflation. This means a diminution in real dollars of money in savings or other low-return investments. Men seem willing to wheel and deal more freely in terms of putting money where it will bring higher returns. The final effect, then, of this conservative approach by women is that their available funds tend to be further restricted.

POSSIBLE REMEDIES

Once women are aware of the disadvantages they face, they can start to consider steps that will improve the situation. One solution to an investment problem is to seek the help of investment-wise individuals. In some cases these may be found within their own family circle. For example: Geraldine Muller is a retiree whose last job was supervisor of a housekeeping crew of a major hotel in St. Paul. The hotel's pension plan plus Social Security gave her an income of about $11,000 a year. Savings and the ownership of a small income-producing property left her in fairly good shape. However, as the years passed the neighborhood surrounding the small apartment house she owned began to deteriorate and its value decreased.

Fortunately, Geraldine Muller had a son-in-law who was a lawyer in active practice in St. Paul. In the course of his dealings, he got to know about investment opportunities in real estate and business enterprises. Mrs. Muller had a serious talk with her son-in-law, described her financial situation in detail, and asked that he help her manage her finances, specifically to help develop investment opportunities for her. He agreed. His first move was to sell the apartment house and re-invest the proceeds in a more promising suburban area. He was also able to take her savings and lend it out to business clients of his who were seeking short-term loans. The return on these investments was considerably higher than she had been getting in the form of interest on her bank savings.

Geraldine Muller was fortunate in having a member of the family who was willing and able to help mitigate the financial squeeze she had been facing. But there are other ways to obtain this kind of help. In some cases banks may offer this service either on a formal or informal basis, depending on the amounts of money involved. Or friends may be able to recommend a lawyer or accountant whose business connections might make it possible for them to develop relatively safe investment opportunities. (For a more thorough discussion, see Chapter 9, Finances.)

Another remedy is to consider a second career (see Chapter 16, Another Job). This route is another means of easing the financial burdens that result from a fixed income in an economy in which the dollar is reducing its buying power from one year to the next.

● *Living Arrangements*

"What?," you may say, "Is this another area where men and women are not equal?" Again the answer must be in the affirmative. Even though patterns are not dissimilar, a man might fit into a household where a woman wouldn't, and vice versa.

Two tendencies exist, distinguished from one another by their degree of flexibility, and relationship with others under the same roof. Some women expect a good deal of personal liberty in their living arrangements. They want to be free to come and go, to be on their own. On the other hand, many women will prefer less independence and more socializing with others.

In some families, the independent type might be able to live happily in a back room, an added-on apartment, or whatever, going their own way without interfering with the son's or daughter's family, or whatever the relationship to the householder.

In other situations, possibly where the family ties are closer, it will be expected—yes, and in some cases welcomed—for the woman, whether mother, aunt, or other relative, to become an active member of the household.

And there is a common arrangement that women make which is much rarer among men. Single women may pair off with other women for both economic and companionship reasons. They may set up a truly "joint" household or elect the kind of independent-but-under-the-same-roof arrangement often employed by younger working women.

Many women begin, at some point in their lives, to think seriously about the advantages and disadvantages of having a roommate.

Rosemary Wallins endured the death of her husband two years ago. She lives comfortably enough in the home they bought 30 years ago, but it's large for one person and, or course, the expenses never end—there's the heat and electricity, the new roof, the house needing paint every few years, and so forth. She's arrived at the feeling that a housemate who could share expenses—and alleviate her aloneness—might be the answer to her problems.

Ann Johnson, a newly retired schoolteacher, has lived single and alone all her adult life—and loved it. She's only starting to have second thoughts about it now for one reason: many of the friends she formerly spent her time with are retiring as well—to Florida, to their children's homes, to retirement villages in Arizona. Suddenly she feels alone, vulnerable, unsure. The idea of a pleasant, companionable woman with whom to share living quarters seems very attractive.

You might expect a person in either of these situations to be a prime candidate for a roommate. But the fact is, while finances and loneliness are solid enough reasons for *considering* a roommate, they are not necessarily valid reasons for taking one on.

If you are thinking of joining forces with someone else in a living arrangement, give some thought to the following considerations.

• How open—and how knowledgeable—are you about dealing with money? Consider that a living arrangement necessitates dividing expenses in a number of ways, often in very open and trusting ways. Will you be able to say no to purchases you might be expected to help pay for but cannot afford? Will you vacation together, sharing expenses? Will you each pay half the rent, even if one entertains more frequently, has more guests, does all the cooking, etc.?

• Do you like the idea of sharing everything with a potential roommate? Church, an exercise group, learning bridge, an investment course? Does the idea of your roommate joining in your activities bring a feeling of frustration, flattery, claustrophobia, increased interest?

• Is the sense—and the reality—of independence very important to you? Or would you prefer to join a potential housemate in her activities? Does the idea of sharing the bathroom or the kitchen annoy you or make you nervous? Think precisely about the actual moments of sharing, not just the general *idea* of it.

• Do you like to talk? Do you enjoy listening to others talk? Do you like to rehash events, reflect on them with someone else? Are there many areas of your life or experience you consider "too private" to discuss even with close friends? Do many people strike you as simply *too* gregarious— all too willing to talk about themselves and their problems, to anyone willing to listen? Do you sometimes find yourself miffed because your interest in the other person is not reciprocated, and you think, "Why doesn't she ask about me?"

• Are you a creature of habit—by choice? Or are you quite unpredictable, taking off for a weekend at a moment's notice, or devouring a fascinating book for days on end, foregoing meals and ignoring interruptions? How would this behavior fare in team living?

• Do you like feeling "responsible" to someone? Or for someone? Does caring—emotionally or physically—play an important part in your sense of self-fulfillment? Or are you more self-sufficient and self-motivated? How would you feel if the other woman were ill and you were called on to do everything for her?

Considerations like these—and the further questions they will undoubtedly spark—can help you to decide not only whether you are a good candidate for a partner, but what kind of partner would be best-suited for you.

Keep in mind one important fact: This is *not* the time to consider which of your acquaintances might *need* a roommate, might *need* the money, might *need* the companionship, might *need* the physical care you could possibly provide. This is the time to consider what *you* want and need from the roommate relationship and who might best be able to provide it for you.

By all means, be a little selfish: consider who is most compatible to the way you live, the way you spend money, the interests you have developed, the priorities you have—and make your decision on that solid basis. Now is not the time to saddle yourself with an incompatible, unsatisfying roommate.

● *Activities*

While the choices open to women after retirement basically are the same as those for men, there are some aspects unique to women worth mentioning.

VOLUNTEER WORK

Today, there are virtually unlimited opportunities for volunteering. The contributions of many worthwhile organizations are made possible by the gift of time and energy made by individuals in their communities. But people in the field will tell you that volunteering seems to come more naturally to women. The reasons for this situation are historical. Traditionally, many nonworking women have gone out into the community and donated their time and expertise in the fields of social work, health care, church work, and more recently, politics and consumer affairs.

In recent years an increasing percentage of men have been volunteering for local organizations—big-brothering orphaned or needy children, counseling young and struggling business organizations, or contributing their business knowhow to the operation of neighborhood improvement and consumer affairs. But volunteering still seems to have a stronger appeal for women who find in it the emotional satisfaction it provides.

FAMILY TIES

Grandmothering is usually a more active and time-consuming activity than grandfathering. Grandmothers can be the fondest baby-sitters and surrogate mothers for their working-away-from-home children.

One obvious hazard in the grandmothering business is the possibility of being exploited by thoughtless offspring. As loving and willing as a grandmother may be, it's unwise to become the always-available rescuer for last-minute baby-sitting, cooking, or housekeeping chores.

SOCIAL LIFE

Retired people have one advantage nowadays that was lacking some years back. There are many more opportunities for joining groups with common interests. City, state, and even federal funds have been made available for neighborhood organizations that offer facilities for dining in groups, usually one meal a day, but also offer additional facilities—everything from game rooms to parties on holidays, Saturday night dances, and so on. Traditionally women alone have not had the freedom of movement possible to men, but this is changing at last. Women, usually in pairs but not always, have been able to enjoy the best available in terms of dining places, theatre, movies, and art functions. I know many women who have become good friends and enriched one another's lives by a happy schedule of being together several nights of the week to enjoy the entertainment and the dining available in their communities.

Some women in their later years have no pressing need for male companionship or company. If they meet men with whom they have common interests and whose company they enjoy, they are perfectly willing to develop an appropriate relationship. But they have no gap in their lives if they live without constant male companionship.

On the other hand, there are women who do feel the need for male companionship. As one 70-year-old put it, "After a while I get tired of female faces. I just feel the need for a man to talk to, to spend time with."

Some women have been resourceful in satisfying this interest. For example, Isabelle Roth, at 68, has been retired for 6 years. Her husband died when she was 58. She's fortunate in having a circle of women friends with whom she spends considerable time. In addition to bridge, dinners out, and so on, from time to time she and one or more of her friends take in some of the art and theatre events at the nearby college. But Isabelle Roth feels that social life without a man is not altogether satisfactory. In an adjoining town lives a widower just about her own age, actually a high school beau. They've just barely kept in contact over the years. Last time she saw him, about four years ago, she attended a dinner given in his honor by a local civic group. Interestingly enough, it had been Leo's son who sought her out and invited her. Leo had been happy to see her and made a big fuss about her turning up at the party. "You know, Isabelle," he explained, "I mentioned to Tim that I was sorry we'd lost touch with each other and it was his idea to invite you. I guess it was pretty stupid of me. I just felt I didn't want to intrude. . . ."

Despite that happy meeting, the relationship was not resumed. So, Isabelle Roth decided to take the initiative. She sent Leo Fields a note suggesting that they have dinner. "I keep thinking of old times," she wrote. "Let's see how it works out. Perhaps we should become friends again."

The evening was a success and gradually the two old friends began to see more and more of each other. Isabelle decided that it had been Leo's shyness that had prevented him from making overtures. She was perfectly satisfied to be the matchmaker.

Women who want men in their lives may find it somewhat more difficult to make the overtures, particularly where something more intimate than casual friendship is the objective. The means of developing those relationships are traditional, well-known, and open to the individuals who have the motivation and the persistence to follow them.

If casual male companionship is all that is desired, why not recruit a brother or other relative for an occasional dinner or evening at the theatre? In some cases, a grown-up son or son-in-law might be a good choice, assuming his wife agrees!

Relationships with men can be very difficult for many women approaching retirement age. Exclaimed one New Jersey widow, "I joined a club for widows and widowers a year ago and am about ready to give up on it altogether. It offers wonderful entertainment, interesting trips at bargain prices, and an opportunity to get out every week, but I'm so annoyed with the whole 'male-female' thing. You'd think at my age women would be past the point of grading men on their financial wealth—or men grading women on the amount of gray hair they still don't have. I'm appalled!"

Some people do think "older folks" should be past that—but why? Is there an age where it is supposed to end? Hardly, even though some people act as though they've reached it. That's precisely why relationships among retirement age and older people can get to be so difficult. For women, especially, often brought up by family and society to attach significance to physical beauty, aging can be particularly trying.

Biases against women "of a certain age," too, can be very restricting. Why is it that a U.S. senator, with his much younger wife, is regarded as a figure of strength to be admired by many, but a sixtyish movie star is viewed as a nut because of her efforts to remain sexually attractive?

Even though it is generally accepted that sexual interest doesn't "retire" at any certain age, sexually active older women (and men, too, at times) are often frowned upon by their younger families and by friends. It's just not an approved activity any longer. And of course, when approval is withheld by others, that can serve as a very strong reason not to continue the activity. One loses self-confidence, even respect. Said a retired woman in Minneapolis, "The last man in whom I was interested, after being introduced to my obviously disapproving family, disappeared within a week. And I can't blame him. My children acted as though I were a foolish schoolgirl unable to recognize a wolf in sheep's clothing. It surprised me at the time so much I didn't react. But you can bet I'll be smarter next time—the introductions will just have to wait!"

Of course, the withholding of approval by others can be even more insidious, indirect, and unexpected. One woman sadly told me a story about her friends who, instead of rejoicing over her developing relationship with a longtime gentleman friend, took to sniping, to criticizing, and to questioning his motives and interest. "They were jealous, I think" she says, looking back. "I was spending less time with them, doing things which they were not able to join, and I had an interest, a joy, that they just couldn't share. And I'm afraid they felt that if *they* weren't happy, why should *I* be?"

As in the example earlier, this woman failed to recognize the signals until it was too late to salvage the relationship. But it taught her an important lesson. In her own words:

"I still value my friends, and understand their feeling of betrayal. And perhaps the gentleman *wasn't* right for me—I had my own doubts, I admit. But the experience taught me something about my responsibility to myself. I had to ask myself: To whom am I responsible? Not my friends and not the gentleman, either. To myself only—first and last. If I was happy with myself, if I felt that I was right and proper in the way I acted, that was all that was important.

"Maybe I'm old-fashioned, because next time I would try to *talk* this out with my closest friend. I know some people say you need never make explanations to others if you're satisfied with yourself inside, but I think it might have smoothed things a bit if I had done it then. After all, I never want to have to *choose* between my women friends and a man. I want both!"

That's a sensitive and perceptive woman speaking. And it took time and a little pain to arrive at her wisdom. With luck you needn't experience the same thing. But the point of the story is to reveal some of the problems that might arise when you try to bring a man into your life. There's no need to compound them, however, with your own self-doubts, worries, fears. You're entitled to the number and intensity of relationships you feel comfortable in managing. After all, it's only by being constantly exposed to active, vital, interested, and interesting older couples that "society" will learn to accept them as easily as they accept younger ones.

● *Surviving Your Husband's Retirement*

Unfortunately, there are no simple, failsafe answers to the problems that may arise when your husband retires. Women who *have* survived offer these suggestions.

Think ahead

First, do some hard thinking about the prospects of retirement—from both your own and your husband's points of view. "If your husband is counting the days til the magic 65," says a retiree's mate from New Hampshire, "you *probably* can count on the transition being relatively pleasurable. But if he's avoiding thinking and talking about it, as my husband did, start worrying. No, better yet, start talking. Help him, however you can, to think seriously about the future, about his own ambivalence, and about the inevitable changes. No need to go into finances and the heavy stuff right now, but do get the word out in the open so he can begin to see it and to deal with it." This good advice is too seldom heeded by retirees and their spouses.

Of course, that doesn't exactly cover the unexpected results of retirement—the husband who had, for example, looked forward to it for years, then was suddenly cast adrift and was foundering.

"My husband was in this category," explained Mary Lonsley of Texas. "Here we had talked and planned about how to spend our retirement—but for the first few months of it Jack was inconsolable. He was distant, uninterested in me or our former plans, and devoured the financial pages with more vigor than ever. I admit *I* felt betrayed and insulted—and I withdrew, too. Jack snapped out of it on his own eventually, but I have the feeling that if I had somehow kept the communications channel open, even if I were doing 99 percent of the communicating, we would have weathered it better."

Marriage counselors and retirement counselors agree on one point: Stay open and stay honest to keep growing together.

Develop activities

For husbands—for anyone who retires—one of the most unpleasant aspects of retirement is the sudden feeling that "there's nothing to do anymore." The lack of structure, routine, organization and, more importantly, the discontinuation of the growing and learning one comes to expect in business can be tough. So, by all means, begin thinking about activities and opportunities you can explore together as well as individually. For many retirees, the ideal answer is travel—it's a learning, leisure, and pleasure experience all rolled into one (see Chapter 15). It's an excellent choice, but by no means the only one. Many retired couples choose this time in their lives to pursue gardening, bridge, volunteer work, music/art education, or fishing—together.

Unless you know you are the kind of couple who enjoys only each other's company, you are wise to allow some private space as well in your lives. Chances are you've already got more than enough independent activities to suit yourself, but it's a good idea to encourage your husband to cultivate one or two, also. More than a few retirement wives talk about their newly retired husbands following them blindly around the house, on social visits, or to the grocery store, just because they don't know how to entertain themselves independently. It's sad and unnecessary. It's not that the men no longer are in charge of their lives, or are incapable of decisive action; they're often temporarily at sea about the change in their lifestyle. An understanding and patient wife makes it easier on *both* of them.

Learn about finances

Now is not the time to skirt around the details of finances and the future. In fact, now is the time for both of you to be hard-headed and honest about your financial picture. Where is your money coming from and going to? Where are all the important papers? Who is your lawyer—and by all means meet him or her, if you haven't done so yet. What are you getting from your husband's company in the way of retirement pension benefits? Who is your company liaison if problems arise? I cannot overemphasize the importance of doing all of this *now*—so that unspoken but niggling worries about money don't crop up to mar the enjoyment of your retirement years.

The fact is, there are many more reasons to rejoice than to worry about at the prospect of your husband's retirement. These hints may help, but much of your mutual success will depend on the kind of relationship you've built through the years. A marriage that has grown apart, with separate lives, little communication, and few shared memories or adventures, will never be repaired by retirement and "spending more time together." But a marriage that has some real strengths, mutual respect and love, individual and shared memories, experiences, and interest in the future will only be strengthened and enriched by a retirement that is truly a beginning.

7
MANAGING TIME

A retirement book that doesn't discuss time neglects a factor that touches and colors everything. What to do with your time, exactly how to spend it, becomes a major consideration after you retire. We become aware that our lifespan has an end somewhere in the future—unlike many young people who seem to live life as though it will go on forever. And, in a real sense, we have less time in which to accomplish long-range objectives. An old economic law applies: the shorter the supply, the more precious a commodity becomes.

● *Using Time*

Some people may not like the idea of time planning. They may feel it brings too much calculation and control to an area that is better left flexible and spontaneous. If this is your feeling, please don't skip over this section completely. You may find some things in it that might persuade even the strongest defender of unstructured time to see virtue in some degree of planning.

Those who were executives or professional people may be familiar with the traditional business approach to time management. Those whose work didn't require such planning may nevertheless be interested in some of the techniques that are used to insure that time doesn't slip by unused and wasted. Without investing too much effort, you may be able to rethink your ideas about day-to-day and week-to-week activities and see whether there may not be some worthwhile adjustments you can make.

DEVELOPING A SENSE OF TIME

We lose time if we cannot observe its passing. In the days before clocks and calendars were in use, time could pass unobserved; consequently people were not in a position to use it effectively. To use time, people must make it visible, almost tangible. We have all kinds of fancy, automatic devices for performing this job for us.

Time unobserved means time lost. Keep track of time.

The individual's sense of time changes at various ages:

AGE	TIME CONCEPT
1 year	No future—only the present
3 years	Awareness of regular hours in the day
4 years	Understands meaning of "today"
5 years	Understands "yesterday" and "tomorrow"
8 years	Can understand "weeks," each of which seems endless
15 years	Basic time unit is the "month"
20 years	A "year" is tangible
40 years	Spans of "years," even "decades"

Note that these are approximations. Some fifteen-year-olds have the point of view of the average twenty-year-old.

Your planning, motivation, and expenditure of effort are all affected by the time distance you can see ahead. Long projects don't fare too well when attention span is short. On the other hand, extensive projects tend to come naturally to those who dip easily into the future.

To get some idea of your own psychology of time, answer the following questions:

1. Have you ever planned an ambitious, long-term project for yourself and then forgotten or neglected it? (Perhaps you were discouraged by the magnitude of the project and the sheer amount of energy required to do it.)

2. Have you ever planned for a trip "next year" and never taken it? Some people resist the one-year span. Planning ahead monthly, even weekly, might be better.

3. Do you refuse an unpleasant task, like volunteering to make a speech on one of your specialties, if the date is near, but accept it if it's many months away? (Nothing wrong with this. Everybody does it. Just don't be surprised when the day comes around.)

4. Do you prefer to buy on the installment plan even when you have

cash at hand? Installment selling is based on the knowledge that for many consumers, the future is less real than the present. But remember, the extra cash you put out in interest and charges is very real.

5. When you have two tasks to do, do you dispose of the unpleasant one first? In this case, you are putting a greater value on the pleasures of the future than you do on the discomfort of the present. Freud gave a name to the willingness to accept present sacrifice for a greater future good. He called it "the reality principle." At any rate, if you derive pleasure from the feeling of finishing off the job, fine.

Use your own sense of time to plan your activities.

Event awareness

A day spent in an absorbing activity—you name it—passes quickly. But an hour in which nothing happens may seem to drag on for ages. This points out the disparity between *clock time,* the actual passage of time as measured by a clock; and *inner time,* the way time seems to pass to you.

Some people think that we ought to plan to increase eventfulness and reduce periods of inactivity. But this can be deceiving. We can lose a great deal of time because we are content with mere "eventfulness"—that is, we are satisfied if a great deal is happening. The real test, however, is not *how much* is *happening* but how much satisfaction we derive from our activities. Avoid being very busy doing nothing.

In keeping your eye on the passage of time, measure against it your progress toward doing the things you want to do and the pleasure of doing them.

Effect of moods

The flow of time, as we see it by the inner clock, is also affected by our moods. When your spirits are low, time drags. That may be one reason why we get so much less done in periods when morale is low than in periods when we are feeling good. Life must have its low moments, and no matter how hard we try, we cannot always raise our spirits by an act of will. However, once you become aware of how your moods affect your performance, you can minimize down-periods by adjusting time use to your moods. Save tough, demanding jobs for when you're "up." And try to realize that those periods of depression are just that—periods that *will* pass.

In moments of moodiness, reset the inner clock by calling on the achievements of the past and your hopes for the future.

Balancing time

One of the distinguishing characteristics of the human race is the ability to conceive of a continuum of time—of the past, present, and future flowing together. In this regard, one could say there were three types of people:

1. *The present-minded.* Of course, we have to live in the present, but there are some who over-emphasize today. They see *only* the present and don't think of tomorrow.

2. *The past-minded.* Some of us may have an especially strong leaning toward the past. The impulse may be to disregard the present in favor of nostalgia and reminiscence—a special hazard for seniors.

In its worst aspect, past-mindedness may mean rejecting a new idea or development. But past-mindedness may have a healthy aspect as well. We set our minds loose exploring—through memory—past experiences that help us meet present challenges more effectively. This describes the true conservative who is not trying to turn back the clock, but wants to preserve the good of the past.

3. *The future-minded.* On the other hand, there are those who discount the past in favor of the future. Sometimes this interest is just a method of escaping from the present and its burdens. It may take the form of day-dreaming—not through memory of realities gone by, as the past-minded often do—but through imaginings of what might "some day" be.

Here again, the psychologist concerned with the time-attitudes that lead to accomplishment would not condemn the dreamer. Healthy people need the emotional exercise of imagination to give them new goals.

Your mastery of time depends on your ability to hold the reins on all three dimensions of time. Those who can keep the dimensions of time in balance respond easily to a new challenge. Given an unfamiliar situation, they don't lose time running around in circles. They ask themselves: "What is the goal I want to attain in the future? Where do I stand now, in the present, with reference to that goal? What in my past and present experience can help me to reach my goal?"

In dealing with the present, try to make use of the right mixture of the past and the future.

SETTING PRIORITIES

Time often presents a problem because we want to carry out activities that can't possibly fit into the same time unit. For example, you may want to get to the night ballgame *and* spend 'the evening with your family.

The ideal solution, of course, would be to find a compromise that makes the two activities compatible. In the case of the ballgame, the answer may be to stay home and watch the game on television; or, take the family out to the ballpark.

When *simultaneity* is impossible, *priority* is the way out. The important thing to remember: *all projects are not created equal.*

Priority involves choice. And wherever there are choices, you must consult a system of values. In short, if you are to use time effectively, *you must know what is important to you.*

Here is an example of how Gene Shear first noted a number of tasks he wanted to tackle, then ranked them in order of importance—which is also the order in which he planned to do them.

ACTIVITIES LIST

Clean up garage
Fix gutter on rear of house
Call Mr. Gridley about showing my shell collection in Town Hall
Call Personnel at Arbuto Plant to see about part-time work
Food shopping with Martha
Visit Paul and help him fix his living-room ramp for his wheelchair
Finish display case and mini-shell collection for Mr. Malden
Talk to Martha about joining the Shell Club in the city
Scrape mud off boots, and wax

Gene Shear's next move was to juggle the items around, to put them in sequence:

TASKS IN ORDER OF PRIORITY

1. Call Personnel at Arbuto Plant to see about part-time work
2. Visit Paul and help him fix his living-room ramp for his wheelchair
3. Finish display case and mini-shell collection for Mr. Malden
4. Food shopping with Martha
5. Call Mr. Gridley about showing my shell collection in Town Hall
6. Fix gutter on rear of house
7. Scrape mud off boots and wax
8. Talk to Martha about joining the Shell Club in the city
9. Clean up garage

From Gene Shear's rearranging of the list, several conclusions could be made. Apparently, getting part-time work is his most important concern, probably tied to financial worries. Next comes his desire to help his wheelchair-bound friend. Finishing the display case is a project for which he is to be paid. Ready cash clearly has its appeal. And then, jumping to the last item, "Clean up the garage," you would probably be correct in assuming that the clean-up job is one that has lingered on his list of things to do for some time. And perhaps it should. One day, when matters of greater urgency have been gotten out of the way, the neglected garage will have its turn. However, don't be surprised if low-priority jobs disappear from your list. It's possible that they don't deserve to be done at all.

When you must choose among activities, base your priorities on your own personal set of values.

Some people get more out of life than others. Why?

It is not that they have more time than anybody else. In any one day, we all have the same number of hours. *The important thing is not how much time you have but what you do with the time you have.*

Clearly time can be a dreadful master, but it also can be a helpful servant. You must master time, regiment it, keep it firmly in its place, have it do *your* bidding.

● *Spending Time*

If you are happy with the way you spend time, that's fine. You can then consider this chapter as a means of reviewing what you are doing and confirming the rightness of your choices.

SIX DANGER SIGNALS

However, some people may not be aware of how satisfied they are with their use of time. And for these, there are signals—things you may say to yourself or others, or feelings—that suggest your time use may be improved.

1. *"I have nothing to do"* If this is your complaint, then developing new lines of action, trying out new activities, and exploring unknown areas, as suggested in many sections of this book, should be your priority.

2. *"I have too much to do"* Some people err in the other direction. With so many desirable objectives in mind, they try to accomplish too

much, take on too many responsibilities, and tackle too many tasks. True, some people—they are called "workaholics"—relish jampacked schedules and a pace that astounds their admiring or possibly uneasy friends. If you fall into the overactive category, ask yourself, "Is this what I want?" If the anwer isn't yes, stop! Take steps to slow down your frantic pace and uncrowd your hectic schedule.

3. *"I'm married to my TV"* Television can be a boon—and is, for people whose health limits many physical activities. But even the most ardent defenders of the medium agree that TV in excess is bad for your eyes, your figure, your muscle tone, and at best is a substitute for living experience. Try to break away from your TV by including a variety of activities in your life—visiting friends, walking in the park, or volunteering your services where they're needed.

4. *"I sit too much"* Even if an incapacitating illness keeps you chairbound it need not rule out anything else. There are no end of absorbing things that can be done while sitting—painting, macrame, stamp collecting, or teaching a child to read or a foreign language to someone who is eager to learn it.

And for some people, sitting is inadvisable for health reasons. A friend of mine with phlebitis made his condition worse by excessive sitting. In general, where exercise is desirable for reasons of health, the ties that bind one to a chair should be broken in favor of walking, swimming, bicycle riding, and so on.

5. *"I'm bored"* Boredom is nature's signal that our capabilities are being underutilized. To the bored person, two words of advice: Do something!

6. *"This monotony is terrible!"* You've just said it. The same places, people, things, and activities create an uncomfortable repetition, a psychic jail. Break out. A lot of pleasure may be had, often just in the trying.

FIVE WAYS TO BEAT THE CLOCK

To come out on top of your face-off with time, bullish tactics are not likely to work. You can't control time by direct assault. A more evenhanded approach is necessary.

1. *Avoid workaholism.* Work addicts—the people who must be at it every moment, who can't enjoy rest and relaxation because they feel guilty—have a compulsion to work beyond need. Their pace can be bad for their health and for family harmony. Workaholics permit ordinary

tasks to drain the time and energy they could devote to less visible but more desirable goals: friends, community, leisure, or hobbies.

Says Richard R. Conarroe, author of several self-help books, "Many people could get their daily tasks done more easily if they would stop working so hard."

Never let yourself be "rushed to death." Remember, you are retired! That kind of pressure should be all behind you. Overabsorption in a task may be blinding you to the passage of time and the need to turn your attention to other matters besides the one at hand.

2. *Get your habits on your side.* One observer of the retiree scene asserts that a quick way to grow old is to be inflexible. "Welcome change," he advises, "even if you have to go out of your way to vary your routine." This calls for an examination of our habits. Some of your daily habits waste time, others save it. Psychologists make the point that habits are of two basic kinds.

Adaptive habits are meaningful, useful, necessary. They help you get done what you want to do—being on time for appointments, setting regular meal times, and so on.

Nonadaptive habits are illogical, unnecessary, and timewasting. You may find that nonadaptive habits are adaptive habits that no longer satisfy a useful purpose. For example, reaching into your vest pocket for a pencil even though you no longer wear a vest is a nonadaptive habit.

Authorities on human behavior agree that old habits can be broken and new ones developed. They don't say it's easy, because it isn't; yet it can be done. Here are two ways of accomplishing it.

First, you can take yourself in hand and read yourself the riot act. When it's a matter of work pace or a tendency to become enmeshed in the unimportant, some individuals can force, persuade, or teach themselves to stop an old habit and adopt a new one.

For most of us, replacing an obsolete habit by a helpful one, or developing a new habit from scratch, is best tackled step by step. Look at the problem the way a time-study engineer approaches a work procedure: The engineer (a) sizes up what's to be done, (b) works out a series of movements that do the job, and (c) whittles away at the procedure till it's efficient. To substitute a timesaving habit for a timewasting one, spot the habits that have outlived their usefulness, and work on a new habit to replace the old and adopt it. Check the time involved; make sure you're getting what you want from your time expenditure.

3. *Suit time to task.* Time is a mercurial substance. Once it's not held in check, it becomes the devil's own job to control it.

Donald A. Laird, in *The Techniques of Getting Things Done*, says, "Quick decisions (in minor matters) strangely enough are more likely to be right than those we let simmer for days." Dr. Laird even recommends tossing a coin to choose between two alternatives on trifling decisions. It's sound advice. Just one word of caution: Don't confuse preoccupation with details with time rightly spent on important matters. Matters of a weightier or serious nature may deserve all the time you can give them— and more.

4. *Do two things at once.* "You can't do two things at once," is a saying as old as the language. It obviously originated before carbon paper and the coaxial cable. *Of course* you can do two things at once. Try it. Take a pencil and do a simple problem in arithmetic, say multiplying 324,515,404 by 2. And at the same time recite a poem you know by heart.

Wherever you can, link activities that can be done simultaneously— for example, outside errands. You can also lump together the tasks that can be handled in the *same place*. For example you can frequently bunch telephone calls or letter-writing.

Start tasks that can proceed alongside one another simultaneously. Where the jobs are to finish at the same time, start the longer operation earlier. Great for gourmet cooks, for example. Another hint is to accumulate little tasks and do them in one sitting. Brief jobs are time killers because it takes a certain number of minutes to get set before starting. Get set once and polish off several at a time.

5. *Salvage time.* "The moving finger writes; and, having writ, moves on. . . ." said Omar Khayyam.

Though we are all likely to agree with the poet, a considerable portion of past time *is* salvageable. For instance, when you use other people's ideas you're using *their* time. You're actually getting the benefit of all the time they spent on thought and development of the idea. By checking other people's experiences you also save time. You avoid the necessity for repeating the time-consuming moves they had to make before they found the right answers.

At the top of the prospect list for time-salvage operations is your own past activity. Make it a practice to review your own past experience. Let's say you spend days investigating the possibilities of a new money-making idea, only to end up in a blind alley. That time is not necessarily lost. A week, a month, a year later, you may get the additional information you need to round out the attempt satisfactorily.

Look for the products of time well spent by others that you can turn to and use. "Formulas for success"—in everything from putting in a lawn to starting a thimble collection—can be learned from books or a next-door neighbor.

Check back on your own past efforts and ideas. Ask yourself whether changed circumstances now make it possible for you to apply them successfully.

Remember, your interests may change, month to month, year to year. With this development go changes in how you will want to spend your time. You may find that time can be reapplied to give your actions better direction and better results.

We become old before our time because we become time's slave instead of vice versa. Don't let that happen. Watch the clock. Make it your servant and add value to living when time is most precious.

● *Scheduling Time*

Making time do your bidding instead of vice versa is a challenging goal. Happily, there is a tool that can make the task easier. It is a device called a *grid*—a chart that helps you plan your activities a week at a time. With a minimum of effort, this tool can help you literally "see" the way you are living your days, and provide a means for analyzing and improving what you've been doing, so that you end up with the most desirable pattern of activities possible.

Of course, your aim *isn't* to lock yourself into a rigid timetable. Used properly, the grid makes for flexibility, as you add the activities, full or part-time, that round out your schedule and get rid of the duds.

An actual case shows how the grid works. John and Rita Ryals are a suburban couple whose lives have been affected by John's retirement. As you will soon see, the grid not only shows John's schedule as a retiree, but shows Rita's after she got a part-time job to augment their income. Rita's experience is noteworthy because it illustrates what happens to a weekly schedule when a full-time housewife takes on an outside job because of her husband's retirement.

A CASE HISTORY

At 55, Rita Ryals and her husband John, 65, live in a two-story, three-bedroom house from which a 25-year-old daughter and a 23-

year-old son, both recent graduates, have moved to start their working careers. Rita and her husband, a construction manager, lived a comfortable life that included a considerable amount of leisure, listening to music, and entertaining.

Rita got up each weekday to make breakfast for her husband and herself, and with the exception of a lunch-and-relaxation period from about one to four P.M., kept going pretty much all the day. Weekends were kept free for leisure activities: reading the papers, relaxing, watching TV, having friends in, and visiting. John's share of the housework was minimal. As a matter of fact, he did no household chores, but on weekends took on the standard jobs of a suburban husband—home maintenance, gardening, and heavy jobs.

But John retired, and John and Rita talked about the need to augment their income, and Rita offered to get a job. At first John was opposed, but as weeks passed, he finally agreed that Rita might look for work. Before Rita started looking for a job, she and John sat down and worked out a suitable way of redistributing the housework in order to free some time. They finally decided that she should seek part-time work only.

After some weeks the hunt paid off. There was an opening in the local hospital for a receptionist-office worker three days a week. The pay wasn't high, but it was sufficient to make a worthwhile addition to their total income. Rita now works Tuesday, Wednesday, and Friday, 8:30 to 5:30 (see Fig. 7-1).

On the three days that Rita works at the hospital, dinner is simple. And "Guess who does the cooking these nights?" asks Rita. You guessed it: John. "And John also shares some of the chores on the weekend. For example, we go shopping together, and from time to time John either prepares dinner or helps clean up the kitchen." (See Fig. 7-2.)

MAKING A SCHEDULE

To help you get started planning your workweek, we've provided a blank grid chart (see Fig. 7-3). If you are averse to writing in books, simply copy the chart by hand or machine.

Take the time to sit down and fill out your chart. This will make it easier to see what you're doing now and how your schedule can be improved. Go through a typical week, from Monday through Sunday, in

FIG. 7-1 Rita Ryals' Schedule After John Retired

	MONDAY	TUESDAY	WEDNESDAY	THURSDAY	FRIDAY	SATURDAY	SUNDAY
Morning	7:00-8:00 Breakfast, dishes 8:00-11:30 House-cleaning, including things done every few months	7:00-8:15 Breakfast, cleaning up kitchen and bedroom with John		7:00-8:00 Breakfast 8:00-11:30 General cleaning	7:00-8:15 Breakfast, cleaning up kitchen and bedroom	9:00-12:00 General cleaning, laundry, weekly changing and washing sheets	9:30-11:00 Church
Afternoon	12:00-1:00 Lunch 1:00-4:00 Errands with John	8:30-5:30 Office	8:30-5:30 Office	12:00-1:00 Lunch 1:00-4:00 Midweek marketing; general shopping and errands	8:30-5:30 Office	12:00-1:00 Lunch 1:00-4:00 Errands with husband	12:00-2:00 Dinner 2:00-5:00 Excursions with John
Evening	5:30-8:30 Cooking, cleaning up kitchen	John prepares dinner. Cleanup: John and Rita relaxing	John prepares dinner. Cleanup: John and Rita relaxing	5:00-6:00 Dinner preparation 6:00-8:00 Dinner, dishes	John prepares dinner. Cleanup: John and Rita relaxing	5:30-7:30 Cooking, clean up kitchen with John	6:00-7:30 Cooking, clean up kitchen with John

FIG. 7-2 John's Post-Retirement Schedule

	MONDAY	TUESDAY	WEDNESDAY	THURSDAY	FRIDAY	SATURDAY	SUNDAY
Morning	Breakfast with Rita Do heavy-duty house-cleaning & mainte-nance	Breakfast with Rita Help Rita clean up & straighten out kitchen & bedroom Gardening	Breakfast with Rita Clean up kitchen & bedroom Do heavy cleaning Work around house until noon	Help with housework & gardening	Spend morning at craft center at church	Help Rita with laundry, heavy cleaning and home maintenance	9:30-11 Church
Afternoon	12-1 Lunch Errands with Rita; bank, Post Ofc., spec. shopping	Gardening Work around outside of house	Special projects in home workshop	12-1 Lunch with Rita Mid-week marketing General shopping & errands	Senior Citizens Center: play-ing chess and so on	12-1 Lunch 1-4 Special errands, coffee with friends	12-2 Dinner 2-5 Excursions, socializing with friends & so on
Evening	5:30-8:30 Dinner, help Rita clean up in kitchen TV	Prepare dinner & clean up Talk: Rita's day at ofc., John's day TV	Prepare dinner & clean up Friends over for bridge	Read evening newspaper Help Rita clean up after dinner TV	Eat out—some-times with friends, or dinner at friends' home	Dinner at home, help Rita clean up TV	6-7 Supper Friends over for bridge or talk

142

FIG. 7-3 Your Schedule

	MONDAY	TUESDAY	WEDNESDAY	THURSDAY	FRIDAY	SATURDAY	SUNDAY
Morning							
Afternoon							
Evening							

Activities to enter on your schedule might include food preparation, dishwashing, shopping, laundry, cleaning, attention to the infirm, pets—any other major time expenditures that fill out your week.

143

your mind, filling in each day's activities. No matter how satisfied you are with your present schedule, you'll find it interesting to review it in light of the suggestions that follow.

These guidelines can help review your schedule:

• *Question all your present major time allocations.* Have you picked the best time for your activities, in terms of (a) best day of the week? (b) best time of the day? (c) minimum amount of conflict or overlap with other obligations, to minimize stress?

• *See that there is a sufficient variety of activities distributed over the week.* The considerations here are to (a) avoid overloading on some days, leaving others with "nothing to do"; (b) distribute your more pleasurable activities, so that, as far as possible, every day offers something of interest to look forward to; (c) avoid putting strenuous activities back to back, to prevent overexertion.

• *Don't overschedule.* Remember your objective in time planning is to win the benefits of retirement. Don't interfere with these desirable goals by creating stresses that result from working under pressure.

• *Be flexible.* Don't hesitate to experiment, shift activities around, add new ones, remove those that haven't turned out the way you'd like.

SPARE TIME

For some people, there is not the slightest doubt about the best way to go with a spare hour or so. Others may profit from the following suggestions.

1. *Relax and enjoy it!* That chunk of time may afford you a great feeling of relaxation. Luxuriate in this rare experience of doing nothing. Nobody is making demands on your time, responsibilities are temporarily suspended, and you feel under no compulsion to fight "the enemy" or do battle for a cause. Breathe deep, let your muscles ease, get in touch with the universe. It's a nice feeling. However, there are other choices that can help pass the time and provide dividends.

2. *Read.* Gladys Johnson of Ridgewood, New Jersey, is a toter of small books and pamphlets. "I get a good deal out of reading in bits," she says. "I always carry a paperback or a brochure or two in my purse. That way I get in a lot of reading. It's perfect for reading poetry, or to really dig into two or three paragraphs of a novel or philosophic thought and really analyze it. I call it reading in depth." Of course, for the traveller, stuck in an airport or train station between connections, the newsstand

offers everything from the daily newspaper to the latest paperback.

3. *Have a list of mental fillers.* "I utilize occasional free bits of time by thinking. I usually have a list of things I want to think about. . . ." Harold Esser, of St. Paul, goes on to explain that his "fillers" are of three basic kinds.

Pleasant: "I re-enjoy a recent experience—a party I attended or an interesting conversation I've had with someone."

Useful: "I try to solve some practical problem. Just yesterday, stuck in a long line at the supermarket, I zeroed in on how to make doors for a cabinet I'm building. It suddenly occurred to me that the best way to swing the doors was by piano hinges. Once that idea came, I was able to mentally redesign the front of the cabinet, and I was so pleased, I almost didn't mind the amount that came up on the printout check."

Remunerative: "I write little things for magazines: bright sayings, humorous verse, and so on. Some of my best ideas come while I have to wait—for a subway to come, or, after it does, waiting to get to my stop."

Some "spare hours" are unavoidable. We all must wait for things or have lapses in our activities. But if you find you have more spare bits and pieces of time than you feel you should have, give some thought to discovering why. If on analysis you find bits of idle time plague you, try to cut down on them by changes in the sequence in which you do things. For example, if you find yourself "always" idle the half-hour or so before your favorite TV program, see if you can't fit in some regular activity or change around the ones that precede the broadcast. Convert that time waste into something enjoyable or otherwise worthwhile.

● *Wasting Time*

One way to save time is to be on the alert for the things that interfere with your satisfactory use of time. Two habits in particular should be avoided as much as possible.

PROCRASTINATION

Putting off doing a job or doing it half-heartedly can make a task look, and often become, inflated and unmanageable. Meanwhile, time passes and little is accomplished.

If you have what seems like an outsize task, break it down into segments and get started on one part of it. Is the task unpleasant? Consider the consequences of not getting it done, and how good you'll feel when you complete it.

If you find yourself dawdling, doing a lot of picture-straightening or other little time wasting preparations, *just get started*. And in some cases when you find it difficult to begin, make a commitment: "Jane, I plan to clean out the garage by three o'clock this afternoon." Or set yourself a deadline. Make a promise to someone that will push you towards completion. And, of course, good planning will always help. At the very least, it gives you a direction and a track to run along.

SEEKING PERFECTION

"The pursuit of excellence," says Edwin C. Bliss, author of *Getting Things Done,* "is gratifying and healthy. The pursuit of perfection is frustrating and neurotic." Says Bliss, "It's also a terrible waste of time."

● *Saving Time*

Some simple approaches serve to optimize your use of time. You avoid having minutes and hours dribble away, and equally important, get the best possible payoff from time available to you. Here's what to do:

SETTING GOALS

A scene from *Alice in Wonderland* illustrates the importance of knowing what you want to achieve in terms of a given task:
Alice comes to a fork in the road and sees a Cheshire cat in a tree. "Which road do I take?" she asks.
The response she gets is a question: "Where do you want to go?"
"I don't know," Alice answers.
"Then," says the cat, "it doesn't matter which road you take."
Decide on your goals to know which road to take. If you are in doubt about your goals, particularly in key areas—spiritual, personal growth, or relationships—write out what you want to accomplish. What achievements would you like to look back on at the end of the current year? Which relationships do you want to improve? Which books of literary, spiritual, or historical interest do you want to read?

Then look at your list of goals. Are they specific? Attainable? Measurable? Compatible with each other and with those of other people involved? And most important, is your heart in them? Are these things that you *really* want to accomplish?

AVOIDING CONFUSED PRIORITIES

One of the major time wasters is not easily discernible because it is disguised. We seem to be working diligently and may even be accomplishing some objectives. However, if the accomplishment is of some trivial kind while more important tasks wait for your attention, time has been misused. Go back on your list of objectives mentioned earlier, mark your most important projects or goals "A", moderately important "B", the least important "C." As long as there are "A" items unfinished, stick with this top category. Only take the "B"s and "C"s as they achieve some degree of priority because the "A"s have been satisfactorily dealt with.

For some people the problem isn't having enough hours in the day, but rather that there seem to be too many. For the people who have time on their hands a solution is to plan one commitment, one project each day. Often the result is that the rest of the day tends to fall into place around it.

"One has to have something to get up for in the morning," explains Dr. Olga Knopf, octogenarian psychiatrist, teacher, and author. "Otherwise one goes to seed."

MATCHING ENERGY LEVELS TO TASKS[1]

Are you aware that your energies have fairly regular peaks and valleys? It is true of everyone. There are times during the day when you feel up to anything; at other periods you would just as soon coast along. If you adjust your activities to your personal daily energy cycle, you will feel less fatigued and accomplish more. Some people have worked all their lives and haven't been aware of this energy-conserving fact about their own bodies.

Industrial psychologist Norman R. F. Maier studied the efficiency of a group of people and charted his findings as illustrated in Fig. 7-4.

[1] The material under this heading has been adapted from *Executive Housekeeping* by Auren Uris (New York: William Morrow, 1976).

FIG. 7-4   Personal Efficiency Chart

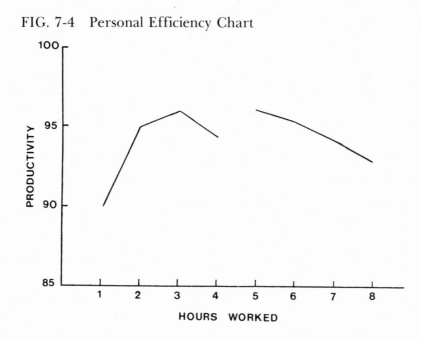

Remember that the curve represents the rise and fall in efficiency of the "average." Your own personal energies may closely resemble those charted, or deviate somewhat. In any event, the same factors apply.

WARM-UP PERIOD.   Note the rise from the morning start. Physiologists explain the warm-up on a partially physical basis. Muscles must be limbered; changes in blood pressure and circulation take place.

FATIGUE DROP.   Fatigue is the usual explanation given for the lowering of efficiency in the course of the working period. In some cases, this tends to be cumulative.

END SPURT.   Although not shown on the chart, there is a tendency for efficiency to increase as the end of the work period is approached. In some cases, a similar increase may occur before breaks in general, such as lunchtime, completion of a task, or the end of the day.

To chart your own ups and downs of daily efficiency, keep a brief record, noting: the hours you feel the peppiest, the times fatigue catches up with you, the periods when you feel most at ease mentally, and the times you find it difficult to work.

Tabulate the results over several days to pinpoint your strong and weak periods. Then tailor your daily activity schedule to your personal chart. For instance, save tough, demanding jobs for high-energy periods. Fit routine tasks into low-energy periods. Fill in mental doldrums with the tasks that almost "do themselves." Tackle new projects, or mentally taxing ones, when your energy peaks are highest.

Some people say, "You can't use time effectively—that is, control it—unless you know how you're spending it." Do you know where your time goes? Even if you think you do, try this experiment. For a week or two, jot down what you do daily and when. Don't worry about the small tasks—just consider your major time expenditures. When the test period is up, take a close look at the list you've made and see how wisely you're spending time. These questions will help you review and evaluate what you've been doing.

- Are you spending time on something less important that could be spent on something more important? You decided what was important in your list of goals. For you, a prime activity at a given time could be to contemplate a tree.
- Are you spending most of each day moving towards one or another of your goals? At least five minutes a day working towards your major goal?
- Of the time you spend on what you "have to do," how much is really necessary? Insofar as you can choose, are you living the life you want to live?

When you begin concentrating on how you use the time you have rather than wishing for more, new possibilities open up.

> I still find each day too short for all the thoughts I want to think, all the walks I want to take, all the books I want to read, and all the friends I want to see. The longer I live, the more my mind dwells upon the beauty and the wonder of the world.
>
> John Burroughs

III

The Four Pillars
of Wellbeing

8
HEALTH

Good health is important at any age, but those in the retirement bracket are especially aware of the consequences of losing it. Their concern is reflected in every survey that is made. Some studies put health first and finances second, others reverse the two items. This shift probably represents the special makeup of the particular group surveyed. Even when interviews show that people feel "in tip-top shape" and "never felt better," there is often an uneasiness expressed about health in the future.

The same emphasis on health is reflected not only in the comments of older adults, but also in the views of the public at large. For example, in one survey conducted for the National Council on Aging by Louis Harris and Associates, it was found that while 21 percent of those 65 and over said poor health was a very serious problem for them personally, a much higher 51 percent of the general public considered poor health as a very serious problem to most people over 65. These figures suggest two things:

1. If you have relatives or friends in the over-65 range, it's possible that you are more concerned about their health than they are.

2. It's not only your own concern about your health that is important, but those around you—friends, family—are also sensitive to the question of your wellbeing. Obviously, this anxiety affects the view of the future and any plans to be made—even if you are years away from age sixty-five.

There's one statement about health that is inarguable: The better your health, the better you feel, the less hampered you are by handicaps, ailments and so on—the better off you are and the freer you are to design and live your life.

However, the experience of countless individuals shows that health problems need not be the overriding factor determining one's lifestyle or day-to-day living. A person who must use a wheelchair can lead a life that is as rewarding as anyone else's. In fact, it's been demonstrated repeatedly that the handicapped person with the right attitude can enjoy the pleasures of everything from eating to travel, from art to interpersonal relations fully as much as anyone else.

Our society has amassed vast amounts of medical know-how and we have the mass media to communicate the knowledge that can keep us healthy. Even so, three ancient obstacles continue to interfere with our wellbeing:

1. *Ignorance.* Joan Hawkins develops recurring headaches. She prescribes liberal doses of aspirin for herself, unaware that hard-to-shake headaches may require expert diagnosis and specific treatment.

2. *Misdirected effort.* Greg Kent "knows" that it is important to keep his weight down. After a month's stay with his daughter, who is an excellent cook, he finds he has put on ten pounds. He undertakes a program of vigorous exercise to lose the excess. He is right about the importance of weight control. But while the solution he has chosen is likely to rid him of a few pounds, it may also worsen his chronic heart condition. Doing the right thing at the wrong time can wreak havoc. Doing the wrong thing at any time can be catastrophic.

3. *Unnecessary fears.* Perhaps this is the worst killer of all. Worry about health can make major inroads on the very thing it is meant to preserve.

The strongest shield against these three obstacles is to understand what promotes health and what can undermine it. This isn't to suggest that you become your own doctor, but rather that you improve your ability to monitor your own wellbeing. No one is in a better position than you are to make the moves that can preserve your health. After all, the best doctor in the world largely depends on the patient's answers in making a diagnosis or checking a treatment.

The idea of having patients share with their doctors the monitoring of their own wellbeing is included in the holistic approach to health care. The holistic idea is a growing one in the health field. It assumes a strong relationship between mind and body, the health of one affecting the health of the other. Holism suggests that mental health, an important consideration for its own sake, may also be viewed as a major influence on your physical condition. But whatever your personal health philosophy, in any health maintenance program, your doctor must be a major bulwark. Selecting the physician who is best for you therefore becomes an important choice.

● *The Patient/Physician Relationship*

Choosing a doctor may be a topic to which you have given little thought. After all, almost everyone has a family doctor. Even if you're moving as a prelude to retirement—well, you can always get a recommendation from a friend, right? Of course, if there's a doctor you're familiar with and who is familiar with you, there are several sound reasons for staying put, medically speaking. For one thing, a doctor who knows your medical history can often do a better job of diagnosing illness, getting to the root of problems, even just making himself or herself understood.

For another thing, there is often a rather steep "start-up" cost in changing doctors, even when medical information can be transferred. Between preliminary examinations, new tests, and so forth, quite a bit of time and money can be invested.

So why bother *choosing* a new doctor? Because finding and getting involved with a good doctor can be the most important investment you make in maintaining good health.

Think of the difference to you between a doctor you can trust—to *hear* your complaints, your worries, your reactions—and a doctor you are fearful of disturbing, of contradicting, of questioning. To whom would you rather entrust the next precious years of your life?

According to Dr. Thomas S. Szasz of the Upstate Medical Center, Syracuse, New York, there are three kinds of patient-doctor relationships:

1. *Passive,* in which the patient puts altogether *too* much faith in the doctor's ability, knowledge, and actions;

2. *Cooperative,* in which the patient at least makes an effort to understand the doctor's plans for his or her health care; and

3. *Mutually participative,* the ideal relationship, in which the patient takes an active interest in informing the doctor as fully as possible, in understanding and agreeing with the essential treatment—that is, actually considering himself or herself part of the medical team.

The *passive* approach is clearly undesirable. Some people prefer the *cooperative* mode, usually because they have had good experience with doctors, or have found one they would (literally) trust with their life. If you opt for the *mutually participative* approach because it suits your idea of what would work best for you, you have to take special care in selecting a physician who will be able to form this type of relationship. Perhaps you can make adjustments and break new ground with your present doctor. If not, you may have to look around for someone new.

JUDGING A NEW DOCTOR

If you are looking for a new physician, you can get names from a variety of sources—medical societies, suggestions of friends or previous doctors, or contacting the administrative offices of local hospitals. After you've made your needs known, you will probably be given the names of several people from which to choose.

Next, you want to establish contact. You can phone and tell the nurse or secretary that you're a potential patient and ask to talk to the doctor briefly at a time of his or her convenience. If this arrangement can't be made—"the doctor is too busy"—it's wise to look elsewhere.

If and when you get the doctor on the phone, tell a bit about yourself and mention any present or chronic health difficulties. This can be helpful if you have some ailment that requires special or immediate attention, and may suggest prompt action on the doctor's part. If things seem satisfactory, ask about fees, house calls, and emergency attention. Eventually, you will firm up your decision by a visit. Does the doctor appear to be comfortable discussing fees, methods of payment, and the like? What about the doctor's appearance? Overweight, smoking, disorganization, or an unsanitary-looking office are all legitimate things to be concerned about. Does the doctor speak in language you can easily understand? Some doctors feel the more medical terminology they use, the more impressed you'll be. Why be impressed with someone who doesn't take the time to clarify things for you?

Does the doctor give the impression that this initial visit is a time waster? If so, you can be sure that sooner or later you'll get the same impression when you're describing your symptoms or worries. Might as well save yourself the embarrassment.

Is the doctor interested in and knowledgeable about the problems of those over 50? Ask directly if you're not getting a sense of interest from what is said. What kind of education does the doctor have? How does he or she keep up with new developments? Is there an affiliation with a teaching hospital? Again, you will probably have to ask these questions directly. Don't be shy—while the doctor may be surprised (that's allowed) he shouldn't be insulted or put off (that's a warning).

Are *you* feeling comfortable, relaxed? Base your decision on that, along with the concrete information you get.

WORKING WITH YOUR DOCTOR

You, too, have some responsibilities as a patient. The more fully and candidly you carry out your part of the partnership, the better you can expect your treatment to be. According to Marvin Belsky and Leonard Gross, authors of *How to Choose and Use Your Doctor,* a smart patient will do any of the following whenever necessary: ask questions, take notes, and seek additional information about his or her body, symptoms, and diseases. You should also offer feedback, including feelings, fears, ideas, suggestions and try to be an observant, accurate reporter. If possible, share experiences with other patients. Recognize that change takes time and don't get impatient. Don't abdicate responsibility for your own health. Learn to criticize constructively. Finally, trust your own feelings and ability to make judgments.

When you've got a real problem, how should you proceed? Follow these steps:

1. *Tell the nurse of your needs.* When scheduling an appointment, explain the reason. If you have to prepare for the visit by stopping medication or avoiding food or drink beforehand, explain this so that the nurse can schedule your visit properly. If you have an existing condition (an ulcer, heart trouble, diabetes, and so on), remind the nurse so he or she can allow enough time for your visit and determine any need for urgency.

2. *Provide a full background and history.* Whatever the reason for your visit, there may be other aspects about you and your life that bear on the problem. Advise your doctor of past illnesses, injuries, conditions; medications you are or have been taking (for how long, and any side effects or reasons for stopping); allergies; and relevant facts about your habits or lifestyle. Don't omit anything just because it seems minor or trivial.

3. *Write down a list of complaints or symptoms before your appointment.*

Try to pinpoint their occurrence, severity, duration, and so on. By doing so, you're less apt to forget or minimize anything that could be of importance to diagnosis and treatment.

4. *Follow instructions, but be sure to ask for clarification, if necessary.* If you're going to be scheduled for additional tests, ask what is involved and the reason for them. Then follow through on them when and as required. If medications are prescribed, take them faithfully as directed. However, be sure to ask what they're for and what the effects and possible side effects may be.

5. *Advise your doctor of any sudden changes in your condition or of any reactions to or effects from tests or medication.* Don't hesitate to call if you experience any unusual or unexpected symptoms. If alerted promptly, the doctor can modify the treatment and alleviate conditions, while continuing to speed your recovery and saving you needless worry and discomfort.

6. *Know your own rights.* You're entitled to ask questions about anything the doctor proposes to do in the course of diagnosis and treatment, and to get a full explanation before any procedures are begun. If you're not satisfied with the answers you get, you're well within your rights to request or seek a second opinion (from a specialist, if needed) before accepting treatment. And, if you don't like the treatment you receive, it may be a good idea to find another physician.

7. *Practice preventive medicine.* Don't wait until something bothers you to call the doctor. Ask your doctor when and how often to have a complete physical examination. The more complete, the better. Go back for recommended checkups, even if you're feeling fine.

A good doctor will be as open and honest with a patient as that patient is with him or her. Getting good medical care is a matter of working well together.

Now that's a tall order, especially for people used to "taking" from doctors, instead of providing any input. But there's no better time to begin than now, while you are at the brink of a new period of your life. It may not be the easiest thing in the world to initiate a new kind of relationship, especially if you are going to stay with a doctor whom you know. But better an uncomfortable, awkward moment or two now in setting the record straight, than experiencing debilitating psychological stress, fear, and resentment when the time comes that you need the doctor's concerned and prompt response.

Becoming a true partner in your own health care is both desirable and satisfying. When you find a doctor who's willing and eager to include you in the effort, you've found a doctor to help and guide your retirement years.

Take advantage of what your doctor knows about your health needs. If you travel or move to a new neighborhood, ask your doctor to put into writing any special details or procedures that would be helpful in an emergency. Of course, when you relocate and make permanent new medical arrangements, your doctor will forward your records on request.

● *Common Health-Related Myths*

Seeking an effective format in which to present the material in this chapter, I discussed the subject with several of my friends. Some comments:

"Tell me whatever you like, but don't depress me. . . ."

"Don't tell me more about health than I want to know, but do be helpful. . . ."

"If you could only help people get rid of some of the phony ideas going around. . . ."

The last suggestion provided a key around which to build the information presented.

Following are a number of commonly held myths relating to various areas of health care and explanations as to why each one can be misleading, worrisome, or even dangerous. The good news here is that your health is not in the hands of the fates. Your own knowledge and efforts can be controlling factors. Learn to distinguish between the facts and fancies of mental and physical wellbeing.

MENTAL HEALTH

MYTH. "I've always been a tense person and I always will be."

FACT. Did you know that after a continuing "emergency response" (another phrase for tension)—a person in a demanding job may experience 250 blood pressure peaks in a single day? Some of these effects become permanent, and blood pressure stays up. But with the depressurizing that often follows retirement, there is a chance that you can lower your pressure count.

High blood pressure can be a contributing factor to stroke, heart attack, and kidney failure. However, it is possible to learn to make yourself relax—to slow your pulse and breathing and relieve the tension in your muscles. And actual recordable blood pressure also can drop to more desirable levels.

One promising method of teaching the body to relax is called the Relaxation Response, as espoused by Dr. Herbert Benson of the Harvard Medical School. (A step-by-step description of the Relaxation Response will be found in Chapter 18 in connection with religious meditation.)

In general, a satisfying schedule that provides exercise and enjoyment can help minimize a bad blood pressure record that was the product of the strains and stresses of the working world.

MYTH.   People who are under stress know that they are.

FACT.   People may be suffering from stress and *not* know it. Strange as it may seem, individuals can suffer debilitating effects without being aware of their own tension.

Be aware both for yourself and others with whom you come in contact that stress may not be visible to the eye. What often happens is that we accept symptoms of stress—irritability, anger, or complaining—as part of a person's general behavior, when actually these moods indicate inner tension.

Where stress is suspected, it helps if the individual tries to figure out the pressure point in his or her life, or relationships that are causing the trouble, and try to alleviate the sources of friction.

MYTH.   Stress is solely a mental state with emotional symptoms.

FACT.   Stress, when it is long-term and out of control, can have specific physical consequences. It may set the stage for ulcers, boost blood pressure, lead to strokes and heart attacks, and aggravate a tendency toward alcoholism.

If you feel on edge or irritable, consider whether these are stress symptoms that may be undermining both your peace of mind and physical health. Don't be misled into thinking that stress is a "normal" part of living. People in high-pressure jobs may have to live with a certain amount of stress. But people without this type of enforced responsibility—in short, retirees—ordinarily have no reason to be stuck with an unacceptable stress level.

You can get some idea of where you stand on the subject of stress by taking the following quiz prepared by two medical experts.

Drs. Robert L. Woolfolk and Frank C. Richardson have developed a self-rating quiz that can give you some idea of your "stress quotient." Here's an adaptation of their questions:

TEST YOUR STRESS QUOTIENT

1. Do you worry about the future?
2. Do you sometimes have trouble falling asleep?
3. Do you often reach for a cigarette, a drink, or a tranquilizer to reduce tension?
4. Do you become irritated over insignificant matters?
5. Do you have less energy than you seem to need or would like to have even though you feel you're in good health?
6. Do you have too many things to do and not enough time to do them?
7. Do you have headaches or stomach problems?
8. Do you feel pressure to accomplish or to get things done?
9. Are you very concerned about being either well liked or successful?
10. Do you perform well enough in life to satisfy yourself?
11. Do you get satisfaction from the small joys or simple pleasures of life?
12. Are you able to really relax and have fun?

Score one point for each yes answer, questions 1 to 9; and one point for each no answer, questions 10 to 12. The psychologists say a score of four or more suggests you may be under significant stress.

MYTH. Zero stress should be your goal.

FACT. If you don't feel any stress in your life, chances are nothing's happening. Stress, in fact, *can* be an indicator of worthwhile involvement in activities, stimulating relationships, and response to challenge. Dr. Hans Selye, international authority on stress, points out that there is "good" stress that tones you up, and "bad" stress that debilitates.

Stress, when unresolved, can indeed be a slow killer in the form of any number of diseases, or a fast one by means of heart attack or stroke.

But most of us, after a full-time working life, are used to some tension and might feel pretty strange without a bit of it. A certain amount of stress has a beneficial effect on memory, for example; it forces the body to produce certain chemical brain stimulants which aid memory processes.

Stress may have mental, emotional, or physical causes. To reduce it, one of the most enjoyable and satisfying things you can do is to participate in some sort of sport or exercise regularly. According to a study by

Dr. O. E. Byrd of Stanford University, 92 percent of 400 physicians surveyed recommended walking, swimming, golf, and bowling (in that order) as prime tension easers.

Relaxation techniques (TM and others) can also be helpful in reducing stress. If you haven't had the chance to read any of the current literature about managing stress, now might be the ideal time. Some suggested titles:

- *How to Kill Stress Before It Kills You*, Matthew J. Culligan and Keith Sedlacek (New York: Grosset & Dunlap, 1976)
- *The Relaxation Response*, Herbert Benson (New York: Morrow, 1975)
- *The Stress of Life*, Hans Selye (New York: McGraw-Hill Paperbacks, 1978)
- *To Bend Without Breaking: Stress and How to Deal With It*, Mary E. Stuart (New York: Abingdon Press, 1977)

MYTH.   Retirees ought to have little reason to feel stress or tension.

FACT.   Nervous tension doesn't disappear with your job.

Work is just one of many sources of stress. And you continue to live with most of them even after you have retired from the stress of work. In fact *change* is one of the greatest sources of stress—and retirement, no matter how potentially pleasant, is a major life change. Any change, pleasant or unpleasant, increases an individual's level of stress. This can mean children moving away from home or getting married, the death of friends or loved ones, moving to a new home or community, and so on. So begin your retirement by a willingness to accept a certain amount of stress. Even if you're sitting in a rowboat fishing, you can be on edge waiting for that big one to bite.

MYTH.   Stress has nothing to do with physical illness.

FACT.   Just as your state of physical health can affect you mentally, so too your mental state can have a direct effect on your physical well-being. Relaxed, optimistic people, even when they do fall ill, recover faster and more fully. And tense, worried people suffer many mentally induced, real physical ills. Headache, dizziness, fatigue, itching, diarrhea, irregular heart rhythm, high blood pressure—all these symptoms and more, while sometimes of solely physical origin, are often the result of stress not properly dealt with. Although with age people become more concerned with their bodies, it is at least as critical to concern yourself with your mental wellbeing.

MYTH. If you're over sixty, you're already as "emotionally mature" as you're ever going to get.

FACT. One's emotional maturity can grow indefinitely. Famed psychiatrist Dr. William C. Menninger developed seven characteristics of what he called an "emotionally mature" person. This is a person who has:

1. the ability to deal constructively with reality;
2. the capacity to adapt to change;
3. a relative freedom from symptoms that are produced by tensions and anxieties;
4. the capacity to find more satisfaction in giving than receiving;
5. the capacity to relate to other people in a consistent manner with mutual satisfaction and helpfulness;
6. the capacity to sublimate, to direct one's instinctive hostile energy into creative outlets; and
7. the capacity to love.

Try testing yourself against this list. Keep in mind that chronological age does not automatically ensure true maturity. Strengthening some of these characteristics in yourself could set an excellent goal for some of your postretirement planning. Again, remember the mind-body link; the emotions, dealt with constructively, can serve you in good stead.

MYTH. Leaving the job means a new freedom, all the time in the world. Result: mental ease.

FACT. That's the old-fashioned view. The great virtue of retirement is that you have the freedom to *marshal* time, to put it to worthy use.

It may seem strange to seek an organized routine when you are about to retire from the structure of your job. But the more structured your life has been until now, the more important it is for you to establish a new routine. It does not have to be rigid, but your time does have to be controlled in order to maintain your sense of purpose in life. You have undoubtedly set some postretirement goals—activities and ways of being you would like to shape into your new life. And you will only reach these goals by means of careful planning. So establish priorities for each day, week, and month. And make sure they are the ones that will bring you the deep satisfactions that are the foundations of mental wellbeing.

MYTH. When you retire, you're on your own. As an employee there was always some help with personal problems—in Personnel, or perhaps your boss or a colleague. Leaving the organization puts all that out of reach.

FACT. These days, help with a broad range of personal problems is more available than ever before.

Any severe blow to your personal life is an occasion to look outward for help. Too many people—through pride, fear, guilt, or shame—insist upon the outdated custom of the "stiff upper lip." Today we recognize that this is neither necessary nor healthy. Whatever crisis you face, there is someone to help, either in a general counseling or service organization or in a group devoted to a specific problem or illness. Your hospital, family doctor, clergy member, or local social service administration can refer you to individual or family counseling, group get-togethers, health care, and home service. Whatever specific difficulty you face, there is no need to suffer in isolation. Getting help when you need it most can mean weathering a crisis less painfully and faster.

MYTH. One thing sure to go as you age is your memory.

FACT. Researchers are finding more and more evidence to show that memory loss is often mistakenly related to biological age.

It's yet another case of self-fulfilling prophecy: worry enough about the possibility and the next thing you know you'll be forgetting everything under the sun. "Memory impotence," says Roy Rowan in *Fortune* (8/28/78), "like male sexual impotence, feeds on the fear of failure. Don't panic."

Of course, some things definitely do cause memory impairment, especially certain drugs and alcohol. Be sure to check your own intake of these if you feel at all concerned about memory retention. To keep memory function supple, *relax*, or tension will block your memory. Practice *association* when trying to remember names, lists, and so forth. Says Harry Lorayne, perhaps the best known memory entertainer and instructor, "It's essential to convert the verbal into the visual. But it's the *weird* pictures you remember." For example, let the mental image of a blue horse remind you to buy some of that cough medicine in the blue box (for hoarseness).

MYTH. Senility is as inevitable as failing eyesight and graying hair.

FACT. The latter two are natural, but senility isn't.

Although the reasons for some people falling victim to this progressive form of mental deterioration are not understood, it is currently recognized that many conditions once assumed to be senile dementia are in reality something else—and many of these can be treated.

Remember that senility in its extreme form is relatively rare. Also keep in mind that some of the classic signs are caused by a number of other disorders, such as tumors, hypothyroidism, nutritional deficiencies, and the misuse of certain drugs, such as alcohol or barbiturates. If a friend or family member exhibits symptoms which suggest senility, a wise move is to seek the guidance of a physician.

Dr. Robert N. Butler, Director of the National Institute on Aging, includes drugs as a common cause of pseudosenility and says that "drugs should be used with extraordinary care by older persons." Another common cause of pseudosenility is depression, which also can be treated.

PILLS AND DRUGS

Choose one:

a. Pills and drugs are dangerous and shouldn't be taken.

b. Pills and drugs, thanks to modern science, can cure almost anything.

Believe it or not, there are people who firmly believe choice *a*; and, there are about an equal number who really believe choice *b*. As is often the case, the truth lies somewhere in between. Pills and drugs, judiciously used, are extremely useful as *preventives* (benamid, for example, to lower the uric acid level of the blood for potential gout sufferers) and as *ameliorants* (aspirin for a common headache). But any drug, if misused, taken in excess, or taken for difficulties for which it is ineffective, is at best a waste of cash and at worst a danger.

MYTH. Name brands in drugs are just a ripoff.

FACT. Often, generic drugs—more or less the same ingredients as the name brand—are almost identical. But although all drugs must conform to standards set by the FDA (Food and Drug Administration), it is generally true that the big pharmaceutical manufacturers that put out name brands have the facilities for greater uniformity of product and better quality control.

Unless you have your own source of authority—a son-in-law who is a druggist, for example—no point in wrestling with the pros and cons of this question. When it comes to taking drugs, tell your doctor to prescribe what he or she thinks is best, but make the point that you prefer generic drugs because of the lower price.

MYTH A.   Vitamins are a lot of hogwash.

MYTH B.   Avoid vitamin pills at your peril.

FACT.   *Both of these views are distortions.* It's easy enough to understand their origins. This is one of the health areas where the authorities themselves are at odds. Some health experts stress the necessity for vitamin supplements. Others say that they usually are unnecessary.

Remember that although it is theoretically possible to get all your vitamin and mineral needs with your normal food intake, there are factors that tend to interfere. Even the best foods lose some nutrients in cooking, and you'd have to eat a great deal of some foods to get from them the prescribed daily requirement of a particular vitamin or mineral.

You may want to experiment with pills as a friend of mine did. She started on a multivitamin and mineral pill as part of her daily diet. After about a month she stopped for a while and then said, "I don't feel quite as energetic as I did before," and returned to her daily vitamin pill.

Some doctors tend to be quite offhand about prescribing vitamins. One doctor I know says, "If you think they'll do you any good, take them," which sounds more friendly than professional.

At a minimum it's a good idea to discuss the subject of food supplements next time you visit your doctor. In addition to recommending a multivitamin, he or she may suggest pills with specific vitamin or mineral content that your particular metabolism or health situation warrants.

MYTH.   Doctors are pill happy.

FACT.   Doctors are rarely pill pushers. But what sometimes happens is that, between a regular doctor and three specialists, a patient is prescribed several different kinds of drugs.

If this happens, stop! Check back with the physicians—*all* of them—to inform them of your drug "diet." It's illogical to expect your doctors to know what others have been prescribing. Be sure to inform your regular doctor and have him take the steps that will orchestrate your drug intake. Also, ask about the possible incompatibility of drugs that have been prescribed and any food or drink, such as alcohol.

MYTH.   "Wonder drugs" work wonders.

FACT.   Americans are becoming more and more aware of the need for caution in drug use. There is no question, of course, that there are times when modern medicines of one sort or another are absolutely vital to health and even life.

Here are some guidelines that can bring you the benefits of drugs, should you have to take them, and avoid the pitfalls:

Make sure your doctor or dentist knows what drugs you are currently taking before prescribing anything else. Since drugs can be more active in older persons, even at reduced dosage levels, older persons are especially prone to adverse drug reactions and interactions.

Make sure you completely understand each drug your doctor or dentist prescribes for you—what it is, what it should do, what its possible side effects could be, and how frequently and for how long it is to be taken.

Be wary of over-the-counter drugs. Self-medication can be dangerous, and no over-the-counter drug is perfectly harmless to everyone under any circumstances. Especially if you are taking any prescription medication, consult your doctor before adding any other drugs to your system.

Never, ever take prescription drugs prescribed for someone else.

When possible, ask your doctor for, and seek out, nondrug remedies for minor ailments. A glass of warm milk, for example, may promote healthy sleep better than a sleeping pill. For many minor symptoms, time and rest are really the only true cures.

NUTRITION

Some people—called food faddists by their detractors—insist that, "we are what we eat." At the other extreme are some individuals, and it must be confessed that these include some members of the medical profession, who feel that as long as you ingest a "balanced diet," you've done all that's required for your good health, nutritionally speaking.

In between these two extremes stand a majority who feel that what's put into a system affects the capabilities of the system—and this applies to nutrition and the human being.

Eating well—and this phrase tends to become a highly individual matter—therefore should be considered a major factor in your personal health program.

MYTH. Food is food and the only thing that matters is getting enough calories and maintaining a good balance.

FACT. Some food products are better than others and you can improve the healthfulness of your diet.

Nutritionists emphasize the virtues of natural foods. You don't have to go to a health food store to get them—just bypass temptingly packaged processed foods and substitute more wholesome foods available right in the supermarket. Nutritionists point out that natural food at its best is straight from the farm or dairy, but even in the supermarket you can select the foods closest to their natural states to ensure maximum nutritive value. For example, buy meat, fish, and poultry fresh, not frozen or canned. Buy breads and cereals made from whole grains. Buy fruits and vegetables fresh, or frozen ones without additional ingredients like sauces or sugar. Buy cheese that is labelled "cheese" and not "cheese food" or "cheese product." And buy plain yogurt and add fresh fruit to it, instead of buying the sugar-laden flavors. But also remember that the food-processing industry makes continuous efforts to improve its products nutritionally, and there are variations in prepared-food quality.

MYTH. Following sound nutritional guidelines in your diet means giving up the dishes you really enjoy.

FACT. Making the switch to a healthful diet can add to most people's eating enjoyment.

Foods that are nutritionally helpful, such as lean meats, fish, fruits, vegetables, and so on obviously can be prepared to satisfy your particular taste. You may want to review your breakfast, lunch, and dinner menus to see whether they are the best possible and the most satisfying.

MYTH. All the talk about diet—you must eat this, you shouldn't eat that—is highly exaggerated.

FACT. Balance is the key to good nutrition, and healthful eating can be a strong bulwark against a range of ailments and health impediments.

Balance and variety continue to be crucial, no matter what one's age. Your body is still growing new cells, and your blood supply and organs need constant nourishment to function properly. You need energy to do the things you want to do. All this can only go on with good eating habits, so shun the temptation to skip and skimp, to eat snacks instead of meals, or to rely on low-nutrition convenience foods. Each day, as well as in the long run, seek a *balance* from among the basic foods. Here are the four categories suggested by the Food and Nutrition Board of the National Research Council:

1. *The meat group.* Two or more servings a day of meat or poultry or fish or eggs.

FIG. 8-1   Recommended Daily Dietary Allowances

	MEN		WOMEN	
	35-55	55-75	35-55	55-75
Age	yr.	yr.	yr.	yr.
Weight (lb.)	154	154	128	128
Height (in.)	68	67	63	62
Calories	2600	2400	1850	1700
Protein gm..................	65	65	55	55
Vitamin A, I.U.	5000	5000	5000	5000
Vitamin D, I.U.	—	—	—	—
Vitamin E, I.U..............	30	30	25	25
Ascorbic Acid mg............	60	60	55	55
Folacin mg..................	0.4	0.4	0.4	0.4
Niacin mg	17	14	13	13
Riboflavin mg	1.7	1.7	1.5	1.5
Thiamine mg	1.3	1.2	1.0	1.0
Vitamin B_6 mg	2.0	2.0	2.0	2.0
Vitamin B_{12} μg	5	6	5	6
Calcium gm	0.8	0.8	0.8	0.8
Phosphorus gm	0.8	0.8	0.8	0.8
Iodine μg	125	110	90	80
Iron mg	10	10	18	10
Magnesium mg..............	350	350	300	300

Designed for the maintenance of good nutrition of practically all healthy people in the U.S.A. Reprinted with permission from Food and Nutrition Board, National Academy of Sciences National Research Council.

2. *The vegetable-fruit group.* Four or more servings a day.

3. *The milk group.* Two servings a day of any kind of milk or cheese or yogurt; occasionally ice cream.

4. *The bread-cereal group.* Four servings a day of any *whole-grain product,* including bread, crackers, cereal, rice, or pasta.

MYTH.   Eating at 100 is the same as eating at 30. It's O.K. to eat anything you can swallow.

FACT.   As you age, your calorie requirements shrink but your nutritional needs stay the same.

Careful selection of the foods you eat can help you squeeze more nutrients into fewer calories. The chart in Fig. 8-1 will serve as a general guideline to your dietary requirements.

MYTH.   Eating "good food," no matter what it is, can help you stay healthy.

FACT. In general, that's true. But with certain people it's desirable that specific diets be maintained to offset the threat of definite ailments. For example, nutritionists have devised an "anticoronary" diet to help potential victims prevent heart attacks.

If you suffer from any ailment that might possibly be minimized through diet, don't hesitate to check with your doctor. But be aware that some members of the medical profession minimize the importance of eating habits in relation to specific problems. Of course, the food faddists go to the other extreme. They feel everything from the common cold to housemaid's knee can be treated by selective dieting or "miracle" vitamins. It's likely the most effective course lies somewhere in between. One person I know whose doctor tried to laugh her off a special diet consulted some books on the subject and devised her own set of foods to favor and to avoid, and then got her doctor to agree—if somewhat reluctantly—that "it might help."

MYTH. Milk is for children.

FACT. At any age you can benefit from the nutritious elements in milk and milk products.

You never outgrow your need for milk, asserts the National Dairy Council. This opinion may have more point the older you get, because milk is one of the easiest and best sources of calcium—necessary, among other things, to prevent osteoporosis, a thinning of the bones common among older persons deficient in calcium. However, one group of medical experts asserts that the fat content of whole milk may contribute to cholesterol buildup. This possibility may be offset: skim milk and the yogurts and cheeses made from it are equally good calcium sources.

MYTH. Protein is the miracle element in diet.

FACT. You shouldn't distort your intake by heavily emphasizing protein or any other single nutritional element. Some "miracle diet" advertising can be misleading, even dangerous. The average American diet (and supermarket) seem to highlight foods that are high in carbohydrates and fats rather than protein. Make a special effort to balance your diet, including an *adequate* amount of protein daily.

MYTH. These days—because of the spiraling cost of food—you have a choice of being rich and undernourished or well fed and poor.

FACT. Even though food prices have been escalating, there are tactics you can use that will get you the most for your food dollar.

Eating right need not break the bank. Since you need to purchase less food each week than you did when the whole family ate together, you may find it possible to indulge in individual portions of nutritious luxuries like shellfish or filet mignon. But even on the tightest budget, you can eat not only right but deliciously. Fresh fruits and vegetables in season cost less—and are usually more nutritious—than out-of-season delicacies. Cottage cheese, peanut and other nut butters, and dried beans and other legumes cost less than other protein-rich foods, and can be the bases of delicious meals. Brown Grade B eggs have the same food value as Grade A eggs.

One major factor in food costs is your ability to shop. There is a whole mystique to supermarket shopping. The following techniques can help you cut as much as 15 or 20 percent from your weekly food budget.

1. Buy specials.
2. Compare quantities and quality of canned goods.
3. Buy the house brands where quantity and quality compare favorably.
4. Get to know the store manager and ask him or her to put you on to forthcoming sales or on-the-spot reductions in perishables like fruit and vegetables. You can often get a good buy when the manager decides to mark down lettuce, melons, grapes, bananas, and so on.

MYTH. A family of one or two usually eats as well as four or six.

FACT. A frequent cause for malnutrition is the "empty nest" syndrome.

With a family of two—or simply oneself—to feed, the good meals prepared for a larger family group may dwindle to convenient snacks from a can. Review your eating habits and make sure that you're not the victim of your own neglect. Obviously one or two people can easily continue to enjoy a nutritious, varied, and balanced diet. But this must be planned.

You have several things working for you. One boon is a freezer. It can literally become a storehouse of food—cooked, raw, or partially cooked—that can enrich your meals day to day. If you don't already, start to prepare several portions of main dishes at a time and freeze the rest for another meal.

In addition to judicious planning and preparation of food, you do have an advantage in your postretirement flexible schedule. Generally you'll be able to make more frequent trips to the store for sufficient foods and produce—and search out the discounted specials of the day, insuring both better eating and economy.

MYTH. Three "squares" a day insures good nutrition.

FACT. According to the American Association of Retired Persons, three "squares" is an ingrained social custom and not necessarily the best way to eat.

Evidence shows that several smaller meals—five or more, spaced at shorter intervals—might actually be healthier. You might try experimenting with the "five smalls" concept for a week or so to see if it agrees with you. Here's a day's sample menu:

Breakfast:	an egg or cereal whole wheat toast milk, coffee, or tea
Mid-morning:	half a grapefruit or orange juice
Lunch:	tuna salad raw or cooked vegetables glass of milk
Mid-afternoon	cup of vegetable soup or bouillon crackers tea
Dinner:	broiled chicken green beans green salad

Be careful, though, if you try this concept, that you don't merely *add* extra, unnecessary food twice a day in addition to normal meals. The point is to cut down on the big meals while adding the smaller ones. Large meals tend to put stress on the heart, authorities point out.

MYTH. When people get older, their sense of taste falters and food no longer tastes good.

FACT. What may falter is willingness to make the effort to prepare the dishes you enjoy.

Be on guard against this tendency. Make eating an occasion of pleasure for all involved. Try new foods; experiment with spices (in moderation) and herbs; enjoy a cocktail with dinner if your doctor sees no problem; try new methods of cooking—crock-pot, one-dish casseroles, foil cookery, or microwave.

MYTH. Maintaining a good diet is simple enough if you can get or make home-cooked meals, but restaurant eating is a problem.

FACT. You can eat healthfully in most any restaurant—if you choose wisely. Restaurants *can* offer more variety and make dining a special occasion. And it can be a welcome change of pace for those who want to get out of the kitchen.

If restaurant eating looms large in your life, you might want to practice what Jim Nechas, a restaurant reviewer, calls "defensive dining." Among his rules are:

1. "All you can eat" doesn't mean you *have* to eat everything in sight. Exercise caution.

2. Solicit recommendations from friends about restaurants. Try not to visit a restaurant you're totally unfamiliar with.

3. Consider how you eat at home. Do you usually have two drinks before dinner, wine with, a cordial afterwards? Is it normal to have a shrimp cocktail, buttered roll, and green salad *before* your main course? Probably not—in which case you shouldn't be eating that way very often at a restaurant, either.

4. Hang the price. That doesn't mean order the most expensive thing because it'll be better for you. It means that, rather than being concerned about the "better buy," or the bigger meal, consider better balance, reasonable portions, and variety. Don't let anyone or any menu dictate what you "should" eat.

MYTH. Alarms and warnings about obesity are exaggerated.

FACT. Most health authorities feel that obesity is one of the primary causes of many physical complaints ranging from fatigue to hardening of the arteries and certain heart conditions. With the help of your doctor, establish your ideal weight. Then, by judicious eating habits, try to reach and maintain it.

MYTH. If you're overweight at 55, it's too late to undo the ill effects.

FACT. It may be more *difficult* to begin to diet, simply because you've had a longer time to let undesirable habits take over, but it's far from hopeless.

Men need about 2,300 calories a day, and women about 1,700 in order to maintain a healthy weight. To reduce, obviously, consume less. But beware of fad diets. Work out your own plan. Remember, though, always check with your doctor before embarking on any substantial change in your diet.

MYTH. When constipation occurs, laxatives are the only solution.

FACT. Dietary habits in many cases can minimize the need for laxatives.

A good intake of fiber can do the trick. Fiber is the nondigestible substance found in many carbohydrates and is Nature's way to bowel regularity. Bran—in cereal, bread, muffins, or sprinkled on any food you choose—is probably the most convenient source of fiber. Also high in fiber are many fruits, vegetables, and nuts. Of course, if you do have some particular medical cause for constipation, consult your doctor and do not try your own remedy.

In typical cases, constipation can be alleviated by including certain types of food in your diet. Prunes, specifically, and most fruits in general can help natural elimination. Some unexpected items can have a laxative effect for individuals. For example, beets fall into this category. You may want to take advantage of this reaction of individual body chemistry should the need arise.

Usually, when an individual is troubled by constipation—and often this is accompanied by hemorrhoids—a doctor will prescribe a lubricant, such as mineral oil, and a hot sitzbath to alleviate discomfort.

SLEEP AND FATIGUE

In recent times doctors and researchers have come to understand a great deal about the physiology of sleep. The sleeping human, in one sense, is hard at work refreshing the circulatory and nervous systems, overcoming some of the stress of the previous waking period, and fortifying himself for activities to come.

In the past, fatigue was considered the simple result of excessive physical labor. If you worked in a coal mine all day or plugged away at any job for twelve or fourteen hours, fatigue was expected. But today we have a greater understanding of fatigue, not only about its chemistry but also its psychogenic origins. The good news about sleep and fatigue is that to a large extent they lie within the control of the individual.

Knowing just how to achieve this control and how to tackle any unsatisfactory aspects that may be getting you down can lead to decided improvement in the level of your energy and alertness.

MYTH. "I sleep well. That must mean I'm getting enough sleep."

FACT. Sleeping well and getting enough sleep are *not* the same thing, says Dr. Harry J. Johnson, well known for his work with the Life Extension Institute.

Remember that it is the *amount* of sleep, as well the *quality*, that matters. As Dr. Johnson says, "If you are getting eight hours of sleep but feel physically fatigued toward the end of the day, try increasing the amount of sleep. I often prescribe nine hours of sleep for patients, and I have seen marked improvement in physical and emotional health."

You yourself are the best judge of how well you are meeting your sleep requirements. Use questions like these to test yourself:

1. Do I feel refreshed when I wake up in the morning?

2. Do I get through an average day without feeling exhausted?

3. If I do tire or get drowsy during the day, does a catnap—anywhere from fifteen minutes to a couple of hours—help me finish the day in good shape?

Dr. Johnson also suggests that if circumstances prevent you from getting the normal seven or eight hours of sleep, you should try to make it up with daytime naps.

MYTH. There is no connection between sleep and mental health; sleep is just a body builder.

FACT. The statement above is a half myth. True, sleep does revitalize the muscles and nervous system. But doctors are becoming increasingly aware of the restorative value of sleep from an *emotional* standpoint.

Don't eliminate sleeping difficulties as a possible cause if you feel edgy and irritable. If you tend to feel at odds with the world, if you sense a trend towards becoming short tempered, or if you feel your responses to situations and people are less than satisfactory, consider the possibility that inadequate sleep may be at least part of the cause.

MYTH. If you have trouble falling asleep, you're in trouble indeed.

FACT. Many people have difficulty in falling asleep, but there are a number of procedures that are successful in minimizing the problem. If you're not one of those lucky people who fall asleep "the minute my head hits the pillow," consider some of these remedies recommended by medical authorities:

1. *Don't* smoke before bedtime or in bed. The latter is a *life* hazard in any event. Many a destructive fire has been caused by a lighted pipe or cigarette dropped onto the mattress by a dozing smoker. In addition, smoking has a stimulating rather than a sedative effect on the body.

2. Avoid caffeine beverages. Coffee, tea, and soda will stimulate rather than calm you down.

3. One partial insomniac says, "I take a warm bath and read in bed. After about ten or fifteen minutes—I make a point of picking not-too-lively reading matter—I turn out the light, and I'm gone."

4. Doris Greene, a Washington friend of mine who finds the hectic life of the capital a keeper-upper, swears by the virtues of warm milk—sometimes with a bit of honey—as a soporific.

5. And for Armin Wolper, of Houston, "TV is just a big sleeping pill for me. When all else fails, I just plump down and let the Late Show put me out like a light."

MYTH.   Older people need less sleep than younger people.

FACT.   It all depends. People of any age group vary individually in their need for sleep.

Dr. Harry Johnson suggests that the best way to find out how much sleep your own body really requires is to forget about "rules." Rather, go to sleep when you feel tired and wake up naturally, without an alarm, for a week or so. Your body will let you know how much sleep is enough. But be sure to do this during a "normal" week—one before which you have not missed too much sleep or during which you are not ill or depressed. For many people, it may take several days or weeks of regular sleep to make up for "sleep debt," and get the body back to its natural rhythm.

MYTH.   The best position for sleeping is to relax on your back.

FACT.   There is no "best" position. Right side, left side, stomach or back—they are all fine.

While in general it doesn't matter what position you get into to start your sleep, there are definite individual preferences. If you aren't sure which position works best for you—there are dozens of things we do automatically for most of our lives of which we are unaware—you may want to experiment. Try the many possible ways to lie down. The four basic ones—on your stomach, your back, right side, or left side—can be further modified. For example, you may lie on your right side with your knees slightly bent. Or, you may bend one leg, keep the other straight.

A friend of mine lessened his insomnia considerably when he discovered that if he lay on his stomach and stretched his arms out under his pillow, sleep came quickly. It's not too bad being a guinea pig, if you are the one running the experiment.

MYTH. "The X Company makes the best mattress in the world."

FACT. Maybe they do, but "the best mattress" is not likely to be determined by the brand name but by its degree of hardness. The consensus seems to be that a firm mattress, which makes it easier to change position during sleep—we all do this about twenty to sixty times a night—is best.

Give some attention to both the mattress and the bed you use. Health authorities seldom say anything that suggests that the design, age, or other quality of the bed makes much difference, while going on at length about the spring and mattress. But in my opinion, there is a mystique about a bed. You too may find as I did that a modern platform bed seems "right." Or your preference may be exactly the opposite: ensconced in an old four-poster, you may sleep like a baby, while you toss and turn on the leanness of a modern platform. Think about it, anyway. Check to see if you have an affinity for the bed you use, and consider changing if you don't.

And getting back to mattresses: if you aren't satisfied with the firmness of the one you have, you may want to insert a bedboard between the spring and mattress to take some of the give out of your present sleeping surface.

MYTH. No sweat if you can't sleep. Pop a pill.

FACT. Sleeping pills are useful, but only if they are taken infrequently, in special circumstances.

You should *never* take sleeping pills—by borrowing someone else's, for example—unless you consult a physician, and have him or her prescribe the type of sedative and the dosage.

MYTH. Don't bother trying aspirin if you can't sleep.

FACT. A recent study at Dartmouth Medical School showed that two tablets taken at night improved sleep for up to three nights in a row.

If you *regularly* suffer from insomnia, you'll have to look elsewhere for relief—and there are plenty of remedies. But for an occasional problem in falling asleep, plain old aspirin can be helpful.

MYTH.   If you have an ailment that requires you to wake up several times during the night, your sleep will always be inadequate.

FACT.   Many people—with prostate or kidney ailments, for example—wake up with varying frequency to urinate. In most cases they adapt to this need and their sleep can be fully satisfactory.

If you do have a need to disturb your sleep—to go to the bathroom, to take medication or whatever—ease the problem by making the activity as simple and convenient as possible. People with bathroom needs have wisely arranged to have the washroom adjoin their sleeping quarters, either by the selection of their living quarters with this factor in mind, or adding a small lavatory.

In some cases, eating or drinking habits may influence the wake-up pattern. Check with your doctor and get advice as to how you may be able to minimize the problem. And remember that you can compensate for loss of sleep during the night by napping during the day. Be sure to work such periods into your schedule as needed.

MYTH.   Insomnia is an unshakeable ailment.

FACT.   For many people, insomnia is an occasional and intermittent interference.

If you find yourself troubled by insomnia for the first time, don't conclude that your doom is sealed. Chances are that some temporary situation—worry over some particular problem or illness of a family member or friend—can cause sleeplessness. In extreme cases, where current circumstances are keeping you awake, you're justified in asking your doctor for drug relief. If you don't want to resort to pills, you may decide to put up with a few nights of broken sleep. You may want to read, take a walk, do a crossword puzzle, or work on a hobby. Companionship can be a welcome alleviant. Your spouse or a family member may be willing, even eager to share your vigil.

MYTH.   Sleeplessness has to be unmitigated discomfort.

FACT.   Talk to some insomniacs and you detect not only annoyance at their inability to sleep as they'd like, but even a note of panic. While lying awake when you want to sleep may be upsetting, it *does* have another, constructive side. Take advantage of some of the discoveries that have been made. Some observers say that the lying-awake state is a kind of twilight zone. The writer Arthur Koestler has described it as a state of reverie in which the mind exhibits unusual qualities.

Many scientists and artists credit this twilight state with creative solutions and inspiration for their work. People find that daily problems, tough decisions that they have wrestled with in vain during their normal waking hours, somehow yield to the special and changed nature of their thinking and awareness.

One expert in the subject of sleep suggests that the suspension of critical judgment associated with the usually dominant left hemisphere of the brain may allow the nondominant right side of the brain, with its more intuitive and emotional processes, to take over.

MYTH. The older you get, the more tired you'll feel after even normal exertion.

FACT. You may *think* you're tired—run down or whatever—but chances are you're bored or tense instead.

Buck the tendency to slow down, or *be* slowed down, merely as a reflection of your chronological age. Of course, if you feel lazy or tired, don't overexert. But don't assume you're "too old" to do what you've done in the past. Studies have shown that older, inactive people over fifty often perceive their bodies to be broader and heavier than they are, and believe as a result that normal physical activity is bad for them. The end results of such lack of movement may be muscular atrophy and lessening of coordination.

MYTH. Living alone has nothing to do with fatigue.

FACT. Studies show that many people living entirely on their own tend to fall into bad eating habits and lose the incentive to exercise—two possible causes of fatigue. And contrary to what many people think, exercise doesn't cause fatigue but basically decreases it. One of the reasons for this is that lactic acid in the blood, which has been thought of as an inducer of "that tired feeling," tends to accumulate as a result of inactivity. Exercise tends to lower the lactic acid blood element and decreases the feeling of fatigue.

Living alone requires more than financial or social considerations. It can also be a health factor. In thinking about living arrangements, the decision to live alone should be made only after due consideration has been given to all the consequences. True, being on one's own has the lure of independence and self-sufficiency, but you don't want to win these at a cost which may be too high to pay.

EXERCISE

People's interest today in many popular activities such as jogging, yoga, setting-up exercises, dance routines for body building, and so on, is far from being a whim. Years of medical study have led to the conclusion that body tone and capability depend directly on physical exercise. The individual who gets in a fair share of physical movement in a day— walking, running, swimming, tennis, golf, and so on—is heavily weighting the odds in favor of good health. And we're not only talking of muscle tone and "feeling good." Heart specialists are among the strongest advocates of adequate exercise. Many undesirable conditions from high blood pressure to overweight can be controlled by a satisfactory physical regimen.

MYTH. The physical signs of age, especially posture changes— stooping over, a shuffling gait—are inevitable.

FACT. Medical science rejects this antiquated idea. "Much of the aches and pains that older people complain of can be eliminated by stretching muscles and giving them a workout," says Dr. Raymond Paris, head of the Center for the Study of Aging in Albany, New York.

"Keep on using it and you won't lose it," is the way some scientists view the solution to the traditional inroads into the good health of older people. One authority says, "Many doctors maintain an active practice with no loss of judgment or stamina into their seventies. People in their eighties remain physically active and lithe. Eighty-year-olds have been hitting the jogging trails. White-haired ladies who have maintained a steady program of walking can reach a pace that leaves younger companions gasping. In short, *inactivity* is the villain." One doctor says, "When you stop moving the years catch up with you."

What actually happens is a combination of slight losses of function compounded by bad habits. As you grow older muscles weaken—for example, at sixty-five people retain only about 80 percent of the muscular strength they had at thirty. Accordingly, it takes a little more effort to get up out of a chair and so on. Then people can become victims of a vicious cycle: the less they move around, the weaker their muscles become.

Unexercised back and shoulder muscles weaken and so the individual develops a stoop. When the muscles that keep your joints straight lose their power, people develop pains in knees, hips, and elbows—and they move even less. An additional consequence of inactivity is a tendency to gain weight, which makes moving around even more of an effort.

Statistics seem to bear out this view. In this country where 45 percent of adults don't exercise, according to the director of the President's Council on Physical Fitness, the ailments that flourish as a result of inactivity are of epidemic proportions. But in "primitive" lands where survival needs force people to continue to work physically, ninety-year old men and women still work in the fields.

For most people, posture is more than a simple matter of appearance. Your outlook on life is, to some extent, reflected by your posture and gait. The man or woman who stands straight and moves gracefuly seems more cheerful and confident—and younger.

Habit can influence the way your body holds itself. This is one area where the exercises can help you improve, if in your case it seems desirable. As a minimum program, the simple resolve to stand straight and walk in a graceful fashion can take you out of the shuffler category and improve not only the way you look but the way you feel. Next time you are out walking, stop. Tell yourself, "I'm going to put on a one-person parade." Put your shoulders back, put your chin up, think a pleasant thought, and set out down the street. You'll not only look better, you'll feel better.

MYTH. If you don't do it in the gymnasium, it's not exercise.

FACT. Any workout you give your muscles, anything you do that steps up your heartbeat and gets you to breathe more deeply, is likely to be healthful.

You may not want to jog, you avoid tennis like the plague, and the last time you tried swimming you almost drowned. But you could cross off dozens of established types of physical activity and still leave enough over from which you could draw one or more that you enjoy. One health authority suggests, "Why not lead a band?" He then points out that many famed conductors and musicians lived to ripe old ages: Stokowski at 83, Toscanini at 89, Pablo Casals at 94. Of course, you don't need an orchestra. Put a record on your turntable, pick up a pencil or whatever you can improvise as a baton, and lead the band. Not only will you be getting exercise, you may even enjoy the music.

MYTH.   Any exercise is good for anyone.

FACT.   Too *much* can be very bad indeed. And then, various kinds of body movements have different effects on the body, desirable for some people, less so for others. Get your doctor's advice in making a choice.

Medical authorities in general, and the American Heart Association in particular, are advocates of exercise as a conditioner and protector. One study by Dr. Ralph S. Paffenberger of the Stanford University School of Medicine showed that as the level of activity went up among the men he studied (Harvard alumni, aged thirty-five to seventy-four), the incidence of heart attack went down. Using 2,000 calories a week as a measure, he found that those who spent less than 2,000 calories a week in exercise were 64 percent more likely to suffer heart attack than those who spent more. The chart shown in Fig. 8-2 provides a rough measure of the connection between exercise and calories used.

FIG. 8-2   Activity/Calorie Use Chart

ACTIVITY	CALORIES/ HOUR	TIME NEEDED TO BURN 2000 CALORIES
Good		
skating (moderate)	345	5 hrs. 43 min.
walking (4½ mph)	401	5 hrs.
tennis (moderate)	419	4 hrs. 45 min.
canoeing (4 mph)	426	4 hrs. 41 min.
Better		
swimming (crawl, 45 yards/min)	529	3 hrs. 47 min.
skating (vigorous)	531	3 hrs. 45 min.
downhill skiing	585	3 hrs. 25 min.
handball	591	3 hrs. 23 min.
tennis (vigorous)	591	3 hrs. 23 min.
squash	630	3 hrs. 10 min.
running (5.5 mph)	651	3 hrs. 4 min.
bicycling (13 mph)	651	3 hrs. 4 min.
Best		
cross-country skiing (5 mph)	709	2 hrs. 50 min.
karate	778	2 hrs. 34 min.
running (7 mph)	847	2 hrs. 22 min.

SOURCE: Reprinted from *Executive Fitness*, by permission of Rodale Press, Emmaus, PA
NOTE: These figures are for a 152-lb. person. If you weigh more, you'll burn up more calories in the same time; if you weigh less, you'll burn fewer.

Dr. Paffenberger also feels that *the way* an exercise is performed is a factor in its value: strolling down the avenue won't do your arteries much good, but a brisk pace that covers a mile in fifteen minutes definitely will.

MYTH. As long as you do exercise, it makes no difference what form that exercise takes.

FACT. Different forms of physical activity offer different fitness benefits. There are two kinds that it is wise to consider. *Heart-lung/cardiorespiratory fitness* develops and protects heart and lung muscles, helps weight loss, improves sleep and sexual activity, and reduces fatigue. *Strength and flexibility fitness* sharpens mental and physical responses and generally makes you look and feel better.

Cardiorespiratory fitness can be achieved in walking, running, cycling, swimming, rowing, and jumping rope—all having the additional benefit of being easily developed into habits essential to permanent fitness. Try alternating some that appeal to you to avoid boredom.

Strength and flexibility fitness comes from the "bending and stretching" variety of exercise—sit-ups, toe-touching, and so on. Swimming and rope-jumping are also strength and flexibility conditioners.

MYTH. Exercise makes you healthy.

FACT. If you're hoping to achieve good health solely from an exercise program, you're barking up the wrong tree.

Look, instead, says Dr. Harry M. Johnson, for a "sense of wellbeing—with or without flawless health." Moreover, be careful about the competitive aspects of the exercise you choose. The more competitive a personality you are, the more you may need to take the competitive element out of your exercise for it to keep you healthy. It's fine if you want to measure your progress. But if you look upon each day's accomplishment as a record to beat the next day, you run the risk of pushing yourself beyond a safe level of exertion.

MYTH. Exercise is for athletes and young people.

FACT. By now the benefits of a continuing program of exercise have been made very clear. Physical activity slows down the development of arteriosclerosis and maintains cardiovascular capacity. This means protection against heart disease, but it also means that organs and tissues throughout the body are better nourished and supplied with oxygen and so can retain their youthful vigor.

And recent studies show that exercise also helps bones absorb calcium. Together with proper diet this can mean forestallment of the onset of osteoporosis—loss of calcium from the bones—that leads to stooped posture and a susceptibility to broken bones that haunts older people.

The benefits of happy, health-giving activity in the form of exercise and so on, are many. The functioning of muscles and bones is tied to the nervous system and the production of hormones. This suggests that exercise maintains or even increases muscle tone and capability and can prevent the slowdown of metabolism that may come with age.

Dr. Lawrence Lamb suggests that exercise may also keep hormones flowing at a youthful level. "It is possible that physical activity is a significant factor in maintaining optimal functioning of the endocrine glands," says Dr. Lamb. The glands are therefore perhaps better able to provide life-giving hormones for continued youth and vigor.

MYTH. The fast pace of contemporary living assures everyone an adequate amount of exercise.

FACT. It depends on what kind of life you're living. If you are a farmer, chances are favorable. City dwellers don't rate as well. A study made of two groups, one living in an isolated Swiss village and another in the city of Basel, as reported by Dr. Jean Mayer, Professor of Nutrition at Harvard, showed marked differences in cholesterol level. People in the village had a high fat intake, and they consumed 100 calories more each day than the urban dwellers. However, the serum cholesterol levels of the physically active men and women in the village were much lower than those of the Basel residents.

If your daily activities don't include an adequate amount of exercise, follow the suggestion of Dr. Michael Mock, cardiologist with the National Heart and Lung Institute. He points out that you can easily work movement into your daily life. For example, avoid elevators and climb stairs whenever you can. Take the stairs down, too. Don't aim for the parking space closest to your destination. Park a distance away and walk. If you live in the suburbs, don't use your car for local shopping, visiting neighbors, and so on.

Look for ways to keep your body in motion. For example, think up projects that get you off the sofa from time to time. Don't be too quick to put phone extensions throughout your house. Even if a phone extension is at hand, walk to the next nearest phone for that extra bit of muscle use.

MYTH. Exercise is hell.

FACT. While many people understandably find routine exercises boring to the point where they simply cannot subject themselves to a regular program, it is quite possible to get a good body-strengthening and muscle-toning workout in a thoroughly enjoyable way.

Folk dancing, for instance, is enjoyed by thousands of people—in cities as well as out in the country. Most areas have groups that have an ongoing program of weekly or monthly get-togethers. Churches or community centers sponsor the programs. Sometimes Ys or schools offer folk or square dancing, putting an auditorium or gymnasium to good use evenings and weekends. And at such occasions you'll find a large percentage of older people, often among the most expert performers, having fun and reaping the benefits of healthful exercise.

Bicycling is another dual-purpose, painless way of keeping fit. Bicycle riding not only builds body fitness, but also takes you places: into town from a country or suburban home; to your shopping; into the country for a one-day excursion. And while you're pedaling, you're building stamina and maintaining your muscle system.

For those to whom the two-wheeler bicycle is undesirable for some reason, the adult tricycle is a happy alternative. In many areas, where road and traffic conditions are favorable, older people have enjoyed the benefits of cycling by using the three-wheeled vehicle. They are stable, require less control than the two-wheeler, and for people who have health problems which make the balancing and control of a bicycle impractical, it can be a fun way of getting around and getting exercise at the same time.

Swimming and walking are two other forms of locomotion and exercise that keep you fit, and represent an alternative to the bend-and-stretch or other type of routine body-fitness program. Walking has one great virtue: it doesn't require special equipment or facility, such as a pool for swimming. My Aunt Harriet, at the age of eighty, got herself a parttime job in a downtown department store. And she walked to and from work—two miles each way. "And they pay me," she said, implying that the benefit of the exercise alone made the job worthwhile.

MYTH. Jogging is a sure way to take you down the road to good health.

FACT. Jogging can cause foot and leg injuries and may aggravate heart conditions.

If you're interested in jogging, first check with your doctor to make sure that there is no reason *not* to undertake the activity. Medical authorities who have an intimate understanding of jogging's effect on the body report that this exercise may affect different leg muscles unevenly.

And one authority says, "Without proper stretching exercises, knee, leg, and feet problems can develop. Preparatory exercises must be undertaken beforehand. They should be done before and after jogging, preferably on a daily basis."

And if your feet have been a problem or you suspect they may become so, it's a good idea to consult a podiatrist in advance. The American Podiatric Association offers a free, four-page pamphlet on the subject of shoes, exercise, and conditioning. It can be obtained by writing to the Association at 20 Chevy Chase Circle, Washington, D.C. 20015. They'd like you to enclose a stamped return envelope.

MYTH. Exercise is good for you because it stirs up your circulation and makes you tingle all over.

FACT. Exercise may do just that for some people. But exercise makes you "feel good" for a more valid reason than is suggested by the stirs-you-up theory. Dr. Gregory Raiport, a Russian medical expert, suggests this cause and effect: When people become older, physical abilities are reduced while the self-image remains the same. This often causes frustration, depression, and feelings of inferiority. In turn, these negative emotions adversely affect bodily functions. This creates a vicious circle that can be broken through physical exercise. A study conducted in the Moscow Institute of Gerontology showed that a group of people whose average age was sixty-six and suffering from depression and anxiety improved significantly when encouraged to do exercise such as jogging, swimming, and brisk walking. They were found to be more optimistic, relaxed, and self-confident, and all reported that they had regained their "taste for life."

Keep in mind that sports and exercise also have a social aspect. Walking, swimming, and exercising with others provide a stimulating social environment and reduce the tendency towards introversion, a trait common to older people. Keep these facts in mind for older friends and relatives. Offer to exercise with them, at least as a starter to get them going.

SEX

I would like to share with you my first exposure to a discussion of sex for older people—a three-day seminar on preretirement education. The woman who conducted the session summed up her major contribution to the subject by telling the somewhat wide-eyed audience, "It's all right, it's all right for older people to have sex!" I agree with the reaction of the woman sitting next to me who whispered, "That's pretty skimpy coverage." I agree there is more to be said on this subject than a reassuring sentence can convey.

Some people have objected to the inclusion of this important topic under health. I have been accused of being uncaring about romance, and the many subtleties of feeling and relationship that sex often creates. But it is precisely my respect for these matters that explains my judgment. Feeling that justice could not be done to the romantic elements, it seems natural to treat sex as a health matter—mental as well as physical—and to offer some useful facts that can remove fears and false notions from a part of our lives that may remain vital in the very oldest of us.

MYTH.   Sex is for the young.

FACT.   "Older people have the same emotional and sexual needs as younger people, with equivalent variations in intensity, kinds of expression, and the need for other persons to express with," says Dr. Mary S. Calderone, well-known educator in the public health field. "As human beings at any stage of life, we long for other human beings to respond to us and to be responsive with—whether in touch, shared pleasures, joys, sorrows, intellectual interchange, or from time to time in sexual responsiveness at many levels including the purely physical." Sex is for people at any age and, at any age, it is made up of many levels of feeling and qualities of relationship.

MYTH.   Aging brings an inevitable end to sexual activity.

FACT.   Aging brings some changes in performance, but no end unless you decide that way.

Ignore the folklore about loss of sexuality, by all means. As Dr. Alex Comfort says, "Sex is a highly undangerous activity." In fact, it's more dangerous to stop than to persist, because depression could result. If you have specific questions about matters sexual, go ahead and ask your doctor. Listen to him or her, unless you start hearing things about "really a little old . . ." in which case you ought to ask another doctor. But in general, you can expect to carry on to the degree to which you're interested.

"Human beings are born with libido and they die with it," says Dr. Stanley R. Dean of the Florida College of Medicine. While sex practices may change—and the sexual acrobatics of the young may not appeal to older people—interest and capability remain. Attach much more importance to the satisfactions and pleasures you obtain from sex, rather than the physical acts that are involved. This principle puts the emphasis where it does the most good—on present feeling rather than on past performance.

MYTH. Those who seek sexual experience after X years are "dirty old men," and "dirty old women."

FACT. Other people's sex practices are no one else's business.

A very good 60-year-old friend told me, "I once drove a very attractive divorcee home from a party. I stopped in front of her house and she seemed to take a long time getting out of the car. I thought she was waiting for me to open the door, and I started to get out when she said, 'Aren't you going to kiss me goodnight?' I said, 'I'd love to but I don't want you to think of me as a dirty old man.' 'The dirtier the better,' she said."

He never told me how the evening ended. But keep this anecdote in mind if you ever are assailed by the fear of being considered a "dirty old" anything.

MYTH. The sex activity of older people is simply a matter of "operating from memory."

FACT. The implication that those in the higher age brackets are simply going through the motions, jaded and without much satisfaction seems to have its basis more in the lewdness of night-club comics than in reality. There are two appetites, lively and capable of giving pleasure, that most people take to the grave: eating and sex.

Understand that sex interest is a highly subjective matter, and that age is only one of several factors that shape it. Dr. Robert N. Butler, author of *Why Survive? Being Old in America,* notes that versatility and capacity to grow persist through the years. And apropos of *improvement* of sexual functioning, Dr. Butler says that Havelock Ellis, who contributed so much to our understanding of sexuality, suffered from lifelong impotence, which was cured in his old age.

MYTH. Sex is largely a physical matter.

FACT. Not only psychological factors, but social ones also influence sexual attitudes and performance.

Dr. Isadore Rubin in *Sexual Life After Sixty* pointed out that in societies in which old age is denigrated, older people tend toward self-rejection. This same type of negative attitude goes on to label sexually active men of sixty or over as lechers, and women over fifty as being sexually over the hill. And since sex and self-esteem are closely related, the damaging effect of social disapproval of sexual activity among seniors becomes clear.

MYTH. When it comes to sexual potency, we are not limited to our own natural resources. There are many products that can turn us into sexual whiz-bangs.

FACT. Stimulants, aphrodisiacs, and gadgets of various kinds are not only generally ineffective, but also possibly harmful.

Don't be taken in by glowing stories of high flying by imbibers of vitamins, tonics, or "love potions" under any name. If you are interested or curious about one or another drug or device, it would be wise not to experiment without the guidance of a professional adviser—doctor, counselor, or sex therapist.

MYTH. Because of age and experience, older people know all about sex.

FACT. Many young people today, because of more open attitudes to which they were exposed in their earlier years, and greater personal freedom to further their sexual interests, are more sophisticated and knowledgeable than their seniors. Some people think sex education is as necessary for over-fifties as for teenagers. Not very flattering, but there it is. If your sexuality, and/or that of your mate or others is unsatisfactory, don't rule out the possibility of seeking professional help. It's better to be informed than frustrated.

MYTH. Too much sex is bad for you.

FACT. There is no evidence that sex is harmful to health, and there is a great deal of evidence that a satisfactory sex life invigorates you physically, mentally, and emotionally.

Don't let yourself be short-changed. Follow your sexual propensities with the same avidity as you would any other absorbing and rewarding interest. Remember, sex, more than almost any other activity, has the potential of making two people happy.

COMMON ILLNESSES

Most health situations are the same for men and women. Both sexes can have hangnails, dandruff, fallen arches, and heart disease. But certain health considerations are unique to each sex. The most common of these, coincidentally, tend to appear later in life: for example, in men over fifty, prostate conditions tend to become quite common. For women, breast cancer and the need for hysterectomies are presently quite common.

Unfortunately, because of the intimate and personal nature of these types of ailments, misconceptions and ignorance are widespread. In this section, you should find the facts that explain away the more common gender-related health myths.

MYTH. Prostate trouble is chronic and incurable.

FACT. Prompt diagnosis and treatment *can* control the noncancerous prostate conditions—infectious and noninfectious prostatitis (inflammation of the gland) and benign prostatic hyperplasia (enlargement of the prostate).

First signs of an inflamed or enlarged prostate are urinary problems—urgency, frequency, burning, difficulty in urinating, and the need to get up often at night to urinate. These signs should be reported to a family physician or urologist.

Inflammation of the prostate is caused by bacteria or chemical and physical irritants. Bacterial or infectious prostatitis, a deep-seated infection that occurs in men under twenty-five, responds to antibiotic treatment (ten to fourteen days of medication), according to Dr. John B. Wear, professor of urology at the University of Wisconsin Medical School. One bout of the disease does *not* mean a future of prostate trouble. Men of all ages get noninfectious prostatitis, which is likely to recur if not completely treated.

Doctors will try to identify and eliminate the specific irritants causing the condition since these are likely to vary with each individual. For older men, benign prostate hyperplasia is a problem; virtually 100 percent of men over sixty have some enlargement of the prostate.

Those who suffer from any of these conditions can help themselves, advises Dr. Wear. Avoid certain foods that exacerbate them: alcohol, cashew nuts, chocolate, cocoa, coffee (including decaffeinated), colas, and tea. Also, cut down on activities that subject the lower part of the trunk to unusual pounding—like bumpy driving, for example—and jar the prostate.

Emotional relaxation and regular bowel habits are important, as emotional tension, constipation, and diarrhea may put a muscular pressure on the gland. Since sexual abstention seems to lead to a buildup of fluid within the prostate, regular sexual release may also help.

MYTH. Prostate trouble means cancer.

FACT. Prostatitis and enlargement of the prostate are *not* cancer. The former condition is in no way linked to cancer, and only a gross enlargement of the prostate may increase the likelihood of a later cancer. While prostate cancer is the second most common cancer among men, survival rates have improved over the past thirty years.

Early detection of the disease does make a difference. For all men over forty, annual rectal exams (where a doctor can feel a tumor with his finger) are advised, says Dr. Wear. He believes men whose fathers or grandfathers had prostate cancer and those with a gross enlargement of the prostate should have the exam every six months.

MYTH. Prostate trouble can destroy a man's sex life.

FACT. Since men with an inflamed or enlarged prostate benefit from regular sexual release (and the clearing of the seminal fluid that collects in the gland), many doctors encourage them to increase their rate of sexual activity. That means, of course, that these conditions do *not* change a man's potency.

According to Dr. William L. Parry, professor of urology, University of Oklahoma College of Medicine, these conditions do not affect a man's fertility. Nor can the female partner catch an infection from the man with a prostate problem, notes Dr. Parry. Prostate trouble should not change a man's sexual self-confidence, and a sensitive doctor can help clear up doubts in this area.

MYTH. Odds favor the average woman having some form of breast cancer.

FACT. One out of fifteen women is, statistically, destined to have breast cancer. While the odds are encouraging, it is still a large enough number to warrant attention. Women should take the time and trouble to educate themselves in the matter of breast care and cancer detection. Ignorance is not bliss: it is dangerous.

MYTH. There has to be an obvious symptom before breast cancer can be diagnosed.

FACT. Recent medical advances make it possible for specialists to diagnose breast cancers before there is even a discernible lump. These examinations—called mammography, xeroradiography, and thermography—are quick and usually painless.

Monthly self-examination, coupled with annual examination by a physician, greatly improve the chances of early detection and treatment. Your doctor should show you how to examine your breasts in the approved manner.

MYTH. Depend on your doctor in dealing with that esoteric subject of "women's diseases." After all, he or she is the expert.

FACT. While it is true that your doctor is more of an authority in health matters than you are, he does not know everything. In addition, a doctor may simply forget to explain something to you or may use language you don't understand.

Aim for an open and honest relationship with your doctor. The closer to equal you feel, the freer you will be to talk about whatever you want to know. Above all, don't hesitate to ask relevant questions. Don't permit squeamishness or embarrassment to prevent you from making inquiries. It's important that you *understand* what is involved in health care, that you are clear on procedures and checkpoints on which health maintenance depends.

MYTH. Hysterectomy means removal of all a woman's reproductive organs.

FACT. The word itself means surgical removal of the uterus. Several different procedures exist, covering a broad range of actual operations.

Don't let yourself be panicked by unrealistic fears of the experiences of other women in general or "by what happened to Ethel." Make sure you understand exactly what is involved in this type of operation. Should you be faced with it, remember that modern medicine has gone far toward alleviating many of the unpleasant side effects women used to experience after hysterectomy.

MYTH. A hysterectomy causes physical changes that interfere with sexual satisfaction, and the end of sexual interest.

FACT. There is no evidence that hysterectomy—with or without removal of the ovaries—changes sexual desire or performance. There may be a general relaxing of the vaginal walls, but doctors can do preventive surgery as a precaution against this.

Anyone who faces this type of surgery should discuss with the surgeon all aspects of the procedure, as well as the operation and postoperative care.

MYTH. Changes in both physical appearance and sexual responsiveness result from a hysterectomy.

FACT. If hormone therapy is carefully planned when ovaries are removed, there should be no dramatic changes due to reduced estrogen levels.

Women who are to face this type of surgery should consult with their regular doctor and their surgeon, both before and afterwards, on the matter of postoperative care.

MYTH. Hysterectomy is an "older woman's disease."

FACT. There are now close to half a million hysterectomies being performed each year, and increasingly on younger women.

Age is just one of several factors that may have to do with the need for a hysterectomy. Some women live to be a hundred after having the operation, some women live to be a hundred without requiring it.

MYTH. Hysterectomies are only performed in cases of absolute emergency—the existence of cancer or other incurable diseases of the reproductive organs.

FACT. Today many hysterectomies are being performed (especially on younger women) in the absence of these medical indications. Several excellent studies have found that at least one-third were clearly unnecessary and another 10 percent or more could probably have been avoided. More recent studies have shown that rate rising close to 50 percent. Many gynecologists have been recommending it as a method of preventing pregnancy, called it "hysterilization," often advocating hysterectomy as a routine procedure "when the patient has completed her family." More specifically, hysterectomies are performed unnecessarily for the removal of small fibroids (instead of a myomectomy, which removes the fibroids and leaves the uterus) or for an abortion in cases where a saline or suction abortion would be appropriate.

If your doctor recommends a hysterectomy, make sure he or she explains to you thoroughly the reasons for believing this procedure is indeed the only possible measure. If you have any doubt at all about the explanation, consult another physician. If you are a clinic patient, be sure to ask to see your medical records. (Some women have been victimized by unnecessary sterilization of all types.) And, by all means, get a second opinion, preferably from another specialist.

MYTH. Most women become severely depressed after a hysterectomy.

FACT. While it is true that some women experience loss and feelings of worthlessness, others have reported a sense of relief, especially if the hysterectomy has eliminated some serious problem or pain.

How you react psychologically will probably depend most on your self-image. If you see yourself as a person with many facets to her existence, a woman who has a variety of roles in life, you will undoubtedly be more able to spring back to your feet more quickly than the woman whose entire existence revolves around her role as wife and mother.

If you do feel depressed, don't hesitate to ask for help. A visit to a social worker or women's discussion group may prove immensely valuable in providing support through the difficult period of recovery. Supportive psychotherapy, by the way, is even more useful before the operation as a preparatory and preventive measure.

ZEROING IN ON BETTER HEALTH

The level of your health can be a plus factor, not only in what you can accomplish day to day, but in the fun and satisfaction you derive from what you do.

A considerable number of misconceptions give many people a distorted picture of their own basic health concerns and prospects for tomorrow. Zeroing in on these misleading ideas can not only help you improve understanding of your present health situation but can assist in maximizing your well-being, physical and mental.

MYTH. Basically, there's nothing you can do about your health; it's largely a matter of luck. Or at best, you can try to lead a "clean life" and hope that will help.

FACT. The American Medical Association has recently swung around to the view that a good deal of illness is the individual's own fault. The AMA has run full-page ads with the headline, "Seven Good Habits

Your Doctor Wishes You Had." The seven good habits:

1. Three meals a day
2. Moderate exercise
3. Adequate sleep
4. No smoking
5. Immunization
6. Moderate weight
7. Alcohol in moderation

As the cornerstone of your own individual health program, adopt these seven AMA guidelines. Their validity rests not simply on the authority of the Association, but on many studies that conclude with the facts reflected in AMA's recommendation.

MYTH. "My golf partner developed an arthritic shoulder and had to give up the game. I'm the same age and, recently, my left elbow began giving me trouble. The doctor told me it is arthritis. Am I in line for the same fate as my friend?"

FACT. Few ailments ever run an identical course in different people. Disorders that incapacitate some people may be tolerated for years by others.

Looking ahead: there is reason to believe that in the near future, cures and alleviants for many diseases—including arthritis—will be found. This is not the fantasy of wishful individuals but the opinion of medical authorities.

Remember back to the twenties when pernicious anemia was considered a hopeless disease? Nowadays, thanks to the development of new liver concentrates and vitamins, treatment of pernicious anemia is almost as simple as taking aspirin.

No matter what ailments afflict people today, or what may strike tomorrow, look for discoveries that will cure or treat the disease effectively and add healthy years to your life.

MYTH. The human life span is programmed to end somewhere between seventy and eighty. People who live longer than the Biblical three score and ten are exceptions.

FACT. Scientists understand human aging well enough to be able to state that the average human life span should be about 100 to 110 years. Said Nikita B. Mankovsky, Director of the Kiev Health Institute, "Nowadays, citizens of the United States and the Soviet Union live thirty to fifty years less than their biological systems could provide. A number of social and environmental factors shorten the average life span. The more successfully these factors can be minimized or eliminated, the longer people will live."

And the Russian health expert makes the point that when, as he expects in the near future, average ages will start pushing into the 100-year-old category, individuals should continue to live healthy, active, and productive lives.

Some people suggest that your life span is influenced by the season in which you were born. Other suggested factors: the order of birth—whether you were the first child or the last, or somewhere in between; genetic influences—whether or not your race is a plus or minus in terms of longevity; and so on. While these factors may be of interest, don't waste time trying to discover your future by means of these "scientific factors" that supposedly dictate how long you're going to live. The pattern of your daily life, the measures you take to fortify your wellbeing, are a more powerful factor in how long—and how well—you live than whether or not you were born on a sunny day.

MYTH. The aging process unavoidably includes a gradual decline of physical functions.

FACT. Scientists no longer believe that aging and frailty necessarily go hand in hand.

Different organs and body systems age differently. For example, the aging rates of the heart, liver, and brain are quite different. What these findings suggest is that if the specific ailments that affect organs can be minimized—for example, stress on the heart reduced by avoiding overweight, liver ailments brought on by imbibing excessive alcohol prevented by moderation in drinking—the human body overall will then function without impairment for longer and longer periods. Some medical authorities feel that the single factor of stress is a major cause of ill health. Where stress can be alleviated, the inroads of ill health can be slowed down considerably.

Getting advice from a physician who knows you is a major move in maintaining your health and faculties far beyond what are considered the "general rule." There are too many exceptions—people in their seventies retaining their physical and mental capabilities—for the traditional ideas about aging to be accepted as the rule.

MYTH. People who work long and hard "wear out their bodies" earlier than others.

FACT. In a study of 40,000 older people, including many individuals of 100 years and over, it was found that most of them began working at 10 or 12 years of age and "retired" at ages of 80 and over.

Your working life undoubtedly plays a part in determining what your health future is going to be. But don't assume that there is a direct relationship between your working experience and the outlook for your general health.

True enough, if you work in a job where you are exposed to debilitating or destructive factors such as fumes, excessive noise, or dangerous chemicals, your health may be adversely affected. But with the exception of factors like these, it's difficult to generalize.

Two men who've been in sales for the same number of years are about to retire. Dick is in robust health, but Harry looks some years older than his sixty-two.

"It's the tension and pressure of selling," his friends tell each other and shake their heads ruefully. But how to explain Dick's more advantageous situation? At least in part, it was not so much the job but the way the two individuals responded to it, how they coped with the tensions, pressures and so on, that explains the difference in the results.

It's unwise for an individual to feel, "My line of work has left its mark." If you were a professional weightlifter that might be so. But in the average case one's work not only was sustaining financially, but most probably regularized your day-to-day living in a way that was beneficial to both your physical and mental wellbeing.

MYTH. There comes a time after which it's "too late" to do anything about failing health.

FACT. This is true only in the sense that the longer you wait, the more difficult it is to get back to par.

If you haven't already developed some kind of a program for body and health building, start now. Dr. Russell V. A. Lee, a gerontologist of Palo Alto, says, "People can expect a happy, productive old age if they prepare themselves in their fifties." We know enough now to make our later years very pleasant ones. Check your preparation. Satisfy yourself that it's adequate.

MYTH. Physicians can't treat a disease until symptoms appear.

FACT. Physicians can spot early warning symptoms of disorders and begin treatment promptly. In addition, there is an approach called *anticipatory medicine,* in which ailments that are likely to bother you are treated—by specific drugs, for example—with the result that they may be significantly retarded or never even develop.

Discuss with your doctor procedures that might be used to minimize the chances of your being troubled by one or another ailment suggested by your physical makeup, genetic background, and so on.

MYTH. If heart disease runs in your family, you're bound to have trouble with it yourself.

FACT. While the genetic element may be an unfavorable factor, things that you can control—maintaining a normal weight, getting adequate sleep, regular and moderate exercise, and avoidance of smoking—may strongly shift the balance in your favor.

Don't let yourself be panicked by general statistics. The medical arts have become increasingly capable of dealing with specific controllable factors—overweight, high blood pressure, cholesterol, exercise—in remedial ways that decrease the likelihood of heart problems.

Your biggest contribution towards minimizing heart problems is to cooperate with a competent physician who will monitor the many factors that have to do with heart function, and if necessary, prescribe the regimen that will increase your odds for good health.

MYTH. Senility is an inevitable consequence of aging.

FACT. Senility in its extreme form affects only a relatively small number of people, 4 percent of those above seventy years of age.

Some people are more concerned about developing mental handicaps as they grow older than they are about physical ailments. Keep in mind that, while some deficiencies may develop with advancing age—weaker eyesight, poorer hearing, memory that may turn up blank spots—these often hit plateaus rather than continue to intensify.

Also reassuring and exciting, medical researchers are working on the chemistry of brain function. Scientists at Massachusetts Institute of Technology have identified a common substance called choline, found in eggs, meat, and fish, that has an almost immediate effect on brain function. Tests have given promising results in treating one disabling brain disorder, and it is hoped that other brain conditions that are important factors in senility, including depression and memory defects, may also respond to this or other therapeutic chemicals.

MYTH. Getting out in the sun is good for you.

FACT. The sun is absolutely essential to our wellbeing, but it does pose one health hazard. Overexposure, particularly to the sun of the tropics and semitropics can produce brown, scaly patches on the skin. And the American Cancer Society reports that too much sun may induce skin cancer, which strikes 100,000 sun worshipers a year. Listen to the health authorities on this one.

MYTH. A good climate can work wonders for your health.

FACT. There are no magical qualities in local natural climates that prevent disease in general, or cure specific ones. However, be aware that some areas are more conducive to convalescence from some ailments, and that people have an affinity for particular kinds of climates. My brother-in-law tells me that his arthritic shoulder becomes much better when he spends time in the Virgin Islands. And a friend of mine who suffers from asthma, particularly in places with high pollen counts or a high pollution index, feels markedly better in Arizona.

A sure way to test out the beneficial qualities of a particular locality, if you have reason to seek out one, is to consult authorities—your doctor or public health officials—and test out by actual exposure an area which promises well for your particular needs.

MYTH. If you're not "regular," you're constipated.

FACT. There is nothing constant or regular about the body's elimination of waste. The myth is reinforced by advertising that refers to constipation as "irregularity."

Remember that many things can interfere with regular bowel movement. Travel, an emotional upset, or unbalanced meals may cause constipation. The body usually takes care of the rhythm of elimination eventually. Actually there's nothing wrong with occasional constipation, skipping a day or two. However, persistent constipation suggests a consultation with your doctor.

MYTH. Diarrhea is nothing serious—it just provides subject matter for comic writers.

FACT. Diarrhea—sometimes called "the other ailment" by constipation sufferers—may range from a nuisance that's temporary to a health problem requiring a doctor's attention.

Diarrhea may result from some food item recently eaten. Some people react to extremes of temperature—for example, very cold fluids drunk along with hot dishes may upset the system. And mental stress may precipitate a seizure. But loose bowels may also signal an infection, or appear as a symptom of some general ailment. If, after several episodes, there is no relief, a call or visit to a doctor is in order. Physical examination and tests may be required to determine the cause and develop countermeasures. In many cases, a simple prescription will ease or terminate the problem.

MYTH. Pain and discomfort are an unavoidable part of many illnesses.

FACT. While pain occurs with many common health problems, from backache to arthritis-caused aching joints, there are medical alleviants. Pain-killing drugs are being developed and improved. Biofeedback techniques are making it possible for individuals to raise the pain threshold and otherwise lessen the feeling of discomfort.

Most recently, electrical devices to reduce some forms of pain are available. These devices, called transcutaneous nerve stimulators, are being produced by many manufacturers. The theory is simple: Apply electricity to skin surfaces and the current will block the passage of pain signals through the nerves. The signal doesn't get to the brain, and no pain is felt. The device doesn't reduce all pain, and it seems to work best on lower back complaints. Study is still required to find out which type of pain benefits the most, the best methods of application, and so on. The devices may only be sold on prescription by a doctor.

Bearing pain in silence is no longer the virtue it used to be when nothing could be done. Don't hesitate to fully inform your doctor if there is a problem. And pain from an unknown cause may lead to a diagnosis that can spot and treat a hitherto unsuspected health problem.

MYTH. Your dental health is fine as long as you can work your way through a steak.

FACT. It's a pretty good sign, but it shouldn't discourage anyone from an essential aspect of dental care—a periodic six-month checkup.

Review your present dental-care setup. Do you have a dentist you're satisfied with? In your opinion, has he or she been doing a good job of maintaining your dental health? Do you feel that he or she has kept up with improvements in technology so that you're not missing out on the latest methods? Do the dentist's equipment and treatment methods seem up to date?

MYTH. Dental care is largely a matter of comfort. If "nothing is bothering you," you're fine.

FACT. There are conditions—such as unhealthy gums—that in the early stages aren't bothersome but can become serious.

Realize that trouble with your teeth doesn't mean simply discomfort or, at worst, a localized problem. Dental complications can adversely affect your entire body, drain your energy, and make you feel sick as a result of infection. The more preventive care and the higher level of care you can get for your dental needs, the better.

MYTH. A slight hearing loss means you are going deaf.

FACT. *Not necessarily*: You may have a serious problem which needs immediate attention, or you may simply suffer a slight loss of hearing and still live to be 110 with adequate hearing. Consult your doctor without delay; the worst thing you can do is worry and fume—assuming the worst—with no basis in fact.

Advancing years occasionally do bring some losses. Your hair started turning grey ten years ago, and you accepted that easily. What bothers one person may be shrugged off by another. Often it's a person's reaction to aging rather than the aging itself that is the problem.

Remember that patterns of aging vary considerably, from one individual to the next. Don't let yourself be haunted by someone else. You may completely avoid Maude's arthritis or Marvin's failing eyesight. And remember, it's the reaction to a symptom rather than the symptom itself that may be the more important problem.

MYTH. "I'm my own best doctor. I'm very good at diagnosing my ailments. Why, one time I developed a bad case of bursitis in my elbow, prescribed hot salt water soaks, and cured myself in a few weeks."

FACT. Sometimes people can make misjudgments and there are no harmful consequences because the problem has been minor. Don't press your luck. Some things can be safely handled on your own: an occasional headache, for example, or a cold. But with the exception of these common ailments, and certainly when unusual symptoms occur or usual ones persist, see your doctor.

MYTH. Just as old people tend to become hard of hearing, they are likely to lose some or all of their eyesight, too.

FACT. Prescription for proper lenses and treatment of eye diseases in the early stages can help maintain your eyesight indefinitely.

Just as you take care in selecting a doctor, look for an ophthalmologist or an oculist on whom you feel you can depend. Both of these specialists are physicians and should have M.D. after their names. You can also go to an optometrist to have new lenses prescribed. An optometrist is licensed but is not a physician. Don't neglect your eyes by accepting poor lighting, for example; don't buy eyeglasses from a store counter, as wrong lenses can do serious damage, don't omit a periodic eye examination. As with your teeth, your eyes should receive periodic attention from the best available specialist, usually an oculist or ophthalmologist.

● *Elective Surgery*

Operations of any kind should not be taken lightly. There should be no hesitation about undergoing emergency surgery for serious internal or external injuries or illnesses and acute conditions. But what about cases that *aren't* urgent, those which doctors call "elective" surgery?

Here's one physician's advice on how to make the best decision:

1. Don't rush into nonemergency surgery.

2. Don't go ahead with an operation without making sure the physician or surgeon does a thorough physical examination, including all necessary blood and other tests, and has time to go over the results with you before surgery.

3. Ask for a complete explanation of the operation, what alternative treatments there might be, and all possible complications. If for any reason you are not satisfied with any explanations, do not hesitate to get a second opinion.

4. If your own doctor is not planning to actually perform the operation, talk to whoever will be doing it.

5. Make sure that whoever performs the operation is (a) certified by the American Board of Surgery and (b) a Fellow or Diplomate of the American College of Surgeons (F.A.C.S. or D.A.C.S.). These certifications should be visible in the office; you can also check board certification in the *Directory of Medical Specialists* at your public library.

6. If you decide to get a second opinion, choose a board-certified specialist, and let him or her know that you're there for a consultation rather than for the operation itself.

7. Discuss all fees beforehand, even if you have insurance. Ask for estimates of hospital and surgical care costs, surgeon's and physician's fees, medications, etc. And check with your health policy administrator.

8. If you do have an operation, try to have it in a hospital that is accredited by the American Hospital Association. If in doubt, don't hesitate to ask your doctor or the hospital office if it has this accreditation.

● *Hospital Rights*

Every year, millions of Americans are hospitalized. For each, it can be an uncertain time. But knowing what to expect and what you're entitled to can help relieve some of that uncertainty. To ensure that patients are treated not as bodies but as human beings worthy of consideration, care, and comfort, the American Hospital Association has drawn up a "Patient's Bill of Rights." According to its provisions:

You have the right to ask for and receive complete and current information from your physician about the diagnosis and prognosis of your case—in language understandable to you. Ask questions and get a social service worker to clarify matters for you if necessary.

You have the right to all information necessary to give what is called informed consent prior to the start of any procedure of treatment. This means that the doctor must explain the specifics of what is proposed, any medically significant risks involved, the period of recuperation, and your alternatives, including nontreatment.

Your consent, if you give it, must be knowledgeable and voluntary. You are well within your rights to say *no* to a specific procedure or treatment, whether that refusal is "irrational" ("I don't want a general anesthetic") or rational ("I would like to get the opinion of a specialist before proceeding further").

You have the right to privacy concerning medical care and your medical records. Discussions, consultations, examinations, and treatments should be confidential and discreet. Any information received from you should not be disclosed to others, even family members, without your permission.

In addition, your medical records should be available only to those directly involved in your case, such as your medical insurance company. However, in the case of an accident, certain nonconfidential information may legally be released to the police—name, address, age, marital status, etc.

You have a right to privacy in another area as well. You can refuse to see any or all visitors. You can also ask to move to another room if someone who shares your present room is disturbing you unnecessarily. In a crowded hospital, of course, this may not be immediately possible, but you are well within your rights to make the request.

You have the right to leave the hospital at any time—even though your bill has not yet been paid. By the same token, you can *refuse* to leave if you disagree with the doctor's instructions to discharge you. You can demand a consultation with another physician before the order is carried out.

You have a right to examine your bill and ask for an explanation of any and all charges on it. Again, you should not hesitate to question the meaning of any item you don't understand. Even if medical insurance will take care of a large part of the bill, there's no sense in accepting liability for payment for something you don't understand or didn't receive.

While the AHA urges its member hospitals to adopt, post, and distribute the "Bill of Rights," no hospital is required by law to conform to it. But it does provide knowledge to all present and future patients of what care and treatment they should ask for as their right. It also suggests that those who haven't had good treatment from a hospital in the past might do well choosing one that subscribes to the AHA code.

● *Recent Discoveries*

In laboratories and medical research centers throughout the country—indeed, throughout the world—scientists and technicians are working on new ways to maintain your health and to cure you if you become ill. We've seen that some of the most dreaded scourges—polio and smallpox, for example—have been licked. Many of today's health threats, one by one, eventually will be eliminated. Death from heart ailments has been on the decline for several years, probably due to our increased knowledge and use of preventive techniques such as early treatment of heart-straining conditions, and of excess substances in the blood that interfere with circulation, such as cholesterol.

Recently the spotlight has been switched on to a new finding that promises further medical advances. A blood element called human leukocyte antigens (or HLA) is a key to procedures that make it possible to predict an individual's susceptibility to specific diseases. Medical writer Gene Bylinsky, in *Fortune*, states that young people can be tested for a certain type of arthritis, and if the HLA test indicates susceptibility, the people can be watched and treated before overt symptoms set in.

More and more emphasis is being given to the general principle behind HLA—prediction and prevention of disease, along with the hunt for specific cures. The outlook for health care is continually improving, giving us the assurance that later years will become increasingly healthy ones—meaning more freedom and less time and money devoted to health problems.

9
FINANCES

Money may not be everything, but it surely plays a big part in making "everything" possible. How and where you spend your retirement years will depend largely on your cash reserve, income-producing investments, and other assets. And your finances, in turn, will depend largely on how well you've planned in the years before retirement.

For some, unfortunately, these pages are going to be like a gourmet cookbook now gathering dust on my shelf. Every time I look up a recipe for a gala dinner, it turns out that I should have started two or three days before—aging, marinating, and so on. But it's never too late to take some constructive action to make the most of your situation, whatever it may be.

Take advantage of financial planning services available to you as early as possible. If you're lucky enough to work for an organization that offers financial counseling, sign up early. Often this type of help is available only in the last year or two of your tenure, and usually in connection with established income and savings—earnings, pension, and social security. But where qualified financial counselors are ready to help, an early start gets your post-retirement finances in the best possible shape.

I'm assuming that most readers are now no more than ten, or at most fifteen, years away from retiring at sixty-five. If you are closer, you can sometimes crowd more planning into fewer years to catch up. However, you'll find no thirty-year investment plans on these pages, nothing about saving for your children's college education, no tips on buying your first home, or setting up a life insurance program. This chapter will concentrate first on shifting your savings and investments into retirement gear, rethinking your housing needs, reviewing and revising your life insurance coverage, and other preretirement financial steps. Second, the discussion will center on the financial aspects of the retirement process itself, and, of course, the all-important matters of making your postretirement income go as far as possible.

● *Preretirement Planning*

Planning the money side of your retirement means figuring out what you have to start with, what you'll have when you retire, what you'll need after retirement, and how to get what you need.

ANALYZING YOUR NET WORTH

In the business world, a corporation's net worth is the value of all its various assets (everything it owns plus all that's owed to it) less its liabilities (the value of everything it owes to others). The firm's stockholders and potential investors are naturally very interested in that figure. Your own personal net worth can be figured in the same way, and you should be doing just that, since it is the most important indicator of your ability to make your retirement a success.

Once you've noted all your assets and liabilities, you will want to examine each of them. If you are looking at an asset, for example, the questions will include the following: Is it producing income? If so, could it produce more? Should it be added to, worked down, or gotten rid of altogether?

For liabilities, there isn't always as much flexibility, but here too you'll find that there are some that should be liquidated, while others may be costing less to carry than the money you'd use to close them out is earning.

A worksheet

Fig. 9-1 is a worksheet you can use to figure your total personal net worth today. It can help you avoid missing some items, and it will give you an organized picture of where you stand. Assets are divided into groups according to their liquidity—how much trouble it would be to convert them into quick cash. This will be a convenient framework for looking at each item to decide where it fits into your retirement plans.

Be conservative in figuring the value of your assets. There's nothing to be gained from putting a value on hopes and wishes, or from insisting that something is worth what you paid for it, rather than a cold-hearted assessment of what you could get for it. For most household assets, for example, we recommend using only half what they'd bring in a "fair sale," on the theory that a fair sale can't always be arranged when the cash is needed.

Actually, most financial advisers suggest that you go through this net worth process every few years, and certainly at important stages of your career and personal development. Like many people, though, you probably haven't gotten around to it yet, so this is a good time to make the first attempt. From here on, however, plan to go through a similar stock-taking every five years or so, to see what progress you've made and what

FIG. 9-1 Your Personal Net Worth

	PRESENT VALUE	GOALS AND PLANS FOR RETIREMENT
ASSETS *"Instant" assets* Cash Checking balances Passbook savings Other _____		
Other "quick" assets 1-yr saving certificates Tax refunds due Collectible debts Deposits with utilities, etc. Company thrift plan, etc. Other _____		
Liquidatable assets (at cash or market value) Life insurance (cash value) Multi-year certificates Government bonds, notes, etc. Stocks, bonds, mutual funds Company annuity or pension fund (cash or loan value) Other company benefits, options, etc. (cash or loan value)		

FIG. 9-1—Continued

	PRESENT VALUE	GOALS AND PLANS FOR RETIREMENT
Liquidatable assets (cont.)		
Other loans due you		
Other _____		
Major fixed assets		
(at quick sale market value)		
Home(s)		
Other real estate		
Going business (your share)		
Cars, boats, etc.		
Other _____		
Other fixed assets		
(at ½ fair sale value)		
Furniture, furnishings, appliances		
Jewelry, furs		
Other valuables (art, silver, etc.)		
Hobby or sports equipment		
Collections (stamps, coins, etc.)		
Other _____		
Total assets		
LIABILITIES		
Short-term liabilities		
(Payable within one year)		
Personal debts		
Charge & credit accounts		
Mortgage & other payments		
Other _____		
Long-term liabilities		
(Payable beyond one year)		
Mortgage balance		
Car & other loan balance		
Bank loans, policy loans,		
Other long-term debts		
Total liabilities		
Personal net worth		

needs doing next. And, naturally, a net worth statement will be particularly valuable at retirement.

Some of the items in this net worth statement you'll be able to fill in easily after consulting a few records. If you have followed advice you must have received several times over the years, and kept a household inventory for insurance purposes, that will be a big help, too. For some items, though, you may have to consult your insurance agent, your bank, your securities broker, company pension plan administrator, and others. Don't feel embarrassed or reluctant about doing this—the chances are you've already paid for this service for many years and you are entitled to it.

Finally, you can go to auctions, read the sales ads, talk with real estate agents, fellow hobbyists, and others to get an idea of the realistic current market values of your possessions. And keep in mind that for most collectibles you "buy at retail, sell at wholesale." What your prized collection may bring in a quick sale may be only a third or a fourth of what you would pay for it as an individual collector, buying piece by piece from an established dealer.

Remember that your net worth at retirement is your "grubstake" for the rest of your life—it's the capital that you'll be counting on to produce the income, and perhaps to *be* the income, on which you are hoping to fulfill the plans you are making.

Evaluating your circumstances

The next step is to look at each item on the worksheet, decide where and how it can best fit into your financial retirement plan, and what steps will have to be taken between now and the big day itself. There's room on the statement to jot down notes about your aims and what's to be done. Later, you can check back on how you've progressed and what is still to be accomplished.

The main role for investments after retirement is the production of income with safety. This means no "sure-fire" schemes for doubling your capital, no dabbling in the commodities market, no plunging in "growth" stocks—in short, no high-risk investments. From here on—or from retirement on, to be more exact—your aims have to be high income and the protection of your capital, with some compromises between these where you can't have as much of both as you'd like.

Now that we know the ground rules, let's look at your list of assets and liabilities. We'll be asking how each item fits in with your long-range retirement plans, what should be done to bring it in line with retirement goals, when the move should best be made, and so on. Some of the answers will be fairly obvious, but some may surprise you.

Instant assets

All your working life, you've been hearing and reading "rules" for how much of your assets should be totally liquid and available—in case you lost your job, in case of illness, and so on. Some sources say three months income, or six months income, perhaps 15 percent of all your assets, or some other figure. Whatever it was, the chances are that in your younger years you could never reach it. You may have felt lucky enough if you could meet your bills every month.

But by now that has probably changed, and if your net worth statement is like most, too much of your assets are in these cash-on-demand low-income forms. You will need an "emergency fund" after retirement, but most financial counselors agree that this needn't be as big as the "rules" for working families call for. Most of your income then will be pretty certain, whether it's in Social Security checks, pension payments, dividends, or comes from cashing in securities.

If you have thousands of dollars in passbook savings accounts, for example, these preretirement years are the time to start putting them to work. Gradually, as you reach retirement age, you should be getting to the point where only enough to cover perhaps two months income is in the form of cash, checking accounts, passbook savings, and so on.

Other "quick" assets

By the same token, you'll want to question every item you've listed under "other quick assets." Chances are that much of this is "lazy money," is not pulling its weight. Deposits with the telephone company or your landlord may not seem like much, but they add up, and you should check to see whether they're really still necessary. The same applies to funds you may have outstanding in no-interest loans to friends and family. It may seem hard and materialistic, but that money should be put to work, too.

LIQUIDATABLE ASSETS

Life insurance

Times have changed. The reasons you bought your life insurance in the first place almost certainly no longer exist. You no longer have small children to protect; your mortgage is probably paid off (and can be covered by a special term policy if it isn't); college tuition, weddings, other big items are in the past, etc. Mostly what your life insurance is doing today is creating an estate—and eating up income in premium payments.

You will want to keep some life insurance after retirement to cover those "final costs" the insurance salespeople are so delicate about. But the idea that you need to protect your family against your loss as a "breadwinner" doesn't make sense any more. With your pension payments properly arranged and other investments set up in the right way, your spouse's income should go on whether you are here or not. And the cash value in your policies, which may be considerable by now, will provide more income if wisely invested than it probably does under the insurance company's conservative formula.

So, make another note on the worksheet, next to insurance. And check with your insurance company about the procedure for cashing in policies. Perhaps, if you're conservative, you can do this in two or three installments. Ask, too, about the possibility of discontinuing premium payments until age sixty-five, then converting the paid-in value of the policy to an annuity. This may be the simplest way to convert your insurance to an income-producing investment, but be sure to ask about the payout details and compare these with other annuity plans. Unless the insurance company will make the conversion to an annuity with no sales charge, you may be better off going to the trouble of taking the money and investing it yourself.

Annuities

An assured annual income over an agreed period of time was once more popular as an investment than it is today. First, the "go-go" atmosphere of the Sixties made common stocks look much more promising, and then the rising inflation rates of more recent years made annuities seem even more of a losing proposition. Not many people near retirement, therefore, have annuities as an important part of their investments today.

But the people who sell annuities haven't given up and have introduced innovations and incentives that may make an annuity a good investment for some of the cash you acquire in your preretirement years, including that from liquidating other investments. The principal advantage of an annuity, of course, and its main reason for existence, is the fact that it can guarantee a payout for life—or beyond, if you choose a survivorship option. You can outlive the proceeds from the planned liquidation of a mutual fund investment, for instance, even if you set the payout period at twenty years or some other long time. But you can't outlive a life annuity, by definition.

To offset the advantages of having a set income that will last as long as you do, however, annuities have some disadvantages. First, if you buy from a commercial firm such as an insurance company, there is a hefty sales commission involved, which eats up some of your principal even before you start. Then, by its fixed terms, the annuity payout has no anti-inflation features at all. And finally, once you begin receiving the periodic payments, there may be no opportunity to change your mind, as there would be with marketable fixed-income securities or other investments.

Nevertheless, annuities may be a proper ingredient in your overall financial plan for retirement. If you decide to invest in one, there are basically two ways to do it. You can pay several installments, each of which will contribute toward increasing the eventual payout. Or you can buy a single-payment annuity, perhaps with the proceeds of the sale of some other investment. You can arrange for the payout to you to start immediately, or at some future time—a "deferred" annuity. Either way, as noted above, one important aim will be to keep the sales cost involved at a minimum. That's what can make the conversion to an annuity of a life insurance policy a good investment.

Savings certificates

These have become popular recently, and there's a good chance you have some. They are, of course, absolutely safe investments and produce a better yield than ordinary savings. But compare them, for example, with government notes and bonds, which are, if anything, even safer, and you may want to decide not to renew some of those that mature between now and retirement. On the other hand, if you are very conservative and will sleep better at night with a good chunk of your funds tied up in savings certificates, there are still things you can do. A series of six-year certificates, with some maturing each year, for example, will give you both a reasonable income yield and a degree of flexibility to make future decisions about what to do with one-sixth of the money each year.

Government bonds

Currently, these rate highly as retirement investments. Right now they produce nearly as much income as many less secure investments. And since the laws governing mutual funds have been changed, you can invest in a mixed portfolio of government bonds without having to plunk down huge amounts of cash—the minimum government bond is $5,000—for each purchase.

Short-term government securities

Treasury bills are very popular these days. They provide high income and almost total liquidity, along with what many retirees seem to find to be the excitement of buying them. (You can use your bank or a fund to do the buying for you at a small fee.) The only potential drawback is the possibility of a drop in interest rates in the future. If you are invested in bonds, that's no problem—in fact it will raise their market value. But if you have been continually reinvesting in six-month bills or certificates, you'll be stuck with whatever is the market rate, at the time. And a drop in interest rates can put quite a dent in your retirement income if these short-term securities have been accounting for a big share of it.

Perhaps you have been investing in high-grade tax-free municipal bonds (the securities of state and local governments, which produce income that is exempt from federal income tax), or in one of the unit trusts or mutual funds that are invested in these. That's perfectly fine as long as your income puts you in a high enough tax bracket to make the net yield on the lower interest they pay worth your while. But if you will be in the lower brackets after retirement, perhaps you should begin to phase out your municipals even before retirement. Several of the organizations that have tax-free municipal bond funds will permit you to transfer funds from that account to their government bond fund or corporate bond fund without any sales charge, and that can be a good deal.

Common stocks, corporate bonds and mutual funds

All of these have a definite place in any diversified retirement portfolio, but very likely not the stocks, bonds and mutual funds you now own. These may have been accumulated with the idea of capital growth in mind, and whether or not that idea has worked out for you, the time has come to modify it. With retirement approaching, you have to start putting assured income first, and deemphasize the hope of growth if it is accompanied, as it almost always is, by increased risk.

There are types of stock, however, that have their place in a retirement portfolio, if your own inclination lies that way. Expanding public utilities, for example, can be expected to pay reasonably liberal and secure dividends, with some moderate growth prospects. Your securities broker or bank can suggest particular stocks that meet these criteria, once you make it clear that you aren't interested in "trading," but are now looking for a stable portfolio. And, of course, there are mutual funds that specialize in precisely these investment aims.

Just a word about any corporate bonds you may own. Some of them may have been bought below par with the idea of capital gains in mind, and some may have had a somewhat uncertain payment record. Again, that was fine when you were aiming to build capital, but will be less so from here on. Capital gains taxes are lower than ever under the new tax law, so this will be a good time to take whatever gains have materialized on both stocks and bonds. After you retire, the difference in tax rates between income and gains won't be nearly as great.

If you want to replace your bonds with others, many advisers suggest sticking to high-grade corporate issues with relatively shorter remaining terms. A bond with ten or fifteen years left to maturity, and a top rating, isn't going to fluctuate as much as one with thirty years to go, even if interest rates change. The same goes, in fact, for the government issues we've talked about above. There are many federal agency issues available with five-to fifteen-year maturities, and payouts a bit above the long-term Treasury issues that first come to mind when government bonds are mentioned. Even if inflation has risen to double-digit rates ten years from now when your bond matures, and interest rates are up along with it, you'll be able to cash the bond at par with no loss and reinvest the proceeds at the higher rates then available.

Retirement funds, profit-sharing, benefits

Today, you may have several choices about what to do with your "vested" retirement funds when you stop working, and it's not too soon to look into these. This will be covered in more detail later, but for now just remember that under the law, pension trustees and similar custodians must be fairly conservative. The interest rates figured into the accumulation and payout tables of your benefits may well be lower than you could do yourself with adequate safety, if there's a way to take the money in a lump sum. At this point, just be sure you don't foreclose that possibility by any moves you make or fail to make while still employed.

Keogh plans and IRA accounts

These can be excellent retirement investments, as they were intended to be. A Keogh Plan (named after the Congressman who first introduced the bill) is a device for putting aside self-employment income, free of tax, for withdrawal during retirement. In effect, it is the self-employed person's counterpart of a noncontributory company retirement plan. We won't go into the rules and limitations here—they are fairly complex and are continually being revised. In fact, they have recently been changed again under the 1978 Revenue Act.

An IRA or Individual Retirement Account is a newer device, intended to let employees of companies without retirement plans build up similar tax-free retirement funds. The annual contribution limits are much lower than for a Keogh Plan, and there are other rules that have already tripped up some of those who have started IRA accounts without a full understanding. These rules have been liberalized by the 1978 tax law changes, however, and the IRA should be a more useful retirement tool in the future.

If you don't have either of these at present, there may still be an opportunity to start one, even for the few years between now and retirement. If so, it can be very worthwhile, if only because of the tax deferral aspects. If you receive artistic royalties, speaking fees, or just about any other income from the performance of services outside of your regular job, you should look into starting a Keogh if you haven't already done so. And, of course, if your employer doesn't have a retirement plan, you should start an IRA if somehow you have overlooked doing so. And both of these are investments you'll want to keep untouched until you begin to draw on them in retirement. In fact, the law insists that you do just that.

A case history

In the course of researching this chapter, I had several long talks with a friend I'll call Ed Trask. Ed is a middle-level executive who is retiring next year at sixty-five, after a career capped by twenty-three years with the same company. He isn't really rich, but partly by luck and largely by design Ed has done a pretty good job of putting his financial house in order for retirement. This presentation of Ed's retirement planning should help to illustrate the information on assets just covered.

First, taking advantage of the 1978 tax law changes, Ed is planning to take his company pension in a lump sum payout, and "roll it over" into an IRA account. He has found a savings and loan association that will let him divide the account into one-, two-, three- and up to eight-year certificates so that he'll be getting a reasonably high interest rate and will be able to defer taxes on each installment payout until he takes it. Ed figures he'll be able to re-invest some of each year's payout and looks on this as a hedge against being locked into one decision on his pension. There's about $80,000 involved here.

For the last ten years or so, Ed has been putting part of his savings into a "municipal unit investment trust," to take advantage of the tax-free interest (which he has been re-investing, as well). There's about $40,000 now, and starting in 1978 and continuing thereafter, he has been sys-tematically converting these unit trusts into shares in a no-load corporate bond fund run by the same firm.

Here's where luck becomes an element, because in the 1978 bond market, corporate yields went up a lot faster than municipal bond yields. So far Ed has been able to get a nice price for his trust units and to buy the corporate fund shares at a high and rising yield. Ed says that's how people get reputations as "savvy" investors.

Ed and his wife Beverly have long been "empty-nesters"—their two kids got married and moved out a while back. Starting a few years ago, Ed stopped paying premiums on a couple of big life insurance policies he has long owned, and is insured for about $60,000, "reduced amount" on the two policies. He has contacted the insurance company and plans to cash in the two policies on the anniversary date following his sixty-fifth birthday, converting the proceeds to an annuity offered by the company. The payout on this won't be ideal, but Ed figures it will be one measura-ble chunk of retirement income that he and his wife won't outlive.

Not everything has gone the way Ed hoped, of course. He figured on selling all of the stocks he has accumulated over many years as a small investor and putting those proceeds into various government agency bonds. But the late 1978 market collapse made him decide to wait, so that part of his plan is unfulfilled. Actually, this may turn out to be all right, too. The 1978 tax law gives capital gains a better break, and Ed figures this time he'll start unloading his stocks as soon as prices are reasonable again, and won't wait to catch the next high.

Altogether, Ed figures he will have realigned about $210,000 worth of assets, an amount that surprises him, and will have an annual income from these of about $15,000 to $19,000, without touching the capital (except for the annuity from the insurance company). But he realizes that he probably will have to be going into the capital and is working out a plan for that, too. Ideally, his objective is to withdraw the last chunk of his holdings as his personal need for cash—or anything else material—becomes irrelevant.

FIXED ASSETS

Your home

If you are a homeowner, this represents probably the largest single investment you've ever made. Your home is one of your major assets and a big potential source of retirement income—or expense. Either way, this calls for some serious consideration of where your present home will fit into your overall financial retirement plan.

Of course, other considerations may override the financial factor in a "cool" analysis. You may be extremely happy and comfortable where you are, with no intention of moving out for any reason. If you're that lucky, no set of dollar figures could possibly offset the immeasurable advantages of staying put.

In that case, though, there'd be little more to say on this subject, so let's assume that, sentimentality aside, you'd be better off to put your house on the market when you retire.

The fact is, today's higher home prices can give you a good start on that line of thinking, plus a nice chunk of cash for investment and living costs besides. And, under the 1978 tax law, you no longer have to wait until you're sixty-five to be able to keep all or most of the proceeds of the sale without paying capital gains taxes. That means you can take advantage of housing market and mortgage rate conditions at any time from here on to make a start on the housing segment of your retirement plans.

BUYING VERSUS RENTING. The real question is—should you buy a home, a condominium, shares in a co-op, or should you count on renting from retirement day on? Solely from a financial point of view, there's much to be said for both owning and renting in retirement, though you may make the final decision on emotional or psychological grounds in the end. Here, in any case, are some of the financial aspects you'll want to weigh on both sides.

First, home ownership is a good anti-inflation investment at any age. If things keep going the way they have been, you'll be able to resell your retirement home for more than it cost you, if you eventually decide to move or start renting. And, barring a financial catastrophe, you'll be secure in it meanwhile. You'll still have all the costs of home ownership and operation, of course, and they are bound to keep going up—fuel, utilities, taxes, and so on. But then, so will rents. In fact, if you are suited to it, buying a place with enough room in it to rent out a small apartment can be a smart hedge against those rising costs, assuming you can always find a tenant.

What about a mortgage on your retirement home? As with other investment decisions, the question is what else you would do with the money. Borrowing against your home (which is what you'd be doing) at 9½ percent interest, for example, and investing the proceeds at 8½ percent wouldn't be much of a bargain. But if you are lucky enough to be able to take over a low-interest mortgage, that might be a better deal than paying all cash. Sometimes, too, there's an advantage to taking on at least a small mortgage, especially in a new community. It gives you an instant relationship with a local bank, and your regular mortgage payments can help establish a higher credit rating for you than an all-cash deal would do.

Remember, also, that the tax advantages of home ownership may be much less important in retirement. If you will be taking the standard deductions, instead of itemizing, for instance, you can forget about the tax break that was built into your mortgage payments and property taxes before. And on the other side of the equation, renting can protect you against the burden of sudden assessments or tax increases that can play havoc with your retirement budget.

One thing is certain—this is a decision you'll be changing your mind about several times before you finally decide. So, put something down in the planning space on your worksheet, but lightly in pencil. And accept the fact that there are going to be some regrets and misgivings whichever way you decide.

CHOOSING YOUR LOCATION. Where you live in retirement will be largely a matter of personal preference, but there's a financial side to that, too. Before you make your final choice, you'll want to check out the tax and living cost situations in the several areas you're deciding among. In general, the "sunbelt" states tend to be better on both these counts, but some are better than others. It will pay to find out not only what the story is on income, sales, and property tax rates, but whether there are any special breaks for seniors and retirement income. Some states give generous "homestead" exemptions on property taxes, but some of these apply only to those with very low incomes. The U.S. Bureau of Labor Statistics, which keeps the records on prices and living costs, can tell you how these costs compare in a great many metropolitan areas around the country. Just drop into any regional office of the Department of Labor or Commerce Department, or a good business library.

You may even decide that living abroad has its financial advantages to go along with its other attractions. If so, remember that your Social Security payments will follow you wherever you live, as will all your other income. The Social Security Administration has a special booklet on receiving benefits abroad which you can pick up at any SSA office. The main point is that without any other sources of information on your postretirement earnings, they'll want to be more closely informed by you about income that might result in reducing your benefits.

For more on housing opportunities and choices, see Chapter 10.

Other real estate

Income-producing property can be an important part of the total retirement income picture. But before you check it off as an item to be left as is, forget what the property is bringing in as a percent of the price you paid for it and think instead about its earnings in terms of what you could sell it for on today's real estate market. It may still look good on that basis, but the comparison may also indicate that you could do better by selling it and re-investing the proceeds in other real estate or in income-producing securities.

If the property is something you originally bought for its capital appreciation possibilities and it produces little if any income, it's in the same class with your other "growth" investments. Now is the time to start taking your profits (if they exist) or to start cutting your losses. Either way, it's getting late to be counting on one more real estate boom, and its time to make this asset, too, carry its own weight in your retirement investment plan.

Other fixed assets

Your car, furniture, household goods, and all those other items of value you've accumulated over the past years undoubtedly add up to a larger total on your net worth statement than you expected. So these too can be part of your retirement planning, and they therefore call for a hard-headed appraisal now, while you can do it at your leisure.

First, there are all those things you've planned to give away or bequeath eventually anyway. Why not start to do it now? Not only will the donees get more pleasure out of them (hopefully), but you'll be able to observe their pleasure, while being relieved of the necessity to maintain, make room for, insure or otherwise spend money on them. And to the extent that your gifts are to approved charities, the tax benefits can be much more important now than they will be later.

For other things, the years between now and retirement may be the best time for a gigantic "garage sale," so to speak. It goes without saying that you won't get as much for anything as you really know it is worth. But selling something when you have time to say yes or no to an offer can bring in a lot more than selling it in those last few hurried months or weeks before you take off for the South Seas. A detailed household inventory can prove invaluable at this point. By marking each item "sell," "keep," "give away," or just "?" you can begin on paper the process of trimming your excess baggage, and getting into shape for traveling light.

Your car and a few other major items will call for special decisions, of course. Should you sell the car now, and start renting one when you need to? Should you run it into the ground from here on and forget about replacement? Or should you buy a good, dependable new or used car just before you retire, so you'll have that item taken care of? The answers to these and other questions will depend on your plans and circumstances, but it's important to answer them before you make decisions that answer them for you, perhaps wrongly.

Next comes the important matter of all personal assets you'll be taking with you into retirement. As a general rule, you'll find it will pay to fix up or replace them now, while you are in a higher income bracket, and the repair or replacement may be to some extent tax-deductible. If you know you will want to continue owning a car, to stick with the same illustration, take care of that matter before retirement. Afterwards, you'll feel the cost more, both financially and psychologically, and this may lead you to make "penny-wise, pound-foolish" decisions.

This advice very definitely doesn't apply, however, to assets you know you will be disposing of. "Cosmetic" fix-ups can often bring a better price—fresh paint, a good cleaning, and the like. But it is a time-honored and sound maxim that you never get back the full investment you put into anything, from a house to a food-freezer or stamp collection, that you are planning to sell. Buyers simply don't appreciate the extent of your efforts and may feel, in fact, that some of them detract from the item's value since they would have done differently.

LIABILITIES

On this side of the statement, for better or worse, most of the questions and answers are much simpler. First, you must determine how much you can pay of what you owe. Second, you must decide which liabilities to reduce before retirement and which ones to carry.

Some of the answers will take care of themselves, depending on what you've already decided to do about the assets to which they're related. If you've decided to sell your home and/or your car, for instance, that will take care of the balances you owe on these. The only thing that remains open is the timing of the shift.

For all of your other liabilities, both short term and long term, there will be one general rule that applies from here on: If servicing the liability (that means mostly interest payments, but may also include credit life insurance, and so on) is costing more than what you are earning on some low-yielding investment, it will pay to liquidate the investment and use the proceeds to reduce your liability. This may not have been the best rule earlier on. Previously, it may have made very good investment sense to pay high interest on a debt in order to keep an investment in an asset with very little income but very large capital gain prospects. But now, the time for that strategy has probably run out.

You will want to keep or even expand some liability items. These may be the years, for instance, to add to or start a policy loan on your life insurance, as an alternative to selling the policy outright. Similarly, a loan against your company thrift plan, if re-invested wisely, can produce higher net income both in the next few years and after retirement, depending on the terms under which it is available.

The point is that while there's no one decision that will apply to everyone, or even to all of one person's assets and liabilities, there are a few guidelines that everyone can use. And the sooner you start this decision-making process, looking at each of your assets as dispassionately as you can, the better off you will be. Don't be afraid to change your mind about decisions you haven't yet carried out. First conclusions may not be the best, and changing conditions can make any decision less attractive than it seemed earlier on. But any decision that's based on thinking things out almost has to be better than one based on impulse or one that's forced on you if you run out of time.

● *The Transition to Retirement*

Let's assume for now that you're planning to retire at the normal retirement age of sixty-five. In most companies and public agencies, that's still the month you turn sixty-five (or sometimes the end of the year or season in which you reach that age). This section, then, is about some of the things to do—your personnel office will probably offer similar advice—in the months before you reach that anniversary.

SOCIAL SECURITY

Application procedures

These days, nearly everybody has been paying Social Security taxes and will be entitled to retirement and health care benefits. To be sure you get yours promptly, you have to make the first move—there's nothing automatic about starting the flow of monthly checks.

Establishing your claim is *usually* simple, but *can* be complicated. Three months before you turn sixty-five, visit your local Social Security office, bringing with you the papers you'll need to satisfy the questions that will be asked about how old you are, whether you're married, and so on. The Social Security people advise calling first to make certain what you need, but usually that means your birth certificate, your spouse's birth certificate, or some other acceptable proof. If there's any question about whether these proofs are available, don't wait for the last minute to start the search.

Amount of benefits

Nor is there any reason to wait for the last moment to get some idea of what your monthly retirement payment will be. Nobody can tell this exactly, of course, because both the law and your income are likely to keep changing, but by making a few assumptions, a reliable estimate can readily be worked out.

To find out your status now, the Social Security Administration has a form to use. You can get it at any SSA office, and many company personnel offices have copies. Or you can make your own copy of the form shown (Fig. 9-2). It's a good idea to send in one of these forms every three years or so while you are working, just to make sure your earnings are being properly credited. But you should certainly do so fairly early in the year before your retirement.

Fig. 9-2 REQUEST FOR STATEMENT OF EARNINGS

Social Security
Number _ _ _   _ _   _ _ _ _
Date of Birth _____ .
                        month   day   year

Please send a statement of my Social Security earnings to:
Name (print) _____
Street & Number _____
City & State _____ ZIP Code _____
Sign your name here _____
(Sign your own name only. Under the law, information in your Social Security record is confidential and anyone who signs another person's name can be prosecuted. If you have changed your name from that shown on your Social Security card, please copy your old name below, exactly as it appears on your card.)

Mail it to the Social Security Administration, P.O. Box 57, Baltimore, Maryland 21203.

Especially if you have never inquired before, it's a good idea to find out how many calendar quarters of Social Security coverage you have piled up during your years of covered employment. This can help determine whether you will be fully insured for the maximum benefit on retirement. To find out, just add a line at the bottom of the card: "Please include the Quarters of Coverage (QC) recorded for my account."

Lastly, you'll want to know approximately what these covered earnings and quarters of coverage will entitle you to receive in retirement benefits. For this, if you are within a few years of sixty-five, add the printed notation "Retirement benefits estimate, please" at the bottom of the card as well. The estimate you receive may turn out to be a conservative one, since it will be based on currently established deductions and earnings limits, and on the assumption that you will stay at your present earnings level until retirement.

How much will you get from Social Security? The exact answer depends on a number of variables, and even when they are all known it will involve some fancy calculations involving your birth date, years of coverage, your highest and lowest covered earnings, and so on. But according to recent changes in the law, those retiring over the next few years will be receiving retirement checks that are a good bit bigger than the "$400 a month" you may have grown used to thinking about as the amount you can count on. Here, for example, are the figures, rounded off, for a retired employee and spouse, for maximum earnings and years of coverage, for retirement in each of the next five years:

Retirement Year	Monthly Check	Annual Benefit
1979	$780	$ 9,360
1980	$855	$10,260
1981	$930	$11,160
1982	$885	$10,620
1983	$930	$11,160

These figures need a few qualifications and some explanation. First, they're entirely unofficial, and carry no guarantee. They assume that the projected increases in taxes and benefits will take effect on schedule and that earnings and inflation rates will continue about as they recently have. Second, they take into account changes that Congress made in the retirement benefit formula in 1977, which may be revised again.

Look at that figure for 1982, for instance. It shows that the maximum benefit will actually drop from 1981, as the new formula is phased in. But Congress also provided that no individual's benefits would be reduced under the new law from what they would have been under the old formula, so there's no telling what the actual figure in your case will be. What seems likely, though, is that whether you reach sixty-five in 1981, 1982, or 1983, your maximum retirement benefit will be about the same—unless the law is changed again.

What if both you and your spouse have worked and have established Social Security records? Usually, the wife's own earned benefits would be smaller than the half of the husband's benefit that she would be entitled to, simply as a dependent spouse. That's because she has probably worked fewer years and usually in a less well-paying job. The result is that her Social Security tax payments all those years are "wasted," and she gets nothing for them. Recently there have been proposals in Congress to assure a working wife at least part of her earned benefits, regardless of her spouse benefit, but so far nothing has come of them. If in your case the combined benefits the two of you have earned would be greater than the benefit for a worker and spouse, you would of course apply separately, but you can't have it both ways, at least today.

Should you apply for benefits early, say at sixty-two? Whether or not you might want to stop working on a regular basis before you reach sixty-five is a highly personal decision, and one you'll have to make on the basis of more factors than we could possibly consider here. But some financial planning experts advise their clients to apply at age sixty-two in any event, whether or not they intend to stop working early. For one thing, your approved application will then be on record, with any difficulties ironed out, and things will go more smoothly when you do actually retire. For another, as long as you go on earning enough each month to cancel out any benefits you might otherwise receive, there will be no reduction in your benefit when you reach sixty-five.

If you apply early and do stop working regularly before sixty-five, benefits will start coming in promptly, with no delay, figured as of the age you stop work. Under the law, you can stop working at any time after you turn sixty-two, but your benefits will be reduced from those shown above. There are two reasons for this. Since you'll start receiving benefits sooner, your expected total lifetime benefits will have to be spread over more years; and your calculated benefits will probably be based on lower total lifetime covered earnings than if you wait till sixty-five.

The advantages of applying early do not apply to Medicare. There are no "early retirement" provisions in the health care section of the law, and these benefits start at sixty-five, regardless of when you actually retire. Thus, Medicare applications won't be accepted sooner than three months before you turn sixty-five, but should be applied for promptly at that time to avoid losing any period of coverage.

COMPANY PENSIONS

Your company pension, if you have one, will probably be your next most important source of retirement income after Social Security (or perhaps the most important, if you have worked many years for a firm with a generous plan, at high salary levels). In the year before retirement, you'll want to explore all the possibilities involved here—how big your basic benefit will be, what options you will have, whether you'll be able to choose to take your benefits in a lump-sum payment, and so on. Your company's personnel office or employee benefits administrator will have all the details but let's look at a few of the questions you should be asking when the time comes.

Your basic retirement benefit depends, of course, on the terms of the plan. Many companies simply pay a certain amount monthly for each year of service, while others use complex formulas based on annual earnings every year you've worked for them, above the amount of Social Security coverage, and so on. Some plans—the nicest ones—pay a percentage of earnings in the five (or three) highest-paid years before retirement. In any event, be sure you know what you can count on from your plan and how the figure was arrived at.

It used to be that most pension plans had only one income option; you took your basic monthly payment for life, or for thirty years, depending on how long you lived, and that was that. The recent Pension Reform Law, however, requires every approved retirement plan to offer a "survivor's benefit" option. Under this, you can choose to have your surviving spouse continue to receive a reduced benefit for life. And some plans, of course, offer as many optional choices as insurance companies and private annuities usually do. Under these plans you can take your benefits for a fixed number of years, for life with a minimum payout guaranteed, in a joint-and-survivor annuity, and so on.

Your decision will depend on the state of your finances and of your health when you retire, how dependent you are on the pension, and other factors you'll have to talk over with your spouse and the company when the time for decision comes. The important point is to be sure to start the talking-over process early enough to be able to make a sound decision. In almost all cases, you won't be able to change it once it's made.

LUMP SUM PAYOUT. What you'd usually be doing here is converting the lump-sum into an annuity of your own, instead of the one the company is offering. Whether or not this is worthwhile will depend on the terms the company is using, what interest rate it uses in its calculations, what its actuarial formula is, and whether you can do better elsewhere. We've talked about the advantages and disadvantages of annuities earlier, and your decision will also depend on what you've decided is the best answer in your own case.

Under the tax laws, one way you can now take a lump-sum payout is by paying tax on it under a special "ten-year averaging" formula. This is a very favorable deal which leaves you the bulk of your withdrawal intact to reinvest and use free of tax as you need it. An alternative method under the law is to "roll over" the lump sum into a special IRA account. This way you pay no tax initially, but pay as you withdraw the IRA proceeds after retirement. One possible disadvantage here is that many approved IRA account vehicles, such as savings bank certificates, will require you to let the investment sit for several years before you can start drawing on it. If you are considering a lump-sum payout, you should certainly also consider whether to take it under ten-year averaging or to put it into an IRA as a form of annuity investment. The only practical way is to figure the tax consequences of both moves in your situation.

CASH FLOW

In addition to its financial statement, the most important report for any business is its statement of net earnings or cash flow—the familiar "P & L" or profit-and-loss account. It tells top management whether it is making or losing money. Your personal cash flow statement, both before and after your retirement, can tell you whether all is well or whether you are living beyond your means and perhaps draining your capital.

Right now, we aren't as interested in how you are doing during your working years as we are in how you'll do in retirement. But your cash flow picture for the preretirement period will be an excellent starting point for looking at the postretirement situation, for two reasons. First, a close look at where your money comes from and goes to now will reveal a lot about how you've become used to living and what has made it possible. Second, the very real figures for an actual year will give you a more realistic basis for estimating the comparable figures for the hypothetical year that's some time ahead. Without this picture of your spending patterns, financial advisers have found, you'd probably be at a total loss in starting on an analysis of your retirement needs and desires.

First, then, sit down and fill in the cash flow worksheet that's shown in Fig. 9-3 for last year (unless that was a very unusual one, in which case you may want to wait a few months and use this year's figures). Remember, this isn't a "budget" in the usual sense. There are no rewards for good behavior, or demerits for bad habits. The cold facts about where your money came from and went in a typical year are what is called for here. (Notice that there are similar columns for an accounting of an after-retirement year, which will be discussed later.)

The first time you go through this exercise, you'll undoubtedly leave out or misstate many items on both sides of the ledger. But with the help of your tax return, bank books, checkbooks, salary stubs, and your spouse, you should be able to fill in most of the gaps and reach a reasonably approximate balance the second time around. Make a serious effort at completeness; it's important for what will follow.

One of the first things you will notice about the form is that it assumes your direct spending won't match your income. There's provision for a "difference," and it's expected that at this stage of life it is a positive one—that you are able to count on a "cushion" each year, made up of your savings, additions to investments and paydowns of debts, charitable contributions, and similar nonconsumption outlays. Again, you won't be able to be exact about this—there's an element of savings in what you spend on life insurance, for example, and an element of spending in some "investments"—but do the best you can.

And notice, too, that the worksheet is to be filled in on the basis of monthly income and outgo. That's because a month is a manageable time period and because many of your income records and bill payments will be available on a monthly basis. For outlays or income items that are irregular or annual, such as insurance premiums, some dividends, and so on, simply divide the annual total by twelve. And for things that vary substantially from month to month—heating and cooling bills, to take an obvious example—use a monthly average.

Postretirement income

Your first move in preparing your postretirement cash flow worksheet will be analyzing your postretirement income. For convenience and accuracy, use the first full calendar year after retirement as the basis. Most of the major income items can be filled in pretty exactly, if you've had the talks with the Social Security people, your company benefits people, and others as suggested. Items like interest will depend on the total investments and savings involved, but can be closely estimated. Dividends and other items will be less solid, but a thoughtful estimate is always better than a wild guess or no figure at all.

FIG. 9-3   Monthly Income and Outgo Report (Cash Flow Worksheet)

	LATEST YEAR	RETIREMENT YEAR
Income		
Salary		
Commissions and bonuses		
Earnings from business		
Royalties, fees, etc.		
Savings interest		
Bonds & bond funds		
Stocks & stock funds		
Rental income		
Social security		
Company retirement		
Other company benefits		
Annuities, etc.		
Keogh and/or IRA		
Veteran benefits		
Other benefits		
Other income _____		
Total Income		
Outgo		
Housing		
Mortgage (interest		
and principal)		
Rent		
Utilities & fuel		
Telephone		
Maintenance & supplies		
Property taxes		
Other _____		
Food		
At home		
Eating out		
Clothing		
Furniture, furnishings		

FIG. 9-3—Continued

	LATEST YEAR	RETIREMENT YEAR

Transportation
    Car payments
    Car expenses
    Public transportation		

Personal care (barbers,		

Health care
    Insurance & plans
    Out of pocket		

Insurance (except health)
    Life insurance premiums
    Property insurance
    Car insurance
    Other insurance		

Leisure (hobbies, sport, travel,
    entertainment, books, sub-
    scriptions, etc.)		

Taxes
    Income & payroll
    Property
    Sales, etc.		

Miscellaneous outgo		
Total Outgo		
Difference		

Savings
Other investments
Contributions to pensions,
    annuities, etc.
Debt reductions (except home
    and car)
Debt increases
Unexplained differences		

Total Difference		

There won't be much similarity between the major sources of income in your working year and your first retirement year. And the total amount is almost certain to be smaller, which should come as no surprise. But if you have been working on a retirement plan, the total from all sources should be substantial enough to make retirement living comfortable.

Postretirement expenses

This, in a very real sense, is what this whole chapter has been leading up to. This will be the moment of truth, when you find out whether your ideas of retirement life have been practical. This, fortunately, is also where you can revise your thinking and avoid some of the mistakes you would have made without the opportunity for planning your retirement budget on paper.

The first thing you will notice as you go through the outgo form item by item is that unless yours has been a very unusual lifestyle, your pattern of postretirement spending is going to be different in many ways from what it has been during your working years. There will be some similarities, of course, but it's the differences that are bound to stand out.

First, there will be the changes that come simply from living on a relatively smaller, mostly fixed income. Whatever your retirement income level, I can guarantee that you will be watching what you spend for many things in ways that you may not believe possible today.

Then there will be the important changes that come simply from not working. You'll spend less on transportation without daily commuting costs; probably less on clothing without the need for suits, uniforms, or other work clothes; and maybe less on eating out without daily lunches and business meals. But you may be spending more on entertainment and leisure activities, from books and movies to travel and sports equipment. The other chapters of this book should give you a pretty good idea of what some of these changes will be or can be.

There will also be changes due to the inevitability of growing older. Health care costs will be the big item here, but your diet will change, too, as will your ideas on what constitute entertainment and relaxation.

Keeping all of this in mind, make a first attempt at estimating your retirement outgo. As you go through the form, you'll appreciate why it is set up in such detail. Without this detail, it's almost certain that many outgo items would be overlooked, and others badly estimated.

Luckily, you have a couple of guides to help you as you go along. The first, as already suggested, is the spending pattern you've been setting up to now. It will change, but as you look at the figures you've put down for each item, you can have a pretty good idea of the limits within which it will change, at least in the early retirement years.

The second guide is the retirement budgets that have been worked out by the government's statisticians, based on their extensive field studies. The Bureau of Labor Statistics (BLS), which develops the Consumer Price Index every month, continually conducts spending surveys to decide what should go into that index's "market basket" of consumer goods and services. Among the groups they study are retired people, and we'll be referring to their findings at several points as we go along.

HOUSING. This is going to be your biggest outgo item, no doubt about that. The BLS says that you will put 35 percent to 36 percent of your total after-tax spending into housing after retirement, compared with about 27 percent to 30 percent before retirement. At this point, you've already made your basic decision about owning or renting and should have an idea about the basic monthly costs that will result. But even with this item nailed down, there's much that you can do to keep other housing costs under close control.

On property taxes, for example, be sure to check into every break you may be entitled to. Exemptions and reductions for retirees are available at every level, from state and county down to village taxes, but their availability isn't always widely advertised.

Energy conservation will become a way of life, if you are paying your own utility and fuel bills. Letting it get a little warmer indoors in summer and a bit chillier in winter will be good for the budget—and probably for the health as well. And don't overlook asking the telephone company about economy or budget service. Most companies offer them, and the yearly savings can add up.

But suppose, despite all your planned economies, that your estimated housing outgo will be just too far out of line. That possibility is precisely why you have put yourself through all this figuring. You may have to go all the way back to your basic plan and choose a more modest housing aim—that, or figure out how to bring your retirement income up to the housing standard you've chosen.

FOOD. Not surprisingly, food will be the second biggest item in your retirement budget. The BLS says that if you are typical it will take up some 24 percent to 28 percent of your total outgo, about the same as it does before retirement. As a basic necessity, food will take a relatively smaller portion of spending the higher your standard of retirement living, but there are ways you can keep the costs down at any level of spending. These include cutting down on expensive restaurant meals, eating a simpler menu at home, or checking the day-old bins at the supermarket, depending on where you are starting from and how serious the need to economize.

Whatever you do, however, don't make the serious mistake that many older people do. Partly out of misguided "thrift," and partly out of falling into lazy habits, they shift to a very limited and inadequate diet. Eating a bit less, the doctor says, is better for almost everybody in the less active retirement years. But that lesser amount should and can be varied and nourishing without being budget-busting. Don't confuse cost of food with nutrition.

CLOTHING, FURNISHINGS, AND PERSONAL CARE. Together, these can add up to a fairly big item—about 12 percent or so of your retirement budget. But this is one subject on which it is difficult to generalize. Some people choose to lounge about in comfortable old clothes on comfortable old furniture, while others will decide to buy new leisure wardrobes, whatever else they have to do without. Either way, enjoy it, as long as you keep an eye on the total cost and don't let it get too far off base.

TRANSPORTATION. In this modern world, transportation is going to be another major budget item in retirement—from 9 percent to 12 percent of total outlays according to the government figures. As with food, that's about the same proportion that the average family spends on transportation before retirement. But also as with food, that means a smaller amount in dollars, based on a smaller total budget. And that, in turn, means cutting corners and saving wherever you can.

If you'll be living in a big city, public transportation may be a wiser choice than owning a car, whatever you thought earlier. There are often "senior" fares available, and trips can be planned more carefully. If you really need a car in a suburban environment, make sure that it's an economical and dependable model. The out-of-pocket costs, including gas, repairs, insurance, and so on, can be only a fraction of those for a "gas-guzzler."

One solution, if you're not certain, may be to keep your car for a while, but keep very close tabs on how much you use it and its total costs.

There's a good chance you'll discover that selling it and relying on a rented car when you really need one will be the best compromise. Your insurance rates are going to be much higher in most cases when you are over sixty-five, and the lower cost of nonowner coverage will be another incentive to rent instead.

HEALTH AND MEDICAL CARE.   As retired people know, this will be a much more important cost item after 65. The BLS figures agree, and its budgets show that health care is likely to take half again as large a share of outlays after retirement as before. That means if you've been spending 4 percent of your budget, it will rise to 6 percent—if 6 percent, it'll go up to 9 percent.

Of course, this is an area in which averages and percentages may not mean too much to the individual. If you are going to be hit with a big doctor's bill and hospital charges for a major illness or surgery, no amount of careful budgeting can prepare for it. But there are things you can do to keep your health and medical costs under some degree of control after retirement.

Medicare has to be your first line of defense. Briefly, here is how that federal health insurance plan for older people works. Starting at age 65 (even if you retire earlier under Social Security), you automatically become eligible for Medicare Part A (hospital coverage), just by applying for it three months before your sixty-fifth birthday—at no cost. This part of the program provides for in-hospital care under a schedule of deductibles and days of care, plus various in-hospital services such as nursing, drugs, X-rays, and so on. Your local Social Security office can supply the details.

Medicare Part B (medical coverage) pays doctor's fees, both in-hospital and under outpatient status, again according to a schedule of deductibles and allowed fees. There's a charge for Part B, but it is small (it was $8.20 a month in 1978, and will be a bit higher every year). Unless you have a fanatical opposition to public health insurance, don't even flirt with the thought of not applying for Part B when you sign up for Medicare. It is subsidized with tax dollars you've been paying in all along, and you couldn't begin to match its rates in the private insurance market. The monthly charge is deducted from your monthly Social Security check, unless you go on working, so it's relatively painless, too.

As we've said, there are deductibles, allowables, schedules, and so on under both parts of Medicare, so you will still have medical bills. In an individual case I know of, a stroke followed by extensive hospital care, rehabilitation therapy, and of course medical specialists' bills, resulted in total costs of around $13,500. Medicare paid $10,900 of this, or a little over 80 percent. As great a break as that was, it still left my friend with bills of about $2,600, which put a big dent in a limited retirement budget. And that's where private health insurance can come in.

"Medigap" insurance, designed specifically to cover the items not included in Medicare, is now widely available, and very heavily promoted. The coverage is available in various forms, and from several sources, some of which can be a much better buy than others. You will want to shop around, therefore, before signing up for it.

One excellent source will be the Blue Cross/Blue Shield plan that covers the retirement region you've chosen. The plans of the various "Blues" may differ somewhat, but they are all broad, dependable, and reasonable. The American Association of Retired Persons (AARP) offers its own plan, through its favored insurance company. This plan is also comprehensive and moderately priced. Many private insurance companies offer similar plans, which vary widely in cost and coverage.

As an intelligent and thrifty retiree, you are not going to be taken in by any high-powered insurance salesperson. Just keep in mind that in any field, the harder the sell, the more likely it is that there's a catch. And there's almost no limit to the lengths some mail-order, out-of-state insurance sellers seem to be willing to go to misinform potential buyers about the coverage of their policies.

In some areas an alternative to medigap insurance can be membership in a "health maintenance organization," or HMO. These organizations contract to cover all of your medical and hospital costs without any schedules or limits. If you are eligible for Medicare, they will require that you carry it, but otherwise their total charge can be less than the cost of insurance, and there are no "fine print" exceptions. The catch is that there are so far only a few HMOs that will accept individual members. But their numbers will be growing, because the government policy is to encourage them. If you have been covered at work by an HMO, "Blue," or private insurance plan, it may be best to continue with it since you will avoid waiting periods, "existing condition" exceptions, and so on.

Notice that nothing has been said here about cutting back on health care costs after retirement. There's no way, beyond adequate insurance coverage, that any sensible person can accomplish that. Keeping these costs under control and avoiding throwing your money away on uneconomical policies, miracle cures, and unnecessary paraphernalia is the best you can plan for.

LEISURE.   One of the chief aims of retirement is, of course, leisure; but how much of it you will be able to enjoy may depend on how well you have budgeted for it and for other claims on your money. Nobody can tell you what the "right" amount to spend on hobbies, sports, entertainment, travel, and so forth will be. If a hammock in the shade is your idea of leisure, you are obviously not going to be spending much. If you are planning cruises and safaris, though, it is going to be important to shop for bargains and set yourself an allowance, just as in any other spending area.

TAXES.   All sorts of these will follow you into retirement, and you may as well prepare to pay them. Fortunately, your income taxes will be much smaller, in most cases, though many of us would be glad to have the income that would keep them high. On this point, the Internal Revenue Service has a number of free booklets containing good tax advice for "Older Americans," "Retirees," "Homeowners," and so on. You can get them from your local IRS office—listed under "United States Government" in any city telephone directory—and they can help you make sure you take every tax break that's coming to you.

In addition, there will be local property, sales, and other taxes. As we've suggested, be sure to check with the local authorities, wherever you settle down, as to any and all exemptions, reductions, rebates, and so on you may be entitled to as a retiree or older person. Some places limit their special tax deals to those who have been residents before passing the particular eligibility milestone. If you know where you are going to be living, check into this and see what you may be able to do to establish residency in advance—if it matters. This could save you money every year of your retirement.

The income-outgo gap

It's almost certain that your budgeted outgo is going to exceed your expected retirement income—certainly on the first go-around, and probably after you've trimmed some of the figures as well. And, in the words of the immortal Mr. Micawber in Charles Dickens' *David Copperfield*— "Annual income, 20 pounds; annual expenditure, 19/19/6, result happiness. Annual income, 20 pounds; annual expenditure, 20/0/6, result misery." Basically, there are two practical ways to avoid this misery—dip into capital, or obtain some more income.

USING YOUR CAPITAL. Many retirees have a morbid fear of touching their capital, but there is actually no good reason for this, if it's done in a controlled manner. Annuity payments, after all, are exactly this—a return in installments of the capital you invested, plus interest. Treating selected investments as "do-it-yourself annuities" can be perfectly sound retirement planning, and your bank, securities brokerage, or fund management can help you work out a withdrawal plan that will keep a more or less steady income coming in for any chosen period of years.

Estate planning is much too complicated and specialized to handle here in depth, but consider this: Money or investments that have been put into irrevocable trusts as part of an estate plan may not be available to you if and when you need them as capital to draw on. Under the new liberalized estate tax laws, you'll find that most or all of your estate will be free of tax, and in that case, revocable trusts, under which you can reclaim your money if necessary, will accomplish the same estate purposes.

WORKING IN RETIREMENT. This alternative may be a positive mental and physical benefit, as well as a financial one, for many people. Finding a job and starting from scratch in a strange locality may not be a simple matter, but there are ways and means here, too. Your former employer may well be interested in using your skills and experience on an "independent contractor" basis that won't reduce your company pension. Some "knowledge" or "information" workers, who carry their skills in their heads, have been lucky enough to be able to arrange to do this on a remote basis, so that they can "go to work" long distance.

Also, despite what you may have thought or been told, there is now no way that your former employer can stop your vested pension payments because you go to work for a competitor after retirement. There are many experienced salespeople, for example, working part-time for former competitors in the area where they've retired. In short, any marketable skills you've acquired over your career can be a real part of your "capital" in retirement to help close the income-outgo gap.

Beyond a point, retirement income you earn will reduce your Social Security benefits. But the amount you can earn annually before that starts is now up to $4,500, and is scheduled to go higher. And what you do earn above that limit reduces your benefit by only one dollar for every two dollars earned. Thus, you could earn a fairly large income before wiping out your benefits entirely.

If your spouse is getting benefits as your dependent, his or her postretirement earnings would have relatively little effect on your total family Social Security income. That is because a dependent spouse also gets a $4,500 annual exemption, and excess earnings beyond that will reduce only the dependency benefit, not your basic benefit, on a one-for-two basis.

On the other hand—and there always seems to be an "other hand" to spoil things—you will have to pay some income tax and payroll taxes on your earnings, will probably have commuting and other costs, and so on. Work all this out carefully before you decide just how much income you can "afford" to earn in retirement without putting yourself back where you started.

Another caution about earnings and Social Security. You may remember hearing something about the fact that crowding all your retirement earnings into a few months of the year can beat the earnings limit. Forget it. Under the changed law, the "monthly benefit" test that made that possible now applies only during the year in which you start collecting. Today, if you have collected benefits for eleven months of the year, then earn over $4,500 in the last month, you will owe the SSA money, and you can be sure it will collect, either by billing you or deducting it from your next year's benefits.

RETIREMENT CHECKLIST

This would be the heading for quite a list if we went into every possible detail. But here's a brief checklist of key items since they can mean cash in your pocket—or out of it, if you neglect them.

NOTIFY YOUR INSURERS. This includes your auto insurance carrier and any others whose premium charges depend on the fact that you are working. Failing to remind the insurance company that you no longer drive your car to work and back, for example, can mean wasted premiums which can be quite substantial in some metropolitan areas.

CHECK LOCAL TAX COLLECTORS. There are a wide variety of small but useful tax breaks available to retired persons in many localities. You might as well take advantage of them, if they exist.

TAX RETURNS. Watch your federal return for the year in which you retire. Depending on the time of the year you stop working, there may be a substantial over-withholding involved. And you will want to check out both itemizing and not itemizing, even if you've always taken the standard deduction before. And, if your income and deduction items turn out as strange as they are likely to in a year in which your lifestyle changes drastically, a note of explanation attached to the return might just forestall a visit with an agent.

A RETIREMENT NET WORTH STATEMENT. And last, but far from least, be sure to make out another net worth statement, as of your retirement. It will tell you how much of your preretirement planning you've accomplished and how much is still left to be done. And it will give you a sound starting point for managing the capital with which you'll be entering what can be a much happier and more satisfying retirement with fewer financial worries.

FIGHTING INFLATION

Sure, you say, maybe everything has been worked out so that there is no longer an income-outgo gap for the first year of retirement. But what about after that, when the income side remains steady but the cost of everything keeps climbing? How does the retired person of set and limited income cope with inflation?

Frankly, not very well. A partial solution lies in the statement of the problem itself. The trick is to have some income that will rise with inflation and as many expenses as possible that don't. And that's not an impossible dream. Social Security payments, for example, will most likely continue to be adjusted upward from time to time for those already retired. They are, after all, a large and growing constituency, and becoming better organized every year.

Some investments can also produce increasing income, such as dividends on well-chosen common stocks. And some of the capital you will be liquidating over the years will also increase in value along with the prices of everything else. All of these will probably still not offset much of the erosion of inflation, but every bit helps.

And every bit helps on the expense side, too. Home ownership, with or without a mortgage, may be a housing bargain, though taxes may still rise. Prepayment of expenses where you can, such as in the health care field, is another step in the right direction. If you are a gardener, raising part of your own food is a good anti-inflation hedge, even while you are still working.

And in the daily course of shopping and paying bills, other savings are possible. Department stores all over the country are making one day a week a discount day for seniors—10 percent off all purchases for people over sixty-five. The Public Service Company of New Hampshire is giving all its customers over seventy a 10 percent discount on their electric bills. Urban and suburban transportation—trains, buses, and so on—have special rates for seniors. Some restaurants, out to get the senior customer, offer discounts. Movies and theatres in many areas offer half-rate tickets to senior citizens. Museums and other art and literary institutions offer lower rates—or free admission—to seniors.

There is just one prerequisite for all these benefits—you must ask for them! Small savings, perhaps, but along with other income-increasing, outgo-decreasing efforts, they pay off.

One more caution: In past years, some people were able (they thought) to eliminate the inflation risk, and most other risks as well, by arranging to retire to a "life-care" institution. In one of these, typically, you pay a lump sum, which may be your total assets, in return for a guaranty of lifetime care. Many of these life-care institutions are excellent establishments, run by religious groups or other nonprofit organizations. Recently, however, inflation has been catching up with some of them, too, and some have come to the brink of bankruptcy. If you decide to choose a life-care retirement institution as a way of avoiding all the financial problems we've discussed here, be very sure to check into its endowment and its financial stability as much as you can before casting your lot irrevocably.

10
LIVING
ARRANGEMENTS

When you no longer are required to show up at a workplace, you may want to consider relocating. It is a key decision because your home takes on an even greater importance after retirement. You are in it more, you use it more, and in a sense, you depend on it more. It has to "help" you by being less of a physical drain, by being more convenient, suiting both your brand new lifestyle and patterns of daily living. For example, a kitchen that requires less stretching and reaching, a bathroom that is made safer because of antislipping and antifalling devices—qualities like these definitely make your life easier and safer.

"Home is where the heart is," is a profound insight. And for house hunters, it suggests a basic guideline: Find out where your heart is, and your search is well along. This section helps you discover where your heart tells you to live—with some important afterthoughts from your rational mind.

In earlier years, your choice of a home was influenced by several major factors: money, the needs of your children, commuting distance from your job, and facilities for activities you favored.

With retirement comes the need to reassess your living arrangements. Finances, health, personal preferences, and family and friends will all play a large part in rethinking your needs.

Clearly, people who are financially well prepared for retirement have fewer restrictions on their living arrangements. Those who are just O.K. must be more careful in their planning. And people whose rent or homeowning costs are severely limited by their finances must look for the most satisfactory arrangement at the lowest possible cost. This pressure may suggest belt-tightening action, such as taking in lodgers, dividing a one-family residence to accommodate a tenant family (if permitted by zoning regulations), or selling one's home and living in a low-rent apartment.

Not only your own health, but also a spouse's or relative's health needs may suggest a move to a therapeutic environment. If someone in your family group can't take the cold, this may be a major factor in setting your sights on a warm-weather area. If a family member suffers from a lung or breathing ailment, a dry climate such as Arizona or Colorado may be in the cards.

"Remember how much we loved Hawaii when we visited there?" Carol Moore tells her husband. "This is our chance, this is time at last to live there—or at least, to try it for a year."

People fall in love with a city, a type of country, or a particular climate. This romance may be based on familiarity, or just a picture in the mind. But like all true affairs, love sets aside objections and even actual drawbacks. "O.K., we can't speak Spanish, and we may not see a theatrical performance or hear a live symphony orchestra from one year to the next. But Fred has been living in that fishing village in Mexico for fifteen years, and he's crazy about it. You've read his letters. And he's asked us to go down there. I say, let's do it."

Not infrequently, home is where children, grandchildren, brothers, sisters, and old friends are. June and Hank Czerny moved from a comfortable Los Angeles suburb to a small town in Nevada because their son had set himself up in a medical practice there. Being near him, his wife, and their twin four-year-old grandsons was the most important fact in their thinking about where to live.

On the other hand, widower Sidney Galt, at seventy, waved aside the invitation of his son and daughter to join them in San Francisco. "It's a beautiful city," he agreed, "and it's got a great deal to offer. But I have friends in Chicago with whom I spend a great deal of time. Nothing could replace that."

● *Case Histories*

To sensitize your own thinking about where to live and the kind of things to consider in making your judgments, here are some case histories that highlight points that could shape your decision.

THREE VINEGARY VIGNETTES

JOHN BLACKWOOD ON THE COSTA DEL SOL. A few years back I rented a condominium apartment for a month in the town of Los Boliches, a small village between the larger towns of Marbella and Torremolinos on Spain's Mediterranean coast.

Shortly after moving in I met a neighbor who turned out to be a recently retired American. He had worked for a Milwaukee construction company and told me with some glee that he had been preparing for his retirement for several years—had studied Spanish, studied up on local history, and had, the year before, spent a heavenly three weeks in the area to make sure that he was right in considering this as a retirement haven.

"How is it going?" I asked.

"Fine, fine."

"Are you living here alone?"

"No, my wife is with me."

"And how does she like it?"

"She doesn't. She wants to go back home."

Obviously Mr. Blackwood had failed in one aspect of his retirement planning. It's doubtful that a protesting and unhappy wife is going to make it possible for him to enjoy his retirement.

Moral: Retirement planning is not only for the retiree. It should involve family—above all, a spouse.

PHIL RUTHER ON THE WEST COAST OF FLORIDA. On a recent visit to Tampa, I got to talking to one of the employees of the hotel. Three years before, he told me, he had come down to Florida with his wife to get away from the cold Vermont winters.

"But we may have to go back north," he said.

"Why did you come down in the first place?"

"An aunt and uncle of mine lived here and when we visited, they persuaded us to come down here to live. It seemed great. It's beautiful country. The trouble is, I find I can't stand the humidity. And then the cost of living here is considerably higher than in Vermont. That's why I'm working in the hotel. I drive guests to and from the airport. My finances just weren't holding up."

Moral: Cost of living and climate are two essential aspects of any area you're considering. Either one can ruin an otherwise good retirement plan. Two of them being unsatisfactory can make a living place untenable.

TOM ZARRA IN RHODE ISLAND. Tom Zarra left a stimulating career and a large circle of friends in Washington, D.C. for a pleasant house and a gorgeous view of the Atlantic off Rhode Island. His dream house had an additional virtue. It was near his favorite daughter and a good tennis club. What more could Tom, an excellent tennis player at the age of sixty-five, possibly want?

Sad to relate, none of Tom's retired contemporaries in the community could present him with the kind of challenge and satisfaction his old tennis buddies had regularly provided. And the younger people who were good enough were tactfully but firmly against playing with such an old opponent. Tom had the embarrassing experience of overhearing a potential partner saying something about " . . . don't want to play with an old guy who's going to have a heart attack." Not playing tennis was a real hardship for Tom. Eventually even his dear daughter joined the people who suggested that he consider moving back to Washington.

Moral: No matter how dreamy a dream house or how gorgeous the view through your living room picture window, if you can't do the things you want to do, it's no place for you.

THREE VICTORY VIGNETTES

THE BOISES' NEW HOME. Emma Boise took early retirement at age sixty-two so that she and her husband, Harold, who had retired two years previously, could move out of the apartment they'd lived in for thirty years in the Rego Park section of Queens, N.Y.

"The old neighborhood certainly isn't what it was when we first moved in," Harold said. "I'd love a bit of the country," Emma agreed. They spent several months looking at houses just north of Westchester. Their limited funds brought them again and again to the frustrating situation of not liking the houses they could afford, and not being able to afford property they liked.

A friendly real estate agent suggested that to get something that met their needs at a price that they could afford, they'd have to go further north, just beyond commuting range of New York City. The agent explained, "Once you have to compete with the commuters for housing, the prices go up."

Finally, in the town of Hopewell Junction they found something promising. An agent almost casually mentioned as they were driving along to look at homes in the $30- to $40 thousand range, "That house we just passed is for sale at $20 thousand." "Back up!" said Emma.

The house had been built about 1850 and was on a half-acre of land that adjoined Wappinger's Creek. There was no one at home but the agent had a key for a lock-box which held the house keys. They entered the house and Emma and Harold looked about at a somewhat run-down but interesting interior. The living room had a fireplace. The kitchen was a disaster, but the four bedrooms upstairs were in pretty good shape.

"The house needs a great deal of work," the agent said somewhat dubiously.

Emma had the feeling that what she was saying was that it required more work than an elderly couple could handle, but both she and Harold were good with their hands.

They looked the house over from basement to attic.

"It would take a lot of work and money to fix the place up," Harold said. "And the general neighborhood isn't particularly choice, although the house has considerable seclusion behind the trees out front. Do you think the owner would take $15 thousand?"

"I'll find out," the agent said. She did, and the answer was yes.

After three months of repairing, modernizing the kitchen and bathroom, ripping out flimsy wall partitions, and doing considerable painting, both inside and out, the Boises, with the help of a local contractor and considerable assistance from their two sons, had converted a run-down house into an attractive and extremely livable home. Spending very carefully, they had been able to make major improvements for a total cash outlay of $12 thousand.

The agent came to visit at the housewarming. "For $27 thousand," Emma said, "we now have a house we probably could sell for $35 thousand." The agent agreed.

Harold said, "Wait until spring when I can start doing some landscaping and fixing on the outside. That'll add another few thousand dollars worth of value to the house."

The Boises had worked out a splendid combination of returns on their investment of cash and hard work: an attractive home that was also an extremely good investment.

THE HALEVYS DISCOVER NEW YORK CITY. Bill and Rita Halevy lived in a pretty Westchester town an hour's run out of New York City. They liked the place and had raised three children there. When the youngest left for college, they looked at each other, "What now?"

Rita said, "How about paying a visit to my sister, Helen. She and her husband have been living in Boulder and love it." "Boulder's a nice town," Bill said, "very scenic, but I don't know. . . ."

Various choices were discussed. Just for the heck of it Bill listed some of the places they'd considered. He found they had talked about living in Spain, Florida, Los Angeles, Miami, Maine, Cape Cod.

Suddenly Rita said, "How about New York?"

"You mean New York City?"

"That's right. I know there are some problems, but. . . ."

With some hesitation, even trepidation, the Halevys started apartment-hunting in Manhattan. Luckily, they found a condominium which they would be able to afford after selling their house, and the monthly maintenance was reasonable.

Two years later the Halevys had become "natives" of New York City. They had met a number of couples whose company they enjoyed, and from their mid-Manhattan apartment the restaurants, theatres, museums, special events, and even Central Park were all within reach.

From time to time friends and relatives came to visit, both from surrounding suburbs and other parts of the country. Their children were also frequent weekenders.

"I can understand visiting New York," was a common reaction, "but is it really practical to live here?"

"As far as we're concerned," Bill said, "this town is the greatest place in the world. It has excitement, color, and you can choose your pace, from fast to easy-going. There's nothing like it. . . ."

ALAN H. OLMSTEAD AT HOME. Some people travel a mile, others ten thousand, to find the place to which they want to retire. But many decide to stay put, to continue living in the same place they've been. Following is an excerpt from a wonderful book on retirement, a personal narrative describing some of the situations that the author, Alan H. Olmstead, faced in the first year of his retirement.[1] One of his most vivid entries describes his feelings about his home. I doubt that any other statement could be as clear or as moving as his. With the author's permission, it's reprinted in full below:

SHOULD RETIRED PEOPLE CHANGE HOUSES?

Monday, Sept. 11. When we came to this house, the wide boards in the floors had been covered with layers of green or maroon floor paint. We sanded them off, down to the clear grain, and then stewed butternut husks, from the tree at the edge of the yard, until we had a brew dark enough to use to stain the floors. This we did ourselves. The maple tree that stands outside the kitchen window, now fifty feet tall, is

[1.]*Threshold,* by Alan H. Olmstead (New York: Harper & Row 1972).

one four of us carried half a mile down from the hill. We didn't believe so large a sapling could be transplanted successfully, but it lived for us. Although we seldom taste the fruit, we planted the russet apple trees by the garage. The black oak in the middle of the lawn provided the canopy for A's wedding ceremony, an August afternoon's midsummer dream of an affair. In our early winters here, it was around the fireplace just to the right of this desk that we gathered for such mid-Victorian family rituals as the reading aloud of *David Copperfield* and *Mary Poppins*. This is the house of our Christmases and our Thanksgivings, the house to which our children came home, with new friends, from their first semesters in college, the house which could open out for our good times and provide suffering corners for our moments of pain. It is also, of course, the house which is beginning to need to be shingled again, even though we told ourselves, when we selected expensive wood shingles thirteen years ago, that that was probably the last roof we would have to pay for. Its vast outer surface will soon be asking for fresh paint. Its interior pipes grow porous; the cost of heat escalates every winter; there really is no hard-boiled statistical way of proving that we can afford to stay here and keep the place livable. But move into something smaller and less expensive and easier to maintain? Only, in present mood, as a dead body.

● *Choosing to Stay or to Move*

One point that emerges clearly from Alan H. Olmstead's statement of his desire to remain in his present home: it can be a highly emotional matter.

Hedi and Oswald Rossi, two dear friends, lived in their large, comfortable home for twenty years. Recently Oswald died at the age of ninety. Hedi's friends and relatives, especially her son, urged her to sell the house and move into an apartment. "Ridiculous," said Hedi, a lively, snappish eighty-two. "I wouldn't be comfortable anyplace else. And I like the feeling of being with Oswald's friendly ghost. . . ."

No logical arguments are strong enough to overcome emotional attachments of the quality of Alan H. Olmstead's or Hedi Rossi's. Hedi, a productive internationally known writer, will doubtless keep on writing her plays, short stories, and TV and radio scripts, relaxed in her secure and familiar surroundings.

No matter how strong your attachment to your preretirement lodgings, however, there are two key points to take into account.

Make sure it isn't just fear of change that's keeping you where you are. For example, Frank and Gert Muller lived in an apartment in a somewhat run-down section of Akron. At the suggestion that they consider moving after Frank's retirement, they offered a dozen reasons for staying with what they had—friends, familiarity with the neighborhood, and easy shopping. But a year later they did move to a Cincinnati suburb: "A change for the better, much better! I guess we were just afraid to leave what we knew for an unknown situation."

Second, no matter what your final decision, at least try to look at the facts objectively. Certainly, accept the wisdom and strength of your emotional reactions. It might very well be the height of folly to give up a home that has all the attributes of a well-fitting glove for a house or apartment that may have everything but the things that satisfy your home-loving soul. But give yourself the benefit of a logical assessment of your situation. The twin checklists below, based on an excerpt from "Your Retirement Housing Guide," a pamphlet published by the American Association of Retired Persons, can assist in this review:

REASONS FOR STAYING

( )   Expenses of my present home are under control and I can meet them in the future.
( )   The mortgage is paid; my house is free and clear.
( )   Property taxes are not expected to increase drastically.
( )   The rent I am paying on my present apartment is within my means and I do not expect it to increase very much.
( )   I don't foresee need for large maintenance expenditures such as a new roof or furnace.
( )   My financial situation is O.K. and I can afford to live comfortably in my present home on a fixed income.
( )   My present living conditions are satisfactory.
( )   Future needs, as far as I can anticipate them, can be met here.
( )   Family and friends live nearby.
( )   I am active in local civic, social, and religious groups.
( )   The neighborhood is friendly, safe, and familiar to me.
( )   I have status in the community, I am a part of it.
( )   I feel comfortable and secure in this home.
( )   I have never seen nor can I imagine a place I'd rather live.

REASONS FOR MOVING

( )   Expenses will increase and my income is fixed.
( )   The house is too large and inconvenient.

( ) Too many stairs to climb.

( ) No bath or bedroom on first floor.

( ) Too many windows to clean.

( ) Maintenance in general requires too much muscle—for example, it's difficult to hang storm windows, mow the lawn, and painting as often as needed.

( ) Bathroom and kitchen need remodeling for satisfactory and safe use.

( ) Heating system (or plumbing, or electrical system) needs replacement.

( ) Rent on my apartment is expected to increase.

( ) Condition of the neighborhood becoming less satisfactory.

( ) Transportation is unsatisfactory.

( ) New construction has made the neighborhood lose its former quality.

( ) A larger population means noisy—and possibly hostile—youths around, both day and night.

( ) Extremes of weather—either hot or cold—keep me indoors too often.

( ) Shopping—because of long trips and need to carry food—is no longer satisfactory.

( ) Friends and relatives have moved away.

( ) Few activities or facilities are of interest to me.

( ) There are a dozen other places I'd rather live (or perhaps just one).

Which approach makes the most sense? Should one go about systematically weighing the pros and cons before making the important decision about whether to stay in the same home after retirement as before? Or should one go along with these strong inner feelings, whether they say either stay or go?

RETURNING HOME

Ruth Rejnis recently did a piece for *The New York Times* about a number of people who retired to areas other than the one in which they had been living. Moves took them to Florida, Arizona, and California—often sunny, icicle-free climes. But the Rejnis piece went on to say that a number of families who had left home, undoubtedly with high hopes for a new and better life, had moved back.

No single explanation covered each instance. For example, there was the case of Frances Bowles, who had moved to the sun belt. She chose to move back to New Jersey from Florida after the death of her husband. She found that being alone in this still somewhat unfamiliar place didn't make for comfortable living and as Mrs. Bowles said, "All my family was up here." Mrs. Bowles wanted to be with them as well as to end their concern for her wellbeing.

And then there were Charlotte and Elmer Stout, who moved back from St. Augustine to Whiting Village in Whiting, New Jersey. After four years, they missed their children and grandchildren.

There were other reasons for returning to the familiar places of their preretirement days. One possibly unexpected reason: the life of ease under a brilliant sun was just not that easy to take. In some cases the sun itself was the culprit: "The heat was intense and the bugs would drive you out of your mind," said one former sun belt lover. He and his wife moved to Covered Bridge in Englishtown, New Jersey after two years of living on the west coast of Florida.

Another comment on the experience of living in the sun belt: "It was too drastic a change."

One refugee from the northeast lived in Arizona for eighteen years before moving back to New Jersey after her retirement. She finally realized she didn't like the desert. "I love the green and the ocean."

Another couple moved from Point Pleasant Beach, N.J., to Florida after their retirement. They wanted a change of scenery, security, relaxation, and sunshine. They may or may not have found these, but what they did find, and what eventually sent them back north, was that "the life was quite dull. People seemed to have nothing to do except sit around and talk or just stare into space."

However, don't be too quick to jump to a conclusion on the basis of these stories. It would be easy to come up with a group of people who had sold out, moved to other parts of the country, and have been perfectly delighted with the benefits of the change.

KEY CONSIDERATIONS

The matter of where you live isn't incidental to your postretirement life. In many cases it is your central concern. The home you live in, its location, both in the community as well as in the geographical sense, can be a major factor in the kind of life you lead. Accordingly, in thinking over whether to stay or move after retirement, considering the following aspects may help you to a decision.

Reasons for staying

Put these down in writing! The feeling that "we couldn't possibly move and leave a community we've been a part of for thirty years" may be wide of the mark. You may have been saying this for years without really examining the facts: a changing neighborhood, the activities you enjoyed when you were younger may no longer appeal, and so on.

Paul and Greta Myers decided to spell out their situation by listing both favorable and unfavorable aspects of their apartment in a midwestern town.

Pros	Cons
Familiar neighborhood	The neighborhood is shabbier
Friendly neighbors and tradespeople	Few of the old-timers left
Comfortable apartment	Apartment has gotten drab and worn
Have status in the community —are respected and known	Less community feeling in present group
Near movie theatre	We seldom go to the movies
Fifteen minute drive to lake for swimming and boating	Haven't been to the lake in three years

Clearly, the Myers's reassessment of their living situation pointed strongly to a living in the past. Present-day realities were harsher than the nostalgic pictures they cherished.

Reasons for moving

Again, pencil and paper can help you discover your own feelings. Here are reasons supplied by retirees:

Better climate	Different lifestyles
Educational facilities	Closer to our children
More like-minded people with my interests	City life, everything from theatres to more exciting pace
Lower cost of living	Country life—relaxed pace

And one venturesome 70-year-old woman said forthrightly, "Change!" She was ready to sacrifice a good deal of the past for some new options in the future.

Timing

A move right now might be a poor decision. Family ties and friends might be lost by a move today. But a year or two—when family members leave, or important friends die or move away—may make the time ripe.

But the reverse decision may be equally wise. Delay a move five or ten years, and you're that much older, perhaps less able to enjoy a new environment. *Now* may be your best time to pull up stakes.

Effects on lifestyle

This can be important enough to deserve special consideration. If you are not altogether satisfied with the various activities that make up a style of life—your socializing, participation in community or other organizations, availability of entertainment, and so on—is it possible that a move to a carefully considered new situation might bring definite benefits?

A fifty-five year old widow told me, "When I moved into this town ten years ago, I thought I had it made: new friends, a good job. But somehow the socializing didn't work out. I guess the people of my age here are interested in different kinds of things. I like good times, activity, doing things. This turned out to be a pretty stuffy place. My job is still O.K., but I feel out of it." This woman moved out west and a year later I heard that it had been a most successful transplant. "Life is really looking up," she wrote.

Calculating the effect of a move on your enjoyment of day-to-day living isn't easy. But if you're dissatisfied where you are, check into the possibilities, speak to people, and finally, visit and decide on the possible promise of a new location.

Considering family

In some cases, the needs and desires of other people enter the calculation. You may be all for packing up and moving—Alaska, Hawaii, or just the next town. But certainly family members—a spouse, or parents who are a permanent part of your household—might have views that should be listened to. This isn't to suggest that there is likely to be a partisan lineup: you want to move and they don't, or vice versa. It's just as possible that they will have views about staying put or where to move that may provide valuable insights for you.

Moving closer to home

"Staying put" suggests literally staying in the same house or apartment after you retire as before. But broaden the concept a bit, and you will find that slight changes can make a difference. Can you move into another apartment in the same building? How about finding a more suitable house just a few blocks away or across town? Could you move to another town just a few miles away? Or, how about remodeling your house—converting it into a two-family dwelling?

In thinking about this decision—go or stay—keep in mind the experiences of others described above. You can often temper a decision by not burning bridges behind you. Rent out your apartment or house, or rent in the new location. See how it works. If it does, fine. Make it permanent. If it doesn't, move back. Perhaps you can rethink the situation at a later date.

Financial concerns

Money talks, it is said. And this is one situation where it pays to listen. What are the financial pros and cons of moving versus staying? What exactly does living in your present house or apartment cost you?

If you live in a rented apartment, then rent is the major expense. But there may be other costs you incur that also should be figured. Garage fees (if you have a car); taxis or other transportation required by the location of the apartment to go shopping, visit people, church, and so on; and services for things like delivery, window-cleaning, and other services not rendered by the landlord must be included.

There may be other costs resulting from the location, size, or other aspect of your apartment. Pin them down to get an accurate total on which to base your thinking (Fig. 10-1).

If you own your home, the figuring becomes somewhat more elaborate. The following worksheet may help you here.

FIG. 10-1   Annual Cost of Living in Your Present Home

Mortgage payment _____ x 12 = $ _____

Electricity _____ x 12 = _____

Fuel (gas, electricity, wood) _____ x 12 = _____

Telephone _____ x 12 = _____

Property taxes   _____

Property insurance   _____

Maintenance and repairs (everything from
    painting to getting the washer fixed)   _____

Lawn and garden care   _____

Cleaning help   _____

Waste disposal   _____

Other   _____

                                Annual total $ _____

Next, look at that total and assume that costs are likely to rise—let's say 8 percent a year if you're an optimist, more if you're a pessimist. Can you *afford* to stay at your retirement income?

I'm not suggesting that money be *the* deciding factor. For example, if you love your home and want to stay, despite an unfavorable financial outlook, then plan the steps that will diminish your costs—trim down on the level of your maintenance, look into ways to cut fuel bills, and so on; or seek additional funds, either by parttime work, or other money-raising methods, or perhaps by cutting down on other parts of your expenditures—travel, entertaining, or whatever.

● *Choosing Where to Move*

Once you've decided that moving is your best option, your next job is to discover where in the world you want to go. As the following material illustrates, you've got your work cut out for you.

CONCERNS
Questions to ask yourself

To make the right decision about a place to live requires a tough but open-minded consideration of your needs, wants, and aspirations. These questions can help you make this important exploration:

1. Do I feel free to move wherever I want—whether it's just across the street (and risk the criticism of those who think you should be more adventurous) or across the ocean (and brook the comments of those who think you're crazy for "cutting yourself off from everything").

2. Am I giving others directly concerned with the move—spouse, other live-in family members—a chance to state their views, and even a vote, if it comes to that?

3. Am I examining the relationships that influence my decision in realistic terms? For example, "I want to be near my brother," says one fifty-five-year old retired stock broker. But actually, the fraternal feelings on both sides have long since petered out, invitations have been perfunctory, and meetings boring. You may have to be quite cold-blooded in your examination of traditional ties to realize that there is no longer a bond of feeling between you and a family member strong enough to influence your domicile selection.

4. Do you have obligations and responsibilities to reconsider? For example, one fond father felt he couldn't move to another part of the country because his son needed him. But the son, twenty-eight and married, might actually fare better if the parental tie were broken.

5. Put aside every single consideration and finish this sentence, "If I could live anywhere in the world I wanted, it would be _____." If you have a spouse, others with whom you expect to live, give them the opportunity to answer the same question. Then, compare your results. Are they different? The same?

Is there some bit of persuasion, or a compromise that could help you benefit from the revealing answers you've gotten?

6. Do you have assumptions about a place to live that bear some questioning? "We've got to move down south," a wife tells her newly retired husband. "You know we can't stand the cold." The statement becomes less restrictive when her husband reminds her that the Hermans across the street live in their pleasant suburban home for six months, and go to Captiva Island for the colder season. Other possible assumptions: "We'll never be as comfortable anywhere else as we are in the old neighborhood." "Our friends have all moved to California, so we should, too." Write your own assumptions—and then question them.

7. Do I have enough information about other places to live to make a sensible choice? Somewhere on the map may be a place that is close to perfect for you. You won't move there if you don't know about it. This question is meant to serve the purpose of getting you to explore—not necessarily physically, but by talking to people, reading, and writing for information to chambers of commerce and tourist bureaus of regions that attract you. When you zero in on a place that strongly beckons, then it is advisable to visit and investigate first hand.

8. Do I fully understand that although matters of the heart, sentimental attachments, and strong personal preferences are important in my decision, in the final analysis the two crucial factors are health and finances? These two factors represent strong negative and positive influences in your thinking. You don't move to snow country if a member of your family can't take cold weather. You do move to an area that is therapeutic for an ailment suffered by one of the family. You don't move into a house that is going to drain your finances. You do consider buying a two-family house where rent from the second apartment will ease your financial situation considerably. Think of the future in relation to these two key factors. Health needs tend to become more stringent. Inflation seems to be a fact of life we won't shake for a long time. Your thinking should project five, ten, and fifteen years into the future.

How to start looking

You may decide to stay in the same place you've been living after retirement as you did before. But once you start looking, your search will have a better chance for success if you go about it optimistically, enthusiastically, and use an effective approach.

Keep in mind that you may end up with an apartment across the hall or a mansion in another country, and that either outcome may be exactly the right one. But whatever the final answer, here are the steps that can lead you along the way. An effective approach is summed up by this incident described to me by a friend.

My husband and I lived in Taipei, Taiwan, for two years, where he was conducting studies in Oriental cultures. One hot morning I was browsing through the English-language section of a major bookstore. The humidity was close to 100 percent, not uncommon. Suddenly I noticed an elderly couple entering the shop. They tried to start a conversation with the Chinese clerk. The woman was talking English with a Hungarian accent, which the clerk struggled to understand. Seeing the problem, I asked if I could be of help.

The woman turned to me. "You're Hungarian!"

"I'm American now," I said, "but I was born in Hungary."

After the business in the bookstore was concluded, the couple thanked me for my help. One thing led to another and I invited them to have dinner with my husband and me that evening. At dinner we learned that Margaret and Andrew had sold their business in Chile and were cruising the globe looking for a place to which to retire. They had been at it for a year, living on ships much of the time. They were enjoying the hunt, taking in the sights as they traveled.

They agreed that Taipei was not a strong candidate for their retirement home. But when they found a place that attracted them, they disembarked and spent time exploring, checking everything from the scenery to the prices to the lifestyles. New Zealand, they agreed, was the most beautiful country they had seen. Andrew would almost have been willing to settle there because of the trout fishing, riding, golf, and the beaches and mountains—almost irresistible to his outdoor temperament. But Margaret had a major objection: the social life, as they saw it, was limited and not attractive to their particular interests. And so they were still hunting.

Next Christmas we received a card from Margaret and Andrew—from Hawaii. That had been their eventual choice. For several years after that, we kept in touch. Hawaii continues to please them.

You may not want to undertake Margaret and Andrew's global approach to finding a domicile. But there are some basic elements in what they did that provide guidelines for anyone who has the opportunity to indulge in a free-wheeling quest.

BE BOLD. They tried to avoid preconceptions, usually based on other people's ideas or tastes. Almost literally, they let the world be their oyster. They didn't hesitate to go off the beaten path in their explorations.

USE MEANINGFUL CHECKPOINTS. They didn't permit the tourist-paradise appeal of a place to blind them to the realities. New Zealand is a beautiful country, but the lack of a single factor they considered essential persuaded them to rule it out. It is important to be very specific—even put down on paper—the things you must have in a community to make it a possible choice.

TEST THE LOCATION.   Any time you consider making a major change in living arrangements, it is highly desirable to test them out. Moving to a new part of the country? Rent an apartment for a while, or stay in a hotel or motel. Use the facilities you are interested in. If swimming is an important factor in a beachfront community, visit the swimming areas and dive in. In addition to temperature, what about roughness, cleanliness, the other people you see on the sands, and the distance of the beach from the neighborhood you're considering? Talk to people and find out about the changes in climate, rainfall, even the wind strengths, at different seasons of the year.

This same objective test should be made of the qualities you think of as essential, including everything from the cost of living in local terms to the institutions and organizations available. In testing out a factor like cost of living, check the price of foods, drugs, and services. How do they compare to your present costs? And if you are interested in religious activity, attend services, talk to the minister, priest, or rabbi. Will you be satisfied in your participation in this particular house of worship?

CONCENTRATE ON ESSENTIALS.   In making as crucial a choice as pulling up stakes and joining a new community, be prepared to compromise on minor matters, but not on major ones. Margaret and Andrew were willing to forego some of the amenities to be found in highly developed lands, but while natural beauty and sports activity were attractive, the absence of social life compatible with their needs was sufficient to rule out a given area.

PLAN CAREFULLY.   Margaret and Andrew gave themselves the time, budgeted their money, and arranged their lives to permit careful planning of their quest. When they finally chose Hawaii, it was the result of months of information gathering, evaluation, and comparison, all vital elements of a planned approach.

HAVE FUN. "I loved house hunting," said a friend of mine. "It's the greatest kind of window shopping in the world." And the Chileans exemplified this same spirit in their undertaking. While not everyone has the money to roam the seven seas in search of his or her paradise, remember that retiring into a new lifestyle requires changes that are worth all your time and energies. And these efforts can be exciting and enjoyable in themselves. If you must do it in any event, you might as well do it right.

AVOIDING BAD INVESTMENTS

A pitfall the dreamhouse-hunter must avoid, if money isn't to be lost and bitter frustration suffered, is the bait put out by developers who may be either unscrupulous or inept. For example, here's a typical mail advertisement. Interestingly enough, such material is slanted both for the young family, newly marrieds, and the about-to-retire couple:

> Dear Friend:
> Here at last is an opportunity that may satisfy your every practical wish and dream. We offer you life in a new community which could bring you everything you yearn for. Location, climate, and lifestyle are ideal along the Florida coast. Greenery, sun-flecked woods, and oceanfront too!
> Beautiful beaches on the Atlantic are only minutes away. Available to you: tennis, boating, fishing, golf, and year-round swimming in our community pools.
> And even this isn't all: the cost of living is low and we boast a favorable tax climate, meaning no personal, state, or local income taxes, and no sales tax on food.
> We offer both homesites and homes with eye-catching architecture at astonishingly low prices. You can purchase property in our community with a low down-payment and excellent financing terms.
> Sincerely,
>
> John D. Doe
> President

John D. Doe may be a person of high principle; his claims may be reasonably accurate. But experience shows that buying into newly developed communities with promised but as-yet undelivered features can be risky. Some of the things to watch out for in this type of situation are described below.

Underfinancing

The developers may start with good intentions, but as their funds diminish, so do their plans. A promised 1,000 acre park dwindles to 10 acres. "Three magnificent golf courses" compress into one—a second-rate one, at that.

Poor construction

Many new owners have been hit by poorly planned or executed home construction. Cement foundations have cracked, electrical or plumbing systems turn up major flaws, roofs leak, cellars flood, and walls crack.

Careless engineering

In some cases, catastrophe results not from poor building practices but faults in original planning. Drainage of large areas is miscalculated so that streets flood and lawns front and back are eroded by unexpected runoff after rainy periods. Sewage systems back up because the soil is too soggy for leeching fields to work effectively. In some cases, bulldozing of trees destroys the natural drainage of an area, and the homeowners suffer the consequences.

Poor installations

Builders of condominiums occasionally have victimized people by promising heaven and delivering hell—or the equivalent—to frustrated buyers who have put down hard cash for which they have gotten endless and sometimes permanent headaches. Elevators don't work properly. A laundry room has no ventilation, so that the tenants swelter or choke in a hot and steamy atmosphere. A promised indoor pool leaks and can't be used. The managers blame the builder, the builder pulls a Judge Crater and can't be found. A promised game and community room is used for storage or remains unfinished.

Poor service

Two round-the-clock door attendants are reduced to one who is often away on other duties. Promised security guards are never hired. Lawns and other areas for which management is responsible go unattended.

Victims of such developments have banded together and tried both by direct pressure and by legal action to get redress. Seldom is there satisfaction in either move.

Lack of buyer protection

The *Wall Street Journal* recently sent a reporter out to an area in Massachusetts to cover the new housing situation there. According to the reporter, a condominium development consisting of town houses four years old was inhabited by unhappy people.

Said one homeowner, "It's a disaster area." She went on to describe how she had to thaw out frozen water pipes with a portable hair dryer and how $2,000 worth of carpeting was ruined when her toilets backed up for the third time. Another owner described how he had to stuff putty into electrical outlets to stop the drafts. Still another one told of his children iceskating on the floor of his flooded garage.

Complaints of shoddy construction and defects in new houses are heard across the country. Inspectors of such properties report major deficiencies in brand new homes. One inspector says that 20 percent of the new homes he has inspected have had "serious defects" requiring more than $500 to fix. A few years ago the Department of Housing and Urban Development inspected a test sample of new homes and found that 24 percent were defective. Said one embittered new home buyer, "Under present laws in the United States, you get more protection buying a toaster than buying a home."

The Federal Trade Commission has brought pressure to bear on some builders. One Los Angeles-based builder agreed to an FTC order to pay for construction defects in over 20,000 homes.

The builders do have an argument, though perhaps not one that will be persuasive for an irate and disappointed buyer. The builders say that consumers are demanding more at a time when the industry in some parts of the country is plagued with shortages of skilled labor and materials. "Under these conditions, there are going to be many houses moved into with things missing from them," says an industry representative.

The builders have taken some steps to deal with consumer problems. The National Association of Home Builders in 1974 formed the Home Owners Warranty Corporation which offers a ten-year insured warranty against defects in new houses. For the first two years, the builder is required to fix most defects. For the next eight years, the insurance company guarantees the house against major structural flaws. The company also pays to fix defects during the first two years should the builder refuse. One thing to keep in mind about this type of insurance: many builders won't participate.

Protecting yourself

What is a prospective buyer to do? The answer is not to refrain from buying a condominium, a new home, or a home in a developing community. Such purchases may be worthwhile, not only in living terms, but as an investment.

Friends of mine recently bought a one-bedroom condominium in Falls Church, Virginia, for $42,000. Six months later, similar apartments were selling for $48,000. That's tremendous appreciation—28.6 percent annually! (Incidentally, this same couple considered buying a two-bed-room apartment but didn't for a very realistic reason. As the wife explains, "As you know, Harry's health is uncertain. And we have two relatives either one of whom would love to move in with us. But they both need help with cooking and cleaning—and I just don't want to turn my apartment into a nursing home." There is a virtue called enlightened selfishness—and my friend has given an exemplary instance of it.)

As long as you carefully follow certain guidelines, your investment can be rewarding.

INVESTIGATION. To get a line on a piece of property you're considering, play the part of an investigative reporter. Here are some of the sources that can help you get the lowdown on a possible purchase.

If it's a group development such as a condominium or community of generally similar dwellings, check with the people who have already bought in. Check with the local Better Business Bureau to see if any substantial complaints against the builder or developer have been made. If you have relatives or friends in the building business, check with them. There may be some general information in the field that can either brighten or dim the reputation of the builders.

All the above points suggest that you have convenient access to the property in question. But what about instances where the house or building lot is in a distant place and you're considering investing because of promotion material you've seen or received. Clearly, investigation may not be simple even though the developers in some cases will offer free transportation, free meals, and other attractions to get you to come to visit the development.

The hitch here is that you get a "visitors' tour." This means you're shown all the good aspects and questionable ones are hidden or glossed over.

As some newspaper and magazine exposés have revealed, some unethical promoters staged situations in order to put pressure on a buyer. In one case the guide for a prospective purchaser received continuing reports "from headquarters" on a walkie-talkie announcing the "sale" of specific lots. And the guide would comment to the prospect, "That lot I just showed you, No. 432, has just been sold. If you want this one, 516, you'd better decide in a hurry. I understand there's another person who's interested."

EVALUATION. After you've checked as thoroughly as you can into the financial help and the good intentions of the developer, evaluate what you've learned. If the evidence suggests shoddy work, unkept promises, or a considerable amount of delayed construction, consider this a poor risk no matter how attractive the property may otherwise seem; no matter how bright a picture is painted for you it would be unwise to buy.

Your investigation may suggest that the developer is highly ethical, other purchasers are well satisfied, and so on. If the selling price is affordable, maintenance costs are reasonable, and the original appeal of the property holds up for you, then seriously consider going ahead.

In some cases the evidence may go both ways. For example, you could find some tenants or homeowners who are well satisfied, others who are not. In this case, if you still want to proceed, do so with caution. Get in writing specific statements from a developer that legally protect you. To make sure the protection is adequate, have a lawyer draw up the document.

CONSULTATION. Before you put your name on a contract or commit yourself in any way, it is wise to get some expert guidance on your side. Don't forget that in the average case, while you are acting alone and on a single situation, the developer has probably handled hundreds of people in your situation. If there's going to be any outsmarting, it will be done by the builder.

Do consult with a lawyer, a builder, an architect, a building inspector, the head of the local zoning board, and the assessor from the bank from which you may be seeking a mortgage (that is, if the developer isn't assisting with the financing).

Remember, though, the information you can get from professionals of this kind won't be the last word. It should be emphasized that any purchase of property represents a certain amount of risk. The purpose of checking with the experts is to minimize the risk.

Last, one recourse the buyer may have is, as far as possible, to arrange payments so that a sufficient sum is owed the builder for some time after the purchaser has taken occupancy. This will give you the leverage you may need to put pressure on a builder who is unwilling to live up to an agreement.

MAKING THE FINAL DECISION

Before committing yourself to the purchase of a new home, there are several points other than the house or condo itself that you should consider.

Social and recreational environment

Earlier chapters of this book have helped you clarify the things you like to do and want to do. Both the dwelling and the community you are considering as a place to live should be carefully evaluated keeping those things in mind. You want to check on everything, from who your neighbors will be—one "bad" neighbor can turn a dream house into a nightmare—to the distance to the nearest racetrack. Remember, it is possible to get just about any kind of information that's wanted. The trick is to ask the right questions. "Will I have appropriate tennis partners?" "How large is the library?" "Can I continue my violin lessons?" "Will there be any other retired teachers to talk to?" "What kinds of chamber music groups are there in town, and how could I get to play in one?" "Where can I continue to sell my quilts?" These are all legitimate questions. The clearer you are about favorite hobbies, sports, or social activities, the more specific your questions will be.

Try to find someone to tell you—before you move—what the unwritten rules of the town are. How one is supposed to entertain and spend money? What are the main social events? Who are the pillars of the community? What is the mood or climate of the neighborhood? Is it pleasant, friendly, or strife ridden and tension creating? Is there opportunity for starting an activity in which you are interested? What are the people like in general? Take your time, enjoy your sleuthing, and use your imagination. Some of the following methods should help you out:

- Subscribe to the local newspapers
- Get in touch with the librarian
- Try doing some business with local establishments
- Get a list of relevant local organizations, from churches to chess clubs, and correspond with them or pay them a few visits
- Find excuses to talk with people, in letters, by phone, in person
- Talk to the local police
- Get in touch with political representatives
- If you are there, drive around the less prosperous parts of town
- Visit some schools
- Pretend to be buying a house
- Attend an auction
- Get yourself invited to the country club

Physical surroundings

If you've been dreaming about the kind of surroundings you think would be perfect, try to test your belief by considering what you'll be giving up by moving.

If you've been dreaming of an endless summer studded with glowing tropical fruit and flowers, remember that if you move south, you give up winter, which gives joy to many people other than skiers and ice skaters. The thing to think about is your relation to the change in climate; winter may have been an integral part of your life since you were born. Will you miss it badly? How will you bear the monotony of constant warmth and sunshine? How will steady heat affect you? Don't go by travel brochures; test these things out for yourself as far as possible. Visit the place in the seasons that may be difficult for you.

Avoiding dislikes

You should pay particular attention in planning your new life to factors that you definitely want to avoid. If you hate the noise of the city, don't resettle near a highway, and carefully weigh the disadvantages of living in a mobile home. If you have been hungering for southern light in your living room, do not settle for a dark parlor even though the rest of your new dwelling is perfect in all ways. It is not good enough for you.

Be imaginative about avoiding what you dislike so you will not have to make major changes later. Consider the case of Barry Riegel, an old friend who loved the country. He bought property on a lake to commune with nature on the weekend. We all used the house a lot, because he needed people to drive him to and from. But it slowly dawned on him that he hated even *riding* in cars. With great relief, he sold his land and moved his abode within the city to a small house in a large garden on the edge of a park. The house is within two blocks of several bus lines and close to the subway. He lived happily in his little house among the roses, walking to a grocery store, using occasional cabs to visit outlying relatives, till the day he died at ninety-one.

You are the best judge of the things you dislike; just make sure you do not leave them out of your calculations.

Don't burn your bridges

Margaret and Andrew, the world travelers described at the beginning of the chapter, showed the wisdom of knowing that something they wanted was not necessarily good for them. They did not settle in the most beautiful place in the world because it was too quiet and didn't afford their preferred kind of socializing.

Your desire for escape from the noise of the city may be real. And yet, living on Block Island or on a horse ranch in Kansas may make you miserable. On the other hand, it may work out perfectly. The very best way of retiring from the city to the country (or vice versa) is to do it gradually, without burning one's bridges.

Accustom yourself to the new without quite abandoning the old. Consider subletting your apartment in the city and renting a cottage in the country, doing research on the new community, returning to the city after a while to give urban living another chance, and letting your decision ripen in your old home.

Or rent out your house in the quiet suburbs, rent a trailer, mobile home, or houseboat, and live like the moving gypsy you suspect nature created you to be. After some time, you may have confirmed that you indeed are a nomad, but you may find that you want to settle down again, either at home or perhaps in a trailer park where the possibility of moving once again is not completely precluded.

Or if you decide to move to the city because you are sick of gardening and want to get a Ph.D. in comparative religion at a university or start the acting career you have always wanted (it has been done!), make the move to the city cautiously, exploring as you go. City research is easy—people in cities keep explaining their way of life to one another in their magazines, newspapers, ads, and books. Try out different neighborhoods. Balance travel time against noise and pollution, cultural facilities against parks.

Changing the level of stimulation given off by your surrounding is the most risky part of moving: nothing is known about how people will react. Watch yourself. Be kind to yourself. Listen to your own voices. Become a good judge of your subjective and objective opinions.

STATISTICS: WHO'S MOVING WHERE

A recent study of population trends reveals some interesting shifts. These migrations are not meant to suggest that you join them, but rather to give you a broad view of where people are moving to and where they're moving from.

The Los Angeles-Long Beach metropolitan area jumped from third to first place in terms of population growth for reasons ranging from climate to possible lifestyles. People from other parts of the country were moving in in sufficient numbers to put this area first in the list of cities.

Chicago, for some time in the number two position, continued in that spot. This suggests that in relative terms at least Chicago is continuing to grow at a sufficient rate to retain its place.

New York City, whose natives think of it not only as the hub of the country but also the center of the universe, long in the number one position, has lost in relative population to fall to third place. The study suggests that some of the reasons for New York slippage had to do with the growth of peripheral suburban centers. Long Island, Connecticut, and northern New Jersey appeal to individuals who have lost their taste for the Big Apple.

In the last decades there has been a notable movement from large metropolitan centers into suburban areas. While to some extent this trend has diminished, there has been an increased flow from suburbs to the countryside. In part this movement is the result of two factors: (1)

individuals to whom suburban living has become less attractive, and (2) rising real estate prices. Would-be homeowners have found that increasing housing costs force them to search further and further away from urban centers for affordable homes. This survey finding is a dramatic break with the past. In the 1960s, for example, metropolitan areas had an annual growth rate four times that of rural areas.

And on a broader regional basis, the study reflects a continuing population dip from the northeast and the midwest to the south and west. As mentioned earlier, population trends are not to be taken as guidelines for one's own home location decisions, but such information does give you something to go on. In some cases, the trends may suggest to some people that they consider a move back to a city which may now be less crowded or to a region whose population is thinning out. This may mean greater availability of housing at reasonable prices.

I recently met a man who, with his wife, had moved back from the west coast to the very home he had sold five years before in New Hampshire. He was very happy with the move, "and I was able to buy my old house back at $2,000 less than I sold it for," he reported.

COSTS AND CONCERNS

To get the full picture of what a move into another home will mean in financial terms, three separate aspects must be considered: (1) the cost of moving, (2) the cost of buying, and (3) the cost of maintenance. This way you will be able to calculate with reasonable accuracy, and with a minimum of oversights, just what your expenses will be.

Selling and moving costs

The moving van may be only a small part of the cost. You will probably find yourself discarding or giving away many items. Some items may be of little or only sentimental value—your mother's chopping board or chipped mahogany picture frames. But some things may have a market value—an old piano, phonograph records, books, old chests, sideboards—for which you have neither the time, patience, nor stomach to undertake the effort that might realize some part of their value.

Even if you try to sell your unwanted goods, you may end up losing. A friend recently told me of having to sell most of her house furnishings because she was moving into a small one-bedroom apartment. "I had a man come in from a second-hand furniture outfit. He offered me a fraction of the value of the pieces, but what could I do? I had to move in a hurry. I accepted." Even when there is more time, and something like a yard, tag, or garage sale is undertaken, you usually have to set low prices to attract buyers.

In both these cases, the loss is represented by a loss of assets. In the course of liquidating, you end up with some cash, but the "real" value of your belongings has disappeared.

Recent capital improvements may prove to be of little value. Ray Quentin, of Muncie, reports that "after years of struggling with a shallow dug well, we finally decided to put in an artesian well, at the cost of about $2,000. I figured that over the years, it would be a worthwhile investment. But when Jennie suddenly decided to retire at 60, we sold the house and moved south. I'm not sure how much of a factor the artesian well was in the sale, but I do feel I lost out at least partially on that cash outlay."

Other major cash outlays may go down the drain when you sell. Another example: "I put in another half a bathroom for the convenience of my mother-in-law, who was living with us. We only had the use of it for about a year. When my mother-in-law decided to move in with her other daughter, we sold the house. That facility didn't mean a thing to the buyer. As a matter of fact, he planned to remove the fixtures and turn the room into a storage closet."

Whether you try to advertise and sell the property yourself—in which case the costs are minimum—or use a real estate agent, some cash outlays are usually necessary. If you advertise, you may be able to hold costs down to just the price of the ads. If you use an agent, a usual cost is 7 percent of the selling price.

Moving itself can be handled in a number of ways, either by professionals or with the help of friends and relatives. If you're doing your own, start collecting boxes, cartons, barrels, and sturdy plastic bags of all sizes. Supermarkets and liquor stores are good places to find cartons. You need smaller cartons for packing heavy things like books. Larger cartons are for clothing, linens, small appliances, and so on. Don't fill a large carton with items so heavy that moving it becomes impossible. Protect fragile items, such as dishes, glassware, and ceramics, with plenty of paper or other pressure insulation. Some people are natural packers and have a sense of how to fill a box efficiently. Let them supervise the others.

If you hire professionals, you will want to get a reputable moving organization. This doesn't necessarily mean the best known or most expensive. "Dependable Fellow With Truck" is the message painted on the side of a large van. The organization consists of the owner and as many of his friends and relatives as he may need for any given job. He has a very good reputation in the community, and will produce references if asked. His charges are less than those of larger outfits.

The point is, suit your mover to your needs. If you have very valuable pieces, then dependability and responsibility become an overriding concern. You'll get the best regardless of price, and make the move with an easier mind.

Here's one recommendation by a couple who have moved several times over a ten-year period: "Make lists of each item and its condition. Don't depend on movers. Some, of shady ethics, have been known to make up an inventory and, next to hard-to-handle pieces, put down notations such as 'Scratched,' or 'Cracked.' If the items arrive unharmed, there is no problem. If the pieces are damaged, they have an out."

Whom to notify

Your local post office makes available a "Change of Address Kit" that helps simplify the mailing changes a move requires. Of course, notify the post office of your new address so that any stray mail will be forwarded automatically. The kit includes cards you can send to business and professional people with whom you correspond or from whom you receive mail (unfortunately, this includes bills). You may want to notify friends and relatives by a more informal note—either a card or letter. Some people like the idea of having a special card printed to announce the move. Here is a checklist the post office kit supplies, with a few categories I've added:

( ) Accountants	( ) Children's camps
( ) Art group or foundation	( ) Church or synagogue
( ) Auto insurance	( ) Clubs, lodges
( ) Banks	( ) Dentists
( ) Book clubs	( ) Department stores
( ) Business contacts	( ) Dividend-check senders
( ) Catalog companies	( ) Doctors
( ) Charge cards	( ) Electric company

( ) Friends, relatives
( ) Gas company
( ) Government agencies,
    Social Security, etc.
( ) Insurance companies
( ) Lawyers
( ) Life insurance companies
( ) Magazines
( ) Milk delivery
( ) Motor vehicle bureau
( ) Newspapers
( ) Organizations to which
    you or family members
    belong

( ) Post office
( ) Professional organizations
( ) Record clubs
( ) Religious groups
( ) Schools
( ) Service station
( ) Stock broker
( ) Stores, local
( ) Telephone company
( ) Town or village government
( ) Union
( ) Voter registration
( ) Waste disposal
( ) Water company

● Community Living

For retired people there is a distinctly different approach to living arrangements called community living. There are many versions of this kind of arrangement, with differences dictated by cost, size, location, and the condition of health of the individuals.

Retirement villages, for example, are often elegant homes and apartments set in carefully maintained grounds, with features resembling country club living—golf, swimming, tennis on the premises, and so on. Good health and healthy finances are usually prerequisites for residency. Nursing homes, on the other hand, are often the only choice of those suffering from poor health and loss of independent action.

In between these extremes are various types of housing distinguished by a wide variety of facilities, services, and residents. The following case histories illustrate some of the many choices open to those considering community living.

RETIREMENT VILLAGES

THE CAINES AT HERITAGE VILLAGE. I've known Mildred and Ed Caine for many years. We were friends and neighbors in Rockland County, a northern New York State area west of the Hudson. Mildred and Ed, delightful friends and charming hosts, are outstanding examples of a couple whose ability to plan has smoothed and enriched their journey through life.

Mildred taught in the Rockland school system and Ed commuted to New York City, where he was a top administrator for the New York State Employment Service. They were both still working when they turned their attention to the matter of retirement and a possible relocation.

I still remember my surprise when Ed informed me that they were thinking of buying a home in a retirement community. At the time I thought their action was highly premature. Of course, they were right, and I lacked their foresight. Let Ed Caine describe how their move worked out—in his own words.

Mildred and I retired just about three years ago. This important step in our lives was not taken without careful thought, much talk, and considerable trepidation. We spent some three years exploring. Starting from a secure financial base (which, of course, is one of the prerequisites for a successful retirement), the major decision we had to make was whether to remain in the community we had lived in for twenty years or move elsewhere. The turning point on this question was that we were both community-involved people and wanted to continue to be able to be so in our retirement. Since there seemed little opportunity for this type of activity in our home setting, we decided to explore what life would be like in the so-called adult communities.

Considerable time was spent in making short visits to adult communities along the East Coast. We had long ago decided that the temperate zone appealed to us far more than warm climates, so we concentrated upon the Middle Atlantic states and New England. Our search came to an end when we found Heritage Village, an adult community in Southbury, Connecticut.

The landscape and architecture are lovely. The units range from one-bedroom apartments to three-bedroom, semidetached homes. They are owned individually as condominiums, while the land and facilities are held in common indivisible shares. Because of the size of the development, the builder established a condominium corporation for every section that he completed, ranging from 100 to 125 units. In total, there are twenty-four condominium corporations.

The Connecticut Condominium Law requires that condominium ownership entail a degree of self-government. Each corporation is headed by a board of directors which elects a trustee. The twenty-four trustees constitute the master association. Local condominium boards delegate to the master association the authority to administer the affairs of the village. A professional manager has been employed and he is responsible for the operation of the village. This includes all repairs, snow removal, lawn and tree maintenance, operation of the recreational facilities, and the myriad operations that are required in a community of some 4,400 persons.

The residents of the village come from a variety of careers with a heavy bias toward the professions, management, and teaching. This diversity has resulted in an interesting mix that produces an environment that is culturally stimulating. A paid activities staff is employed to arrange and organize functions, trips, concerts, and so on that are self-supporting.

It should be noted that there is ample opportunity for recreation for those who are not so gregarious. Swimming, hiking, the library, and music are available for those who are not comfortable in group activity. The proximity of the village to New York City permits taking advantage of its cultural opportunities.

This was the environment we found when we purchased our home in Heritage Village eighteen months before our retirement. It was our view that by "having our feet in both camps" we could make an adjustment without trauma. We sold our old home, moved our furniture (after considerable pruning) to Heritage Village, rented a small furnished apartment in our home town, and spent our weekends, holidays, and vacations in our "retirement home." This enabled us to sample the activities and to meet the residents of the village. During this period we made many acquaintances. What was planned for as a smooth transition was accomplished in reality. When retirement day came, we simply started living here fulltime.

We found the selection we had made all we had hoped for. The village provided us with a choice in the type of homes available. We had selected a model at a location that suited our taste and need for some privacy. Our home is built on a single level. The plan provides a kitchen with dining area, two bedrooms, and a large living-dining room around it. In the kitchen, a clerestory window and patio doors enable us to see the sun rise and set. The house had to meet the test of having a wood-burning fireplace. Our second bedroom has been converted into a den-music-sitting-guest room and is our favorite spot when we are home alone for the evening.

In my view, a key to successful retirement is the ability to keep oneself usefully occupied and absorbed in life. It struck me that retirement activity falls into two major categories, as probably does all human extra-vocational affairs. A person can receive or give, or do both; be entertained or render service, or do both. In fact, I am convinced that a happy retirement for active people is a judicious combination of both categories.

Because it gave us the opportunity for receiving and giving, Heritage Village is proving to be an almost ideal retirement residence. The opportunities for entertainment, for physical, social, and cultural activities are large. The residents use their skills and backgrounds to enrich the cultural life of the village. For example, a retired teacher conducts a lecture series on poetry. A former professor from Antioch conducts a Shakespeare cycle; plays are heard on tape and discussed. An opera group does the same for grand opera; Gilbert and Sullivan operettas are also done. Lecture series too numerous to mention are sponsored by village organizations, such as the library, the men's club, and the women's club. Artists promote exhibits and sponsor classes. On the lighter side, dances and dinners are promoted. Concerts are held frequently, and we are fortunate to have available the talent at Yale University. Organized trips are available to the Long Wharf Theatre in New Haven, the Bushnell in Hartford for symphony and ballet, and to the Goodspeed Opera House. Mildred and I partake of these to the extent that we wish or have the time to.

The life here also offers many opportunities for service. Many residents serve as volunteers in nearby hospitals, state institutions, and public schools. Others have found their niche in helping to govern the village, as members of condominium boards and committees. A fair number of residents participate in the town government as elected or appointed officials.

Shortly after we began living in the village, I decided that I would like to work with the village's volunteer ambulance service, which the residents had organized. After eight months of training, which included ten hours of hands-on experience in the emergency room of a hospital, I earned my state license as an emergency medical technician. I now serve as vice-president and director of recruiting of the ambulance association, and teach an occasional class in first aid. Mildred works in the women's exchange half a day a week and has become something of a merchandising expert.

Both of us had decided early on that we did not wish our activities to be limited to the village. Mildred joined the Southbury League of Women Voters and soon found herself chairing a group studying the financing of the education system of the local school district. She expanded her studies to include local land use. Recently she was appointed a member of the Town's Inland Wetlands Commission, a statutory board concerned with the protection of wetlands. These activities, added to time spent studying the piano, keep her quite busy.

Two years ago I was invited to join the town's Economic Development Commission, an agency concerned with attracting suitable business enterprise to the town. Recently, I was asked to lead a Long Range Study Committee to project how the town would grow and to propose measures to guide its growth along desirable directions.

To round out our life in retirement, we plan about six weeks of travel each year, either in this country or abroad. Travel lets us get away from the routines that develop even in retirement and prevents the growth of the ivory-tower syndrome that could so easily develop in our enclave.

No human society is free of problems. The village has its share of them, and while not all are solvable, patience, intelligence, and a concern for others helps ameliorate some of the difficulties.

Inflation has been a problem for those on fixed incomes, as taxes and operating costs have steadily increased. A few of the residents are having financial difficulties and may seek less costly housing.

Some residents are unable to adjust to condominium life. There are rules that have to be followed in a community of this sort. For example, a resident cannot change the exterior of his home, nor may he or she modify the landscape, without prior approval. Those who cannot adjust usually leave. There are the usual number of residents who say they could run the village better but refuse to take a part in doing so. Human nature is not left behind in retirement.

The most serious difficulty is dealing with the emotional problems of the sick, the widowed, and the lonely. We do have a few cases of alcoholism, depression, and withdrawal. The village does not provide medical care, nor does it plan to do so. Some residents leave on their own initiative for more appropriate types of service such as living-care or total-care facilities.

There is a growing concern about the mental health problem and several committees have been organized to tackle this difficulty. I have been asked to work in this field.

This then is a brief description of our life in retirement. We are happy, active, engaged, and feel useful. This is not to suggest that all of us living here are cut of the same cloth. Some may be engaged in playing golf, or bridge, and are quite happy doing so. The important thing is that it is possible to work out your own life style within reasonable bounds and to live happily within the parameters of an organized community.

The Caines are an excellent example of the benefits of thoughtful, well-considered action. Clearly, the well-managed facilities of Heritage Village, its appeal to the financially comfortable, the community minded, and leisure oriented, would make satisfactory surroundings for many.

The approach taken by the Caines in making their choice is especially noteworthy. They discussed their ideas of what they wanted, and didn't want, in the way of a place to live. This meant not only clarifying their feelings and ideas, but also the elimination of misunderstanding and disagreement that might otherwise arise. Well in advance of the need for action, they began the moves that would eventually help them hit their target. Accordingly, they were spared the pressures and possible miscalculations that result from action and decision in haste.

Having selected the general area in which they wanted to live, they visited and considered a number of possibilities. Their assessments included not only location, but also the appearance, management, facilities, and services of the installations they viewed.

They moved into Heritage Village on what was essentially a trial basis, going so far as to rent a small apartment in their home town, and spending week-ends and holidays in their retirement home. By "having our feet in both camps," as Ed Caine put it, they were able to sample the activities and meet other Village residents. As a result of this toe-in-the-water approach, they were able to understand and adjust to the elements of their new life without bumps or shocks.

The other factors that explain the Caines' happy adjustment to retirement living reflect their personalities and interests. They are worth noting. From the things Mildred and Ed have become involved in, it is obvious that they are participants. They are active—some people of lesser energy might say almost too much so—in a range of tasks and responsibilities that they enjoy and that enrich their lives. They believe in community service and seek it out. And they vary the mix of undertakings, adding travel, visiting their children and grandchildren, and other projects to their personal programs.

Note that Ed Caine indicates that some residents, for one reason or another, fail to find Heritage Village as satisfactory a home site as Mildred and Ed do. One person's Eden may be another's bore. There are those who, because they require more personal services or fail to find in the village services and facilities that satisfy them, move on to what they regard as greener fields.

THE BERMANS AT SPRINGVALE INN. Lillian and Irving Berman had been living in the Springvale Inn for just a few months when I interviewed Irving. A retired schoolteacher, he is eighty-five. His wife is some years his junior. His impressions were fresh and notably favorable.

With some pride, Irving told me that he had worked until just recently. Until the age of seventy he was a teacher and administrator in the New York school system. Taking mandatory retirement at seventy, he continued to teach for another fourteen years as a substitute. A major requirement was an annual physical examination which qualified him for another year's stint on a substitute basis.

But finally he and his wife decided it was time to move out of their Queens home in which they had lived for almost forty years. They tried several places before deciding on Springvale. Here's the way our conversation went:

Uris: Tell me about some of the other possibilities you explored.

Berman: There was a place in Ramsey, New York. It was a beautiful building, and the cost was $31,000 a year for the both of us. I can tell you right away, the food was terrible and it was not only the food that turned us off. There was no place to walk outside the building and a few blocks away there was an industrial area. That's why Springvale appealed to us so much. The buildings—they are three stories high—are surrounded by woods, and there are roads and paths.

Uris: What are the costs compared to the Ramsey place?

Berman: Much less—$1,022 per month. We brought in our own furniture. There would have been an additional charge of $25.00 a month if the furniture had been supplied.

Uris: I see the apartment is very attractive.

Berman: Yes. We have these two large rooms and a complete bathroom. We don't have a kitchen, but we do have a refrigerator and a two-burner electric stove. Fine for occasional cooking and snacks.

Uris: How did you find Springvale Inn?

Berman: We did some exploring on our own. Then, since I'm a retired teacher, I wrote to the NRTA—that's the National Retired Teachers Association—and asked them to send me a list of places for senior citizen residents, not nursing homes, in this general area. I told them what we were looking for and they sent me a list with about twenty-five possibilities.

Uris: Before we go on with that, tell me about your wife. Is she a teacher also?

Berman: No. She had been doing a lot of work in the community.

Uris: Does she like Springvale as much as you do?

Berman: She loves it. We were very lucky to find this place.

Uris: Was there a waiting period before you could move in?

Berman: We came here March 1 and we had several long talks with the administration. They asked us whether we would like to move into a furnished apartment on a trial basis for a month and we did.

That sold us and we moved in shortly after that—August 1. Moving out of an apartment—we lived in Queens for forty years—was very difficult. So much stuff to have to decide about—what to throw away, what to give away, and so on.

Uris: Tell me about the services available.

Berman: We get two meals a day in the dining room and the food is excellent and more than we can possibly eat. There's maid service once a week and that's fine for my wife because, on doctor's orders, she isn't supposed to do laundry or heavy housework. All this is included in our monthly rent. And another thing is the maintenance around the apartment. If we have anything that goes wrong, with the plumbing, for example, or the electricity, there's a man here in a short while to make the repairs. About meals, I can tell you: they're served three times a day to 160 people. That's the number of residents in the inn.

Uris: Any other services?

Berman: The administration puts out weekly and monthly bulletins of activities; once a week there's a van to take people shopping. We do our own buying and bring the bundles out to the van. Also, there are trips scheduled for sightseeing and recreation. For example, a group of us went to see *The Sound of Music* recently and there are trips to museums, and so on.

Uris: On what basis do they select the residents?

Berman: People from fifty years and up are eligible, either singles or couples, but no families and no pets. And these are people who are in good physical health, ambulatory.

Uris: What happens if there's some kind of accident, or other physical problem that comes up? For example, what about a resident who might have an accident that would confine him to a wheelchair?

Berman: Well, of course he'd be rushed to a hospital.

Uris: What about his return to the inn?

Berman: If they can't get around by themselves, if they're not ambulatory, they have to leave.

Uris: Tell me about the administration. Who runs the inn?

Berman: The Bethel Springvale Corporation. They run two hospitals, but the operation of the inn is separate and it's a nonprofit organization.

Uris: Are the operations here subsidized in any way?

Berman: Not that I know.

Uris: Is there anything here you would change if you could or is there anything about the setup that the administration itself plans to change?

Berman: The only thing I would suggest—not so much food.

Uris: I guess if you must have a complaint, that's the best one to have.

Berman: They're very good here about taking suggestions. You can make suggestions about the dining room or the maintenance or any of the activities; they always listen.

Uris: How about your life here in general? Socializing and so on?

Berman: It's very pleasant. Most people are very friendly. Just one sign—there's going to be a wedding here next week, two singles decided they want to get married. Needless to say, it's caused a lot of interest and excitement.

Uris: I realize you've been at the Inn a comparatively short time. How about the other residents? Do they like it as much as you do?

Berman: This place was built about 1964. I've talked to many people who moved in at the beginning. They're as happy here as we are—after many years.

Uris: Anything else?

Berman: The other night they had what they call an ice cream party. Music and dancing. And recently, we had observance of the Jewish holidays—about 25 percent of the people here are Jewish. It's nonsectarian. Everybody joined in. They served cake, wine, and fruit. A wonderful celebration.

Uris: Do they have a health program?

Berman: No regular program, but a nurse is available if needed. And there is a hospital close by. Lillian and I have our own health program. We walk five miles a day on the paths through the woods around the buildings.

A particularly interesting aspect of Lillian and Irving Berman's successful housing hunt is the role played in it by the National Retired Teachers Association.

Other organizations may provide similar help. In some cases, writing to a local chamber of commerce will do it. In larger towns and cities, organizations for older-age groups often will furnish housing information concerning local facilities. The AARP at 555 Madison Avenue, New York, NY; or 1225 Connecticut Avenue, N.W. Washington, D.C. 20036; or its western headquarters, Times Building, Long Beach, CA 90802 will also provide information to its members, or to those who intend to join.

The Bermans seem as happy in their two-room apartment as the Caines are in their larger quarters. One explanation is that the Bermans have always been city people, used to apartment living. The Caines are suburbanites, for whom the open spaces of Heritage Village are pleasant and familiar. "Comfortable surroundings" is a subjective term and depends on what you're looking for.

Like the Caines, Lillian and Irving Berman explored. This gave them a basis for comparison. When they finally found Springvale Inn, its attractions shone by contrast, not only in terms of cost, but physical setting, programs, and so on.

And speaking of comparison, it is notable that the corporation that owns the Inn also operates, adjacent to it, a complex of thirty garden apartment buildings on thirty-five acres. Accommodations, for people over fifty-five, include efficiencies and one- and two-bedroom apartments, unfurnished. These are rented on a two-year lease, from $165 to $335, which includes heat, gas for cooking, hot water, and parking. No services are provided, except for free transportation to shopping, movies, concerts, and so on. Social activities are arranged mostly by the tenants with cooperation of the management. And there is emergency twenty-four-hour help available by phone.

Many urban and suburban communities have housing facilities similar to the Springvale Apartments, sometimes partially subsidized by state or city, sometimes backed by religious organizations.

GOVERNMENT-SUBSIDIZED HOUSING

Following World War II, the government got more deeply into the housing business, largely because of the tremendous housing shortages of the postwar period. In the following years, government-assisted building continued, not only for the economically disadvantaged, but also for older people with low incomes who were becoming victims of substandard living quarters because of the rising cost of living and loss of purchasing power resulting from inflation.

The first White House Conference on Aging held in Washington in 1961 further fueled awareness of the housing needs of seniors. Funds for construction from both federal and state treasuries became available to cities and local governments.

As a result of extensive government sponsored building, housing specifically set aside for senior citizens became a major solution for many. Every state in the union eventually participated in this important assist to its older population. A description of one such housing project appears below. Although it is unusual in that it stands in one of the highest-rent districts in the country, in many ways its facilities, operating policies, and population are similar to government-subsidized housing elsewhere.

For the person about to retire, knowledge of public housing can be useful in planning moves, either in the present or in the future. Even if this kind of living is not likely for you, it can be helpful to have some idea of the facilities, services, and lifestyle a facility of this kind makes possible. At the very least, it can represent a revealing comparison to other housing choices.

A HOUSING PROJECT IN MANHATTAN. In 1975 the New York City Housing Authority, assisted by funds from federal sources, opened a twenty-story building at 341 East 70th Street. One notable feature of the new apartment stucture: it was right in the middle of one of Manhattan's most expensive neighborhoods.

It seems likely that behind the decision to build subsidized housing in this area was the concept of "mingling"—mixing upper- and lower-income bracket people, supposedly with heightened social awareness for both groups. Whatever the reasoning, the concept was successful. After some preliminary edginess, the new unit and its 250 tenants was integrated smoothly into the neighborhood.

The twenty-story structure contains 150 apartments and a community center, the latter operated by the Lenox Hill Neighborhood Association (LHNA), an eighty-five-year-old community group which had pushed for the project from the beginning, to satisfy local needs.

Seventy-five of the apartments are studios for single occupants. Bath and kitchen are included. Fifty-five are one-bedroom units for two people—husband and wife or two family members. Fourteen are two-bedroom apartments for a family group of three. The head of the household must be over age sixty-two. Three apartments are set aside for project personnel. Three two-bedroom apartments are rented to LHNA for an experimental program in group living.

The rooms are unfurnished. Tenants must do the furnishing on their own, sometimes with help from other agencies.

REQUIREMENTS FOR OCCUPANCY. Because of the low rent and desirability of the apartments, 341 E. 70th Street has a long waiting list of would-be tenants, who must satisfy a number of criteria. The person or family must be residents of the Yorkville area, specifically within the zones covered by the postal zip codes 10021 and 10028, and must be living under unsatisfactory housing conditions.

There is a top limit for income—$7500 annual income is approximate top limit for a person seeking a studio apartment; $9,000 is approximate total for couple seeking a one-bedroom apartment; $10,000 for two-bedroom quarters. No more than 25 percent of income may be charged for rent, and the actual amount is keyed to income. Rent includes gas and electricity. Applicants must be no younger than sixty-two but lower ages may be acceptable if the individual is handicapped.

Screening and qualifying of applicants is done by the New York City Housing Authority itself. Eligible applicants are then sent to 341 for a meeting with the Housing Assistant who "rents"—that is, matches applicants to apartments available.

The long waiting list referred to earlier means literally thousands of people who have applied for residence in 341. Since the New York Housing Authority has dozens of housing projects, ordinarily when people apply, they are asked to specify their first, second, and third choices. Because of the desirability of 341 housing, most applicants don't indicate other choices. However, when faced with the alternative of a long waiting period or the possiblity of city housing in adjoining neighborhoods, applicants often take other locations.

SERVICES AVAILABLE. For many of the residents, a key feature in their house is the elevator. Of course you would expect one in a twenty-story structure. But for many tenants, past experience was with a five-story walkup, typical of older houses in Yorkville.

No housekeeping services are available normally. Everyone is on a do-it-yourself basis. However, if individuals have difficulties, and either temporarily or continually require help in cleaning, doing laundry, and so on, assistance may be forthcoming through the good offices of the Lenox Hill Neighborhood Association.

The building does have its own maintenance staff who tend the grounds, care for the building, and do small jobs like opening or closing a stuck window; electricians, plumbers, and others are available as needed.

Tenants, who tend to be service and security conscious, are assured twenty-four-hour coverage with the help of a resident adviser—who is employed by the Lenox Hill Neighborhood Association—to take care of any emergencies during night and early morning hours. Security is further assured by housing police who maintain a periodic patrol. Since

341 is not large enough to warrant its own force, regular police from a nearby precinct round out the protection.

Construction features in the apartments themselves further assure the comfort and safety of residents: bathrooms are tiled with nonskid material; bathtub and toilet have handrails.

A "good-neighbor" alarm can summon assistance at the pull of a string. A resident in distress can trigger a siren that goes off in the hall at the same time a signal light over the outside door flashes on. A person who suddenly feels faint, or who falls, or—occasionally—who becomes stuck in the bathtub, gets instant help from neighbors who have a tacit group-help pact.

For health emergencies of less urgency, a registered nurse from nearby New York Hospital comes in once a week to listen to descriptions of symptoms, to make referrals to sources of help, and to take medical histories to assist in future diagnosis and treatment.

Tenants continue their status as long as they can maintain themselves and their apartments—with or without assistance. Where help is required, it is usually forthcoming by cooperation between 341 administrators and the Lenox Hill group. The same principle of independence applies to handicapped people, who qualify for admission if services they need can be arranged for.

LIVING AT 341 EAST 70TH. The population of approximately 230 people in the project constitute a community. Not only do the people live together, but due to the Senior Citizens Service Center operated by the Lenox Hill Neighborhood Association, they *eat* together—lunch served daily, Monday through Friday; *play* together—bridge and bingo; *learn* together—German conversation and lectures; *create* together—arts and crafts; and try to *stay healthy* together—nutrition, health talks and swimming.

Fig. 10-2 shows a typical week's schedule.

Not indicated in the program are special events—group trips to points of interest in the city and environs, for example. One such recent venture was to a rustic camp in Connecticut, where for $20.00 residents enjoyed round-trip transportation, meals, room accommodations, and fun and games on the site. Other specials are dances and parties— holiday celebrations or individual events, birthdays, anniversaries, and so on—usually in the service center.

FIG. 10-2 Typical Schedule

CENTER HOURS: 9:30 AM to 4:00 PM—Mon.-Fri.
NEW MEMBERS REGISTRATION: Mon. & Wed. 1 to 3:30 PM
ACTIVITIES AT MAIN BUILDING, 331 E. 70 St.
CARD CLUB: Mon.-Wed.-Fri. 3rd Fl. 1-5 PM; BINGO: Thurs. night
LUNCH: Served Daily, Monday thru Friday: 12:00 Noon

Monday, Oct. 2	Tuesday, Oct. 3	Wednesday, Oct. 4
10:30 Sewing Club	10:15 Calligraphy	10:30 Sewing Club
11:00 Food Committee	11:00 "Fitness Fun"	10:45 Lecture Series
1:00 German	11:30 Social Action	10:45 Nutrition &
Conversation		Health
1:00 Horticulture	1:00 Oil Painting	1:00 Current Events
1:00 Bridge Club &	1:00 Bingo	1-2 Begin. Spanish
Instruction		1:00 Choral Group
1-5 Card Club		1-5 Card Club
2:00 Piano Lessons		2:00 Tai Chi Chuan
2-3 Swim		6-7 "Learn to Swim"

Thursday, Oct. 5	Friday, Oct. 6
10:00 Arts & Crafts	10:00 Crafts for Men
11:00 Communal Sing	10:30 Sewing Club
1-2:25 French	11:00 Slide Show
1-3 Woodshop	11:15 Sunshine Club
1-3 Ceramics	1:00 Oil Painting
1:15 Travelogue	1:15 Pokeno Party
2-3 Swim	6-7 "Learn to Swim"
2:30 Adv. Spanish	
7:00 Bingo	

PROBLEMS. In a project such as 341, with its people averaging about age seventy, it may be slightly disconcerting but certainly revealing to review the kinds of complaints and problems that ruffle the group mood.

Cold weather brings to the housing assistant—actually, acting administrator—requests for more heat. The administrator explains, "We set thermostats at 70 degrees F, which is above a normal setting. Older people simply seem to require higher temperature levels. We try to oblige." In the warm weather, there is an opposite discomfort. The service center is air conditioned, but individual apartments aren't. Residents may have air conditioners installed on their own—and then must pay an additional $7 a month for electricity.

A frequent request is for a doorman at the main entrance. It is not a desire for class, but security that is wanted. No public housing has a doorman. Partly as a response to this type of demand, 341 and other projects encourage tenant patrols, consisting of about three people. These units cover the project from 6 PM to 10 PM usually in two shifts of two hours each. The unit has a person in charge who is paid—$75 every two weeks. Others volunteer their services free of charge.

There is a continuing need for information and answers to questions. The population at 341 wants help with Social Security problems, requests for rent adjustments, and reassurance about personal health symptoms.

"Part of my job," explains the perceptive young woman who is the housing assistant, "is hand holding. It's perfectly understandable with our group. However, it's important not to make them overly dependent, and when they have real difficulties, to get them professional help."

Apparently there is considerable cliqueing. The subgroups seem to form on the basis of such things as education or social background. Sometimes the factor of past cultural exposure—travel or patronizing the arts—provides the basis for a clique. Such divisions, while harmless in themselves, do tend to interfere with formation of total group identification and participation in group activities. Also, for the shy individual or the nonjoiner, cliques tend to represent social-freeze-out areas that make for isolation. The service center administrators try to minimize the problem by judicious programing, offering activities for a range of interests and tastes. And special efforts are made to draw loners into one or more of the activities offered.

There is a specific, seldom-publicized problem that troubles members of a senior group such as the residents of 341. It is intangible, an element of mood and climate. But it tends to be basic and prevalent, and accordingly, an element in everyday living that must be reckoned with. Here is how this problem emerged in the course of a meeting with an official of 341.

"Health," said the Housing Assistant, "is a constant preoccupation, and a major subject of conversation. Most people are health conscious, and quite sophisticated about ailments, symptoms, and so on."

Individuals fall short of "practicing medicine without a license" but diagnoses and prescribing of countermeasures for suspected ailments are ongoing activities. And underlying this concern about health is what can be described as a "who's next" syndrome—a morbid consideration of the mortality rate in an older population, an involvement in the ailments of friends and neighbors, and depression when a death takes place.

A preoccupation of this kind is clearly undesirable. And there is no doubt that for some people, it exists in or out of a group situation. But in the context of housing, it is suggested that people who live closely in a senior-dominated community may have to make efforts to offset the negative influence of others in order to enjoy the positive elements of group living—for example, availability of peers, entertainment, and educational and recreation facilities.

NURSING HOMES

Nursing homes have had a bad press recently. Not that the criticism wasn't deserved—some of these facilities are dreadful places operated by unscrupulous persons solely for their own gain and offering a minimum of care to the residents.

But as sometimes happens, the media overdramatized the situations and gave all nursing homes a bad name, at least in the public mind. Fictional treatment of nursing homes also served to darken the image. In books and on the stage, the nursing home was represented as a final and terrifying alternative, often with a pathetic protagonist fighting desperately to "stay with the family," or "live in my own place," while callous children or relatives persisted in committing them to one or another icy institution.

Well, hospitals are not particularly nice places, and we all rightfully should try to avoid them, but they do fill an essential need. When they must be used, one should seek the best available.

What is a nursing home?

The term "nursing home" is an umbrella for a range of institutions that differ in size, modernity, and appearance, but all are devoted to housing the aged, ill, or infirm. The stay of an individual resident may vary from a few weeks—for convalescent care, generally—to the balance of his or her life.

The typical home is licensed, by the state alone if it accepts only private patients, or by the federal government if Medicare and Medicaid coverage is involved. Licensing standards vary widely among the states, and most states require less in professional care and personnel than the federal government. A major reason for the unacceptable conditions revealed by investigations of the mid-seventies was laxness of licensing agencies in enforcing standards. A facility that has both federal and state approval is more likely to be operated in a satisfactory manner.

Occasionally you find a so-called nursing home run as a cottage industry. An individual with two or three spare rooms may solicit residents who require some degree of medical attention, and provide it personally—if a trained nurse, for example—or engages the services of a local professional. Of course, rents will be considerably higher than for the same space without the medical services, minimal though they may be. Such facilities may, in special instances, be satisfactory, although completely unsupervised by a licensing authority. Essentially, you are gambling on the character of the person or people who run the establishment, as well as suitability for your particular candidate.

Finding the best facility

The person interested in exploring the possibilities of nursing-home care has several starting points. A doctor or other medical professional familiar with the needs and economic situation of the individual may suggest one or more homes. These of course should be considered. But however well intentioned, no one else's opinion, even a professional's, should be accepted as the final word. Put these recommendations high on the list—but appraise the institution as carefully as you would any other before making a choice.

Other people's opinions are of two kinds: the person may have first-hand knowledge of the facility—for example, because a family member is or has been there; or, he or she is going by the reputation of a place, which can be misleading.

Jean Baron Nassau,[1] with considerable experience to her credit, asserts that reputation can be a misleading basis for judgment. She feels that even a good reputation should be checked on. Of course, unfavorable comment might serve the useful purpose of deterring you from

[1]*Choosing a Nursing Home*, by Jean Baron Nassau (New York: Funk & Wagnalls, 1975).

wasting time in a pointless investigation. The friend who says, "An ex-neighbor of mine has been staying at the X Home for months. I've visited her, and everything I've seen looks fine," has certainly provided a lead worth following up.

Almost every classified phone book has a listing under "Nursing Homes." In a typical instance, some of the institutions also had space advertisements. Here is one:

> Dignified, Painstaking Professional Care
> A Modern Setting of Graciousness and Charm
> Unexcelled Standards, Country Setting

Certainly the ad says the right things. What you make of it depends on your faith in advertising, but you should check further on appeals like these. Other advertisements offer inducements that are more substantial and easier to verify. Claims like these, whether in the yellow pages, brochures or anywhere else, hold out a bit more promise than "charm and character":

> "Accredited by the joint commission on accreditation of hospitals; active medical board does planning and implementation of all professional services; specially trained nursing staff for advanced rehabilitation."

A phone or written request to departments of health will usually bring you a useful list of facilities. Specify that you are interested in licensed long-term health care institutions in your area.

In this instance, too, accept the listing merely as a point of departure for investigation. The particular requirements being sought are a primary basis for selection. For example, a nursing home that has outstanding physical therapy and rehabilitation services may be a good bet for a person who requires these, but they have little importance for someone who doesn't.

The interests and requirements of the resident are a primary guide for judgment. In general, there are nine factors to consider during an appraisal visit:

ADMINISTRATORS. Try to meet and talk with not only the "official greeter," who obviously will represent the institution's effort to put best foot forward, but other behind-the-scenes people, such as the director of programs.

BUILDINGS AND FACILITIES. This includes not only structures, but also their setting and their physical state and maintenance.

EQUIPMENT. This item covers everything from comfortable seating outside the buildings to the public rooms and medical equipment in the infirmary or hospital. Perhaps you won't give equal weight to a park bench and an X-ray machine, but they both deserve attention.

MEDICAL PERSONNEL. The people who are involved in the physical care of residents are often a key to the general excellence of the home. Try to meet and talk with both top and front-line people. The chief of the medical corps may be a fine, well-intentioned person, but if the home is staffed with untrained and poorly supervised employees, the actual experience of the residents requiring medical services is likely to be unsatisfactory.

SOCIAL SERVICES. For some residents, this may be a major point of judgment. Individuals in nursing homes may have emotional problems having to do with their relationships with other residents, their health, or friends and relatives on the outside. A trained and capable social worker may be able to ease anxiety or anger, fear, or frustration of an upset resident, and in some cases, act as a bridge between resident and friends and relatives on the outside.

If possible, ask to talk to the person in charge of social services, establish your interest or concern, and see how satisfactory or otherwise are the responses you get.

DIET AND NUTRITION. Talk to the dietitian if you can, and if possible, in terms of the particular requirements of the potential resident. Will he or she be able to get the strictly controlled food intake a medical condition may require? How will this be done? Are there specific procedures that assure this type of personal attention? A walk through the kitchen, with an explanation of how the food is served and brought to the residents, will give you some idea as to whether eating will be a pleasure and an assist to health, or a source of disappointment and physical deterioration.

RECREATION AND ENTERTAINMENT. For people in a nursing facility, activity is not just a matter of "keeping busy," but also a factor in mental health. Ask to see a printed program of weekly activities or other evidence of an ongoing program. If your candidate has special interests—in an art or craft—will instruction or a workplace be provided? Are trips outside the home scheduled for those who are interested and physically able to make them? Does the entertainment include "live" elements, as well as TV and canned music?

COST. Before Medicare, Medicaid, and health insurance, families of nursing-home residents were sometimes forced to pay out their last cash reserves to maintain a family member in a facility. Even now, in special cases, or those in which coverage does not take care of special needs, destructive financial drains may be imposed to buy the benefits of nursing home care.

In some cases, special funds in the form of Supplemental Security Income (SSI) may be available to the disabled and indigent. Your local Social Security or welfare office can give you information as to the availability of funds from this source.

And some institutions offer contracts that are similar to insurance coverage. The resident turns over all or part of his or her assets, and in return, is guaranteed care for life. Such arrangements are obviously susceptible to misuse and exploitation. The individual may have little recourse if the "permanent care" which has been contracted turns out to be less than satisfactory. The advice of an attorney is suggested before undertaking any such agreement.

A certain amount of shopping around may turn up a facility that offers as much as, or more than, a more expensive place, at a lower figure. If government funding is available to help defray expenses— either through subsidy to the facility, or Medicare and similar benefits—you may be able to get helpful counsel from people at the agency involved.

EVALUATING A HOUSING FACILITY

With the Caine and Berman case histories, along with the New York City project and the section on nursing homes as background, the worksheet below offers a convenient tool on which to note key aspects of a particular facility in which you are interested. If you have two or more places in which you are interested, using Fig. 10-3 for each one makes for easy comparison.

FIG. 10-3   Housing Evaluation Worksheet
Name of facility or development:_____
Location:_____
General description: _____
Description of house or apartment being considered: _____
_____
Restrictions (screening rules by owner or administration—age, income, number of people permitted in family unit, pets, and so on): _____
_____

FIG.10-3—Continued

Total cost per month or year—including any extras or special services required:_____

Net cost to you—if government or insurance coverage will pay in part:

_____

Medical or health services:_____

Dietary or nutritional services—meals, special menu: _____

_____

Group facilities available—swimming pool, game rooms, garden, and so on: _____

House services available (such as housekeeping, meals, and so on): ____

_____

Maintenance services (plumbing, painting, electrical, and so on):_____

Security (guards, fire alarms, and so on):_____

Transportation services: _____

Programs and activities sponsored by administration:_____

_____

Programs and activities developed by residents:_____

_____

Shopping (nearby?) short-term needs—food, drugs, newspaper stand, and so on:_____

Shopping, long-term needs—department stores, furniture, other major items:_____

Entertainment (movies, theatre, and so on): _____

Cultural facilities (libraries, museums, art galleries, and so on):_____

_____

Public transportation—if it is a factor for you: _____

Local job opportunities—if anyone in your family unit is interested in full- or parttime work:_____

Your appraisal of the atmosphere of the place, attitudes of administrators, and so on: ( ) Friendly ( ) Businesslike ( ) Distant, aloof ( ) Formal, correct ( ) Surly, disinterested   Other: _____*

Availability or absence of any other factors that may be of interest to you:

_____

If space on form doesn't allow all your comments, don't hesitate to jot them down on additional sheets of paper.

*This appraisal item is included even though there may be some difficulty in pinning down the answer. The intention is to help you give consideration to an intangible but important factor.

Sources of information

Pamphlets and books produced by individual authors and sponsored by organizations offer a wide range of information and detail about housing opportunities and related matters. Since new books, studies, and surveys are appearing regularly on the subject of housing for retired people and related groups, you may very well find additional sources by consulting your local library.

Best Places to Live When You Retire, Frederick Fell, Inc., 386 Park Ave. South, New York, NY 10016.

Builder's Guide to the Retirement Home Market: A cyclopedia of market facts, Douglas Fir Plywood Association, Tacoma, WA.

Choosing a Nursing Home, Jean Baron Nassau, Funk & Wagnalls, 53 E. 77 Street, New York, NY 10021.

Foreign Retirement Edens, Martha Ligon Smith, the Naylor Company, San Antonio, TX.

Furniture Requirements for Older People, National Council on the Aging, 1828 L Street, N.W. Washington, D.C. 20036.

Guide for the Selection of Retirement Housing, National Council on the Aging, 1828 L Street, N.W. Washington, D.C. 20036.

Helping to Serve the Aging In Their Own Homes. Community Council of Greater New York, 225 Park Avenue South, New York, NY 10003.

Housing for the Elderly, Robert Cummings, University of Southern California, Los Angeles, CA 90007.

Housing the Aging, Wilma Donahue, University of Michigan Press, Ann Arbor, MI 48109.

National Directory on Housing for Older People, National Council on the Aging, 1828 L Street, N.W. Washington, D.C. 20036.

Planning Housing Environments for the Elderly, Louis E. Gelwicks and Robert J. Newcomer, National Council on the Aging, 1828 L Street, N.W. Washington, D.C. 20036.

Retirement Communities—for Adults Only, Katherine McMillan Heintz, Center for Urban Policy Research, Rutgers University, Building 4051, Kilmer Campus, New Brunswick, NJ 08903.

Sunbelt Retirement, Peter A. Dickinson, E. P. Dutton, 201 Park Avenue South, New York, NY 10003.

Woodall's Retirement and Resort Communities Directory, Clark & Woodall Publishing Company, 500 Hyacinth Place, Highland Park, IL 60035.

11
RELATIONSHIPS: FRIENDS, FAMILY, PETS

"One of the things that makes my retirement a breeze," says a newcomer to the ranks, "is my group of friends. They have fortified me at every turn, reassured me, and helped me over rough spots with their encouragement and counsel."

You've just heard from a lucky man. Family and friends can be a source of strength and confidence in the preretirement period, and later on as well. People whose intimates rally round and provide support can count themselves fortunate.

There's no mystery to the fact that life becomes pleasanter when you live a full, rich social life. Friends and companions make your days fuller and more enjoyable. Friends may be a responsibility too, perhaps, but it's seldom that the advantages and satisfactions of friendship don't outweigh the occasional irritations.

A seven-year study of approximately 7,000 people by Dr. Lisa Berkman of the University of California shows that people with few social contacts—lonely, isolated people—tend to die at a younger age. They seem to be more prone to heart disease and cancer, for example, than those with satisfying social contacts.

The implication is clear: Maintain an active circle of friends. Not only do friends enrich your social life but the very texture of living becomes richer and warmer, and your life may be significantly prolonged.

However, the plain fact is, not everyone is blessed with loyal friends or helpful relatives. The alternative can be troublesome. Jim Herman, newly retired at sixty, told me, "What I find amazing is the way everybody's attitude towards me has changed. My daughter treats me like a rickety codger. My nine-year-old grandson likes me better because I'm around more. But my *wife!* She acts as though I'd developed some communicable disease! The only one I'm still sure of is my dog Foxy."

To some people, one of the most unexpected consequences of retirement is the realignment of relationships. "Why should that be?" the surprised ones ask. "I'm still the same person I was yesterday!"

Precisely because retirement may result in some boat-rocking in the area of your relationships, you have an opportunity to review and improve the whole pattern. Some contacts that you have been maintaining perhaps should be let go. Some that were uncertain perhaps should be strengthened. And some alliances that you may not have had might be developed and nurtured to the point that your life works better and feels better.

● *Dealing with Altered Relationships*

It is one of life's dismaying coincidences that, at retirement, when the benefits and reassurance of good relationships would be a pleasant and stabilizing factor, they seem to slip away. You can't assume that the contacts—both personal and job-related—that have been a substantial part of your emotional and social life will remain unchanged.

Ordinarily, you don't have to concern yourself with analyzing the nature of your friendships. One definition I've always liked: "A friend is a person you know all about, and like anyway." After retirement, however, many people are forced to make a reappraisal of their friendships because they tend to change. But you can put yourself in the desirable position of making a virtue of necessity. Seeing the situation in these terms, you have a wonderful opportunity to revamp the structure of your relationships, almost as you would remodel a house, so that they become more what you want them to be.

REVIEWING RELATIONSHIPS

Some years ago a friend of mine who had recently been widowed went off for a month's vacation. The reason was, she said, "To think." There, in a quiet resort in the Pennsylvania Poconos, she devoted a great deal of time to thinking about her relations with people. In the course of her widowhood, the whole pattern of her contacts and feelings about others had altered.

She returned more relaxed and "feeling much wiser." Her thoughts about friends, relatives, and suitors had made it possible for her to come up with some new insights. She realized that some people she was seeing were unsatisfactory contacts:

"The time with them was really wasted. In one case I didn't enjoy being with the other person. In another instance, I realized I was spending considerable time with a relative towards whom I felt some obligation—and shouldn't have."

And finally, she was able to make up her mind as to which one of three men she had been seeing was really a desirable prospect for a permanent relationship. From this woman's experience you can get some idea of the benefits of reassessing how you feel about the people you know.

For example, you'll find that it takes two to relate in a friendship as well as in a marriage. There's bound to be trouble if one person does all the giving, the other the taking. You can learn the kind of people that turn you on and those that turn you off. You may also find out if you like assertive individuals or quiet ones. You'll see whether you prefer to spend long periods of time with members of your own or the opposite sex. You may be surprised, once you think about it, just what your feelings are about people in different age brackets. You may discover that you like to be with older people, or younger ones. Or perhaps your favorite age group is the one you yourself are in.

Chances are this "friendship review" is the first one you've ever made. And you'll be doing it now in your mature years. You may be surprised to find that your present values may differ considerably from those of ten or twenty years ago and you may see old relationships with a fresh eye. In one case the result will be to set even greater store by old friends. In another instance, you may suddenly realize an individual with whom you spent a lot of time is no longer the source of interest and enjoyment he or she once was. As a result you may decide to change the pattern of your contacts.

The procedure we've been talking about is a delicate one. A reasonable goal to set yourself would be a partial clarification of the pattern of your friendships and contacts. If along with this you are able to straighten out your feelings about one or two key people, you'll definitely be ahead of the game. But don't be disappointed if you find you can't dot all the i's and cross all the t's. What you can expect is that with this new approach towards people, you can, over the next months and years, further clarify your relationships.

A major purpose of this review is to have you end up with both the quantity and quality of relations with others that satisfy you. Whether you "upgrade" acquaintances into friends or "downgrade" friends into occasional companions, you want to be certain that you keep working at your relations with others until you have the kind of friends and the number of them that can provide satisfactory enrichment.

For some people—widows, widowers, and those who have been divorced—a key relationship is one that brings into one's life a particularly close intimacy and presumably a special kind of happiness. If this is your situation, you may want to undertake a reassessment of the people in your life who represent this kind of contact.

In one case—as was true of the friend whose Pocono vacation was the setting for her soul-searching—you may decide to concentrate on someone you already know to develop a deeper relationship. In another case, you may feel that at present there's no one in your life who can satisfy this particular need. If this is your conclusion, the obvious answer is to make the social moves that will help you meet worthwhile prospects.

This is not always a simple quest. I have talked to people who have spent exasperating lengths of time trying to meet individuals with whom they could develop a special relationship. They've enlisted the help of friends, relatives, joined organizations, gone traveling, all without notable success. The best possible counsel in this matter: don't give up. Chances are you have an opposite number who's as eager as you are. Keep looking with the hope that the more active your search, the more favorable the outlook.

POSSIBLE PROBLEMS

As noted earlier, the simple fact of retirement will probably cause some disruption in your relationships. In your efforts to redevelop these in a satisfying, rewarding way, there are some things to watch out for and, if possible, to avoid.

Your children's attitudes

Once you have that gold watch in hand, some people think you've lost half your brain. No work to go to? No challenge or stimulation? Obviously, mental deterioration will rapidly set in, right? Of course you know differently, but it's amazing how strong stereotypes can be.

Your children may put a figurative cane in your hand when you retire—they may start telling you what to do, how to live, how to spend your money, where to live, and how often to visit the doctor.

Other times, your children may see you in one way: *available*. "Watch the dog this weekend while we're away, Dad?" "Pick Sherry up from dancing class at 3:30, Mom?" Or even, "Why don't you both come and live with us? That way Mom won't feel too guilty about getting a job and not being home every night in time to cook dinner."

Don't let your children's lopsided view influence your own clear picture of yourself.

Your own attitude

You probably know someone—almost everybody does—who took his own retirement to mean he was no longer worthwhile as a person and a friend. Why? He felt old, used-up, out-ot-the-mainstream, and even uninterested in many of his former pursuits. That last scared him perhaps more than any other postretirement phenomenon, and he recoiled from others—and doubted himself—as a result.

Never happen to you? Ask yourself this question: How do I feel about "retired people" as a group? In his book, *Self-Creation*, Dr. George Weinberg asks ten questions that may help you to start thinking about your own reactions and how they affect other people as well as yourself. Check your answers to these probing questions:

1. In what ways do you discriminate against old people? For instance, do you condemn your husband as a "poor old man" or talk differently to older people from the way you do to younger ones? Do you say that other people your age who try to have a good time are making fools of themselves?

2. Do you have ways of buying friendship from younger people? Volunteering gifts and services you'd never expect them to offer you?

3. What dispensations do you grant the young—and not yourself? Do you, for example, always show up on time, but "understand that the young people have better things to do?"

4. Do you believe you're too old to understand certain things (politics, perhaps, or new clothes styles or the new movies)? And do you use this as an excuse not to pay attention to what's going on around you?

5. Do you conceal your personal problems because you feel you have no right to bother young people?

6. Do you try to establish yourself as an expert on life and give constant advice to young people?

7. Do you dwell on the past and ask sympathy because your life is over?

8. Do you criticize the modern world, calling it immoral or decaying? Do you maintain that you have no place in it?

9. Do you invade the privacy of the young, trying to live their lives instead of talking and thinking about your own?

10. Do you demand that young people listen to long speeches that you make—and get upset if they interrupt? Are you really listening to what they say?

Don't be surprised or guilty if the answers to Dr. Weinberg's questions suggest that you are not very well adjusted to either older or younger age groups. Most of us tend to become self-conscious about our age, and this sensitivity, understandably enough, is a factor in the way we relate to others.

Fortunately, there is a simple factor that minimizes the problem for us. We don't have to be concerned about adjusting to groups in the abstract, but to flesh-and-blood individuals. You may be wary of young people but may develop a perfectly fine relationship with a neighbor's teenage kids. You may be uncomfortable with older people but find that your ninety-year-old aunt is one of the most fascinating people you know.

Lack of assertiveness

Some people let themselves be shanghaied into friendship. For one or another reason, they let themselves be "pressed into service" and end up doing things they'd rather not.

A retired couple—the Jennifers—told me of their experience that exemplifies this point. They had joined a church group in the new community into which they had moved, and were well pleased. The church members were bright and friendly and the minister was an excellent example of a congregation-oriented religious leader who made the group lively, stimulating, and a constructive social force. They became especially friendly with a couple about their own age. Visits were exchanged, and the newcomers felt they were fortunate in getting to know Heather and Ron. But after a few months, it became clear that the time spent together as a foursome was pretty much scheduled the way Heather and Ron chose. The Jennifers found themselves doing considerable hiking, visiting places of historic interest, and attending every auction within a hundred miles—all fine activities in which they had little interest.

It was Mrs. Jennifer who finally blew the whistle: "Jack, there is absolutely nothing wrong with hiking, visiting landmark sites, or going to auctions. But by now I have fallen arches, my eyes glaze over when I see those metal commemorative plaques, and if I see one more trunk or chest of drawers, I'm going to faint dead away!"

Eventually, the Jennifers were able to see less of Heather and Ron. They still see them, but less frequently, and half the time it is Ruth or Jack Jennifer who plan the activity.

Closing yourself off

"We stayed on in our old neighborhood," a Cleveland accountant told me, "while many of our friends moved out. I suddenly realized that there were few people with whom Ginny and I could spend time."

The group of people you describe as friends ideally should not shrink in numbers. This suggests an arbitrary principle, that you should have X number of friends to call your own. If one moves away, why, you find a replacement. That kind of arithmetic is *not* intended. A more sensible way of looking at your contacts in terms of quantity is to understand that making friends is a continuing process. No reason to stop at any point and say, "This is all I need."

In the course of your activities, you meet people, all kinds of people. Those with whom you develop a common interest or a mutual liking are obvious candidates for closer contacts, and possibly friendship. In this way, your social circle becomes a lively and growing thing, well calculated to provide the warmth and pleasure that friends add to existence.

Trying too hard

The process of "making friends" is more complicated than the phrase suggests. You certainly don't make friends by recipe, like making a pudding. In the typical case there are a number of interactions, some decidedly subtle, which consist of two phases. You and the other person first reveal yourselves—your likes, dislikes, interests, background— everything from naming your home town to your business or professional training.

Second, if what you say and the other person says creates a mutual appeal, then there is a tendency to "want more." And so you might want to bring your spouse over, talk of seeing each other again, meet for a drink, dinner, or whatever.

Occasionally, in the process just described, one or the other person may become overeager, may want the contact to develop significantly more strongly than the other person. What happens then is that the delicate balance of mutual interest becomes changed into a pursuer and pursued. And this augurs ill for a good relationship.

Undoubtedly your years of socializing have given you a sense of the give-and-take of first meetings. No matter how eager you are to develop friendly relations—indeed, the more eager, the more circumspect you may have to become—be moderate in your advances.

If you're in the market for romance, and the person you're attracted to is a suitable candidate, don't let yourself be misled by the old Hollywood movies, in which the hero, by brash if tasteless tactics, sweeps the heroine off her feet and eventually into his arms. These days, it is possible to be open without being insensitive, clever without being crude, and persistent without becoming a nuisance.

A disillusioned lady of great charm told me, "The other night I was at a house party where I met a heart-stopping man. I have an instinct for this kind of thing, and I must confess I made it clear—in a discreet way—that I found him decidedly interesting. What I got in return was a cold shoulder, and as a result, the evening was considerably less than a triumph for me. Next day I learned from my hostess that not only was my temporary dreamboat married, but that to public knowledge he had at least one girl friend. I guess my eagerness must have suggested that I was applying for admission to his harem. Sure guessed wrong on that one."

The moral is, the person you might like to make into a friend, or even an acquaintance, may not be in a situation to respond to overtures for any of a number of reasons. Don't be upset by lack of a looked-for response. It may be caused by factors over which you have no control. But remember, don't create a negative impression by seeming overeager. Easy does it. If the basis for a friendship exists, let it develop at its own pace, naturally.

● *Evaluating Friendships*

The words *friends* and *friendship* have occurred often in this chapter. At this point it is desirable, for purposes of clarity, to try to be somewhat more specific about what a friend is and isn't, what friendship should and shouldn't mean.

A FRIENDSHIP TEST

Of course, there is no scientific device for evaluating that tremendously complex and delicate state we call friendship. The test which follows makes no pretense of validity. But, depending on the reliability of your own judgments, it can provide a crude measure by which you can rate current relationships based on the way you interact with the other person. In addition, the tool gives you information you can use to judge *potential* friendships—those started that have a possibility of growth.

FRIENDSHIP TEST

With respect to a particular friend (you may want to note his or her name here to pin down your thinking), answer the following questions.

Indicate your answer by scoring a zero if the statement is untrue, 5 is right on the mark, and 2, 3, and 4, for degrees in between. Circle the appropriate numbers.

Name of person _____

	To what extent true?
1. I enjoy and find pleasure in his/her company	0 1 2 3 4 5
2. I feel relaxed and at ease with him/ her	0 1 2 3 4 5
3. When we are together we communicate easily—	
a. in words	0 1 2 3 4 5
b. nonverbally (on same wavelength)	0 1 2 3 4 5
4. We have a good deal in common—	
a. We enjoy mutual interests and doing things together	0 1 2 3 4 5
b. Occasionally, one or the other of us has a spontaneous crazy idea, which we then have fun acting on	0 1 2 3 4 5
c. We are concerned with each other's feelings	0 1 2 3 4 5
5. We have pleasant memories of things done together, which we re-enjoy by occasional reminiscence	0 1 2 3 4 5
6. I like and approve of—	
a. what he/she does;	0 1 2 3 4 5
b. how he/she does it	0 1 2 3 4 5
7. Trust: I feel I can tell him/her anything—	
a. without fear of it being told to anyone else	0 1 2 3 4 5
b. without fear of being made to feel guilty	0 1 2 3 4 5

To what extent true?

8. I admire his/her mind in at least one aspect;
   for example, wit, creativity, sharpness, maturity   0 1 2 3 4 5

Scoring: Add up the individual scores or ratings, and use the scale that follows to get a rough measure of your feelings about the person:

0–10: Doesn't seem to be much here on which to build a friendship. Perhaps this individual belongs, as far as you are concerned, in the permanent acquaintance category.

11–20: Has some good points. Perhaps more contacts might add substance to the relationship, but you shouldn't make firm assumptions.

21–30: Seems to be good potential here. With some work—more frequent meetings, exploring new areas of mutual interest and activity—this person may become a very good friend.

31 and over: The closer the rating comes to 65, the more likely it is that this person has the qualities to which you respond, and most likely, vice versa. If there are any big surprises in your score, go over your addition first, then check over your ratings question by question. If there are no errors, you may want to consider the possibility that there is a difference between what you *think* you feel and what you actually do feel.

A major purpose of the Friendship Test is to spark your overall review of your relationships. If there are changes you want to consider—people with whom you would like to build better ties, or those whose ties you would like to loosen—insights reached by use of the test can help clarify your thinking.

CONTINUING BUSINESS FRIENDSHIPS

The varieties of friendships you can look forward to in retirement are as endless as the people you know. And it's important to go ahead and get together with as large a variety of acquaintances as possible. Many retirees are concerned about the loss of one group of friends right at the start: business associates.

"What will we have in common in another two months?" lamented one about-to-retire manufacturing equipment salesperson. "What will we find to talk about when we get together?"

The answer to that question is simple—whatever you'd talk about with anyone else.

The point is, there is no need to get out of touch with business friends once you retire—if you're still interested in seeing them. In fact, many is the person still working who feels, as one put it, "a little hesitant about calling friends who have retired. I don't know—maybe they no longer give a damn about the company—or professional acquaintances. I hate to intrude on *their* lives at this point."

The message should be clear: it's usually up to *you* to make the decision about continuing friendships with people at work. That may call for a little thinking, however.

Ask yourself if you really are interested in those people—whether they interest you or entertain you, whether you are truly comfortable with them (and vice versa), whether they fulfill your social needs now. Don't hang onto them simply out of habit or out of a fear that if you let them go you'll never find any others. Now is the time to consider yourself first, to decide whether the relationship is important to you on a personal level.

If it is, there are lots of ways to maintain it. As you might have guessed, though, the first step is usually yours—and perhaps it will be up to you most of the time. Keep an eye out in newspapers for news of your company. When you read something interesting, make a phone call to chat about it. Call or drop in—by prearrangement—for some "quick advice" on a matter you know the person to be knowledgeable about or interested in. Drop a postcard from exotic, or not-so-exotic places you travel to. Said one retiree, "My phone was ringing off the wall when I returned from my last trip down South. I passed through the home town of a formerly close business friend, and on a whim I sent him a picture postcard of Main St., saying 'They're still talking about you all over town!' He just loved it!"

Arrange for a standing lunch date "the third Wednesday of every month" to be broken only with advance warning. Or, clip articles of mutual interest from magazines and send them with a note to the person.

You don't need to be unusually creative—or spend a lot of time or money—to keep up old ties if you're really interested. But do yourself the favor of deciding whether you're sincerely interested in that person on a personal level, rather than for old-times' sake. You may be surprised by your feelings when you confront them candidly. Said one retired gentleman from a small town in Georgia, "I thought I'd miss the dickens out of Joe, Tom, and Barney—everyone, in fact, who was part of work. But you know what? I was happy to get out of the plant, and all the smells, noise, and mess. I associated them with it all so strongly, I didn't want to be reminded once I left."

THE AGE BARRIER

There's a lot of comfort and companionship to be derived from association with friends your own age, of course. People who have shared similar experiences in working, in raising families, and in the world can provide much security and even help in your retirement.

But you're missing something educational and inspirational if you dismiss "young people" as not worth your efforts, like the fiftyish bachelor who claims, "Young people don't have time for me. I'm too slow for them, and I don't understand their priorities and their interests, anyway. We have nothing in common. The hell with 'em!"

Of course, most people aren't quite as hard-hearted about their own relations—especially those pearls called grandchildren. But you segregate your friends by age at your own peril. Granted, some of today's younger generation haven't developed the sensitivity and maturity you've learned to appreciate, and you may have a lot of company in dismissing "college-kids" altogether. But then again—look at all you might teach them about manners! Seriously, many people agree that it's their younger friends and acquaintances who "keep them young" through constant exposure to new ideas, values, and activities.

There are things you can do to keep your contacts with people of different ages at a satisfactory level. Enjoy meeting friends of your children, nephews, and nieces.

You can enroll in college or evening adult courses, volunteer for certain activities, or join organizations open to all ages. Try just taking walks around your community and striking up converstions with other gardeners, joggers, or dog owners. A shared interest is always a good way to open up a relationship with another person of any age.

● *Making New Friends*

One thing likely to cause uneasiness for people about to retire and move is the thought of creating new friendships in a new place. Tom Jones is moving to a retirement village in Florida from New York City. Alma and John Thompson are relocating to Los Angeles to be near their children and grandchildren. Mary Philipson is moving in with her family across town.

Each person or couple is uprooted, even if the miles aren't numerous. Each wonders, with some justification, if he or she will lose old friends, meet new ones, and be able to cope with the initial loneliness of transition.

Getting acquainted in a new neighborhood, no matter the location, is essentially a series of simple steps. After one is settled into the new spot—and even during the process of settling—you come into contact with people in three phases.

NEED. The requirements of daily living dictate contacts you must make. You have a dog and you've got to find out the leash laws in the area, so you question someone you see walking their dog. Or you would like to have a morning newspaper delivered, so you call the newspaperman to inquire about the details. Or you want the lawn mowed, so you ask the teen-aged son of the family next door if he'd be interested. Presto! You've contacted several people already. It's a small circle, but a solid beginning.

AFFINITY. You make contact with some people because of mutual interests. For example, you stop to chat with the man down the block whose rose bushes are as gorgeous as yours—almost! You notice someone else on the block who is a widower just like you—and strike up a conversation one morning when you're both picking up your mail.

These are likely prospects for new friendships because you have something in common. It may not turn out to be worth pursuing after some testing, but chances are it'll be easy enough to have a warm, friendly, enjoyable relationship with people like this because of your common interests. With some, you will find it simple and natural to build on those interests into a deeper friendship, with others an acquaintance will be satisfactory.

RECIPROCITY. Eventually, your circle ideally includes all kinds of people, in various degrees of closeness. Relationships will be formed not only from people who entertain or interest *you*, but also the people who give you, and to whom you give in return, interest and stimulation.

Many people believe that old friends are the best, that only those who have grown with you can possibly share your emotions, hopes, fears. Others, more open and accepting, find that some of the greatest rewards of growing older are the opportunities to share their lives and dreams with new-found friends.

The experience of finding a potential friend, developing a relationship in a considerate, sensitive manner, and enjoying the full fruits of shared confidences and experiences is one that is never limited to the young. In fact, says one fifty-five-year old grandmother: "I met Marlene only two years ago, and I don't know how I managed without her for all these years. We're kindred spirits—and we knew it within fifteen minutes of meeting each other. Believe me, this feeling is totally unexpected—and not to be missed for the world."

Some people feel that appreciation of the qualities of real friendship grows more acute with age. Said one candidly: "When I think of how cavalierly I treated 'friends' at thirty, I blush. The ones I've developed later in life are better friends—perhaps because *I* am, too."

SUGGESTED TECHNIQUES

Many years ago, Dale Carnegie, in his book *How to Win Friends and Influence People,* spelled out "rules" for making friends. For many people today, however, the making of friends is a more complicated problem than Dale Carnegie envisioned. Still, there are some things you can do, some guidelines to follow, that can enlarge your circle of friends.

Acquaintances

The number of acquaintances one meets day to day is impossible to count. Ever find yourself wondering about some of them—"If only we had the occasion to talk more, we'd probably find a lot in common," or "I have a feeling that this person would be really interesting if only I knew him better"?

It might be a novel idea in the next couple of months to review your list of casual acquaintances and mine it for possibilities. With the amount of free time you anticipate after retirement, this might be the perfect opportunity to get something going.

One retiree in a new condominium in Arizona told a thought-provoking story: "My wife and her three friends had been playing Monday afternoon bridge for months on end. I puttered around the house, took a nap—the usual. One afternoon one of my wife's friends took a look at me and said in a stage whisper to my wife, 'My husband Jim is sitting home all alone watching football highlights on cable TV. And we're fresh out of beer.' Don't you think I was down in that apartment in ten minutes with a few beers and pretzels to share? That afternoon began what has continued to be a warm and easy friendship between Jim and me—one that might have stayed forever at the 'Hi, how are you' stage if not for the sensitivity and concern of Jim's wife."

What about the friends of your wife—or husband—that you've never really made an effort to cultivate? You just might get something going.

Beyond your family circle

When work, family, and home take up most of your time, there may be a tendency to socialize principally with your family, perhaps only with a spouse. And this may hold true, too, when money is tight. As satisfying as family relationships may be, contacts with others provide a larger support network that enables you to weather loss, separation, and change in your circle of friends in the future.

You don't have to have scheduled meetings with John and Mary, or Bill and Sue on a regular basis. You can maintain friendships with occasional phone calls, notes in Christmas and birthday cards, and letters. When you have more time, you can pick up the relationship without having to start from scratch. If money is the problem, remember that a coffee-and-cake get-together with good conversation may be as satisfying as a night-on-the-town reunion. Your friends, too, may well be feeling the money pinch.

You're not out for the big numbers. Admittedly it is the *quality* of social contacts that counts, not *quantity*. And by all means avoid accumulating "friends" who contribute more headaches than pleasures to your life. No one can afford this extra weight.

Still, you shortchange yourself if you say "I have more than enough friends" and close the book on other relationships. It is harder to restore the capacity for friendship if it has been confined to the same small group for a number of years.

James J. Lynch, professor of psychology and scientific director of the Psychosomatic Clinic, School of Medicine, University of Maryland, and author of *The Broken Heart: The Medical Consequences of Loneliness*, suggests that people consider their investments in human companionship as of even greater importance than their investments in other aspects of their lives. The view certainly will get agreement from those who are lonely.

And don't fall into the age-segregation trap. People whose ages are more than ten or even five years apart may assume they have nothing in common. As noted earlier, this just isn't true. It will benefit them to have younger friends as well as those of the same age and older. There is considerable stimulation in variety, different viewpoints, values, and so on.

Join new groups

Membership in a group—religious, social, special interest, or whatever—gets people together on a regular basis. The advantage of belonging to a group is that there are always others to talk with, pass the time with, share laughter or feelings with, and visit with.

In looking for an activity that brings you in contact with others, try to become involved in one that you can enjoy in later years. If you are an avid tennis player, that doesn't mean you should give up tennis as you hit the higher age brackets. There are people who ski, play tennis, even ride in their eighties. But consider pursuing other interests, where age is no barrier. Anything from saving stamps to ham radio can offer endless pleasure to be shared with others.

REVIVING OLD FRIENDSHIPS

Relationships vary in importance at different times of life.

Circumstances and attitudes have an inevitable way of changing. And people find themselves wondering, "Whatever happened to old Jerry? When we bought our first house, he and Marge lived next door and we used to have cookouts together, have lots of fun. But we moved away after a couple of years and just never kept up with them."

Even a relationship that has suffered from neglect can be salvaged. Keep a couple of points in mind when reconsidering old friendships.

For one thing, was the lapse all your responsibility? Chances are, each had a fairly equal share in the neglect. So don't get mired down in feeling guilty for what is now water under the bridge.

Never renew a friendship with an apology. Put your call, letter, or whatever on a positive note. Which would *you* rather hear at the other end of the telephone tomorrow morning:

"Hello, Anne? I'm so sorry I haven't gotten in touch with you all these years. Seems like I've been so busy and you know how the time flies. . . . I really feel badly about it—you know, the way we just drifted apart—but thought I'd give you a try."

Or:

"Anne? Hi, this is Mary Jones from Peoria. Of course it's been a long time, and I thought before we got any older, I'd give you a call and see how you are. So how are you? And how are Joe and the kids?"

Some people hesitate to take the initiative in following up on a lapsed friendship for fear of seeming overly assertive, or possibly self-serving in some devious way. "Why is he calling me?" is anticipated as a question in the mind of the other person. So they decide, "Well, I'll write him a note, and if I don't hear from him in a month, then I'll know he's just not interested. I certainly don't want to push myself on him, that's for sure."

But you owe it to yourself to have a little more perseverance than that. As long as you've made the first contact, go ahead and make the second one if necessary. The person you're getting reacquainted with may be shy, unsure of himself, or worried about a change in finances or situation (perhaps he's lost his wife and feels you'll be uninterested if you can't make it a foursome for cards the way you used to, for example).

Don't assume the relationship will remain the same as it was before. As I mentioned above, chances are you will be rudely shocked by some of the changes you find. People change their outlooks and their attitudes, not to mention their spouses!

So give yourself—and the other person—lots of room to be different. Just talking over the differences can keep you going a few months, before you even have to decide whether you really care for the "new-old" friend enough to want to pick up the pieces.

Most renewed acquaintances *are* successful, from what people tell me. And you know what I hear most every time old friends stop to talk about it? "Wish I'd done it ten years earlier—the first time I thought about it." Or, "Why didn't we do this sooner?" or "Wish we'd never lost contact in the first place."

The impulse to pick up the phone or write a note to rejuvenate an old friendship is one impulse to which you should definitely succumb.

● *Family ties*

The word *family* is surely inadequate for the great variety of relationships that it includes. It must cover everything from a husband and wife to a couple with ten children to brothers, sisters, cousins, aunts, uncles, and so on, and so on. It's not really possible to generalize about families because they differ so widely in makeup. In your own case, in thinking about relationships, don't forget to examine your feelings about the individuals who make up your constellation of relatives.

If your parents are living, your feelings about them may be warm and loving. You may enjoy their company, and vice versa. On the other hand, for the adult there can be no surprise in the fact that when it comes to relatives, negative feelings may be strong. The old cartoon character Andy Gump put it neatly when he voiced one of his favorite aphorisms: "Of all my wife's relations I like myself the best."

But the important element in taking stock is to draw a line between what is expected and what is real. True, blood is *supposed* to be thicker than water. You're *supposed* to love and respect parents, love and cherish children, and hold siblings in high and loving regard. We all know, however, that this often is not the case.

For example, Tom Bruckner dislikes his father: "He threw me out of the house when I was sixteen. I've seen him maybe half a dozen times in the last ten years. Frankly, I don't care if we never meet again."

Kate Benson has never forgiven her mother for playing favorites: "My sister Elizabeth was the apple of her eye. Nothing was too good for Betty. I not only got short shrift, but mother made no secret of the fact that she considered me an ugly duckling, which she took as a kind of personal insult."

The point here is to have a realistic awareness of your true feelings. If they are negative, it's far better to accept the fact, regrettable though it may be, and not try to glorify a relationship that means little to you.

On the brighter side, most of us do experience some kind of satisfying emotional bond with a family member. The following case histories detail a few of these.

CASE HISTORIES

CARL AND MARIAN.   Perhaps nothing in the world is more beautiful than the relationship—open, warm, loving, and giving—between a man and a woman who've shared most of their adult lives. Carl and Marian are two people I know who tell me more—wordlessly—about real love in marriage than any couple I've ever seen. They do disagree, sometimes loudly, and they don't share *everything* under the sun. He never did learn to appreciate roses, for example, but he *did* learn to appreciate her interest in them. Sounds easy, perhaps, but it's a rare gift to be able to accept and even foster your mate's pursuit of a hobby or concern that doesn't move you. He rarely goes to flower shows with her, but then again he enjoys listening to her descriptions of the people who frequent them. She's smart and sensitive enough to save technical jargon for like-minded friends, and instead tells him about shrub and hedge landscaping ideas, the price wars that develop, and so forth.

Marian and Carl each seem to feel that the other one provides food for thought, a lot of laughs, and a lot of comfort when times are tough. In fact, they look to each other for most everything important in their lives. Their feeling for one another is one of the most inspiring advantages of a long life you could ever want to see. And within many marriages, the opportunity for growth and love like theirs exists.

What are some of the ways they've fostered and increased their lovely relationship? They accept and encourage their differing interests; they listen to each other; they talk to each other; and they try new things.

And none of it is terribly odd or difficult, either. Just a basic, but sincere and continuing, effort at consideration and caring for the other person.

GRANDFATHER FRED. Fred is the 70-year-old grandfather of two boys, John (age 5) and Norman (age 12). He has a great time with each of them, but in a different way. John is a "corker." He's always on the move and keeps his grandfather going at top speed whenever they're together. They go fishing, take trips to the grocery store, take the dog for walks, or whatever seems to suit the weather and the mood. Johnny talks a blue streak, too, and grandfather is perhaps the only person in the family who lets him. He listens, too—laughs in the right places, agrees when necessary, and acts horrified when called for.

It's that listening ability that means so much to Johnny. This child has never encountered anyone else in the world who seems to like what he says so much. That's why, when grandfather comes calling, Johnny always responds.

Norman is a different sort of grandson. He's already the intellectual student, and far quicker and brighter than his grandfather was at that age—or so grandfather says. That's why he's such a great listener here, too, but that's not the only reason Norman feels so comfortable with him all the time. It's more likely because grandfather wants to know all the details behind Norm's experiments, helps him design good work benches, picks up interesting books about Norman's interests, and cares about the results of tests, experiments, and so forth.

Grandfather, needless to say, gets a lot of emotional return out of these relationships—he doesn't stick around merely to babysit! But in both cases, even with the great divergence in activities with the boys, they respect him as someone who is their real and individual friend, who understands and cares about each of them. How does grandfather maintain this image?

He listens to what they want to talk about. He doesn't talk "down" to their level. This means he doesn't monitor his responses, his feelings, or try to minimize his sense of play. He accepts their opinions and enjoys them, and he likes to do things with them—not just talk. He lets them know he values their opinions and feelings, and he brings his own ideas and experiences into the conversation. Again, nothing "out of the ordinary" here—if that phrase can be applied to a real love that shows itself in interest and respect for someone else.

NORA AND JEANNE. Then there's the case of Nora, 40, and her 66-year-old mother, Jeanne. If you can talk about "average families" and "average life," that would describe Nora and Jeanne until the last couple of years. Then Jeanne lost her husband and moved closer to Nora and her family for a bit of added security and companionship. And where the relationship between the two of them might easily have grown strained and unpleasant because of the increased contact, it has instead blossomed to one of genuine beauty and love. Nora has been finding out just what makes her mother "tick" on a personal level, and Jeanne is slowly and surely beginning to understand what a fine and good daughter she has raised.

Exchanging recipes is the least of their sharing—they talk about Nora's childhood, her father and Jeanne's husband, and other family concerns. Nora learns about and begins to appreciate Jeanne's ever-increasing interest in the Orient and things Oriental; Jeanne, under Nora's expert tutelage, develops an interest in local politics and even a hankering to be a part of that scene. Their relationship is mutually supportive, loving—and, for really the first time—fully adult. They accept each other on an adult basis and give and take what is available from each.

What happened in the relationship that drew Nora and her mother Jeanne closer together? First was proximity. While this can be a dangerous factor if abused, in their case it created a feeling of added security and companionship. Their conversations are built on openness and trust. That's what is meant by the statement that Nora has been "finding out what makes her mother 'tick' on a personal level."

The interaction is mutual, too. Note that Jeanne, too, is getting a better insight into the true qualities of her daughter. They appreciate each other's interests and show their feelings by being supportive to one another, showing their affection. Their mutual acceptance of each other is on a nonjudgmental and approving basis.

Why these anecdotes of seemingly idyllic relationships? Simply to show that they are always possible—even in this imperfect world. Remember that *you* form half of any relationship, and that if problems become difficult, you may look towards the wrong person to solve them.

Forming, reforming, and reviving family and friend relationships are perhaps the greatest opportunities available to anyone approaching retirement age. It's a shame to think that you might leave the responsibility to someone else when the time, the resources, and the will are uniquely yours.

DEALING WITH DEPENDENCY

One aspect of family ties should not be ignored. With aging, the ability of a relative—mother, father, uncle, or aunt—to get on alone may be lessened. A once-proud parent, debilitated by sickness or age, can no longer live alone, despite desperate efforts to do so. What's to be done by concerned family members?

You could get live-in help for the relative—a companion to take care of basic wants. Or, someone could come in to do the necessary chores of shopping, cleaning, cooking, and helping with personal matters. You could move the relative to smaller quarters if the size of the house or apartment is a major part of the difficulty. These quarters might be especially designed for a wheelchair or to accommodate another handicap. Perhaps you could arrange to have the person live with relatives, whether permanently in one household or taking turns with two or more. Another possibility is to arrange for residency in a nursing home where practical and health needs will be taken care of by trained personnel.

None of the choices are good. They are all expensive, and in the first two instances, require people of a particular temperament, capable of relating to and caring for the frail elderly. These qualifications, unfortunately, are very rare. And as for the last choice, this may be the most traumatic for all concerned. (But there are big variations in such homes. See the section on nursing homes in chapter 10). Many elderly people see their entry into a nursing home as the last mile of their lives, and understandably, shrink from the thought of one.

The point is, the emotions in this situation are so intense that making practical decisions is difficult. People who are forced by circumstance to deal with such considerations must look within themselves, as well as at the objective facts, in order to decide.

In most dramas on this theme, there is a scene in which family members—sons and daughters, for example—discuss the matter. And the fact that often emerges is that each person is caught in a basic conflict:

the tug of the family bond—the long history of a close and often loving relationship—versus the practicalities of everyday living:

"We can't take Mom to live with us because we have no room. The kids are noisy and we'd have to shush them all the time, and they won't be able to bring their friends home."

"Sure the Six Oaks is a lovely nursing home. We just can't afford it. It would mean paying out money Mona and I have slaved for for fifteen years. . . ."

"You were Pop's favorite, he treated me like a dog. You take care of him."

In coping with this potentially searing problem, try not to feel guilty. It's biology, not you, causing the problem. Try to strike some acceptable compromise between the practical and the emotional, between what you want to do and what you can do. If possible, invite in a third party—most desirably, a professional: a psychologist, a minister, or a doctor with special qualifications (a geriatrician) who can bring third-party objectivity and perhaps additional wisdom to the situation.

● *Pets*

People seem to be divided into two groups, pet lovers and pet haters. And I must address myself to the latter group—with a certain amount of nervousness. You see, to some extent I belong in that category myself. True enough, when my family was growing up, we always had cats around, adding a lively note to our semirural surroundings. And when I was a child, spending summers on a farm in Connecticut, one of the joys of the place was the companionship of a Scotch collie named Jack.

But as a city dweller, my feelings about mobile pets have turned a bit negative. I have been depressed by the basic incompatibility of dogs and cats as apartment house denizens. Now, having made my position clear, I must further explain that I have become very much aware of the strong bonds between people and their pets. And I have seen how much a pet can add to what otherwise might be a socially and emotionally barren existence. And it is this observation that accounts for a section on pets in the chapter dealing with human relationships. Pet people will find the association perfectly acceptable. I hope the others will modify their resistance for the benefit of the many to whom a canary or a tank of fish can mean a brighter, warmer day. In fact, I know people—some who are housebound, some who live alone and are practically friendless, some who get affection or even contact from no other source—who find in a cat or dog a major element in their emotional lives. Depend on one thing—tears shed for the death of a pet come from the heart.

Perhaps Benjamin Franklin's dictum will be the clincher. He said: "There are three faithful friends—an old wife, an old dog, and ready money." The pages that follow are about dogs, cats, and whichever of God's creations people take a liking to.

WHAT THEY GIVE AND RECEIVE

No chapter that purports to talk about love, friendship, or companionship could fail to take into account some of the more domesticated members of the animal kingdom. Pets, as most anyone who owns one will tell you, can be one of the greatest little pleasures of life.

Who could possibly beat Fido or Rover for sheer joy at your arrival day after day? Who could top Tabby for providing hours of entertainment with a ball of yarn or a ray of sunshine? And that's only dogs and cats, the more common pets. Lots of other people swear by their more exotic pets, from birds to snakes to hamsters to fish to turtles.

Of course, pets have their disadvantages. If you're considering your first, it's wise to be fully aware of the possible drawbacks right at the start.

Care

Any pet in the world means work. You have to feed it, or walk it, or clean its cage, or change its litter box, take it to the vet at least annually and, not least important, give it attention daily. Are you prepared to sustain interest in your pet—even after the novelty wears off? Do you have the time, the health, the dexterity, and the space necessary for the pet you want to house?

A further consideration of care involves travel. Do you plan to and want to? If you're looking forward to retirement to satisfy your travel urge, postpone the pets till you can do them justice. (Nevertheless, in the pages ahead you'll get some tips on traveling with your pet.) Even frequent weekend trips can saddle pet owners with both the hassle and the expense of locating temporary quarters for their animal. And it's unfair to the animal to be repeatedly left to wonder if your absence means he's been abandoned.

Friends and relatives are not likely to have the same high opinion of your peerless pets that you do and will not appreciate being asked to care for them in your absence very often. And boarding your pets is a chancy proposition. It's difficult to be sure of the quality of care, and whether the quality is good *or* bad, it tends to get quite expensive if you're going to be away for more than a few days.

Basically, the decision to own a pet means a responsibility both in time and effort. Don't shortchange yourself—or the pet—with less than a whole commitment.

Expense

Though you may receive your pet free—a gift from a friend, for example, or a pick from the pound—your expenses are just beginning. And you can count on them to last as long as your pet does. Food is, of course, the major ongoing expense—dogs and cats naturally being more expensive than birds, fish, and other smaller animals. The cost of food you buy for your pets can differ greatly, depending on brands, the proportion of meat to filler, and how much "people food" you allow your pet. But whatever the amount, it's continuous.

Another cost will probably be veterinary bills—and they can be shocking if you're not prepared. Usually they're highest when your pet is young—shots, check-ups, spaying—and then again with older pets who develop all sorts of chronic and expensive illnesses. It's a good idea to talk to someone who already owns the kind of pet you're interested in, just to get a ball-park idea of the kind of expenses involved.

Housing

If you live in a private home, or an apartment or condominium where pets are already permitted, housing is no problem for your pet. But fewer and fewer apartment managers are allowing pets these days, and it's a trend that is spreading to many other kinds of communities as well—for example, retirement complexes. If you're looking forward to buying or moving in the future, your pet may well be an insurmountable stumbling block. Be sure to check into existing regulations about pets in places like these *before* you decide to move. And beware of places where you "hear that the management casts a blind eye or deaf ear to pets," even though the rules specifically prohibit them. Perhaps that applies only to pets of people who have lived there a number of years; perhaps it applies to fish and birds but not cats; perhaps to cats but not dogs. And in the final analysis, do you really need the added worry and insecurity of knowing that you are violating the rules of the place you live in and might be harassed or even evicted?

With all these headaches, why would anyone even *consider* taking on such a burden voluntarily? For one reason, and one reason only: the companionship pets provide and the interest, warmth, and affection they can add to your life.

"Having a pet—in my case, a cat," says one two-year retiree, "has returned more to me in entertainment and enjoyment than any amount of money I might have put into it. Just knowing the house isn't empty when I return from shopping, or an evening out, or even wake up in the mornings, somehow makes things a bit more pleasant. My cat is relatively painless to take care of—he's an "inside" cat so I never have to worry about him. Keeping him in the house saves on vet bills, too, as he doesn't get worms or get into fights with other cats. I don't even have to worry if I plan to go away for a weekend. My cat is so smart (actually, all cats do this!) that I can leave enough food and water for two days, and he eats a little bit at a time and gets along fine. Though he pretends to be very aloof, he's always happy at my return and lets me know it in his own ingenious ways. I don't know—I never expected to get attached to an animal this way, but somehow I'm hooked. It's kind of nice to be interested in someone besides myself every day!"

"Of course, no animal beats a good dog for showing affection," asserts a retired banker in New Jersey. "But that point about thinking of someone else for a change is true. I enjoy the responsibility, the discipline of having a dog, maybe because I've had a lot of responsibility all my working life and am used to it. Knowing I need to walk my dog twice a day, at least, doesn't bother me at all. In fact, it's opened up whole new avenues of interest—pardon the pun. I like to read, and I often tuck a book in my pocket when I take the dog to the park in the morning. He romps around for half an hour and I have a chance to read and think and get some fresh air—all at the same time! It's a perfect combination—one I certainly never considered before I got my dog."

The benefits of pet ownership are highly personalized, as you can tell. Chances are, if you've resisted owning a pet until now, it was with good and sufficient reason. But it might be a good time to reconsider that decision in the light of your approaching change in circumstances. More free time and more discretion in spending your money might make it the right time to indulge yourself. And indulgence it is—one that, according to most anyone who's already succumbed, you shouldn't miss.

TRAVELING WITH PETS

"Every time I go away for a while, and board my dog at a kennel, I find she's a total wreck when I return. I don't know what they do to her—the place has a good reputation—but between the high cost and the aftermath, I've decided that she is going with me on my travels."

The dependency of a pet is one of the drawbacks of pet owning. Many people are able to make adequate arrangements for care when necessary. Many others find traveling with a pet the preferred choice.

A word of caution: Even though you have decided to take your pet along, circumstances might force you to rethink your plans. For example, a pet's feebleness due to advancing age, illness, or recent recovery from an illness or surgery might suggest deferring the trip or changing the arrangements. A pregnant animal also is not likely to be a good traveler. And in some cases, nervousness that makes adjustment to the shocks and strangeness of travel difficult might also suggest second thoughts.

If the trip is either long or arduous—even a five-hour ride in a plane can be a strain—consider cutting down on food intake in the four or five hours before departure. Water intake should also be tapered off.

For short hauls, in a bus or taxi, for instance, you'll need some kind of carrier. And in trains or planes, the creature's comfort and safety are increased in a well-suited cage or box, clean, ventilated, and of appropriate size. Experts suggest that if you're going to use a new carrier, buy it in advance and give your pet the opportunity to become familiar with it. Many airlines sell their own pet carriers which they require you to use, so check before you get to the airport. And remember—pets ride in baggage compartments of planes, which aren't heated or pressurized as well as passenger sections.

If you are planning to cross national borders with your pet, find out in advance from your travel agent or the travel bureau of the country which you will be visiting what papers you will need. Requirements differ.

A friend of mine recently was bringing her dog into New York City from the midwest. She brought him to a vet, got a series of shots, then got two documents, one stating that rabies shots had been administered, the other a certificate stating that he was in good health as of the date of examination. Just remember that some countries—notably Great Britain—enforce a six-month quarantine on pets, regardless of any innoculations or other preventive treatments.

For some creatures, the kindest move you can make is to ease the anxiety of the trip by use of tranquilizers or sedatives. Consult your vet for a prescription, since dosage is important. Amounts of the drug are influenced by the size and disposition of your pet, and by the length of trip and means of transportation.

If you're traveling by car, you're in charge. But if your pet is going to end up in the baggage compartment of a plane, train, or boat, you must arrange for proper cleaning and feeding. You should supply the food and utensils for serving, with instructions as to frequency and amount to be offered. Also prescribe the amount of water to be offered, and simplify matters by attaching all items to the carrier. Any special instructions should be *clearly* spelled out.

Your pet should wear an identification tag with its name, destination, and your name and address, both at home and the place you'll be staying. This same information should be attached to the carrier.

Both the safety and the comfort of your pet will be furthered if you can arrange for it to get a brief workout from time to time. In case of layovers at a waystation, you yourself may be able to get to the baggage compartment and enlist the attendant's help in handing your pet over to you temporarily for a brief walk.

Don't underestimate the nervousness your pet may feel in unfamiliar surroundings. A visitor to Fire Island, on New York's Great South Bay, took her cat along for a one-week stay. On the way back to the ferry for the return to the mainland, the terrified creature, unused to the bumping of the handcart in which it was being conveyed, clawed its way out of the flimsy carton in which it was housed and disappeared. The distraught owner, after two hours of searching, eventually had to return without her pet. Two weeks later it returned to the house at which it had been staying, and eventually was restored to its delighted mistress.

Be sure to use a leash for cats, dogs, and other restrainable pets when in unfamiliar territory.

Of course, check in advance with any places you plan to stay and with any conveyance you expect to use. Make sure they have the accommodations you will need, along with the willingness to accept your pet. In many cases, a hostelry will provide service—someone who will walk your dog, feed your cat, or at least put food down for it—if you must be away for some time.

IV

Rights and Responsibilities

12
LEGAL RIGHTS

"Prospects for over-fifties are certainly looking up," an about-to-retire executive told me. "Just in terms of favorable legislation, people in the retirement brackets have advantages and protections that are unprecedented."

And it's quite true. In part because of the social changes in the 1960s that made minorities come out fighting for their rights, and in part due to the passage of laws by a Congress enlightened (and pressured) by lobbying on behalf of older age groups, you have protection in several areas that reinforce your social and financial security.

● *Three New Laws . . .*

Our nation's lawmakers, many of whom are well past sixty-five, have become increasingly sensitive to the situations and needs of people over fifty. Over the last few years they have approved three major laws aimed at protecting the rights and benefits of older Americans. These are:

1. The *Employee Retirement Income Security Act* (ERISA), passed in 1974. The major purpose of the law is to insure that the pensions employees had been counting on all their working lives would be available to them at retirement.

2. The *revamped Social Security Act,* passed in late 1977. While increasing the Social Security tax for both workers and employers, the amendments put the Social Security system back on the right financial track, increased the benefits for some, and allowed retired employees to earn higher levels of income and still qualify for maximum benefits.

3. The 1978 Amendments to the *Age Discrimination in Employment Act.* Congress decided that workers should no longer be forced to retire

at age 65. This act provided that employers could not require workers to retire prior to age 70, except for tenured professors and high-level executives. The law also barred mandatory retirement for federal employees who are able to continue working even past age seventy.

● ... and How They Help You

What do these three new laws mean to you and how do they affect your retirement? For one thing, they allow you to more effectively plan your retirement. The new schedule of Social Security benefits and the fact that most people will have their guaranteed pension benefits will give those planning for retirement a good idea of what financial reserves will be available. In addition, as long as you are physically and mentally qualified, you can continue working an additional five years and put away extra income that could mean the difference between a rewarding retirement or one marked by financial stringency.

Finally, the new age discrimination law means that your working life will not be cut off prematurely. Up to the age of 70, Americans need not fear an arbitrary decision that will deprive them of their jobs, or indeed of their rights to promotions, scheduled raises, and so on. What's more, Congress is already considering a new law that would prohibit mandatory retirement at *any* age. It should not be too long into the future before you have complete freedom to decide when you wish to put your working life behind you.

But the laws will only benefit you if you make the most of them. This means that you must know what your rights are. This chapter is intended to provide you with a basic knowledge of the laws that affect you as you grow older and to show you how they can be put to good use. In addition it sheds light on other subjects that you should know about as you near retirement, including wills and special tax breaks that favor older Americans.

● The Age Discrimination in Employment Act

CASE HISTORY

Here is a case that illustrates how the new Age Discrimination in Employment Act protects you against discriminatory firing.

Jim Williams, age 62, had been working for Jones Plastics, Inc., for almost thirty years. Starting as a sales representative, he became regional manager of the firm's Pittsburgh office. Jim and his wife Martha had been putting away money since his third daughter married five years ago. They planned to save for a condominium in Florida and join several of their friends who had bought homes in the same community.

One day, Jim received a memo ordering him to report to the firm's executive offices for a conference with a senior vice president. In a polite but firm tone, Jim was told that his services were no longer needed. The VP thanked Jim for his contributions to the company but said that the firm was planning to reorganize its sales force and Jim did not fit into their plans.

Jim could hardly believe what he had heard. How would he tell Martha? What would happen to their retirement plans? How, at age 62, could he find another sales job that would give him the opportunity to save enough for that condominium he and Martha were dreaming about?

Months later, Jim finally did find another job, but one that did not pay nearly enough to allow him to save for his retirement. The dream of retiring to Florida had to be abandoned.

What happened to Jim and thousands of other Americans in similar cases would not have happened at all had they known about their rights under the Age Discrimination in Employment Act. The original law, which went into effect in 1967, bars discrimination based on age in hiring, firing, salary, and other conditions of employment. Had Jim known about his rights under the law, he could have filed a complaint with the Department of Labor. Jim's employer would have been investigated and if no business-related reason could be found for the firing (say poor sales performance), the company would have been pressured by the government to rehire Jim. If the firm refused, either the government or Jim could have sued the company to recover lost wages and damages. Jim's retirement plans still could have come true.

There is really no excuse for workers not to know what their rights are under the law. Government regulations require almost all employers to post notices in their plants, factories, and offices outlining the rights of workers under the age discrimination act.

Previously, the age bias law protected workers ages 40 to 65. But the amendments passed by Congress in 1978 extended the protection of the law to workers until they reach 70. The new law took effect on January 1, 1979.

PROVISIONS

The new amendments to the age discrimination law extend protection from forced retirement up until the time employees reach seventy. Another provision of the law explicitly states that employers may not use the terms of a pension, retirement, or other type of benefit plan to force workers into early retirement. This is significant protection. Previously, many company pension plans provided that companies require employees to take early retirement and the Supreme Court had upheld the right of employers to abide by the terms of these plans. The Court said that an airline's pension plan could require an employee to retire at age 60. But the new law nullified the Supreme Court's ruling. It states: "No such seniority system or employee benefit plan shall require or permit the involuntary retirement of any individual (between 40 and 70) because of the age of such individual." Again, the law makes one exception to this rule. Collective bargaining agreements in effect on September 1, 1977, can continue to require the retirement of workers 65 to 69 years of age up until termination of the agreement or January 1, 1980, whichever comes first. But after January 1, 1980 no more involuntary retirement will be allowed.

The new law does not affect *voluntary* retirement. Thus, if your company's pension plan or personnel policy gives you the *option* of retiring before age 70, that option is still open to you. But the firm cannot force you to retire before age 70.

EXCEPTIONS

If you are a tenured university professor, a high-level company executive, or policymaker, you can be forced to retire at age 65, but not before. The exception for university professors expires on July 1, 1982. While there are currently no time limits on the exception for executives, chances are Congress will rescind this provision before too long. The wording of the law refers to "bona fide executives."

Here's how the act defines a bona fide executive: "Typically the head of a significant and substantial local or regional operation of a corporation, such as a major production facility or retail establishment, but not the head of a minor branch, warehouse or retail store, would be covered by the term bona fide executive." The exception also applies to individuals who occupy high policymaking positions. "This group of employees is limited to those individuals who have little or no line authority but whose position and responsibility are such that they play a significant role in the development of corporate policy and effectively recommend the implementation thereof." Examples would include a chief economist or chief research scientist.

In addition, if you are an executive or occupy a high policymaking position, you must also have held that post for at least two years before you reach age sixty-five and you must be entitled to an annual employer-financed pension of at least $27,000. All of these "tests" must apply to you in order for your employer to legally require you to leave work at age sixty-five

WHEN FIRING IS LEGAL

Reasons other than age

The most important provision of the law to workers nearing retirement is the ban on firing because of age. This does *not* mean that an employee cannot be fired at age 63, 67 or 69 for "reasons other than age." For example, Sam Noble, 64 years old, was a plant supervisor for National Steel Co. Productivity in Sam's department had fallen off considerably in the last few years. Moreover, Sam could not keep costs within budgetary limitations and was consistently late in filing reports. Finally, the National Steel plant manager informed Sam that he was being discharged. Sam sued the company, claiming age discrimination, but the court ultimately dropped the case. The company produced as evidence Sam's performance evaluation form. It showed that he was no longer able to perform his job satisfactorily, and in the court's eyes that was ample justification for the firing. Age discrimination, said the court, had nothing to do with Sam's discharge.

Age as a BFOQ

Poor job performance is not the only exception to the ban on firing because of age. A worker in the protected age category can be legally fired if the employer can show that "age is a *bona fide occupational qualification.*" Thus for example, employees working at particularly hazardous or dangerous jobs—such as firefighters, police officers, and certain others—can be fired before age seventy when their physical and mental reactions have slowed to the point that the public's or their own safety is in question. But this exception to the law has been narrowly applied by the courts. In most jobs, age is *not* a bona fide occupational qualification.

Likewise, the act does not prevent an employer from discharging a worker because of poor health if his condition results in numerous absences or if it impairs his ability to perform satisfactorily.

OTHER PROTECTION

While the ban on mandatory retirement prior to age 70 will have great impact on retirement plans, you should not overlook the other age protections of the act extended to you if you are between 40 and 70. You cannot be denied a job, demoted, or denied a promotion solely because of your age.

For example, for many years John Waldron had been an effective teacher and school administrator, but had never attained his goal of becoming principal. John was 64 years old when the principal's job suddenly became vacant, but because John was only one year away from retirement (under the former law), the school board refused to even consider John for the promotion. John sued the school board claiming that he possessed the best qualifications, yet he was denied the principal's job only because of his age. The court agreed that the school board was guilty of age bias. And though by the time the suit had been completed John had retired, he was given back wages for the year he would have been principal and an adjustment in his pension benefits to reflect the higher salary.

If you should decide to take early retirement and then change your mind, you will not have an easy time getting back into the labor force. But you should remember that potential employers cannot deny you a job because of your age if you qualify. In fact, if help-wanted ads indicate preference for younger workers by stating, for example, "ages 25 to 35" or "young," that may be an indication of age bias, and the advertiser is open to a legal complaint.

PROCEDURES FOR FILING COMPLAINTS AND SUITS

As a result of a government reorganization, age discrimination complaints are no longer handled by the Department of Labor. Beginning July, 1979, jurisdiction for enforcing the age bias law shifted to the Equal Employment Opportunity Commission, the agency that also handles discrimination based on race, color, sex, religion, and national origin. If you have an age bias complaint, go to the EEOC office nearest you. If your state has its own antidiscrimination agency, you may have to file your complaint there first. Keep in mind that it's important to get your complaint in quickly since there is a time limit on age bias suits. Individuals may file suit on their own behalf, but must file a charge of unlawful discrimination (1) not less than sixty days before taking court action and (2) within 180 days of the alleged violation (this is extended to 300 days if a state takes action under its own discrimination law). When EEOC or the state agency gets your complaint, it will notify your employer or former employer, investigate, and attempt to work out an out-of-court settlement. If no agreement can be reached, EEOC may sue the employer on your behalf. The agency can decline to handle the case, leaving it up to you to decide whether you want to hire an attorney and sue.

SUMMARY OF YOUR RIGHTS

Following is a list of your rights under the new Age Discrimination in Employment Act:

1. 1978 Amendments to the law prohibit your employer from forcing you to retire before you reach age 70 unless you are a tenured university professor, executive, or occupy a high policymaking position.

2. The new law does not prohibit you from taking early retirement if you choose.

3. Companies may not use the terms of a pension, retirement, or seniority or insurance plan to force you to retire before age 70.

4. In general, the law does not allow your company to discharge you because of your age if you are between 40 and 70, whether you are one year or ten years away from retirement.

5. You lose your protection under the law if your job performance has fallen off, if age is a special or bona fide qualification for your particular job, or if illness disrupts your ability to carry out assigned duties.

6. The law prohibits your company from discriminating against you because of age in hiring, promotion, demotions, and wages.

7. If you have an age bias complaint, you may file it with your local office of the Equal Employment Opportunity Commission or state fair employment agency.

8. Don't procrastinate. If you miss the deadline for filing complaints and suits, you may lose the opportunity to take legal action.

9. If you are unsure as to whether you have been the victim of age discrimination, consult your local EEOC office.

10. Your office or plant bulletin board should have an age discrimination poster outlining your rights under the law.

● *Employee Retirement Income Security Act*

Millions of Americans would not have the financial security they need to see them through their retirement years if Social Security were their sole source of income. Fortunately, many have put in years of service for employers with pension plans, and these years of labor will pay off when they retire and start receiving the pension benefits they have earned.

But up until Labor Day, 1974 (the day the Employee Retirement Income Security Act or ERISA became law), even those individuals who seemed to qualify for pension benefits under the terms of their company plans could not be sure of a pension when they retired. What happened was that many were being denied benefits accumulated over the years because they failed to read the "fine print" in their plans and had to forfeit their pension because of some technicality in the terms of the plan.

In other cases, those individuals or plan trustees responsible for managing the funds of many plans were not investing the money prudently. And so, when it came time for some employees to retire, there were not sufficient funds in the plan to pay out all the benefits due. Inevitably, many retirees were denied thousands of dollars in pension benefits they had counted on to see them through their years of retirement. Many had to go back to work, if they could find jobs, in order to make ends meet. In individual cases, hardships were extreme.

PROVISIONS

These are just a few examples of the kinds of abuses that were prevalent before Congress acted in 1974 to protect the pension and other benefit plan rights of employees, retirees and their beneficiaries. However, it is important to understand the limitations as well as the benefits of the legislation. ERISA, as the law is commonly called, does not *guarantee* a pension to all Americans. Nor does it require companies to set up pension plans for their workers. What the law does do, however, is to protect the rights and benefits of workers who *are* covered by pension plans. In particular, ERISA sees to it that workers are not required to satisfy unreasonable age and "years of service" rules in order to qualify for participation in a company pension plan. The act also insures that employees who work for a preestablished time period under a pension plan are assured of at least some pension benefits upon retirement, and makes certain that there will be sufficient funds in the plan to pay out pension benefits when they are due.

In addition, ERISA insures that plan funds are carefully managed and provides that employers must notify plan participants and beneficiaries about their rights and obligations under the pension plan. The act also sets up a government-backed insurance program so that the benefits of workers in defined pension plans (benefits are preset) are protected in case the plan terminates as a result of bankruptcy or insufficient funds.

Pension eligibility

Many people actually begin thinking about retirement in their early years of employment. That is the time when most employees become eligible to participate in their firms' pension plans.

Pension plans usually require employees to meet certain age and service prerequisites before they qualify to participate in the plan. Generally, ERISA says that if a pension plan bases eligibility for participation on age and service, participation may not be denied beyond the time an employee reaches age 25 and completes one year of service. (A year of service is a twelve-month period during which the employee has worked at least 1,000 hours.) For the most part, a plan may not exclude an employee because of age. For example, a new employee who happens to be around 40 or 50 may begin participation in the new employer's pension plan. However, defined benefit pension plans (benefits are established before retirement) can deny a new employee participation if he or she is five years or less away from the normal retirement age set by the plan. (For example, if the employee is 62 years old, the company need not include him in the pension plan.)

Once you become eligible to participate in a pension plan, you begin to earn credits toward your pension based on your years of service with the same employer. After you have put in a certain number of years with your employer, the law requires that you receive the right to a specified amount in benefits which you have earned. You actually do not receive the benefits until you retire even if you leave the company before retirement. The right to accumulated pension benefits, based on the number of years of service with your employer, is called "vesting."

ERISA requires that employers who make all the contributions to sustain their plans must use one of the following types of vesting schedules:

CLIFF VESTING. An employee becomes fully vested (entitled to 100 percent of pension benefits) after ten years of service. Under this formula, there is *no* vesting prior to the completion of ten years of service.

GRADED VESTING (5-15 YEARS). Employees get 25 percent vesting after five years of service, plus 5 percent for each additional year of service up to ten years (50 percent vesting after ten years) and an additional 10 percent each year thereafter. All in all, an employee would be fully vested after fifteen years, but would be entitled to some benefits if he leaves his employer after five years or more.

RULE OF 45 (BASED ON AGE PLUS YEARS OF SERVICE). There is 50 percent vesting for an employee with at least 5 years of service and when his or her age and years of service add up to 45, 10 percent for each year thereafter.

Because the various vesting schedules may seem complex, your employer is required by law to notify you as to what type of vesting schedule is being used by your pension plan and to explain the operation of the plan in understandable language.

Once employees are vested, their rights to pension benefits are nonforfeitable. This is one of the significant protections provided by ERISA.

Here is an example of how it helps to insure your benefits.

Steve Leonard had been employed for over 15 years as a financial analyst for Gould & Kline, one of Wall Street's top investment firms. He felt his career was stagnating, and that it was time for a change. One day Steve was offered a job with one of Gould's competitiors, Continental Financial Services. He accepted the offer. Soon after Steve began working for his new employer, he received a letter from Gould advising him that he had forfeited his accrued pension benefits. Gould's pension plan stipulated that if any employee leaves the company to work for a competitor, he will automatically forfeit his right to pension benefits.

Naturally, Steve Leonard was irate and immediately contacted his attorney. The attorney told Steve the type of forfeiture clause written into the terms of Gould's pension plan was illegal. And so Steve sued Gould to recover his vested pension benefits. The judge ruled that ERISA was enacted to protect the pension rights of employees from the kind of action taken by Gould. The court ordered Gould to restore Steve's pension credits. At age 65, Steve will begin receiving his full pension benefits.

To be sure, there are some exceptions to the law, and in some cases vested benefits are forfeitable. For example, if your plan is funded by your employer, the plan may provide that vested benefits are not payable if you die before retirement (unless a survivor annuity is payable). This exception, however, is not applicable to plans that are funded by employees. If employees have contributed to the plan, benefits are payable to the beneficiary of the participant who dies before retirement.

Protection from loss of credits

Before ERISA was enacted in 1974, it was not unusual for an individual to lose the pension credits he or she had earned after years of work because of an interruption in employment (break-in-service) due to illness, layoff, plant shutdown, or other reasons. As a result, employees then had to begin earning pension credits as if they had just qualified for the pension plan, even if the break was only for a short period of time.

Even with ERISA, you can still lose all your pension credits because of an interruption in employment. However, the law does offer some new safeguards that narrow the circumstances under which this can occur. The law, in general, does not permit pension plans to recognize as a "break-in-service" periods of time that are less than one year. A one-year break is defined as a twelve-month break during which an employee has less than 501 hours of service or worktime.

One important point to remember is that if your pension benefits have already become fully vested, then a break, no matter how long, cannot be used to eliminate your benefits. But again, if you are not vested, whether your pension credits are wiped out as a result of a break will depend on when you return to the job and the type of pension plan you participate in.

Pension plan insurance

It's a good idea to check the break-in-service provisions of your plan before you take any leave of absence or, indeed, if any break in service is in the offing. That way you'll know just where you stand. Here is how ERISA protects your pension benefits, even against company failure.

Joan Gilroy, an employee of the ABC Manufacturing Co. for thirty years, had no idea that the company was in deep financial trouble. It was 1957 and Joan had just passed her sixty-third birthday. Naturally, she was already thinking about retirement and was looking forward to a pension of $200 a month to supplement her Social Security benefits.

One day, without warning, Joan and her fellow employees received a notice from top management. It said that ABC was going out of business. What's more, there was no money left in the firm's pension fund. Joan and about 100 other employees with vested pension rights would not receive one penny for all their years of service with the company.

Prior to the enactment of ERISA, there was little Joan Gilroy and many other Americans facing the loss of their pension benefits could do. But ERISA created a pension plan insurance program making this kind of situation unlikely. The law requires all employers with defined benefit pension plans to pay a premium for pension plan insurance to a new government agency—the Pension Benefit Guaranty Corporation. Should a pension plan fold as a result of a business failure or merger, without sufficient funds to pay out all due benefits, PBGC will pay your monthly vested pension benefits up to a maximum amount set by law.

Your right to information

One of the most important rights you have under ERISA is the right to see plan documents. The law says that plan administrators—those individuals responsible for your pension plan—must provide you with information on how the plan is set up and what your benefits are under it. In addition, these documents must also be forwarded to relevant government agencies such as the Labor Department and the Internal Revenue Service. They inspect plan documents to make sure pension plans are in compliance with the law. Here's a rundown of the various types of forms you are entitled to see as a participant in a pension plan:

SUMMARY PLAN DESCRIPTION. The document furnishes you with information on the benefits provided by the plan and how it operates. It includes eligibility requirements for participation and benefits and provisions for nonforfeitability of benefits. In addition, it lets you know what circumstances may lead to disqualification, ineligibility, loss or denial of pension benefits, and sources of the plan's financing. Finally, it tells you how to present claims for benefits and what avenues are open to you should you be denied a claim for benefits.

SUMMARY ANNUAL REPORT. This document outlines financial information concerning the value of the plan's assets and liabilities and other data pertaining to the financial integrity of the plan.

In addition, a plan administrator must supply you as a participant or beneficiary, upon your written request, with a statement of the total benefits you have accrued, your accrued benefits which are vested, if any, or the earliest date on which your accrued benefits will become vested. What's more, you must automatically be supplied with information detailing the nature, form, and amount of deferred vested benefits when your employment with your company ends.

ENFORCING THE LAW

While ERISA created the framework for protecting your pension rights, it's up to you and the government to make sure the law is observed by those responsible for operating your pension plan. Say, for example, you are declared ineligible for a pension benefit you feel you have earned. What legal recourse do you have?

First, keep in mind that pension plans are required to have some mechanism for handling disputes. For example, if your firm operates a plan, it will notify you of the procedure for seeking a benefit that may have been denied you or how to get information you feel you are entitled to. If you are not satisfied with the response, there are other avenues open to you. You can contact the Department of Labor office in your area and file a complaint against the administrators of your pension plan. The Labor Department can sue the plan to correct any violations of ERISA.

Even more important, you can sue the plan's administrators on your own to force your plan's administrator to supply you with certain plan documents; to enforce your rights under the plan and recover any benefits that may have illegally been denied you; to clarify your rights to future benefits; or to stop the plan from violating ERISA reporting requirements, vesting and participation rules, or the mishandling of the plan's funds.

KEOGH AND IRA PLANS

Before ERISA became law, a worker whose company did not have a pension plan or who was not self-employed (and thus eligible for the so-called Keogh Plans), was out of luck. (A Keogh Plan is a pension or profit-sharing plan established by a self-employed individual. Generally, a self-employed person can put away a portion of earned income—15 percent or $7,500—whichever is less, on a tax-deferred basis that earns tax-free income until it pays out benefits at retirement. Self-employed individuals who set up "defined benefit" Keogh plans can make higher annual deductible contributions.) ERISA, however, allows an employed individual not currently covered by a pension plan (other than Social Security and railroad retirement plans) to set up a tax-deferred individual retirement plan called an Individual Retirement Account (IRA). An IRA is a retirement program which allows you to set aside a portion of your earnings which, along with the income from this investment, will not be taxed until you begin withdrawing benefits, usually sometime after you reach age 59½. The law allows you to make a yearly contribution to your IRA of up to $1,500, or 15 percent of your compensation, whichever is less. Compensation includes wages, salaries, or professional fees and other funds you received for services rendered.

To find out if you qualify for an IRA and how to set one up, contact your local savings bank or office of the Internal Revenue Service.

SUMMARY OF YOUR RIGHTS

Here is a list of the major rights and safeguards provided by ERISA:

1. It makes information about your plan accessible to you.
2. It protects your plan's assets from mismanagement and misuse.
3. It provides you with the right to appeal the denial of your claim to pension benefits.
4. It gives you the right to sue the administrators of your pension plan in federal court.
5. It establishes standards for eligibility for participation in a pension plan.
6. It safeguards your right to the pension benefits you have earned.
7. It protects at least some of your pension benefits in case your pension plan terminates or merges.
8. It allows you to start an Individual Retirement Account (IRA) if you're not covered by a pension plan, and realize tax benefits.

● *The New Social Security Act*

Social Security is a government-operated insurance program which provides many benefits to those who qualify, including disability, retirement, survivors and health benefits, and so on.

To most of us, Social Security has long been synonymous with retirement. That's because most of us pay Social Security taxes all of our working lives in order to enjoy retirement benefits and health insurance under Medicare. The number of people affected by Social Security, according to government figures, is tremendous. Of all workers in the United States, some 90 percent are currently earning protection under Social Security (employees of the federal government and some state and city employees are *not* covered by Social Security). Moreover, 22.8 million people 65 and over benefit from health insurance coverage under Medicare.

Even though many people are or will be affected by Social Security, few know how the complex set of regulations governing Social Security eligibility and pay outs works. In fact, there are many misconceptions about Social Security that should be cleared up right at the outset. Here are a few:

MYTH. Most people automatically qualify for Social Security retirement benefits no matter how long they worked during their lives.

FACT. You must have a minimum number of work credits to qualify for benefits.

MYTH. You must wait until you're 65 to begin taking advantage of Social Security benefits.

FACT. You can begin collecting retirement benefits when you reach age 62.

MYTH. If you continue working, you cannot get any Social Security benefits.

FACT. You can work part-time and still collect full benefits.

MYTH. If you've earned the maximum amount covered by Social Security, you will get the maximum amount of monthly benefits.

FACT. Most people do not qualify for maximum benefits.

MYTH. If you decide not to retire at age 65, you will not get Medicare health benefits.

FACT.   You can continue to work beyond age 65 and still qualify for Medicare.

MYTH.   Medicare health insurance protection is entirely free.

FACT.   You do have to pay for Medicare protection.

The following discussion should give you a clear understanding of how the Social Security and Medicare systems work, just how changes in the law that went into effect in 1978 apply to you, and what your obligations and benefits are under the law.

MONTHLY RETIREMENT BENEFITS

The government does not provide you automatically with Social Security benefits when you reach age 65. In order for you and your family to qualify for Social Security, you must have credit for a certain amount of work under the system. Just how many work credits you need depends on your age. And, you must actually apply for benefits at your local Social Security Administration office.

Social Security credit is measured by "quarters of coverage." As a result of changes in the Social Security law, beginning in 1978, employees and self-employed individuals will get one quarter of coverage for each $250 of covered annual earnings. What's more, no more than four quarters of coverage will be credited for a year no matter how much more than $250 you earn. The $250 yardstick does not remain constant. It increases automatically in the future to keep pace with annual wages changed by inflation. Prior to 1978, an employee generally earned one quarter of coverage if he or she earned wages of $50 or more in a calendar quarter. This method of computation is no longer in effect.

If you should stop working before you have earned the required number of credits, you will not be entitled to Social Security benefits when you retire. However, if you stop working, and then return to work, the credit you already earned will be on your record.

Another point to keep in mind is that having sufficient credit means only that you and your family have the right to some benefits. Just how much your monthly retirement check will be will depend on your average earnings over the years. Figure 12-1 shows you how much credit you need in order to qualify for retirement benefits. (There are different tables for credit needed to earn survivors' or disability benefits. Check with your Social Security office for details.)

FIG. 12-1 Work Credit for Retirement Benefits

IF YOU REACH 62 IN	YEARS YOU NEED
1975	6
1976	6¼
1977	6½
1978	6¾
1979	7
1981	7½
1983	8
1987	9
1991 or later	10

Basis for determination

Traditionally, the amount of a monthly Social Security benefit check was based on a person's average earnings under Social Security over a period of years using the actual dollar value of the person's past earnings. This method remains in use for workers who reached 62, became disabled, or died before 1979.

However, a new method of calculating benefits took effect for workers who reach 62, become disabled, or die after the end of 1978. This method provides that actual earnings for past years *will be adjusted* to take into consideration changes in average wages since 1951. Adjusted earnings are averaged together and a formula is applied to the average to determine the amount of benefits.

Why was the new method adopted? Mainly to make sure that benefits reflect changes in wage levels over your working lifetime and have a relatively constant relationship to preretirement earnings. Under the old method, benefits for future retirees were rising faster than wages and were draining the government's Social Security resources. However, in order that no one nearing retirement will be disadvantaged by the new method, the new Social Security law contains a guarantee. That is, retirement benefits for workers who reach age 62 after 1978 but before 1984 will be calculated two ways: under the old method using benefit rates that were in effect as of January 1979 and under the new method. The benefit rate paid will be the higher of the two calculations.

Your contributions to Social Security are taken out of your wages while you continue to work. And, the tax bite increases each year. For example, in 1978, you paid Social Security contributions on all wages up to $17,700. The yearly earning figures for contribution purposes increase to $22,900 in 1979, $25,900 in 1980, $29,700 in 1981, and so on. According to the government, this means that a worker paying increased Social Security contributions can be sure of higher benefits later because a higher level of earnings will determine a higher benefit pay out.

One of the most widespread misconceptions about Social Security is that if you've earned the maximum amount covered by Social Security, you will be entitled to the highest benefit. This is not true. Your Social Security benefits at age 65 will be far less than the maximum allowed. The reason for this is difficult to explain.

Basically, the maximum retirement benefits to a worker who became 65 in 1978 are $459.80 a month based on average covered yearly earnings of $8,257 (even though the top benefit is $502 a month).

The reason the average can be no higher now is that the maximum covered earnings were lower in past years. Those years of lower limits must be figured in with the higher ones of recent years to arrive at your average covered yearly earnings and this average determines the amount of your check.

If you are going to retire between 1978 and 1983, at age 62 or 65, and you have been earning the maximum amount allowed, you can expect to receive monthly benefits as shown in Figure 12-2. (This does not include future cost-of-living allowances. If you retire at 63 or 64, and earned the maximum amount, your benefits will fall somewhere between the figures on this chart.)

FIG. 12-2   Sample FICA Benefits

YEAR OF RETIREMENT	AT AGE 62	AT AGE 65
1978	$367.80	$459.80
1979	381.90	477.40
1980	391.80	489.80
1981	400.60	500.70
1982	410.30	512.90
1983	420.10	525.10

Is there any way you can tell now what your retirement check will be even if you don't plan to retire for several years? The answer is that until you apply for benefits, you won't know. However, you can estimate ahead of time. The formula is set down in a booklet called "Estimating Your Social Security Retirement Check," available free of charge from your Social Security office.

Another popular misconception about Social Security is that you cannot get benefits if you retire before 65. This is not true. You can retire at 62 (but no earlier), 63 or 64 and still earn benefits, but at a reduced rate. If you retire at age 62, you will get 80 percent of what you would have been entitled to if you had waited until 65. If you retire at 63, you get $86^2/_3$ percent of what you'd receive at 65; at 64, it's $93^1/_3$ percent. It is also very important to remember that this reduction is permanent. The amount will not increase when you do reach 65. In addition, payment amounts are also lowered if a wife, husband, widow, or widower starts getting payments before 65.

You'll remember that the recent changes in the age discrimination law allow many employees to put off retirement until they reach age 70. If you decide to go this route, how will it affect your Social Security benefits? Anyone who delays retirement beyond age 65 and does not apply for Social Security benefits will have future retirement benefits raised by 1 percent a year for each extra year worked—up to age 72. (3 percent for those who reach age 65 after 1981 up to age 70). But there are also disadvantages. For example, you will lose five years of benefits and will be paying Social Security taxes during this time.

Part-time work

You have just noted two options that you have as you near retirement. You can stop working completely at age 62, 63, 64, or 65 and begin to collect Social Security benefits; or, you can defer retirement and not apply for Social Security until you reach age 70. But there is another option. You can continue to work and still get Social Security benefits. You can receive all the Social Security benefits you are entitled to if your earnings do not exceed an annual exempt amount. In 1977, the ceiling was $3,000 for everyone, but in 1978 the amount was raised to $4,000 for people over 65 and $3,240 for those under 65.

However, some words of warning. If your earnings go *over* the amount, you lost $1 in benefits for each $2 of earnings above the ceiling.

For example, Dave Smith earned $4,000 in 1978 while collecting Social Security. He is entitled to his full wages plus his entire Social Security benefit because his earnings did not exceed the allowable limit.

Judy Small earned $4,500 in 1978. Since this is $500 over the allowable amount, she loses $250 in Social Security benefits (one-half of $500).

In addition, under the old Social Security law, there was a monthly exception to the earnings limit which allowed benefits to be paid for months of low earnings regardless of annual earnings. Under the new law which took effect in 1978, the monthly exception only applies to the calendar year in which you retire. It allows you to receive a Social Security check for any month in which you do not earn more than $334.34. After that, monthly earnings are no longer considered in determining whether or not benefits will be paid.

For example, Pete Wilson retired in September of 1978 at age 65. He continued to work part-time, earning $250 in October, $400 in November, and $100 in December. Pete received his Social Security check for October and December but not for November.

After 1978, the amount of allowable earnings not subject to any reductions (for those who retire at 65 or later) goes up as follows: $4,500 in 1979, $5,000 in 1980, $5,500 in 1981, and $6,000 in 1982. After that, it will continue to rise with inflation.

APPLYING FOR BENEFITS

You can apply for Social Security benefits either in person at your local Social Security office, or by phone if your office is far from home. You will be asked to supply the following information: (1) your Social Security card or a record of your Social Security number; (2) proof of your date of birth. The Social Security office prefers an official record of your birth or baptism recorded early in your life, such as your birth certificate. If this is not possible, you should submit the best evidence you have; (3) your latest income tax form. Bring with you your latest W-2 (Wage and Tax Statement) form. If you're self-employed, you need a copy of your latest self-employment tax return.

If your husband or wife is also applying for benefits, he or she will need the same documents. Also bring along a copy of your marriage certificate if you have it. If either of you was married previously, you should have information on the duration of your previous marriage. In order to start getting your Social Security checks the month you retire, you should apply two or three months ahead of time. In some cases, divorced spouses are eligible for benefits if they apply. Present law requires that the marriage have lasted for a minimum of ten years.

RIGHT OF APPEAL

If you believe the Social Security benefits you are receiving should be higher, you have a right to appeal. Go to your Social Security office and request that the decision on your benefits be reconsidered. If you disagree with the results of the reconsideration, you can ask for a hearing before an administrative law judge. If you still disagree, you can ask for a review by the Appeals Council. If the Appeals Council declines to review your case, or if it rejects your claim, you can file a civil action in a Federal Court.

In addition, you have the right to be represented by a qualified person at any stage of your claim. The Social Security Administration will send you and your representative notices of its decision.

SUPPLEMENTAL SECURITY INCOME

In addition to the Social Security program, the federal government operates a supplemental security income program. Its purpose is to provide a minimum monthly income to needy people with limited income and resources who are 65 or older, blind, or disabled. The benefits available are $177.80 per month or $266.70 for a couple. For further information, check your Social Security office.

● *Medicare*

Medicare is a health insurance program under Social Security which provides millions of Americans 65 years old and over and many severely disabled people with help in meeting the high costs of medical care.

Actually, Medicare is made up of two health insurance plans. Part A, hospital insurance, takes care of in-patient hospital treatment and follow-up treatments in a skilled nursing facility or at home. Part B, is the medical insurance plan, which helps to take care of doctors' bills and related expenses.

How do you become eligible for Medicare? First, you qualify for Part A coverage at 65 by applying for Social Security or railroad retirement benefits. Keep in mind that in order to qualify, you must apply even if you continue working past 65. In fact, it's a good idea to apply before you reach 65 so that you have a better chance of meeting all requirements, and you will be assured of coverage promptly at 65.

Your application for Social Security also entitles you to coverage under Part B, the medical insurance segment of Medicare. However, because you will have to pay a premium for Part B coverage, you can elect on the application form not to be covered under this part of the program. If you do opt for Part B coverage, the premium will be taken off your monthly Social Security check. The most recent premium was set at $8.20 a month, but it is increased annually because of inflation.

Despite the cost, Part B coverage is a bargain and generally should not be turned down. Keep in mind that it is subsidized by the federal government and provides coverage at a fairly low cost. What's more, most private medical policies for older individuals are structured to supplement Part B coverage.

Another factor to note is that you automatically become eligible for hospital or Part A coverage if you have worked long enough under Social Security or railroad retirement. However, if you are over 65 and do not have enough work credits, you can still buy hospital insurance (Part A) for $63 per month if you also have medical insurance. The premium rises with increases in hospital costs.

Medicare is open to everyone at 65, regardless of income. Don't mistake it for Medicaid, which is a separate program only for the "medically needy," as spelled out by state law and administered by state welfare agencies.

PART A, HOSPITAL INSURANCE

Part A, or the hospital insurance part of Medicare, provides benefits for a certain number of days in each "benefit period." A benefit period starts when you enter the hospital and ends when you have been out of the hospital or nursing facility for sixty consecutive days.

INPATIENT HOSPITAL CARE. Coverage is up to ninety days in each benefit period. You will have to pay the hospital deductible, or the first $160 (current amount). Medicare pays the remainder of the cost for the first sixty days of hospital care. From the sixty-first day through the nintieth day, you pay $40 per day (again, this amount is likely to rise because of inflation). In addition, Medicare assumes a large part of the costs for stays in skilled nursing facilities and for home health care.

Covered services under the hospital insurance plan include the cost of semiprivate rooms, meals, regular nursing services, and the cost of special care units, such as intensive care. Also included are the costs of drugs, supplies, appliances, equipment, and more. For home health care, services covered include part-time skilled nursing care, physical therapy, and speech therapy.

PART B, MEDICAL INSURANCE

Part B of Medicare pays part of the costs of doctors' fees, outpatient hospital care, and other services. There is a $60 deductible, which means you have to pay the first $60 of your medical expenses in each calendar year. After you have paid the deductible, Medicare pays 80 percent in reasonable charges for all other covered medical expenses. You can get detailed information on eligibility for Medicare, covered services, and costs, from your Social Security office.

● *Wills*

The next subject to be dealt with is a departure from Social Security to what might be thought of as individual security. The law makes it possible for you to dispose of your personal belongings, financial assets, and other holdings after your death in a manner most satisfactory to you. Since many people have strong and definite feelings about the matter of the disposal of their property, it is important to know some of the laws that apply in your own case.

BENEFITS OF HAVING A WILL

Although the making of a will is a subject some people would probably rather not confront, a will can be very important to the people you love. Generally, a will represents your instructions on how you want your assets distributed after your death. What happens if you die without a will? The state steps in and divides your assets without you having any say in the matter. The manner in which assets may be distributed varies depending on the individual state. But here is an illustration of how property may be distributed if an individual dies without a will.

Should the husband die, the wife gets half the estate and the remaining half is evenly divided among the children. If the husband and wife die at the same time, the children get equal shares of the estate. If there are minor children, they become wards of the state until guardians and trustees are named by the state. Should an entire immediate family die at the same time, and no relatives are living, the entire estate is assumed by the state in which the husband lived.

WRITING YOUR WILL

If you would rather not leave it up to the state to distribute your assets (and most people would not and do not), you must make a will. Remember how important a will can be to your survivors. In addition, the will may even save money. If state policy is to distribute your assets in fixed percentages, your surviving spouse will be unable to claim the full marital deduction. If the court appoints a bonded administrator, the cost of the bond will be deducted from your estate.

True, you will have to pay for the cost of drawing up the will and probably for legal advice. But generally, the costs of a will are not steep depending, of course, on which lawyer you use. If you want counsel or opinion on personal matters, then the maturity of the person you choose may be an important qualification. And since a will must meet all the requirements of state law or else it will not be valid, ascertain whether or not the candidate is conversant with the laws of your state.

If you have any thoughts of writing your own will or using a printed form, be extremely cautious. Requirements for recognizing the validity of homemade or holographic wills vary from state to state. Even where they are recognized the language of the will may cause problems for your survivors. However, if you like the idea of a do-it-yourself will, you may want to draw one up and find a lawyer to review it—presumably at a lower fee.

The will you leave does not automatically entitle your survivors to what's included. First, survivors must authenticate the will or prove that the document is the actual statement of how you want your property distributed. This process takes place in probate court. Witnesses are brought to testify to the will's execution. The executor (or the administrator of your will) must show the court that all your bills and taxes have been paid. Final distribution of your property to those named in the will cannot be made until all claims against your estate have been settled.

After you've had a will drawn up, make sure to look it over from time to time. Your financial status can change over the years, and so can the status of some of the heirs named in your will. Some of the items that may affect your will are as follows: (1) a change in your personal life, such as a marriage, divorce, or the death of your spouse; (2) the death of any beneficiaries named in your will; (3) new heirs that you may wish to include, such as grandchildren; (4) the death or relocation of your executor; and (5) a change in your residence—if you move to a new state, your will must be changed to comply with the laws of that state and you must also establish legal residence; (6) a change in federal or state laws governing wills; (7) a change in your financial status may cause you to increase or decrease the sum to certain beneficiaries; (8) your personal feelings about a beneficiary.

Although it may seem like a small matter now, you may not know what to do with the will once it's been drawn up. Some people put wills in such odd places as behind paintings and under rugs. If you hide your will too carefully and it cannot be found, a court may rule that you purposely wanted it destroyed. The best place to keep your original will is at home in an accessible place (like your desk). You should also give a copy to your lawyer. Make sure your spouse or closest relative knows where you put both the copy and the original.

● *Tax Relief*

In planning for your retirement, you will certainly want to consider how much Uncle Sam will take out of your limited, and probably fixed, income. Fortunately, Congress has amended the tax laws over the years to provide special benefits for persons near or at retirement age. Many Americans in this age group pay no tax at all, and those who do are treated to special exemptions and credits. Remember, changes in the tax laws and regulations that affect you are made every year. In order to make the most of your tax benefits, you must keep up with these changes.

EXEMPT INCOME

The following sources of income generally are not subject to federal taxes and need not be reported on your return.

SOCIAL SECURITY. Lump-sum or monthly Social Security benefits paid out by the U.S. government are not taxable.

RAILROAD RETIREMENT BENEFITS. Basic railroad retirement benefits are not taxable.

PUBLIC ASSISTANCE BENEFITS. If you should receive public assistance benefits, such as benefits for the blind, you do not have to report this as income.

COMPENSATION FOR SICKNESS OR INJURY. Payments received for the following are generally not taxable: damages for sickness or injury; worker's compensation paid because of sickness or injury; Federal Employee's Compensation Act payments; compensation for the permanent loss of use of a part or function of the body; and benefits received from an accident or health insurance policy for which you pay premiums.

GIFTS AND INHERITANCES. Gifts, bequests, or inheritances are, in themselves, not income and not taxable. But if these items later earn you taxable income, such as dividends, interest, or rentals, then the income is taxable.

VETERANS' BENEFITS. If you are a veteran, any benefits you and your family receive under any law administered by the Veteran's Administration is not taxable. The exemption would cover, for example, pension benefits and disability compensation. Generally, veterans' proceeds and dividends are also not taxable.

WHEN YOU NEED TO FILE

A question that frequently arises when a person reaches age sixty-five and earns a limited income is, do I have to file an income tax return? The answer, courtesy of the IRS is, if you reach age sixty-five, even if you owe no tax, you must file a return if your gross income exceeds a certain level, depending on your marital status. The amount changes almost yearly as Congress continues to make changes in the tax laws. You should check with your IRS office if you are in doubt as to your need to file a return.

One important point to remember is that even if you are not required to file a return, it may be to your advantage to do so, if there was income tax withheld from your pay. If you file a return and claim your personal exemptions, you can get a refund for the withheld tax.

SPECIAL AGE EXEMPTION

For the 1979 tax year, taxpayers were entitled to claim a personal exemption of $1,000; if you were married, you were also entitled to claim an additional $1,000 exemption. What's more, you can claim a $1,000 exemption for each individual who qualifies as your dependent.

However, if you are age sixty-five or older on the last day of the tax year, you can claim an additional "age" exemption (of $1,000). If your spouse is sixty-five or older on the last day of the tax year, and you file a joint return, you can claim both a regular exemption of $1,000 and an age exemption of $1,000 for your spouse.

Here's an example of how those exemptions accumulate if both you and your spouse are sixty-five or older. Tom and Beth Norman were both over sixty-five at the end of the year and are filing a joint return for the calendar year. Tom is allowed personal exemptions of $1,000 for himself and for Beth. Moreover, since both Tom and Beth are over sixty-five, he can claim an additional age exemption of $1,000 for both himself and Beth. All in all, Tom is allowed total exemptions for the year amounting to $4,000.

If you file a separate return, you can claim the exemption for your spouse only if he or she had no gross income and is not a dependent of another taxpayer.

Keep in mind the amount you can claim as personal and age exemptions will continue to rise as Congress amends the tax laws.

CAPITAL GAINS EXEMPTION

The tax laws grant preferential treatment to persons fifty-five and older who sell their homes. If you sold your home during the year, you can exclude from your gross income all or part of the gain of that sale if (1) you were fifty-five or older before the date of the sale; (2) you owned or used the property as your principal residence for a period totaling at least three out of the previous five years; and (3) you or your spouse have not taken advantage of this exclusion previously. You can exclude your gain from the sale of a home only once during a lifetime.

If these prerequisites apply to you, you can exclude your entire gain if the adjusted sales price of the home is $100,000 or less. In other words, you will not have to pay taxes on any of that amount. However, if the adjusted sales price is more than $100,000, you can exclude only part of the gain from your gross income. (The "adjusted sales price" is defined as the amount you realize from the sale after commissions and other selling expenses minus certain fixing-up expenses.)

TAXABLE INCOME

Despite all the tax benefits that are coming to you if you are sixty-five or older, you still must pay taxes on all income you receive that is not specifically excluded. The following common sources of income *are* taxable.

COMPENSATION FOR SERVICE. This category would include wages, salaries, fees, commissions, bonuses, tips and other payments you may get for your services.

INTEREST. Most income from interest payments is taxable.

DIVIDENDS. According to the IRS, most dividends on stocks are taxable income.

RENTAL INCOME. Generally, whatever amounts you get from rent and royalty income must be reported.

PENSIONS AND ANNUITIES. If you did not contribute to the cost of your pension or annuity (in other words, the pension was fully funded by your employer), the payments you receive are fully taxable.

If both you and your employer contributed to the cost of your pension or annuity, and you will recover your contribution within three years after the date you receive your first payment, no parts of the payments you receive are taxable until the cost has been recovered. However, after your cost has been recovered, all amounts you receive are included in gross income.

If you do not recover the cost within three years, then each payment you do receive has two parts: (1) a return of your cost which is not taxable, and (2) taxable income. Again you should ask your tax preparer or IRS representative to find out how to compute what you owe.

● *Sources of Legal Information*

This chapter contains only a brief summary of all the information about federal laws that affect you when you reach sixty-five or when you retire. The laws and the regulations that implement them are many thousands of pages long and obviously cannot be fully covered. Yet, in each area discussed here—including age discrimination, pensions, Social Security, Medicare, and taxes—there is more information available to you if you decide you care to seek it out.

Each government agency or department that implements a law discussed here has a district office in almost every major city around the country. If you live, for example, in New York, Boston, Chicago, San Francisco, or other large city, there is a federal office to visit, call, or write. What's more, if you live in proximity to these cities, you can contact the federal office there for help. The federal offices in these areas have specially trained people who should be able to give you fast and helpful answers to your inquiries. They also stock hundreds of pamphlets and booklets available free of charge that explain your rights, benefits, and duties.

If you should have trouble reaching your local government office, you can call or write to the agency headquarters in Washington, D.C. Here are some addresses:

For inquiries on your rights under the age discrimination law, contact: Equal Employment Opportunity Commission, Office of Public Affairs, 2401 E. St., N.W., Washington, D.C. 20506; telephone (202) 634-6930.

For information on your rights under the pension law (ERISA), contact: Department of Labor, Office of Information, Publications, and Reports, Room S1032, 200 Constitution Avenue, N.W., Washington, D.C. 20210; telephone (202) 532-7316.

For help with Social Security or Medicare, contact: Department of Health, Education, and Welfare, Information Center, 200 Independence Avenue, S.W., Washington, D.C. 20201; telephone (202) 245-6295.

For tax information, contact: Internal Revenue Service, Public Affairs Division, 1111 Constitution Avenue, N.W., Washington, D.C. 20224; telephone (202) 566-4021.

13
HOME SAFETY

Personally, I'm very much aware of safety as a subject of crucial importance. As a production supervisor for the Celanese Corporation, I had the responsibility for maintaining safety in a workplace for up to 150 employees. I became aware of the dangers of carelessness and inattention and the serious accidents that might result from a machine breaking down, a shelf tipping over, an employee slipping, and the threat of fire. Being sold on the need to educate employees about safety practices and the elimination of hazards in the workplace, my department won the prize several times for greatest reduction in accidents and best overall safety record.

And I became very much aware of the threat of home accidents. I have two sisters, each of whom suffered a broken hip as a result of a fall. By diligently applying safety practices at home, you can avoid physical injury, possible medical bills, and damage to or loss of property. This in turn will mean the peace of mind you deserve to enjoy your retirement years.

In general, the two basic causes of accidents in the home, or anywhere for that matter, are *unsafe acts* and *unsafe conditions*. An example of the former would be using an electric hairdryer while showering; an example of the latter would be inadequate lighting on a steep stairway. And, of course, a combination of the two—such as climbing on a broken step ladder while wearing high-heeled shoes—can be lethal.

You can train yourself to be aware of both kinds of hazards and to eliminate them before they cause trouble. Following is first a section on the causes of slips and falls, and second a room-by-room checklist of unsafe acts and conditions to watch out for.

● *Identifying Hazards*

Safety experts say that slips and falls are second only to motor vehicle accidents in frequency. Even more frightening, the death rate from slips and falls is well over twice as high as that for fires and burns. However, with a little care and concern, causes of slips and falls at home often can be identified and eliminated.

Some of the best spotters of situations that cause falls are phrases spoken frequently. Pay close attention to statements like the following to give you an assist in eliminating the factors that cause falls.

1. *"That's the second time I've tripped over that darn thing."* This is a sureshot revelation. It may be a telephone wire, a badly-placed piece of furniture, a decoration in a walkway, or a loose board or tile in the floor. When you hear that complaint, pinpoint the offending object and move, eliminate, or cover it.

2. *"These high heels will be the death of me."* Don't be too quick to let the blame for a hazard fall on footwear. For women with high heels, this ear-opener suggests a torn rug or a hole or some other imperfection in an underfoot surface. Even low heels in men's and women's shoes may get caught in a floor declivity. Patching or resurfacing may be indicated here.

3. *"Don't stub your toe."* This is a giveaway for a projection in the way of foot traffic. It may be a floor-mounted electric outlet or a piece of construction material that's come loose. Whatever it is, when you eliminate it, you prevent those head-over-heels falls that can be painful, costly, or even permanently damaging.

4. *"It's a bit dark."* In a stairwell, inadequate lighting may lead to banged-up knees or a bone-breaking tumble. Look over the areas where you hear a complaint about poor lighting. In some cases, increases in wattage can help matters. In others, illumination sources may be long overdue for a cleaning. But this situation is serious enough to warrant a new lighting fixture, if other remedies are insufficient.

5. *"Watch your step."* If you have to say this, it means trouble. This warning is used where there's a step down, just inside a door, for example. Or a step up, on a ladder with loose or broken rungs.

Another hazard under this heading: Large chips out, or other imperfections in cement steps, or loose or broken boards in wooden ones may lead to a turned ankle and a dangerous fall.

6. *"Oops!"* Another general tipoff to the existence of falling hazards

are the accidents that *almost* happen. You slip and barely manage to save yourself by exceptional agility or by grabbing some convenient support.

The next person may not be that lucky. So check into the "almosts" in the slips and falls category, and eliminate the hazard once and for all. A near miss in any accident category targets a hazard to eliminate.

● *Room-by-Room Checklist*

The following lists can assist you in going through your home and correcting hazardous conditions. In some cases, the remedy requires that you install a safety device, such as a hand-hold in tub or shower. In others, the remedy may involve changing some unsafe behavior.

In addition to the hazards listed, burglary and vandalism are also discussed. Your peace of mind depends on assuring the safety of your home not only when you're on the premises, but also when you're away.[1]

KITCHEN

The kitchen is a busy place, with lots going on. Here's what to do to keep your kitchen from becoming an accident scene:

• Keep aerosol cans and pressurized containers away from the stove, because excessive heat can cause them to explode.

• Don't store caustic cleaners, drain openers, or other poisons under the sink or at other low levels where small children can get at them. Even if none lives with you, you may have a pint-sized visitor now and then.

• Be careful in handling your sharp knives and other sharp instruments. For example, knives are safer stored in a rack rather than tossed loosely in a drawer. And pointed or sharp utensils are best washed and dried separately, rather than left exposed in a drainer.

• If you use electric appliances, such as toasters or percolators, make sure no cord runs over any burner that may be turned on, melting insulation and posing the possibility of shock.

• Immediately clean up spills that reach the floor to avoid slips or falls.

[1]This section is adapted from *Executive Housekeeping*, by Auren Uris, New York: William Morrow & Co.

• Don't overload shelves; they may pull loose and fall.

• Don't overreach in trying to get objects from high shelves or cabinets. Use a sturdy stool or ladder.

• If a glass or bottle breaks, avoid cuts by using a brush and dustpan. Wipe up the slivers with a damp paper towel or use a vacuum cleaner.

• If there are youngsters coming to visit, especially toddlers, beware of their ability to reach up and pull. This applies to handles of pots or pans projecting out over the edge of a range, or the dangling electric cord of an iron.

• If you're going to do anything unusual with an electric appliance, unplug it first. For example, reaching into a plugged-in toaster with a fork can get you shocked before it gets the toast unstuck.

• Keep pot holders handy for picking up hot items.

• Avoid leaning over the stove, especially in loosely fitted long-sleeved garments.

• Keep the fire extinguisher handy for small flash fires. Make sure you keep it out where you can grab it quickly, not in the back of a crowded cabinet.

• Avoid storing napkins, bags, and plastics in or near ovens.

BATHROOM

Like the kitchen, the bathroom, because of its construction and use, tends to harbor special hazards. Here are some things to make your bathroom safer:

• Regulate the hot water at its source (your own hot-water tank if you own your own home) to prevent scalding.

• Install a nonskid bottom, either a rubber mat or other similar protection, in your bathtub or shower.

• Place a small nightlight near the bathroom door.

• Provide sturdy handholds near tub and shower to give support when moving around or in and out of the facility.

• Have a satisfactory means of disposing of used razor blades—either a slot in the back of the medicine chest or other closed container.

• Use plastic cups, bottles, and so on, to prevent breakage that inevitably results when glass crashes against a tile floor. If shampoo or other cosmetic comes in a glass container, pour it into a plastic bottle for bathroom use.

• Keep all potentially dangerous drugs, including everything from aspirin to rubbing alcohol, safely out of reach of youngsters.

• Have a first-aid kit available with the usual recommended list of items—antiseptic, Band-Aids, bandaging materials, and so on.

• At least one person in the family should know the rudiments of first aid. (If not, it's a good idea to enroll in a course offered by your local Red Cross.)

• Keep appliances away from bathtub or shower area to prevent lethal electric shock.

• Get rid of old prescription drugs.

• Store medicines for external use on separate shelves of your medicine chest.

LIVINGROOM, BEDROOM, AND DININGROOM

Of course, there's a wide range of possible hazards in these three rooms, and they vary greatly depending on the kind of home you have. You will want to be sure of the following things:

• The electric wiring in each room should be adequate to handle the load. (If your TV picture shrinks when your furnace or refrigerator turns on, wiring may be inadequate.)

• There should be a phone extension near your bed.

• Have plenty of electric outlets so that octopus connections are unnecessary.

• Always keep the spark screen closed when your fireplace is in use and—temporarily or otherwise—no one is in the room.

• There should be sufficient space for air circulation around your TV or hi-fi to prevent dangerous overheating.

• Keep enough large ashtrays for smokers in the house or for visitors.

• Keep matches and lighters out of the reach of children.

• Use a metal tray under fondue pots or chafing dishes to protect against a possible overflow of blazing alcohol.

• Keep candles away from blowing curtains.

• Use extension cords only for temporary convenience, never as permanent wiring.

• Avoid using hair spray or other spray containers near a flame or while smoking.

• Windows, particularly those that are close to the floor, should be guarded to prevent anyone from falling out.

ATTIC, CLOSETS, AND STORAGE AREAS

Every home has closets of one size or another and, of course, some suburban homes have attics and storage rooms. All too often objects and materials are shoved, stuffed, and piled in an attempt to get the maximum into the minimum. Here are some safety tips for storage areas.

• Avoid accumulating paper and combustible materials.

• Keep oily polishing and waxing rags in tightly closed metal containers.

• Use only nonflammable cleaning materials.

• Store paints and solvents in their original containers and keep the total to a bare minimum.

• Keep combustibles away from the furnace or other sources of heat.

• Have the furnace, heaters, vents, and chimneys inspected and serviced regularly.

• Make sure the fuses are of the proper size for the circuits they protect.

• Store gasoline for your lawn mower in a safety can.

• Keep stairways and landings free of accumulated paper and other stored materials.

STAIRS

• Locate lightswitches at entryways.

• Remove throw rugs from landings.

• Paint or tape bottom steps with a bright, highly visible color, particularly in basement area.

• Replace rickety railings, bannisters, and treads.

• Check stair runners and fasten down any loose spots.

FIRE HAZARDS

To make your home as fireproof as possible, try to eliminate hazards and encourage all to follow the basic rules of fire prevention. The following guidelines are for each member of your household.

• Keep matches, lighters and lit candles out of the reach of children. If you use candles, be sure that they are well seated in holders and kept away from hangings that could be blown toward the flame.

• Be especially careful with combustibles: paint thinner, turpentine, and so on. Keep them away from open flame and heating appliances.

• If you use portable room heaters, make sure that they are kept away from inflammables. Turn them off when leaving the room.

• TV sets or other heat-generating appliances should not be kept in a confined area. Circulation space is necessary to prevent combustion from overheating.

• Lack of fireplace control is an obvious but sometimes overlooked hazard. A sturdy fire screen is an absolute must. Making sure that it's in place, particularly if the room is left unoccupied, is another essential.

• Combustibles such as waste paper, trash, and so on should always be kept clear of the heating plant.

• Spontaneous combustion can happen. Keep cleaning materials in well-ventilated areas. Also keep waxing and polishing cloths in closed metal cans.

• Smoke-activated alarms can be lifesavers, sounding off in the presence of smoke or intense heat.

• Smokers not only risk lung damage but also burn down houses; don't permit smoking in bed.

• Don't permit the use of lighted matches in looking for items in closets or attics—or for gas leaks!

• It's a good idea to have fire-fighting or safety-assisting equipment. Certainly you should have a small fire extinguisher in the kitchen. However, don't depend on your ability to overcome any fire that's started to get out of control. It's wiser to call the fire department than try to conquer the flames yourself.

• Plan an escape route from your room and home, and practice using it. Work out an alternate route, just in case.

• Close your bedroom door before going to sleep. If fire should break out elsewhere in the house, the closed door may keep flames, gases, or smoke away long enough for rescue to reach you. Flames terrify, but gas and smoke are equally dangerous.

• Never open a hot door. If you smell smoke or think there is fire in the house, touch test the inside of a door. If it is hot, don't open it. Go to the window and wait for rescue there.

• If your home has two or more floors, a portable rope or chain ladder may permit escape from upstairs windows when other routes are blocked. Rehearse all family members on the proper use of such escape routes.

• Fire drills? Certainly. You must take these contingency plans seriously. Let everyone know what to do in case of fire—how to get out of the house, how to call for help, and so on.

● *Vandalism*

In some communities, vandalism is virtually nonexistent. In others there's a good chance that if you leave your home unguarded just for the time it takes to go to a movie, there will be damage when you return.

Happily, minimum efforts can reduce the hazard considerably:

HOUSE SITTING.   The practice is sufficiently well established to have proved itself. People who are going away for a vacation arrange to have someone occupy their house or apartment. Says one New York City apartment dweller, "I paid a young couple to live in my apartment for a month. Of course it was an added expense, but it was worth it just in terms of mental ease."

LIGHTING. Vandals, like cockroaches, hate light. Spotlights at doors and entrances and one or two lights left on inside the home can keep vandals and other human predators away.

BEWARE THE DOG. Families that have watchdogs feel quite secure about the vandalism threat. Families who don't have dogs sometimes can have the benefit simply by posting a "Beware of the Dog" sign.

AFTER THE FACT. Occasionally vandalism presents you with a peculiar problem. If you catch the perpetrator in the act, especially if it's a neighbor's child, what do you do? An official working on a big-city antivandalism program says: "The best punishment for vandalism is to insist that the vandal clean up the mess or pay for any costs of restoration, replacements, and so on."

Since some of the measures you might want to consider for the next home safety hazard—breaking and entering—also apply to vandalism, read those recommendations with the vandalism threat in mind, as well.

● *Burglar-Proofing Your Home*

A couple I know lives on the second floor in a garden apartment complex near Los Angeles. Being very security-minded, they ended up with five locks on their front door. Their planning, however, left something to be desired. One night, they woke up to find an intruder in their bedroom. All their security efforts had been for naught. The burglar, using a lightweight ladder, had entered by way of the terrace at the back of their apartment. The burglar was quickly given all the valuables the frightened couple could lay their hands on.

The husband said, "I hope you'll leave now," and pointed to the terrace. The burglar, clad in a stocking mask, shook his head. "I'm not going out that way. It's too risky." And so—irony of ironies—they had to open each one of the locks to let the burglar *out* of the apartment.

As you can see, taking wrong or inadequate precautions against burglary is almost as bad as taking none at all. While it is hoped you don't feel the need to lock yourself up like jewels in a bank vault, you should take a good, realistic look at your situation with an eye to security. Here are some hints.

MAINTAIN PRIVACY

There are some people—like the proverbial Joneses whom everybody is trying to keep up with—who want to make their affluence known. If they get a new color TV, the neighborhood knows about it.

This kind of publicity may be fine for the ego, but it wreaks havoc with security. You don't have to be paranoid about it, but the less fanfare, the less general knowledge of the special assets and valuables in your home, the better.

For collectors, zero publicity is a special problem and a special need. For example: Paul Harvey of Chicago recently sold a small but expensive collection of musical instruments. Even some of his best friends hadn't known of the existence of the collection. And this fact alone may explain why, even though Paul Harvey's apartment house had had several burglaries, his unit was not one of them.

An experienced Philadelphia detective says, "Many people invite crime by making the interiors of their homes visible. A potential burglar might be tempted by objects separated from him only by a window. And, of course, criminals are not always looking for loot. The naked woman-in-the-window has been celebrated as a come-on in newspapers and movies alike. So, particularly at night, make it impossible for anyone either at street level or from dwellings across the street to look into your home. Draw window shades, venetian blinds, or curtains."

PROTECTIVE HARDWARE

Entire books have been written on the variety of locks and other mechanical window and door fasteners that are available. There are several factors involved in getting the full benefit of such devices.

Keys

Carelessness with house keys accounts for a substantial number of burglaries. Obviously the strongest lock manufactured protects nothing if a would-be burglar has the key. There are a number of ways in which keys can find their way into the hands of criminals.

Never put identification tags on your keyring or keyholder. If you lose your keys it's better to just forget about them than risk the possibility of their turning up in the possession of an individual who will either undertake to burglarize your house or might pass them along to another individual for that same purpose.

Once an individual has a key and knows the door it fits, he or she is in a position to make the few preliminaries—known as "casing"—that will tell enough about your personal habits to know when is the best time to rob your house.

And criminals can be extremely clever in their timing. Again and again people have left their homes for a short interval—shopping, for example—and come back to a house turned into a shambles when a burglar with possibly an assistant has gone through it looking for valuables.

Although observant neighbors can be helpful in deterring or even spotting burglars in action, even they can't always know what's going on. An experienced burglar may put on a uniform and identify himself as an employee of a utility company, or show up at your door with a bundle of groceries, supposedly from your supermarket.

Another problem with lost keys: A clever operator can induce you to leave your house free and clear for his entrance. Having your keys and the address, he can eventually get your name and telephone number, call and tell you that he has found your keys at the supermarket, drug store, or wherever, and ask you to come pick them up. He can be in a phone booth with a view of your front door. As you leave to get your keys back, he moves in and cleans out your valuables.

Experts recommend separating house keys from car keys. Failing to do this might mean that if you park your car in a commercial garage, someone might make a duplicate of the keys and trace your address through the vehicle registration you probably carry in your car.

When you have extra keys made in a shop, watch the person at the lathe to see that an extra one isn't struck for the benefit of the person doing the job or a confederate.

Locks

No lock is completely burglar-proof. An experienced professional, given surprisingly little time, can open almost any lock on the market.

One apartment dweller felt she was perfectly safe because of a series of locks she had installed, plus a strip of galvanized channel iron that prevented the insertion of a bar between the door and the door frame.

To her astonishment, she came home one afternoon to find that her apartment had been burglarized. The ingenious criminal had simply jammed a crowbar between the center panel of the wooden door and broken it away from the rest of the door. With that large panel out, he didn't even have to open the locks but simply slipped through the large rectangular gap created by the removal of the panel.

But locks are a valuable deterrent. They buy time and they do make the would-be break-in artist have to work harder. It's not so much that criminals mind a bit of hard work, but they're likely to pass up the tough target for one that seems to offer less resistance.

Some of the more common types of household locks are described below.

COMMON SPRINGBOLT DOOR LOCK. Unfortunately, this one is easily pried open. This is the type of lock you see burglars and private eyes alike on TV opening by inserting a strip of plastic and pressing against the beveled face of the bolt.

DEADBOLTS. These come both horizontal and vertical, and are more effective than the springbolt. Just make sure that when you have a device of this kind installed, it extends at least one inch into the strike plate. Anything less might make it easy for an intruder to force.

DOUBLE-CYLINDER LOCKS. These have a cylinder on the inside and a cylinder on the outside. If you double-lock the door from the inside, a key is needed to permit you to open the lock and the door. The advantage of this device is that an intruder would also need a key to get in or out. If this kind of lock is installed in a glass-paneled door, an intruder can't break the glass and reach in and open the door from the inside. A key is still needed.

This type of lock does have one major disadvantage. In case of fire, it's possible that the people who don't know where the keys are—children or guests—might be trapped. Or if the flames cut you off from where you've put the key, you may not be able to open the door.

Some people overcome this drawback by locking a double-cylinder lock only when there's no one at home, leaving the key in the lock when there are people at home.

SLIDE BOLTS. Slide bolts are useful second locks for exterior doors. They are cheap and easy to install. Make sure you get a heavy style where the bolt is strong enough to offer real protection. Locate the device at a convenient height with the bolt projecting at least one inch into the door frame. Properly installed, the bolt should slide smoothly and easily.

CHAIN LOCKS. In many instances, they're a false security. They're often installed in such a way that a few short screws hold one or the other side of the unit. In that case, if this becomes the sole bar between your home and a burglar, the intruder has only to throw his full weight against the door to snap the lock.

PEEKING SYSTEMS.   You may not want to have your own TV monitor to see who's standing on your doorstep, but the simple fisheye lens in the center of your door is a wise investment that helps you look over anyone seeking entrance to your home.

Clever criminals can come up with many dodges for gaining entrance to a house or apartment. Never open the door to any would-be visitor you don't know. This should be true no matter how well dressed he or she may be. Never open the door to a stranger who "just wants a drink of water" or "would please like to use your phone." If the stranger seems to be genuinely in need of help, offer to make the phone call yourself.

If you've had the foresight to have a peephole installed, use it. If the caller is unknown to you, have him or her establish identity to your complete satisfaction. Ask for credentials or other documents. If an ID is waved in front of the peephole and you don't really see it, ask to have it slipped under the door. Don't be too concerned about hurting the caller's feelings. Your own self-protection is worth that and more. You can apologize later if you feel it's necessary.

Needless to say, the same measures that can make your front door impregnable should be used to secure a back door or any other walk-in entrances to your home.

And with the thought in mind that partial security is no security at all—an efficient burglar will always head for the easiest means of entry—don't be satisfied with burglar-proof doors and leave even a single window unprotected.

WINDOW LOCKS.   There are almost as many of these as there are locks for doors. Different windows require different devices.

A common lock for a double-hung window—that's the kind that slides up and down—is a fitting with a turnscrew that can be fastened to one half of the window and turned to pressure the other half in such a way as to jamb them both and make them relatively unmovable.

One do-it-yourself window lock for a double-hung window is easy to make: You drill a quarter-inch hole through the window sash and in the frame. Then insert a metal bolt or pin that will fit the hole from the sash into the frame. Now the window cannot be moved.

If you use this type of protection, you can make it easy to raise or lower the windows by drilling similar holes at two or three points in the frame.

A common but not particularly effective type of lock for the double-hung window is the half butterfly that locks the top of the bottom window to the bottom frame of the top one. A turn of the lever engages a strip of metal into the other part of the lock, which now prevents the window from being slid open. But this lock is susceptible to manipulation by a screwdriver or a similar tool. Also, because of the usually flimsy fastening of the parts to the window-frame, a pry bar or even a sharp, snapping yank can separate one or the other half of the lock.

In general, don't be satisfied with the *appearance* of safety. Three locks may not be safer than one, if each has some weakness that will not elude a criminal.

And, equally important, *use* the devices you have. Even if a chain lock is not the last word in protection, it's better than nothing at all. Don't open your door to a stranger unless the chain is in place. Use your peep-hole before responding to a ring, to give the individual the once-over. And, if in doubt, *don't* let a naturally unsuspicious nature lead you to assume that that nice-looking person, well groomed and smiling, couldn't be a thief.

Professional advice

If you own objects of value or if security is a special preoccupation, it would be wise to have a locksmith come in and make suggestions for securing the various entrances to your house or apartment.

Since these services and devices can be expensive, you may want to get more than one estimate. Also, rather than accepting what is recommended offhand, have the expert go into some explanation for the suggestions. Your objective is to get the most satisfactory protection at the lowest cost.

And if you shy at the thought of this type of professional help, a visit to your local hardware shop can also turn up some worthwhile guidance. Describe the sites for which you want locks, bolts, and so on, and have the clerk show you what's available and explain the advantages and disadvantages of each item.

One minor precaution can improve the quality of the help you get. In effect, go to the top. If you have a clerk who doesn't know much about these hardware items, ask for a more experienced one, or possibly the owner. Along with your purchases, ask for instructions on installation. In many cases you can do the installation procedures yourself; they're fairly simple. But if no one in your household has this kind of skill, perhaps a neighbor-artisan or a local maintenance man may be able to do the job.

Alarm systems

These are not necessarily costly. Some start at $50 but may go up to as high as $1,000. If you're considering such a system, make sure you get what you pay for. You don't want to become complacent because you're depending on a system that doesn't work or one that even a dumb burglar could circumvent. If you have a system that makes a lot of noise when it's set off, or sends a signal to the police or a private security firm, make sure that it's pretested and in working condition at all times.

If you have an alarm system advertise it, say the burglary experts. A decal or sign on your door or window stating, "This house is protected by . . ." definitely deters burglars.

Robert McDermott, once a New York City detective, more recently a top executive for the Holmes Security Corporation, offers this helpful information:

Most city apartment burglaries are done by picking locks; suburban entries are by force—breaking a door or a window. City robberies usually occur from one to three in the afternoon, Monday through Thursday. In the suburbs, nights and weekends are prime break-in times, especially in the summer. Burglars also find some situations most inviting: an empty garage, no lights on at night, a pileup of mail or newspapers or other deliveries that suggest that nobody's home. Avoiding each of these conditions may deter the would-be burglar.

INSURANCE COVERAGE

"Crime insurance isn't your first line of defense; it's your last!" So says Mel Mandell in his book on home security, *Being Safe.* True enough, nothing can really compensate for the disruption and upset of a burglarized home. And of course, trauma or physical injury can't be made to disappear even on payment of insurance—and we're not considering the extremes of rape, permanent injury, and death. However, the loss of physical assets—jewelry, artwork, electronic equipment, and so on—can be shattering without the alleviation of insurance. There is considerable variation in the type of insurance that's available and its cost, since, among other things, insurance is state regulated, although federal legislation has also been passed in some insurance areas. As some city dwellers know too well, it's difficult to obtain insurance in high-crime metropolitan districts.

But it's wise to be insurance-minded. Somehow the financial and emotional bite of a robbery is mitigated by someone handing over a check to cover losses, at least in part. Talk to an insurance agent or producer, and get an expert answer as to how much and what kind of coverage you can get.

BURGLAR-PROOFING QUESTIONNAIRE

This quiz can either increase your peace of mind, or guide you to take the steps that lead in that direction.

	Yes	*No*
1. Doors:		
a. sturdy, no glass panels near doorknob?	( )	( )
b. well-lighted outside to deny low visibility to house-breaker?	( )	( )
c. equipped with a peephole?	( )	( )
2. Door locks:		
a. at least two locks on each outside door?	( )	( )
b. at least one lock on each outside door of the deadbolt variety, or a "police" (bar-type) lock?	( )	( )
c. do you have a chain lock, installed properly?	( )	( )
3. Door keys:		
a. can you vouch for the responsibility of each person who has them?	( )	( )
b. are they kept separate from car keys, to prevent duplication?	( )	( )
c. if you were to lose your keys, would you replace locks—particularly if you have valuables among your possessions?	( )	( )
4. Windows:		
a. do you block visibility of windows (by using drapes, drawing blinds) with sight access from the street or other outside points?	( )	( )
b. do you have bars on windows with ladder or other physical access from outside?	( )	( )
c. do you always lock windows that have any possible access from outside—fire escapes, for example—when no one is at home, and lock windows in distant part of your apartment or home even when you are present?	( )	( )

5. Deliveries—
   a. keep deliveries made to your door to a minimum (use the package room of your apartment house, if there is one). ( ) ( )
   b. keep all but the delivery people you know outside the door, on the theory that the less familiar strangers are with your premises, the better. ( ) ( )
   c. don't open the door for unexpected deliveries, but ask to have packages left outside. (A standard mode of entry of a robber is to fake being a messenger.) ( ) ( )

6. Do you have a mutual surveillance pact with one or more of your neighbors, and if you haven't, will you try to arrange one, right now? (The benefits as well as the responsibilities are usually mutual.) ( ) ( )

7. Watchdog or mechanical or electrical alarm system: do you have a guardian, canine or otherwise, that can alert you to prowlers? If not, should you have? ( ) ( )

8. Are you wary:
   a. toward strangers who show up on your doorstep, even if they look neat and cleancut, and tell a persuasive story to justify your letting them into your home? ( ) ( )
   b. do you always use the chain lock when conversing with a caller you don't know? ( ) ( )

Every *"yes"* answer is a correct answer. Any questions not answered *"yes"* suggest a device or security practice you should inaugurate to increase your personal security. It goes without saying that every family member should observe precautions, in the best interests of security for all.

Of course, you have to be realistic. You can't become paranoid about home security, see every stranger who comes around as bent on breaking and entering, lose sleep worrying about whether the particular system of locks on your doors are the best available, or, as one man did after spending a considerable sum on a burglar system, develop the fear that his particular unit was a dud, and wouldn't work when he needed it.

But too many people are at the other extreme—they take no precautions, and are careless in their security practices. The best course is to do everything you reasonably can, then relax, because you've earned your peace of mind.

V

Enriching Your Life

14
PERSONAL
APPEARANCE

The two-character play, "The Gin Game," by D. L. Coburn, entranced Broadway audiences for an extended run. The characters, Fonsia Dorsey and Weller Martin, are in a nursing home where Weller has been a long-time resident and to which Fonsia comes as a new tenant. When we first see Weller Martin, a man in his seventies, he's dressed in baggy pants, an unpressed shirt, and his hair seems to have been combed with a rake. Then he meets Fonsia, and they soon become interested in one another.

By the second scene, Weller Martin is transformed. He's now wearing a pair of pressed pants, a shirt and attractive tan cardigan, and his hair, obviously having gotten his benign attention, lies neatly on his head. The result: Weller Martin now looks like a man in his early sixties. His bearing and appearance attest to a new youthfulness.

It shouldn't take a Broadway production to persuade people that personal appearance can be changed for the better—very much better—with comparatively little effort. Interestingly enough, some people who are perfectly willing to accept the principle, hesitate to apply it to themselves. Attention to appearance can make men and women look not only more attractive, but younger, more vital, and more interesting.

The question, "How old would you be if you didn't know how old you are?" is less a joke than it is a revelation. Your age is a self-image— the way you see yourself—and the way you see yourself influences the way you attend to your dress and grooming. How we deal with changes that occur in our appearance as we age influences not only the way others see us, but equally important, the way we see ourselves.

In our youth-oriented culture, aging—particularly its physical signs—has been taken as a fall from grace. Fortunately, this attitude is fading. We are not only retaining our youthfulness in a physical sense, but we are learning how to dress and groom ourselves to the same end. Accordingly, we can better our appearance at any age.

And some people are well able to appreciate mature attractiveness. Recently, a friend and I were walking along Fifth Avenue when we came abreast of three ladies, each with a cane and all probably in their early eighties. My companion said, "Look at that beautiful woman!" The first of the trio—they were all well-groomed—heard and turned to us. Her blue eyes were alert, her expression alive, and she smiled, out of sheer pleasure at hearing the compliment. No question, she *was* beautiful and she knew it.

Attractive people at any age look good because they do not let themselves look any other way. Some of them probably have to work harder at their looks than others, but anyone who is willing to make the effort can achieve the benefits. You want the self-confidence and satisfaction that come with a good appearance.

● *Dress*

No aspect of appearance conveys more about people than their clothes. Clothing is the first thing noticed about another person. And, because of this, lasting impressions are made. Clothing expresses social status, an individual's sense of style (or lack of it) and, most importantly, it shows how a person feels about himself or herself.

There is an idea at large that older people dress badly. The sad fact is, it is often true. Most people seem to hit a holding pattern during middle age that sets the pattern for the way that they dress for the rest of their lives. Perhaps the inertia is an effort to stay young, or a failure to remain flexible and change as circumstances suggest.

To dress well does not require a large and expensive wardrobe, but rather knowing in what you look and feel best. For some people this comes naturally, but for others it is an acquired ability. If you believe that being well dressed can add something to your retirement (it most definitely can), then taking the time to develop a well-coordinated, workable wardrobe can be a very worthwhile (and enjoyable) investment.

Enjoyable seems to be the key word in describing both the selection and the wearing of a well-planned wardrobe. In the years of retirement, a person has more time to devote to shopping and selecting clothing. For most women this attention to shopping is not a new experience, but to men it may seem strange. It really needn't be if you plan your shopping expedition carefully.

SHOPPING FOR CLOTHES

First of all, check your closet and see how you are set for the activities in which you are interested right now. And during this process, check on colors—what you have that will either mix or match with what you might buy. Then, make a list of the things you have that don't go with anything else you own, and then shop for the connecting pieces. For example, men, maybe you have a favorite blue suit that is great for dressy occasions, but stays in the closet at all other times. Look for a green or a blue-and-green plaid blazer that will go with the pants. Or, a pair of contrasting slacks—gray or light blue—that could go with the jacket.

Perhaps you women have a brown velvet suit that's fine for formal occasions, but you don't have many of them. Look for a tan or tweed jacket that would go with the skirt, or some coordinating sweaters or scarves.

Always have at hand a record of your complete measurements, as well as a list of your sizes in everything from gloves to pajamas.

If your spouse or friends have established themselves as good guides, call on them to accompany you on the clothes hunt. If not, take advantage of the shopping service offered by many large department stores, if you are unsure of your tastes and needs. These people are well trained and can be great time savers. The drawback is that the stores that can afford to have them are usually expensive. If you are hunting for a particular item, call first. Five minutes on the phone can save you a couple of hours of fruitless searching.

Consult clerks who seem to reflect a sense of style similar to your own. You have to talk with them and match their opinions with your own to judge. In making the decision to buy, let your head take a bigger share of responsibility than your emotions. Emotions change, but reason remains pretty much the same. And be sure that any clothing you choose fits comfortably. The best-looking slacks in the store won't be worn if they're too tight. If you are unsure about an item, leave it in the store and return later to see if you still want it.

Shop for bargains. Comparison shopping for clothing makes as much sense as comparison shopping for any other product. Clothes can be a sizable investment—get the most and best for your money.

It is unrealistic for older people to expect their clothing to fit as it used to. If your body is in peak form through proper exercise, nutrition, and attitude, physical changes may be slight and have little effect. For others, it can make a difference. Age tends to make people lose a bit in physical stature. This can be further exaggerated by poor posture. Then the individual must either make a special effort to improve his or her posture, or to purchase clothing that will hang correctly with the stoop. The body also may become heavier because of an unbalanced diet and the fact that older people need fewer calories. The ideal solution is to develop the best body shape possible through diet and exercise. Then choose clothing that deemphasizes extra weight and is not too tight for proper comfort.

Shoes may be a problem. Some people may need special footwear for comfort and health. Fortunately, the manufacturers of orthopedic shoes now make much more fashionable foot gear. All shoes should fit properly and give maximum comfort. There is never any question that function should come before form: older people's feet are more susceptible to corns, callouses, and bunions, all of which are caused or greatly aggravated by ill-fitting shoes.

USING COLOR TO ADVANTAGE

The color of clothing is a major factor in its attractiveness. Proper color can make the difference between being dressed and being well dressed. A problem that some older people may run into in choosing clothing is a loss of the ability to distinguish colors. This obviously affects their ability to mix and match colors. In such a case, ask for help in verifying your color choices.

In the bad old days, when a person passed some undefined age, he or she was expected to forsake all color in dress for drab blacks, grays, and browns. Unfortunately, this idea is still around, and most of the people who believe that older people should be subject to some special "color code" are the older people themselves. As with any other aspect of dressing, the choice of colors should depend on personal preference based on climate, purpose and style of clothing, and a sense of good taste.

GUIDELINES FOR WOMEN

For many women, selecting clothes can be a trial; for others it is a joy. But for all it is more difficult to find the appropriate clothes in later years.

Here are some ideas that can help.

The most important thing any garment should do is accent a woman's good points. If she has nice legs, she should show them off. If a color is flattering, it should be worn, no matter how bright or startling. For example, older women forget how receptive their natural coloring is to bright hues. Gray hair and light complexions look fantastic with vibrant reds, deep burgundys, and even bright pastels.

Also, clothing can play down a woman's negative aspects. If her upper arms are flabby, she would be wise to wear long sleeves. If her figure is not her strongest point, wise choice of colors and style can diminish the drawback. For example, many women who feel that their figures are not right for slacks are surprised by how slacks in colors such as black, dark green, and navy hide figure flaws.

A fad, no matter how appealing, should be approached with caution. Anything exaggerated such as low-cut or backless dresses, deep skirt slits, bare midriffs, or anything overly dramatic should usually be avoided. There are better and more mature and dignified ways to make one's presence felt. For example, well selected accessories—a striking pendant or an unusual hairstyle—can create a desired effect.

Usually, simple clothing looks best and is more versatile. The lines of simple, tailored clothing seem to particularly suit the older woman. A tailored tweed suit can enhance your dignity, or a simple black evening gown can create a sense of drama. In getting fashion information, don't rely on the fantasy of fashion magazines, but watch how other women interpret it—in the street and shops—then add your own originality and flair.

Blouses and skirts are the real staples of almost any woman's wardrobe. Women who are good shoppers purchase classically styled blouses in basic colors and good fabrics. They literally will last years. Advice from one knowledgeable dresser: "When you find a style that looks good, is versatile, and wears well, buy one in every color."

A well-made suit is one of the most versatile outfits a woman can own. It can be the "emergency kit" in any wardrobe. The dress is a little more difficult to use as a wardrobe builder because it is harder to change its look with accessories. However, it is still a "must." For daywear, a dress should be as basic as possible, yet not matronly nor severe. For evening, your taste is your limit. Here is one area where a woman can really indulge. No woman is ever too old to want to look glamorous—and never too old to *be* glamorous.

The coat is probably the single most expensive item in a woman's wardrobe. Versatility should be the most important factor. A woman should ask herself, "Can I wear this with a dress? With pants? Could I wear it out at night? Will it do all this and still provide the proper warmth?" If a coat can do all this, buy it. It will last several years.

To work a little versatility into the wardrobe, purchase jackets that will go with other outfits you already have. Here is where some trendiness can be indulged in.

Many older women still feel uncomfortable wearing pants, while others have adopted them as a uniform. In some cases, pants can be a foundation in any well-dressed woman's closet, affording ease of freedom. Pants should be well cut, long enough to cover the top of the shoe, and in a color flattering to the figure. There is also no reason an older woman should not wear a pair of well-cut jeans, now that they've become a uniform worldwide for males and females. The same standards apply to shorts should the climate dictate them.

GUIDELINES FOR MEN

Many men couldn't care less what they wear, or so they claim. The truth is, it's human nature to want to look good. For many the pretense of not caring is a coverup because men feel on shaky ground when it comes to selecting and coordinating clothing. But since the ability to choose and wear clothes well is an advantage and pleasure, why forego it?

Most men have come to depend on some sort of uniform as a wardrobe staple. This uniform may take the form of a gray flannel suit or the coveralls of a carpenter. Nothing will be more comfortable or dependable. And after years of this comfortable existence, it is difficult to have to rethink and then buy clothes for a different life. For example, a man who has spent his entire life encased in a three-piece suit can have problems feeling at ease in shorts and a golf shirt at one in the afternoon.

Another problem is that many men aren't shoppers. Whether by choice or by necessity, they have become dependent on the women in their lives to select and purchase their clothes. These men are at a disadvantage when it comes to selecting what to wear for a new life.

To be well dressed and able to navigate through a clothing store unassisted, a man needs information. Men's fashion magazines are one source, but the best information comes from just paying attention to what looks good on other men. The actual development of a wardrobe that will be practical and look good takes time and thought. The first consideration should be comfort. If a garment doesn't feel good, it will not be worn, and is a bad buy. Clothes should be bought with specific activities in mind. Along with comfort, the way clothes fit is important. The two do not always go hand in hand. A garment may be comfortable, but if it doesn't look as though it fits correctly, it will not enhance appearance.

Clothing of good quality will last longer, be much easier to care for, and give the man who wears it confidence that he looks good. If a person is a careful shopper, even the best clothing is no more expensive in the long run.

The clothes you select should be easy to care for. To lead a more relaxed life, maintenance of clothing should not become a major expense or time consumer. You should not expect anyone else to assume any unnecessary caretaking.

Hats are mainly a functional accessory these days—to keep your head warm in winter, cool in summer, dry in the rain, and so on. Keep trying them on in the store until you find one that is an appropriate shape and color you look good in.

Men can now indulge in a myriad of shirt styles. This freedom can cause problems. Rarely should a shirt other than the most basic be chosen unless a complete outfit is also being bought or the shirt can easily be coordinated with the existing wardrobe. With shirts a major consideration is upkeep. Unless you have the money for proper commercial laundering, select only "no-iron" shirts that can be machine laundered and dried at home, if possible

If you add a suit to your wardrobe, it is one area where for best value, conservatism should be the rule. For most any occasion, a basic dark blue or a dark narrow pinstripe suit is proper, and here is where the clothing dollar should be spent. A good basic suit of conservative cut can be one of the most versatile items in a man's wardrobe and will last for years. With such a suit, a dark blue blazer, and perhaps a light-colored blazer for warm weather, a man is well equipped for most occasions. For more formal events, renting is the best policy.

Trousers should be selected on the basis of fabric quality and fit. And no matter what a current fad dictates, trousers look best when they just cover the tops of your shoes.

For many men, retirement is the first time casual clothing has played a major role in their total wardrobe. As with all other facets of dressing, quality will show. Basically, the major criteria should be based on the activity involved. For real sports activities—golf, bicycle riding, or tennis—man-made fibers can be uncomfortable because they're generally less absorbent than natural fibers. Many older people will also need softer and more pliable fabrics than younger people to compensate for any loss of movement caused by disease or the effects of aging. Often garments made of knitted natural fabric can add the needed ease.

Shoes should be comfortable and durable. Suitability for wear with several outfits and in diverse situations should also be considered, but style should not be short-changed for the pleasure it affords. Again, quality shoes, although expensive, are a better investment than bargain shoes which may not fit properly, nor last.

In general, clothes should be bought with specific activities in mind. One way to check the completeness of your wardrobe, as well as to make sure that a change in the weather or a special event doesn't find you with "nothing to wear" is to look over what you've got from the viewpoint of both weather and activities—warm weather, cold, beachwear, "go to town" clothes, a party suit, jacket and slacks and so on.

● *Hygiene*

The basic part of any grooming routine is a bath or shower, which for almost everyone should be a daily experience. It's especially important for mature people since they shed many more dead layers of skin that need to be removed. Consider these moves to make the bath as effective and safe as possible:

1. Keep the bath water in the warm range. Water close to body temperature is a good standard. If it's too hot, the water can dry out your skin; water that is too cold can be a shock to your body.

2. If you prefer a shower, it can be more effective in cleansing and, since it takes less time, can be far less drying to your skin.

3. Bath oil keeps skin from becoming too dry from bathing.

4. Use as mild a soap as possible. Confine deodorant soap to the underarm area.

5. A bath brush, loofah, or polyester cleansing pad may be used periodically to remove accumulated dead skin cells.

6. Pat your body dry gently.

7. Immediately after drying is the best time to apply body lotion for maximum benefits of the moisturizer.

8. Apply deodorants, antiperspirants, antifungal sprays, powders, or any prescribed topical drugs immediately after your bath or shower.

9. During a bath or after a shower is also the best time to shave since hairs have been softened by a combination of water, heat, and steam.

● *Skin and Hair Care*

The idea that a few wrinkles or grey hairs destroy a person's appearance fortunately has lost credibility. Regardless of what cosmetics manufacturers would have us believe, there is no way to reverse the effects of aging. But there are things that can be done to make your skin as healthy as possible and to make it look its best.

SKIN

Women are more familiar with the benefits of skin care and so generally have healthier skin in later life than men the same age. Only recently have men realized the benefits of a well-planned skin-care program. For some men, it may be difficult to break the bad habits of a lifetime, or to get over the commonly held idea that a man need not—or should not—take care of his skin.

The unattractive things that can happen to the skin are due to a combination of factors. Some we have control over, others not. These factors can be sorted into some basic areas: Sun; the drying effects of climate, natural and manmade wear and tear from stretching of the skin; and the natural tissue breakdown caused by aging. Fortunately something can be done to minimize their effects.

Protection from the sun

Wear a protective sun-screen at all times. Some double as a moisturizer. Limit drastically the time you spend in the direct sunlight. Wear protective clothing and hats combined with a strong sun-screen, frequently applied, when you must be in the sun for extended periods.

Neither young nor old skin can take the punishment that goes with developing a dark tan. The best tan is no tan. Avoid the sun as much as possible—walk on the shady side of the street and always wear sunglasses outdoors. At the very least, the delicate and highly vulnerable area of skin around the eyes should be protected by a sunscreen and sunglasses whenever you're out on a sunny day.

The other most exposed area of the body, the hands, should also be protected with a sun-screen at all times. Age spots on the hands and arms are a direct result of exposure to the sun. Further protection for women can be had by choosing any makeup containing a sun-screen. For men there are bronzers and aftershave conditioners.

Protection from dryness

Using a moisturizer can protect your skin. The optimum time to apply it is right after cleansing. Also, a moisturizer should be applied before you use any hair dryer. Hot air will dry skin as well as hair.

Moisturizer should be gently patted on, not rubbed into the skin. Patting greatly reduces wear and tear on the skin. Replenish the moisturizer after every cleansing and at any time the face feels or appears dry. At night, when sleeping in an overheated or air-conditioned room, or in any very dry climate, a heavy moisture film or barrier product should be worn and don't forget the skin around the eyes. For those particularly prone to dry skin, a humidifier in the bedroom may be a partial solution.

Protection from stretching

When washing the face, use as little manipulation as possible. Your face doesn't need scrubbing. Washing using only the fingertips is a good method. And, when cleansing the face, avoid any pulling of the skin in the eye area. Any eye rubbing habit should also be broken.

Another culprit is smoking. Aside from being generally bad for the health, it causes many small wrinkles because of associated facial movements. (Just another good reason to quit.)

There are many, many skin care products on the market, some of which make exaggerated claims concerning the benefits they bring. Your doctor, pharmacist, or beauty consultant (at better department stores or hairdressers' establishments) can help guide you to the products best suited to your needs.

HAIR

The basic step in making hair look its best is to keep it clean.

Warnings against washing the hair often are exaggerated. There is hardly any way that washing can damage hair, even when washed daily, if a few precautions are taken.

The best rule to follow is to wash the hair as often as needed to keep it looking its best. If it does not hold the style you want, it needs washing. If there are even slight hints of oiliness, it needs washing. And if you suffer from dandruff, wash your hair long before the flakes dot your collar. Washing means more than just shampooing and then rinsing with water. Other important parts of a good hair program are conditioning, deep-conditioning, and drying.

Actually, the best way to treat gray hair is to first learn to live with it, and then turn it into an asset. Why would anyone prefer a head of mouse-brown hair to a mane of shimmering silver, white, or pewter? With most people it is the style, not the color, of their hair that looks dated. Well-styled hair means, for either sex, a precision, professional haircut that can be easily cared for at home, usually by means of frequent washings.

Routine Care

Following are some hair-care suggestions to help you keep looking your best.

1. Use a gentle shampoo since the hair actually doesn't get that dirty. It should also be acid balanced (the label will indicate) to keep the hair at its normal slightly acid level. A good shampoo for those with no special scalp problems is baby shampoo diluted one to one with water.

2. A quick lather followed by a thorough rinse is sufficient.

3. Few people have hair oily enough to need the second lather most manufacturers prescribe. It may only contribute to dry the hair and scalp.

4. The shampoo and rinse should be followed by the application of a conditioner to make the hair easier to comb when wet. It also adds emollients.

5. The conditioner, like your shampoo, should be acid balanced. Experiment with several brands as they tend to perform differently for different people. Follow the directions on the label closely and remove the conditioner thoroughly by a complete rinse.

6. Never brush your hair when it is wet. It is most vulnerable then and easily damaged or pulled out. A wide-toothed comb can help re-move excess water.

7. Your hair, especially if it tends to be very dry, may periodically need the added benefits of a deep-conditioner. These include hot oil, henna, and heavy creams, and usually need to be left on the hair for a longer period than a regular conditioner. You need to experiment with various products to see which work best for you.

8. If you have dandruff that regular shampooing does not keep in check, first consult a doctor to be sure it is not a skin disorder. If not, try using a specialized dandruff shampoo. If several of these are ineffective, you may need a prescription preparation. Your hair will still need a conditioner as dandruff is a skin problem, not a hair problem, and many dandruff shampoos tend to dry the hair.

Hair Loss

Hair loss is another early sign of aging for either sex, but is usually more dramatic in males. Baldness usually begins in men in the late twenties, and little can be done to prevent it when it is natural.

Baldness is generally inherited, and so is part of one's chromosomal makeup. However, it isn't always hereditary; it can be caused by disease, emotional trauma, dietary deficiencies, stress, allergic reactions, and skin disorders. Fortunately, when these conditions are corrected the hair will grow back.

An unfortunate aspect of balding and its effect on the appearance is the attempts (often futile) that men make to hide it. Throughout history remedies have been put forth that promised to prevent, cure, or hide baldness. For those who feel that covering up the problem is the best way to achieve their ideal appearance, several approaches are available:

HAIRPIECES. The oldest method of disguising baldness, other than worthless potions and ointments, has been the use of a toupée or hairpiece. If the hairpiece is a good one it can be virtually undetectable. A well made hairpiece is expensive and must be well taken care of for best results. Despite the claims that many manufacturers make, hairpieces do restrict their wearer's activities to some extent. It is still not possible or desirable to sleep, swim, shower, or perform other strenuous activity wearing a hairpiece. Hairpieces made of real or synthetic hair can give excellent results but if they do not look absolutely natural, reconsider the whole idea.

HAIRWEAVING. In hairweaving, human or synthetic hair is woven into a fiber net secured to existing hair. This produces a natural look and in no way restricts the activity of the wearer. As the wearer's own hair grows, the woven-in hair becomes looser and must be secured periodically. This requires the services of a skilled person and must be done in a salon or barbershop.

SURGERY. The most drastic "cures" for baldness are hair transplants or implants. In hair *transplanting*, plugs or hanks of about ten to twenty hairs are taken from the sides and back of the head and transplanted into the areas where hair is sparse. Several sessions (often painful) are required before enough hairs will have been transferred to make a real difference. Results are permanent and in some cases satisfactory. But cases of unpleasant consequences—notably infections—have proven real problems.

In a hair *implant*, tufts of artificial hair are surgically inserted into the bald areas of the scalp. As with a hair transplant, the results can be very natural, but as with other foreign objects, the body may reject the artificial hair. With either procedure there may be pain and both require a good deal of time. They are also expensive. As one ages, there is a greater risk of infection and other side effects that may occur with any kind of surgery.

The best way to deal with baldness may be to turn it into an asset by accepting it as a natural process. Some efforts at concealment just don't work. Nothing looks worse or exaggerates baldness more than long strands of hair on the sides of the head combed over the top to hide a bare pate. The next worse offense is wearing a hairpiece that is obviously a fake.

Consultation with a good barber or hair stylist can produce a haircut that will deemphasize baldness or, in some cases, emphasize it even more by incorporating it into one's style or look. Once a new style is decided upon, products such as shampoos containing proteins (which can plump up the hair shaft) can make the hair look thicker and therefore more abundant.

For some people—a very few—a radical hair cut or even total baldness can work to provide the image they feel best projects their personality. (Consider the cases of actors Yul Brynner and Telly Savalas.) Adding a well-styled and groomed beard and/or moustache can also be tried to balance the face and complement baldness.

To color or not . . .

Perhaps the most frequently considered hair treatment is dyeing or coloring. Graying is a natural sign of aging; the hair follicles stop producing the pigment that gives the hair its color. Graying can also change hair texture since the absence of pigment can leave it more brittle and less oily. Using a good hair conditioner solves this problem.

For those who intend to color the hair, here are some considerations. A professional does the job best. Do it yourself only if you're skilled with home dye products. No matter how skillful a coloring job is, it may be detectable, but still preferable, even though the hair looks slightly artificial.

Remember that solutions used for permanents and dyes can be irritating and may cause temporary hair loss if both are used at once. Always follow instructions to do a patch test on your forearm 48 hours before using on your hair or scalp. Some hair dyes have harsh ingredients and may cause allergic reactions—if you are prone to allergic responses, you should check with your dermatologist first.

A note of caution: hair dyes containing Diaminazole are suspected by the FDA of being carcinogens. Manufacturers have rushed to alter their formulas, in most cases replacing the suspect Diaminazole.

● *Cosmetics*

The best way to learn how to use makeup well is to consult a professional. Large hair salons and even department stores in large cities have trained makeup artists who (for a fee) will devise an individualized plan. In general, if you like the things that a salon does for your hair, you will also like what they can teach you about makeup. This method can be expensive, so get the most out of it. Ask many, many questions and have the makeup artist do a chart of all the techniques and products being used.

A less expensive method to educate yourself about makeup is to learn from the people behind the cosmetic counters in department stores. They are not just average sales personnel. The larger cosmetic companies spend millions of dollars every year to train them. Keep in mind that they are there to promote their company's products, but don't hesitate to ask questions. You'll find them helpful and knowledgeable.

One of the biggest stumbling blocks you'll face in choosing makeup is the amazing array of products. Once again, salespeople are more than happy to assist you in sampling their products. The one drawback is that you'll find the best-trained sales people work for the companies with the higher-priced lines. Remember that makeup products often have similar formulas and ingredients, regardless of price. And so it can be easy to find cheaper products that will closely match the more expensive ones. It is just a matter of experimenting.

No matter what your age, always select makeup that's compatible with your skin. If there is chance of an allergic reaction, first check the list of ingredients to see if there are any you're sensitive to. Some cosmetic firms have introduced product lines geared specifically to the needs of older women. These are usually unscented, devoid of any ingredients that may be irritating, and in general are much more gentle in their formulation.

Makeup for men has not retrogressed to the practices common in the seventeenth century, when gentlemen regularly resorted to the powder and rouge box. But today's adult males routinely use assists that make male cosmetics a multi-million dollar industry. Shaving creams, after-shave lotions, colognes, and underarm deodorants, have provided wives and sweethearts with a happy solution to birthday and Christmas presents, and satisfy male interest in grooming that exists in almost every bird and animal species.

● *Cosmetic Surgery*

In a recent year, over 1.5 million people underwent some form of cosmetic plastic surgery—face lifts, nose reshaping, breast reconstruction, and so on. Despite these statistics, it should not be forgotten that plastic surgery *is* surgery, and holds all the risks any surgery does. For adults, this means that the success and safety of any cosmetic surgery is related to their general health and age.

With cosmetic surgery, the psychological aspects must also be considered. No matter how prepared people may think they are, the end result may be a shock. No matter how much you may desire to alter the shape of your nose, bags under your eyes, or the sag of your breasts, it is hard to accept these changes. A great deal of thought, lengthy consultation with surgeons, and possibly a talk with a psychological counselor should be taken before a major decision is made.

Why is the operation wanted? If you have been considering surgery for a long while, or if the condition is very irksome, you may be ready. If, however, you want an operation just to follow the trend, or because someone you know has had successful surgery, more thought should go into the decision. A major problem is that expectations are generally set too high. Skillfully done cosmetic surgery helps you look better, but never flawless. People may only notice that you "look more rested," or that you just look better but they don't know why. It is not a question of erasing years but of repairing some of the damage done by aging. One reputable cosmetic surgeon tells his prospective patients, "Remember, the operation may change the way you look, but it will not solve any of the other problems that you may have in life." However, a successful face lift may help you have more confidence to deal with other problems. People may feel better about themselves. This, in turn, can enrich your retirement years.

SELECTING A SURGEON

An important task once corrective surgery has been decided upon is finding a qualified surgeon. You can ask your family physician for a recommendation or contact your local medical board. Another source is the American Society of Plastic and Reconstructive Surgeons (29 East Madison, Chicago, IL 60602.)

Make sure that any surgeon you consult is accredited by the American Board of Plastic Surgery. Your local medical board can give you this information.

A good plastic surgeon will interview you thoroughly concerning your general health, your reasons for seeking plastic surgery, and your mental ability to deal with the procedure and its results. He or she may also make sketches, take photographs, and make precise measurements of the area to be treated. An important factor in choosing the surgeon is the rapport the two of you are able to develop.

TYPES OF RECONSTRUCTION

Plastic surgery has progressed greatly in recent years. Virtually all of the body exterior can be altered by some form of plastic or reconstructive surgery. For people of retirement age, most plastic surgery is directed toward the facial area, mainly because it is one of the first parts of the body to be affected by age. There are many forms of cosmetic surgery.

Rhinoplasty, or nose reconstruction, can lengthen, shorten, change the general shape, or remove bumps or irregularities along the bridge of the nose.

Chin surgery can be performed to change the line of the chin, to remove excess fatty tissue, to build up the chin with silicone implants, and define the jaw line by tacking up slack jowls or by working on the jaw bone. The shape of the ears or the amount they stick out from the head can be corrected.

Mammoplasty is correction of the shape of the breasts, by implanting silicone to enlarge the breast or by removing breast tissue to reduce the breast. Sagging breasts can also be surgically corrected. Women who have had a cancerous breast removed may elect, in time, to have it reconstructed.

Rhytidectomy, or facelift, can reduce the sagging look that comes with age. The surgeon makes an incision from the temple to behind the ear and separates the skin from the underlying tissue. The loose skin is then pulled back to reduce sagging jowls and to soften wrinkles. The excess skin is them trimmed off and the incision sewn up. When done well and in moderation, results can be excellent. When the change sought is extreme, the result can be shocking to both the patient and friends. A key judgment must be made—jointly by doctor and patient— just how far to go. Another form of plastic surgery that is often done at the same time as the facelift is the blepharoplasty or eyelid surgery in which the fatty tissue and saggy skin that develops around the eyelid is removed in much the same way as a facelift.

Other measures that can prove effective in making wrinkles less apparent are dermabrasion and chemabrasion. Both of these procedures can remove scars and wrinkles. In both cases the idea is to remove the damaged skin so that new skin can replace it. In dermabrasion the skin is abraded with an electric wire brush or a steel burr; in chemabrasion the skin is removed by burning off the top layer with chemicals.

Many of the smaller operations can be performed in a doctor's office. Some major ones entail a series of operations and may take years to complete. The more common are not very complicated and involve only a relatively short recuperation.

The basic question for the would-be patient to answer: "Will what I get be worth what I am paying?" The cost of plastic surgery may be prohibitive. As surgery goes, plastic surgery *is* expensive. In some cases medical insurance may pay for some of the expenses, and plastic surgery is now deductible from your income tax in the same way as any medical or surgical expense.

Many people considering plastic surgery are concerned about whether the treatment will last. Just as people have different rates of aging, they also experience different time spans for cosmetic surgery. Some of the factors affecting this, are weight, age, whether you smoke or drink, how much your skin has been exposed to the sun or stretched and, very importantly, your emotional health. A facelift may retain its cosmetic qualities for anywhere from four to eight years. Following the advice of your doctor is the best way to insure that the results of plastic surgery will last as long as possible.

● *20-Point Personal Plan*

If you believe that a different appearance would make your life happier and more satisfying, then by all means work at making the changes you desire. Following is a list of twenty suggestions. Check the ones you would like to achieve and then get to work!

1. Lose weight.
2. Gain weight.
3. Develop an effective exercise plan and stick with it.
4. Work on developing some simple physical traits (habits?) that can vastly improve your looks—stand straight, smile, breathe properly, and so on.
5. Clean out your closet—get rid of things that no longer enhance your appearance whether because of color, style, fit, or attitude.
6. Do another closet cleaning to get rid of the things such as shoes that have always hurt, ties that are tattered, evening gowns from New Year's Eve 1952, and the like.
7. *Really* clean out your closet. Pitch out the whole uncoordinated mess and start from scratch. But know it will take time, money, and patience to do this.
8. If you wear hats, don't for a while. If you never wear one, buy a smart looking one and wear it.
9. Sign up for a series of professional skin treatments.
10. Consider a new hair color. Even better, have any gray highlighted.
11. Purchase some fashionable eyeglasses (tinted perhaps?) or

try contact lenses. Soft lenses are much more comfortable than the original hard ones.

    12. Go to your hairdresser or barber and treat yourself to the works.

    13. Make an appointment with a *new* hair stylist and let him or her choose a new look for you.

    14. If you're male, start a beard or moustache. If a woman, have a professional apply individual false eyelashes.

    15. Buy a really fun item of clothing or accessory. *Indulge.*

    16. Sign up at a health spa.

    17. If you are really serious about it, take the plunge and consult a plastic surgeon.

    18. Make an appointment with the best makeup artist in town.

    19. Select a new perfume, after-shave or cologne.

    20. Invest in a good wig or hairpiece.

One final thought: admire the good points of your appearance, add to them as far as possible, and make the most of them.

15
TRAVEL

The travel industry in recent years has experienced a virtual explosion. More and more people have the time, money, and inclination to go further and faster than ever before. And a large segment of the traveling population is composed of older people out to savor the experiences of flying or cruising and gaining the social, cultural, and historic benefits of the many corners of the world.

Because of the special importance of travel in the lives of retired people—and the often considerable cost involved—the subject is treated at some length. Whether you long to circle the globe or are delighted to drive two hours to spend a weekend at the beach, careful planning and thorough preparation can make your trip the true stuff of which dreams are made. For retirees, travel often represents the carrying out of plans nurtured for years but put off for lack of time, money, or interest—which may come in later life.

Some organizations offer services to older people, such as special trips catering to the preferences of this large group. Usually these services center on group tours—travel by air, sea, or land to one or more places with an array of attractions. But all the ingredients that make a trip memorable may exist in going only a short distance. A retired secretary I know who has lived in Brooklyn all her life now makes two trips a year, to a small resort in the Pocono mountains. She and her husband, a retired music teacher, "have the time of their lives." Their obvious enjoyment matches the pleasure and rewards of a world tour.

● *Developing Travel Goals*

"I love to travel. To me it's the most exhilarating activity in the world. . . ." Two people can make that statement and you'd be astonished at how different the images are that they have in mind.

For one person a wonderful trip means a luxury tour with gourmet meals, the best hotels, and "high society" people as fellow travelers.

To another traveler, the reasons for enjoyment go something like this: "I loved my trip to Florence. I did it in the cheapest possible way. I flew over in a group tour and stayed in a pensione that had been recommended by a friend. But the important thing was the beauty of the city itself. It's called a living museum and that's what it is . . . the paintings, the statues, the history. There were a dozen thrills a day going around to the museums. And the Uffizi . . . What an experience!"

You may be like the person who enjoys luxury travel or the one who loves the culture and history of a place. No matter what category or what your interests, the important thing is to pin down what *you* really want.

One travel agent told me, "I'll plan any kind of trip a customer wants. For example, I have one man who loves rugs and carpets and planned what I'd have to call 'an Oriental rug trip' for him." And then, laughing, she said, "I also have a customer (his name is Francis)—I'm very fond of him—and his interest seems to be adding new countries to his list. For example, I was talking to him about getting him from country X to country Y with a stopover at country Z. But Francis said, 'I've already been to Z. I don't want to go there.'"

Some people like the experience for its own sake; they enjoy moving about and seeing the world change before their eyes.

"The minute we landed in Morocco," Henry Paulsen of St. Paul says, "I knew I was in a different world. Everything was different: the people, their language, their dress, the streets. Camera in hand, I hesitated. Not because there was nothing to shoot. On the contrary, there was a picture in every direction." Others rhapsodize about the Grand Canyon and our country's many national and state parks.

IN SEARCH OF ONE'S ANCESTORS

Alex Hailey's book describing his adventures in tracing his ancestry back to its African beginnings created an upsurge of interest in geneaology. Everybody—or almost everybody—was doing it, finding deep pleasure and a sharpened self-identification in going back to lands of their ancestry. Are you satisfied with your appreciation of your family tree? Why let your family tree be a tree of ignorance rather than of knowledge?

A VISIT TO THE OLD COUNTRY

Pan Am ran a series of TV commercials showing people going back to the countries of their ancestors. Doing this can give you the thrill in many cases of seeing the places—and sometimes the people—you have heard relatives talking about in your younger years. And, of course, the "old country" need not mean England, Italy, or Denmark. For some New Yorkers it means a trip to Tucson, for some Californians, it means visiting Hadlyme, Connecticut.

But going back to Grandma's home town—or one's own—may have two possible outcomes. Morris Jacobson emigrated from a suburb of Riga, Latvia, with his family at the age of five. Some fifty years later, a man of some wealth and much nostalgia, he decided to go back. His three older sisters were beside themselves with excitement to hear what had happened. The night after his return they congregated in the Jacobson living room to be regaled with a description of the places and sights they so well remembered.

Morris looked at them and smiled ruefully: "Remember the river we played in as children? It's just a stream that I could throw a stone across. And the schloss! Remember, it used to stand as big as a mountain? It's a very small castle indeed. . . ."

On the other hand, Amy Wilson had been corresponding with cousins in Troon, Scotland, for years. When her husband died, her mother's sister, aged ninety-one, had her cousin Hugh write and ask her to come visit. With some misgivings—she didn't like to fly—she finally agreed and a date was set. The flight turned out to be exhilarating. After landing at Prestwick, she finally made it to the home of her Aunt Mary. Excited greetings were followed by a round of visits, events, and encounters that kept her in a happy whirl for two weeks—"the best two weeks of my life!" she told her friends on her return to Boston.

A SPECIAL YEARNING

Many people harbor for years an ambition to get to see a special place, undertake an activity special to a particular area. For history buff Leon Leonard it was to visit Corsica, Napoleon's birthplace. He loved the bleak beauty of an unusual island and the historical relics of his greatest personal hero. "Just think," he told friends, "in Calvi there was a plaque on a building, marked because Napoleon's *great-uncle* had lived there. And the people keep the spirit of the Little Corporal alive. Go into a shop and you see ballpoint pens with Napoleon's head capping the handle. . . ."

Visits to a Shaker village and the baseball Hall of Fame in Cooperstown add extra thrills for the buffs. This kind of dream trip, a realization of a fantasy, or the concretization of a dream, can belong to a sports person: "I've always wanted to play St. Andrews," says a confirmed golfer. An art lover: "I yearn to see the Rodin Museum in Paris." "I always wanted to visit Fortnum & Mason," says a gourmet. "What a thrill to be in a shop that has the most exotic foods—and in triplicate."

DEFINING YOUR OWN DREAM

Why not take advantage of a strong interest you have that can start you on a voyage of exploration and realization? Spend some time thinking about the things that give you your biggest thrills. Do you have an absorbing interest in Biblical history? How about a trip to the Biblical lands? Are you interested in marine life? Do you collect shells? Then why not consider a trip to the several ocean shores known as prime places for shell beach combing?

I talked to a friend of mine about his travel plans. "I've been in most of the usual places in Europe and Scandinavia. Not much interested in Africa or the Orient."

I asked, "Fred, aren't you a Gilbert and Sullivan buff?"

He agreed he was. I suggested, "How about a trip to London when the D'Oyly Carte company performs there? You could get tickets for each of the operas."

"I've been to London twice, but it was off season for the G & S company," Fred mused.

Fred took the trip. He sent back a postcard: "London is a different city from previous visits. Walked over the Hungerford Bridge to the National Theatre. Heard 'The Mikado,' 'Iolanthe' and 'Pirates of Pensance'. Next week, 'Yeoman of the Guard.' Bliss!"

A nature interest suggests travel. Talk to bird watchers and they grow lyrical over a trip to Wisconsin to see the yellow-headed blackbird and the marsh wren; or a visit to Hawk Mountain in Pennsylvania to view the soaring flight of hawks in mountain updrafts.

Similarly, rockhounds, people who collect geological specimens, find tremendous thrills in chipping away at outcroppings in areas known for the availability of interesting and, in some cases, valuable gemstones.

Perhaps you aren't a birdwatcher or a rockhound. Perhaps you haven't heretofore been interested in exploring woods for floral or plant specimens, or beaches for shells and marine relics. But many people, given the time, have developed interests like these and found travel a logical related activity, taking them to new places in an exciting and rewarding quest.

The results of a special-interest trip can be fantastic. Zero in on a particular interest, one associated with a particular place. Plan a trip to that place, at a time when that interest can be satisfied. Then go!

● *Saving Money*

The important development that has transformed travel from an activity of the rich to a common experience for the person of average means is, first of all, the relatively low cost of air fare, and second, the package tour. Competition, national and international, has affected air-line prices, and group travel is much less expensive than the same trip you might undertake on your own.

You may want to look into the package tours offered by the travel departments of service organizations. For example, the National Council of Senior Citizens has a travel service, as does the American Association of Retired Persons. Off-season tours, off-hours and off-day rates, and cheaper round-trip rates can slim down fares on bus, train, and plane.

DOUBLE OCCUPANCY

"X dollars per person, double occupancy." That's the way almost all group tours are billed. Husbands and wives or friends traveling together have a clear advantage not only on cruises but also in hotels, whose management traditionally dislikes singles because they can't get as much for a room.

Where does that leave the unattached person? The answer is, in the red—for a sizeable percentage of the tour cost. For example, a recent tour billed at $700 per person, double occupancy, cost a single person $950.

In some cases the tour sponsors will "match" singles. But one travel agent says, "Generally, only a minimum effort is made to pair people. One organization will help two people get together on the basis of whether they're smokers or nonsmokers, but once that affinity is established, the travelers either have to take their chances or establish a phone or correspondence contact to test compatibility."

"Among older people," says another agent, "you might have as many as ten to twelve single individuals in a group of forty." It's an encouraging percentage, suggesting that if you are a traveling single, you might be able to team up with another person, which will serve not only to lower the cost, but also might make the trip more pleasant. Of course, the best arrangement is to go with friends, or persuade a relative whose company you enjoy to join you.

PACKAGE TOURS

The lowest-cost trips are package deals for a minimum of three weeks or a multiple of three weeks. Currently, for example, one travel organization offers a three-week package tour of Spain's Costa del Sol, including airfare, a studio apartment in a condominium, entertainment—shows, movies, and even local professors lecturing on the history of the country—for $449. The same accommodations are available at $549 for six weeks.

The destinations of such tour packages often are warm-weather climates such as Costa del Sol (Spain's Mediterranean coast), Portugal, Greece, Tunis, Sorrento, Guadalajara in Mexico, Tangiers, Florida, and Hawaii. In recent years, Puerto Rico has been included in this low-cost travel arrangement.

There are many ways to cut down on costs. And you may feel freer to pursue these inexpensive trips if you accept the view of a veteran who spends about two months a year away from home. "There is no connection between enjoyment and what you pay." As a matter of fact, many people get extra satisfaction out of ending a description of a fun-filled, happy excursion with, "And it only cost me X dollars!"

Money is *always* an object. If you consult a travel agent, do two things: (1) give the top amount you want to spend to make sure you're being realistic, and (2) when tentative plans are being developed, ask: "Is there a cheaper way to get there, a less expensive hotel, or any frills that can be eliminated?"

A couple I know—inexperienced travelers in their late fifties—spent $1,400 on a ten-day stay in Bermuda. Recently they made a trip to St. Croix. Using the two suggestions above with their travel agent—a different one this time—their two-week stay came to under $1,000.

DISCOUNTS

One of the ways in which you can cut down on travel costs: many carriers give senior citizen discounts. While the availability and amount of the discounts tend to vary—and sometimes tend to appear and disappear according to circumstances that have to do with such factors as the season, level of passenger load, and attitude of the regulatory agencies—it's always worth checking. For example:

Currently, several airlines in the United States give discounts to people over 65. American Airlines offers a 40 percent discount on all flights within the U.S. Transworld Airlines—TWA—gives a one-third discount on its flights. In most cases, there is a time limit. TWA's offer is good within five days of flight time. Other airlines—United and Western, for instance—offer confirmed reservations no earlier than one calendar day before departure. Most discounts apply to the regular economy fares and multiple stopovers. In some cases there is no advance purchase restriction. In all cases, passengers claiming the senior citizen discount must show proof of age—a driver's license, passport, or birth certificate—when purchasing tickets.

And airlines are not the only fare discounters. Buses and railroad lines also may have discounts on particular trips. Contact the information offices and ask for their special discount travel offers—both in general, and for senior citizens.

SHOULDER- AND OFF-SEASON TRAVEL

Some people prefer to travel during the *"shoulder season"*—the few months before and after the peak season. For example, in Florida, April and May are the shoulder season after the winter rush; and about the middle of September to October is the preseason "shoulder." There are advantages that are gained by the people offering group tours in the shoulder season. One is that accommodations are more available than they will be during the height of the season. And second, and as a result of the first, rates are lower.

There are real bargains in the third season—*"off-season"* travel. For those who don't mind the bare beaches of Bermuda in January or February, swimming pools that are empty because of 60 degree temperatures, and sparsely-tenanted hotels, costs are lowest in the off-season. And some travelers report exciting and uncrowded trips—Moscow or Leningrad in winter, for example.

● *Travel Insurance*

Most travel brochures, discreetly or otherwise, suggest that you consider taking out "travel insurance." That phrase covers several specific types:

HEALTH. It is just as easy to become ill or have an accident on holiday as at home. Unfortunately, Medicare does not cover people outside the United States. Some companies describe their coverage as "Accidental death and specific loss benefits," and "Accident medical expense benefits." Your travel agent or travel line can suggest how to get the insurance. And, sorry to relate, some insurance companies have a "maximum issuing age"—sixty-eight in one case.

BAGGAGE. There is always the possibility of a bag or suitcase being misplaced or stolen during your trip. Few carriers or travel services take responsibility for lost or damaged luggage. Some policies cover both baggage and personal possessions.

TOUR INVESTMENT PROTECTION. Several things can happen in connection with a trip that may mean a loss of money.

If you become ill a week before departure time of a package tour, you may stand to lose some money. True, tour packages usually have a cancellation clause that supposedly permits a traveler to get out of the contract for any reason, from illness to simply a change of mind. However, in the average case any cancellation for less than thirty days—the number of days varies from package to package—yields only a partial return of your fare.

One recourse is to check the cancellation clause and if you are going to opt out, do it before the cancellation penalty period. The other option is to cover yourself by insurance. Just one additional caution—even if you have cancellation insurance, if it's for you and your spouse traveling together, and if one person gets sick, the other person may not be covered. Before buying, see if separate policies may not be advisable.

Another change of plan that can affect cost is the necessity to return home earlier or later than the return date specified. If this happens, the special group rate—for example, for a twenty-two- to forty-five-day excursion fare or an economy ticket—may require exchange for passage at a higher rate. For example, one traveler on a group tour to southern France had paid $495 for a three-week package. He had to pay $421 one-way economy fare from Nice to JFK.

● *Safety*

Insurance is usually a nice thing *not* to have to collect. Particularly in the case of auto travel, when injuries can be severe, it's better to play it safe than reap the benefits of the best insurance coverage.

And since many people depend on their cars for holidays, it's a wise move to stay with the safe road rather than the risky one. According to the National Safety Council, turnpikes are far safer than rural roads. Still, the figures indicate the need to stay alert, to drive defensively, and to *keep with the speed limits*—even on the turnpikes.

Here is how the National Safety Council recently rated the turnpikes in this country according to their incidence of fatalities:

Worst Turnpikes	*Fatal Accident Rate**
West Virginia Turnpike	4.3
Saw Mill River Parkway, N.Y.	3.3
Pennyrile Parkway, Ky.	2.5
Kansas Turnpike	2.3
Cumberland Parkway, Ky.	2.3
Daniel Boone Parkway, Ky.	2.2
Delaware Turnpike	1.9
Western Parkway, Ky.	1.9
Oklahoma Turnpike	1.5
Richmond-Petersburg Turnpike, Va.	1.4
Merritt-Wilbur Cross Parkways, Conn.	1.2
Massachusetts Turnpike	1.2
Ohio Turnpike	1.2
Garden State Parkway, N.J.	1.2
Atlantic City Expressway, N.J.	1.1
Kennedy Memorial Highway, Md.-Del.	1.1
New Jersey Turnpike	1.1

Best Turnpikes	*Fatal Accident Rate**
Dallas North Tollway, Texas	0.0
Maine Turnpike	0.0
Audubon Parkway, Ky.	0.0
Green River Parkway, Ky.	0.0
Purchase Parkway, Ky.	0.0
Dallas-Ft. Worth Turnpike, Texas	0.3
Hutchinson River Parkway, N.Y.	0.4
Florida Toll Roads	0.4

Best Turnpikes	Fatal Accident Rate*
Florida Turnpikes	0.5
Illinois Tollway	0.6
Pennsylvania Turnpike	0.6
Indiana East-West Toll Road	0.7
New York State Thruway	0.8
Connecticut Turnpike	0.9
Bluegrass Parkway, Ky.	1.0
Bert Combs Parkway, Ky.	1.0
New Hampshire Turnpike	1.0

*Based on 100 million vehicle miles. The rate for *all* turnpikes in 1976 was 1.0.

● *Mini-Vacations*

Some retirees take a different approach to travel. Rather than spending two or three weeks at one shot, they take a series of mini-vacations—three-and four-day trips to various locales, all within two hundred miles of home. Says one ambitious traveler: "In July my wife and I are camping out in a state park—that's for me. In August, it's the mountains and music. And in October, we're heading for some big city fun."

But a range of locales isn't the only benefit of mini-vacations. There are several others. For one thing, you can get ready to "take off" more easily. Usually you don't have to take so many clothes, which cuts down on the packing. A mini-vacation is also less of a strain; in a practical sense, there is less at stake. As for that home you're leaving, all you have to do is stop the newspaper delivery and ask a neighbor to take in the mail. A breeze compared to the more detailed preparations for the long vacation.

Then there is the matter of costs. Mini-vacations can be comparatively inexpensive. Limiting excursions to a two-hundred mile radius, for example, cuts down on the cost of to-and-from travel. And you can do off-season traveling. Not only will prices be lower, but if you are crowd-shy, you will also encounter fewer vacationers.

This doesn't mean that you have to, or should, cut down on things you really want to do. Travel often gives you an opportunity to live it up in ways you might not consider during the rest of the year, due to budget considerations. And a financial note: the costs of a series of mini-vacations can be spread out over the year. Mini-vacations can also provide a change of pace when it's most needed. It's nice to get away during the first hot days of summer, for example, but if you take all your time away from home then, you can't give in to that urge to get away during the fall or winter months.

Where will you go? You may have some ideas already, but consider the whole range of possibilities. Read the travel pages of your newspaper and send for the available free brochures. Consult your local library for information on places to visit within two hundred miles of your home. Write to the Chamber of Commerce in the areas you want to visit and request all the information available. Don't forget to sound out friends and neighbors. They may have some recommendations based on their own travel experiences.

● *Planning Your Trip*

Before sending in your deposit or hopping in the car, you should make sure that you have explored all the possibilities and decided on each element of your trip.

A PLANNING CHECKLIST

The following checklist can help you in this undertaking. If you are traveling with one or more companions, have each one also go through the list and then compare your selections.

HOW TO GO
( ) By one's self   ( ) Affinity group
( ) With companion(s)   ( ) Escorted tour
                           Other: _____

MEANS OF TRANSPORTATION
( ) Air   ( ) Car
( ) Train   ( ) Bike
( ) Bus   ( ) Motorcycle
( ) Ship   ( ) On foot
Other (Canoe, camper, and so on):_____

DESTINATION

( ) A new place
( ) A distant place
( ) Somewhere nearby
( ) Beach and ocean
( ) Countryside
( ) A city (London, San Francisco, New York)

( ) Woods, forest, and so on
( ) Lake country
( ) Farm
( ) Summer resort
( ) Winter resort
Other: _____

OBJECTIVES OF TRIP

( ) New experience
( ) Excitement, stimulation
( ) Rest and relaxation
( ) Communing with nature
( ) Socializing
( ) Cultural experience (drama, music, dance)

( ) Aesthetic experience (contemplating art, architecture, and so on)
( ) Share new experience with friend or spouse
( ) Education
Other: _____

ACTIVITIES

( ) Swimming, sun bathing
( ) Underwater sports: snorkeling, scuba diving, and so on
( ) Tennis, golf
( ) Winter sports: skiing, ice skating, etc.
( ) Boating
( ) Enjoying entertainment (theatre, night clubs)
( ) Visiting old friends or family
( ) Gourmet dining
( ) Gambling, horseracing
( ) Hiking

( ) Landscape painting
( ) Museums and galleries
( ) Visiting places of historic interest
( ) Visiting places of family interest
( ) Pursuing a personal interest or hobby (collecting antiques, gemstones, and so on)
( ) Shopping for anything from clothes to artworks
Other: _____

COST

( ) Little as possible
( ) Cost is no object
( ) Somewhere between the two extremes
( ) I can afford or want to spend $ _____

LENGTH OF TIME

( ) Long weekend
( ) 1 week
( ) 2 weeks
( ) 3 weeks
( ) a month or longer
Other: _____

BEST TIME TO GO

( ) Spring   ( ) Autumn

( ) Summer   ( ) Winter

Specifically when: _____

TYPE OF ACCOMMODATIONS

( ) Stay with friends or relatives   ( ) Resort complex

( ) Modest hotel(s)   ( ) Campsite

( ) Medium posh hotel(s)   ( ) Rent or swap private house or

( ) Luxury hotel(s)   apartment

( ) Motel: Average   ( ) Housekeeping cottage or guest

( ) Motel: luxury   house

Other: _____

Bob and Clare Idakus of Denver sat down together, and after comparing notes and discussing their ideas, checked off the following:

> *How to Go*—With companion
>
> *Means of Transportation*—Air
>
> *Destination*—A new place; a distant place; a city
>
> *Objectives of Trip*—New experience; excitement, stimulation; share new experience with spouse
>
> *Activities*—Live entertainment; gourmet dining; museums; shopping
>
> *Cost*—Somewhere between "as little as possible" and "cost is no object"
>
> *Length of Time*—2 weeks
>
> *Best Time to Go*—Autumn, first two weeks in September
>
> *Type of Accommodations*—Modest hotel

As a result of putting their ideas down on paper they were able to talk in terms of specific cities that provided the activities and satisfied the objectives of their trip. They discussed a number of places, and finally chose Florence. One factor for the final choice was that a neighbor had a sister living in Florence. This not only gave them the advantage of a contact there—someone with whom they spent several enjoyable days and evenings—but also, someone through whom they were able to arrange for tickets at the Opera, where they saw, of all things, a performance of *Boris Godunov* in Italian, but also, an evening of ballet, starring some of Italy's best dancers.

The checklist can also help you spot inconsistencies in your travel thinking and planning. For example, Ida Darnay of Toronto, used the planner and discovered that she had checked "Beach and ocean" under

Destination and "Cultural experience" under *Objectives*. She realized there were few beach-and-ocean locations that had a rich potential for culture. She rethought her wishes, and finally opted in favor of a divided trip, ten days on Cape Cod and ten days in Boston.

DEALING WITH TRAVEL PROFESSIONALS

It's important to understand something about the travel business. There are many organizations and individuals, some largely invisible, which play a major part in the travel business.

Wholesalers

These persons or organizations have the financial means and the clout to reserve large amounts of space on airplanes, cruise ships or in hotels. They deal in wholesale lots—obviously the rates to the wholesaler are less than to an individual traveler, and that is where their profit lies—selling through agents at a price high enough above their cost.

The wholesaler puts together a package including the three basics of a tour: transportation, hotel, and sightseeing (or an entertainment program of some kind). The wholesaler then advertises the package in print and by brochures sent to all possible points of distribution, including travel agents.

In some cases, the brochures are where the trouble starts. Everything from confusion about terms to major misrepresentations can give a distorted picture of what you will actually get for your money. For example, a brochure will show a bikini-clad girl and a bronzed giant in a pair of bathing shorts running down a sun-drenched and beautiful beach. The only trouble is, in the period that the tour is scheduled, the temperature on that particular beach hovers in the sixties and bathing is "out of season."

Travel Agents

The travel agent is the person who does the actual booking of your trip. If you are interested in a package tour, he or she will consult with you on a selection, then contact the wholesaler, who does everything including the airline ticketing. In some instances the agent may handle the tickets, particularly if you have some special requirement, but all of the reservations and confirmation of space have already been handled by the wholesaler. And usually, the price of the package tour as set by the wholesaler includes a commission to the travel agent.

However, when you want the agent's services for other than a package tour, he or she, once you've made your choice, will contact the airline, ship, or railroad, contact the hotels, arrange for you to be picked up by limousine at the airport to transport you to the hotel and take care of any reasonable services you want during your stay. Everything from a conducted tour to special admission for a limited-admission site, landmark, or point of interest will be arranged. A good agent will take care of all the details and supply you with a typewritten agenda that makes it easy for you to know almost hour-by-hour where you'll be and what you'll be doing. Or an agent may be asked only to take care of travel arrangements, if the traveler prefers to take care of housing or other requirements.

An agent can also develop a complete individualized package tour for you. While the cost will undoubtedly be higher than that of a wholesaler's package, you'll have the advantage of getting pretty nearly what you want.

The agent's profit lies in getting a percentage of whatever the bill comes to for the traveler. In other words, the agent is paid, let's say, 10 percent by the airline, hotel, and so on for the booking.

Travel agents can do you wrong two ways, one perhaps unintentional, the other unethical. An agent may recommend to you a vacation spot that's a personal favorite, although you may find it to be all wrong for you.

In some cases, there is an advantage to an agent to book a particular tour or a specific hotel. And don't forget—the agent is paid 10 percent of your booking by the carrier or hotel, so the higher your costs, the higher the agent's commission.

Choosing an agent

A good travel agent can make a great difference in how your trip turns out. Although there are always variables over which no agent could possibly have control, a knowledgeable, experienced travel expert can work wonders for you and your plans. If you don't already have an agent with whom you're satisfied, use guidelines like these to help select one.

RECOMMENDATIONS. An agent who has proved himself or herself by satisfactory service to someone you know is likely to do as well for you.

Try to get a little more from your friend than "I can recommend X wholeheartedly." Ask questions such as: What's the reason for the high esteem? What did the agent do that seemed to make the trip especially successful? How good was he or she at translating the traveler's wishes into specific suggestions? What guidance was provided that proved to be wise and helpful? Did the agent try to plan *your* ideal vacation or someone elses?

PERSONAL INTERVIEW. Make an appointment to meet face to face to discuss your plans. If the agent is "too busy" to see you, that's a bad sign. He or she probably is also too busy to serve you. If you get a turn-down of a request for an appointment, keep looking.

RAPPORT. "I wouldn't stick with the best travel agent in the business," says one much-traveled, seventy-year old woman, "if I didn't like her and our dealings weren't pleasant."

That mystical quality known as rapport is a great easer and improver of communication. When mutual good will is built up, any transaction is apt to go better. Since you have the choice, why not deal with someone with whom you've developed a pleasant and friendly feeling?

COMMUNICATION. Occasionally you find an agent who seems to have better ideas for where you should want to go than you do. This is a good individual to avoid. But the trouble may be difficulty in understanding; and it's even possible that part of the trouble is on your side. When talking to the agent, don't hold back on the basic facts that help the agent to be intelligent about your requirements. For example, be honest about the amount of money you want to spend. One agent told me: "A couple came in the other day and the husband informed me that his wife 'hates buses' and he 'loves luxury hotels.' But when it came to pricing out a tentative trip I had planned, it was obvious that their money ideas couldn't support their expensive tastes." Avoid misunderstanding by giving the agent some idea of anything else relevant, from the state of your health to the amount of time you want to devote to the trip.

Another important aspect of communication is the agent's ability to help you clarify your ideas. People may want to travel but be unsure of where they want to go, how they want to get there, how long they want to stay, and so on. In this situation, a misguided agent may pressure you to accept his or her ideas. A better agent will try to help you clarify your thinking. One way this can be done is to describe places and activities to which you can respond. For example, an agent might say, "There are two hotels I have in mind in Bermuda. One is very large, in the center of the island, and there's a great deal of activity; it's very social; people dress for dinner.

"The other place consists of a group of attractive cottages on and near the shore. There is a center building that has a very nice restaurant, a bar, a lobby with adjoining rooms in which you can play bridge with fellow guests, and so on. It's less expensive and more quiet. Which of these places comes closer to the kind of thing you would most enjoy?"

PHYSICAL SURROUNDINGS. There are some factors you *can't* use as a basis for selecting a travel agent. For example, a slick, plushy office may make you feel better, but it's no guarantee that the person you'll be dealing with is more expert or more helpful than someone in a less pretentious place. People who know the agency business say that no matter how big an agency is, you're still dealing with an individual agent—and that's the key factor. A small agency—a one-, two-, or three-person office, for example—can do as well for you as an outfit with more space and personnel, and you may get more personal attention.

AVOIDING PITFALLS

The Nassau County (New York State) Department of Consumer Affairs runs an active complaint bureau. Conversations with Tracy Brown, the person in charge of handling travel complaints, turned up information that can help the traveler avoid being bilked, fooled, or otherwise taken advantage of. Here's what Brown has to say:

"Ninety-nine percent of the complaints we get have to do with charters. One reason is that, because of the variety of services involved in package travel, the individual is at the mercy of all kinds of people, from hotel clerks to tour guides. And strangely enough, there seems to be no agency, governmental or otherwise, that can do much to improve matters."

It should be added that package tours are not limited to charter carriers. And while complaints about airline service tend to be more severe with charters, scheduled service comes in for its fair share of criticism too.

Unequal substitutions

Of course, when it comes to air travel itself, the Civil Aeronautics Board (CAB) controls the airlines and generally does a good job. The majority of complaints are not with the air portion of a trip but with the services involved in what is called the "land portion."

For example, Hatty Cooper and her friend Maddie Collins are on a package tour where they've been promised accommodations at the famous XYZ London Hotel. When they get to Heathrow Airport they're informed that the XYZ is booked solid.

"But that's impossible," protests Hatty Cooper. "The brochure plainly stated the XYZ Hotel."

"Yes, it did," says the representative, "but there's an asterisk with a footnote in fine print that says 'or similar accommodation'. . . ."

Hatty and Maddie are shuttled to the "similar" accommodation and first glance is sufficient to tell them it simply isn't on a par with the luxury hotel originally promised.

The advice from the experts is that when you're on a charter you often get the "similar accommodation" and it seldom matches the glowing description of the first choice. But you can ask your agent to confirm a booking to make sure you get what you ask—and pay—for. The charter-wise people will tell you, "Expect things to go wrong and you won't be upset—because they often do."

The Federal Trade Commission, after an intensive investigation, has pinned down a number of ways in which the package plan traveler is likely to be disillusioned by the bright exotica of the travel folders. The FTC points out disappointments like these: landing in the wrong city; finding booked lodgings incompletely furnished or otherwise deficient (in lighting, cleanliness, and so on); being bumped on a flight because of overbooking or other contingency; a "no-more-rooms-available" shrug from a hotel deskclerk; or a sudden change in plan, such as elimination of one part of the tour or visit to a particular site (if it's something you've counted on, it may be a major frustration).

And in some last-minute cases, rearrangements of an itinerary because of "special circumstances" may mean a higher fare or additional charge. Your best protection against these "bait and switch" tactics is a reputable wholesaler and your travel agent's assurance that if anything like that does occur, strenuous efforts will be made to recover any unscheduled charges you may have been forced to pay.

Poor scheduling

Another unfortunate practice of some charters is when the brochure says, "Enjoy a glorious week in glamorous Luxembourg"—or whatever—"Leave June 26—Return July 3." The simple arithmetic of the offer suggests a one-week tour. But what actually may happen is this. The plane is scheduled to leave at 11 P.M. There's a long delay due to mysterious circumstances and the plane finally leaves at 3:30 A.M. Notice that technically you've already lost one day.

There's a further delay because of a stop in Washington that no one told you about. Up in the air everything goes smoothly enough and finally you're down at the airport. Your group is then transported to the hotel and—happy to relate—it's one actually mentioned in the brochure. But things aren't quite as rosy as you could hope. The room isn't ready and won't be until three or four hours later. And finally, when you get into the room you discover that this so-called posh hotel may have some elegant chambers elsewhere, but the ones for charter passengers are undoubtedly the worst there are.

The point is, aside from the disappointing room, that a big chunk of a day has already been wasted—between the plane delay and the wait to get into the room. And that's a significant part of your one-week trip.

Mislabled accommodations

To most older Americans the word "first class" has an aura of quality and excellence. This reputation is based on travel as it used to be. These years "first class," when it relates to hotels, motels, and in some cases transportation facilities, is less than satisfactory. The reason is that "first class" is not a specific designation. It's just someone's opinion, or, even less reliable, someone's claim. And the fact is, while the meaning of "first class" has degenerated in this country, it has come to mean even less elsewhere. Many a startled traveler has found himself being ushered into what was described as a first class hotel in some small town. And while it might be the best the town affords, it may be just one or two cuts above what might be called a "fleabag" back home.

However, some countries do protect the traveler. Committed to a program of tourism for their country, they do maintain standards. These are emphasized not only in terms of accommodation on trains and buses but also by hotel ratings given by the government agency for tourism. Most European countries control costs in hotels and restaurants—Belgium, Holland, Italy, France, for example.

WHAT TO TAKE

What you take with you on your trip depends, of course, on how you go, where you go, when you go, and what you plan to do when you get there. The following general guidelines may help you decide what's best for you.

Luggage

This is obviously a highly individual consideration. Generally, there are two types of luggage: (1) hand luggage, usually one or two pieces at most, may be anything from a small suitcase to an oversize purse, and (2) heavy baggage, anything from steamer trunks to larger suitcases or garment bags. Some large bags—both hard and soft—either have wheels or can be made more mobile with the help of a temporary wheeled attachment.

There are two schools of thought on "soft"—fabric or foldable plastic—versus "hard"—leather, fabric-and-board construction. Favoring the former are lightness, low cost, and disposability. "I use a light-weight plastic garment bag for two or three trips, then toss it out and buy a new one," says one traveler.

Favoring the "hard" luggage are appearance and durability. Also, they tend to protect the contents and resist being pierced by collision with sharp points or edges in processing by baggage handlers.

Clothing

Selecting a travel wardrobe is often a guessing game. You try to anticipate all your needs and prepare for them. By and large, people take too much. But that is understandable. In some cases, you have to prepare for *all* six basic weather conditions: hot, moderate, and cold temperatures and either high or low humidity.

No attempt will be made here to suggest clothing lists of the two-evening-dress, four-changes-of-underwear variety. But these tips can help keep the packing problem within reasonable limits.

If you're traveling to Canada or cross-country in the U.S., try to get information on probable weather conditions. Ask your travel agent, a friend who has made the trip, or even the chamber of commerce of the locality about the normal range of weather and temperature in the area at the time of your visit.

Try to have one set of clothing for each expected situation. This choice will reflect not only the weather but also the things you expect to do. If you are going on a trip to the Grand Canyon, sturdy outdoor clothing is indicated. If you're coming to New York and expect to take in a Broadway show or the Metropolitan Opera, you may want to wear evening clothes for the occasion. All-purpose clothing or outfits that can be made dressy with a blouse or shirt and informal with a different item can be very useful. Also, synthetic fabrics make life easier. Underwear you can handwash and suits or dresses that come back from a cleaner looking brand new can cut down on the number of changes you need and the number of items you need pack.

Sundry personal items

It's *not* a good idea to take along expensive jewelry. However, if you want to take some pieces along don't pack them in your large suitcases. Carry them on your person or in hand luggage, and don't leave luggage unattended at any time (with or without jewelry). *Never* leave expensive items in your hotel room. Instead, ask the hotel management to keep valuables in their safety deposit box.

A blow dryer can save you time and money. If you dry your hair, ask the hairdresser or barber, if you'll be away for any length of time, to help you procure the hair coloring you are currently using. For a special formula, ask for a bottle, premixed. And if you go to a hairdresser, hand over the coloring, to be applied.

For the blow drier, electric shaver, or other electrical items, remember that if your travels will take you to places using a different type of electrical current, an adapter is necessary. Your agent can tell you if you'll need one, which your hardware store will probably be able to supply.

A popular travel item is the small electrical gadget that heats water or other liquids. You plug it in and hang the heater element inside the glass or other small container to make tea, coffee, or soup (from a mix) in your room.

"I live in the quietest suburb in the whole state of Minnesota," says one travel-prone pensioner. "But occasionally when I'm abroad, I get a noisy room, or one where the street lights glare. I prepare myself both with ear plugs and an eye-mask, and I'm all set." One person travels with a small, comfortable pillow—those in hotels are too puffy, too hard, or somehow just "not right." In your own case, review the items that make for your comfort and convenience that you can reasonably pack.

Pack an extra pair of eyeglasses, get a prescription from your eye doctor, or a copy of the prescription filled by the shop that supplied your glasses. And if sunglasses are advisable, particularly if you use prescription lenses, similar precautions are advisable.

Finally, various sizes of plastic bags—preferably of the see-through variety—can be a help in handling clothing and segregating certain items like shoes or a damp bathing suit. When unpacking and packing in hotels, particularly one or two day stopovers, it's easier to pop them in and out of luggage than the individual items.

Medical supplies

In addition to a small first-aid kit, do take along a headache remedy, lotion for bug bites, your own personal prescription drugs, plus prescriptions in case you run out, insect repellent, and antidiarrhea remedies (check your doctor). And in not-so-civilized areas, take along toilet paper, soap, and toilet seat covers. If you plan to do your own laundry, a small traveler's wash line, an iron, and laundry soap or detergent will be necessary.

Don't forget drugs you take regularly or those you might require occasionally—headache remedies, pain easers for a bad back, antacid tablets for an upset stomach. In your travels, you may have no trouble in getting suitable medicines, but you can't count on local sources. Foreign pharmaceutical items and practices are somewhat different from ours. And there may be no sure substitute for a prescription your doctor has given you.

Ann Jones, a travel writer for *The New York Times* suggests that a traveling personalized medicine kit contain aspirin, vitamins (especially B complex and C vitamins the body loses under stress), a standard antibiotic that your doctor should prescribe, soda mints or similar antacid, and Lomotil (the drug most commonly used for relief of diarrhea) for which your doctor may have to give you a prescription. And, depending on where your travels will take you, add antihistamines (for anything from bee bite to hay fever), salt tablets, quinine, or a snake-bite kit.

Ann Jones also suggests: "Write down all the aches and ailments you have suffered in the last six months and what you took to cure them." Add these remedies to your kit, and you've done a reasonable job of protecting yourself against normal health contingencies.

MEDICAL ASSISTANCE ABROAD

Getting sick in a foreign country can be an unsettling experience. Local doctors may speak no English, charge exorbitant fees, or be considerably less than reassuring. Even a cold or other minor ailment can become a problem if the traveler hasn't brought along appropriate medication, and local drugstores (if you can find one) don't carry American brands.

IAMAT

A new service offers a double safeguard against such contingencies. For $12, you can obtain a medical kit that contains medication for ten common travel illnesses, with explicit instructions for use, plus a membership in the International Association for Medical Assistance to Travelers (IAMAT).

The membership can be a most valuable service. IAMAT has established centers in key foreign cities throughout the world, which are listed in a directory provided to members. If you become ill, you call the listed center (usually in a major hospital) for the name of an internist or specialist from a panel of physicians on twenty-four-hour call. All participating doctors have professional qualifications which meet standards set by IAMAT, speak English or another common language, and have agreed to charge a standard fee for their services.

The medical kit (with the membership) can be purchased from Medi Kits, Inc., 25706 Elena Road, Los Altos Hills, California 94022. Membership in IAMAT can also be requested without buying the kit. It is free, since the organization is entirely supported by voluntary contributions. Write IAMAT, Suite 5620, 350 Fifth Avenue, New York, N.Y. 10001; telephone (212) 279-6465.

Medical ID card

The personal medical ID card, with your complete medical history on microfilm, can reduce the risks of emergency treatment if you get sick or have an accident while away from home. This is especially important if you have allergies or health problems that might go unrecognized by an unfamiliar physician. A microfilm insert on the wallet-size "MD" card provided by one service gives all vital data, such as previous operations, allergies, blood type, phone numbers of relatives to notify, home doctor, Blue Cross number, and so on. Conditions that should be known immediately, such as cardiac problems, diabetes, etc., are printed in readable type on the face of the card. If the emergency facility has no viewer for reading microfilm, the attending physician can call collect to a number on the back of the MD card, and personnel at the MD center will provide all the necessary information. Cost of an MD card is $5 plus $.50 postage. (Obtainable from Meridian Buying Corporation, 6 Silver Spring Road, Ridgefield, Connecticut 06877.)

Specialized health care

Health organizations that focus on a special ailment can be of help both before and during your trip. For example, Diabetes Travel Services Inc. offers counseling and information on all aspects of travel for diabetics including special tours and cruises. When you join ($15 for one year, $25 for a two-year membership), you receive a subscription to the DTS monthly newspaper, cruise and tour information, discounts on travel products, a diabetic ID Alert Card available in English and forty foreign languages, a hot-line phone number for assistance in an emergency travel situation or for fast help in planning travel, question-and-answer advice from the DTS advisory board composed of physicians and dietitians, and diabetic recipes. For further information, contact DTS at 349 East 52 Street, New York, N.Y. 10022; telephone (212) 751-1076.

If you are affiliated with other health organizations—heart, lung, kidney, and so on—contact their central office to see if they offer help similar to that supplied by DTS.

TRAVELING FOR THE HANDICAPPED

A physical handicap, even confinement to a wheelchair, should no longer keep anyone at home when they long to travel. A dear personal friend, immobilized by polio, made a world tour in his wheelchair—and enjoyed every minute of it. A second friend, Brooke Waring, a well-known painter, during a cruise to Europe fractured a bone in her leg in a tumble on shipboard. Her first thought was to return home. But Brooke and her husband Alan Lewis had counted heavily on the pleasures of the voyage. And so, fitted up with a cast and assisted by a wheelchair, they proceeded to enjoy the entire tour as planned:

"People were absolutely marvelous," Brooke says. "I was treated like royalty, perhaps even better. It was the most enjoyable trip ever."

Traveling in a wheelchair clearly has its inconveniences. And people with any infirmity that interferes with locomotion, sightseeing, and so on, may hesitate. But one thing is clear: those who want to travel, who respond to the siren song of distant shores and entrancing sights, will travel—no matter what.

And, important to note, help is available. Most transportation organizations—bus, train, plane—stand ready to offer aid to the handicapped—the frail, elderly, wheelchair travelers, and so on. Amtrak, our national railway system, offers its assistance this way:

"Amtrak encourages handicapped, elderly, and other passengers who need special assistance in stations or on board trains to call the toll-free reservations number in advance of travel. Whether it's assistance with baggage, with a wheelchair, boarding a train, or special food service, we will be better able to help you if we have advance notice of your travel plans."

Other lines and transportation companies offer similar help, if notified in advance.

OFFICIAL PAPERS

Passports

Some travelers keep their passports in a wallet along with cash—to insure constant alertness against theft or loss. As seasoned travelers know, losing a passport while abroad can bring a pleasant trip to a grinding halt while hectic efforts are made to get a replacement. Sometimes it seems as though direct intercession by the White House is the only way in which snarled red tape can be untangled.

If you have never had a U.S. passport and qualify for one, get an application from your local agency, or Passport Office, State Department, 1425 K Street, N.W., Washington, D.C. 20524. Fill it out and present it *in person* to the nearest State Department Passport Agency, or the Clerk of your County or State Court.

With the application, you need: (1) proof of citizenship—birth certificate, naturalization papers, or a previous U.S. passport; and (2) two photos, full face, three inches square. Ordinary snapshots are usually not acceptable. Since the procedure requires several weeks, it is best to apply well in advance of your trip.

You may renew a U.S. passport that is no more than eight years old through the mail. Ask for the special form (DSP-82 Pink Form) available for this purpose, and fill it out carefully, as directed.

It's a good idea to have individual passports, even if you're traveling with family members. In the event of separation—a spouse might have to return home on some urgent matter—obvious complications would result.

Even those with considerable travel experience may get careless. Before you start your trip, note your passport number and date of issue, and put this note in your purse, wallet, or other safe place. Don't pack your passport in a piece of luggage. If it gets lost, you have a passport problem, along with the rest of it. And don't leave your passport in your hotel room. It just isn't safe there. Keep your passport on your person or in your purse at all times—where it will be both safe and handy.

Visas

A visa is permission granted by a country to cross its borders. Many countries don't require one. For example, you can travel visaless through Western European countries. But Iron Curtain countries, and others—Asia and the Middle East—require them. To obtain a visa, apply to the nearest consular office of the country you intend to visit and they will explain their requirements. Usually, the process is a formality but does take time. Again, it's a good idea to get visa clearance well in advance.

Travel agents will acquaint you with visa requirements and usually will do the paperwork necessary to get one for you.

Vaccination certificates

In some cases, countries require visitors to have proof of immunizations against specific diseases. Your travel agent or the embassy of the destination country can tell you the requirements.

What happens when you come into the customs area is that there is a passport and baggage inspection and a health check. In the latter, the visitor isn't examined but his or her papers are proof of immunization against yellow fever, smallpox, and so on.

Currently, a smallpox vaccination certificate is no longer required when you *return* to the U.S., unless you have been in a place reporting smallpox in the previous two weeks. The same regulation holds for most European countries.

In some countries, certain types of shots are *desirable* but not mandatory. For example, in Israel, tetanus and typhus immunizations fall in this category. Again, ask your travel agent about the situation in the countries whose borders you will be crossing.

DEPARTURE CHECKLIST

Once you're ready to go, the following checklist can help you verify that none of the basic necessities of your trip will be left behind.

( ) Money. Cash, travelers checks, personal checks—make sure they're in your purse or pocket. Don't pack cash, or other valuables for that matter, in your large suitcase.

( ) Tickets. Do you have them, all of them, either in purse or pocket where they can be reached easily?

( ) Passport. Like your cash, it should be readily available, which means on your person or in your purse.

( ) Medicines and first aid. If you use special prescription drugs or hard-to-get items, local shops may not stock what you need. A small first-aid kit can save emergency dashing about.

( ) If you are a list-maker, noting clothing and accessories can help you make a final check to prevent forgetting important items. If lists aren't for you, check as you pack, using the time-season-activity test; do you have the items you need for morning and evening wear? hot or cool temperatures? all your snorkeling gear? etc.

( ) Gifts. Any presents you intend to take along to distribute to friends or relatives en route or at your destination.

( ) Have you notified those who should know what your schedule will be—how, where, and when you can be reached? If you haven't, reach for the phone and call the one person who can spread word to others.

( ) Newspaper delivery suspended?

( ) Have you arranged for mail either to be held at the Post Office or picked up by neighbors?

( ) Count your pieces of luggage. Are they all assembled? (Too many travelers go off, leaving one or more pieces forgotten in the bedroom, hall, and so on.)

( ) Does a trusted friend, relative, or neighbor have a house key in case of emergency?

( ) Have you arranged to have your plants watered—or boarded out?

( ) Have you arranged with a friend or neighbor to—
(1) Keep a watchful eye on your house?

(2) Take special measures that might be necessary—for example, get a plumber if a water pipe breaks, and so on?

( ) Gas off? People who use gas invariably wonder midway in their trip about this question. Reassure yourself one final time before you leave.

( ) Faucets checked? Possibly water turned off at main valve?

( ) Windows and doors closed and locked?

( ) All security measures, electrical and mechanical, in "on" position?

( ) All other gas and electric equipment—range, air conditioner, thermostat, etc.—in "off" position?

ALL ABOARD! It's a big planet out there. The experience of travel—new places, faces and things to do, adds spice to life, opportunities for collecting, making friends, and having something to tell the grandchildren about.

The expense needn't be large. Your adventure can be just as great in the next state as it would be across the oceans. Bon voyage!

16
ANOTHER JOB

426

Ideally, your retirement schedule will be packed with rewarding activities and so you may have neither the financial need nor interest in another job. But some people do feel that they want to go back to work.

Despite your dollar income—usually made up of pension and Social Security benefits—you find you need more money to maintain your standard of living, or to achieve adequate security for the future. For example: Belle and Phil Ampter, after Phil retired, felt that they were reasonably well off—even counting inflation. But their fortunes suddenly took a downward turn. A heating system in their house that they hoped would keep going for several years suddenly broke down and had to be replaced. Shortly thereafter, a daughter left her irresponsible husband. She turned to them for "temporary help," but the immediate effect was another dollar drain that left them short of cash. The decision for Phil to look for a job was reached by mutual agreement.

Another factor that may influence your thinking is that you may just feel better about yourself and things in general when you have a job. Some people—and they are usually those who have had successful careers—are lost without the settings, situations, and contacts of the workplace.

Grace Haller retired from the vice-presidency of an advertising agency. "The happiest day of my life," she assured her colleagues at her farewell celebration. "Of course, I hate to leave you all, but. . . ."

It seems that Grace Haller had miscalculated. The "happiest day of her life" ended up being the start of a highly uncomfortable year. No matter what she did in the way of passing time—and it included everything from frenetic socializing to a European tour—she ended up with the realization that she missed work too much not to want to return to it.

Some retirees plan a range of activities—perhaps concentrating on sports or a craft—but after some months or years, they aren't satisfied with their activity schedule. One obvious possibility—and it often turns out to be a satisfactory solution—is to get back into the job market, even if only part-time.

Les Borden was quite confident that the lifestyle and life schedule he had worked out for himself and his wife, Lucille, would keep them both happy and fulfilled. He had depended heavily on his near-professional golf game to give him a rewarding life.

But there was something lacking in the formula. Les realized that golf, as a *diversion* from work, was a fine relaxant as well as a source of pleasure, but as a major activity, it left him with a feeling of only partial satisfaction. Gradually, he became aware of a gap in his day-to-day life. He came to realize that the one thing that would really fill that gap with any degree of certainty was a job that would keep him busy, if not all week, at least a substantial part of it.

Working may also contribute a stabilizing element in your life that may prove to be essential. For example, I walked into a mid-Manhattan bookstore recently to make a purchase. The man at the cashier's desk was talking to a customer as I walked up with the volume I wanted, and I was struck by the cashier's pleasant, interested manner. When my turn came, he was equally attentive.

"How come you're enjoying your job so much?" I asked, a shot in the dark we all indulge in every once in a while to make contact. The cashier smiled, came around the counter—I was the only customer at the moment—and said: "I retired about three years ago. My wife died two years ago, and I found that I spent most of my time watching TV and drinking. When I got to the bottle-a-day level, I decided I'd better do something."

"Were you in the book business before?"

"No, I was general sales manager for a chemical company. But I've always liked books, I applied for a job here, got one, and I love it."

"Great," I said. "I love success stories." We shook hands warmly.

In some cases, as was true of the cashier, a job is therapy, a constructive factor that eliminates the devils summoned by idleness and apathy.

Please note that this chapter speaks in terms of a "job" rather than in the more ambitious phrase "second career." The emphasis is on "a job" because, for most people, this is the practical light in which the possibility of getting back into the job market is viewed.

There are some who may see in retirement merely a milestone

marking a switch from one phase of employment to another. This is perfectly legitimate—if it's what you desire. For some individuals, the world of work holds satisfactions and rewards not easily duplicated by any other type of activity. For this group, career planning may indeed go into a new phase on retirement. The suggestions and considerations made here will apply to either the job hunter—temporary job, part-time job, or whatever—as well as those who continue to look to the world of work for a major satisfaction.

● *How Working May Affect Social Security Payments*

Just one reminder if you're thinking about wage-earning after retirement: an individual drawing Social Security benefits may earn $4,000 a year without any decrease in payout. But over that amount, every two dollars earned means a one-dollar deduction. (That $4,000 figure is subject to change, year to year. Check your local Social Security office for the latest update.)

Here is fuller information, as supplied by the Department of Health, Education and Welfare, Social Security Administration:

Because Social Security checks are intended to replace, in part, lost earnings, monthly payments generally are reduced if earnings go above a certain level in any year. The measure used to decide whether benefits must be reduced or stopped due to earnings is called the "retirement test."

The retirement test applies to everyone who gets Social Security checks except those who are 72 or older. At 72 a worker can get checks regardless of the amount of his or her earnings (70 starting in 1982).

Your right to hospital and medical insurance under Medicare is not affected by your earnings.

You don't have to retire completely to get Social Security checks. But if you expect to work while getting benefits, it's important to know how your earnings will affect your Social Security checks.

If you are under 72 (age 70 starting in 1982) at least part of a year and expect to earn over a certain amount, some or all of your Social Security checks should be withheld. In this way, you won't have to pay back money later. Then if your earnings drop, benefits can be started again.

In general, you can receive all benefits due you for the year if your earnings do not exceed the annual exempt amount. This limit in 1979 was $4,500 for people who are 65 and over by the end of the year, and $3,480 for people under 65. If your earnings go over the annual amount, $1 in benefits is withheld for each $2 of earnings above the limit.

If you earn more than the exempt amount. Even if your earnings are well above the exempt amount for the year ($3,240 if under 65 in 1978, or $4,000 if 65 through 71) some Social Security checks may still be payable. The basic rule is that $1 in benefits is withheld for each $2 you earn above the exempt amount.

If you work as an employee. It doesn't matter when the wages are actually paid in determining whether you can get a benefit for a particular month. The controlling factor is when you *earn* the money. If you're *self-employed,* the main consideration is whether you are active in your business and performing "substantial services."

Unlike employees, who usually know how much they have earned in each month, self-employed people often do not know whether they will have a profit or a loss until the end of the year. The money a self-employed person receives from his or her business in a given month may vary considerably and often may be for work during some earlier month.

For these reasons, we don't use a monthly earnings figure to decide whether a self-employed person is "retired." Instead, if you're self-employed, the law considers you "retired" if you don't perform "substantial services."

What "substantial services" are. Our decision as to whether your services are substantial depends on several factors: the amount of time you devote to your business; the kind of work you do; and how the work compares with what you did in the past.

Checks for a family. If you are getting checks as a retired worker, your total family benefits may be affected because of your earnings. This means we'll withhold not only checks payable to you, but also those payable to your family.

Earnings for the whole year count. You must count your earnings for the whole year in figuring the benefits due you for that year. For most people, this means January through December.

● *Identifying Your Capabilities*

The world is full of activities that delight some people and are abhorred by others. Consider selling, for example. Many people love it—they find it stimulating, challenging, a good way to meet people.

Others shrivel up at the mere thought of having to confront someone and, as they see it, "beg" for an order, or try to "wheedle, cajole, or persuade" a customer to buy.

Before you can identify the activity that will be right for you, you have to do some self-analysis. It's easy to voice the key questions: "What are my major interests?" "What do I really *like* to do?" It's *not* easy, however, to answer these deceptively simple but meaningful queries. However, there is a second order of questions easier to answer, that can lead you to the same self-understanding and self-evaluation: "Shall I look for a job in the field I left when I retired?" If the answer is no, try these: "What kinds of activities give me my biggest kicks?" "What do I do that gives me my greatest feelings of accomplishment?"

Here's a practical question that may shortcut your decision: "What work could I do that would pay me the most for the smallest time expenditure?" And here's a bit of fantasizing that can be helpful: "If I could do anything in the world I wanted, what would that be?"

Your gut feeling about the future may steer you away from past interests, even be at variance with things that preoccupy your present. Consider the case of Jack and Pearl De Camp

Jack had been a teacher, specializing in working with retarded and brain-damaged children. Pearl was a social worker, employed by a private agency to counsel clients.

When Jack faced retirement, he and Pearl had a series of talks about their future. Pearl wanted to continue working, if not in her present job, in one similar, and Jack also felt he wanted to stay involved with helping people.

Out of their conversations eventually came an idea—"Pretty far fetched, you know," Pearl said, and Jack agreed—that they try to start a mental health center in their county. They had enough friends and neighbors in difficulties to make them realize how crucial emotional problems were in the lives of people.

After months of interviews, following up leads, getting various professional opinions, they were able to start things moving. Psychiatrists practicing in the area, one of high standing in his professional association, became interested. Local civic and political figures became involved. Eventually they started getting funding—some from philanthropic and some from government sources. And a county-wide mental health organization was started in a small private home donated by a retired 80-year old doctor. It was perfectly natural that Jack was asked to be the administrative head, and Pearl became assistant to the chief psychiatrist.

The De Camps, as a result of good thinking and hard work, had made a highly successful work transplant, with both monetary and emotional rewards.

Try to avoid jumping from the frying pan into the fire represented by the phrase, "just a job." If the activity you're seeking is intended primarily to earn money, look for the most remunerative opening you can find. But if you can be more choosey, and your essential purpose is to get into something that will mean high levels of satisfaction, cater to your deeper interests and abilities. If you feel drawn towards politics or a more serene but absorbing field like museum work, follow up your instinct.

Some people find that completing the phrase, "The perfect job for me would be . . ." helps to sharpen their thinking. Here are some answers that people have supplied:

- working outdoors
- working with animals
- using craft skills
- use of an interest in antiques
- working with people in trouble
- some aspect of government
- contact with education of the handicapped
- anything in which I'm in charge of my own turf

● *Exploring Job Possibilities*

At the outset, you must be realistic about your chances in the job market, neither over- nor underestimating the odds in your favor.

On the less positive side, in the average case, older workers must spend more time job-hunting than those in the younger age brackets. A major reason is that business today is increasingly technical—computerized, automated, and machine-dominated. Many jobs require skilled, professional, and specialized workers with recent training.

However, many things work for you. A survey by the National Association of Manufacturers indicates that older workers do better on the job than younger ones. They stay at the same job longer, their attendance is better, and their safety record is superior. Moreover, you have given good and long service to one or more employers. In the course of your career, you have learned to work in an organization, team up with others, and direct your efforts toward group goals. You wouldn't have made it through to retirement age if you weren't considered an effective employee—at whatever level. Your age and your sense of responsibility should be plus factors to the average employer. In your life on the job you have acquired many capabilities. These include the specifics of past jobs—if you were in the purchasing department, you understand the ins and outs of working with suppliers; if you were a typist you know not only how to make a typewriter produce, but understand office routines. Also, you understand the limits and obligations of the world of work.

These assets can mean a great deal to an employer, who in hiring is seeking many of the qualities not yet achieved by the young.

Older people have been helped by legislation as well as by social change to have a better chance for employment. Fewer areas are off limits for the over-forty group. Here are types of opportunities to consider:

PART-TIME WORK

Part-time work is becoming more common on the business scene. Some authorities believe that the trend for the next two decades will be toward more part-time employment. The practice is already well established—currently, about 20.5 million people, or one out of every five employed Americans, work less than thirty-five hours a week.

The workweek is being sliced up horizontally, vertically, and in various other bits and pieces. This way, employers can attract qualified people that might not want full-time jobs. There are other mutual benefits. The Labor Department reports that part-time employees generally provide higher productivity, greater loyalty, and less absenteeism than full-time employees. Employees like the less demanding, more flexible arrangement.

One 58-year old woman operates paper-cutting equipment in a bindery. Her hours are 9 A.M. to 2 P.M. and allow her to be home when her 8-year-old grandson returns from school. She is much happier than when she was a full-time department-store clerk.

A 78-year-old former postal supervisor in Chicago has a three-day-week job as bank clerk. He has been at it for the last twelve years and asserts the job has saved his health and marriage. "My wife got tired of having me around the house," he says. "She said, 'If you don't get out soon, I will.'" In the Continental Illinois National Bank & Trust Co., where the retiree works, one-third of the 1,500 part-timers are over 65.

In some cases, people may work one, two, three or four days a week. Other schedules are for five days, even six, but mornings only or afternoons only. And thanks to a concept called "Flextime," employees are permitted to work staggered hours. For example, an employee may come to work six hours a day—any six hours—within set limits, such as 8 A.M. to 6 P.M. This flexibility makes it possible for employees to arrange their days to include everything from convenient shopping to golf, hiking, or whatever.

TEMPORARY WORK

"Temps"—as people who are hired for limited periods are called—originated in the office field. Peaks of workload during the month—billing, for example—required extra help for a few days or weeks. It became obvious that other business needs clearly could be met by temporary workers. Now companies hire temporary help for everything from selling to research to maintenance.

Another need for temps is created by regular employees out on vacation, out sick, or on a leave of absence. It is the vacation-caused temporary vacancy that may create a special opportunity: apply for temporary work in medium to large companies, where a wave of vacationers may leave departments understaffed.

People prefer temporary work for a number of reasons. They want to get back to working after a long hiatus, but they want to do it toe-in-the-water style, to see how they like it. Or, they may want to try a variety of jobs, as a means of zeroing in on a final choice.

FULL-TIME WORK

Retirees have been swelling the ranks of full-time employees. The reasons for the increase range from the need to increase family income because of inflation, to the antidiscrimination laws that impose penalties on employers for failing to hire qualified people, regardless of age.

Recent legislation requiring employers to give seniors equal treatment has caused an upheaval in business tradition, and seniors have come out ahead. Cold objectivity requires a qualification: despite all the publicizing of victories of minorities in the world of work, it must be admitted that there is still considerable tokenism.

Companies, either fined for lack of "affirmative action"—that is, rosters that actually reflect equal hiring, promotion, and pay opportunities for minorities—or fearful that they would be, have bent over backwards to prove their fair-mindedness. This has meant better opportunity for all minorities, including senior citizens. Not only have more seniors been hired, but they have been given equal treatment in terms of training and even opportunity for advancement.

YOUR OWN BUSINESS

Many men and women dream of having their own business—being the only boss in an enterprise they enjoy and, best of all, being financially independent.

Why not? Unfortunately, the question is not merely rhetorical. There can be strong reasons for going into business for yourself—and for *not* doing so. Many have—successfully. But others have found the going rough, frustrating, and in the end, financially devastating.

The U.S. Small Business Administration (SBA) lists ten characteristics it feels could help you make it on your own:

1. initiative
2. a positive, pleasant attitude
3. leadership
4. organizing ability
5. industry
6. responsibility
7. the ability to make good decisions
8. sincerity
9. perseverance
10. high level of energy

To these ten, people who have been through the mill would add: luck, willingness to work harder for yourself than you would for anyone else, and a fallback position, so that if things don't pan out, you won't be either emotionally or financially crushed.

At the outset, you have to face up to some discouraging statistics. According to the SBA, approximately 20 percent of small businesses fold in the first year, 20 percent fail in the second, and another 10 percent drop out during the third year.

Explaining the high mortality rate in detail would mean producing a complete handbook on how to run a small business, which is beyond this context. But there are major reasons for failure that can be considered as warning sings.

POOR MANAGEMENT. The person or people undertaking the business are unfamiliar with standard practices, don't know how to read a profit and loss statement, don't really grasp the concept of effective and economic operation.

LACK OF CAPITAL. Either because of overoptimism or failure to assess needs, people start businesses with insufficient funds. After laying out the money for the startup, the entrepreneur may find almost all available funds have been used and there's nothing in reserve to keep the business going for a year or two.

IMPROPER PURCHASING. In some businesses—such as running a clothing shop—purchasing the right types and quantities of clothing may mean that you have a store full of inventory that your customers don't want or that you have failed to stock adequate supplies of what is wanted. Part of business knowhow is an instinct for what will sell and what won't.

IMPROPER MARKETING. The ability to attract and hold customers requires a range of skills from advertising to pricing display and maintaining good relations with the customers when they do appear.

POOR LOCATION. You can have a lot going for you in the way of attractive well displayed stock, and you may have the most pleasant sales manner, however, if your shop is outside the heavily travelled parts of town, if you're too close to established competition, your chances for success are considerably lessened. A low-rent location is usually a poor bargain for a retailer.

One irony about running your own business: any losses you suffer for whatever reason, you must stand alone. But Uncle Sam is always ready to share as a partner in your profits.

At the end of this chapter you will find more information about resources available to you if you're interested in starting your own business.

POLITICS

At the local level, this is pretty much a wide open field. Anyone who wants to get involved in partisan politics—especially near election time— just has to get in touch with the people at the headquarters of the party of his or her choice.

You may be interested in serving in local government. Some small towns are rather one-sided politically—either with a heavy Democratic or Republican majority—so that participating in the government means becoming active in the majority party. Occasionally, one finds a local government that is more or less nonpartisan. But at any rate, there are nonpaying jobs that can give you experience you may want—serving on a zoning board, or some other appointed post.

Of course, if you want to run for elective office—a town trustee, or member of the governing board, called by whatever name—then you must work toward being nominated by one of the local political groups. This could conceivably lead to election to a post with salary.

SPORTS

The "physical" people also have talents on which to base some productive, satisfying, perhaps even remunerative activity. Tennis, golf, swimming, can be a major interest for those with a high level of ability gained over many years of practice and experience. Becoming a sports "pro" at a local club may lie within the realm of possibility for the qualified skiier, tennis player or golfer who is also a good teacher.

And team sports are not ruled out by any means. Coaches, trainers, other aiders-and-abetters of basketball, softball, baseball, even football, groups can find an area of interest, excitement, and satisfaction in working with young people.

VOLUNTEER WORK

Every community that has a hospital or a home for the aged, the blind, or the infirm can usually use all the volunteers it can get. In some cases, there are organizations that directly sponsor volunteers—the Red Cross, for example. And in such cases, the organizations will sometimes provide the background or technical training of a particular kind to equip the volunteer for a specific duty.

Caring for the sick, the infirm, and the needy, may not be everyone's cup of tea, but many of those involved in this work find it to be rewarding and enriching.

For many, the appeal and potential rewards of volunteer work are great. You should, however, choose your work carefully in order to find the area in which your particular talents are best put to use.

The possibilities are vast. Hospitals, churches, community organizations, school-affiliated activities—they all can use you. But be selfish in this one decision: choose a field for which you have a special affinity.

Investigate the possibilities before applying. Visit the premises, talk to one or more administrators, communicate your needs or interests, and see to what extent the organization can meet them.

Volunteers sometimes step right into trouble. They start with high hopes that are soon shattered. Said one disheartened man: "I wanted to work with a local ecological group. I'm a chemist by training, and thought I might be able to do some planning or investigation. When I turned up on my first day, I was put to work cleaning up an office and putting stamps on envelopes. Sure that kind of work has to be done. But I didn't have it in mind for me." Discuss in advance the type of job or jobs you would like—and when you actually show up make sure that the administrator puts you in the spot that was agreed on.

Both for your sake as well as for the organization's make sure there is a fairly clear understanding about the time you are offering. This doesn't mean an inflexible program. But it does mean that if hours are to change, they remain within specified limits.

People who have never done volunteer work are sometimes surprised by relationships among the workers. Said one person: "I was very happy the first day or so I turned up to work with handicapped people on a recreation program. But then I realized that someone who I thought was doing the same work I was began acting very bossy."

If there is to be a person you "report to," who is in a sense a designated supervisor of your work, get this fact clear in advance. Don't assume that a bossy person is just being superior. In some cases that individual may have been misled by promises or assumptions as to what he or she would be doing.

Finally, don't be surprised if your first try at a volunteer assignment proves less satisfactory than you hoped. If you feel you've given it a fair trial and you aren't meeting *your* objectives, rethink your situation, see if there isn't another opportunity—perhaps in the same organization—that will deliver more of what you are seeking.

FREELANCING

If you have creative talents, freelancing can be an ideal compromise between working at a nine-to-five job and setting yourself up in business. It's an "in-business-for-myself" arrangement without all the risks of ownership. People who can write, paint, design and make jewelry, have a way with a camera, and so on can find remunerative outlet for these talents. For example, many book publishers use freelance editors to prepare manuscripts for publication. Naturally, experience is important here. Advertising agencies use the talents of people who have a way with promotional copy to write everything from a bright line for an ad to promotional brochures. Ad agencies also use freelance artists for ads that appear in newspapers and magazines. Firms that put out catalogues sometimes prefer artistic renderings to photographs for items they sell.

Department stores and boutiques buy everything from jewelry to handmade dolls, from pillows to dried-flower arrangements. Photographers have taken themselves out of the amateur ranks by selling their pictures to newspapers, magazines, doing baby pictures, and covering weddings or other social events. Painters who do portraits well have gotten commissions to do everyone from the highschool principal's dog to the founder of the local factory. And performing artists, pianists, dancers and actors have given lessons to aspiring youngsters.

COMMUNITY SERVICE

Every community has a life of its own, and its vitality requires the participation of people. To some extent, community life is represented by organizations and institutions: an art center, a museum, a youngsters' sports center—in some communities the "Y" organizations fill this area—historical society, "improve-the-neighborhood" groups, and theatrical groups.

Closely allied to community life are church and so-called "service" organizations. The list varies from community to community, and in large cities, from neighborhood to neighborhood. No matter where you live, it's likely that there is some civic or church activity going on that may be of interest. Of course, these are volunteer jobs, and unpaid except for expenses.

Perhaps, in your community, there is a need for some kind of service that would interest you. For example, Henry Stagg was dissatisfied by the level of education his twelve-year-old granddaughter Sabena was getting in public school. Sabena was a very bright child, and her school studies were not enough to stretch her. In the community was a university-sponsored research laboratory where many scientists and technicians worked—chemists, physicists, geologists, and biologists. Henry Stagg decided to try to persuade the scientists to volunteer their Saturday mornings to teaching and working with youngsters who were interested in learning more about science. It took a lot of doing, but Stagg was finally able to persuade the authorities to sponsor the Saturday program on school premises. Eventually, the program, which became extremely successful, expanded to include local artists and crafts people. Stagg ended up as administrator of the program, with a salary paid for out of local educational funds.

● *Job Hunting*

In matching yourself with one or more prospective activities, remember that someone will be making a judgment about the suitability of the fit between what you want and your qualifications for it. Presumably you have already decided, perhaps if only in a general way, on the kind of activity you want. But if you're not fully qualified by objective measures, this doesn't mean abandoning your objective. Consider the case of Bentley Leehan.

Bentley, retired at 60 from an advertising agency, decided he wanted to continue working, but not in advertising. He had had some contact with videotape production, and wanted to get into that field. He looked up a business acquaintance who was a partner in what is called a post-production house. The firm processed, edited, and prepared for viewing both videotape and film. "No openings," Bentley was told. But he persuaded his acquaintance to take him on just as a learner, at no salary. After some months Bentley had caught on in a big way, and he was hired on a regular basis by the firm.

Whether your primary objective is money or self-fulfillment—and please remember that the two are *not* mutually exclusive—the more sophisticated your approach, the better your chances of getting what you want. This may seem obvious but for many people, job hunting is a difficult, even unnerving experience—even for those who have held down a job for years.

Talking to people in the job market at every level, it becomes clear that many applicants haven't the faintest idea of how to go about selling themselves to an employer. The problem of nonpaid employment is easier, but even here the possiblity still exists of missing a desired target because of ignorance. The following material can help you refine your thinking and expand your awareness of the actual process of looking for a job.

HOW TO LOOK

No matter what kind of job you're seeking, it's essential early on that you find people or organizations that are in a position to hire you. How do you find these prospective employers? Some of the ways are traditional, some off the beaten path. But to organize the best possible approach, the broader your range of methods, the better your chances. And there's another "rule" of job hunting: the more energetic and enterprising your hunt, the greater your chances become—both to find the kind of emloyment you're seeking, and of doing so in the shortest possible time.

Ads

Almost every newspaper carries classified help-wanted ads. Check *all* the newspapers in your community, not only the one you yourself read. Also, be sure to check the trade and professional journals in the activity areas in which you're interested.

Should you place an ad in the positions wanted section? It can be costly, of course, but it's usually worth a try, just to test out what happens. Exactly what you say in your ad will be a major factor in the results you get. Usually, the newspaper employee who takes your ad will be glad to help with the wording.

You'll save yourself some postage and wasted effort if you carefully read the ads you're answering and try to figure out what the employer is seeking. Unless your experience and qualifications are pretty much in line with what's wanted, don't respond. However, if you have a very strong and persuasive story that may just be good enough to get the employer to take you on with the thought that you may actually work out better than the kind of person the ad described, then go ahead and try.

Employment agencies

These have a mixed reputation, but many of them are worth a try. Agencies tend to specialize, so look for those handling the kinds of jobs you're interested in.

Remember that agencies are essentially brokers. They can't hire you. Their stock in trade is contacts with companies that have vacancies. Don't waste time with agencies that don't seem to be interested in you or helping you find the kind of job you want. Some firms may try to convince you to take a job considerably below your earning capacity. Others will try to "string you along" even though they don't have anything to offer you. Don't waste your time.

Definitely worth a visit is the State Employment Service office in your community, or the one that's closest to you. Of course, in bad times these services get jammed up, but they're worth at least one visit. And in some cases they may be able to make constructive suggestions.

Following leads

Another possibility is job leads supplied by friends, relatives, neighbors, or a chance conversation in an employment agency. A good lead is one that spotlights a specific job opening of the kind you're interested in, in a specific company. And sometimes the tip comes along with, "The person to see is Mrs. Winifred Mayhew . . ."

Included in those who may be able to offer more than just kind words are personnel directors or other people who interview you. Even if they can't use your services they might know of some people who can. One sure way to find out is to ask:

"Mr. Smith, I'm sorry you don't have anything suitable for me right now. But now that you know my qualifications and background, can you suggest anyone who might be a good prospect for me to call on?"

It's a common experience for people who ask this question to have the interviewer pick up the phone and make an appointment for them right then and there. Even if you're not this lucky, you may get specific guidance to other prospective employers.

HOW TO APPLY

Resumes

A job hunt usually brings a request from a prospective employer for a resume. Resumes don't get people jobs, but they do get you in to see an interviewer—an essential preliminary.

For retirees, a resume may pose two problems: one is age; the other is a possible period of time during which you were not working. Fortunately, neither need be a handicap. As long as you are under seventy, age cannot legally be a deterrent to employment. The anti-discrimination laws are on your side.

The second problem was faced by Dick Richards, of Akron. Looking for a job at age sixty-seven, he had not worked for four years. What could he do about this in his resume and in talking to interviewers? He was open and direct, explained his nonworking as a result of temporary retirement, then went on to sell himself on the basis of ability and experience.

As far as the resume is concerned, the answer is simple. Since the main purpose of a resume is to get an interview, negative elements should be minimized. They are dealt with more logically in the conversation with a prospective employer.

Legal restrictions prevent most employers from discriminating against individuals in hiring on the basis of age. This fact generally forces interviewers not to ask questions that touch on this qualification. It isn't that the questions themselves are illegal, but that an applicant might claim discrimination and offer the delving into age as proof.

An employer hires you because he feels you will do a good job—strengthen a weakspot on the staff, supply experience, or perform a task that needs doing. In the course of an interview, don't be concerned with possible gaps or weakpoints in your qualifications. Emphasize what you have that the employer can use, needs, and will benefit from.

A SAMPLE RESUME. Here is a type of resume recommended for people interested in rejoining the job market. It avoids the problem, posed by others, of specifying previous employers in connection with *periods worked*. Note also that the "Education" item at the bottom gives the degree earned without specifying the year.

It's not that the applicant's age is to remain a dark secret. The intention is simply to diminish the importance of the age factor for the interview.

It's generally advisable to accompany a resume that is mailed or left with a prospective employer with a cover letter explaining what the applicant and the employer might have to offer one another.

Chris Anders, Sales Executive
901 West Oak Street
Los Angeles, California

Marketing–Developed and supervised a continuing series of research projects throughout the United States. Developed sales-potential measurements for given areas. Summed up findings in the form of written reports, and made recommendations for sales improvement in covered areas, programs for new territories.

Sales Promotion–Worked up sales-promotion programs for a broad range of products, with heavy concentration on toys and adult games. Helped plan newspaper and trade-journal advertising and point of purchase promotions. In many instances, succeeded in raising the volume of sales 20 per cent within a year's time. (This statement documented in backup pages of this resume.)

Sales Management–Hired, trained, and supervised sales staffs ranging from ten to one hundred ten men, on national basis. Developed communications network between field and H.O.—call reports, regular summary letters, and so on. Particularly successful in starting new products.

Sales–Heavy experience in wholesale selling to department stores. Also, have sold at retail.

Order Clerk–Received, processed, and expedited orders. Worked with the head of the department to develop an order control system that was eventually adopted, and considerably increased efficiency.

Previous Employers

F & L Sales Company	Sales executive
Sales and Marketing Corp.	Sales promotion manager
J. K. Adams Toy Company	Salesman and sales manager

Education–University of Pennsylvania—B.S.

References–as indicated on last page

Letters

The mails can help you uncover prospective employers. Job hunting by mail has one special virtue: it does not conflict with other job-hunting activities. You can carry out a mail campaign evenings and weekends.

The most effective approach is a letter aimed at employers for whom your qualifications will be most relevant. A resume or other material may be enclosed, but it is the pertinence of the letter you write and its direct appeal to the reader that bring the desired result.

The communication you send has one purpose, and one purpose only—to get you a job interview. It's *not* supposed to get you a job. Essentially, it's what magazine writers call a "query letter"—one written to sound out or to create interest.

A woman who had had considerable experience with the purchasing of printing decided she would like to work in a large company as liaison between the company and its suppliers of printing services. She talked to old friends in the printing field and finally came up with the names of six large companies who were major users of printing. Out of the six letters she sent off she got three interviews—and eventually a job with one of the companies.

Make up your mailing lists from your own and friends' knowledge of the trade or industry you wish to enter. There are "list companies" that may be able to sell you mailing lists of employer categories you're interested in, but these can be costly. In the average case the yellow pages can give you a serviceable mailing list of the category of company you want to reach. The companies that belong on your lists should be selected on the basis of the kind of job you're after. Then, just as in selling a product, you should know something—at least the essential points—about the company that you're "calling on."

To a considerable degree, the "pull" of a letter depends on its getting to the desk of the appropriate person in the prospective company, often the personnel director, but perhaps the head of a particular function—engineering, production, marketing, and so on.

There's a simple way to learn the name of the person you should be addressing. Telephone the company, and ask the name of the person in charge of the function in which you're interested. Such inquiries are routine. Where telephoning is prohibitive because of distance, write and ask the personnel department for the information.

A SAMPLE LETTER.   Here's a sample letter that succeeded in its objective, getting a face-to-face meeting with a prospective employer:

Mr. Samuel J. Ruthven, Director of Purchasing
Acme Office Furniture Company
116 Maltese Drive
Cincinnati, Ohio

Dear Mr. Ruthven:

Mr. Val James of this city suggested that I write you about an upcoming vacancy in your purchasing department. As the enclosed resume shows, I have had some purchasing experience in your field. While working as assistant head of the purchasing department of a Los Angeles furniture company, I developed some successful techniques for value analysis and inventory control that would improve the profitability of operations for the company that applies them.

While I've been retired for the past three years, I am now interested in returning to the business world. I would be glad to meet with you at any convenient time to discuss the possibilities. May I hear from you?

Sincerely

Interviews

"The interview is the climax of the job hunt," says one experienced personnel director. Remember, the resume and all the preliminaries you may have gone through in finding a prospect don't get you the job. You're only hired after you've had a chance to sit down with a potential employer and persuade him or her that you're the right person for the job.

Being successful in an interview doesn't necessarily mean you walk off with the job. In some cases, deciding *not* to take the job is the right move. But if you do like the sound of what's being offered, remember that the employer wants nothing so much as to be sold! Be sincere and direct. Act in a way that comes naturally. Make sure all your questions are answered. Don't forget that you, too, are seeking information. You want to make sure the job is suitable.

"Sell the benefits"—what the company will gain by hiring you. Here's one person's approach: "Mr. Rogers, am I correct in concluding that lack of creative design is a major problem for your company? If so, I'd like to spend a few minutes suggesting how my training and interests can be applied to your needs in this area."

Let yourself come through. In the course of the conversation help the interviewer develop a picture of your experience, special qualifications, ambitions, and expectations for the future. This isn't the kind of thing you put in a resume, but it is often the basis on which people hire. The interview is your chance to talk yourself up.

Anticipate questions about your motivation. Most interviewers are interested in finding out what makes an applicant tick: Why are you going back into the world of work? How important is money to you? Would you do better with a low-pressure job or could you take pressure in stride?

Finally, understand the best way to represent a weak point. In some cases a return to work after a period of retirement may seem to be a handicap. The important point to remember is, this can be minimized. Compare, for example, the more favorable second sentence with the weakness of the first:

"Yes, I've been off the job market for three years."

"I've devoted the last three years to becoming more mature, developing a greater responsibility, improving my ability to get along with people. And I'm happy to say my job skills are as good now as when I left my last job."

WHERE TO LOOK

The Government. New Labor Department rules make it easier for older, low-income persons to obtain part-time federal jobs. The Department has amended its Senior Community Service Employment Program to include older Americans with low incomes in the program, which offers approximately 40,000 jobs nationwide to people age 55 and older. Jobs are offered in a variety of different activities: daycare centers, schools, hospitals, senior citizens' centers, and conservation and restoration projects. What is available does fluctuate with funding so that opportunities change, month to month.

HEALTH-CARE FACILITIES. Hospitals, nursing homes, health centers, and other health-care facilities offer entry-level jobs which require minimal education, skills, and experience. Generally, little or no previous experience is necessary to qualify. Hospitals and nursing homes usually prefer to train their own personnel to hiring people who have had some related experience.

Starting salaries for entry-level jobs—covered by the unions, in which membership is usually required—range from $8,100 to $9,100 per year. Union benefits, which include health and hospitalization insurance and a pension, begin three months after joining the union.

YOUR FORMER EMPLOYER. Mack Trucks, Inc., uses their own retirees to conduct tours of its plants for visitors. Baltimore's Union Trust Co. of Maryland opens a "bank within a bank" a few hours a week for use by its own employees and has two retired tellers at the windows. The Cross Company uses retired experts to inspect custom built machinery parts, compile training manuals, and advise on the handling of overseas shipments. The Firestone Tire and Rubber Company has opened its employee-suggestion program to retirees on the theory that it could benefit from their many years training and experience. This doesn't mean steady employment, of course, but retirees whose ideas are accepted receive 10 percent of the first year's gross savings or increased profits up to a maximum of $25,000.

Check the personnel department of your former employer and see if there are any similar programs for retirees. If not, you may want to suggest one yourself.

DEVELOPING AN OLD SKILL. In your work experience, you undoubtedly have developed one or more capabilities that are now marketable. These skills may be manual or otherwise. For example, the "ability to sell", is as specific and desirable as the ability to paint a house or build a cabinet.

If necessary, put down on paper the skills you have acquired in your years of experience, both specific ones, like bookkeeping or typing, and those which are not as definite but still valuable—such as "an ability to work well with other people."

DEVELOPING A NEW SKILL.   It is assumed that the capabilities mentioned in the point above are those that have been developed and applied in previous work you've done, but there may be skills just as valuable which you've never used commercially or professionally. For example, a hobbyist who has developed a keen eye for antiques and knows some history and the value of items might find an eager employer in an antiques shop.

YOUR COMMUNITY.   Here you concentrate less on what you have to offer and more on your environment to find and develop opportunities. Look around your neighborhood, community, or city and consider every business and organization as a potential employer. How can you fit in? What contribution could you make to a local manufacturer, life insurance company, bank, or book shop?

FRIENDS AND RELATIVES.   There is a long history of jobs people have gotten working for friends and relatives. One retiree says, "That would be my last recourse. I'd never work for a friend of mine. It's liable to destroy the friendship or at least interfere with it."

It's a possibility, but if they're not potential employers, friends or relatives may be able to put you on to business contacts or openings that could lead you to worthwhile employment.

STARTING AS A VOLUNTEER.   Many people have started as volunteers and ended up either in the same organization with a paying job or else have learned enough as a result of their volunteering to be able to get a job with another organization. Don't lose sight of the fact that a volunteer job, which may have a great deal to recommend it in itself, may also be a foot in the door for eventual paid employment.

YOUR INTERESTS.   In some cases, the person who is looking for income-earning work has just one guiding principle: take the first job that comes along, if it pays enough. And if the financial pressure is on, that may be the height of wisdom. But if the job-seeker has some freedom of choice, the appropriate thought may be, "At this stage in my life, I'm going to hold out for work that gives me some kind of pleasure."

This principle would lead a person who enjoys selling to turn down an offer of employment as a stock clerk and hold out for one in the sales field. Or it would persuade a person for whom tennis or golf are exciting and involving to look for a job that kept him in the sports milieu—as a pro in a country club, a customer service representative for a sporting goods manufacturer, and so on.

● *The Second Time Around*

In a recent article, *Psychology Today* pointed out that a study of career satisfaction showed that a sizable number of people were disgusted with their jobs. "Years ago," said one executive, "I made a bad mistake and I'm paying for it. I'm trapped."

Ending your career with one organization may make it possible to test your aspirations and abilities once again—in other arenas. Al Baylor was a member of a real-estate family with large holdings in a mid-western city. He was expected to join the firm when he graduated from college—and did, as an assistant in the renting office.

But he didn't like his work, and five years later served notice of his intention to leave. His Uncle Kerry, head of the firm, tried to dissuade him: "You're foolish. In a few years you'll be a top executive here. And why are you leaving, anyhow?"

"I'm interested in painting. I want to devote all my time to it."

"Ridiculous. Would you rather be a second-rate artist or a first-rate real estate executive?"

Al Baylor left no doubt about his answer. He quit and enrolled in the best art school he could find. He struggled along, supporting himself by part-time jobs, from hacking to construction work. He got married, and when his wife became pregnant, their financial situation forced him to reconsider his situation. After months of soul-searching, he phoned his Uncle Kerry and asked for another chance.

"Of course," was the answer.

Al Baylor stayed on in the firm, a successful and respected executive. But at age 55 he took early retirement, able to do so because of his pension and good investments in real estate properties.

He told his wife, "Now I'm ready to take another crack at my art. I never felt I gave it a good enough try."

At this date, Al Baylor is still struggling to make it big in the art world. He has had some success, some recognition—and a great deal of satisfaction.

"Uncle Kerry wasn't all wrong," he says, "and I wasn't either. I would rather be a second-rate artist than a top-notch business executive . . ."

His years of working made it possible to have a second chance, and the deep pleasure of doing something he wanted to do. For many, retirement may have this second-chance opportunity.

● *Selected Bibliography/Small Business Operations*

Allen, Louis L., *Starting and Succeeding in Your Own Small Business*. Grossett and Dunlap, 1978, $3.95.

Baumback, Clifford M., and Lawyer, Kenneth. *How to Organize and Operate a Small Business*. Prentice-Hall, 1979, $15.95.

Simon, Arthur C. *How to Start a Business and Make it Grow*. Future Shop, 1978, $9.95.

Steinhoff, D. *Small Business Management Fundamentals*. McGraw Hill, 1974, $13.95.

Tate, Curtis E. *Successful Small Business Management*. Business Publications, 1978, $15.50.

Taylor, John R. *How to Start and Succeed in a Business of Your Own*. Reston Publishing Company, 1978, $12.95.

U.S. Small Business Administration. *Checklist for Going Into Business*. 1977, free.

U.S. Small Business Administration. *Incorporating a Small Business*. 1976, free.

17
HOBBIES

In talking to retirees about what they do with their time, it appears that those people who have a hobby seem to make out better than those who don't. And the value of a hobby goes beyond merely filling time or providing an outlet for excess energy. To many hobbyists, their interest provides for them a continuing challenge and the promise of reward.

If you don't have a hobby now that you're sufficiently enamored of to devote more of your time to after retirement, it may be wise to do some exploring. But don't wait until you've retired to test out the possibilities. Begin as soon as possible to seek out a new interest. Read books, visit places, and speak to people that can provide information. The more firmly established your interest before you retire, the better are your chances for a successful retirement.

One interesting aspect of hobbying is that in almost every case, there is a professional aspect. Consider stamp saving. There is a group of professional philatelists who devote a major part of their energies—and indeed, of their lives—to collecting the colorful engravings, in some cases worth thousands of dollars.

And there are related activities which are part of the fun, the pleasure, and sometimes the profit. The involved stamp collector will travel, correspond with other like-minded people, and attend conventions and conferences which are held over the world in pursuing his or her special interests.

And for some people—those who like to teach—there is the opportunity to give courses, usually at local institutions, on philately in all its many aspects.

I've selected stamp collecting not as a typical example but one that many people might think lends itself less well to enriching one's life compared to more active hobbies, such as woodworking, for example, which involves a greater element of creativity. Stamp collecting may seem somewhat limited—but that precisely is the point. For the person interested, *any* avocation can furnish the avenues and directions that can lead to great rewards.

● *Selecting a Hobby*

APPROACHES

Different people will, of course, approach a hobby in different ways, depending on how much they want to put into and take out of the activity.

A pastime

The language offers us the word "pastime," which can be used to describe the first or most superficial degree of involvement. The dictionary describes a "pastime" as "something that amuses and serves to make time pass agreeably: a diversion."

There's nothing wrong with activities that make time pass pleasantly. For some people and for some lifestyles this degree of interest in a hobby may be just the thing.

Creative outlet

For some people, the kind of hobby that produces something tangible is particularly satisfying. Painting, knitting, writing, cooking, woodworking, and so on are all in this category. They allow the practitioner to become involved to whatever degree he or she wishes and still end up with something to show for the effort.

Recognition or status

For individuals who become expert in a particular field there is to be found ego satisfaction and the pleasure of being recognized as expert or authority. For example, Fred Matthias, who became interested in the local history of his community, became a recognized authority on the early colonial and post-colonial history of Rockland County, New York.

CONSIDERATIONS

You may already be pursuing an art, a craft, or be a collector and find your involvement completely satisfying. Even if you are, you may be interested in reviewing your choice. There are several facts of life you must consider before making your final decision.

Physical ability

A friend of mine in Massachusetts welds metal as a hobby. He has made many unusual wrought iron pieces, both artistic and utilitarian. He is a man of strong physique and the physical exertion required is well within his capabilities. I have another friend who's confined to a wheelchair. For him, welding would be at best awkward, at worst unsafe. However, he enjoys tremendously collecting rare books, limited editions, first editions, and so on.

Natural affinity

Some people seem to have an *affinity* for certain kinds of materials, for certain kinds of work. One woman loves to work on leather. Another is completely absorbed in clay modeling. The leather worker hates the feel of clay. To the clay modeler, leather is just an uninteresting medium. In selecting a hobby or in developing an interest in one, it pays not to fight these natural tendencies.

Available facilities

A person who lives in a studio apartment in a city is not going to get far with a hobby of making furniture that requires a cabinet saw, power tools, and the freedom to make the noise required in woodworking.

However, the facilities for practicing your hobby need not necessarily be limited to your own apartment or house. For example, I have several friends who design and make jewelry. Their "studio" is the local YWCA, which gives courses and has bench space available. Sometimes space may be "borrowed" or rented reasonably—a neighbor's basement, for example.

Cost

If your funds are severely limited, this may be a major factor.

Certain hobbies are more costly to pursue than others. If you are interested in making jewelry you may not be able to work in gold—especially at current prices—but perhaps you can work in silver. If this less expensive metal is still outside your budgetary resources, then possibly you can work in copper.

In figuring the costs of a hobby, tools, materials, space (for a studio, for example), and services (some hobbies may require electricity) must all be taken into account. All other things being equal, it's wise to choose the hobby that is the least expensive for you. Admittedly you don't want to sacrifice an activity for which you have an especially strong feeling and undertake one that's inexpensive but also unrewarding. You may have to make a trade-off and compromise between cost and your natural interests.

Returns

The final returns from a hobby may include anything from your becoming an expert and winning national or international recognition, to the socializing that certain hobbies, such as ham radio, make possible.

Hobbies also can become a source of income. In some cases, this may be a deciding factor. If you have a natural interest in ceramics and find that you have a flair for the craft to the point where you can exhibit and sell your wares, the crowning virtue of being able to augment your income may put this ahead of any other possible avocation.

The following chart can help you rate the suitability of a hobby already chosen or guide you in the direction of one or more possibilities. Pick a type of activity and score it as indicated.

	Defin-itely	Some-what	Not at all
1. Is it in line with physical ability?	( )	( )	( )
2. Is it in line with your natural interests?	( )	( )	( )
3. Are facilities for practicing the hobby available?	( )	( )	( )
4. Are the costs of the activity within reasonable limits?	( )	( )	( )
5. Is there a possibility of cash benefits? That is, making your hobby a source of income?	( )	( )	( )
6. Is there a possiblity of some side advantage— socializing or travel?	( )	( )	( )

Rate yourself *10* points for each *Definitely;* *5* points for each *Somewhat;* *0* for each *Not at all*. Score each answer and add up the total. Here are some indications suggested by your score:

50–60: A very good possibility for you.

40–50: Possible, but look into the negatives suggested by the low-rated items.

Below 40: Look further.

● *Some Hobbies to Consider*

Of course, no list of hobbies, however long, can possibly include all the highly original and unique activities that the term covers. You may remember the Californian who built a huge, modernistic structure out of beer cans some years ago. Perhaps beer-can architecture isn't for you, but for the individual who dedicated years of his life to this activity, it was an absorbing and obviously satisfying undertaking.

At any rate, some of the more popular kinds of hobbies are listed below for your information. Remember, no one else can say what's right for you, and no one else's success or failure can guarantee the same results for you. The right hobby can be a major factor in your happy adjustment to the retired life.

VISUAL ARTS

Most people have some potential in the visual arts, even if (some people say *especially* if) they can't draw a straight line. If you are interested, you can do it—reasonably well. Consider taking a course or two in the basics, just to get started.

Painting

• Sketching and drawing—foundations for any kind of artwork, as well as being absorbing in themselves.
  • Painting—oils, acrylics, water color.
  • Specialized media—etching, lithography, silk screen.
  • Special subject matter—animals, still life, landscapes, seascapes.

Sculpture

• Clay modeling—pieces can be made permanent by firing in a kiln or by reproduction through a casting process.

• Carving—stone, wood, plastic.

• Metal—originals in clay or wax can be cast in metal. In addition, metal welding, bending, and joining are popular with contemporary artists.

• Woodblocks and linoleum—for printmaking

• Decorative woodcarving—details on furniture and around the house.

Graphic Arts

• Photography—this covers a vast range of possibilities. You can try anything from photojournalism to marine landscapes. And, picture taking is often an important adjunct to other interests, from travel to collecting dolls.

• Dried-flower pressing and framing.

• Montage, collage—fabric, paper, memorabilia, photographs old and new, and anything else your ingenuity can turn up.

• Batik—a method of dyeing a print into fabric using wax.

PERFORMING ARTS

Music

• If you play an instrument, join an amateur group—quartet, local orchestra, and so on.

• If you can carry a tune, join a choral group—church, local musical society, and so on.

• If you love music, like to be where it is made, and enjoy the company of musicians, there may be a need in a local group for a manager, assistant, or a nonplayer who can donate time and services to the group's activities.

Theater

Community or other nonprofessional theater groups are flourishing. And every such group is usually eager for new members, who will have a chance to participate in any of a dozen theater arts.

• Acting

• Backstage work—set construction, lighting, and so on.

• Promotional activities—publicizing and advertising the group's performances.

• Business manager or treasurer—guiding the group's financial affairs.

Dance

• Ballet, modern dance, yoga, tap dancing, aerobic dancing, even belly dancing are offered at gymnasiums, Y's, and adult education centers.

Specialties

• Magic—you can practice to become a magician and please yourself, amaze your friends, and entertain the neighborhood kids. Magic shops that sell equipment that makes the impossible easy usually have proprietors who can start you off. Or, contact a practicing magician, who most likely will be willing to answer a few questions that can get you going.
• Picture talks. If you have a collection of slides in connection with a special interest—travel, architecture, whatever—organizations often want speakers for their meetings. If you enjoy talking about your hobby, you can have ready-made audiences.

CRAFTS

The list is almost endless. Anything the human hand can grasp, any material available on the planet, has been hammered, beaten, sawed, knit, or shaped by an imaginative artisan. The suggestions below are just a few of many.

Woodworking

• Furniture—chairs, tables, dressers, shelves, buffets, beds, sideboards, outdoor pieces, and so on.
• Cabinets, chests, trunks, builtins, lamp bases, and so on.
• Boxmaking—from a simple rectangle for holding cigarettes to an inlaid container for jewelry.
• Picture frames.
• Specialty items around the house—from bathroom counters to kitchen gadgets.

Jewelry making

    • Gold, silver, copper—rings, earrings, pendants, pins, necklaces.
    • Wood—carved or shaped, for items of personal adornment.
    • Metal—not necessarily precious—iron, pewter, and so on.
    • Assemblages—necklaces of beads, minerals, ivory, ceramics, and shells. Parts may be collected or bought.

Ceramics

Different methods of forming ceramic materials into vases, pitchers, dishes, masks, statuettes and so on.

Needlework

    • Sewing, knitting, crocheting, needlepoint, and so on. People have been delighting themselves and others with the products of these crafts—everything from apparel to afghans, bedcovers, wall hangings, and so on.

Dolls and dollhouses

Many adults are fascinated by the world of dolls, and they make them—from stuffed fabric, wool, wood, and ceramics. There also has been a recent surge of interest in making and collecting dollhouses and the miniature furniture and accessories that go with them.

Imagination is the only limit. People have made furniture from cardboard and lamps from driftwood. Look about you for inspiration.

COLLECTING

This is possibly the most widespread of all hobbies. Many people started collecting with only an offhand interest that turned into a major preoccupation. Here is a partial list of possibilities:

    • Stamps
    • Coins
    • Books—rare, first editions, and so on
    • Shells
    • Dishes
    • Bottles
    • Pitchers

    • Animal replicas (pictures, sculptures of horses, owls, armadillos, and so on)
    • Netsukes (small Japanese toggles used to fasten items to kimono sashes)
    • Nature items—rocks, fossils, pressed flowers

SPORTS

Sport-Fanning

There's no such word or phrase, but its meaning is clear. Many people derive great excitement and pleasure from watching sports. Our country is notable for the diversity and number of sporting events. You don't have to have a card or any special qualifications to make it as a fan. All you need to join the hundreds of thousands of absorbed and cheering onlookers is interest and some knowledge of the game. Whether you watch it live or on television, you're guaranteed hours of pleasure that can make a welcome addition to other interests and activities. The most popular sports that have a proven record of fascination for onlookers:

- Baseball
- Football
- Basketball
- Soccer
- Ice Hockey
- Horse racing
- Track and field
- Swimming
- Bowling

Not quite so popular, but fully capable of gripping your attention before, during, and after the fact:

- Horse shows
- Gymnastics
- Skiing
- Ice skating
- Boat racing
- Archery

Active participation

The popular "civilized" sports like golf, tennis, and boating are good possibilities. But there are many others that just might be of special interest to you:

- Fishing
- Hunting
- Canoeing
- Hiking
- Skiing—downhill and cross country
- Swimming
- Scuba diving
- Snorkeling
- Bowling
- Swimming
- Ping-Pong
- Paddle tennis
- Squash
- Handball

NATURE

A love of nature gets countless people into the great outdoors to observe, collect, enjoy one or more of the following:

- Birds
- Animals of all kinds
- Trees
- Wildflowers
- Rocks

- Marine life
- Fossils
- Orienteering
- Archeological digs

COOKING

It should be obvious to everyone that interest in the culinary arts is growing by leaps and bounds. Television programs feature master chefs, cooking courses in everything from Chinese pastries to Mexican beverages are offered, and new and exotic kitchen gadgets seem to appear in stores every week.

If cooking appeals to you, learn the basics (if you don't already know them) and then try to find a specialty you really enjoy.

AUTOLOGUE

People who talk to themselves may be targets for good natured joshing or critical comment. But some time ago I wrote a book entitled, *Discover Your Inner Self*, which described at some length some serious applications of the procedure of talking to oneself or, as I referred to it, conducting an autologue.

In an autologue a person talks to himself or herself in the ordinary way a runner may say, "Pick up the pace, Bill, or you'll be out of it;" or a troubled person may say, "Quiet down now and take it easy. Some clear-headed thinking is called for now, not panic."

This book is out of print and no longer available, but from time to time, however, I come across people who have read it and found it of interest. Recently I received a letter from a reader. I reprint it here because it suggests an unusual and novel occupation, an unusual way of spending time productively. Note the writer is somewhat immobilized because of physical problems. The activity he describes is not in the least limited by the handicap.

Dear Mr. Uris,

I retired several years ago, and in recent months a combination of arthritis and incomplete recovery from a broken hip limits my movements drastically. TV became my chief preoccupation, but after a while eye difficulties as well as boredom had me cut down. I was hurting for lack of activity, when a friend lent me a copy of your book, *Discover Your Inner Self*. The idea of talking to myself—as a form of entertainment, as well as for some of the other purposes you suggest—started me on a project: a personal reminiscence. It's been an absolutely fascinating and rewarding experience. I bought myself a cassette recorder and began, going as far back into my childhood as I could. I have now filled about 50 tapes with all kinds of recollections. I enjoyed doing it. Others—my son and his wife, and their teen-agers—have listened to several hours of it, and the questions they asked started great conversations. And I find myself listening to my own voice, remembering incidents and events of my past. They make me realize I've had a pretty exciting and rewarding life. It's added a whole new dimension to my existence. . . .

Autologue or photography, stamp collecting or painting, making ceramic trivets or becoming a baseball fan who knows the batting averages of his favorite stars for the past five years—the world of hobbies is vast, an unending treasure trove—available if and when you want it.

BIG PROJECTS

Some absorbing hobbies are unclassifiable. They involve special materials, of course, and may require specific skills. But the end product is so unique as to break the ordinary limitations of the craft. Just a few examples:

• An exact scale model of the Empire State building.
• A six-foot-high doll house completely furnished with miniature kitchen utensils and books in the living room.
• A drawing of a family tree that takes up an entire wall of a room, complete with branches, names, and dates.

In this area you can let your imagination run loose. The more the idea reflects your unique feeling and thought—and the more unusual the end product—the more rewarding it's likely to be.

● *Getting Started*

No matter how exciting a new hobby seems at the very beginning, don't get in too deep without being sure that you really are enjoying it and it is delivering other benefits you expected.

For several reasons you don't want to overcommit yourself at the start. For example, costs may be great. Second, you don't want to devote a lot of time to something and find that it's turned out to be a drag rather than a source of pleasure.

A good way to test out your new interest is to work along with someone already involved. Chances are there's someone in your community who may be doing the activity you're interested in. One particularly fruitful approach is to contact local schools and find out if there are courses given in say, wood carving. Communities that have art councils may help you find a professional, that is, a wood sculptor or a craftsperson who does the kind of carving in which you are interested. My experience is that most artists or artisans enjoy a real show of interest and are pleased to help others develop a skill in their area of expertise.

You might even ask if the artist would mind if you used the tools just to get the feel of them. Perhaps take a piece of scrap wood, a mallet and a chisel or gouge, and make a couple of cuts. See if the physical aspect of the work pleases you, the feel of the gouge biting into the wood, the clean sliver slicing off the block and leaving a smooth, nicely grained channel in its wake.

Further, you might ask the artist about costs and try to get any advice or information that would be of interest—the kind of work place you would need, how noisy the work is (in case you have close-by neighbors), and any other tidbits that may be helpful.

Once you do get started on your hobby, it's best to get a teacher. True, many fine artists and craftspeople have been self-taught, but a good teacher can save you time and get you to a higher level of proficiency than possibly you could achieve on your own.

In large communities there are art and craft schools that you may want to investigate. In small communities, even if there are no organized classes, it's perfectly acceptable to contact a person pursuing the activity you're interested in, either professionally or as an amateur, and ask whether he or she might be interested in taking you on as a student for a while, for a fee.

In the average case the very first attempts at any new activity can be disappointing. The pleasure in many hobbies comes from the proficiency you acquire. Keep the trial period open long enough—and it will vary from person to person and from hobby to hobby—to feel it's been a fair trial.

Some people are able to get considerable enjoyment out of an activity which they're not very good at. These are the happy putterers who seem to be less interested in mastering a hobby than they are of just keeping occupied. There's nothing wrong with this, but there are additional rewards in working to achieve even higher levels of accomplishments.

● *Related Activities*

MORE THAN ONE HOBBY?

There are individuals who become interested in two or more activities related to their original hobby. They find that occasionally spending time working in another area of interest sharpens their awareness of both activities.

Sometimes, the interests may dovetail. Perhaps you might say that clay modeling—making heads, torsos, abstract sculpture—and making ceramics are basically not that different. However, they are different enough to yield entirely different kinds of satisfaction and somehow they utilize different parts of your feeling and different aspects of your creativity. Or, if you are involved in an activity like jewelry making, you may want to also develop an interest in silversmithing, which involves making silver vases, mugs, boxes, and so on.

One man I know who is both a jeweler and a silversmith, tells me, "I find that one craft seems to feed the other. I feel I'm a better jewelry designer because I develop a different feeling about metal when I make large pieces, and when I do my silversmithing my experience in designing and making jewelry helps me in developing the design and decoration."

Some avid hobbyists I know seem to delight in the fact that they have an interest in hobbies that are very different. One woman is quite an expert in leather craft. She makes belts, sandals, purses and pocketbooks, which are of sufficiently professional quality to be sold through local stores in her community. In addition, she makes something she describes as "soft caricature." These are figures and heads of, usually, famous people. She has done a large life-size head of Winston Churchill out of various materials—buttons for eyes, cloth of various textures for eyebrows, skin, and so on.

She says, "Sometimes I am just not in the mood for doing my leather work. It's a strange thing, but I find that when I'm particularly light-hearted the sense of play I have when I work on the soft sculpture is particularly enjoyable."

Perhaps this woman thinks of her leather working as a vocation and the soft creations as an avocation. The flexibility she has in going from one activity to another satisfies different moods and different needs.

TALKING ABOUT YOUR HOBBY

In almost every community, you'll find a thoroughly involved hobbyist who so dotes on his or her work that it bubbles out in the form of endless conversation. Of course, talking about an absorbing hobby is one of the pleasures it delivers. But you don't want to cloud the benefits of the activity by having it interfere with relationships with others.

Most people will be glad to hear—once—about how much you enjoy your hobby and the exacting quality of your last piece of work—or acquisition, if you're a collector—but don't overdo it. If you see that your listener is starting to fidget or is looking over your shoulder hoping for an interruption, be generous enough to change the subject or permit the other person to do so.

However, there is one move you can make that is almost sure to provide as much conversation about your hobby as you like: make contact with fellow hobbyists. Form a club, if you like. Or, if this is not to your taste, get together with one or two people of similar interests on an informal basis, but sufficiently often to give you—and them—the chance to talk about your hobby to your, and their, hearts' content.

There's another subtle but powerful factor that has to do with a benefit you can derive from being able to talk about a hobby:

You change your retiree status. You can say quite simply when the conversation gets around to "And what do you do . . .?" "I deal in antiques," 'I'm a philatelist,' or whatever. One man answers the question by saying, "I have the fifth largest collection of netsukes in this country." He reports, "It impresses the hell out of people—including me."

● *Reaping the Rewards*

Occasionally you find a person *practicing* a hobby rather than *enjoying* one. The potential rewards are lacking—in part because the individual remains unaware of the extent of the pleasure and reward that is possible.

In an amusing and helpful book about retirement[1] Peter Schwed, one-time Chairman of the Board of Simon and Schuster, describes how his wife, Antonia, received the best possible return on her investment in her hobby.

> My wife looked over a YWCA catalogue one day and decided to take a course. Among her many other attractions and attainments, she is an imaginative sketcher and extremely adept with her hands. So she chose to study and learn enameling, which is the creation of artistic objects such as jewelry, sculpture, wall hangings, bowls, and so forth, by fusing enamels (colored powdered glass) to the surface of a metal (such as copper or silver). She proved to be very good at it from the very beginning, and loved doing it so much that she bought a kiln, which was installed in a spot in our apartment where it was least likely to get in the way, or incinerate our children or our cat. Beautiful one-of-a-kind pieces started appearing all over the house and, while my wife kept most of them and our daughters absconded with some, a number of others were displayed in group shows and in art galleries. Some time later, the sponsors of her enamels course at the Y, the Craft Students League, asked Toni to become the teacher of a course of her own and, for the past half dozen years, she has been doing that as well as continuing with her own enameling.

Then Schwed goes on to describe Antonia's feelings about her beloved activity:

> One evening Toni gingerly removed a champleve pendant from her kiln, hovered over it watching the colors change as the piece started to cool, and said: "You know, I think I'm set for life. I simply love doing this, and it occupies my time and imagination whenever there's nothing else on tap that I have to do or want to do. You can leave me sketching a design in the morning as you go off to your office, and I can get so intent upon working out the piece that I keep at it all day, and you have to tear me away from it when you come home. With a little bit of luck and my enameling, I don't think I'm ever going to have to wonder what to do with my time."

[1]*Hanging in There!* by Peter Schwed. Boston, Houghton Mifflin, 1977.

● *Further Information*

Sixty-Four Hobby Projects, Brown and Olsen. 1969, TAB Books, Blue Ridge Summit, PA 17214.

Treasury of Hobbies and Crafts, Michael Estrin. 1973, Key Books, 147 McKinley Ave., Bridgeport, CT 06606.

Housebook: Unique Hobbies, In press, Jonathan David, 68-22 Eliot Ave., Middle Village, NY 11379.

At Your Leisure, Craig MacDonald. 1978, Beta Books, 10857 Valiente Court, San Diego, CA 92124.

Hobbies: A complete introduction to crafts, collections, nature studies, Alvin Schwartz. 1972, Simon & Schuster, 1230 Ave. of the Americas, New York, NY 10020.

Choosing Your Retirement Hobby, Norah Smardige. 1976, Dodd, Mead & Co., 79 Madison Ave., New York, NY 10016.

Crafts and Hobbies, Garry Winter. 1971, Arco, 219 Park Ave. South, New York, NY 10003.

18
RELIGION

Phoebe Bailey, a top executive of AIM—Action for Independent Maturity—says it is her opinion that "religion is one of the most neglected subjects in the whole field of retirement."

In many different cultures, the need for a spiritual life is enhanced in older people. A recent study of a Levantine group shows that while the younger generation devotes its time and energies to the day-to-day problems of living, the outward behavior and inner life of the older people are devoted to the service of Allah. As anthropologist D. L. Gutmann states in his report, "The older men of the tribe shave their heads, adopt special garb, give up tobacco, devote much time to prayer and dwell on God's mercy while forgetting their own grossness and stupidities."

Perhaps this type and degree of religious devotion would be unusual for most Americans. But it should be noted that in some areas in this country, people devote more time to church-going as they come into their sixties. They take literally the injunction of the Bible, "Cast your burden on the Lord and He will sustain you."

Religion is a highly personal matter, difficult to discuss objectively. But even confirmed churchgoers might find it worthwhile, in their retirement years, to reexamine their feelings and interests. And some seniors who don't think of themselves as religious—especially in church-going terms—spend more and more time in a search for the meaning of life and their response to that meaning. Some people, seeking an updated answer to the question, who am I?, may find themselves dipping into the writings of theologians and philosophers.

There is good reason for such fresh thinking. As Rabbi Bernard Mandelbaum puts it:

> We are put here on earth with many possibilities for goodness and happiness, but we whittle them away and live only partial lives. Man

seeks a purpose and values with which to guide himself. Yet in the rush of daily events, the clamor of his surroundings, the bigness of everything around him, he loses sight of the goals that can give purpose to life and confuses the values that can give it direction.[1]

The retiree is in an advantageous position: he or she is reasonably well rid of the "rush of daily events" which Rabbi Mandelbaum points to as a basic distraction of the average person. And, as he suggests in the title of his book, adding life (meaning, zest and pleasure) to one's years can be as rewarding as adding years to your life.

● *Meditation*

In his book, *The Relaxation Response,*[2] Herbert Benson describes what he calls "a method of repetitive prayer that purifies the intellect by means of a positive attitude, emptying it of all thought, image, and passion." An early religious sect provides a prescription for such an approach:

> Sit down alone and in silence. Lower your head, shut your eyes, breathe out gently and imagine yourself looking into your own heart. As you breathe out, say, "Lord, have mercy on me." Say it, moving your lips gently, or simply say it in your mind. Try to put all other thoughts aside. Be calm, be patient, and repeat the process frequently.

This spiritual exercise includes four elements that are considered essential to effective meditation. These are, according to Benson:

A QUIET ENVIRONMENT. One must "turn off" not only internal stimuli but also external distractions.

AN OBJECT TO DWELL UPON. This may be a word or sound that is repeated, providing an aural object. For those preferring a visual object, a symbol or even a stone may serve.

A POSITIVE ATTITUDE. The meditator is supposed to empty his or her mind of all distractions. Thoughts, images, and feelings interfere and should be allowed to pass or otherwise be rejected by the mind. "A person should not be concerned with how well he or she is doing," counsels Benson.

[1]*Add Life to Your Years,* by Rabbi Bernard Mandelbaum. New York: Grosset & Dunlap, 1973.
[2]*The Relaxation Response* by Herbert Benson. New York: Morrow, 1975.

A COMFORTABLE POSITION.   Since it's desirable for the individual to remain in the same position for at least twenty minutes, it's important that a comfortable posture be found. Usually a sitting position is recommended. If kneeling, squatting, or swaying seems more appropriate—the swaying movement traditionally serves the purpose of keeping the practitioner from falling asleep—adopt the stance you prefer.

In modern times meditation has taken a popular turn which divorces it somewhat from early religious origins. Meditation is a means of shedding the tensions that contemporary flesh is heir to as a means of achieving a more relaxed mind and body. Here is a technique used to develop a deep level of relaxation at the Beth Israel Hospital of Boston:

1. Sit quietly in a comfortable position.
2. Close your eyes.
3. Deeply relax all your muscles, beginning at your feet and progressing up to your face. Keep them relaxed.
4. Breathe through your nose. Become aware of your breathing. As you breathe out, say the word, "one," silently to yourself. For example, breathe in . . . out, "one"; in . . . out, "one"; etc. Breathe easily and naturally.
5. Continue for 10 to 20 minutes. You may open your eyes to check the time, but do not use an alarm. When you finish, sit quietly for several minutes, at first with your eyes closed and later with your eyes opened. Do not stand up for a few minutes.
6. Do not worry about whether you are successful in achieving a deep level of relaxation. Maintain a passive attitude and permit relaxation to occur at its own pace. When distracting thoughts occur, try to ignore them by not dwelling upon them and return to repeating "ONE." With practice, the response should come with little effort. Practice the technique once or twice daily, but not within two hours after any meal, since the digestive processes seem to interfere with the elicitation of the Relaxation Response.

● *Supportive Benefits*

Being religious-minded or joining a religious organization is a matter of personal preference. For some, religion can be a rewarding and major preoccupation. Others may turn elsewhere for their philosophical conjectures. But there are some benefits that make it worthwhile to reconsider one's religious views. And this need not be with the intention of changing present attitudes or habits. On the contrary, such thoughts may convince you that your present attitudes are exactly what you want them to be. Nevertheless, here are two benefits that people ascribe to their religious convictions.

SHARED BELIEF. When you join a religious group, you develop a community of interest with others. This makes not only for a sense of belonging, but also usually yields social enrichment—new contacts, friends, activities to participate in with others.

SPIRITUAL COMFORT. We must sometimes bear blows that are almost intolerable, probably the worst being the loss of a loved one. People with strong religious convictions often are better able to bear a bereavement that, unsupported by religious conviction, might have broken them.

EVERLASTING LIFE. One of the strongest appeals of religion is the concept of everlasting life. The traditional religions that speak of life after death in a spiritual hereafter have, for many people, lessened the fears of death and dying.

● *Religion and Your Family*

Religion is a personal subject, and yet it also can be a family affair. It's likely that regardless of the religious interests of your own children—they may be devout church-goers or have grown away from any religious interest—your own religious practices may rub off to some extent on your grandchildren.

Traditionally it often fell to the grandparents to provide religious education and indoctrination. Old paintings show scenes of a white-haired grandfather teaching the grandson in his lap the Hebrew alphabet. Another depicts a grandmother hearing the catechism lesson of twin boys. And, of course, holiday feasts at Grandma and Grandpa's are a way of life for many people.

In some cases an older person's interest in religious practices may be the link by which an appreciation of spiritual values is passed along to later generations. And this may be done in an informal, subtle way, or perhaps more directly, by a grandparent, with the approval of the parents, taking grandchildren to church services, Bible class, or other religious activities.

● *Exploring Religious Activities*

If the subject of religion has some aspects that you have not fully explored, you may want to follow up with some specific activities. Fig. 18-1 is a list of things you might want to consider including in your retirement life. The two columns to the right give you the opportunity to follow through.

Note under "Implementation" what action you can take to pursue the interest. For example, if you are interested in prayer, read about the

FIG. 18-1 Choice of Activities

	Implementation	*Talk to*
1. Prayer, alone or with others		
2. Bible reading		
3. Other religious reading: books, magazines, newspapers		
4. Listening to religious programs on radio or TV		
5. Attending church services		
6. Praying with others		
7. Religious discussion group, or Bible study class		
8. Discussing religion with children, possibly your own grandchildren		
9. Visits to churches or shrines		
10. Writing spiritual reflections		
11. Doing good works— volunteering charity, philanthropy		
12. Other		

subject, refresh your understanding of why people pray, how they pray, and so on. Or, discuss the subject with others.

Put down the names under "Talk to" of individuals or organizations in which you might find people who could help you pursue your interest.

One final note: In his book, *Threshold,* Alan H. Olmstead makes the point that a normal American Sunday, often crammed full of things there isn't time for during working days, has become the most highly pressured day of the week. Retired people, who benefit from the de-pressurizing of Sunday, might find themselves in a position to completely reschedule what they do on this day. As Olmstead says, "Perhaps Sunday has been liberated. It occurs to me: I might even, some Sunday, be able, have time, to go to church."

● *Suggested Reading*

Change Your Life Through Prayer by Stella Terrill Mann is intended to teach readers how to pray, when to pray and what to pray for. (Bantam, Des Plaines, IL 60016, $1.75)

The Emergence of Christian Science in American Religious Life by Stephen Gottschalk attempts to understand Christian Science within the context of American religious thought and culture. (University of California Press, Berkeley 94720, $4.95)

Every Whit Whole, The Adventure of Spiritual Healing by Michael Drury examines Christian healing as an integral part of Christ's doctrine and offers practical approaches to trying it for oneself. (Dodd, Mead, NY, NY 10016, $5.95)

The Experience of Inner Healing by Ruth Carter Stapleton provides further insights, testimonies and personal histories of the power of "Charismatic renewal." (Bantam, Des Plaines, IL 60016, $2.25)

A Great Treasury of Christian Spirituality by Edward Alcott is a collection of spiritual writing, ancient, medieval and modern, highlighting the process of Christian growth. (Carillon Books, NY, NY 10017, $4.95 and $8.95)

The Interpretation of Otherness: Religion, Literature, and the American Imagination by Giles Gunn explores the implicit and explicit religious dimensions found in literature and literary criticism, concentrating on American literature, and discusses several works in detail. (Oxford University Press, NY, NY 10016, $14.95)

The Jesus Book edited by Michael F. McCauley brings together hundreds of sayings, epigrams, thoughts, poems and reflections on Christ. Illustrated. (Thomas More Press, Chicago, IL 60601, $12.95)

Searching for Truth: A Personal View of Roman Catholicism By Peter Kelly is a design for anyone within and without the church, concerned with the future of Christian faith in the world. (Collins & World, Cleveland, OH 44111, $8.95)

The Seven Mysteries of Life: An Exploration in Science and Philosophy by Guy Murchie presents spirituality and philosophy in everyday terms by a visionary who emphasizes the unity of all things. (Houghton, Mifflin, Boston, 02107, $17.95)

The Seven Storey Mountain by Thomas Merton is Merton's autobiography and search for faith and peace in a world that first fascinated and then appalled him. (Harcourt, Brace, Jovanovich, NY, NY 10017, $4.95)

The Spiritual Journey of Jimmy Carter: In His Own Words compiled and with an introduction by Wesley G. Pippert is a compilation of the President's religious thoughts that provides a candid portrait of the man in the Oval Office. (Macmillan, NY, NY 10022, $8.95)

Stories of God: An Unauthorized Biography by John Shea explores revelation, tradition, literature, history and human behavior to show how stories of God can be understood to make God present to us now. (Thomas More Press, Chicago, IL 60601, $4.95)

The Uncomplicated Christian by LeRoy Dugan offers four springboards to spiritual progress plus seven simple steps to put them into daily practice. (Bethany Fellowship, Minneapolis, MI 55438, $1.95)

Understanding the New Religions edited by Jacob Needleman and George Baker seeks to explore the meaning of the "new religions" and their relationship to American life. (Seabury Press, NY, NY 10017, $8.95 and $17.50)

You Can Beat Those Spiritual Blahs by Lew Miller offers a personal strategy for a rejuvenated faith based on the Second Book of Peter. (Accent Books, Denver, CO 80215, $2.95)

19

CONTINUING
EDUCATION

Albert Edward Wiggam, in his *Marks of an Educated Man,* tells this anecdote:

> One summer night to the home of a bored and disappointed man in his middle years comes a visitor who enchants him with tales of travel, adventures, remarkable friends, books read and written, and lovely deeds performed for and encountered from others; and also with his wisdom, wit and loving-kindness. When at length the disappointed man emerges from the spell long enough to ask the visitor who he is, he replies, "I'm the man you might have been."

Perhaps it isn't necessary to tell this dolorous tale to emphasize the advantages of experience and education. For the person facing retirement and considering plans for making this period of life a full and happy one, the opportunities of continuing education may take on new significance.

There is no doubt that interest in education is expressed widely—though sometimes in other than realistic terms—by a large segment of the adult population. Here is how one source describes the situation:

> Many American adults, perplexed by the rapidly changing world around them and more or less dissatisfied with their own situation in it, frequently engage in unproductive wishful thinking. "I wish I had finished high school!" "If only I had a million dollars!" "If my figure were like hers!" "If I could play the piano the way he can!" "I wish I could write—what great things I'd have to say!" "If I'd had the opportunities he has, how successful I would be!" "If I had the money to finish college, then I would qualify for a promotion."[1]

[1]"The New York Times Guide to Continuing Education in America," edited by Frances Coombs Thomson. New York: Quadrangle Books, 1972.

Not all these wishes can be satisfied by study, training, and the acquiring of knowledge or a skill. But for many who want to *do* something about these yearnings instead of day-dreaming, there are far-reaching rewards that training and education can offer by transforming dreams into reality.

The concept of continuing education suggests that learning need never cease. There always can be, in every person's life, room for education. If this is so, why aren't more of us perpetual scholars? The fault usually lies with the stereotype with which education is identified.

● *Common Misconceptions*

Learning is sometimes thought of as something that is done *to* a person, a kind of information-stuffing operation not unlike the stuffing of a goose. Another view is of competitive groups of people pinned down in neat rows and kept on their good behavior by an authoritarian teacher. And then, final threat, each student is "marked," rated on his or her performance in a way that may affront abilities and undermined self-respect.

None of these factors need exist in a learning situation. Ideally, learning should be stimulating, rewarding, enriching—and fun.

Another mistaken idea that keeps some people from the halls of learning is the fear of being too "old" to learn. "Education is for kids," says one preretiree to whom some courses of study were recommended. Behind this kind of tunnel vision often lies the fear that, "You can't teach old dogs new tricks—and I feel I'm in the old-dog category."

But people in the highest age brackets still have the capacity to learn. Studies show that there is a decided variation in the rate at which people acquire and retain information and skills, but these investigations also suggest that age is not a determining factor in ability to learn. Contrary to the adage, you *can* teach an older dog new tricks. What matters is whether the dog—at whatever age—*wants* to learn the tricks. As a matter of fact, over 60 percent of the individuals involved in learning today (teaching, academic and informal course students) are over the age of fifty. These adult Americans actively seek a broad range of educational services to adjust to changing life situations. They are interested in acquiring new skills and interests so that they may take part in activities where they feel wanted and needed, to fulfill their desire to be of service and, in many cases, to earn additional income.

Interestingly enough, preliminary fears of not fitting in, of seeming out of place among a younger group, usually disappear quickly. The reason is that, as the learning group begins to function, the mature approach and experience of the older students becomes a welcome addition. And there is mutual pleasure as the younger people find themselves on a peer basis with the more mature students.

It should be made clear that education should not be confused with "busywork," activity undertaken for the sake of "looking busy." There are enough things to be done in this world that will yield a profit—material or otherwise—to make busywork unnecessary. Nor is there a need to favor an activity, such as education, because it is status-charged. Fortunately, education in one's later years has much more in its favor than the fact that it "looks good."

● *The Value of Education*

FULFILLMENT OF NEEDS

The 1971 White House Conference on Aging identified four categories of educational needs of particular interest to those people no longer holding down regular jobs who are seeking some worthwhile replacement for remunerative activity. The Conference statement emphasizes the practical benefits of late-in-life learning:

> 1. *Adjustment needs.* Trying to cope with a new and unfamiliar life situation involving, perhaps, reduced income, increasing social isolation, flagging energies, and the feeling of being superfluous. These adjustment needs are the object of a number of educational approaches.
> 2. *Identity needs.* Finding new outlets for skills and interests previously absorbed by a job in business or a place in the community and reestablishing the feeling of being a recognized and appreciated individual. These identity needs are part of a whole process of maintaining or recovering one's sense of self-worth.
> 3. *Participation needs.* Developing appropriate means of pursuing one's role as a significant element in a participatory democracy; to help advance the social, economic, and political interests of the cohort of retired citizens through the electoral process; and to feel that one is making one's own contribution to the well-being of the larger society. The politics of aging and consciousness-raising among hitherto passive senior citizens have been popular parts of the new curriculum.

4. *Fulfillment needs*. Seeking to be of service, to be useful and wanted, to feel that one is part of a community and a productive member of society. The idea that upon retirement life can begin anew, not peter out, is the exciting ingredient of several approaches to the concept of new careers for older people. Yet, so little is known about productive opportunities for persons past fifty, and little information on the subject is being offered by institutions of higher education.

PREPARATION FOR RETIREMENT

In a study "Never Too Old to Learn" by the Academy for Educational Development, it is pointed out that people of retirement age may have difficulty in setting personal priorities. Many become excessively preoccupied with problems of health and income. Some start with romanticized expectations about their retirement years, such as the continuing satisfactions of extended travel, if they can afford it, or the full-time pursuit of recreation. They do not always fully understand why they are dissatisfied with a lifestyle that they may have been awaiting eagerly for decades. For hundreds of thousands of people who have the foresight to learn how to plan their finances, build their interests, and their point of view, retirement comes as a welcome event. For others, unprepared for retirement, it comes as a psychological disaster. Education—particularly in the preretirement period—can make the difference.

The AED study goes on to describe a concept that can be helpful to you in thinking about continuing education:

> A new educational philosophy, lifelong learning, is reforming the way the public thinks of schooling and the way educators think of their mission. Whereas "education" has traditionally been defined in terms of formal schooling, this new approach has brought the recognition that learning is a continual, lifelong process, not one that stops at adolescence. As a result, postsecondary institutions have begun to develop programs that better integrate education with other aspects of life. These programs include work-study arrangements, which encourage undergraduates to incorporate periods of employment into their course of study, and external degree arrangements, which allow people of all ages to create their own program of study with degree requirements established in consultation with an advisor. The external degree programs are paving the way for granting academic credit for life experience.

However, no one should permit other people's enthusiasm—including mine, the federal government's, or an organization like the Academy for Educational Development, which has a vested interest favoring formal education—to be persuasive. How do you feel about continuing education for yourself? Are you interested? Are there benefits for you?

In his book, "The Lifelong Learner," Ronald Gross sets down what he calls the characteristics of those for whom learning has a natural appeal.[2]

- You are open to new experiences, ideas, information, and insights. You like to make things happen instead of waiting for life to act on you.
- There are always things you'd love to know more about, appreciate better, or learn to do. In fact, you never have the feeling that you know everything, have every skill, you'll ever need to know.
- You feel better about yourself when you are successfully learning something new.
- You've learned enormously from certain important experiences which don't usually rate as "subjects."
- You often learn a great deal in ways other than taking courses.
- The kind of life you want to lead five years from now requires that you begin to learn new things now.
- You believe that investing in your own growth is the best investment in your future—occupational or personal.
- You have been attracted by, or perhaps are already enrolled in, one of the new kinds of educational programs for adults offered by colleges and universities around the country.

In addition to Ronald Gross's list, there is another approach that can help you decide whether the classroom or other settings for learning are for you.

Is there a subject you would like to know about that would help you in some planned activity—a hobby, travel, and so on? For example, speaking another language, learning the history of some place, or possibly a craft you want to practice with greater expertness?

Is there a subject that would enrich something you're already doing? For example, if you're a movie fan, some colleges give courses in contemporary films. These could add substantially to your appreciation and enjoyment. A course in cooking could make you an even better cook—

[2]*The Lifelong Learner*, Ronald Gross. New York: Simon & Schuster, 1977.

with potential increased dining pleasure for all concerned.

Is there a subject that would boost your ability to earn money? This might be anything from typing and shorthand to a training program for radio and television repairs.

Is there a subject that has enticed and enthralled you, but which you've never pursued? Such a study might satisfy strong intellectual curiosity. Astronomy, for example, has brought just this satisfaction to many adults. For others, philosophy and psychology have put them on familiar terms with fascinating areas of knowledge. Impractical subjects? Certainly, in everyday terms. But when you are of retirement age, subjects like these shed light on mysteries that touch on our place in the universe—ultimate questions which we now have the time and perspective to examine anew.

It there a subject that would help you solve a current problem? For example, a course in home care for older people may help you better cope with problems arising from having an aging person in your household.

● *Where and How to Go*

PLACES TO LEARN

Interests and purposes like those just discussed don't inevitably lead you to an institution of learning. Books or tapes on almost any subject might make it possible for you to go it alone, and that's fine. Self-education may be the best kind. But in adopting an approach to learning, just make sure you consider the major possibilities:

• Local schools—high schools, colleges, universities.

• Organizations that offer courses—Ys, community organizations, special interest groups. For example, Asian societies in large cities give courses in Far Eastern philosophy, culture, and so on.

• Extension courses—special adult courses offered by institutions of higher learning.

• Correspondence courses.

• Community study groups—in areas like literature, religion, art, and so on.

• An employer's own education-training programs—some organizations can properly boast programs aimed to improve the intellectual and skill capabilities of employees. For some larger companies, the curricula are varied, supported by audio and video equipment, films and film strips, and well-qualified instructors. Not all courses are open to everybody. Employees can explore their interests with a counselor in the training department. Studies that are strongly job-oriented may depend on learning-by-doing and be restricted to those who can immediately apply what is learned.

Some educational groups—The American Council on Education and the University of the State of New York—are backing a move to give credit for company courses because, as they see it, these may be in essential respects comparable to college courses.

• Self-study—You design your own course, with the help of materials from your local library or other source of books, tapes, records, and so on. Television, potentially a fantastic educational medium, in some localities offers series of information programs. Subscription TV (STV) and Cable TV (CATV) expand the range of programs available both on networks and local stations. The arts are given their due—symphony, ballet, theatre. Interviews with political, literary, and performing-arts figures can refresh and fill out interest in these subject areas. In some areas, colleges and universities televise certain courses of study regularly. Tuning in on these programs not only provides mental and cultural stimulation, but also helps you keep tuned in to the times.

CREDIT FOR EXPERIENCE

Hundreds of colleges and universities throughout the country have encouraged adults to resume their schooling. To make the open door even more attractive, the adult student is being offered life-experience credits—that is, credit for what has been learned outside the academic world. This credit may reflect experience gained in a paid job, in volunteer work, or any "teaching" environment. In the College of New Rochelle, 125 adult students have earned up to thirty credits for writing their life stories.

For example, Lenore Altman has three children, all grown up and away from home. Her husband makes a fair salary as a heavy-equipment salesman, and plans to retire soon. She took one year of college during World War II, when she worked in Washington, D.C.

Lenore Altman has just enrolled in a New York State program. She has gotten credit for part of her Washington college courses, for teaching handicrafts to children, for experience as a publicity agent and fund raiser for several hospitals, and for a series of articles she did as a theater reviewer for the local newspaper in her town.

"I expect to get my degree—a Bachelor of Arts—in about a year," she says. "I'll be thrilled to have it. I've seen too many doors closed to my friends who wanted to go back to work and didn't have a college diploma."

If you want to know more about prospects and possibilities of going back to school for a degree, check with the institutions in your area. Each of them has an advisor who can give you the information and guidance that will help you decide whether this is for you.

FINANCIAL AID

Some employers have an active interest in underwriting the educational interests of employees. Their motivation may be described as benevolent selfishness. Says one personnel director of a large electronics equipment firm:

"Any time an employee betters himself or herself educationally— whether it is job-related or not—we feel the company is going to benefit in the long run." And the long run may include a postretirement interest.

It is this type of thinking that explains why many business and government organizations are willing to pay for some or all of the costs of an employee's schooling or training. Here are some figures from a recent study.[1]

Benefits Paid	No. of Plans
100% plus some or all fees	51
90% plus some fees	2
85% plus some fees	1
80% plus some fees	2
75% plus some or all fees	21
66⅔% plus some fees	2
50% and some fees	10
Sliding scale	24
Other	18

Some companies pay only for courses that are job related: for example, a technical writer on the staff of a research and development unit in a chemical company would be reimbursed for a course taken to

[1]*Industrial Relations News*, Chicago, Ill. 60606

improve his writing skill, but not for a course in Development of Jazz in the 1970s.

Although job-relatedness is generally a criterion for payment with most companies, only a few stick to precise definitions. The majority of plans permit all the courses required for a degree, although some plan administrators grumble when employee-students ask for reimbursement for a course like music appreciation or the history of art.

You have to query your own personnel people in order to find out just what the limitations may be in your own company. In some cases, these same individuals can help you plan a course of study according to your needs.

● *Educational Options for Retirees*

People feel differently about formal education. For some going to school—in the later years of their education—seems a waste of time. "It wasn't until I got out of college," says one successful manager, "that I began to learn in the world of work itself what I had to know to get ahead."

However, there's more to learning than that segment of it that helps people in their wage-earning activities. Many individuals are fascinated by the process of learning itself, the opportunity to acquire new ideas and outlooks. For one such person a study of history is absolutely fascinating: "That's where we came from; that's how the world became what it is today," says one fifty-year-old student who is taking history courses at a local university.

There's no limit to the fields available to the continuing student. Music, art, psychology, philosophy, any and all of these have their devotees, people who in continuing their education find fascination, uplift, even excitement in the process of learning.

Opportunities for continuing education exist in almost every community regardless of size. In a town in northeastern Massachusetts with only a few hundred residents, there is nevertheless an arts and crafts center formed by local people that teaches everything from drawing to weaving. "When a retired professor moved into the community," reports one of the citizens, "someone thought up the idea of having him give a course in contemporary history, based on reading current newspapers and news magazines."

INSTITUTE FOR RETIRED PROFESSIONALS

One movement in continuing education is particularly noteworthy because it is becoming more and more popular all over the country. This development, known as the Institute for Retired Professionals (IRP), started in the New School for Social Research in New York City. Highly successful, other centers of education in other communities became interested in IRP at the New School. Almost a hundred institutions of higher learning sent representatives to observe the IRP programs. There is a growing number of IRP-oriented activities now available from Maine to California. A description of the IRP program as it now exists at the New School provides a revealing and useful picture by which to measure other educational opportunities available to you.

"Many of the people," said the spokesman, "have built a second life around IRP. Their enthusiasm and commitment is unusual. . . ."

These are the words of Fred Plant, a retired Vice President of Block Drug Company, of Jersey City. Plant is himself a member of the Institute for Retired Professionals, and took on the job of doing public relations for the group. His personal enthusiasm comes through clearly as he describes how the organization works:

"A unique quality of IRP is that the members themselves plan and implement the programs. There are no guest lecturers in our meeting rooms. Everthing is done 'in house.' "

Although the IRP approach is limited to "professionals"—at first that meant people with advanced degrees, but later those with a regular college degree qualified—the basic idea promises to spread to a broader base of operation.

For example, the pilot group was formed at and affiliated with the New School for Social Research in New York City. However a recent survey shows that thirty-eight institutions are at various stages in the development of programs for retired professionals and executives. All these programs use IRP's self-administering, self-implementing idea. And from responses in the survey, it becomes clear that the IRP approach can be used by groups without the requirement of advanced education. Two elements explain the high level of involvement of IRP members: (1) the program is developed, administered, and run by members themselves, and (2) each member is expected to participate in an active way in the learning sessions.

For example, in a typical class, the "faculty" consists of a chairperson and co-chairpeople who run the proceedings. In a course such as The

Detective Story, each member of the group will be asked to read an example of the genre, and write a paper that describes and critiques the book. A general discussion then follows the reading of the report on the book. In some courses "students" will be asked to read and research different related areas, this variety later being reflected in the discussion in class.

Origin of the program

In the spring of 1962 Dr. Hy Hirsch, a retiree, approached the New School with an idea for a new kind of continued learning program for retired professionals and executives. The school agreed to conduct a three-year experiment if Hirsch could recruit retirees who were willing to pay the first year's fee of $35. When he brought in sixty-five checks from retirees, the IRP was launched.

By the end of the first year Hirsch had gathered a group of 180, who came from many walks of life, to be leaders, teachers, and participants. At the end of the third year, the program was judged a success and IRP became a permanent department of the school. By 1978 membership had risen to almost 700 members, with a volunteer faculty from the member group numbering about 100. Council seats on the IRP policy-making body are contested for in an annual election.

Courses of study

Admittedly the Institute for Retired Professionals—although the term "professional" has been watered down somewhat to accept anyone with a college degree—represents a group of higher than average education and possible interest.

To satisfy the varying demands for the student body of approximately 700 people requires about 70 classes. These classes are run by the members themselves, organized around a chairperson and possibly one or two assistants.

The groups meet weekly or biweekly for an hour and a half in morning or afternoon sessions. There is no paid teaching staff. The members are leaders and learners alike.

Assignments are made to individuals who then become "experts" in a given area. For example, in one literature course a student was assigned to study the novels of Theodore Dreiser and several others were given research to do that related to the life and times of Dreiser. All the students were also given assignments that would make it possible for them to participate in a discussion on the subject. The woman who had the primary job of studying Dreiser's novels wrote a paper reporting on her research. After reading her report to the assembled group, the general discussion started.

"And that's where the fun and worthwhile aspects of learning come in," says one loyal IRP member. "It's the participation, the give-and-take of the discussions that create interest and involvement and leave us feeling that we really learned—more so than if we just sat and listened to a lecture."

A sample curriculum

A sampling of the titles of some of the courses included in the IRP curriculum gives some idea of the wide range of interests of the group:

RETIREMENT
Life and Living for Retirees
Making the Best of Our Years
The Seventh Stage
Yester-Morrow
Yoga for Retirees
You and Your Health

THE CONTEMPORARY SCENE
Contemporary Affairs
Current Scene
Foreign Policy
Issues and Action
News & Views
Periodicals
Speaker's Choice
Sunday Magazine
The Travellers
World of Business

LITERATURE AND THE ARTS
Aesthetics
American Nobel Prize Novelists
Biography
Contemporary Poetry
Contemporary Literature
Literature of the Ancient World
Our Musical Heritage
Playreading
Shakespeare
The Culture Scene
The Dectective Story
The History of the Dance
The Novella
The Political Novel
The World of Art
The Writings of Camus
Theatre

LANGUAGE STUDIES
French Conv.
French Playreading
German Literature
Hebrew Conv.
Italian Conv.
Russian Conv.
Spanish Conv.

THE SOCIAL SCIENCES
Cultural History
Jewish History
Social Science Study
Modern Thought
The Other Side
Today's Economics
Uses of Power in History
  and Today

THE SCIENCES
Adv. Science Seminar
Bio-Med. Problems
Handwriting Analysis Seminar
What's New In Science

WORKSHOPS
Chamber Music
Chess
Classic Guitar
Creative Dramatics
Fiction
Music Workshop
Non-Fiction
Paper Sculpture
Pencil Sketching
Photographers
Recorder Consort
Sketching & Painting
The Singers
Vocal Experiences
Watercolor/Acrylic

● *Related Social Activities*

Of special interest in connection with IRP is the manner in which the program, originally purely educational, has expanded to meet related needs.

Of course, the wish to make friends with those having the same interests is common to all large groups, but the need of retirees is unique, for many opportunities to socialize have been drastically reduced. However, because of the contacts the IRP students make in the classroom, it was found that common learning interests provide new dimensions for friendship.

In addition to spontaneous friendships that have developed, each class or learning group has a social secretary who plans get-togethers honoring the individuals who have volunteered to do the actual business of running classes.

OTHER PROGRAMS

Obviously there are many other kinds of formal education available to adults. Colleges, universities, and some high schools give courses which may be taken selectively. And, of course, extension programs and high school night courses have been a staple in adult education for decades.

In addition to studies available at regular seats of learning, churches, community centers, and Ys throughout the country are also seeking to satisfy the hunger of the population for continuing education. Many Ys, for example, give courses under the general heading of Educational Program for Retired Adults.

A survey of the people taking courses of this type shows the typical attendee has the equivalent of a high school education, a sufficiently strong base on which many courses are offered in everything from contemporary events based on an analysis and discussion of newspaper headlines to courses in poetry reading.

In one large community center in Boston a program consisting of forty courses was offered to senior citizens at fees ranging from $5 to $15 per course. As in the IRP program, the courses were given in the morning and afternoon. This program is simply explained: These are the times when other community groups, housewives and students, cannot attend elective educational programs and of course it's to the advantage of the institution to use its facilities as fully as possible.

20
RETIREMENT PROBLEM-SOLVING

Most people, by the time they face retirement, have their lives pretty much under control. This doesn't mean that postretirement will be a problem-free period, but that present day-to-day difficulties tend to be pretty much in hand and unexpected crises are relatively few—a reflection of a stable and mature controlled existence.

But as you approach retirement—and certainly after you have reached it—new situations may arise and things you didn't think of as problems develop a cutting edge. For example, a simple question like "How old are you?" once could have been fielded and answered with little hesitation. Now the same words may have implications that make you hesitate to respond.

Or, while you were working, you were pretty much insulated from the sights, sounds, and crises faced by your neighbors. But now that you're home most of the time, the fact that there's a heavy drinker next door may pose a trying and immediate problem for you.

● *Problems You May Encounter*

How you meet these new challenges and handle these new problems will have a great effect on your wellbeing. This chapter presents some of the problem situations you may begin to encounter as you reach retirement age, and some suggestions for how to handle them.

VISITING YOUR FORMER WORKPLACE

Almost always, you will be confronted with the possibility of going back to the place you used to work, either to finish up some business with the personnel office, or perhaps just for a visit. Former colleagues may invite you to join them for lunch, or you may just feel like revisiting the scene of your old "crimes." Should you go?

Of course, you know better than anyone else what your own situation is, but some general advice based on the experiences of many is—go if you wish, but don't expect everything to be the same as it was. Once you are no longer actively involved with the day-to-day business at work, your relationships also change. Your former coworkers may be delighted to see you, but your involvement with them is simply not what it was. Don't blame people for these changed attitudes. Even the strongest of friendships grow out of the circumstances that tie people together. It's not insincerity nor a betrayal of past feelings, but change in ourselves and in our lives that weaken past relationships.

MEMORY ON PAPER: A JOB COLLAGE

One outlet for your job-nostalgia may seem at first a bit strange to you, but many people have tried and enjoyed this combination artistic endeavor and trip down memory lane.

What's suggested is making a collage, a collection of items mounted and framed to go on the wall of your den, living room, or wherever. Two steps take you to the finished product, a wall hanging that will gain in value and meaning with the passing years.

Of course, you can keep your job memorabilia in a scrap book or other repository, but there is a special effectiveness in being able to see the items all together. They reinforce one another, intensify memory.

First, dig into your drawers, files, photo albums, or in these same places of friends and colleagues who may have items you may have missed or simply don't have. In some cases, the records of particular items may be available from the personnel department, or the files of the organization's house organ. Some of the items you might want to include:

• Announcement of your arrival in the organization. It might be in the form of a memo, bulletin-board notice, or a piece in the house organ.

• Notice of promotions, job changes.

• Any news items having to do with your job, your department, in which you had a special interest.

• Photographs of colleagues, organization officials, organization events, shots of you at work, grounds or buildings important to you.

• Events in which you figured as a participant or committee member covered by a printed program. These might be anything from the annual dinner, Christmas party, picnic, and so on.

• Your retirement dinner or celebration—announcements, photos, coverage in the organization paper or magazine, local press, and so on.

• Farewell memos from friends, colleagues, officials.

Anything that's on paper, or that is small or flat enough to paste down, that brings back your working days can be used. One such collage I saw featured facsimiles of a friend's first and last paychecks—showing the increase in salary over a 24-year period. Another one included a photo in color of the company building, which had been used for the cover of the annual report. Once you've collected your memorabilia, you're ready for the next step.

Get a piece of cardboard—any light board that is reasonably stiff will do—that is large enough to take the items you've collected; 16 by 20 inches is a good size for display, but collages can be made any size within the limits of your wall space. One consideration—if you want to frame the finished work, a very large frame with glass can be expensive.

With the cardboard before you, spread out all the items you want to use. At this point, feel free to arrange them any way you please. They can be laid out in rows, curves, a patchwork of swirls or mixed shapes. Some items you will want to have visible in full—a photograph of your department in the early days, for example, when there were only a handful of people in it, but each one a cherished friend. But other items can be partly obscured, just showing the important part of it. For example, an anniversary dinner given for a company official might be represented by a menu of the affair, which you might want to display only in part—the heading, a few lines of the program—the rest of it covered by a photograph of the guest of honor.

After you have a fairly good idea of just how you want the various items to show in your collage, start pasting them in place on the cardboard. Use an adhesive such as rubber cement that will be permanent and won't discolor the pieces. The wrong adhesive will yellow paper or cause it to turn brittle and crack after a while. Check with a supplier to make sure your collage will be able to withstand time at least as long as your memories will.

Framing is desirable for two reasons: first to preserve your collage, and second, to make it look even better. If you observed the caution made earlier, and avoided making the collage grossly oversize, framing can be relatively inexpensive. Plastic frames—those made of clear plastic, with front and sides one unit—are one good possibility. Check in second-hand stores and flea markets. Old frames, with glass, can often be picked up cheaply. It will help if the dimensions of your collage are close to those of standard frame sizes. Sometimes adjustments can be made by cutting down a frame or trimming down the backing on which the collage is mounted.

Then drive your nail, hang your collage, and your happy past will always be with you.

TELEVISION

Television is our latest and most personal form of mass communication. It has shaped our mid-twentieth-century culture, brought pleasure to countless millions, added one more growth industry to our economy, and through its advertising potential, helped numberless providers of goods and services find quick access to new markets.

For retired people, the magic box poses something special in the way of both opportunity and as a problem. Because it can be a too-perfect answer to, "How shall I spend my time?"—because it is inexpensive, convenient, and potentially fascinating—you may have to give it special consideration. It may be advisable, as a matter of fact, to have to think about it intensively enough to be able to come up with a personal viewing policy. If you feel that your use of TV would benefit from fine-tuned thinking, here are some suggested guidelines.

Time limits

Is it possible that your TV watching is too much of a good thing? You may find continuing sequences of programs that interest you keep you glued to the tube. A quick mental calculation may show that you spend an astonishingly large number of hours a day at it.

A "reasonable amount" of viewing for one person may be twice too much for another. A person whose TV viewing takes up periods lengthy enough for it to become a major element in daily activity and preoccupation, may be short-changing other aspects of life. TV has a great deal to offer. But if it cuts into time that in your case might better be spent with other people, in contributions to the welfare and happiness of others—through volunteer work, for example—then a realistic answer may have to be found to the question, "How much is too much?"

The malady known as "middle-aged spread" has a companion called "TV muscle tone." This ailment is distinguished by loss of healthy muscle tone and a general debility resulting from lack of movement and exercise.

A second result of too much TV can be eye troubles. The complaints may range from ordinary eye strain to damage resulting from the particular circumstances of over-exposure along with poor room lighting. For example, watching the TV in an otherwise dark room can result in vision setbacks that may require medical care.

Selective viewing

One practical control that can prevent the misuse of TV is to pick and choose judiciously from among the daily offerings. The chance to see your favorite stars, the outstanding entertainers of the day, in your own home for free is irresistible. But why not go through the day's or week's offerings, and pick just those entertainment shows that really grab you? Some experienced and wise viewers may say, How else would you go? The answer is, some people either channel hop, each hour or half-hour selecting the "best there is," mediocre though it be; or tune in on their favorite channel and stick with it, hour after hour. The pre-selection mentioned seems like a preferable alternative.

One of the unquestioned values of TV lies in its potential to educate and inform. The minutes spent on educationally worthwhile viewing—documentaries, contemporary history and events, some of the series on public TV—can enrich us permanently.

And news programs, when they are at their best—which usually means a minimum of sensational police-news coverage—can be an excellent way of keeping abreast of our changing times.

Review

Despite good intentions, even with a guiding plan, actual TV watching can get out of hand. The natural fascination of the medium, like eating peanuts, may be hard to control once started. It can be helpful every once in a while to keep a record of actual time spent. Then, total the hours. If they don't seem excessive to you, fine. But if the figures amaze and distress you, watch yourself in the days ahead. Is inertia—or lack of a desirable alternative—keeping you tube-bound? Consider summoning up the resolve that turns off the set and returns your mind and body to worthwhile pursuits until the next good program comes along.

Of course, as a member of the writing brotherhood, I consider reading as a prime adjunct or replacement for anything going on TV.

WAITING IN LINE

Queueing up, unfortunately, is part of many essential activities, everything from supermarket shopping to airline travel. And postretirement, you may be doing more of this kind of thing. Standing and waiting is a boring (in)activity at best. When you add a tendency toward muscle weariness or foot problems, standing in line becomes a bit of torture that most of us would like to do without. Next time you're queued up—perhaps at an airline counter waiting to see if there's room on the flight you want, or you have a cartful of groceries you want, desperately, to get through the check-out counter—see if these ideas can help:

Sharing

If you're with a companion, perhaps you can take turns with the actual standing and waiting. While one of you is "serving" the other can be free to walk around or perhaps sit and relax. Ten-minute stints can make even a long wait a lot pleasanter.

Holding a place

In some situations, particularly if the tension levels are low, you may be able to get the person in line behind you to keep your place. A pleasant request to that person, "Do you mind keeping my place? I'll be gone for just a few minutes," may get an agreement. Don't delay your return to the point where your place-holding acquaintance gets to the service point. If this happens the next person in line, who may not have been too happy about the arrangement you originally made, is likely to enter an objection. And, of course, the whole point of this arrangement is to avoid arguments and hassles.

Sitting

Whether it's train or bus tickets or other travel situations, people with luggage often may use a large sturdy suit-case to sit on, thus delivering that blessing known as "taking a load off your feet." One hardy soul, a woman waiting in line at a notoriously slow government agency, brought a light-weight folding chair to ease the waiting ordeal. In the English tradition there is a gadget known as a shooting stick, which is a combination cane and monopedal seat. In some circumstances, particularly where there is soft ground underfoot which will accommodate the point of the support, you may be able to find or borrow one of these.

In some cases you can by-pass the entire standing bit. Popular restaurants commonly have lines of people waiting to be seated at meal times. Making a phone reservation in advance may well save you the wait. Or, tell the maitre d' to find you at the bar when your turn comes.

In other instances where arrangements can be made over the phone, take the time to prevent the necessity of standing and waiting. It's not only easier on the feet and body muscles, it's also a boost to one's self-esteem.

CONVERTING FREE TIME INTO MONEY

This isn't about converting lots of free time into lots of money; that is a subject touched on in Chapter 16, dealing with possibilities of employment after you've retired. The situation discussed here is the one that confronts you when you find that, despite reasonably good use of your time, you still find gaps in your daily rounds.

Our feelings about doing something for which we get paid persist after retirement. And some of us may feel a little aggravating twinge when we realize we have three or four hours a week—more or less—for which we seem to have no immediate use, that are just going to waste.

If you like the idea of trying to change a few hours and minutes into a few dollars and cents, here are some approaches that may just make it possible.

Make something

Is there some item or object that you can make that no one else around can, or that you can make better than anyone else? People who have been able to give an affirmative answer to this question have had in mind anything from baking bread to building bird (or doll) houses. Selling? Well, that's usually the tough part, but still possible. One person simply circulates the word among friends and neighbors that the fruits of his or her labor are up for sale to a deserving few. Others have gotten permission from neighborhood storekeepers to put a notice up announcing the availability of the item—with a phone number, or, "Leave your name and number with Mr. Smith, the proprietor, and I will contact you."

Do something

You may want to go scouting around for people who need services that you can supply during your free hours. A lot of the services are traditional—anything from baby-sitting to lawn care. But one retiree, whose hobby is gourmet cooking, helps neighbors prepare one or two dishes for weekend partying. Another man, who has taught himself to be a much-better-than-average calligrapher, has called on the personnel departments of two or three of the big plants in his neighborhood and has arranged to fill in his time by making up colorful presentation documents—for special awards, anniversaries, presentations, and so on, as needed by the organizations.

Think of something

Few people are ever so busy they can't think. Retired people aren't likely to be in this category at any rate. But there are some *subjects* for thought that people may keep putting off for a number of reasons: they may be intimidating, or require heavy concentration and a quality of time—quiet, unpressured—not always available.

How about scheduling thinking time in these free periods in your daily activities? This is an act that might not be practical for some people—their minds just don't work that way—but might work extremely well for others. Why not try it? At least you'll find out which of the two types of thinkers you are.

The kinds of subjects suitable for this approach may be long range, or may be immediate and concerned with the here-and-now of remunerative activity.

With the object of money-making in mind, consider questions like these:

Is there any use to which the empty back acre of my property could be put? Or, my wife and I have done an excellent job of redecorating our house. Everyone who sees it, raves. Is there any way of commercializing this capability? Or, I have a pick-up truck. Are there things I could do with it for which I could charge—transporting things like single furniture pieces, particularly those that are too heavy or large to fit in a car trunk?

Pinpoint some unused asset you have, either a skill or a physical item—equipment, land, tools powered or otherwise, that may be put to use. Look for a money-making idea, some way of doing something, some needed service that can be translated into salable form.

Test something

Some efforts may have cash possibilities, but you can't be sure until you try. Let's say you hear about someone in the next town raising earthworms in his cellar and making some cash thereby. The idea tempts you. Or maybe it is selling encyclopedias by telephone. Could you do it? If you have the free time and are interested, spend part of that time experimenting. That way you'll be able to avoid going all out for a scheme that had drawbacks you couldn't have anticipated. A trial can tell you either way.

YOUR STATUS

"People come up to me and say, 'Didn't you used to be Eddie Fisher?'" Eddie Fisher, the well-known singer and entertainer of the fifties, makes that rueful statement that suggests that at 49 he's a has-been.

A similar sense of being out of it sometimes threatens the retired person. If a stranger at a party asks what you do and you say, "I used to be a pipefitter," you have in one sense "declassed" yourself. You know you haven't lost your know-how, just your employed status.

You continue to be the person you were, certainly in a professional sense. Just as the retired pipefitter could with perfect propriety say that he's a pipefitter, you can properly refer to yourself as an architect, salesperson, or whatever.

If in subsequent conversation you want to make the point that you are no longer active or that you are engaged in other pursuits, that's fine. But don't put yourself down, or intimate in what you say, do or think, that just because you no longer have an employer, you're somehow reduced in value.

Consider the case of Will Bentley, who was a senior administrator in a large electronics firm. When he's with a new group of people and the conversation turns to professional activities, Bentley says, "I'm recently promoted out of IBM. My work now keeps me busy sixty hours a week." Then he goes on to talk about the many things he does—everything from his activity in the volunteer fire department to turning out beautifully finished furniture for his own use and occasionally for a fortunate customer who is given the privilege of acquiring an original Bentley piece.

Bentley's attitude of having been promoted from one job into another is a realistic and positive way of looking at the change of activity that retirement brings. When you feel you've been "promoted" into retirement, the negative feelings that occasionally are associated with concluding years of regular employment disappear.

YOUR AGE

There is a woman named Edna Fuller who gives dancing lessons in a Los Angeles suburb. She's popular both with her own students and their mothers, who are eager to have them acquire a dancer's grace and occasionally hope for a professional career.

You'd have trouble guessing Edna Fuller's age. She looks to be in her early 50s, but from her birth certificate you would learn that she is 67. She tells the following story:

"I started dancing late in life, at 19. Some of my dancer friends said it was foolish to expect to get anywhere starting then. But I'd developed a sudden fascination for dancing and was resolved to pursue it.

"However I did accept one bit of advice from my well-meaning friends. When I was interviewed for entrance into my first dancing school I was asked how old I was and I answered 15—quite believable because my figure hadn't matured.

"After 3 years of dance lessons I was ready to enroll in a school with much higher professional standards. At this point I was almost 24 and again my friends told me that I'd have trouble if I gave my right age. So when I was asked I replied that I was 18."

Edna Fuller went on to become a successful professional dancer, but at each phase of her career, continued to set the clock back. When she was 45 she said she was 30, and so was accepted into a touring ballet company, with which she stayed for 10 satisfying years.

At this point Edna Fuller was ready to leave the company and start her own dancing school. She was given a farewell birthday party—which she celebrated as her fortieth, although at this point she was 55.

"And here I am with my own school, which I'm happy to report is very successful, and when I look back I have to laugh when I think that if I hadn't lied about my age none of the pleasures, as well as the more trying, vivid experiences of a professional dancer, would have been mine."

Dr. Ralph M. Crowley in the *NRTA Journal* tells a somewhat similar story about his mother, Ada Fuller Crowley, who was widowed at 50. She devoted her next 4 years to obtaining an M.A. in sociology, but had difficulty getting a job. Realizing the difficulty, she changed her age from 54 to 44 and soon thereafter got a job as a social worker with a welfare agency near Chicago.

Her career continued and she continued to get choice jobs, giving her age as 10 years less than it actually was. Dr. Crowley concludes by saying, "Anyone should lie about his or her age as long as there exists such a ridiculous, barbarous custom as mandatory retirement at age 65." Of course, the federal antidiscrimination law now makes it illegal for organizations to discriminate against people because of age in hiring as well as in other job areas.

But there is another area in which the question, "How old are you?" may also be critical, and unfortunately no legal restriction prevails. This is in the area of social intercourse. For example, Paul Henley—not his real name since he talked to me in confidence—said: "As a widower, I'm interested in making friends with members of the opposite sex. I recently met an attractive woman of about 50. On our first date she asked, 'How old are you?' Usually feeling no need to disguise the fact, I responded that I was 67. I noticed that she blinked and dropped her eyes. I interpreted this negative reaction correctly, because even though we'd had a most enjoyable evening she put me off when I asked for another date."

The disappointment and annoyance of Paul Henley and all those who deal with people who consider age a kind of numbers game should be faced up to and dealt with realistically. In this area there is no cut-and-dried way to proceed. In Paul's situation where there is some thought of developing a close relationship, it's probably advisable for people to level with one another about their ages. If knowing one's real age makes that much of a difference to the other person, then it's a test they have failed. An individual who judges a potential friend or intimate on the basis of a number rather than in terms of the person's manner, appearance, the degree of rapport created, and so on, is probably not worth having as a friend in the first place.

Then how should one respond to the question, "How old are you?"

First of all, you can tell the truth. Even in cases where you may feel defensive or suspect that giving your correct age will have a negative effect on the listener, this may be the desirable course.

For example, you would select this option with a person with whom you might want to have a close friendship and you may not want to start this relationship with an untruth. In some cases there may be a procedural or legal reason for being truthful. Qualifying for certain privileges may depend on your being 65 or over, for example. In such a case practicality may be the deciding factor.

Or, you can sidestep the question. "Oh, I never give away state secrets," is the way one 70-year-old puts off giving a direct answer.

In some cases this retort also contains an implied rebuke—which may very well be intentional. In casual relationships the matter of numerical age may be completely irrelevant. And an individual may have every right to be annoyed by what amounts to a prying question.

This type of rejoinder permits of many variations: How old do I look? Or, I really don't remember. Or, Do you have a favorite age? Whatever it is, that's mine.

As mentioned, you may incorporate a rebuke, humor, or simply a crisp turndown of the question.

When the question of age arises it obviously can come in a wide variety of situations and people. Telling the truth about your age and evading an answer are not the only choices.

You can increase the figure to a humorous degree. One individual, hardy at 60 and looking in his early 50s, dismisses the age question by saying, "I'll be 102 on my next birthday." It's an answer that's more subtle than you might think. In addition to making a joke of the question, the answer tends to embarrass the questioner because it says in effect, "You asked the question to verify your suspicion that I'm old, and by exaggerating I seemed to confirm your suspicion in an ironic way."

Finally, you can just plain fib and give a low "estimate." This is a common recourse which many people find easy to justify. Some people say, "I'd be losing a lot of opportunities if I gave my real age, so I lop off 5 or 10 years."

Another justifies taking 7 or 8 years from her true age by saying, "I know I look 45 and feel younger. I think that's a better measure than my chronological age."

When you come right down to it, the best answer to "How old are you?" is the one that does best for you, the one that will eliminate an obstacle, temporary or otherwise, and make you feel better about a situation. But remember, you have every reason to be proud of your age and, in most instances, shouldn't feel reluctant to disclose it.

EMERGENCY ASSISTANCE

The retiree who lives alone and loves it may be fully justified in that feeling of pleasant independence. But if advancing age or physical handicap represent a threat to safety, it's desirable for the individual living alone to have some kind of safety arrangement which will summon assistance quickly and surely if it's needed. In some cases an alarm system makes it practical for an elderly person to live by himself or herself rather than to enter a nursing home. Several kinds of emergency communication systems have been developed.

Lifeline

This is a system installed in the home, an electronic device that automatically can make four calls if a button is pushed. One of the calls can be to a relative who lives reasonably close by. The other three phone call recipients might be a neighbor, doctor, or a local rescue squad.

For individuals who have heart trouble or other medical problems, a push button may be kept on the individual's person in the form of a pocket-sized transmitter.

Information on this system may be had from Marketing Technologies Corporation, 3410 Tuscawaras Street West, Canton, Ohio 44708.

Microalert

This system may be worn on a chain around the neck or on the wrist. It consists of a match-box-sized battery-powered radio transmitter which can trigger a telephone response from as far away as 300 feet with the touch of a finger. Even if the person is outdoors, prerecorded phone messages may be made.

The prerecorded messages might be as follows:

• *To a friend or relative*: "Joe isn't feeling well. Will you please come immediately. Also, notify Dr. Jones, whose telephone number is 456-7300."

• *To a police department*: "There is a medical emergency at the home of Joseph Smith, 717 Main Street. Please send help immediately."

• *To a doctor*: "There is an emergency at the home of your patient, Joseph Smith, 717 Main Street. Please call the police department and make sure they got the message and are on their way."

For. more information on this aid-summoning device, write to Microalert Systems International, 3030 Empire Avenue, Burbank, CA 91504.

Informal arrangements

In addition to commercial services, those who may need emergency help may design their own systems.

For example, an elderly voice teacher who lives in New York City has among her students a young woman who lives just a block away. "I have Mara ring my doorbell when she's out walking her dog in the evening. We have a code. She rings three times. If I'm all right, I press the button that activates the door buzzer once. If I want her to come up, I press the button twice." One evening there was no answer to the ring. The voice student let herself in with the doorkeys provided, and found that the teacher was too sick to get out of bed, but had already arranged for a doctor to call. The young woman made the ailing teacher comfortable in the meantime.

An elderly St. Paul resident lived on the third floor of an apartment house. The friendly family on the floor below had an ingenious young son who rigged up a battery-operated buzzer. The activating button was fastened to the windowsill of the retiree's living room, and the connecting wire was dropped out the window and into the family's living room, where the buzzer was fastened to the windowframe. A ring of the bell brought a family member to investigate.

A 92-year-old widow living in Cincinnati had two of her four married children living in the area. They agreed among themselves that twice a day a phone call would be made to see how Ma was doing. Each took a weekly turn. Occasionally, excessive fatigue, in one case a fainting spell, made it impossible for the widow to answer the phone. The daughter and her husband hurried over and stayed until the woman's strength returned.

In similar ways, friends, relatives, neighbors, and in some cases service people who pass by regularly may be asked to check up on people living alone who are in frail health. One Connecticut citizen asks his mail carrier—who had been a fifth-grade student of his in public school—to look in on him briefly as he delivers the mail.

PROBLEM DRINKING

Your neighbor, Greg Peele, retired six months before you did. One afternoon you're going over your accounts and Greg appears at your door, a bit unsteady but grinning.

"Hey, mind if I hide out in your place for a while?"

Without waiting for an answer he comes in and drops into a chair.

"I gotta get myself together." He laughs and shakes his head. "Phil from down the street stopped in for a quick snort. Boy, that guy can put away the booze. I gotta get sobered up or Harriet is gonna chew me out when she gets home."

What can you do?

If Greg's over-imbibing is a rare occurrence, you might smile along with him and give him some black coffee as a start of sobering him up.

But it's possible that Greg's problem is the reverse of temporary. You've seen him in the yard through your window, obviously suffering from the effects of too much alcohol. And sometimes he comes down with a temporary ailment that his wife, Harriet, describes as the flu. It seems to put him out of action for a couple of days.

When a friend has a drinking problem there may be little you can do. In some cases it takes an extremely strong tie to stand the strain and the impositions that often result. What should you do about the problem? What would you do if Greg Peele were your neighbor?

One writer—Mary Ellen Chamberlin—in the magazine, *Women in Business,* feels that in friendship one should not ignore the alcoholic. Chamberlin, herself a former problem drinker, cautions against lessening "the painful consequences" of drink. This usually leads to a worsening of the addiction. Other experts agree that the common response of going along with a drinker—smilingly accepting or covering up for the weakness—is likely to make matters worse.

Certainly this is one of the more complicated problems a friend can face. Yet psychologists warn that when you refrain from pointing out the seriousness of the problem you can actually reinforce it.

How can you deal with a drinker, whether family member or friend? Taking Chamberlin's advice, which squares with that of other experts, don't make little of the problem. Instead, level: "Greg, you know we've been good friends for a long time. We've done neighborly things for each other over many years. But yesterday helping you sober up, frankly, was an unpleasant experience. You ought to think about what you're doing to yourself—and to your family and friends."

Try to be matter-of-fact. Avoid righteousness or preachiness. Keep your voice even, don't raise it or get angry if you can help it. Your introducing an emotional note in the form of anger or a rebuke may be playing to the problem drinker's need for punishment. If the individual shows up again saying in words or actions, "See, I've been bad again. Tell me how wrong I've been," you could be provoking the very behavior you don't want to occur.

Be careful with your choice of words. Refer to a *drinking problem*. Don't use the word *alcoholic*. Even experts find it difficult to agree upon the definition of the word and it conjures up the image of a drinker which the individual may reject out-of-hand. An individual may be willing to accept the phrase *problem drinker* and would deny vehemently being an alcoholic. Talk, then, about a person having a problem that affects family and friends and puts a strain on relationships.

Suggest that your friend seek help from a professional, AA, or the National Council on Alcoholism. By doing so you emphasize the seriousness of the problem. But once or twice is enough—don't repeat the suggestion. After all, the basic problem belongs to the drinker.

Let it be known now that you can't be depended on to cover again. The more you do, the easier it is for the friend to further the addiction. If you can, also discourage others from assuming the burden.

Don't try to gloss over the situation to other friends or family, who have a right to know. You don't have to be accusatory or even say, "Drunk again." Just state what is obviously true. "Well, when Phil brought him into my house this evening he was practically helpless. I did the best I could for him, but he's got a problem that really should be looked after."

Mary Ellen Chamberlin points out that the drinker may not welcome the truth as you see it. You may, in fact, be told to mind your own business. But he or she is causing you to have a problem. It *is* your business—as a friend. If you ignore the problem when it affects so many people, you are really not fulfilling your responsibility to yourself and the others who are involved.

ACTIVITIES

When you worked on a rainy day—or a snowy one for that matter—it only posed a transportation problem. But in retirement, inclement weather can make a prisoner of you. A good way to avoid this is to have on hand a schedule of things that can be done indoors that are of sufficient interest to avoid the "make work" syndrome, and satisfy your feeling that you're just not marking time. Following are some suggestions:

1. Mend china (keep broken pitchers, plates, etc. around for just this occasion).

2. Make phone calls to old friends and relatives, preferably those not talked to for some time.

3. Once and for all, do that nuisance job that has been bugging you for months—putting a new washer in a leaky faucet, putting another bracket under a loose shelf, straightening out your files, going through your wardrobe and disposing of things you'll never wear, and so on.

4. Review your daily and weekly schedules to see if:
a. you're getting the things done that you want to do;
b. you're not doing things that you've gotten bored with, or no longer satisfy any real need or purpose. Any discrepancies either way suggest some juggling that puts your activities in line with current intentions.

5. If your spouse or other family member is at home, ask yourself—or the other person, for that matter—whether there are any matters you could profitably discuss, from the state of your finances to plans for your next trip.

6. Straighten out a few drawers—in your desk, bureau, workbench, and so on.

7. If you're in your own home, go up to the attic and check the roof—particularly if you've suspected you might have the beginnings of a leak.

8. Check your storage areas. Could you organize your storage better to make it easier to find things? Are there any stored materials that are not standing up too well to the passage of time and the conditions of storage, and should be disposed of, or better protected? And how about a treasure hunt? You and I have both read of valuable items uncovered

in dusty attics—furniture worth hundreds of dollars, rare books, and bric-a-brac that may have lost its value to you but which might make an antique dealer drool.

9. And how about some deferred reading—a book you bought or borrowed some time ago with the thought that you'd get to it some day. Is this the day?

10. Finally, how about some of those other "some day" tasks or chores? Maybe you've been meaning to stack the wood for the fireplace or go through those old photographs and put them in the album.

Whatever you choose, satisfying activity on a rainy day can make those days some of the nicest of the year.

TENSION AT HOME

Absence may make the heart grow fonder. It also can reduce some of the tension that may build up between two people who, because of one or the other's retirement, now must spend 24 hours, 7 days a week, together. This problem of a newly retired person being seen as an intruder into the spouse's domain and privacy is a standard problem discussed in most preretirement programs.

The retiree who finds himself or herself in the situation where proximity becomes a source of annoyance and tension had better look for constructive courses of action.

The first, and most desirable, is to discuss the matter with the other person. Recognizing the problem, putting it on the table, can give both parties a chance to express their feelings and discuss ways to alleviate the problem. A conversation like this may go as follows:

> *Husband:* Remember—before I retired—how you used to go on about how great it would be for us to be able to spend more time together. I guess it was true for the first few weeks.
>
> *Wife:* But now the honeymoon is over. We just seem to be getting into each other's way, and on each other's nerves.
>
> *Husband:* I'm afraid it's true. Certainly something we didn't anticipate. What do you suggest we do about it?
>
> *Wife:* I think somehow we're going to have to stop acting as though we are chained together—and have some activities apart.
>
> *Husband:* That's a great idea!

With this constructive approach, the couple sets up a more realistic and acceptable design for living for two.

For some couples, however, this "talking it out" approach may not work. If this is the case, one or the other person may have to take the initiative and try a short-term separation. In other words, take a walk, go to the movies, visit a friend, or fix something—preferably out of sight of the other person.

Longer-term measures may involve working on or developing separate hobbies or even taking an occasional one-day vacation alone.

If the irritations, arguments and ill feelings seem to grow rather than dissipate, the good offices of a third party may be in order. Consider getting help from some of the logical sources: someone in your church skilled in dealing with marital relations, a respected friend or relative whose wisdom and maturity have proven themselves before, or a professional counselor in a community organization, such as a mental health center. Whatever you do, don't allow tensions to mount so that the only recourse is a blow-up.

● *A Problem-Solving Technique*

Occasionally, you may run into a problem that defies a simple solution. In that case, it helps to have a problem-solving procedure to follow in order to arrive at the best possible answer. The technique discussed below may be applicable to some situations you will encounter.

IDENTIFY THE PROBLEM

In some cases, the problem is obvious. If things in general are fine but a super-tight budget is dragging you down, then you can label your problem *finances*. Or, if an unpleasant home situation is souring an otherwise happy retirement—you and your wife could do very well on your own but you're providing room and board for your ailing mother and the burden is becoming painful—again, it's easy enough to pinpoint the problem. However, in some cases identification may not come quite so easily. The symptoms of the difficulty may be perplexing. Or actually more than one cause may fog up your identification efforts.

For example, Bill and Myra Dutcher live in a large, old-fashioned apartment on West End Avenue in New York City. The neighborhood has deteriorated from its former elegance, but since Bill and Myra have his father staying with them, the large apartment makes it easier for them physically. The father has his own room and bath, which helps considerably.

Bill Dutcher works as a consultant with an engineering firm in

Poughkeepsie. Commuting isn't easy. It takes about two hours on good days to drive the distance one way.

Myra's life isn't much easier. In addition to taking care of the house and feeding and caring for Bill's father, she also has a part-time job in Roosevelt Hospital. A year after this living arrangement started Myra and Bill had a confrontation that grew out of a minor incident. Bill's father, trying to heat a meat loaf that had been left for him, burned himself and dropped the platter. When Myra came home she found the old man nursing the painful burn, a mess on the kitchen floor, and their dinner gone. As soon as Bill's father had gone off to bed, Myra, boiling with suppressed anger, told Bill they'd better have a talk.

Bill said, "I realize my father is a serious problem for us."

But Myra had a broader view: "He's only part of the problem, Bill. Let me tell you this. We're both capable of enjoying life a great deal more than we are at present, and it's not just your father. As much of a burden as he is, if that were the only thing, we could live with it. But your job with crazy hours and that long commute, and my job with pressures at the hospital are just too much for us to cope with. We've got to re-think our whole situation. And frankly, I don't care if we have to break up house here and move to the North Pole, we've got to take the steps that solve all three situations."

ANALYZE THE SITUATION

Myra Dutcher has done a realistic job of identifying the problem that confronts them. From that beginning, in order for the Dutchers to come up with a solution, they have to analyze exactly what is wrong.

The problem isn't Bill's commuting. It's the four hours tacked onto a long day, his erratic coming-home schedule, that's exacerbating the situation. The problem isn't just Bill's father living with them, but also the problem of physical care, the emotional drain of his continuing needs, and, trying to make some kind of enjoyable life for a man who is ailing.

The problem isn't only Myra's being overloaded with a part-time job on top of everything else, but also having responsibilities that constitute a further drain on her energies and resources.

DEVELOP SOLUTIONS

If you've gone through the first two steps properly, you should have a clear idea of exactly what's wrong. If the problem is a single major one—housing, finances, health, or whatever—try to figure out and put down on paper, if that helps, what could help maximize your eliminating the problem. For example, in the case of Myra and Bill Dutcher, the couple developed solutions for each of the three aspects of their unhappy home situation. Here are the notes they made:

BILL'S FATHER

1. Have a housekeeper or a capable person come in, probably part-time, to take care of his needs—feeding, bedmaking, conversation, and so on.
2. Talk to him about the desirability of nursing home care.
3. See if Bill's sister would agree to share the burden of his care.

MYRA'S WORK PROBLEM

1. Give up the job. Take another one at the hospital that is less demanding. Cut down on the hours.
2. Get another kind of work with less responsibility.

BILL'S WORK PROBLEM

1. Get a job in New York City.
2. Move to the country, as he has always tried to work at home two days out of the week.

Choose and implement the best solution

Each of the suggested solutions for the problem has advantages and disadvantages. Spell these out, again putting your thinking down on paper if you think it will help. Usually the pros and cons are obvious, although there may be some "X" factors, those which you can't accurately estimate. For example, in the case of getting someone to come in to tend to Mr. Dutcher, while this would lessen the burden, mostly Myra's, a negative factor would be the cost, and secondly, as people will tell you who have used this type of solution for care of an ailing relative, the kind of people who do this work are sometimes problems in their own right—not as responsible as they should be, not as considerate as one would like in the care of the person, and so on.

However, spell out the benefits and the drawbacks of each possible solution and select the most promising one or ones.

Obviously, your next move is to put the solution you've chosen into effect. In some rare situations, you may be unable at the moment to develop a course of action that offers a sufficiently large benefit to warrant using. In that case, two common choices are to select the most promising course on the principle that doing something may be better than doing nothing. Or, you simply may have to wait until, either one of the factors in the situation changes, or you come up with a new solution.

Whatever you do, remember that the manner in which a thing is done is often a major element in its success or failure. So if you decide to make a change, implement it with all you've got—enthusiasm and hopefulness. No matter what the problem or the odds, if you can inject these qualities in your action, you help stack the cards in your favor.

● *Evaluating Your Retirement*

There are three times at which your perspective on retirement changes. These moments can be put to good use; they can become viewing sites from which to assess yourself, your reactions to the change from being an employee to being "at liberty." How are you making out? How have you responded to the changes? How resilient have you been, how successful your planning? How well have you been able to exploit the potential of your new situation? The three quizzes in this section help you consider these revealing questions on the first day of your retirement, six months later and, finally, one year after you've retired.

For each question, check the statement that most closely suits your feeling and situation.

THE FIRST DAY

This is the first day of your new freedom. You have awakened to a world in which clocks no longer push you, your job responsibilities no longer occupy you. Your job worries now belong to someone else.

1. You feel—
   ( ) at loose ends
   ( ) happy, liberated
   ( ) resentful, grumpy
   ( ) numb

2. Your expectations—
   ( ) were off target, you underestimated the shock of the transition

( ) were on the button, things are going pretty much as you expected

( ) seem to have been pessimistic, you expected to feel terrible but you feel fine

3. You—

( ) look forward to a busy day and week

( ) don't know what to do with yourself

( ) say to yourself, "I'd better cobble up some kind of activity or I'll go batty"

( ) desperately try to recall what people—personnel counselor, author of a book on retirement, your friend who retired last year—told you to do your first day home

4. Fortunately—

( ) you have mapped out a program that will occupy you for at least the first few weeks, start you off in the right direction

( ) somebody gave you a book on "How to Retire." You dig it out, read it, and find it helpful

5. You look to the future—

( ) optimistically

( ) pessimistically

( ) very optimistically

( ) very pessimistically

( ) with a "wait-and-see" attitude

REVIEW. Don't be surprised at any of your answers. After all, you are undergoing a major change. Retirement is one of the major rites of passage in today's world.

Now for specifics:

1. Any answer you may have given to the first question is understandable. The preferred answer is "happy, liberated." However, there may have to be a brief shakedown, let's say a few weeks before the transition takes place. Just keep in mind the "happy, liberated" response and accept it as a goal. If, after a reasonable period of time you are not able to adopt a constructive view of your situation, there is a possibility that your planning, particularly your scheduling, has not been adequate. This is the first area for you to reexamine in case there is a significant delay in your reaching a favorable frame of mind.

2. This question is a measure of how realistic your thinking about

retirement has been. Clearly, being "on the button" in terms of acceptance is the desired answer. Either of the other two answers suggests some
shaky thinking, leading to feelings about retirement which realities are
not likely to support. Therefore, if things are not going "pretty much as
you expected" think over the things that surprised or disappointed you.
Give some thought to *why* your expectations are off target. Such probing
can be a learning process to help you modify unrealistic use of the past
and put you on a more constructive path in terms of what lies ahead.

3. The preferred answer here is the first, "Looking forward to busy
times ahead." If your answer is any other but that, there are two possible
remedies at hand: (a) your plans for day-to-day activities have not been
clearly thought out; (b) your actual scheduling has been too loose, gives
you too much free time between tasks.

If either of these reasons apply, rethink your objectives. For example, have you neglected new educational objectives (studies in a formal
situation also have a social advantage—you can meet other people)? Is
there volunteer work you might undertake that could bring you considerable satisfaction, and be of great help to others? Finally, are there
activities which might bring you some income and have the second virtue
of a satisfying work program?

4. Either answer you gave to this question is OK. If you checked off
the first answer, keep in mind that it refers only to the first weeks of your
retirement. The important thing here is to use this preliminary period as
a test run, as a time for evaluating your program. If it's all you can hope
for, if you are completely satisfied with it, there's no reason not to extend
it into the future. And if there are gaps or activities which are less
challenging or rewarding than you had hoped, this is the time to start
making constructive changes.

5. This is a key question because it pinpoints the mood you have at
the start of your retirement. The preferred answer is one that reflects an
optimistic attitude.

The "wait-and-see" reply has certain virtues. It suggests that the
person is being realistic, is taking nothing for granted. For example, an
individual may find the first few days of retirement sufficiently satisfactory to suggest that the future will be more of the same. For most people,
this outlook will lead to an optimistic view of the days ahead. But the
"wait-and-see" person is saying, "Yes, things are going fine right now, but
after a month or two I may find myself getting bored, restless, or in need
of new things to do." No objection to this attitude. The only suggestion

here is that the "wait-and-see" person, after the "waiting," really "sees"—that is, takes stock of the situation with the idea of strengthening any weak points.

SIX MONTHS LATER

Six months have passed. First feelings have matured, perhaps adjustments have been made, changes gotten used to. In effect, you've completed your shakedown cruise. How are you doing, how does the world look to you now?

1. You feel—
   ( ) that you are still groping
   ( ) you don't know what to do with yourself
   ( ) the day you retired, the world came to an end
   ( ) the day you retired was the start of one of the happiest periods of your life

2. Your relationships with people—
   ( ) are O.K.
   ( ) are deteriorating in number
   ( ) are deteriorating in quality
   ( ) were never better

3. Your daily activities are—
   ( ) just O.K.
   ( ) unsatisfactory
   ( ) a workout, not much more
   ( ) exciting, challenging

4. You are—
   ( ) able to solve daily problems as they come up
   ( ) in need of help and can't seem to get it
   ( ) puzzled by this item! Problems? You don't have any

5. Your financial situation is—
   ( ) O.K.
   ( ) just passable
   ( ) poor
   ( ) very satisfactory

6. Your health—
   ( ) is no problem

( ) is as good as you can expect
( ) requires attention, and you are getting the help you need
( ) you've been getting careless, not taking good care of yourself

7. In general, your life is—
( ) zestful
( ) a drag
( ) busy and rewarding
( ) spotty—good and bad

8. You look to the future—
( ) optimistically
( ) very optimistically
( ) with a "wait-and-see" attitude
( ) pessimistically
( ) very pessimistically

REVIEW. Now check the replies reflecting your status after six months of retirement. From this new time perspective, what do you see?

1. The preferred answer is the last one, that retirement in fact is one of the happiest periods of your life. If this answer doesn't come close to describing your situation, some self-examination is called for:

If you are still groping, the indication is that you have to come to grips with a basic problem. True enough, it is one that can bedevil a person at *any* stage of life. But in retirement, you're under a certain amount of time pressure to come up with possible answers.

So, if you are still groping in terms of what you want and what you want to do, have a brass-tacks talk with yourself, or consult with people whose opinions you respect. Reexamine the possible things you could be doing, the activities that would bring you the sense of satisfaction and self-fulfillment that make life pleasurable.

In one case, such a review may lead you to remember things you've done in the past that you might want to get back to. In other instances, it may be going off into a completely new direction that will bring things into your life that make for zestful experience.

2. For most of us, a great share of living involves other people—whether we work with them, play with them, or love them. Check back on your answer to this question. If you didn't answer "OK," or relationships were "never better," the best suggestion that can be made is to reread Chapter 11: the views and information in those pages, will help to

direct your thinking in ways that will lead you to repair or create a better and more satisfying social life.

3. This question gives you another opportunity to check that important area, your daily activities. The best answer, of course, is "exciting, challenging." If it's anything less, then, regardless of previous planning—or perhaps because of inadequate planning—your day-to-day program isn't working out as well as it should. You will find the other chapters in Part V a helpful source in which to find ideas and methods for enriching your days.

4. The first and third choices are both favorable. But if you feel that the second choice, "need help and can't seem to get it" comes closest to the mark, indications are that you must persist in your attempts to get help until you succeed.

What kind of help and where do you get it? If problems are specific—finances, health and so on—it won't be difficult to zero in on organizations or people who can offer guidance. You may be able to get help in the financial area from a friend who knows how to handle a buck, an officer of your bank, perhaps an accountant who understands problems of personal income and investment. Problems with health can take you to any one of the sources for health information that start with your own personal physician, or to a clinic in your local hospital.

However, if the "problems" that hang like a cloud over your retirement are less well defined and if you have trouble identifying what they are, the source of help is equally uncertain. But a good place to start might be a mental health center in your community where trained professional people can help you see your own situation clearly and identify areas of dissatisfaction.

5. This question on your financial situation gets right to the point and, of course, it's a vital one. Here it is, six months after you've retired. Are you satisfied with the way your finances are holding up and with prospects for the future? The "very satisfactory" answer is very satisfactory. But if your answer is *poor*, or you would have to use some other word meaning that the going is rough, you may want to review your financial planning. I suggest that you reread Chapter 9 and consider the steps that can help strengthen this crucial aspect of your retirement.

6. The answer to view with alarm on this question of your health is the last one, that you've been getting careless. I personally react negatively to any suggestion that "the body is just like a machine." But, as reluctant as I am to accept this comparison, I would have to agree that,

like other mechanisms created by man, the human body needs taking care of at a consistently high level. The better your self maintenance, the more favorable your outlook for a healthy future. Health care in terms of diet, exercise, physical checkups, and following the recommendations of your doctor should get top priority in your day-to-day and long-range plans.

7. This question gives you the opportunity to take a broad overall view. It is a reflection of the appropriateness of your planning for your pleasure and comfort needs. The real point of this question also involves how high a standard you hold for yourself and your ability to enjoy life.

For example, let's say you answered the question by saying "my life is spotty—both good and bad." That may be a realistic appraisal and many people would say, "that's the way it's got to be." The poet who said "Into each life some rain must fall" certainly didn't bar the period of retirement from this dictum. However, if there are areas of dissatisfaction along with the good parts, there are two possibilities worth considering: (a) think back over the happenings or areas that you have to label "bad"—can you do anything about these? eliminate? minimize?; (b) review the things in your life that come under the "good" heading—can you expand or add to these? Remember the old saying, "You can have too much of a good thing"? Forget it. In this case, the more the better.

8. Here at the six-month mark, what answer did you check off as to your appraisal of the future? If it was anything other than optimistic, that's unfortunate. But don't accept these less-than-satisfactory prospects with a shrug or the feeling that the thing to do is grin and bear it.

The good thing about the future is that, within reasonable limits, it is under your control. You certainly can't do anything about the past. You may not be able to do much about the present. But the future is largely unformed and the pattern can often be changed in a favorable way by: (a) rethinking objectives; (b) applying intensive and creative thought to how these objectives can be reached; and, finally, (c) putting into operation the moves and methods that will start you in the directions you want to go.

FIRST ANNIVERSARY

Looking back, you realize that the past year has been one of transition. The shakedown period is over, you're now on a regular run. How are things going?

1. Your financial situation—
   ( ) you're just holding your head above water
   ( ) your planning has worked out, and your income–outgo ratio is satisfactory
   ( ) needs improvement; you must either trim expenses or develop new sources of income

2. Your health is—
   ( ) fine
   ( ) as good as can be expected
   ( ) suffering from your own carelessness or neglect
   ( ) not satisfactory, but you're getting the help you need

3. Your state of mind is—
   ( ) awful
   ( ) ups and downs
   ( ) tranquil
   ( ) terrific

4. Your lifestyle—
   ( ) is fine, rewarding
   ( ) needs an injection of zest—new friends, new adventures, change of scene
   ( ) would benefit from rethinking altogether, which you are doing
   ( ) is a shambles and you see no hope for it
   ( ) is a shambles, and you are getting professional help—counseling, etc.—to improve it

5. Your relationships—
   ( ) have never been better
   ( ) are skimpy
   ( ) neglected on your part
   ( ) are poor because friends, family neglect you

6. Your daily program, your life day to day—
   ( ) is full of rewarding activity
   ( ) lacks interest or variety
   ( ) is monotonous
   ( ) sparkles with new enterprises, challenges, surprises

7. You look to the future—
   ( ) optimistically

( ) very optimistically
( ) with resignation
( ) despite setbacks, with resolve to keep right on pushing
( ) pessimistically
( ) very pessimistically

REVIEW. Your assessment of yourself and your situation after one year of retirement could be crucial. If this review is made realistically, you can do the planning from this vantage point that could insure a satisfactory retirement in the years to come. These questions should have been answered with particular care.

1. Your financial plans at this point have had the opportunity to be tested. You can now see whether your estimates of income and expenses were realistic. Also, you can now see whether your financial planning matches the lifestyle you've adopted.

In this instance, however, even the second answer, which is the most favorable, deserves reconsideration in view of changes in the economy. For example, if prospects are for inflation—as has been the case since early in the 70s—then it might be unwise to assume, because the first year looks good in your financial records, that the income–outgo balance may not start to tip unfavorably. Project into the future and see whether, in view of the changes in the economic picture, your financial situation is likely to remain favorable. If your financial resources threaten to be a less satisfactory foundation for your expenditures, you may have to consider: (a) moves that will make it possible to reduce expenses if that's indicated; or (b) methods for increasing income. This may involve anything from reconsidering your investments to calculating the advisability of including a certain amount of your capital in your operating funds, or seeking a source of earnings.

2. Your health in the first year of retirement represents a special and significant period. While you've been relieved of the work pressures, you've been living in a new situation which undoubtedly also has tensions and strains even though they may be more subtle than the old nine-to-five squeeze.

If your health is "fine," then chances are that you're living right. Just keep on with more of the same. This is another area where anything less than a satisfactory record suggests that you reexamine your planning, health procedures, and so on, and make the moves indicated that promise to improve matters for tomorrow.

3. The question on your state of mind echoes those asked the day after retirement and six months later. But now, a full year has passed. Has your answer changed? Would you say your state of mind is more satisfactory now than it was six months ago? If the comparison is favorable, that is, you feel better about yourself and your situation now than you did earlier—Victory! You're doing fine. But if your answer suggests that you're going downhill even slightly, do a little fence mending. Try to pinpoint the areas that account for the falling level of satisfaction, whether it's in the area of relationships, activity or whatever. The table of contents in this book may suggest specific chapters that can help you rethink and replan the areas where improvement is possible.

4. This question on lifestyle is clearly related to the previous question on your state of mind. The difference is that the lifestyle question tends to be more specific. You can think about it in more tangible terms.

In a way, your lifestyle is a payoff point where several key matters come together—finances, health, friendships, hobbies, etc.

Check your answer to this question. And if you can't honestly give the first answer, "fine, rewarding," reread Chapter 5, lifestyles to which you can compare your own. As a result, you may be able to come up with a pattern that will prove more satisfactory.

5. How have your relationships stood up under the test of this first year of retirement? One particular area to review: what about your business friends? Have you been able to maintain contact with those people whose friendship you once valued and enjoyed? Or, under the old principle that absence not only doesn't make the heart grow fonder, but seems to erode friendships, have you lost touch with people whose friendship you valued?

In this subject area, Chapter 11 provides a discussion that stimulates your thinking and the "Friendship Test" quiz can help you be specific about individual relationships.

A special consideration here are your family relationships. Retirement almost invariably affects these. In this first year of your changed life, you may see relationships grow closer or deteriorate with the passage of time. For example, your children may have actually seen more of you. You may have enjoyed being with them more than ever before.

As with friendship, family relationships optimally are based not on the traditional "shoulds" and "ought-to-be's" but on real feelings. Just as you can't force your feelings (you may find time spent with one child happy times indeed and those spent with another, boring and tension inducing) your relatives may have positive and negative feelings about you.

Family relationships fare best when they are natural and can be pursued by both parties without strain. Don't be surprised if your retirement has had an affect on your feelings for your relatives and friends. In the end, it may be best to adjust to these changes. Obviously, where they are positive, take advantage of the warmer feelings. And where your retirement has watered down the relationship, either accept the new state of affairs or consider moves that may possibly lead to better ties.

6. This question deals with your daily activities. From the perspective of a year's testing—and possible adjustments made after the six-months quiz—you can now decide whether your planning in this area is working out.

If things have been going the way you want them to, fine. If not, settle down to a replanning session—yes, using pencil and paper. Put down what you've been doing, where you feel the lapses are. In this connection, Chapter 7 may provide a number of useful ideas. You should find help both in rethinking and replanning your daily program if you are less than satisfied with the way things have been going.

7. After one year of retirement, it's as though you are standing at a lookout point where you can see both the past and beginnings of the future taking shape. Use this view to help you move ahead in the most rewarding way possible. Your answer to question 7 can give you a clue as to what you should do, if anything, about making adjustments for happier days in the years ahead. If you are optimistic about the future—suggesting that the past year has been a happy one—then you're in the catbird seat, and have every reason to be pleased with what you've been doing and happy about your prospects.

However, if your assessment is less than favorable, if the future doesn't hold the promise of satisfaction and happiness that you want for yourself, then benefit from the past year. Use your observation of what you've done and failed to do, of the activities that have paid off and those which have yielded disappointments, as a basis for redesigning your life for the road ahead. Even minor adjustments can make major improvement.

21
STAYING YOUTHFUL

The aim of keeping young does not in any way belittle the virtues of maturity. The older person, wise in experience, balanced in judgment, understanding and compassionate in his or her views and values, is indeed the pinnacle of the human growth process.

What's intended in this chapter is to describe steps that some people have taken that won't make you *young*—but can make you *youthful*—which means strengthening those qualities of youth that can enrich and add excitement to life.

"I feel younger now than I did in my twenties," says Jim Woodrows, a 68-year-old St. Paul architect. His alert manner and lively interest in his work and developments in his field support his assertion.

Woodrows is not the first man to note that feelings of youthfulness are not confined to the young. A psychiatrist supplies a fact that helps explain Woodrows' observation: "None of us," he says, "perceives himself as aging."

And the psychiatrist makes another illuminating point: "Aging," he says, "is a set of expectations; expectations we have of ourselves as aging persons, and expectations others have of us in terms of our aging."

From this expert's statement one might go on to suggest that people who *expect* to be old, thereby become old. On the other hand, those who expect to retain the desirable qualities of youthfulness—freshness, vigor, spirit—may very well succeed in avoiding "old age" forever.

"I'm 80 years young," says the octogenarian—and it may not be an idle boast. He is voicing a view that too few people understand: Youthfulness is not a *period of life,* but an *attitude toward life.*

Too many people are inclined to cash in their chips prematurely. They suspend effort, regard the opportunities of living with a passive eye. What a waste! A waste of talent, developed over the years. A waste of judgment, carefully honed by experience. A waste of capability to create and achieve. Says one self-confident 70-year-old: "I didn't get this smart just to call it quits. I intend to accomplish more in the next five years than in the past twenty." He's got the right attitude.

The world of retirement can be exciting, challenging, rewarding. Make the most of it, not only now but for as many years as you like! To paraphrase an oil company slogan: Expect more of yourself, and you'll get it.

● *How People Stay Young*

We all know one or more people in our own circle of friends who are advanced in years, yet undiminished in vigor. Such individuals are often cited:

"Tom could pass for a man ten years younger."

"Harriet has more vitality than all her contemporaries put together."

"Ray has the sharpest mind of anyone around, including the new college crowd."

Confronted by outstanding examples of retained youth and vitality, one can't help wondering: "How come some people can be as alert and productive at 60 as at 30?"

GENETIC FACTORS

"His father was active at 80," goes one school of thought. "It must be in the blood."

Gerontologists agree that favorable heredity may help longevity. But considerable evidence shows the potency of environmental factors. A study by Philip M. Hauser and Evelyn Kitagawa indicates that education and affluence affect one's life span. Analyzing a group of 340,000 Americans, the researchers found that males with less than four years of school had a death rate 40 percent *higher* than those who had completed one or more years of college. And those with less than $2,000 income during 1959 had a death rate 2.5 times as high as those in families with an income of $10,000 or more.

Facts and figures of the Hauser-Kitagawa study furnish just one more proof that environmental factors *can* influence the life span. None of us is necessarily a helpless victim of his or her genes.

MODERATE LIVING HABITS

Perennial youthfulness is often attributed to sensible living: diet, exercise, moderation. Yet those who examine the backgrounds of dynamic individuals soon discover that many live quite immoderately. Sir Winston Churchill with his brandy and cigars was one. No formula covers all cases. The deeper one digs, the clearer it becomes that the causes of retained youthfulness are complex.

REJUVENATION THAT WORKS

Remember the phrase by Satchel Paige noted earlier? "How old would you be if you didn't know how old you are?" It makes us realize how much our thinking about ourselves and our age is dominated by the dates on our birth certificates.

In your case, how old would *you* be if you didn't know the number of years you've lived? In some cases the answer might be, younger than you actually are. I have interviewed many people about their feelings about their age. From time to time I have encountered individuals—and how lucky they are—who have said in effect, "I felt much younger at 60 than I did at 50," or, "... 70 than I did at 60." How is it possible to reverse the laws of nature? Can one truly grow younger? The answer is: it *is* possible.

Let me anticipate an objection at this point. People with whom I've discussed this concept mentioned it sooner or later. "You're just telling us to violate that old dictum, 'Act your age.'"

That statement means something quite different from what I'm saying. Acting your age means don't *pretend,* don't behave in unrealistic ways. For example: Don't try to dance with the physical abandon of a 20-year old at the age of 60. This doesn't mean if you have the sense of rhythm for it and the physical capability that you shouldn't try the current steps, whether it be a waltz, the hustle, or tomorrow's yet un-named rage.

It doesn't mean buying a badly fitting toupee at the age of 50 and trying to pass in the swinging singles crowd.

Nor does it mean dressing in inappropriate garments that, it is hoped, give the appearance of youthfulness but, alas, may make quite evident the lack of it.

Ashley Montagu, the well-known authority on people, was asked, "How do you manage to keep so young?" His answer:

"The trick is simple. Die young as old as possible." Montagu went on to say, "This means to preserve the spirit of a child, of youthfulness . . . an open-mindedness that is free to consider everything, a sense of humor, playfulness."

● *Four Aspects of Youthfulness*

There are four areas of concentration which account for a large part of a person's youthfulness.

PHYSICAL VIGOR

The ways and means of retaining or achieving youthful vigor and physical resilience are discussed elsewhere in this book as well as in many other sources. Anything and everything that you do along the lines of diet, exercise and health care that help maximize your physical well-being are all to the good.

MENTAL VIGOR

A simple way to illustrate what is meant here is to examine the men or women in the higher age brackets who are "set in their ways," have a diminished interest in the world around them, and have settled into more or less rigid patterns of behavior, human interaction, and so on.

But the youthful older person is marked by flexibility, freedom, and a lively interest in people, things, learning, exploring, and sometimes just keeping up with today's world.

ATTITUDE

There is another element that is somewhat related to mental vigor but is different in some respects. It involves one's values and one's view of other people's. This is marked by an openness towards other people's ideas, a reluctance to make judgments, particularly derogatory ones, of others, and an interest in and sometimes an acceptance of the new and the different.

The person with a youthful attitude tends to be venturesome and interested in exploring either new places, people, or ideas. This person is not bound by the limiting attitude that has seen everything, knows everything, and is usually disinterested in anything outside his or her ken.

BEHAVIOR

Attitude is the way people feel. But in the pursuit of youthfulness, it's what people do that adds an additional important element.

The great psychologist Carl Jung at one point in his career became intrigued by the lives of children. He valued their spontaneity, their openness, their creativity. "What a wonderful world they live in," he thought, "to be able to play so single-mindedly and enjoy the make-believe."

In his admiration he developed a professional curiosity in trying to recapture the spirit of childhood. And so he spent a great deal of time in playing—as young children do. He built mudpies and sand castles. He tried to bend with the spontaneity and freedom that the untrammeled child does.

And evidently his methods produced a result. He was able to understand the world of childhood—its vastness, its freshness, its excitement. And to some extent he was able to bring into his every-day life this appreciation of living, this view of the world that children have that is often outgrown too early and usually lost irretrievably and forever.

Ashley Montagu in his professional life also was impressed by the virtues of the young in terms of living experience. He said, explaining his view: "My task in life, among other things, is to make not adults of children but children of adults. In other words, to rescue those adults who have become ossified, as it were, in what they call 'mature ways.'

"My point is that one should never mature in the sense of reaching some stereotyped system of ordinates which bind one in a straitjacket of behavior according to the demands prevailing in a particular family or a particular segment of society."

Other observers along with Montagu feel that there is an unconscious conspiracy to douse the glow of childhood and youth that seems so wonderful and promising but eventually is stilled by "reality."

Perhaps you know of young people or were one yourself, of whom it is said, "He (or she) was such a promising youngster—made model trains, painted so beautifully, wrote poetry, and so on, and so on." It's not necessary to go into the forces that finally eliminated these latent talents—everything from our educational system to economics is given as the villain of the piece. Whatever the reason, the important thing here is that it need no longer be assumed that aging means achieving the antithesis of youthfulness.

The fact is, no one is on a one-way trip towards physical, mental, and emotional rigidity. The proof lies in the experience and the testimony of people who have either maintained the freshness and alertness of spirit despite their years, or those like Jung and Montagu who showed the way towards turning back the clock and achieving in later age those youthful qualities that not only make you feel younger but make the world around you and your life more attractive, more rewarding—more worth living. This is not to suggest that everyone should spend his or her retirement years making mudpies or playing games. It is the sponteneity, the excitement with which children go at their play that is desirable. The goal of keeping young is intended only to help the mature individual *continue* to use capabilities at their highest possible level, unweakened by failing health, professional obsolescence, worry, and tension.

Put in positive terms, what is sought is the continuation, despite calendar age, of a high energy level, of creative activity, and of satisfaction with work that is generally typified by the energy, enthusiasm, buoyancy, and drive of youthfulness. The objective is to make the latter years continuingly vital and useful, rather than a period of decrepitude and failure.

● *A Program for Youthfulness*

If you feel that your life could benefit from a healthy injection of youthfulness, the following guidelines may help get you started on your own personal "get-young" program.

LEARN FROM OTHERS

Learning anything is easier if you can observe other people who, one way or another, exemplify the skill, behavior, or knowledge in which you are interested.

It can be of definite help to study people over fifty who, in your opinion, represent successful instances of youthfulness and who exhibit the behavior you identify as putting them in the youthful category.

From among the people you know, select the ones whose youthfulness belies their age. It may be a friend, neighbor, or member of your family. One way or another, something about them is calculated to make you think or say, "How youthful X seems." X, a man or woman, is doing something that makes him or her seem younger than chronological age. Exactly what is it? Dress, manner, speech, quality of ideas, interests, associations, activities, or some other factors may be the answer.

Once you've decided, your aim is to express the quality shown by the model—the way he or she dresses, for example—in your *own* personal terms. Let's say Paul Grey, at 61, projects a flamboyant image because of the way he dresses. *Specifically,* how could this behavior be applied by others? This question, posed to two people, turned up these answers:

Ada Rutgers: "I would wear red slacks and a pink blouse to a picnic."

Carl Dewer: "I would wear a turtleneck and sports jacket to the theater."

Of course, I'm not suggesting that all there is to the principle of learning from a model is to observe behavior and go and do likewise. A mechanical application of this idea would be both ineffective and silly. What is intended—and what will work—is to borrow a leaf from the book of those who seem to have caught on, who offer an image of youthfulness, in ways that seem appropriate for you. If the matter of dress is one where you feel you can make a change for the better—then proceed to do so. If the model's style of dress isn't suitable for you, then just skip it. Look for models exhibiting other aspects of youthfulness that you feel you can apply.

And, just as there are kinds of behavior that register attractively and youthfully, there are those that suggest aging. Spotting these negative impressions, identifying exactly what the behavior is that makes the poor impression, and avoiding these can also help.

BREAK YOUR OWN RULES

You may be doing fine in the youthfulness department, and be satisfied with the way you feel and look, both to yourself and others. But if you see room for improvement—that means change.

Resistance to change is always with us, even when the change is for the better. The reason seems to be that the human psyche has a strong penchant for inertia. Mostly we like things to remain the way they are.

And this tendency means that, even when improvement is in the offing, we hold back, hemmed in by inertia and ingrained habits. This is why, in contemplating modifications in your style of dress or your interests, it may not be easy to strike off in new directions. However, awareness is one of the strongest assists you can have in making a change.

Expecting a certain amount of difficulty, anticipating your own resistance—for example, to making new associations, getting to know new and possibly more stimulating people—may take a special effort. But once you make that effort and break out of an old pattern, the excitement and, it is to be hoped, rewards that result from the new state of affairs will keep you going and motivate you to continuing efforts.

ACCEPT NEW EXPERIENCES

Some avenues of opportunity that can enhance the youthful quality of your lifestyle don't necessarily involve breaking out of old patterns. You may not have to undertake anything sensationally new and different to achieve the lift that comes with novelty. Some changes may represent only minor alterations from the past, but still they can add the stimulation that enhances the feeling of youthfulness.

For example, Fred Miller was an instructor at a junior college, giving a course in criminal justice. He taught this subject one night a week. Over a period of time he became aware that on the floor below, an area of the college devoted to crafts, was a room devoted to lapidary. Once or twice he passed by the workroom where people were being taught how to cut and polish gemstones. One time he even went in to watch the instructor illustrating a particular technique for getting a perfectly smooth facet by using a flat-faced wheel.

Somewhere along the way, Fred Miller fell into a slight depression. Thinking about it, he realized that his feelings were generated by disappointment with his work and with his achievement.

"I'm just a hack teacher," he told himself. And just putting his feelings into words confirmed, in a sense, the justification for his depression.

At this critical juncture, something special happened. One night, on his way to his own classroom, he passed by the lapidary workshop. On impulse he walked into the room and started a conversation with the instructor. The latter's enthusiasm was infectious and Fred Miller suddenly became interested in semiprecious stones—the special satisfaction of taking a rough, dull pebble and transforming it into a colorful, gleaming gem.

Fred Miller signed up as a student in the first lapidary workshop he was able to fit into his schedule. From there, he was able to develop an absorbing interest strong enough to suffuse everything else he did.

The change was visible to others. One neighbor confided to another, "The way Fred's been acting lately, he's either inherited a million dollars or found a new girlfriend."

MEET YOUNGER PEOPLE

There is a way of reacquiring a more youthful set of values. It's so simple it may seem trite. But it does work—if done judiciously:

For example, Mae Bruno was a magazine editor in Cincinnati. At the age of 45, she felt young enough but realized that the patterns of her social activity had pretty much frozen. She had a small circle of good and old friends, but began to realize that they bored her from time to time. "And I'm sure they must feel the same about me," she thought.

Good fortune in the shape of a new younger editor made it possible for her to brighten her life. The new addition to the staff was a 35-year-old woman, Louisa Lord, who, it turned out, had a vast assortment of friends and a large range of interests.

Mae had lunch with the new editor shortly after she joined the staff. Stimulated by the younger woman's liveliness, she followed up with a suggestion that they have dinner and go to a movie one evening.

From this beginning, Mae was introduced to a number of Louisa's friends, mostly in the younger age range. Caught up, then, in this new circle and the kinds of interests represented—movie-going, occasional dinners out, and just as interesting, dinners in with each hostess or couple did something unusual in the way of food preparation to make the occasion special—Mae's life headed for new heights of interest.

Things—discussions, interests—that Mae Bruno had not had in her life for years reappeared. She enjoyed lively talks about current events, strong feelings pro and con about everything from women's liberation to how well or badly the government was functioning. All these brought a new luster to Mae Bruno's life. The fact that Louisa Lord's friends included some interesting unattached men was no detriment to the whole process of rejuvenation that Mae felt her life was undergoing.

PARTICIPATE IN A SPORT

Perhaps you're the unathletic type. Your greatest claim to anything that approaches exercise may be a reasonable amount of walking each day. But as far as anything requiring more physical exertion than that—forget it.

But if you haven't been athletic in the past, you may want to reconsider your attitude toward participation sports now. The reason for this line of thinking is that the right kind of sport—one for which you are physically suited—can supply the physical stimulation that keeps the body young and refreshes the mind.

Walking, if undertaken with consistency and a certain amount of vigor, is not to be discounted. If this proves to be the "sport" that keeps you physically vigorous and active, fine. But you may want to consider other possibilities—all, of course, with proper approval and guidance from your physician. You don't want to undertake any physical regimen, as attractive as it may seem, that your body is not capable of performing.

The types of sport that qualify here are some of the obvious ones like tennis, golf, and jogging; and some that are more exotic—anything from horseback riding to canoeing or sculling, if you live near appropriate bodies of water. Another possible side benefit from some of the athletic avenues you may want to explore: They can lead you into groups of people with whom you can share your interest. This social side of some activities can be a worthwhile addition to your youth-retention program.

TRAVEL

Travel has been recommended as a cure for everything from the blahs to a broken heart. Miraculously, it's a remedy that can work for a whole range of things. Now consider travel as a means of reviving your youthfulness. Why should travel be able to accomplish this challenging objective?

One of the reasons that the process of moving about this globe is efficacious for so many ills is that it removes us from the restrictions of our everyday life. Without being aware of it day to day, we're bound by habit, by the patterns of living and working. Travel—even if it's into the next town—frees us from many of our normal limits. Most of what we see is new and different—new places, new faces; in some cases, new customs, new types of food, and new types of activity.

And it is a major quality of youthfulness: the world around us seems fresh and unexplored. When we are very young, we live in a world that is made up to a large extent of unknown factors. It is our inexperience that makes the world unfamiliar. And it is exactly this feeling about our surroundings that travel recreates for us. Literally, as when we were young, we are—during our travels—in unfamiliar territory. The unexpected is always possible. New and stimulating experiences are very much in the cards.

And so most travels, psychologically, are travels in time. No matter where we go, we're taken back to the fresh, unjaded view of things that we used to have.

Just one word of caution to people who may turn to travel as a means of refreshment, emotionally and psychologically. Don't mistake going through the motions for the real thing. The individual who, by boat, train and plane, ends up 5,000 miles from home might just as well be at home if, when arriving at his or her destination, the schedule followed is one that keeps the traveler snugly in the hotel, consorting with the same travelmates day after day—seeing, hearing, smelling, or tasting nothing new.

In other words, for a voyage to be beneficial, it should be marked by the traveler's willingness to venture to seek out the artistic, cultural, and social elements in the unfamiliar town or city.

To clarify just a bit further, the suggestion here doesn't mean throwing yourself into the Humphrey Bogart type of foreign intrigue. You don't have to walk down dark alleys or risk high-crime areas in order to savor the uniqueness of distant places. Your new experiences can come from completely safe activities, but those which expose you to the elements in your new environment that are different from those at home.

In some cases it may be useful to consult people who can help you develop a flexible program of activities that will give you the fresh experience you're seeking. Your travel agent may be able to help. People who have been to the places you plan to visit may be able to furnish useful information. Certainly the individuals in the place you're visiting—the hotel clerk or manager or the local tour information office—if asked the proper questions, can give you helpful answers.

AVOID EXCESSIVE NOSTALGIA

There is a habit of mind that psychologically ages people. It may seem paradoxical, but it's the tendency to look backward to one's more youthful days with unmitigated approval.

For example, Clem Lorayne is a supervisor in a warehouse of a chemical plant. At age 62, he's thinking of retiring in about a year or so.

He wants to take this early retirement because he and his wife are eager to move out to New Mexico, an area they've always loved. But although he doesn't know it, Clem is likely to have a problem not only adjusting to his new situation but also in keeping from growing old in a hurry. He suffers from the "good-old-days" syndrome. On the job he frequently harks back to the times—five years ago, ten years ago, or more—in which any one of a number of things were "done better." Somehow the good old days were replete with everything from better beer to better decisions on the job.

On a recent morning Clem came back to his office, muttering under his breath after a session at the front office. "They want me to start a whole new system of identifying materials," he explained to his assistant. "It's as complicated as hell and I predict it's going to cause more confusion than anything else. This simple system we devised ten years ago was much better."

In some situations there's a good deal to be said for holding on to the methods that are tried and true. In this situation, the new method was needed because of the increased number of inventoried items, the much more rapid cycle of materials turnover and, finally, the fact that the whole system was to be put on a computer.

But Clem harks back to the "good old days" not only on the job but at home. He's a great critic of everything new. He has a whole vocabulary for belittling innovations. He hates touchphones and prefers the old dial: "This new phone is too gadgety for me." A new system of checkout actually speeds up the line at the supermarket counter but, according to Clem, "That new younger manager is just out to do something slick."

People who can avoid Clem Lorayne's attitude stand to benefit substantially. The reason is that we retain youthfulness not by clinging to the values and attitudes we used to have but by tapping into the elements in our surroundings that reflect the new, the different, and the innovative. These make up the fresh and youthful elements of the world around us that, when kept up with, reinforce a youthful attitude toward life and living.

DON'T "LET YOURSELF GO"

One reason that youthfulness tends to disappear prematurely is quite simple: people let themselves "become old." This isn't meant in a physical sense but in a psychological one. In some cases the old-age drift is quite clear. People refer to themselves as being old and then, understandably, they exhibit the behavior that makes the statement true.

And unfortunately there are people about us who—usually unintentionally—push us toward the old-age brackets. They give us this unwelcome assist by what they do. Their thought, however well meant, is shown by unnecessary offers of help—everything from carrying a suitcase to threading a needle when you're sitting there with a little gadget that makes it a cinch to pull the thread through the needle's eye.

You may not want to rebuke these well-intentioned people. As a matter of fact, some assistance may be welcome. But don't hesitate to discourage offers of help that you don't want. And, try to avoid things in your own behavior that will encourage people to respond to you as an "older person." The signals can be clear. For example, appearance can be a particularly effective one. The individual who shuffles around in carpet slippers and an old bathrobe when receiving friends or relatives shouldn't be surprised if the visitor becomes solicitous of the host's ability to manage.

Nothing that's been said here should be interpreted as encouragement to behavior that is phony. It's not a suggestion that people "put on a front" of trying to act in some way that contradicts basic realities. What is suggested is that you be aware of the strong hidden forces that tend to propel individuals into "old age" unnecessarily and prematurely.

BE GUIDED BY YOUR SELF-IMAGE

There is a psychological factor that works strongly in your favor. Almost invariably, people feel younger than their chronological age. This fact can be a decided help in the fight against what is often a put-down: the way you think you look to others. A continuing self-censorship grows when you worry too much about others' opinions of your clothes, habits, activities, and so on.

As a result of that judgmental eye we feel is on us, we tend to turn ultraconservative. A woman may reject a dress style because it makes her look "too youthful"—in others' eyes. Understandably, she wants to avoid any negative reactions from friends or relatives that might suggest she is committing that sin known as "trying to look younger than she is." Presumably the virtue that matches that vice is summed up in the phrase, "Look your age."

But there's a perfectly good way to resolve the matter of your appearance and how it is affected by what you wear, your grooming, and so on: When in doubt as to whether, for example, a blazer and ascot might be criticized as showing poor taste—"wanting to look like a college boy"—have a trial run in front of the mirror with the item of apparel. Then ask yourself *not*, "What will others think of the way I look," but "How does it look to me?". And here you let your feelings about yourself and your own youthfulness guide your answer. Look at that image in the mirror. Compare it to the way you want to look, your own sense of your age, and if you feel it's in keeping with the youthful you—buy!

KEEP PHYSICALLY FIT

In addition to any or all other things you do to avoid the somnolence of aging, an essential is optimal health. One of the principal supports of youthfulness is the physical ability that helps support the appropriate energies and drive.

Diet, exercise, and medical checkups are the three supports of maintaining your health at the highest possible level. And there is an extremely important point to keep in mind in connection with health practices. As time passes, individuals tend to let down—in almost anything. A once highly successful diet still delivering benefits may be abandoned by an individual, not by intention but just because of a gradual slippage.

What this means is that at any one given time a review of these three key elements—eating habits, exercise, medical review—may lead you to improvements. In other words, reexamination may show that an area of activity that gave you a good level of exercise has deteriorated badly. For example, you used to play tennis fairly frequently, but your tennis partner moved away. The last time you checked with the manager of the courts, the convenient hour you used to play was no longer available. For one reason or another, the sport that was keeping you fit is now less available to you.

But a review that highlights this fact now makes it possible for you to reconsider your exercise situation. Perhaps going back to tennis isn't necessarily the only situation. If you can't reestablish a satisfactory program of tennis-playing, consider some other activity that you can perform on a regular basis that you will enjoy as well as benefit from in health terms.

In some cases, just looking around you to see what your community offers may be the simplest and most direct way of rebuilding a healthful activity. For example, a new facility that has become available either in your town or possibly an adjoining one, such as a new swimming pool, gymnasium, or both.

And eating habits tend to get out of whack from time to time. Maybe you or your spouse have gotten tired of cooking. The result is that you've been eating out—and really not as well in terms of nutrition and balance as used to be the case. Poor diet can be a major cause of lower levels of energy and a resulting general deterioration of lifestyle.

Just review in your own mind, briefly, your present eating habits. If you have any doubts about the adequacy of food intake, you may want to do some replanning of where and what you eat, consult your doctor or, possibly, a dietician if you have access to one.

It should be emphasized again that the aim of this chapter is not to make the point that aging is a terrible thing, to be fought tooth and nail. The intention is to keep life more interesting and more rewarding by approaching it with youthful anticipation rather than with the view of a person who has let chronological age mar the potential of daily living. In the words of J. P. Richter, "Nothing is more beautiful than cheerfulness in an old face."

Special Information

ORGANIZATIONS AND SERVICES

With the increase in numbers, political clout, and financial resources of the Over 50 segment of the population, more and more organizations have sprung up to meet its special needs. The groups, associations, and agencies discussed in this section have as their primary purpose service and information.

In researching this chapter, I met a lot of nice people—in person, on the phone, and through the mail. Most of them, from a young woman in California who works for a legal-services group that helps the elderly poor, to a man in Washington, D.C., who arranges cruises for well-heeled retirees, seemed committed to their jobs and eager to provide information.

When Mary, a member of the Gray Panthers, described the inter-generation housing project the Boston chapter is backing—housing for young and older people together—her enthusiasm was infectious. And Tom Clark, of West Virginia, was obviously pleased that the American Association of Retired Persons (AARP) had sent him, at no cost, a list of retirement facilities in the three states of his choice.

Lillian Jones, a preretiree in Columbus, Ohio, praised *Dynamic Years*, a bi-monthly publication of Action for Independent Maturity (AIM). She told me, "I can't wait to read it. And the photos are great."

George Shreiber, a personnel manager in Houston, Texas, who does retirement counseling for his firm, said, "I always recommend *Fifty Plus* [formerly *Retirement Living* magazine]. It's dynamite."

Magazines are but one benefit of membership in a preretirement or retirement group. Since different people want different things from group membership, it's not surprising that the organizations described cover a wide range of activities. But there is one benefit of membership that applies to everyone: loneliness can cut down on life, and membership cuts down on loneliness. Many people report a feeling of belonging, of contact with others, that they find exhilarating.

Recent research confirms that sociable people live longer than nonsociable types. Dr. Lisa Berkman, of the University of California, reported that people who had few social contacts were two to four times as likely to die from the major causes of death as those who maintained strong social ties. Thus, Dr. Berkman's research suggests that good personal relationships—including those to be found in membership in social, religious, political and/or retirement groups—holds out the promise not only of a pleasant, but a longer, life.

You may choose to join a music group or a political group that marshals evidence to present before the House Select Committee on Aging, which, under the leadership of septuagenarian Representative Claude Pepper, works for legislation to benefit the elderly. Whatever you're looking for, your chances of finding just the right group are being increased by the growing number of organizations.

Not all groups are open for general membership. Some are professional or research organizations, others provide information and referrals for services. There is also a list of toll-free numbers you may want to call for specific information if questions or problems arise. The section concludes with information on how to find groups and services in your community.

If you decide to join a preretirement or retirement group, you may find, as Cathy Linde of Portland, Oregon, did, that, "I enjoy my group contacts and the magazine they send me. You see, the people in the group, and the stars and celebrities pictured in the magazine, show me an important thing—I'm not the only one who is getting older. . . ."

● *Membership Organizations*

GENERAL MEMBERSHIP

AARP
American Association of Retired Persons
1909 K Street, NW
Washington, DC 20049
(202) 872-4700

AARP is the largest and oldest retirement organization open for general membership. Founded in 1958, membership as of late 1978 numbers some 12 million people 55 or older, employed or retired, who are serviced by a staff of 300. AARP, in affiliation with NRTA (National Retired Teachers Association) offers the most comprehensive array of services designed for older people. The annual membership fee is low, and includes the member's spouse in all benefits through dual membership.

AARP publications include *Modern Maturity* magazine, a professionally edited, full-color general interest magazine considered favorably in the field. The AARP *News Bulletin* provides members with a monthly update on legislative developments of interest to older people and reports on outstanding community services performed by chapters and individuals.

AARP also publishes *Better Retirement Guidebooks*, free to members, on such subjects as crime prevention, legal affairs, taxes, health, housing, and consumer affairs.

The Legislation and Government Affairs Program run by AARP works with members of Congress on bills affecting older citizens and develops federal and state legislative objectives in such areas as retirement income, health insurance, nursing home standards, housing requirements of the elderly, and credit discrimination.

The Church Relations program works with a variety of Protestant, Catholic, Jewish, and Interfaith coalitions to increase and improve their services for and with older people.

AARP's Consumer Program operates the National Consumer Assistance Center (NCAC) in Washington, D.C., which provides assistance to members and nonmembers in resolving consumer problems. NCAC handles questions and complaints either directly, or by referral to a more appropriate agency.

The Defensive Driving Course, developed by the National Safety Council, teaches AARP members to drive in hectic traffic. Graduates of the course are awarded certificates which entitle them to a reduction of auto insurance premiums in most states. AARP offers its own program of automobile insurance as well. And AARP members may become teachers of this driving course.

The Generations Alliance Program, composed of AARP members and young people in the community, offers an agenda of "rap sessions" and community service projects.

The Health Education Program provides information related to the health and well-being of older adults, as well as preventive screening and testing for arthritis, cancer, and diabetes.

AARP's Institute of Lifetime Learning works with such other organizations as the Coalition of Adult Education Organizations, the American Association of Community and Junior Colleges, and the American Association of State Colleges and Universities to expand learning opportunities for older people.

The Tax-Aide Program provides capable older adult counselors from the community to assist other older people in obtaining maximum tax benefits by helping them with the preparation of their annual income tax returns. In states which give special credits and rebates to older residents, counselors help older adults of all income levels to obtain direct cash rebates as well.

AARP will also provide state-wide lists of retirement communities and nursing homes on request.

Additional AARP services include:

1. The Purchase Privilege Program, which offers members discounts at a number of leading hotel/motel chains and auto rental companies.

2. The Travel Service, which offers low-priced domestic and world-wide tours designed to meet the needs of older people.

3. The Pharmacy Service, which offers prescription medicines, vitamins, and other health-related products at reasonable prices, available in AARP pharmacy centers or delivered to the home by mail.

4. Mature Temps, which specializes in placing retired people in temporary jobs.

5. Insurance information about policies developed for older people, including renewable automobile, tenants and homeowners, and health insurance, and life insurance without health qualifications. While the Colonial Penn Franklin Insurance Company, through which AARP offers medical insurance, has been criticized for using AARP as a sales agency, its Mature Care 65 health plan offers comprehensive coverage at a moderate cost.

The organization has delineated its aims and services in a statement that is noteworthy because it also echoes the thinking of other membership-supported groups in the field:

• AARP works to secure more equitable treatment for people 55 or over, actively employed, semiretired or retired. It constantly searches for ways to improve retirement conditions.

• Through the strength of its membership, AARP gains benefits for members which they could not gain for themselves.

• The AARP group health insurance plans are open to all AARP members and their spouses, regardless of age, and are noncancelable while the contracts are in force.

• AARP members are eligible for a broad range of low-cost benefits and services, including the bimonthly magazine, *Modern Maturity*, and the monthly *AARP News Bulletin*. Annual membership is $3, $8 for three years.

AIM
Action for Independent Maturity
(A division of American Association of Retired Persons)
1909 K Street, NW
Washington, DC 20049
(202) 872-4850

AIM offers several kinds of retirement planning services. Included are individual and group AIM memberships; a Retirement Planning Seminar; a Retirement Planning Lecture Series; film-and-discussion programs on mid-life problems and concerns; Retirement Preparation Training Programs; a one-day consciousness-raising Retirement Planning Workshop; customized training programs, and a series of guidebooks on preretirement and retirement areas of interest.

AIM was formed in 1971 by the Board of Directors of AARP to develop and promote a comprehensive program to help people in their retirement from industry.

AIM membership is open to all employed people, ages 50 to 70, and their spouses. AIM sees itself as a "spokesman for the middle years." Its goal is to help its more than 450,000 members "learn how to live better right now, while planning intelligently for the future."

AIM publishes *Dynamic Years*, a bi-monthly magazine of general interest to preretirees. It is the only preretirement magazine in the country. AIM guidebooks provide material on physical fitness, household and personal security, legal and medical matters, single living, and other aspects of preretirement life. Like AARP, AIM offers a pharmacy service, group health insurance plans, and life and automobile insurance information. In addition, AIM provides consumer information and advice, and conducts preretirement preparation training programs to help organizations improve the effectiveness of their preretirement programs. Some people belong to AIM and AARP simultaneously.

RELATED ORGANIZATIONS. Some of the purposes and services of AARP and AIM have been described. In the section on organizations open to specific professional groups, NRTA, the National Retired Teachers Association, will be discussed. It is helpful, at this point, to explain the relationship among these three groups. NRTA was founded in 1948 and is the parent organization; AARP was founded ten years later, in 1958; and AIM was formed in 1971 by AARP.

Today, NRTA and AARP are separate organizations which work together and have parallel structures, though they share functional staff. Each has a National Board of Directors consisting of national officers and members of the executive staff. The organizations are divided into regions, with area vice presidents and at least two staff members administering the regions. The volunteer State Director and one or more assistants work most closely with the local chapters and units. AIM is the retirement planning program division of AARP.

In addition to many national programs, NRTA and AARP individually and jointly sponsor a number of community service programs. Some are in the form of courses; others are designed to provide opportunities for members to become active in programs serving the community.

Gray Panthers
3700 Chestnut Street
Philadelphia, PA 19104
(215) 382-6644

Founded by Maggie Kuhn in 1971, the organization now has more than fifty local Panther groups, composed of some 10,000 persons over 65 and young people, joined together in consciousness-raising and activist projects to combat ageism in society.

The group believes that "older persons in this society constitute a great national resource, which has largely gone unrecognized, undervalued, and unused. The experience, wisdom, and competence of older persons are greatly needed in every sector. Creative and innovative ways must be found to enable older people to make their contribution."

The group applies its action-oriented philosophy to problems involving war and peace, poverty, hunger, racial injustice, and judicial reform. Having absorbed the Retired Professional Action Group in 1974, members testify at legislative hearings, trying to improve the legal, medical, and financial status of older adults. Local chapters develop their own community projects, such as intergeneration housing, now being established by the Boston Panther groups.

In addition, the Gray Panthers maintain an information and referral service and conduct seminars and research on age-related issues. When an important court case involving the rights of the elderly comes up, the Panthers call on the National Senior Citizens Law Center for back-up support, briefs, and appeals.

If you are interested in trying to bring about changes in the treatment of, opportunities for, or services available to, seniors, either in your local community or in state or national legislation or programs, this is a group to think about seriously. The Gray Panthers, unlike most other groups, are militant and aggressive—a dynamic force for change. Of course, they work cooperatively with other organizations to improve conditions for senior citizens, and those interested in their welfare.

NAMP
National Association of Mature People
Box 26792
Oklahoma City, OK 73118
(405) 523-2060

NAMP is the newest general membership group to be formed for individuals 55 and over. It seeks a "healthy competition" with AARP, and many people are members of both groups. NAMP is currently strongest in the midwest and west, though it is expanding eastward. It provides a wide variety of services for older adults, such as recreational activities; group travel programs; financial guidance and counseling; educational programs and activities; health, auto, and life insurance; prescription drug services; free traffic court appearance certificates (similar to AAA's); and discount buying assistance.

In addition, NAMP testifies before state and federal legislative bodies, conducts a charitable program, and publishes the quarterly, *Best Years*.

NASC
National Alliance of Senior Citizens
Box 40031
Washington, DC 20016
(202) 338-5632

Founded in 1974, NASC now has 16,500 members organized into 150 regional groups. Its purpose is to inform members, and the American public at large, of the needs of senior citizens and of how well or poorly these needs are being met by programs and policies of government and other specified agencies. To this end it compiles statistics, maintains a library for political and general research, and represents the interests of senior citizens before Congress and state legislatures.

NASC maintains a Golden Age Hall of Fame, honoring individuals for outstanding service to the senior community. Its Advisory Council is composed of experts in the following fields: Adult Education; Budgeting; Consumerism; Crime; Economics; Election Laws; Employment Security; Environmental Protection; Family Life; Farm and Rural Life; Gerontology; Health Care; Housing; Nursing Homes; Nutrition; Organized Labor; Pension and Retirement Benefits; Planning and Zoning; Political Action; Productivity; Psychologist on Aging; Retirement Centers; Rural Transportation; Social Security; Sociologist on Aging; Taxation; Urban Transportation; Veterans Affairs; Volunteers; Welfare.

NASC publishes *Senior Independent*, a bi-monthly magazine, and an annual *Senior Services Manual*.

NCSC

National Council of Senior Citizens
1511 K Street, NW
Washington, DC 20005
(202) 347-8800

NCSC, founded in 1961 and employing a staff of 120, is an organization of private individuals, 3800 autonomous senior citizens' clubs, associations, and other groups totaling a membership of 3 million people. It is nonprofit and politically nonpartisan.

The organization was formed by a coalition of groups—church, trade-union, social welfare, and recreation—interested in having medicare-type legislation passed. The executive board, consisting of sixty-five people, includes representatives of these founding groups.

NCSC tries to have those who are members through their senior citizens' club membership become individual members, to qualify for benefits such as supplemental Medicare insurance, prescription drug program, travel assistance, and a monthly newspaper. Senior citizens' clubs get a monthly packet that includes the monthly newspaper, guidelines on current legislation, and information on local activities which they might be interested in supporting—stage legislation, for example.

The objectives and principles of NCSC are:

• to promote the interests of senior citizens in the United States in harmony with the national interest

• to encourage greater opportunities for voluntary civic service for senior citizens

• to act as a clearinghouse for the exchange of information, ideas, and experiences among affiliated members and groups

• to engage in fact finding and analysis of issues, to publish the results of such studies, to provide a responsible and articulate voice for senior citizens, and to conduct other types of public relations activities

• to provide leadership training opportunities for senior citizens by conducting workshops, institutes, and other types of educational programs

• to be nonprofit and to promote social welfare by attempting to influence legislation, but never by endorsing or supporting any candidate for public office

• to take such other action as is consistent with the interests and needs of senior citizens

NCSC sponsors educational workshops on topics such as reduced costs of drugs, better housing, Medicare, and Social Security. It distributes films, news releases, and special reports, and maintains a library on Medicare, nursing home standards, and related issues. Its publication, *Senior Citizens News,* appears monthly.

SPECIFIC PROFESSIONAL GROUPS

NARFE

National Association of Retired Federal Employees
1533 New Hampshire Ave., NW
Washington, DC 20036
(202) 234-0832

Founded in 1921, NARFE now has 275,000 members—retired U.S. Government and District of Columbia employees, their spouses, persons drawing annuities as survivors of retired government employees, and present employees eligible for optional retirement. NARFE reviews and promotes preretirement programs provided by government agencies, sponsors and supports legislation in the best interest of civil service employees, and is interested in a wide range of problems involving aging and the aged. Members receive the monthly publication *Retirement Life*.

NRTA

National Retired Teachers Association
909 K. Street, NW
Washington, DC 20049
(202) 872-4700

NRTA is a seminal entity among retirement groups. It was founded in 1948 by Ethel Percy Andrus, who had been principal of a California high school. Aware of the lack of preparedness of the average teacher about to retire, she sought to provide in her organization some of the supports she felt were needed. Insurance was one of the benefits she felt was desirable and not generally available to people of retirement age. She was able to make arrangements for this coverage, and added other benefits—travel, health information and so on. Dr. Andrus described the general purpose of NRTA as, "Putting spunk into those who need to get their lives moving again!" It was also her belief that "creative energy is ageless," and, speaking of retired people, she said that, "Years of experience, understanding and skill are reserves of energy and power that must be put to work."

Becoming aware of the similar problems and needs confronting other retirees, she helped found the affiliated general-membership organization, American Association of Retired Persons.

Today, NRTA claims 525,000 members—66 percent, or two out of three, retired teachers. They are organized into 2,100 local groups. In affiliation with AARP, NRTA services include group hospital-surgical insurance, group travel, pharmacy service at reduced cost, consultation and information, Institute of Lifetime Learning, consumer information, health education, tax-aid, crime prevention, and church programs. NRTA maintains a speakers' bureau and compiles statistics.

SCORE

Service Corps of Retired Executives
1441 L Street, NW
Washington, DC 20416
(202) 382-5558

This volunteer program sponsored by the U.S. Small Business Administration includes 8,600 members. Retired businessmen and women make their managerial skills and experience available to owners/managers of small businesses in need of management counseling and are reimbursed for out-of-pocket expenses. SCORE publishes *Insight: Management Assistance Newsletter,* as well as a *Counselor's Guidebook.* Companies wanting this kind of help contact SCORE directly, or their local SBA office.

TROA

The Retired Officers Association
201 N. Washington Street
Alexandria, VA 22314

Men and women who are or have been commissioned or warrant officers in any component of the Army, Navy, Air Force, Marine Corps, Coast Guard, National Oceanic and Atmospheric Administration, and Public Health Service compose the association's 245,000 members. TROA assists retired officers, their dependents, and survivors with their retirement problems and service status, and sponsors a scholarship program and a retiree employment service. Members receive *The Retired Officer Magazine* monthly.

SENIOR CITIZENS CLUB MEMBERSHIP GROUPS

The organizations in this section are open through Senior Citizens Club membership. Also see National Council of Senior Citizens (NCSC) on page 552.

GRCSC

Golden Ring Council of Senior Citizens
22 W. 38th Street
New York, NY 10018
(212) 840-2111

The council consists of twenty-five clubs in New York City and twenty-five in states other than New York. Its purpose is "to promote better living conditions for elderly people, social activities in the clubs, and social action to improve legislation." The council sponsors an essay contest for high school students on the topic of Social Security.

JASA

Jewish Association for Services for the Aged
222 Park Avenue South
New York, NY 10003
(212) 677-2530

Around 4,000 members, participating in thirty local senior citizens groups, benefit from the services of JASA, a social welfare organization whose objective is, where possible, to keep older adults in the community and provide the services necessary to enable them to maintain themselves there. Services include information and referral to appropriate health, welfare, educational, social, recreational and vacation services; personal counseling; financial assistance; health and medical service counsel; counsel on housing; securing of homemaker service; conducting of group educational and recreational activities through senior citizens associations; referral to summer camps; day camp activities for the elderly; legal services; protective services; reaching out to the isolated; and volunteer service opportunities. JASA also sponsors Sheve House and Brockdale Village, housing-for-the-elderly projects, and trains students from the New York University School of Social Work, Hunter College School of Social Work, and Yeshiva University of Social Work.

PROFESSIONAL/RESEARCH ORGANIZATIONS

The following are organizations which look at aging from the professional, rather than the personal, point of view. They are included here to let you know what is being done in the field of aging research, and to give you sources to which to turn for technical information. National as well as international associations are included.

AAAR

Association for the Advancement of Aging Research
309 Hancock Building
University of Southern California
Los Angeles, CA 90007
(213) 746-6019

AAAR is an organization of professionals in the field of gerontology, which, in combination with concerned lay people, works to organize and promote research into the biological origins of aging and the effects of aging on the quality of life for the elderly.

AAAR, founded in 1968, surveys research programs exploring mechanisms of aging, maintains an information bank on this research, and conducts meetings on the molecular biology of the aging process.

AF

Andrus Foundation

The Andrus Foundation is supported and encouraged by the NRTA and AARP. Established in 1973, the Foundation honors the late Dr. Ethel Percy Andrus, the retired educator who founded the National Retired Teachers Association and American Association of Retired Persons.

The Andrus Foundation supports research projects in social gerontology—the study of the social and psychological aspects of aging—with grants to university-based projects throughout the United States.

Foundation-supported research covers a range of aspects of the older person's life, from improved training for older drivers to physical fitness programs and help for the senior job-seeker. Some typical projects for which grants were made:

1. A Duke University project on geriatric training for medical students enrolled in family practice programs.

2. An attitude study at North Carolina State University indicating that the negative views some adolescents have toward aging can be changed through education.

3. A Brandeis University study of how Social Security and pension legislation can adversely affect an older person's job opportunities.

4. A project at the University of Southern California with the long-term goal of improving service delivery to the elderly by insuring that professionals delivering these services are properly trained.

In general, AF sponsors academic research aimed at making life more productive and meaningful for older people.

AGE

American Aging Association
c/o Denham Harman, M.D.
University of Nebraska College of Medicine
Omaha, NE 68105
(402) 541-4416

AGE, founded in 1970, is an organization of laypersons and scientists in the biomedical field dedicated to "helping people live better longer" by promoting studies directed toward slowing down the aging process. It also informs the public about the progress of aging research and about practical methods of achieving a long and healthy life. In addition, the group works to increase knowledge of gerontology among physicians and other health professionals.

AGS

American Geriatrics Society
10 Columbus Circle
New York, NY 10019
(212) 582-1333

AGS is a professional society whose 8,000 members include physicians, physiotherapists, occupational therapists, social and welfare workers, as well as superintendents of hospitals and homes for the aged. Its purposes are to encourage and promote the study of geriatrics and to stress the importance of medical research in the field of aging. The group bestows two annual awards for achievement in geriatric medicine.

AGS publishes the Journal of the *American Geriatrics Society* and the *AGS Newsletter,* both monthly.

ARI

Aging Research Institute
342 Madison Avenue
New York, NY 10017
(212) 682-2245

ARI was founded in 1953 to engage in, encourage, and support research studies of the fundamental aspects of the aging process, including studies of the embryonal, mature, and aging cells in all their phases. The organization is concerned with research into the prevention, diagnosis, and treatment of disease during advancing years and in furthering the work of doctors engaged in geriatric research and clinical geriatrics.

ASGD

American Society for Geriatric Dentistry
11 East Adams
Chicago, IL 60603
(312) 341-0909

ASGD is devoted to the maintenance and improvement of oral health in the elderly. The group promotes the continuing education of practitioners of geriatric dentistry, nursing home administrators, hygienists, nurses, and students in related fields. ASGD is affiliated with the American Dental Association.

GS

Gerontological Society
One Dupont Circle, Suite 520
Washington, DC 20036
(202) 659-4968

Founded in 1945, GS is an organization of physicians, physiologists, psychiatrists, pharmacologists, geneticists, endocrinologists, and other professionals interested in improving the well-being of older people. The group promotes the scientific study of the aging process, publishes information about aging, and works to bring together all groups interested in older people. GS publishes The *Gerontologist* and the *Journal of Gerontology,* both bi-monthly.

IAG

International Association of Gerontology
Section of Biological Ultrastructure
The Weizmann Institute of Science
P.O Box 26
Rehovot, Israel

This association of national gerontological societies, founded in 1950, supports research in the biologic, medical, and social fields carried out by gerontological associations, and promotes cooperation among their members. It advances the training of highly qualified professional personnel in the field of aging and works to protect the interests of gerontological societies internationally. IAG publishes *The Gerontologist.*

IFA

International Federation on Aging
1909 K. Street, NW
Washington, DC 20049
(202) 872-4700

Founded in 1973, in part through the efforts of AARP and NRTA, IFA is a federation of nongovernmental, nonpolitical, nonsectarian, nonprofit voluntary organizations from twenty countries that serve as advocates for the elderly and/or provide services to them. Its purposes are to "serve as an international advocate for the aging; exchange information on a cross-national level of developments in aging of primary interest to the practitioner; assist in the creation of associations of the aging; sponsor conferences and symposia." IFA publishes *Aging International*, quarterly, as well as special reports and handbooks.

ISCA

International Senior Citizens Association
11753 Wilshire Boulevard
Los Angeles, CA 90025
(213) 472-4704

ISCA members include individuals over 50 years of age and professional groups. Founded in 1903, ISCA provides coordination on the international level "to safeguard the interests and needs of the senior citizens of the world." It sponsors international conferences and publishes a quarterly newsletter.

NAHD

National Association for Human Development
1750 Pennsylvania Avenue, NW
Washington, DC 20006

Founded in 1974, NAHD seeks to assist people over 60 years of age in establishing and maintaining physical and emotional health and vigor. It operates model demonstration projects as well as evaluation, research, and training programs. Presently concentrating on physical fitness, it conducts an "Active People Over 60" program. NAHD also gives local workshops and nutrition seminars. The organization publishes a quarterly digest, a training manual, audio-visual and media-oriented materials, and a bibliography.

NASUA

National Association of State Units on Aging
1828 L Street, NW, Suite 505
Washington, DC 20036
(202) 466-8529

NASUA, although not itself a governmental agency, is the coordinating organization of the fifty-six State Units on Aging, which are official state—and territory—agencies. It acts as a center for the exchange and dissemination of information on the problems and progress of older people among federal agencies, other national organizations concerned with older Americans, and the State Units on Aging.

The organization also provides information on federal regulations and policies in time for the states to plan for and respond to them. Thus, through NASUA the State Units on Aging are able to act collectively as a force to improve the status of older Americans.

NASUA maintains a liaison office in Washington to respond to federal laws and regulations, and an information clearinghouse on State Aging Units activities. It also issues a variety of reports on State Unit programs and accomplishments.

NCBE

National Center on the Black Aged
1424 K Street, NW
Washington, DC 20005
(202) 637-8400

NCBE is a nonprofit organization, funded primarily by the federal Administration on Aging, concerned with problems affecting the black elderly. It serves as an information clearinghouse and conducts education, training, and research and development programs.

NCOA

National Council on the Aging
1828 L Street, NW
Washington, DC 20036
(202) 223-6250

Founded in 1950, NCOA includes members from business, organized labor, and the health professions, as well as social workers, clergy, educators, and various private and government agencies. It works with and through other organizations to develop concern for older people, as well as methods and resources for meeting their needs. NCOA provides a national information and consultation center; holds conferences and workshops; and sponsors an annual award for outstanding contributions on behalf of older people.

NCOA has a library of more than 5,000 volumes on aging, with emphasis on psychological, economic, and health aspects. It maintains the National Institute of Industrial Gerontology, the National Institute of Senior Centers, the National Media Resource Center on Aging, and National Voluntary Organizations for Independent Living.

NCOA publishes: *NISC Memo,* monthly; *Perspective on Aging,* biennial; *Current Literature on Aging,* quarterly; and *Industrial Gerontology,* quarterly. It also publishes numerous books, brochures, and pamphlets.

NGS

National Geriatrics Society
212 West Wisconsin Avenue, Third Floor
Milwaukee, WI 53203

Founded in 1953, NGS is an organization of public, voluntary, and proprietary institutions providing long-term care and treatment of the chronically ill. Membership is composed of hospitals, sanitariums, homes for the aged, nursing homes, and similar institutions with a geriatric program. NGS promotes the maintenance of proper operational standards and qualified administration of facilities caring for the aged.

NGS cooperates with public, voluntary, and private agencies in matters pertaining to geriatric education and assists and advises members in the solution of problems arising in geriatric institutions. It publishes *Views and News,* monthly, and a *Nursing Procedures Manual.*

● *Special Interest Groups*

CONSUMER AID

CPC

Consumer Protection Center
200 H Street, NW
Washington, DC 20052
(202) 676-7585

Founded in 1969, this consumer self-help program is jointly sponsored by George Washington University Law School and WRC-TV in Washington, D.C. It acts as mediator between the consumer and party complained against. If special services are required, the consumer is referred to appropriate federal, state, and local sources to enable him or her to receive a quick and satisfactory resolution to the problem. In addition, law students working with the television station are developing programs to expose fraudulent and deceptive practices uncovered by complaints phoned in to the HELP Center.

CPC also provides legal and mental health counseling to the elderly through Senior Citizen's Storefront. People 55 years old and above are taught substantive law in areas that most directly involve the elderly. Since its inception, the Center has acted on approximately 30,000 complaints.

NCAP

National Consumer Assistance Program run by AARP (American Association of Retired Persons). See page 546.

CULTURAL INTERESTS

CPG

Club for Philately in Gerontology
2525 Centerville Road
Dallas, TX 75228
(214) 327-4503

In affiliation with the Gerontological Society, the members—gerontologists, physicians, educators, clergymen, stamp collectors, and dealers—formed the club in order to increase interest in aging through philately; to identify and compile lists of stamp issues pertaining to the aged; to encourage issuance of commemorative stamps honoring the aged; to provide for exchange of information and to publish educational materials.

NCAEE

National Committee on Art Education for the Elderly
Culver Stocton College
Canton, MO 63435
(314) 288-5221

This group, which includes individuals and organizations interested in promoting better art education opportunities for the elderly, works to promote research and development in art education; to expand art education's role in our society at the critical time in a citizen's life when the work ethic is replaced by a leisure ethic; to encourage quality program opportunities in art education for the elderly; to urge the establishment of programs, facilities, and personnel in existing organizations which are either partially or entirely geared to serve the elderly.

LEGAL PROTECTION

LCE

Legal Center for the Elderly
842 Pacific Street
Placerville, CA 95667
(916) 622-4636

This center provides direct services to clients over 60. Like the many other centers in other states, it is funded through HEW's Administration on Aging, and helps people with problems concerning Social Security, Medicare, divorces, and wills. Priority is generally given to low-income individuals. For the center in your area, call your State Agency on Aging. (For the phone number of your state agency, see next section.)

LSEP

Legal Services for the Elderly Poor
2095 Broadway
New York, NY 10023
(212) 595-1340

Attorneys here provide advice on legal problems of the elderly. Funded through the Legal Services Corporation and HEW's Administration on Aging, its purposes are to conduct research, litigation, and educational programs. LSEP maintains a library and has published numerous reports, articles, and papers.

RELATED TO NURSING HOMES AND RETIREMENT FACILITIES

AAHA

American Association of Homes for the Aging
1050 17th Street, NW
Washington, DC 20036
(202) 296-5960

AAHA's 1400 members—voluntary, nonprofit, and governmental homes for the aging, as well as other interested individuals and organizations—strive to protect and advance the interests of the residents. AAHA works with the government in developing plans for basic curricula for administrators of homes, and it conducts institutes and workshops on current concerns, such as accreditation, financing, the meaning of institutional life, and planning for the residents of the future. AAHA publishes a *Directory of Nonprofit Homes for the Aged: Social Components of Care.*

AHCA

American Health Care Association
1200 15th Street, NW
Washington, DC 20005
(202) 833-2050

AHCA is a federation of fifty state health care associations, embracing 7,600 members. It conducts seminars and conferences as continuing education for nursing home personnel; maintains liaison with governmental agencies, Congress, and professional associations; compiles statistics, and maintains a 2,000 volume library. AHCA publishes the *Journal of the American Health Care Association* bi-monthly, pamphlets on health career opportunities and *Thinking About a Nursing Home.*

The Church of the Brethren Homes and Hospitals Association

1111 E. Kansas
McPherson, KS 67460
(814) 793-2104

The administrators and board members of the twenty-two Brethren Homes for the Aged and its one hospital meet to discuss their common concerns and to develop programs of service to aging people.

NAJHA

National Association of Jewish Homes
    for the Aged
2525 Centerville Road
Dallas, TX 75228
(214) 327-4503

Composed of 105 nonprofit charitable Jewish homes, retirement or nursing homes, geriatric hospitals, and special facilities for Jewish aged and chronically ill, NAJHA conducts institutes and conferences; undertakes legislative activities, and compiles statistics. It is affiliated with the National Conference of Jewish Communal Service and the American Association of Homes for the Aging.

RRWA

Retirement Research and Welfare Association
215 Long Beach Blvd.
Long Beach, CA 90801
(213) 432-5781

RRWA compiles, and distributes upon request, comprehensive lists of retirement facilities in each state. Information about the retirement homes and convalescent and nursing facilities is supplied by the administrators, and inclusion in the lists does not represent an endorsement or recommendation. However, with each list supplied, RRWA includes tips on how to select an appropriate retirement facility. It is a private, philanthropic, nonprofit organization established to sponsor and conduct research and welfare activities in the field of aging.

RELATED TO PENSION PLANS

CREF
College Retirement Equities Fund
730 Third Ave.
New York, NY 10017
(212) 490-9000

CREF is made up of 450,000 policyholder members who are on the staffs of colleges, universities, independent schools, foundations, libraries, and scientific and research organizations. Its purpose is to provide members with a variable annuity, based on common stock investments, which will keep up with rising living costs.

NASRA
National Association of State Retirement Administrators
302 Public Safety Building
Montgomery, AL 36130
(205) 832-5080

An association of administrators of statewide public employee retirement systems, NASRA encourages nationwide review of pension and retirement programs, sponsors conferences, and provides technical and information services to members.

NCPERS
National Conference on Public Employee Retirement
    Systems
275 East Broad Street
Columbus, OH 43215
(614) 221-7845

The purpose of NCPERS, an association of national, state, and local public employee retirement systems, is to promote and safeguard the rights of the members of those systems. It also serves as liaison with the U.S. Congress.

● *Government Agencies*

FEDERAL AGENCIES

ACTION
806 Connecticut Ave. NW
Washington, DC 20525
(202) 254-7310

ACTION administers, develops policy for, and provides funds to community agencies to run the following programs for low-income people over 60: Foster Grandparents, which gives participants the opportunity to aid children with special needs; Retired Senior Volunteer Program (RSVP), which develops volunteer service opportunities in hospitals, schools, and courts; and Senior Companions, in which other older adults, with special needs, are helped by volunteers.

AOA
Administration on Aging
330 Independence Ave., SW
Washington, DC 20201
(202) 245-0724

This agency, a subsidiary of the Department of Health, Education, and Welfare (HEW), administers programs under the Older Americans

Act, including aid to state and community groups which assist the elderly in solving the problems that develop along with advancing years.

COA
Clearinghouse on the Aging
330 Independence Ave., SW
Washington, DC 20201
(202) 245-0188

This subsidiary of the Department of Health, Education, and Welfare (HEW) provides information on the problems on aging, including health care, state and community programs, nutrition, physical education, and protection.

NIA
National Institute on Aging
9000 Rockville Pike
Bethesda, MD
(301) 496-5345

One of the National Institutes of Health, NIA conducts and funds research into the biological, medical, and behavioral aspects of aging.

STATE AGENCIES

Your State Agency (or Unit) on Aging is the place to turn for information on topics related to aging. A main function of each agency is to provide the elderly with information and referral to local services qualified to deal with their problems. Following is an alphabetical (by state) list of these agencies for the U.S. states, territories, and possessions.

ALABAMA
Commission on Aging
740 Madison Avenue
Montgomery, AL 36130
205-832-6640

ALASKA
Office on Aging
Department of Health &
  Social Services
Pouch H
Juneau, AK 99811
907-586-6153

ARIZONA
Bureau on Aging
Department of Economic
  Security
111 West Osborn
Phoenix, AZ 85004
602-271-4446

ARKANSAS
Office on Aging & Adult
  Services
Department of Social &
  Rehabilitative Services

7107 West 12th Street
Little Rock, AR 72203
501-371-2441

CALIFORNIA
Department of Aging
918 J. Street
Sacramento, CA 95814
916-322-3887

COLORADO
Division of Services for
  the Aging
Department of Social Services
1575 Sherman Street
Denver, CO 80203
303-839-2651

CONNECTICUT
Department on Aging
90 Washington Street
Room 312
Hartford, CT 06115
203-566-7725

DELAWARE
Division of Aging
Department of Health & Social
  Services
Newcastle, DE 19720
302-421-6791

WASHINGTON, DC
Office of Aging
Office of the Mayor
Suite 1106
1012 14th Street, N.W.
Washington, DC
202-724-5623

FLORIDA
Program Office of Aging
  & Adult Services
Department of Health &
  Rehabilitation Services
1323 Winewood Blvd.

Tallahassee, FL 32301
904-488-2625

GEORGIA
Office of Aging
Department of Human Resources
618 Ponce de Leon Avenue, N.E.
Atlanta, GA 30308
404-894-5333

GUAM
Office of Aging
Social Service
Department of Public Health
Government of Guam
P.O. Box 2618
Agana, GU
745-9901-x324

HAWAII
Executive Office on Aging
Office of the Governor
State of Hawaii
1149 Bethel Street
Room 307
Honolulu, HI 96813
808-548-2593

IDAHO
Idaho Office on Aging
Statehouse
Boise, ID
208-384-3833

ILLINOIS
Department on Aging
431 East Capital Avenue
Springfield, IL 62706
217-785-3356

INDIANA
Commission on Aging and Aged
Graphic Arts Building
215 North Senate Avenue
Indianapolis, IN 46202
317-633-5948

IOWA
Commission on Aging
415 West Tenth Street
Jewett Building
Des Moines, IA 50319
515-281-5187

KANSAS
Division of Social Services
Services for the Aging Section
Department of Social Services
  and Rehabilitation Services
State Office Building
Topeka, KS 66612
913-296-4986

KENTUCKY
Center for Aging Services
Bureau of Social Services
Human Service Building, 6th Fl.
275 East Main Street
Frankfort, KY 40601
502-564-6930

LOUISIANA
Bureau of Aging Services
Division of Human Resources
Health & Human Resources
  Administration
P.O. Box 44282
Capitol Station
Baton Rouge, LA 70804
504-389-2171

MAINE
Bureau of Maine's Elderly
Community Services Unit
Department of Human Services
State House
Augusta, ME 04333
207-289-2561

MARYLAND
Office on Aging
State Office Building
301 West Preston Street
Baltimore, MD 21201
301-383-5064

MASSACHUSETTS
Department of Elder Affairs
110 Tremont Street, 5th fl.
Boston, MA 02108
617-727-7751

MICHIGAN
Office of Services to the
  Aging
300 E. Michigan Avenue
P.O. Box 30026
Lansing, MI 48913
517-373-8230

MINNESOTA
Minnesota Board on Aging
Suite 204, Metro Square
  Building
Seventh & Robert Streets
St. Paul, MN 55101
612-296-2544

MISSISSIPPI
Council on Aging
P.O. Box 5136
Fondren Station
510 George Street
Jackson, MS 39216
601-354-6590

MISSOURI
Office of Aging
Division of Special Services
Department of Social Services

Broadway State Office Building
P.O. Box 570
Jefferson City, MO 65101
314-751-2075

MONTANA
Aging Services Bureau
Department of Social &
  Rehabilitation Services
P.O. Box 1723
Helena, MT 59601
406-449-3124

NEBRASKA
Commission on Aging
State House Station 94784
300 South 17th Street
Lincoln, NE 68509
402-471-2307

NEVADA
Division of Aging
Department of Human Resources
505 East King Street
Kinkead Building, Room 101
Carson City, NV 88710
702-885-4210

NEW HAMPSHIRE
Council on Aging
P.O. Box 786
14 Deport Street
Concord, NH 03301
603-271-2751

NEW JERSEY
Division on Aging
Department of Community Affairs
P.O. Box 2768
363 West State Street
Trenton, NJ 08625
609-292-4833

NEW MEXICO
Bureau of Aging Services
PERA Building, Room 515
Santa Fe, NM 87501
505-827-2802

NEW YORK
Office for the Aging
New York State Executive
  Department
Empire State Plaza
Agency Building #2
Albany, NY 12223
518-474-5731

NORTH CAROLINA
North Carolina Office for Aging
Department of Human Resources
Administration Building
213 Hillsborough Street
Raleigh, NC 27603
919-733-3983

NORTH DAKOTA
Aging Services
Social Services Board of
  North Dakota
State Capitol Building
Bismarck, ND 58505
701-224-2577

OHIO
Commission on Aging
50 West Broad Street, 9th fl.
Columbus, OH 43215
614-466-5500

OKLAHOMA
Special Unit on Aging
Department of Institutions
Social & Rehabilitative
  Services

P.O. Box 25353
Oklahoma City, OK 73125
405-521-2281

OREGON
Human Resources Department
772 Commercial Street, S.E.
Salem, OR 97310
503-378-4728

PENNSYLVANIA
Office for the Aging
Department of Public Welfare
Health & Welfare Building
Room 511, P.O. Box 2657
Seventh and Forster Streets
Harrisburg, PA 17120
717-787-5350

PUERTO RICO
Gericulture Commission
Department of Social Services
P.O. Box 11368
Santurce, PR 00908
809-722-2429

RHODE ISLAND
Department of Elderly Affairs
150 Washington Street
Providence, RI 02903
401-277-2858

SAMOA
Territorial Aging Program
Government of American Samoa
Office of the Governor
Pago Pago, AS
Samoa 3-1254 or 304116

SOUTH CAROLINA
Commission on Aging
915 Main Street
Columbia, SC 29201
803-758-2576

SOUTH DAKOTA
Office of Adult Services
& Aging
S.D. Department of Social
Services
State Office Building
Illinois Street
Pierre, SD 57501
605-773-3656

TENNESSEE
Commission on Aging
Room 102, S&P Building
306 Gay Street
Nashville, TN 37201
615-741-2056

TEXAS
Governor's Committee on Aging
Eighth Floor, Southwest Tower
211 East Seventh Street
P.O. Box 12786, Capitol Station
Austin, TX 78711
512-475-2717

MARIANA ISLANDS
Office of Aging
Community Development Division
Government of the Trust Territory
of the Pacific Islands
Saipan, Mariana Islands 96950
Overseas Operator 2143

UTAH
Division of Aging
Department of Social Services
150 West No. Temple
Box 2500
Salt Lake City, UT 84102
801-533-6422

VERMONT
Office on Aging
Agency of Human Services

State Office Building
Montpelier, VT 05602
802-244-5158

VIRGINIA
Office on Aging
830 East Main Street
Suite 950
Richmond, VA 23219
804-786-7894

VIRGIN ISLANDS
Commission on Aging
P.O. Box 539
Charlotte Amalie
St. Thomas, VI 00801
809-774-5884

WASHINGTON
Office on Aging
Department of Social &
  Health Services
OB-43G
Olympia, WA 98504
206-753-2502

WEST VIRGINIA
Commission on Aging
State Capitol
Charleston, WV 25305
304-348-3317

WISCONSIN
Bureau on Aging
The Division of Community
  Services
One West Wilson Street
Room 685
Madison, WI 53702
608-266-2536

WYOMING
Aging Services
Department of Health &
  Social Services
Division of Public Assistance &
  Social Services
New State Office Building, West
Room 288
Cheyenne, WY 82002
307-777-7561

● *Publications*

The publications listed below are official organs of the groups which publish them, though many are of interest to nonmembers as well, and some are available on a subscription basis. Looking through a few copies in your local library will determine whether you might like to receive one or more on a regular basis. The publications of professional research interest, of course, do not have mass appeal, but the magazines of general interest are professionally and attractively done. Addresses of the organizations which publish these organs are supplied earlier in this section, where objectives of each group are discussed.

GENERAL INTEREST

TITLE	FREQUENCY	ORGANIZATION
AARP News Bulletin	monthly	American Association of Retired Persons (Washington, DC)

TITLE	FREQUENCY	ORGANIZATION
Best Years	quarterly	National Association of Mature People (Oklahoma City, OK)
Dynamic Years	bi-monthly	Action for Independent Maturity (Washington, DC)
Modern Maturity	bi-monthly	American Association of Retired Persons (Washington, DC)
NAMP Newsletter	bi-monthly	National Association of Mature People (Oklahoma City, OK)
Senior Citizens News	monthly	National Council of Senior Citizens (Washington, DC)
Senior Independent	bi-monthly	National Alliance of Senior Citizens (Washington, DC.)
The Network	quarterly	Gray Panthers (Philadelphia, PA)

PROFESSIONAL/RESEARCH INTEREST

Aging International	quarterly	International Federation on Aging (Washington, DC)
Current Literature on Aging	quarterly	National Council on the Aging (Washington, DC)
Industrial Gerontology	quarterly	National Council on the Aging (Washington, DC)
Journal of Gerontology	bi-monthly	Gerontological Society (Washington, DC)
Journal of The American Geriatrics Society	monthly	American Geriatrics Society (New York, NY)
Journal of the American Health Care Association	bi-monthly	American Health Care Association (Washington, DC)

TITLE	FREQUENCY	ORGANIZATION
National Institute of Senior Centers Memo	monthly	National Council on The Aging (Washington, DC)
The Gerontologist	bi-monthly	Gerontological Society (Washington, DC)
The Gerontologist		International Association of Gerontology (Rehovot, Israel)
Views and News	monthly	National Geriatric Society (Washington, DC)

● *Guidebooks*

There is a surprising number of well-written pamphlets available on a wide variety of subjects of interest to preretirees and retired people, generally at very low cost or free with membership. Contact the organizations mentioned below for lists of titles and price lists.

SERIES	AVAILABLE FROM
Subjects include: consumer affairs, estate planning, health, household and personal security, legal affairs, medical matters, nutrition, physical fitness, taxes and wills	American Association of Retired Persons (Washington, DC)
	Action for Independent Maturity (Washington, DC)
	National Association of Mature People (Oklahoma City, OK)

SINGLE SUBJECTS	AVAILABLE FROM
Directory of Nonprofit Homes for the Aged–Social Components of Care	American Association of Homes for the Aging (Washington, DC)
Health Career Opportunities	American Health Care Association (Washington, DC)
Senior Services Manual (annual edition)	National Alliance of Senior Citizens (Washington, DC)

● *Hotline Chart*

*Toll-Free Numbers to Call for Information
and Assistance*

QUESTIONS ANSWERED ON	TELEPHONE NUMBER	HOURS	SERVICES PROVIDED
Cancer (American Cancer Society)	800-638-6694	24 Hours, 7 Days	Information and individual client research and referral on virtually any cancer-related question or problem. The number listed here is the source of referral to the closest of twenty-three Cancer Information Service Offices around the country.
Community Services (United Community Services of Metropolitan Detroit)	800-552-1183* (in 313 area only)	24 Hours, 7 Days	Information and referral on all questions relating to the aging. Counsellor to the aging on duty during daytime hours.
Consumer Products (Consumer Products Safety Commission)	800-638-2666	8:30 AM–8 PM EST, Mon.–Fri. (recorded response at other times)	Product safety information; product recall information. Evaluates specific consumer complaints, and in some cases investigates. Distributes consumer safety publications.
Food Stamps (New York State Dept. of Social Services)	800-342-3710 (New York State only)*	8:30 AM–4 PM EST, Mon.–Fri. (Recorded response at other times)	Information and referral on food stamp program; Medicaid; adult residential care; other age-related problems.
Homes For The Aged (New York State Office For the Aging)	800-342-9871 (New York State only)*	9 AM–10 PM EST, Mon.–Fri. (recorded response at other times)	Referral and information on housing, paying for medical care, legal aid, Social Security.
Meals on Wheels*			These programs are all administered locally. The quickest referral to the nearest agency can be obtained from your State Unit on Aging.
Special Needs (Action)	800-424-8580 ext. 39	9AM–5 PM EST, Mon.–Fri.	Referral to local agencies for older adults with special needs. Also administers Foster Grandparents (RSVP) and Senior Companions programs.

*For the phone number of your State Agency on Aging, see page 568.

QUESTIONS ANSWERED ON	TELEPHONE NUMBER	HOURS	SERVICES PROVIDED
Venereal Disease (Operation Venus)	800-523-1885	9 AM–10 PM EST, Every day	Information and referral on venereal disease.

● *Community Groups and Resources*

As the ratio of older people to younger people continues to increase, so do the groups and services designed to meet their special needs. On all levels of government, staff and resources exist to answer your questions and get you the help you require.

But suppose you want to find out—in an informal way—what's available in your own small town or rural or suburban community. You don't need technical information, such as your local Department of Social Services can provide, or Social Security or Medicare. You want to know if there's a social Senior Citizens Club, or which nursing home in the county is supposed to be the best, or whether there's a local discount-buying group for older adults. Who's likely to have that information?

There are many sources close at hand. Check these out for personal knowledge of the groups and services in your area.

CITY, COUNTY, OR STATE OFFICE FOR AGING. Here you can find information and referral to specific sources of help for individual problems.

CHURCHES. Churches of any denomination are likely to know about activities for older adults in the community. Many have established programs specifically for older people, either independently or in association with the Church Relations Program run by AARP (American Association of Retired Persons). Church personnel are also likely to be familiar with retirement facilities and nursing homes in the area.

HOSPITALS. The hospital nearest your home certainly knows about nursing homes and other health-related facilities in the community. And, chances are, the hospital's social services staff is familiar with Senior Citizens Clubs in the community and knows of any out-reach programs designed to attract older adults.

LIBRARIES. Your local library undoubtedly receives publications from local, as well as national, senior citizen clubs and organizations. The library bulletin board may well be sporting flyers and announcements of activities of interest to seniors. It's worth taking a look.

BUSINESSES. The major employer in your area knows about pension plans, retirement groups, and the like. And chances are, the personnel office of a major company has been asked to contribute to fund-raising efforts of local senior citizens groups. It's certainly worth one phone call to find out.

COLLEGES. The college or university near your home may have its own Department of Gerontology. If it does, that will be the most complete, nongovernment source around. Even if it doesn't, college students often volunteer in local nursing homes and senior citizen organizations. Talk to someone in the Gerontology Department or to the Coordinator of Student Volunteers.

ORGANIZATIONS. Many community social service organizations are directly involved with senior citizen activities. Even those that are not are likely to know what's available. For example, some YMCAs and YM-YWHAs conduct preretirement courses and lectures. In some cities, the Salvation Army has programs for older adults. Some chapters of the National Council of Jewish Women support nursing homes, housing for older adults, and senior citizen clubs. In some areas the Community Council or local unit of United Way is directly involved in, or knowledgeable about, senior citizen activities.

WORD OF MOUTH. Friends and neighbors of retirement age, or those with parents of retirement age, are also a good source of first-hand, reliable information. You know whose judgment you can trust, so you might as well make use of it.

Whether it's a social club, a local politically active group, or a national association with discount buying, travel, and insurance plans, a retirement group can add important, even essential dimensions to both your daily life and long-range considerations of lifestyle.

RECORD KEEPING

Perhaps your family unit includes a spouse, an additional relative, or other member. But whether one person or several, like a business concern, you have an income and outgo and capital—the accumulation of assets produced by past and present earnings. Like any business, you must handle financial matters efficiently. Record keeping involves not only finances but personal matters as well—a will, for example, or general family information that is essential when there is a shift of responsibilities.

● *Benefits of Record Keeping*

There are several practical benefits to converting a flood of paper into a systematic set of records. First, a good set of records simplifies the process of updating and prevents the confusion of a disorganized set of incomplete or haphazard notes.

Another important benefit is psychological: You can take satisfaction in the feeling that your paperwork is neatly organized, that you won't go floating off in a sea of bills, cancelled checks, records of purchases and indebtedness, and so on. Fast retrieval is another plus. If you need an item quickly you will be saved the exasperating searches through drawers full of accumulated paper. And when tax time comes around, you can lay your hands on the papers you need.

Finally, a systematic approach may make you aware of an area that needs attention, such as not knowing the contents of a safe deposit box neglected for many long months. In other words, your control of the activities which you are recording tends to focus on possible weaknesses which can then be improved.

In the event of illness, travel, or sudden emergency, well-kept records can make it possible for members of the family or a trusted friend to handle your affairs.

● *Storing Records*

The facts and figures of your finances, the amount and nature of your assets, and all kinds of valuable personal data should be kept in a safe and accessible place. This might be a small metal box in a wall safe or file cabinet, or perhaps a safe deposit box in your bank.

Some parts of your personal records may be confidential. In that case, you might want to insure privacy by letting only one or two other people know their whereabouts. In any case, the three basic elements of effective storage are clear, precise records, a safe and accessible place for them to be kept, and, finally, one or two other people besides yourself who know where the records are and how to get them when necessary.

● *Essential Forms*

In the pages ahead, you'll find forms to serve as a complete, at-a-glance record of your important papers and planning. To these you may want to add special record-keeping aids reflecting a personal interest. For example, if you are a collector, you may want to include in your private papers an itemized history of acquisitions and sales. Here is a simple form devised by a wood sculptor that could easily be adapted by any artist or artisan:

Name or Description	Type of Wood	Date Started	Date Finished	Acquirer
Sea Venus	Pine board	May 10	Sept. 3	Luyten Gallery

Many of the forms that follow were designed by the staff of the Research Institute of America. I want to thank this organization for its permission to adapt them. Other records were developed from professional sources and have been acknowledged in the appropriate places.

HOUSE RECORDS

For your family's convenience and for your information at tax time, you may want to obtain a specially prepared chart of your mortgage payments. This chart will indicate the amounts out of each payment that go for interest and amortization and the net amount due on the mortgage up to that particular payment. Your local bank can tell you how to get this kind of chart. Or, the person or institution holding a mortgage, if any, will supply such a record.

Mortgage and real-estate-tax record

Owned in name of: _____

Purchase price: _____ Cash: _____ Mortgage _____

MORTGAGE

Held by: _____

Address: _____

Person you deal with: _____

Phone No: _____

Where mortgage is located: _____

MORTGAGE TERMS

No. of years _____ Rate of interest _____

Monthly payment of _____ includes _____ for

interest and _____ for amortization.

Prepayment clause: Years _____ penalty _____

DEED

Type:

Where is it:

TITLE

Guaranteed _____ yes _____ no _____

By whom _____

TAXES (as of_____ 19_____)

County _____ Due date _____

Town _____ Due date _____

School _____ Due date _____

Deed and plot plan

It can be helpful to have a plot plan of your house and property on hand. In some cases, a previous owner may pass this important piece of paper along to you. Usually the deed for a piece of property describes boundaries with respect to established marks or topographical features. A copy of your deed, or at any rate the description of the property, may be obtained from your town clerk.

To get a plan of the property developed from the description in the deed may require the services of a surveyor. If you're unsure about the boundaries or if you possibly plan to subdivide or to sell, it's worth the investment to have a survey made, including overall lot measurements, setback, yard dimensions, and, of course, location of your house with respect to boundaries.

Street _____

Plot Number _____

Town of _____

County of _____

Assessed valuation _____

Date acquired _____

Easements _____

Remarks _____

Property improvement record

Most householders, particularly those who have owned their homes for some time, have added improvements from the first day of occupancy. These improvements, of course, increase the value of the house. Having a record of permanent improvements also can help minimize the amount of capital gains subject to tax that may be involved if you sell your house.

Bring the following table up to date, and note each future "investment" as you make it. Include permanent items, such as storm windows, lighting fixtures, landscaping and the like. (Do *not* include maintenance costs, such as the bills for painting or decoration.)

Date	Item	Cost

Evaluation of contents

For a number of reasons—insurance purposes and as an aid in moving or distributing your estate—it's a good idea to keep an updated inventory of the contents of your house.

Contents	Cost	Value
Living Room		
Library or Den		
Dining Room		

Contents	Cost	Value
Kitchen, Pantry, etc.		
Bedrooms		
Bathrooms		
Clothing		
Jewelry		
Personal Belongings		
Basement		
Garage and miscellaneous		
Table and Bed Linen		
Silverware		
Total		

INSURANCE RECORDS

Life insurance

While many people of retirement age have no life insurance either because of costs or because their bequests to heirs will be made in other forms, many do have insurance. It's important for these people to keep a record: in the event of death, it informs heirs and executors of insurance benefits that are available, as well as whom to contact and how to file claims. Second, if the insured person is incapacitated, other family members will be able to refer to this record so that policy premiums may be paid as they fall due. Also, the information you've entered on the form enables you to evaluate the adequacy of your coverage from time to time.

Insured	Company and Agent	Policy Number	Location of Policy	Amount of Insurance	Premium	Premium Due Date	Beneficiaries	Form of Benefit Payments

Health and accident insurance

A record of your personal insurance coverage helps you tell at a glance the extent of your coverage—the amount and for how long. It also provides a record if by any chance policies are lost. Also, you have the basic information at hand if you keep the policies elsewhere, such as in a safety deposit box. The form may be used to schedule premium payments.

Insured	Policy Number	Company and Agent	Amount of Insurance	Type of Coverage	Premium	Premium Due Date	Expiration Date	Remarks

Property and liability insurance

The newspaper boy trips on your front path, breaks a leg, and sues you for damages. Are you covered by insurance? Where's the policy? Is it paid up to date?

Your neighbor claims you built your new tool shed partly on his property. Can you disprove it? Where is your property line? Do you have a record of it?

You suffer fire damage to your home. It's covered by insurance, but you have to move out and rent other quarters for the time being. Who pays the rent? Do you know that for a nominal sum you can obtain an "additional living expenses" rider to your policy to protect you in just such an emergency?

Of course, questions like these should be discussed with your insurance agents. Even with the new, more "readable" language found in insurance policies, they are still complex documents. The record forms in this section can help you organize your thinking and may point out areas where you need more—or less—coverage.

Fire and theft insurance

Carelessly, someone drops a lighted cigarette on one of your favorite chairs. Before you can spot the damage, the chair is ruined. Of course, it's covered by fire insurance—or is it? And if so, for how much?

In addition to fire insurance for the house itself, most homeowners have found it desirable to insure the contents of their homes, including furniture and other furnishings as well as jewelry and furs. An extract from the standard fire insurance policy tells you why it's important to keep an inventory of your possessions:

"If fire occurs, the insured shall give immediate notice of any loss thereby in writing. Make a complete inventory of the same, stating the quantity and cost of each article, and the amount claimed thereon."

Filling out the forms on the following pages will assemble that information for you. In addition, keep these points in mind:

1. Check with your insurance broker to find out whether, in your state, the insurance company reimburses for original cost, depreciated value, or replacement value. Only on that basis can you decide exactly how much insurance you need.

2. Carry only enough theft insurance to cover the amount of property that could be carried off by an intruder.

3. Make certain that household appliances are covered by fire insurance. Some policies exclude items like dishwashers and clothes washers from both house and contents insurance.

Unfortunately, due to the rising crime rate, some apartment dwellers and homeowners find it difficult to get theft insurance.

Type of Policy	Policy Number	Company and Agent	Location of Policy	Amount of Coverage	Premium	Remarks

Type of Coverage	Company and Policy No.	Location of Policy	Expires
Fire (Contents)			
Smudge Endorsement			
Explosion			
Windstorm			
Burglary—Theft			
Hold-Up			
Personal Effects			
Stamp Collection			
Fine Arts			
Musical Instruments			
Floaters: Fur			
Jewelry			
Scheduled Property			
Personal Property			
Total			

Automobile insurance

Cars can be stolen, can be involved in accidents, and need to be kept in safe running condition. And, of course, they must be paid for. Keeping records can help toward these ends. If younger members of your family are also car owners, encourage them to keep similar records.

Make of Car _____

Year _____

Type _____

Date of Purchase _____

Purchase Price _____

Model _____

Weight _____

Engine No. _____

Cylinders _____

Serial No. _____

Car License No. _____ Expires _____

Operator Lic. No. _____ Expires _____

Financed by _____

Address _____

Down Payment _____

Amount of Monthly Payment _____

Balance Due _____ Due _____

Insurance Company _____

Name of Agent _____

Location of Policy _____

Amount of Premium $_____ /(yr., mo.) _____

FINANCIAL RECORDS

Bank accounts

Retired people have a special need for keeping complete financial records. First of all, you want them for your own benefit. In addition, if other people are going to be required to review and assess your financial situation, having the facts down in black and white is essential. Also, there's the question of loss.

Losing a savings bond is not a very serious matter *if* you have a record of the bond number, the issuing agency, and the date of issue. Nor will you be greatly inconvenienced by losing a savings account passbook—*if* you know the account number. Whether or not there is an "if" to help you out depends on whether you have recorded all the facts. Make such a record without delay.

Do you have a joint account? Do you know that in the event of death, the survivor is *not* permitted to touch the money until certain legal requirements are satisfied?

Do you have another account from which your family could obtain funds to tide it over an emergency?

A REMINDER. Many banks block joint accounts when they receive notification of death of one of the joint owners. It is a good idea to ask your bank to write you a letter stating its policy in this respect. If the bank does block such accounts, each spouse may wish to set up a separate emergency account in his or her own name.

Name and Address of Bank, Credit Union, Savings and Loan Association	Account No. and Type of Account	Other Signers on the Account	Location of Passbooks

Safe-deposit record

Renting a safe-deposit box assures you and your family of a secure place to keep important documents, records, and personal possessions. However, when you fill out the rental forms, be aware that if a renter dies, there are specific rules governing access to the box and its contents which vary from state to state. Many renters assume that should they die, a joint box holder or authorized deputy can immediately remove necessary documents from the box. This is *not* always the case. A number of states consider that a deputy's authority or a power of attorney ceases when a renter dies, and the safe-deposit box is sealed upon death. You should ask the bank officer the following questions:

• After death, does the surviving tenant have access to the box? If not, how long does it take before access is permitted?

• Who can enter an individually rented box after the tenant dies? How is authorization obtained? How long does it take?

• What restrictions are placed on access to the box's contents?

• Is a tax inventory required before free access to the box? If so, how long does it take?

• What are the rules on removing a will from the box of a deceased renter, whether individual or joint? To whom can the will be delivered? How long does the process usually take? What are the rules on removing life insurance policies?

What belongs in your safe-deposit box—and what doesn't? As a general rule, only those documents and valuables which are irreplaceable or can be replaced with difficulty or expense need to be kept in such a depository. Items which can be replaced with minimal inconvenience, such as passports, or which are frequently needed for reference, such as cancelled checks, might better be kept in a good file case, preferably a metal one with a lock.

Preferably in Safe-Deposit Box:

Abstracts	Court Decrees
Adoption Papers	Deeds
Birth Certificates, Originals	Insurance Policies
Bonds	Inventories for Insurance
Certificates of Deposit	Purposes
Contracts	Jewelry (valuable)
Copyrights	Marriage Certificates, Originals

Military Discharge Papers	Savings Certificates
Mortgages	Stock Certificates
Promissory Notes	Treasured Photos or Negatives
Naturalization Papers	Trust Agreements
Patents	Valued Letters
Pension Certificates	Wills

Name and Address of Bank	Box No.	Names and Addresses of Persons with Access	Location of Keys

*Based on material developed by Action for Independent Maturity

Tax-deductible expenses

Many people use bank statements or cancelled checks as a record of expenditures. But some deductible outlays may not show up on your checking account and you may suffer an actual loss from failing to record them. While the Internal Revenue Service doesn't like the idea of allowing deductions not backed up by a cancelled check or other tangible proof, an auditor might allow a written record; and, if necessary, the record could lead you to verify a deductible payment that had been made.

Item	Amount	Date

Keep a separate list of the *contents* of your safe deposit box and any *special instructions* regarding the contents in an accessible place.

Investments

BONDS & DEBENTURES

Kind	Interest Rate	Number Owned	Serial No. of Certificates	Purchase Price	Maturity Date	Value	In Whose Name(s)

STOCKS

Company	Number of Shares	Serial No. of Certificates	Date Acquired	Cost Per Share	In Whose Name(s)

OTHER INVESTMENTS

Kind (Promissory Note, Mortgage, Contract, etc.)	Payable by Whom	Principal Amount	Terms of Payment	Date Due

Loans

	Lender	Amount	Date Made	Loan Period	Method of Repayment	Special Information
1						
2						
3						
4						

IN CASE OF DEATH

Immediate concerns

There are a number of vital facts that a family will need immediately in the event of the death of the major income earner. The more completely you fill in the following charts and tables, the easier it becomes for others in the family who must assume the responsibilities.

Executor _____

Address _____

Notify _____

Will is located _____

Life insurance policies are located _____

Safe deposit box located at _____

Address _____

Box number _____

Keys _____

Bank account _____

In name of _____

Family vita

Name _____

Birthdate _____

Location of birth certificate _____

Citizenship by _____

Location of papers _____

Social Security Number _____

Location of Armed Services discharge papers _____

Name _____

Birthdate _____

Location of birth certificate _____

Citizenship by _____

Location of papers _____

Social Security Number _____

Location of Armed Services discharge papers _____

Name _____

Birthdate _____

Location of birth certificate _____

Citizenship by _____

Location of papers _____

Social Security Number _____

Location of Armed Services discharge papers _____

Name _____

Birthdate _____

Location of birth certificate _____

Citizenship by _____

Location of papers _____

Social Security Number _____

Location of Armed Services discharge papers _____

Professional advisers

Do others know the name and address of the family lawyer? Doctor? Accountant? Situations may arise where such information is vital. Revise and update as necessary.

Doctor

Name _____
Address _____
Phone No. _____

Name _____
Address _____
Phone No. _____

Attorney

Name _____
Address _____
Phone No. _____

Name _____
Address _____
Phone No. _____

Insurance Adviser

Name _____
Address _____
Phone No. _____

Accountant

Name _____
Address _____
Phone No. _____

Clergyman

Name _____
Address _____
Phone No. _____

List below an individual on whom your family may rely in case of emergency.

Personal Adviser

Name _____
Address _____
Phone No. _____

Veterans' survivors' benefits

Apply for benefits to the Veterans Administration Regional Office or state veterans assistance office.

(a) NATIONAL SERVICE LIFE INSURANCE. You will need the following papers:
1. Certified copy of death certificate
2. Certified copy of widow's birth certificate
3. Forms VA 21-4125 and VA 1501 (A-D) obtainable from VA

(b) BURIAL BENEFITS. You will need the following papers:
1. Certified copy of death certificate
2. Certified copy of military discharge
3. Statement from undertaker showing the amount of itemized funeral expenses and by whom paid
4. Form VA 21-530 obtainable from VA

(c) DEPENDENCY AND INDEMNITY COMPENSATION. Widows or children of deceased veterans, if the veteran has died in service or from a service-connected disability, may be entitled to certain income benefits. If you or your children are eligible, you will be required to provide the following papers:
1. Certified copy of death certificate (include certified death certificate of prior spouse, if any)
2. Certified copy of marriage certificate (include certified divorce decree of any prior spouse)
3. Certified copy of each child's birth certificate
4. Certified copy of military discharge
5. Form VA 21-534 obtainable from VA

(d) DEATH PENSION. The same papers required for dependency and indemnity compensation are required for death pension benefits. Form VA 21-534 is also used.

If you file for more than one veterans' benefit, it is not necessary to provide more than one copy of any form or paper.

NOTE: Survivors' benefits are subject to change under federal law.

Other sources of survivors' benefits

A. Most workers covered by compensation insurance are entitled to benefits under varying conditions. Was your job covered by State Workmen's Compensation Insurance?　　　　　＿＿Yes ＿＿No

B. There are several other possible sources of survivors' benefits. If you think or know your survivors are entitled to benefits under any of the following, check the appropriate space:

Employer's Insurance Policy	＿＿Yes	＿＿No
Life Insurance Policy(s)	＿＿Yes	＿＿No
Health/Accident Policy(s)	＿＿Yes	＿＿No
Auto/Casualty Insurance	＿＿Yes	＿＿No
Trade Union	＿＿Yes	＿＿No
Fraternal Organizations	＿＿Yes	＿＿No

If so, list organizations:＿＿＿＿＿＿＿＿＿＿＿＿＿＿＿＿＿＿＿＿

Information for burial certificate

1. Name, home address and telephone number
2. How long in state
3. Name of business, address and telephone number
4. Occupation and title
5. Social security number
6. Armed Service serial number
7. Date of birth
8. Place of birth
9. U.S. citizen
10. Father's name
11. Father's birthplace
12. Mother's maiden name
13. Mother's birthplace

Important documents regarding deceased

1. Death certificate and certified copies for burial permit, insurance and other purposes
2. Will
3. Birth certificate or other legal proof of age
4. Social security card

5. Marriage certificate
6. Divorce decree, if any
7. Citizenship papers, if naturalized
8. Military discharge papers
9. Insurance policies
10. Bank books
11. Deeds to property, automobile title(s)
12. Income tax returns
13. Disability claims

Persons and places to notify

1. Doctor or Health Maintenance Organization
2. Funeral director or memorial society
3. Institution to which remains may be donated
4. Memorial park
5. Relatives and friends
6. Employer of deceased
7. Employers of relatives who will miss work
8. Insurance agents
9. Attorney, accountant or executor of estate
10. Religious, fraternal, civic, veterans' organizations
11. Newspapers regarding notices

Funeral preferences

Choice of mortuary: _____
                 Name   Street   City   State

Disposition of Remains:
Interment _____Crypt _____Inurnment _____Ashes Scattered_____
Name of Cemetery, Columbarium, etc.: _____
Do you own: Plot _____Crypt _____Niche _____? Location of deed_____
Service at: Mortuary_____Church _____If church, name: _____
Type of service: Private _____For friends _____Memorial service later_____
                 Location _____
Service to be conducted by: _____
Fraternal orders, lodges, organizations to be notified:

Name	Person to be notified	City	Phone
1.			
2.			
3.			

If you belong to a memorial society:

_____
Name

_____
Street   City   Phone

If you have donated your remains to a scientific institution or hospital:

_____
Name

_____
Street   City   Phone

Location of documents

This section will provide a list of the locations of your most important documents, papers and assets, any or all of which may be needed in the event of accident, illness or death.

Location of Important Papers of

_____and_____
              Husband   Wife

Indicate in space provided the location of the following important papers by inserting appropriate letters: (H) Home Files, (D) Safe-Deposit Box, (S) Safe, (O) Office (X) Other (Specify).

	Husband	Wife	Jointly Held		Husband	Wife	Jointly Held
Wills				Life Insurance Policies			
Birth Certificates				Home Insurance Policies			
Marriage Certificate				Health/Accident Policies			
Divorce Decrees				Auto Insurance Policies			
Military Records				Social Security Records			
Stock & Bond Certificates				Pension Plan Certificates			
Deed(s) to Property				Records			
Mortage(s)				Other: (Specify)			
Title to Automobile(s)							
Income Tax Returns							
Tax Receipts							

Wills & Estates

WILLS. The importance of both spouses having up-to-date wills cannot be overemphasized. The individual who makes no will forfeits any assurance that his or her property will be distributed according to his or her wishes—and also may cause unnecessary difficulties and possible losses for survivors. When a person dies without a will the distribution of the estate is governed by state intestacy laws which, being "standard," may not fit the best interests of a particular person or family.

All seniors should review their wills periodically to see that they take into account changes in the family situation and tax laws. For example, your will should be updated if you have moved to a different state, if you have already disposed of some property mentioned in your will, if the size and nature of your estate have changed, or if new potential heirs have been born or others have died.

	Date of Will	Location	Executor	Attorney
Husband's			Name _____ Address _____ Phone _____	Name _____ Address _____ Phone _____
Wife's			Name _____ Address _____ Phone _____	Name _____ Address _____ Phone _____

TRUSTS. List any trusts you have created or any trusts created by others under which you possess any power, beneficial interest, or trusteeship.

_____

_____

_____

_____

INDEX

Earl Ashmitt
Box 491
Ballarei, JA
ZD 448